HANDBOOK OF RESEARCH ON ARTIFICIAL INTELLIGENCE IN HUMAN RESOURCE MANAGEMENT

Handbook of Research on Artificial Intelligence in Human Resource Management

Edited by

Stefan Strohmeier

Professor of Management Information Systems, Chair of Management Information Systems, Saarland University, Germany

EE Edward Elgar
PUBLISHING

Cheltenham, UK • Northampton, MA, USA

Published by
Edward Elgar Publishing Limited
The Lypiatts
15 Lansdown Road
Cheltenham
Glos GL50 2JA
UK

Edward Elgar Publishing, Inc.
William Pratt House
9 Dewey Court
Northampton
Massachusetts 01060
USA

A catalogue record for this book
is available from the British Library

Library of Congress Control Number: 2022931121

This book is available electronically in the **Elgar**online
Business subject collection
http://dx.doi.org/10.4337/9781839107535

ISBN 978 1 83910 752 8 (cased)
ISBN 978 1 83910 753 5 (eBook)

Printed and bound by CPI Group (UK) Ltd, Croydon, CR0 4YY

Contents

Figures

Tables

Contributors

William J. Becker, Associate Professor of Management, Pamplin College of Business, Virginia Tech, Blacksburg, VA, USA.

Constant D. Beugré, Professor of Business Administration, Delaware State University, Dover, DE, USA.

Chulin Chen, PhD Student in Industrial and Organizational Psychology, University of Minnesota, Twin Cities, MN, USA.

Raphael de Barros Fritz, PhD Student, Passau University, Passau, Germany, and SJD Student, Tulane University, New Orleans, LA, USA.

Alberto Fernández, Associate Professor of Computer Science, Center for Intelligent Information Technologies and Applications (CETINIA), University Rey Juan Carlos, Madrid, Spain.

Carmen Fernández-Martinez, PhD Candidate/Researcher, Center for Intelligent Information Technologies and Applications (CETINIA), University Rey Juan Carlos, Madrid, Spain.

Peter Fettke, Professor for Business Informatics, Saarland University, Saarbrücken, Germany, and Research Fellow, Principal Researcher, Research Group Leader, German Research Center for Artificial Intelligence (DFKI), Saarbrücken, Germany.

Sandra L. Fisher, Senior Research Fellow and Lecturer, Münster School of Business, Münster University of Applied Sciences, Münster, Germany.

Felix Gross, PhD Student and Research Assistant, Chair of Management Information Systems, Saarland University, Saarbrücken, Germany.

Jake T. Harrison, Pre-Doctoral Student Researcher, Department of Management, Jon M. Huntsman School of Business, Utah State University, Logan, UT, USA.

Christopher J. Hartwell, Associate Professor, Department of Management, Jon M. Huntsman School of Business, Utah State University, Logan, UT, USA.

Garret N. Howardson, Research Psychologist, U.S. Army Research Institute for the Behavioral and Social Sciences, Fort Belvoir, VA, USA.

Richard D. Johnson, Associate Professor, Washington State University, Pullman, WA, USA.

Charlotte Köhler, Department of Information Systems, Freie Universität Berlin, Berlin, Germany.

Cornelius J. König, Professor of Work and Organizational Psychology and Vice-President for Internationalization and European Relations, Saarland University, Saarbrücken, Germany.

Richard Landers, Associate Professor of Psychology, John P. Campbell Distinguished Professor of Industrial and Organizational Psychology, University of Minnesota, Twin Cities, MN, USA.

Markus Langer, Research Associate, Department of Work and Organizational Psychology, Saarland University, Saarbrücken, Germany.

Sven Laumer, Professor of Information Systems, Schoeller Endowed Chair for Information Systems – Digitalization in Business and Society, Friedrich-Alexander Universität Erlangen-Nürnberg, Nürnberg, Germany.

Christian Maier, Assistant Professor of Information Systems, Chair of Information Systems and Services, University of Bamberg, Bamberg, Germany.

Jorge Martinez-Gil, Research Project Manager (Data Science), Software Competence Center Hagenberg, Hagenberg im Mühlkreis, Austria.

Florian J. Meier, Schoeller Endowed Chair for Information Systems – Digitalization in Business and Society, Friedrich-Alexander Universität Erlangen-Nürnberg, Nürnberg, Germany.

Stefan Morana, Junior Professor of Information Systems, Junior Professorship of Digital Transformation and Information Systems, Saarland University, Saarbrücken, Germany.

Franziska Raudonat, Algorithm Accountability Lab, TU Kaiserslautern, Kaiserslautern, Germany.

Maarten Renkema, Assistant Professor of Human Resource Management & Innovation, University of Twente, The Netherlands.

Dianna L. Stone, Research Professor, University of New Mexico, Albuquerque, NM, USA, and Affiliate Professor, Virginia Tech, Blacksburg, VA, USA.

Stefan Strohmeier, Professor of Management Information Systems, Chair of Management Information Systems, Saarland University, Saarbrücken, Germany.

Sarah E. Tuskey, Post-Doctoral Researcher, Pamplin College of Business, Virginia Tech, Blacksburg, VA, USA.

Kai von Lewinski, Professor of Law, Chair of Public Law, Media and Information Law, Passau University, Passau, Germany.

Tim Weitzel, Professor of Information Systems, Chair of Information Systems and Services, University of Bamberg, Bamberg, Germany.

Lena Wolbeck, Associate Researcher, Department of Information Systems, Freie Universität Berlin, Berlin, Germany.

Katharina A. Zweig, Professor of Computer Science, Head of the Algorithm Accountability Lab, TU Kaiserslautern, Kaiserslautern, Germany.

Preface

For some time now, I have been convinced that Artificial Intelligence (AI) in Human Resources (HR) constitutes a particularly intriguing, manifold, and relevant field of research that deserves more scholarly attention. I thus more than welcomed the suggestion of Edward Elgar to publish a handbook that broadly covers the topic of research on AI in HR and am grateful for the opportunity to be (a participating author and) the editor responsible for this volume.

Since AI in HR currently constitutes a rather nascent field of research, established and accepted approaches, frameworks, or conceptualizations for researching AI in HR are largely missing. It was therefore not without challenge to structure the field and recruit authors that were both willing and able to explore and map this *terra incognita*. I am pleased and grateful that the authors of this handbook have taken on this pioneering work and now can provide initial systematic insights into current research and implications for future research on AI in HR. Thanks for accepting me (and my idiosyncrasies) as editor.

In preparing and editing the handbook I received valuable support. Beyond contributing his own chapter, my PhD student Felix Gross supported me in the entire process from identifying potential authors to sending the final manuscript to the publisher. My assistant, Khanda Adams, helped me in reviewing and formatting the manuscripts. Caroline Kracunas, my contact at Edward Elgar, always had an open ear for my questions. Thanks for your support.

Now, I would like to extend a special welcome to the readers of this handbook. I am convinced the book provides a wealth of useful insights. The handbook covers a broad range of AI fields relevant to HR, and not only considers AI fields that are currently en vogue, such as machine learning or natural language processing, but also lesser known, yet innovative and relevant, AI fields such as affective computing or robotic process automation. Moreover, beyond presenting different AI fields, the book also covers normative issues such as the explainability, fairness, accountability, and legitimacy of AI in HR, and offers guidance on how to research AI in HR and, vice versa, how to employ AI for research in HR. The structure of the book enables readers to selectively read chapters of individual interest, or else gain a comprehensive overview of AI in HR by working step by step through the chapters. In sum, the handbook offers a first systematic introduction into researching AI in HR and provides multiple starting points for readers' own work. Thanks for your interest and enjoy the book.

Stefan Strohmeier

1. Artificial intelligence in human resources – an introduction

Stefan Strohmeier

Artificial intelligence (AI) constitutes an important field of computer science that is additionally related to different further scientific disciplines such as philosophy, mathematics, statistics, anthropology, psychology, neurology, biology, or linguistics (e.g., Russell & Norvig, 2021). Starting in the 1950s, AI shows a long and volatile history of successes and setbacks (e.g., Delipetrev et al., 2020). Based on ever increasing ("big") data stocks and computing power, in the 2010s particularly machine learning, an important field of AI, took an upswing that led to intriguing improvements in a lot of domains such as machine translation, robotic vehicles, or game playing (e.g., Russell & Norvig, 2021). In the wake of these successes, AI induced growing attention, discussion, and also application in numerous domains, among them the human resource (HR) domain. In the HR domain it is expected that AI will massively expand augmentation and automation towards complex tasks such as communication and decision making and even entire management (e.g., Strohmeier, 2020; Strohmeier & Piazza, 2015). Following discussions and developments in practice, research also started to consider AI in HR. The current overall state of research, however, is that it is nascent and scattered over different disciplines, and is far from systematically accompanying and guiding practice. To trigger and support such research, the current handbook thus aims at providing a systematic introduction to research on AI in HR. To introduce readers to the handbook, the current chapter elaborates on the basics of AI in HR and subsequently delineates the objectives, structure, and contributions of the handbook.

BASICS OF AI IN HR

As AI in HR constitutes a multifaceted and complex phenomenon, it is frequently not well understood (e.g., Long & Magerko, 2020). The following section thus briefly introduces the basics of the field, by elaborating on the *definition*, *categorization*, and *history and state* of AI in HR.

Definition of AI in HR

Regarding a definition of AI, there is a large set of suggestions uncovering different understandings (see e.g. the review of definitions by Monett & Lewis, 2018, the discussion of definitions by Wang, 2019, and the versatile reactions to this in Monett et al., 2020). Existing AI definitions are often based on similarities between AI and natural intelligence (NI). That is, AI is defined as a technology that is "similar" to NI, while there are, however, differences in the ways in which NI and AI are seen as similar (Wang, 2019). Early definitions refer, for instance, to structural similarities of AI and NI ("AI is structured like the brain of a natural intelligent being") or behavioral similarities of NI and AI ("AI behaves like a natural intelligent being"). Since such similarities are narrow and restrictive, more frequently functional similarities ("AI provides functions like a natural intelligent being") are employed for defining AI (Wang, 2019). Aiming at researching and exploiting the *functions* that AI provides to HR, a functional definition approach thus seems adequate and the following working definition can be suggested: *AI designates the set of digital technologies that mimic certain functions of NI, such as perceiving, learning, knowing, or reasoning, to augment or automate human tasks, which conventionally require such functions of NI to be performed.*

This definition needs several clarifications: First, with the definition component of *"mimic certain functions of NI"* the above definition is premised on the idea that there is a similarity between NI and AI. This similarity of providing intelligent functions, however, is restricted and in need of concretization. A frequent metaphor for illustrating the restricted similarity refers to the comparison of natural flying with artificial flying (e.g., Russell & Norvig, 2021). Taking birds and helicopters as examples, both show the function of flying. However, both realize this function through very dissimilar procedures. A first clarification, thus, is that similarities of NI and AI refer to the results rather than to the procedure of gaining these results. Moreover, as helicopters for instance are able to fly backwards while birds are not, the results also differ. In this sense, AI uses procedures dissimilar to NI ones to produce results that are similar to NI results but are not identical. Second, with the definition component of *"functions of NI"* the scope of the AI concept sensitively depends on the understanding of the "NI functions" concept. A broad understanding that encompasses any cognitive activity as an NI function would imply that, for instance, "calculating" constitutes a function of NI. This, however, would in turn count spread-sheets, which augment and automate the human task of calculation, as AI, even though spread-sheets conventionally are *not* seen as AI. AI literature, thus, uses a conventional set of functions of NI such as sensing, reasoning, learning, or knowing (e.g., Russell & Norvig, 2021) to determine AI, rather than systematically determining the function concept and, based on this, determining AI. The definition is thus not fully selective in separating technologies conventionally understood as AI from further technologies. Third, the definition component of *"NI"* includes human intelligence as a core category, yet goes beyond by explicitly allowing for further categories such as general biological intelligence (Wang, 2019). Fourth, with the definition component *"set of digital technologies"* AI should be understood as a set of different technologies, rather than as one homogeneous technology.

Categorization of AI in HR

Recent attempts to categorize AI (e.g., Corea, 2019; Golstein, 2020) uncover the complexity and versatility of the field that evades any simple and neat internal and external delineation. Nevertheless, in order to create a basic understanding of the field, in the following the *strength, paradigm, convention*, and *function* of AI are employed as criteria to roughly categorize AI in HR.

Categorization by strength
Strength designates the overarching level of intelligence expected from AI, while in a rough categorization narrow, general, and super AI can be distinguished (e.g., Bostrom, 2014; Russell & Norvig, 2021; Searle, 1980). *Narrow AI* (also known as *weak AI*) aims at tackling a more or less defined, single human task. While narrow AI can even outperform humans in

this specific task, it is not able to perform any other human task, even if more trivial. Narrow AI is frequently associated with the position that AI can only act *as if it would be* intelligent, that is, thinks, has a mind, and so on (Searle, 1980; Bunge, 1956a and 1956b). *General AI* (also known as *strong AI, artificial general intelligence [AGI], full AI*, or *human-level AI [HLAI]*) aims at tackling *any* task that humans can perform based on NI. General AI is frequently associated with the position that AI actually *is* intelligent – that is, actually thinks, actually has a mind, and so on – therewith raising issues such as machine consciousness, self-awareness, and intentionality, which on their part raise subsequent issues such as machine rights and responsibilities (Russell & Norvig, 2021; Searle, 1980). *Super AI* (also known as *artificial super intelligence*) aims at qualitatively and quantitatively outperforming humans in any task and beyond, allowing the performance of tasks that cannot be completed by humans due to their NI restrictions (e.g., Bostrom, 2014). Beyond the issues raised by general AI, super AI raises further issues such as self-triggered exponential growth ("explosion") of AI or machine dominance over humans (e.g., Bostrom, 2014). At the moment, only narrow AI can be realized, and there is ongoing dispute as to whether general (let alone super) AI *could be* or even *should be* realized (e.g., Russell & Norvig, 2021; Bostrom, 2014; Wang, 2019).

Based on this, *all* current applications of AI in HR necessarily are narrow AI. (For this reason, the above definition of AI shows an explicitly narrow understanding.) The current discussion on AI in HR, however, ignores this at times and (at least implicitly) assumes the existence of non-narrow varieties of AI, for instance in the popular discussion of whether "AI will take over HR" (e.g., Hmoud & Laszlo, 2019; Lin et al., 2018).

Categorization by paradigm
A paradigm designates the basic approach that AI takes to achieve results, while in a rough categorization symbolic and connectionist AI can be distinguished (e.g., Russell & Norvig, 2021). *Symbolic AI* (also known as *good old-fashioned AI [GOFAI]*) is a paradigm within which humans build a model of reality by using symbolic representations such as words or phrases and AI employs or manipulates this symbolic model to achieve results. Since such symbolic models are conventionally built by humans, they are "hand-crafted" and usually effortful. Symbolic AI was the dominant paradigm in earlier phases of AI research, thus explaining the designation of "good old-fashioned AI" (Haugeland, 1985). *Connectionist AI* (also known as *sub-symbolic AI* or *non-symbolic AI*) is a paradigm that uses representations of reality such as pixels or structured data to let AI itself learn a model of reality by connecting known inputs and outputs.

Both AI paradigms are discussed and applied in HR. Knowledge-based search and matching engines in recruiting, which use a symbolic knowledge base ("ontology") for improving search and matching results, constitute an example of current symbolic AI in HR (e.g., Martinez-Gil et al., 2016). HR analytics applications that use artificial neural networks to predict future employee absenteeism constitute an example of current connectionist AI in HR (e.g., Ali Shah et al., 2020). While systematic empirical studies on the adoption of AI paradigms in HR are missing, there are clear indications that applications in HR follow the general trend and a clear majority of HR applications refer to connectionist AI (see section "History and state of AI in HR").

Categorization by convention

Conventions are historically emerged agreements on categorizing AI, as for instance manifested in AI textbooks, journals, conferences, and departments. The background for this categorization thus is historical rather than theoretical (Wang, 2019). Conventional AI fields are rather distinct, are based on different foundations, and use different methods to solve different problems (Russell & Norvig, 2021; Wang, 2019). As a consequence, the different fields do not necessarily collaborate on a regular basis. This fragmentation evidently detracts from a unified discipline of AI (Wang, 2019). Moreover, as they have their own designations, such as "computer vision" or "natural language processing", these fields label themselves as "AI" only if the public opinion on AI happens to be positive (Russell & Norvig, 2021), as is the case at the time of writing this chapter. Though there are conventions of categorizing AI, it comes as no surprise that there is no complete consensus, and that existing categorizations somewhat differ. This brings about the question of which fields to consider. As this handbook aims at a comprehensive consideration of AI in HR, the following fields of AI that show actual or potential relevance in HR are considered: First, this of course includes the well-established "classic" AI fields of *computer vision, knowledge representation, reasoning, machine learning, robotics*, and *natural languages processing* (e.g., Russell & Norvig, 2021). Second, this includes three further fields of AI that show direct relevance for HR. A first additional field refers to *evolutionary computing* (e.g., Eiben & Smith, 2015). Occasionally, evolutionary computing is understood as a sub-category of machine learning (e.g., by Sammut & Webb, 2017); as it however differs from machine learning in its basic approach, it is counted as an AI category *sui generis* by this handbook. A second additional field refers to *affective computing* (e.g., Picard, 2000 and 2015). A third additional field refers to *robotic process automation* (e.g., Czarnecki & Fettke, 2021). By incorporating more and more AI functions, robotic process automation currently just establishes itself as field of AI. While other categorizations by convention are admittedly possible, these fields are seen as relevant and thus are briefly introduced in the following.

Computer vision constitutes a field of AI that aims at mimicking the visual perception of humans (e.g., Russell & Norvig, 2021). Computer vision learns patterns in existing digital images and videos as recorded by cameras and employs these patterns for sensing new digital images or videos. Core objectives refer to "seeing", "understanding" what is seen, and sensing complex visual information (e.g., Russell & Norvig, 2021).

Knowledge representation constitutes a field of AI that aims at mimicking the internal mapping of facts by humans (e.g., Russell & Norvig, 2021). Knowledge representation systematically ascertains intended knowledge and subsequently formally maps it in knowledge bases using knowledge representation techniques such as ontologies. The core objective is providing knowledge bases for reasoning and for solving problems (e.g., Russell & Norvig, 2021).

Reasoning constitutes a field of AI that aims at mimicking the internal thought processes of humans (e.g., Russell & Norvig, 2021). Reasoning employs *reasoners* (also *inference engines*), which infer logical consequences from a set of facts as for instance stored in a knowledge base. Core objectives are providing new information and solving problems (e.g., Russell & Norvig, 2021).

Machine learning constitutes a field of AI that aims at mimicking the acquisition of new knowledge by humans (Jordan & Mitchell, 2015). Machine learning employs existing data to "learn" knowledge inherent in these data and map this knowledge in a model. The overarching objective is improving human and machine performance in a certain application domain based on the provided knowledge (Jordan & Mitchell, 2015).

Robotics constitutes a field of AI that aims at mimicking the physical manipulation of (parts of) the world by humans (e.g., Russell & Norvig, 2021). Robotics employs physical *robots* that use sensors, such as cameras, radars, or lasers, to enable the perception of their environment, and effectors, such as wheels, legs, or grippers, to assert the intended physical forces. The overarching objective is purposefully changing the physical environment (e.g., Russell & Norvig, 2021).

Robotic process automation constitutes a field of AI that aims at mimicking the performance of operational work processes by humans (e.g., Czarnecki & Fettke, 2021). Robotic process automation employs non-physical (i.e., software) *robots* that first "learn" and subsequently automate human process performance, thereby autonomously interacting with operational software, further robots, and humans. The core objective refers to automating (and thus accelerating, improving, and cheapening) process execution (e.g., Czarnecki & Fettke, 2021).

Evolutionary computing constitutes a field of AI that aims at mimicking biological problem solving (and therewith general natural rather than specific human intelligence) for finding an acceptably good solution within a large set of alternatives. It therefore aims at providing heuristics for finding solutions for problems too complex for straightforward mathematical optimization (e.g., Eiben & Smith, 2015).

Natural language processing constitutes a field of AI that aims at mimicking the language-based communication of humans. Natural language processing employs speech recognition, natural language understanding, and natural language generation. Core objectives refer to a direct communication between machines and humans, and beyond to autonomous learning of machines from extensively available written human knowledge (Russell & Norvig, 2021).

Affective computing (also *emotion AI*) constitutes a field of AI that aims at mimicking the human perception and expression of emotion (Picard, 2000 and 2015). Affective computing thus recognizes, reacts to, and simulates human affects such as fear, anger, joy, surprise, or disgust. Core objectives refer to improving the interaction of machines and emotional humans, and thus the respective outcomes of the machine–human interaction (Picard, 2000 and 2015).

It is important to note that the above fields are not neatly separated, autonomous areas of AI research and application, but quite contrarily show complex overlaps and interactions. To give a rough impression of this, Figure 1.1 shows core *supporting* (an AI field supports another AI field by improving and/or expanding it) and core *enabling* (an AI field enables another AI field by transferring methods to a new application domain) *relationships*.

This uncovers the prominent position of machine learning that enables or at least supports diverse other fields (e.g., Jordan & Mitchell, 2015). Machine learning, for instance, enables affective computing by allowing for learning models of human affect based on voice, gesture, and other data, that can be used for automated affect recognition. Machine learning becomes even more prominent if evolutionary computing is categorized as a sub-field of machine learning (as e.g. by Sammut & Webb, 2017). Further supporting relationships refer for instance to reasoning and knowledge representation, since the former regularly employs knowledge bases of the latter as input. Moreover, relationships further uncover robotics process automation and robotics as "composite" AI fields that are based on the support of several other AI fields. As a consequence of such overlaps and interactions, existing applications of AI in HR are not necessarily unambiguously assignable to one field of AI. For instance, HR sentiment analysis (e.g., Costa & Veloso, 2015) can *be* and actually *is* assigned to machine learning, natural language processing, or affective computing. Beyond such categorization ambiguities, there are however true composite applications of AI in HR that rely on the functionalities of multiple AI fields. For instance, physical robots for conducting job interviews (e.g., Inoue et al., 2020) evidently rely on robotics *and* natural language processing.

Supporting or Enabling Category	Supported *or* Enabled Category								
	Computer Vision	Knowledge Representation	Reasoning	Machine Learning	Robotics	Robotic Process Automation	Evolutionary Computing	Natural Language Processing	Affective Computing
Computer Vision						○	○		○
Knowledge Representation			○						
Reasoning									
Machine Learning	●	○				○	○	●	●
Robotics									
Robotic Process Automation									
Evolutionary Computing				○					
Natural Language Processing						○	○		○
Affective Computing						○	○		

○ *Supporting Relationship*   ● *Enabling Relationship*

Figure 1.1   Intertwining of conventional AI categories

All the above AI fields show basic application potentials in HR. Even though systematic empirical insights on the adoption of AI in HR are missing, distinct differences regarding the application of different AI fields are to be expected. Machine learning, for instance, is by now already more broadly applied in HR, while robotics, for instance, is just beginning to be used (see section "History and state of AI in HR").

Categorization by function
Functions designate the categories of NI that AI intends to mimic. In the following, a pragmatic categorization based on different existing categorizations in NI literature (see e.g. the overview on NI theories by Kaufman et al., 2013) and AI literature (see e.g. the categorization by Russell & Norvig, 2021) is employed. As core NI functions mimicked by AI, *cognitive* (i.e.,

perceiving, reasoning, knowing, and *learning), practical* (i.e., *deciding, acting,* and *solving*), and *social* (i.e., *communicating* and *empathizing*) *intelligence functions* can be distinguished.

Perceiving refers to the sensing and interpretation of external signals to represent and understand one's environment. *Reasoning* refers to the internal act of logical thinking to gain knowledge. *Knowing* refers to the internal representation and understanding of issues, such as facts (propositional knowledge) or skills (procedural knowledge). *Learning* refers to acquiring such new knowledge. As perceiving, reasoning, knowing, and learning are interrelated and refer to the acquisition, production, and representation of knowledge they can be categorized as core *cognitive* functions of NI (e.g., Brody, 2004).

Deciding refers to choosing between different alternative actions under uncertainty. *Acting* refers to performing a purposeful activity, be it by active doing or passive tolerating. *Solving* refers to finding the best – or at least an acceptably good – solution among a large set of different alternatives. As deciding, acting, and solving constitute three interrelated functions to realize humans' ideas and objectives to assert themselves, survive, and progress in their environment, they can be categorized as core *practical* functions of NI (e.g., Sternberg, 1985).

Communicating refers to transferring information and meaning in a verbal or non-verbal manner. *Empathizing* refers to recognizing, understanding, and reacting to the emotional states of humans. As communicating and empathizing constitute two important functions of starting, maintaining, and improving social relations they can be categorized as core *social* functions of NI (e.g., Kaufman et al., 2013).

The above functions can be used to categorize applications of AI in HR. However, because of the interrelations of the different functions, AI applications regularly mimic several interacting functions, rather than one isolated function. For instance, as the result of learning is knowing, an AI application that mimics learning necessarily also implies that it mimics knowing. Given the mentioned lack of empirical studies, insights on which functions are relevant in HR applications are missing, yet a broader relevance can be assumed based on existing application examples. For instance, expert systems mimic human knowing and reasoning (e.g., Lawler & Elliot, 1996), machine learning mimics human learning, knowing, deciding, and acting (e.g., Ali Shah et al., 2020), evolutionary scheduling mimics human solving and deciding (e.g., Apornak et al., 2021), robotic process automation mimics human learning, deciding, and acting (e.g., Papageorgiou, 2018), and conversational agents mimic human communicating (e.g., Sheth, 2018).

Integrated categorization
In order to provide an integrated overview, in the following the above criteria are employed together to allow for an integrated categorization – with the exception of the criterion of strength, which has only one existing category ("narrow AI") (see Figure 1.2).

This integrated categorization initially classifies the conventional AI fields according to the primary paradigm they mainly follow. With knowledge representation and reasoning, only two fields refer primarily to symbolic AI, while all other fields refer primarily to connectionist AI. Moreover, the integrated categorization uncovers the primary and secondary functions of NI that AI intends to mimic. The focus of the different fields is shown by their primary function. However, given the interrelations of NI functions, primary functions are regularly accompanied by secondary functions. For instance, machine learning shows the primary function of "learning" new knowledge from existing data. As the resulting knowledge however is mapped in a model, a first secondary function is "knowing". Moreover, as machine learning can learn how to decide based on data on past decisions or to solve a problem based on past solutions, "deciding" and "solving" constitute further secondary functions. Finally, if data contain solutions to problems or tasks, machine learning can learn these solutions, which if automated can be seen as autonomous "acting" as a further secondary function. In this way, different fields show different functional foci, which in sum add up to a broad set of relevant NI functions that can be mimicked by AI.

| | by Paradigm | | by Function | | | | | | | | |
| | Symbolic | Connectionist | cognitive | | | | practical | | | social | |
by Convention			Perceiving	Knowing	Reasoning	Learning	Deciding	Acting	Solving	Communicating	Empathizing
Computer Vision		●	●	○		○					
Knowledge Representation	●			●							
Reasoning	●				●						
Machine Learning		●			○	●	○	○	○		
Robotic Process Automation		●					○	○	●	○	
Robotics		●	○	○			○	○	●	○	○
Evolutionary Computing		●					○	○	●		
Natural Language Processing		●	○	○						●	
Affective Computing		●	○	○							●

● Primary Paradigm or Function   ○ Secondary Function

Figure 1.2   *Integrated categorization of AI*

History and State of AI in HR

History

General AI shows a longer history that is characterized by cyclical ups and downs (e.g., Haenlein & Kaplan, 2019; Delipetrev et al., 2020). With the seasonal metaphors of "AI summer" (phase of positive expectations, attention, and investment) and "AI winter" (phase of negative expectations, disregard, and disinvestments), AI even has its own terminology to name the ups and downs of public opinion (e.g., Haenlein & Kaplan, 2019).

The beginning of AI is regularly dated back to the 1950s. In the subsequent *foundation phase* the basics of AI were researched and developed (e.g., Delipetrev et al., 2020). While there was a certain focus on symbolic AI in this phase, pioneering work in connectionist AI, particularly artificial neural networks, was also done. This led to a first AI summer. However, to the best of our knowledge HR research and practice did not participate and engage in AI in this first phase. By and by the – at times bold – expectations and promises of the foundation phase turned out to be exaggeratedly optimistic, thus bringing about the first AI winter in the 1970s (e.g., Delipetrev et al., 2020; Haenlein & Kaplan, 2019).

In the 1980s, a shift towards expert systems (also knowledge-based systems) induced a *symbolic phase* and led to a second upswing of AI (e.g., Delipetrev et al., 2020; Haenlein & Kaplan, 2019). Based on knowledge representation and reasoning, expert systems aim at mapping the expertise of a domain and use it for providing information and decision support to non-domain experts. Although with a certain delay, HR also participated in this second summer of AI, as diverse attempts to develop "HR expert systems" show (e.g., Chu, 1990; Extejt & Lynn, 1988; Hannon et al., 1990). Again, the high expectations of this second phase were finally not met. Being symbolic and thus "hand-crafted" AI, expert systems require high development effort, are dependent on experts and modellable expertise, and frequently have to be developed company-specific (e.g., Haenlein & Kaplan, 2019). In the wake of these difficulties, expert systems were not broadly adopted in HR and other domains. A new AI winter emerged.

A new upswing, the third by now, started with the dawning of the 2010s. Constantly growing ("big") data stocks and constantly increasing computing power enabled a massive shift to connectionist AI, especially machine learning (e.g., Delipetrev et al., 2020). This *connectionist phase* brought about intriguing improvements in a broad range of domains, such as machine translation, robotic vehicles, or game playing (e.g., Russell & Norvig, 2021), and led to a new AI summer. Like many other domains, HR is participating in this AI upturn, as manifested in broad discussions on and expectations of AI in HR (e.g., Ernst & Young, 2018; IBM, 2018; Oracle, 2019; PWC, 2017), in new AI-enabled HR conceptions such as "big HR data" (e.g., Garcia-Arroyo & Osca, 2021) or "HR analytics" (e.g., Madsen & Slåtten, 2017), and, of course, in practical applications of AI in HR such as natural language processing in recruiting or machine learning in selection.

State

To roughly delineate the current state of AI in HR, the paradigms, categories, and sub-categories of AI in HR are grouped into a life-cycle model of digital technologies (Gartner, 2021). The model assumes that digital technologies pass through ideal-typical phases over time, which are characterized by clearly different levels of expectations of the respective technology. These start with a trigger phase (a technological breakthrough triggers the respective technology), which is followed by a peak phase (overenthusiasm and unrealistic high expectations reinforced by media), a disillusionment phase (overexaggerated expectations cannot be met, expectations plunge again reinforced by media), and finally two recovery phases (ongoing elaboration of the technology allows for a more realistic assessment, improvement, and finally a productive application) (Gartner, 2021). Even though the model is not without critique (e.g., Dedehayir & Steinert, 2016), its application allows for deriving some interesting insights on the current state of AI in HR. As systematic empirical studies of expectations on and adoption of different paradigms, categories, and sub-categories of AI in HR are lacking, the grouping was realized based on expert estimates by the respective authors of this handbook (see Figure 1.3).

First, as already indicated by the above definition and categorization, AI is not a homogeneous block of technology, but decays into different paradigms, categories, and sub-categories. These imply different application potentials, different use cases, and different consequences in HR. A first insight thus refers to the heterogeneity of AI in HR. Consequently, the respective (sub-)categories should be carefully distinguished, rather than lumped together as "AI", therewith employing an attention-grabbing but heterogeneous and, thus, ambiguous concept.

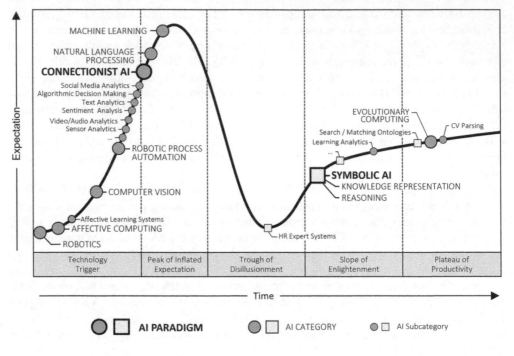

Figure 1.3   Current state of AI in HR

Second, on the paradigmatic level the model clearly predicts and maps the summer and winter phases of AI. The last AI winter referred to symbolic AI and its passage through the phase of disillusionment. Even though not all (sub-)categories of symbolic AI could be transferred into productive applications, there are nevertheless examples where this has been achieved, such as knowledge- (ontology-) based search and matching engines in recruiting (e.g., Martinez-Gil et al., 2016). This is evidence for the model assumption that continued development can lead to productive application of a technology after a disillusionment phase. The current AI summer and the high expectations of AI, contrarily are clearly driven by the connectionist paradigm and its versatile (sub-)categories. A second insight, thus, is that connectionist AI constitutes the dominant paradigm of current interest and expectation, while, however, applications of symbolic AI in HR also exist.

Third, the current high expectations do not apply equally to all categories of connectionist AI but refer mainly to three categories. Machine learning receives the most attention. Based on the current intensive discussion on "HR analytics" and related concepts, diverse forms of machine learning based analytics incur a lot of attention (e.g., Giermindl et al., 2021; Lengnick-Hall et al., 2018). Moreover, natural language processing, in particular in the form of conversational agents ("chat bots"), also gets a lot of attention in professional discussion. With a certain lag, and currently just emerging, robotic process automation is also attracting a growing amount of attention. A third insight, thus, is that the current high expectations of AI mostly refer to three connectionist AI categories.

Fourth, in HR, AI as a whole still constitutes an emerging rather than a mature technology. However, on a sub-category level there are AI applications that have already been adopted productively. This refers to sub-categories such as parsing of CVs in recruiting, knowledge- (ontology-) based search and matching in recruiting, or evolutionary computing in staff rostering. Although these applications are being more frequently adopted, they are not the focus of current attention and therefore constitute "stealth" applications of AI in HR, being mostly "beneath the radar" of current discussions. A fourth insight, thus, is that AI already has some established applications in HR and, thus, is more than just an academic mental exercise.

Fifth, the current discussion additionally largely overlooks potentially relevant AI categories that might become productively applicable in the future. This first refers to *robotics*, which has broad potentials for HR applications, be it as hybrid robots that beyond their primary manufacturing or service tasks (e.g., Steil & Maier, 2017) also perform secondary HR tasks such as performance appraisal, or as proprietary physical robots exclusively built for HR purposes such as job interviews (e.g., Inoue et al., 2020; Nørskov & Ulhøi, 2020). Moreover, as HR deals with humans and, thus, with human emotions, *affective computing* also promises obvious and broad potentials – for instance for identifying and managing employee stress (e.g., Richardson, 2020) or improving the performance of employees by considering and improving their emotional states (e.g., Lee, 2019). Perhaps even more mid-term opportunities (yet also threats) in HR will be offered by *computer vision*, which could be used not only for the prediction and prevention of work accidents (e.g., Liu et al., 2019) but also for the systematic surveillance of employee performance (e.g., Lebedeva et al., 2019) and even general employee behavior (e.g., Alom et al., 2014). A fifth insight, thus, is that there are more relevant categories of AI in HR than recognized and considered in the current discussion.

Sixth, as demonstrated by HR expert systems, there are also setbacks in applying AI in HR. In the wake of the second AI summer ("symbolic phase"), expert systems aimed at providing information and decision support in domains with rather qualitative procedures and expertise. HR, thus, initially seemed an ideal candidate for expert systems, and there were large expectations and promises. Consequently, there were practical attempts to develop and apply HR expert systems (e.g., Hannon et al., 1990). Only the practical attempt of developing HR expert systems uncovered the huge effort of "hand-crafting" knowledge bases and further problems such as the limited availability of experts and knowledge. While there still are current scholarly attempts to capitalize on the expert systems concept in HR (e.g., Angela et al., 2020; Bohlouli et al., 2017), expert systems have so far not been able to get rid of the negative image acquired in the second AI winter, and they currently show low expectations and adoption in HR. A sixth insight therefore is that applications of AI in HR have, of course, no guarantee of success and require the willingness to take certain risks.

Seventh, the model predicts that the current "hype" phase of connectionist AI in HR will be followed by a disillusionment phase, in which expectations literally plunge. As there are evident indicators of overenthusiasm in the current AI discussion, it is important to expect and accept coming disillusionment as a "normal" phase that can be followed by recovery and the productive application of AI (Gartner, 2021). Since it produces and increases *over*enthusiasm, the ongoing active "hyping" of AI in HR – as practiced by certain authors, consultants, and vendors at the time of writing this chapter – is clearly counter-productive. A seventh insight, thus, is that the current enthusiasm will expectedly be followed by disillusionment. The latter needs to be accepted and overcome through ongoing efforts to productively apply AI in HR, rather than precipitately giving up on it and therewith "throwing out the baby with the bathwater".

HANDBOOK OF RESEARCH ON AI IN HR

With the above delineation of AI in HR, an intriguing, relevant, and manifold field of research appears in outline. The current section thus briefly and roughly provides an overview of current research on AI in HR to derive the objectives of this handbook and subsequently introduces its structure and chapters.

Existing Research and Objectives of the Handbook

So far, there is no established community of researchers (let alone established conferences or journals) that is specialized on AI (or one of its fields) in HR. Existing research is scattered over different disciplines and numerous outlets. While recently there have been some serious reviews of this research, these are restricted to specific disciplinary perspectives and boundaries, as well as to specific aspects of AI in HR. Existing reviews refer to:

- generic AI in general HR (Vrontis et al., 2021),
- generic "algorithms" in general HR (Cheng & Hackett, 2021),
- machine learning in
  - general HR (Berhil et al., 2020; Garg et al., 2021; Strohmeier & Piazza, 2013),
  - personality traits prediction (Azucar et al., 2018),
  - learning (e.g., Du et al., 2020; Romero & Ventura, 2020, among others),
  - recruiting (Siting et al., 2012; Freire & Castro, 2021), and
  - turnover prediction (Ekawati, 2019; Zhao et al., 2018),
- affective computing in learning (Yadegaridehkordi et al., 2019),
- computer vision in employee safety (Liu et al., 2019),
- fairness of AI in
  - general HR (Robert et al., 2020) and in
  - recruiting and development (Köchling & Wehner, 2020).

Gaining an overview of current research on AI in HR, thus, is complex and cumbersome. Scanning existing research nevertheless allows some initial insights on its state and allows deriving objectives for the current handbook.

First, existing research appears to be *multi-topical* in the sense that a broad range of topical issues are covered. Besides the technical issues of developing AI artifacts for HR (e.g., Pessach et al., 2020) and the managerial issues of applying AI artifacts in HR (e.g., Black & van Esch, 2020), diverse further topical areas such as the psychological (Hmoud & Várallyai, 2020), ethical (e.g., Loi, 2020), and legal (e.g., Barocas & Selbst, 2016) issues of applying AI in HR are addressed. Such multi-topical research is mandatory: While particularly the managerial issues of applying AI constitute a core domain aspect, it is clear that, first, application issues are dependent on the preceding technical issues of developing appropriate AI artifacts and, second, both development and application issues are inseparably superimposed by ethical, legal, and psychological issues, among others. The current handbook thus aims at an integrated consideration of the relevant issues of AI in HR.

Second, and related to the above, existing research appears to be *multi-disciplinary* in the sense that diverse disciplines participate. Relevant contributions stem for instance from computer science (e.g., Fernández-Martínez & Fernández, 2020), information systems (e.g., Ochmann et al., 2020), law (e.g., Barocas & Selbst, 2016), economics (e.g., Chalfin et al., 2016), ethics (e.g., Loi, 2020), industrial and organizational psychology (e.g., Langer et al., 2019), and human resource management (e.g., Charlwood, 2021), while the last – even though being the core domain discipline – seems not to lead the field. This research is *multi-* yet not *inter*disciplinary, as the different disciplines involved take little or no notice of each other, and do not regularly cooperate. This is particularly true for the two core categories of methodical-technical disciplines, which deal with the development of AI in HR, and managerial-behavioral disciplines, which deal with the subsequent application of AI in HR. While at first glance such a disciplinary division of labor seems obvious and promising, existing research shows that it is not. Methodical-technical disciplines often lack domain expertise. This yields AI artifacts that just do not fit domain opportunities and requirements (e.g., Strohmeier & Piazza, 2013). Vice versa, managerial-behavioral disciplines often lack technical expertise. This yields – at times blatant – misconceptions of AI, leading to both exaggerated hopes and promises and exaggerated concerns and caveats regarding AI in HR. To improve this situation, participating disciplines must close their respective gaps in expertise and/or cooperate with other relevant disciplines on an *inter*disciplinary basis (e.g., König et al., 2020). The current handbook thus aims at interdisciplinary research with the relevant disciplines considering and learning from each other.

Third, existing research appears to be *multi-functional* in the sense that it covers diverse HR functions. Relevant contributions refer for instance to recruiting (e.g., Johnson et al., 2021), selection (e.g., Liem et al., 2018), scheduling (e.g., Apornak et al., 2021), compensation and benefits (e.g., Petruzzellis et al., 2006), learning and development (e.g., Maity, 2019), performance management (e.g., Ahmed et al., 2013), or HR administration (e.g., Chichester & Giffen, 2019). However, following a general pattern of (applying and then) researching new digital technologies in HR (Strohmeier, 2007), recruiting and selection once again appear to constitute the pioneer and focus functions of current research. However, aiming at research that comprehensively and systematically maps the application domain of HR, future research should not only care for HR (sub-)functions that already show certain AI applications, but also and in particular for opening up HR (sub-)functions that so far do *not* show AI applications. The current handbook thus explicitly aims at covering all the (sub-)functions of HR.

Fourth, existing research appears to be *multi-technical* in the sense that it covers *all* conventional AI fields. Relevant contributions refer to reasoning (e.g., Kumar et al., 2014), knowledge representation (e.g., Martinez-Gil et al., 2016), machine learning (e.g., Ali Shah et al., 2020), evolutionary computing (e.g., Apornak et al., 2021), robotics (e.g., Inoue et al., 2020), robotic process automation (e.g., Papageorgiou, 2018), natural language processing (e.g., Sheikh et al., 2019), and affective computing (e.g., Lee, 2019) in HR. However, there appear to be striking differences regarding the intensity and frequency of research in these fields. A massive core focus refers to machine learning – thereby not seldom even *equating* machine learning with overall AI (e.g., Tambe et al., 2019). In comparison, research in other AI fields, such as robotics, computer vision, or reasoning, falls significantly behind. As research on digital technologies generally tends to follow trends in practice (e.g., O'Leary, 2008), current research on AI in HR echoes the current attention patterns of practice. However, as AI in HR is heterogeneous, and as diverse AI fields either show future application potentials or even current applications in HR, the current handbook explicitly aims at a systematic consideration of all AI fields in HR – whether or not they are currently "*en vogue*". Because connectionist AI in HR may be facing a phase of disillusionment and, beyond, connectionist AI as a whole may be facing a new "winter" (e.g., Floridi, 2020), it is necessary that research does *not* follow the volatile ups and downs of public opinion, but instead conducts constant and sober work on what AI can or cannot really do in HR.

Structure and Contributions of the Handbook

Structure
The current handbook consists of four parts:

> Part I: Applications of Artificial Intelligence in Human Resources
> > Part I.1: Applications of Machine Learning in Human Resources
> > Part I.2: Further Applications of Artificial Intelligence in Human Resources
>
> Part II: Consequences of Artificial Intelligence in Human Resources
>
> Part III: Normative Issues of Artificial Intelligence in Human Resources
>
> Part IV: Research Issues of Artificial Intelligence in Human Resources.

Part I deals with actual and potential *applications of AI in HR*. To this end, the above conventional categorization of AI fields is employed for structuring the different chapters. Doing justice to the distinct importance of machine learning (also) in HR, Part II is divided into two sub-parts. A first sub-part (Part I.1) deals with applications of machine learning in HR (CHAPTERS 2–8), while chapters are oriented towards employing machine learning on core HR data types and in core HR functions. A second sub-part (Part I.2) maps further relevant AI fields ranging from HR knowledge representation and reasoning to HR affective computing (CHAPTERS 9–13). This allows mastering the heterogeneity and scope of AI in HR and enables readers to selectively read chapters of individual interest, or else gain a comprehensive overview on AI in HR by working step by step through the different chapters. *Part II* deals with the *consequences of AI in HR*. As AI is seen as a trigger for the digital transformation of HR, a chapter elaborates on the direct transformations of HR to be expected from applying AI in HR and the indirect transformations of HR to be expected from applying AI for augmenting and substituting employees in their work (CHAPTER 14). *Part III* deals with *normative issues of AI in HR*. As ethical, social, and legal issues superimpose the development and the application of AI, four chapters deal with the explainability, fairness, accountability, and legitimacy of AI in HR (CHAPTERS 15–18). *Part IV* deals with *research issues of AI in HR*. As this volume is research oriented, this part refers both to researching AI in HR and to employing AI for research in HR (CHAPTERS 19 and 20).

Given the early state and manifoldness of research on AI in HR, this structure provides interested researchers and practitioners with a comprehensive overview of the field and, beyond, provides interested researchers with multiple starting points for their own work, in the hope that these will be taken up in the future.

Contributions

To provide a general orientation, the following section briefly introduces the chapters of the handbook.

CHAPTER 2 *"HR machine learning – an introduction"* written by me (Stefan Strohmeier) delineates the basics of machine learning by providing a definition and elaborating on the process, algorithms, and data of HR machine learning, as well as on its potentials and challenges. Based on this, the chapter examines research on HR machine learning and derives implications. In doing so, the chapter aims to act as an introduction to Part I.1 and lay the foundations for the following chapters on machine learning on different HR data types and in different HR functions.

CHAPTER 3 *"HR machine learning on text data"* written by Felix Gross deals with machine learning on the specific data category of unstructured HR texts. The chapter delineates basic machine learning technologies for text data and discusses their application possibilities in HR. Based on this, an overview on current research is given and an outlook for future research options and directions based on existing text data potentials is given. As the vast majority of existing data are unstructured and as comprehensive text data exist in HR, this constitutes a first important extension and specialization of HR machine learning.

CHAPTER 4 *"HR machine learning on audio and video data"* written by Carmen Fernández-Martinez and Alberto Fernández deals with machine learning on the specific data categories of unstructured audio and video data. The chapter delineates technologies for video, audio, and multimodal processing. Moreover, common HR use cases are outlined and open research issues and challenges are discussed. As audio and video data are increasingly available and employed, this constitutes a second important extension and specialization of HR machine learning. Since machine learning on video data largely overlaps with "computer vision" the chapter also addresses the latter AI field.

CHAPTER 5 *"HR machine learning on social media data"* written by Jake T. Harrison and Christopher J. Hartwell deals with machine learning on the specific data category of social media data. The chapter discusses the diverse data sources offered by different social media categories and uncovers how machine learning can be applied to capitalize on these data in different areas of HR, such as predicting personality. Based on this, core research directions are derived. As social media is widely adopted and is comprised of diverse data that are potentially valuable for HR, this constitutes a third important extension of machine learning.

CHAPTER 6 *"HR machine learning in recruiting"* written by Sven Laumer, Christian Maier, and Tim Weitzel deals with the opportunities for utilizing machine learning in recruiting, especially to automate the finding and evaluation of candidates. Following an introduction on machine learning and recruiting, the chapter offers a systematic literature review and develops a HR recruiting machine learning model. Based on the insights provided, various future research opportunities are put forward that would improve the usage of machine learning in recruiting, such as broadening the perspective of fit, using common recruiting data sets, and avoiding discrimination.

CHAPTER 7 *"Machine learning in HR staffing"* written by Florian J. Meier and Sven Laumer deals with using machine learning for predicting developments relevant to staffing – in particular for predicting future net employee requirements, reserve employee requirements, future hires, and future attrition of employees. After introducing the staffing function conceptually, the chapter systematically reviews existing research contributions regarding their orientation, objectives, data basis and algorithms employed, achievements, and challenges. Based on this, the consequences for practice and research are discussed.

CHAPTER 8 "*Machine learning in personnel selection*" written by Cornelius J. König and Markus Langer introduces machine learning in the field of selection – therewith tackling a current core HR application of machine learning. After initially introducing the approaches to using machine learning for selection purposes, the chapter reviews existing empirical research on the potentials and the challenges. Based on this, the chapter provides suggestions for future research, in particular research that will provide evidence for the validity of machine learning approaches to selection, explore the human–AI interface, and examine the reactions of users, applicants, and other stakeholders.

CHAPTER 9 "*HR knowledge representation and reasoning*" written by Jorge Martinez-Gil deals with current applications of symbolic AI in HR, thereby treating the interrelated AI fields of knowledge representation and reasoning together. The chapter uncovers how current knowledge bases and reasoners are employed in HR, with a particular focus on searching for candidates and matching them to positions in the process of recruitment. Besides introducing the technical realizations and applications, the chapter elaborates on future tasks such as automating the building of knowledge bases and using them beyond recruiting, for instance in HR development.

CHAPTER 10 "*HR robotic process automation*" written by Peter Fettke and me (Stefan Strohmeier) deals with the application of software robots to further automate the operation of already implemented digital applications in HR and therewith closing existing automation gaps. To this end, the problems that robotic process automation address and the solutions that it offers are described. Based on this application, potentials and challenges of robotic process automation in HR are derived along with the state of current research and implications for future research on the topic.

CHAPTER 11 "*HR evolutionary computing*" written by Lena Wolbeck and Charlotte Köhler deals with the application of algorithms inspired by biological evolution for solving HR problems that are too complex for straightforward optimization. To this end, the chapter gives an overview on the family of evolutionary algorithms. Based on this, various applications of evolutionary algorithms for solving HR problems, in particular in scheduling and re-scheduling employees, are highlighted. Finally, current and future developments in evolutionary computing within HR are reviewed.

CHAPTER 12 "*HR natural language processing – conceptual overview and state of the art on conversational agents in human resources management*" written by Sven Laumer and Stefan Morana deals with natural language processing, in particular conversational agents, as applied in HR. The chapter first introduces the technology of conversational agents. Subsequently, a conceptual overview on the application possibilities of conversational agents in HRM is elaborated. Based on this conceptualization, the chapter reviews relevant research contributions and derives perspectives for future applications and future research on natural language processing and conversational agents in HR.

CHAPTER 13 "*HR affective computing*" written by William J. Becker, Sarah E. Tuskey, and Constant D. Beugré deals with the recognition, stimulation, and expression of human emotion by AI. It elaborates how these functions can be applied to improve and transform HR. Based on an introduction to the current state and likely future of affective computing, the chapter explores several application areas of affective computing in HR, among others in personnel selection and performance management, and derives avenues for future research on affective computing in HR.

CHAPTER 14 *"Consequences of artificial intelligence in human resource management"* written by Maarten Renkema deals with the desired and undesired consequences of applying AI in HR. To this end, it develops a framework that offers a categorization of the effects of AI in HR and of the research on these effects. This allows for discussing the effects of AI and highlighting exemplary research. The chapter thus offers insights into (research on) how HRM can be transformed by achieving desirable consequences, while avoiding undesirable ones, when applying AI in HRM.

CHAPTER 15 *"Explainability of artificial intelligence in human resources"* written by Markus Langer and Cornelius König deals with the problem of the opacity of AI in HR both for humans applying AI in HR and for humans affected by it. The chapter introduces, discusses, and further develops the concept of eXplainable Artificial Intelligence ("XAI") as a means of overcoming the opacity of AI in HR. Based on this, suggestions for future research on XAI in HR are provided. As opacity and incomprehensibility undermine acceptance, and thus the adoption and success of AI in HR, XAI constitutes a crucial requirement of future applications.

CHAPTER 16 *"Fairness of artificial intelligence in human resources – held to a higher standard?"* written by Sandra L. Fisher and Garret N. Howardson deals with the problem of fairness of AI in HR decision making. While the biases of human HR decision makers are well known (and frequently more or less accepted), public opinion is highly sensitive regarding potential discrimination or errors in AI-based decisions. The chapter thus reviews different perspectives on the fairness of AI in HR decision making, discusses differences in judging the fairness of humans and machines, and derives implications for research and practice to contribute to a fairer AI in HR in the future.

CHAPTER 17 *"Accountability of artificial intelligence in human resources"* written by Katharina A. Zweig and Franziska Raudonat deals with the problem of the attributability of AI results in HR. If machines augment or even automate human tasks, in particular decisions, positive as well as negative consequences emerge, leading to the question of who is accountable for them. The chapter thus reviews different approaches to conceptualize accountability of AI in HR, and employs the "long chain of responsibilities" and the "five role model" to discuss responsibilities and uncover the complex accountability structures of developing and applying AI in HR.

CHAPTER 18 *"Legitimacy of artificial intelligence in human resources – the legal framework for using artificial intelligence in human resource management"* written by Kai von Lewinski and Raphael de Barros Fritz deals with the legal regulations of AI in HR. Given the large variety and diversity of relevant regulations worldwide, the chapter employs a three-times-three matrix to structure the field: on one axis, labor law, data protection law, and anti-discrimination law, on the other axis, the technological level, the implementation level, and the application level. This allows the systematic discussion of regulations based on concrete examples of different national regulations. In doing so the chapter offers a structured overview on central legal regulations.

CHAPTER 19 *"Design considerations for conducting artificial intelligence research in human resource management"* written by Richard D. Johnson and Dianna L. Stone deals with approaches to researching AI in HR and provides guidance to researchers regarding their choice of an adequate research design. To this end, quantitative non-experimental design, qualitative non-experimental design, experiments, and quasi-experiments are introduced and evaluated regarding their strengths and weaknesses for research on AI in HR based on illustrative current examples. The chapter thereby offers support for choosing adequate research designs in future research on AI in HR.

CHAPTER 20 *"Employing artificial intelligence in human resources research"* written by Chulin Chen and Richard Landers deals with the potential of AI for use in HR research. Given AI's improved capabilities to detect associations and relationships within data beyond traditional statistical tools, its scholarly applications are on the one hand obvious and promising yet on the other hand imply many challenges regarding validity, reliability, and ethics. Focusing on machine learning, the chapter provides guidance on how AI can be used to advance research on HR topics, reviews existing HR applications, and highlights research gaps and future research directions.

REFERENCES

Ahmed, I., Sultana, I., Paul, S. K., & Azeem, A. (2013). Employee performance evaluation: A fuzzy approach. *International Journal of Productivity and Performance Management, 62*(7), 718–734.

Ali Shah, S. A., Uddin, I., Aziz, F., Ahmad, S., Al-Khasawneh, M. A., & Sharaf, M. (2020). An enhanced deep neural network for predicting workplace absenteeism. *Complexity, 2020*, Article 5843932.

Alom, M. Z., Karim, N. T., Rozario, S. P., Hoque, M. R., Bin, M. R., & Ashraf, S. L. R. (2014). Computer vision-based employee activities analysis. *International Journal of Computer and Information Technology, 3*(5), 942–947.

Angela, O. A., Anichebe, G., Uchenna, U. I., Modesta, E., Ogbene, N., Michael, I. U., & Chukwunweike, A. J. (2020). Advancement in e-recruitment towards expert recruitment system (ERS). *International Journal of Progressive Sciences and Technologies, 23*(2), 471–481.

Apornak, A., Raissi, S., Keramati, A., & Khalili-Damghani, K. (2021). Human resources optimization in hospital emergency using the genetic algorithm approach. *International Journal of Healthcare Management, 14*(4), 1441–1448.

Azucar, D., Marengo, D., & Settanni, M. (2018). Predicting the Big 5 personality traits from digital footprints on social media: A meta-analysis. *Personality and Individual Differences, 124*, 150–159.

Barocas, S., & Selbst, A. D. (2016). Big data's disparate impact. *California Law Review, 104*, 671–732.

Berhil, S., Benlahmar, H., & Labani, N. (2020). A review paper on artificial intelligence at the service of human resources management. *Indonesian Journal of Electrical Engineering and Computer Science, 18*(1), 32–40.

Black, J. S., & van Esch, P. (2020). AI-enabled recruiting: What is it and how should a manager use it? *Business Horizons, 63*(2), 215–226.

Bohlouli, M., Mittas, N., Kakarontzas, G., Theodosiou, T., Angelis, L., & Fathi, M. (2017). Competence assessment as an expert system for human resource management: A mathematical approach. *Expert Systems with Applications, 70*, 83–102.

Bostrom, N. (2014). *Superintelligence: Paths, dangers, strategies.* Oxford University Press.

Brody, N. (2004). What cognitive intelligence is and what emotional intelligence is not. *Psychological Inquiry, 15*, 234–238.

Bunge, M. (1956a). Do computers think? (I). *The British Journal for the Philosophy of Science, 7*(26), 139–148.

Bunge, M. (1956b). Do computers think? (II). *The British Journal for the Philosophy of Science, 7*(27), 212–219.

Chalfin, A., Danieli, O., Hillis, A., Jelveh, Z., Luca, M., Ludwig, J., & Mullainathan, S. (2016). Productivity and selection of human capital with machine learning. *American Economic Review, 106*(5), 124–127.

Charlwood, A. (2021). Artificial intelligence and talent management. In S. Wiblen (Ed.), *Digitalised talent management* (pp. 122–136). Routledge.

Cheng, M. M., & Hackett, R. D. (2021). A critical review of algorithms in HRM: Definition, theory, and practice. *Human Resource Management Review*, *31*(1), Article 100698.

Chichester, M. A., Jr., & Giffen, J. R. (2019). Recruiting in the robot age: Examining potential EEO implications in optimizing recruiting through the use of Artificial Intelligence. *Michigan Bar Journal*, *98*(6), 34–37.

Chu, P. C. (1990). Developing expert systems for human resource planning and management. *Human Resource Planning*, *13*(3), 159–178.

Corea, F. (2019). AI knowledge map: How to classify AI technologies. In *An introduction to data* (pp. 25–29). Springer.

Costa, A., & Veloso, A. (2015). Employee analytics through sentiment analysis. In SBBD. *Proceedings of the 30th Brazilian Symposium on Databases* (pp. 101–112).

Czarnecki, C., & Fettke, P. (2021). Robotic process automation: Positioning, structuring, and framing the work. In C. Czarnecki & P. Fettke (Eds.), *Robotic process automation: Management, technology, applications* (pp. 3–24). De Gruyter.

Dedehayir, O., & Steinert, M. (2016). The hype cycle model: A review and future directions. *Technological Forecasting and Social Change*, *108*, 28–41.

Delipetrev, B., Tsinarakli, C., & Kostic, U. (2020). *Historical evolution of artificial intelligence: Analysis of the three main paradigm shifts in AI*, Publications Office of the European Union.

Du, X., Yang, J., Hung, J. L., & Shelton, B. (2020). Educational data mining: A systematic review of research and emerging trends. *Information Discovery and Delivery*, *4*(48), 225–236.

Eiben, A. E., & Smith, J. E. (2015). *Introduction to evolutionary computing*. Springer.

Ekawati, A. D. (2019). Predictive analytics in employee churn: A systematic literature review. *Journal of Management Information and Decision Sciences*, *22*(4), 387–397.

Ernst & Young (2018). *The new age: Artificial intelligence for human resource opportunities and functions*. https://assets.ey.com/content/dam/ey-sites/ey-com/en_gl/topics/alliances/ey-the-new-age-artificial-intelligence-for-human-resources-010978-18gbl.pdf, accessed January 20, 2021.

Extejt, M. M., & Lynn, M. P. (1988). Expert systems as human resource management decision tools. *Journal of Systems Management*, *39*(11), 10–15.

Fernández-Martínez, C., & Fernández, A. (2020). AI and recruiting software: Ethical and legal implications. *Paladyn. Journal of Behavioral Robotics*, *11*(1), 199–216.

Floridi, L. (2020). AI and its new winter: From myths to realities. *Philosophy and Technology*, *33*, 1–3.

Freire, M. N., & de Castro, L. N. (2021). e-Recruitment recommender systems: A systematic review. *Knowledge and Information Systems*, *63*, 1–20.

Garcia-Arroyo, J., & Osca, A. (2021). Big data contributions to human resource management: A systematic review. *The International Journal of Human Resource Management*, *32*(20), 4337–4362.

Garg, S., Sinha, S., Kar, A. K., & Mani, M. (2021). A review of machine learning applications in human resource management. *International Journal of Productivity and Performance Management*, volume ahead of print.

Gartner (2021), *Gartner hype cycle*. https://www.gartner.com/en/research/methodologies/gartner-hype-cycle, accessed January 20, 2021.

Giermindl, L. M., Strich, F., Christ, O., Leicht-Deobald, U., & Redzepi, A. (2021). The dark sides of people analytics: Reviewing the perils for organisations and employees. *European Journal of Information Systems*, 1–26.

Golstein, B. (2020). *A brief taxonomy of AI*. https://www.sharper.ai/taxonomy-ai/, accessed January 20, 2021.

Haenlein, M., & Kaplan, A. (2019). A brief history of artificial intelligence: On the past, present, and future of artificial intelligence. *California Management Review*, *61*(4), 5–14.

Hannon, J. M., Milkovich, G. T., & Sturman, M. C. (1990). *The feasibility of using expert systems in the management of human resources*. CAHRS Working Paper Series. Paper 384.

Haugeland, J. (1985). *Artificial Intelligence: The very idea*. MIT Press.

Hmoud, B., & Laszlo, V. (2019). Will artificial intelligence take over human resources recruitment and selection? *Network Intelligence Studies*, *7*(13), 21–30.

Hmoud, B., & Várallyai, L. (2020). Artificial intelligence in human resources information systems: Investigating its trust and adoption determinants. *International Journal of Engineering and Management Sciences*, *5*(1), 749–765.

IBM (2018). *The business case for AI in HR*. https://www.ibm.com/downloads/cas/AGKXJX6M, accessed January 20, 2021.

Inoue, K., Hara, K., Lala, D., Yamamoto, K., Nakamura, S., Takanashi, K., & Kawahara, T. (2020). Job interviewer android with elaborate follow-up question generation. In *Proceedings of the 2020 International Conference on Multimodal Interaction* (pp. 324–332).

Johnson, R. D., Stone, D. L., & Lukaszewski, K. M. (2021). The benefits of eHRM and AI for talent acquisition. *Journal of Tourism Futures*, *7*(1), 40–52.

Jordan, M. I., & Mitchell, T. M. (2015). Machine learning: Trends, perspectives, and prospects. *Science*, *349*(6245), 255–260.

Kaufman, J. C., Kaufman, S. B., & Plucker, J. A. (2013). Contemporary theories of intelligence. In D. Reisberg (Ed.), *The Oxford handbook of cognitive psychology* (pp. 811–822). Oxford University Press.

Köchling, A., & Wehner, M. C. (2020). Discriminated by an algorithm: A systematic review of discrimination and fairness by algorithmic decision-making in the context of HR recruitment and HR development. *Business Research*, *13*, 795–848.

König, C. J., Demetriou, A. M., Glock, P., Hiemstra, A. M., Iliescu, D., Ionescu, C., … & Vartholomaios, I. (2020). Some advice for psychologists who want to work with computer scientists on big data. *Personnel Assessment and Decisions*, *6*(1), 17–23.

Kumar, K., Kumar, A., Abhishek, K., & Singh, D. K. (2014, April). Automation of HR interview system using JESS inference engine. In *2014 Fourth IEEE International Conference on Communication Systems and Network Technologies* (pp. 1102–1105).

Langer, M., König, C. J., & Papathanasiou, M. (2019). Highly automated job interviews: Acceptance under the influence of stakes. *International Journal of Selection and Assessment*, *27*(3), 217–234.

Lawler, J. J., & Elliot, R. (1996). Artificial intelligence in HRM: An experimental study of an expert system. *Journal of Management*, *22*(1), 85–111.

Lebedeva, E., Zubkov, A., Bondarenko, D., Rymarenko, K., Nukhaev, M., & Grishchenko, S. (2019). Evaluation of oil workers' performance based on surveillance video. In *International Multi-Conference on Engineering, Computer and Information Sciences (SIBIRCON)* (pp. 432–435). IEEE.

Lee, M. F. (2019). Working place monitoring emotion by affective computing model. In *International Conference on Frontier Computing* (pp. 51–54). Springer.

Lengnick-Hall, M. L., Neely, A. R., & Stone, C. B. (2018). Human resource management in the digital age: Big data, HR analytics and artificial intelligence. In P. N. Melo & C. Machado (Eds.), *Management and technological challenges in the digital age* (pp. 1–30). CRC Press.

Liem, C. C., Langer, M., Demetriou, A., Hiemstra, A. M., Wicaksana, A. S., Born, M. P., & König, C. J. (2018). Psychology meets machine learning: Interdisciplinary perspectives on algorithmic job candidate screening. In H. J. Escalante, S. Escalera, I. Guyon, X. Baró, Y. Güçlütürk, U. Güçlü, & M. van Girven (Eds.), *Explainable and interpretable models in computer vision and machine learning* (pp. 197–253). Springer.

Lin, M., Ling, X., & Chao, C. (2018). Will artificial intelligence take HR's job? *Journal of Modern Commerce*, *8*, 61–63.

Liu, Y., Wang, Y., & Li, X. (2019). Computer vision technologies and machine learning algorithms for construction safety management: A critical review. In *ICCREM 2019: Innovative Construction Project Management and Construction Industrialization* (pp. 67–81). ASCE.

Loi, M. (2020). *People analytics must benefit the people. An ethical analysis of data-driven algorithmic systems in human resources management*. https://algorithmwatch.org/en/wp-content/uploads/2020/03/AlgorithmWatch_AutoHR_Study_Ethics_Loi_2020.pdf accessed April 20, 2020.

Long, D., & Magerko, B. (2020). What is AI literacy? Competencies and design considerations. In *Proceedings of the 2020 CHI Conference on Human Factors in Computing Systems* (pp. 1–16).

Madsen, D. Ø., & Slåtten, K. (2017). The rise of HR analytics: A preliminary exploration. In *Global Conference on Business and Finance Proceedings* (Vol. 12, No. 1, pp. 148–159).

Maity, S. (2019). Identifying opportunities for artificial intelligence in the evolution of training and development practices. *Journal of Management Development*, *38*(8), 651–663.

Martinez-Gil, J., Paoletti, A. L., & Schewe, K. D. (2016, August). A smart approach for matching, learning and querying information from the human resources domain. In *East European Conference on Advances in Databases and Information Systems* (pp. 157–167). Springer.

Monett, D., & Lewis, C. W. (2018). Getting clarity by defining artificial intelligence – a survey. In V. C. Müller (Ed.), *Philosophy and theory of artificial intelligence 2017* (pp. 212–214). Springer.

Monett, D., Lewis, C. W., & Thórisson, K. R. (2020). Introduction to the JAGI special issue "On defining artificial intelligence" – commentaries and author's response. *Journal of Artificial General Intelligence, 11*(2), 1–4.

Nørskov, S., & Ulhøi, J. P. (2020). The use of robots in job interviews. In T. Bondarouk and S. Fisher (Eds.), *Encyclopedia of electronic HRM* (pp. 208–213). De Gruyter.

Ochmann, J., Zilker, S., & Laumer, S. (2020, June). Job seekers' artificial intelligence-related black box concerns. In *Proceedings of the 2020 on Computers and People Research Conference* (pp. 101–102).

O'Leary, D. E. (2008). Gartner's hype cycle and information system research issues. *International Journal of Accounting Information Systems, 9*(4), 240–252.

Oracle (2019). *AI in human resources. The time is now.* https://www.oracle.com/a/ocom/docs/applications/hcm/oracle-ai-in-hr-wp.pdf, accessed January 20, 2021.

Papageorgiou, D. (2018). Transforming the HR function through robotic process automation. *Benefits Quarterly, 34*(2), 27–30.

Pessach, D., Singer, G., Avrahami, D., Ben-Gal, H. C., Shmueli, E., & Ben-Gal, I. (2020). Employees recruitment: A prescriptive analytics approach via machine learning and mathematical programming. *Decision Support Systems, 134*, Article 113290.

Petruzzellis, S., Licchelli, O., Palmisano, I., Bavaro, V., & Palmisano, C. (2006). Employee profiling in the total reward management. In *International Symposium on Methodologies for Intelligent Systems* (pp. 739–744). Springer.

Picard, R. W. (2000). *Affective computing.* MIT Press.

Picard, R. W. (2015). The promise of affective computing. In R. Calvo, S. D'Mello, J. Gratch, & A. Kappas (Eds.), *The Oxford handbook of affective computing* (pp. 11–20). Oxford University Press.

PWC (2017). *Artificial intelligence in HR: A no-brainer.* https://www.pwc.nl/nl/assets/documents/artificial-intelligence-in-hr-a-no-brainer.pdf, accessed January 20, 2021.

Richardson, S. (2020). Affective computing in the modern workplace. *Business Information Review, 37*(2), 78–85.

Robert, L. P., Pierce, C., Marquis, L., Kim, S., & Alahmad, R. (2020). Designing fair AI for managing employees in organizations: A review, critique, and design agenda. *Human–Computer Interaction, 35*(5–6), 545–575.

Romero, C., & Ventura, S. (2020). Educational data mining and learning analytics: An updated survey. *Wiley Interdisciplinary Reviews: Data Mining and Knowledge Discovery, 10*(3), Article e1355.

Russell, S., & Norvig, P. (2021). *Artificial intelligence: A modern approach* (4th ed.). Pearson.

Sammut, C., & Webb, G. I. (Eds.) (2017). *Encyclopedia of machine learning and data mining.* Springer.

Searle, J. R. (1980). Minds, brains, and programs. *Behavioral and Brain Sciences, 3*(3), 417–457.

Sheikh, S. A., Tiwari, V., & Singhal, S. (2019). Generative model chatbot for human resource using deep learning. In *2019 International Conference on Data Science and Engineering (ICDSE)* (pp. 126–132).

Sheth, B. (2018). Chat bots are the new HR managers. *Strategic HR Review, 17*(3), 162–163.

Siting, Z., Wenxing, H., Ning, Z., & Fan, Y. (2012, July). Job recommender systems: A survey. In *2012 7th International Conference on Computer Science & Education (ICCSE)* (pp. 920–924). IEEE.

Steil, J. J., & Maier, G. W. (2017). Robots in the digitalized workplace. In G. Hertel, D. L. Stone, R. D. Johnson, & J. Passmore (Eds.), *The Wiley Blackwell handbook of the psychology of the internet at work* (pp. 403–422). Wiley Blackwell.

Sternberg, R. J. (1985). *Beyond IQ: A triarchic theory of intelligence.* Cambridge University Press.

Strohmeier, S. (2007). Research in e-HRM: Review and implications. *Human Resource Management Review, 17*(1), 19–37.

Strohmeier, S. (2020). Digital HRM: A conceptual clarification. *German Journal of Human Resource Management, 34*(3), 345–365.

Strohmeier, S., & Piazza, F. (2013). Domain driven data mining in human resource management: A review of current research. *Expert Systems with Applications, 40*(7), 2410–2420.

Strohmeier, S., & Piazza, F. (2015). Artificial intelligence techniques in human resource management – a conceptual exploration. In C. Kahraman & S. Çevik Onar (Eds.), *Intelligent techniques in engineering management* (pp. 149–172). Springer.

Tambe, P., Cappelli, P., & Yakubovich, V. (2019). Artificial intelligence in human resources management: Challenges and a path forward. *California Management Review*, *61*(4), 15–42.

Vrontis, D., Christofi, M., Pereira, V., Tarba, S., Makrides, A., & Trichina, E. (2021). Artificial intelligence, robotics, advanced technologies and human resource management: A systematic review. *The International Journal of Human Resource Management*. https://doi.org/10.1080/09585192.2020.1871398

Wang, P. (2019). On defining artificial intelligence. *Journal of Artificial General Intelligence*, *10*(2), 1–37.

Yadegaridehkordi, E., Noor, N. F. B. M., Ayub, M. N. B., Affal, H. B., & Hussin, N. B. (2019). Affective computing in education: A systematic review and future research. *Computers and Education, 142*, Article 103649.

Zhao, Y., Hryniewicki, M. K., Cheng, F., Fu, B., & Zhu, X. (2018). Employee turnover prediction with machine learning: A reliable approach. In *Proceedings of SAI Intelligent Systems Conference* (pp. 737–758). Springer.

PART I

APPLICATIONS OF ARTIFICIAL INTELLIGENCE IN HUMAN RESOURCES

PART I.1

APPLICATIONS OF MACHINE LEARNING IN HUMAN RESOURCES

2.   HR machine learning – an introduction
Stefan Strohmeier

BASICS OF HR MACHINE LEARNING

Machine learning (ML) constitutes a core field of artificial intelligence (AI) that allows for direct applications but also supports and enables further categories of AI such as computer vision, robotics, robotic process automation, or natural language processing (Jordan & Mitchell, 2015; see CHAPTER 1). This section briefly introduces the field by elaborating on the *definition, process, algorithms*, and *data* of ML in HR.

Definition of HR Machine Learning

Beyond HR ML there are further terms such as "data mining" (e.g., Strohmeier & Piazza, 2013), "predictive analytics" (e.g., Jain, 2018), "knowledge discovery in databases" (e.g., Jantan et al., 2009), or "data pattern recognition" (e.g., Strohmeier & Piazza, 2010) that are used in HR. Depending on individually differing definitions, these terms are synonymous or at least largely overlap with "ML". Taken together, the components of these terms can be used to uncover core characteristics and derive a working definition. First, "learning", "discovery", and "recognition" point out a process of acquiring new knowledge. Second, "machine" points out that this knowledge acquisition process is performed automatically by algorithms. Third, "data" and "databases" point out that this knowledge acquisition process is based on data. Fourth, the terms "pattern" and "predictive" uncover that the intended knowledge refers to generalizable regularities in the data, which can be used for predictions. Based on these terminological components the following working definition can be derived: ML designates the *automated acquisition of new knowledge about general regularities based on learning algorithms and data*.

Process of HR Machine Learning

The process of ML refers to the set of timely and logically ordered tasks to be performed for realization. Based on existing general ML process models (cf. the reviews by Azevedo & Santos, 2008 and Mariscal et al., 2010) a reference process of HR ML can be suggested (see Figure 2.1).

As a first task, *domain understanding* refers to acquiring systematic background knowledge on the specific HR task and purpose that an ML application should serve. This knowledge subsequently has to be converted to and described as an ML problem. Creating domain understanding thus implies the development of a *use case*, which is a general idea of which type of algorithm to apply on which type of input data to generate which type of model to fit which type of HR purpose.

As a second task, *data understanding* aims at auditing potential input data (e.g., Abdallah et al., 2017). Auditing is necessary since input data frequently are of secondary nature and thus of unknown characteristics and quality. Understanding data comprises the identification of the format (form of physical provision), the quality (number and kinds of problems), and, in the case of structured data, the level (measurement types and resulting analysis possibilities) and characteristics (distribution, location, dispersion, and binary correlation) of input data (e.g., Abdallah et al., 2017).

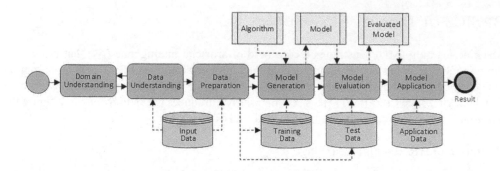

Figure 2.1   Process of HR machine learning

As a third task, *data preparation* refers to manipulating raw input data into a form ready for analysis (e.g., Abdallah et al., 2017). In the case of structured data, this implies numerous activities on the level of data fields (such as the selection, re-coding, cleansing, or transformation of data fields) and of data records (such as the selection, sorting, merging, balancing, or sampling data records). In the case of unstructured data, datatype-specific preparation steps are necessary. Text data, for instance, require tokenization and lemmatization of raw texts, among other steps (see CHAPTER 3). A last sub-task refers to partitioning input data into training data, which are used to generate the model, and test data, which are used to subsequently evaluate the model. This task is frequently lengthy and effortful.

As a fourth task, *model generation* refers to applying an algorithm to training data to generate a model. A model maps the regularities that the algorithm detected in the input data and can thus be used to gain information on new cases. Besides isolated models, sequences of several models that combine different ML functions can also be generated.

As a fifth task, *model evaluation* refers to assessing the quality and thus applicability of the generated model (e.g., Webb, 2017). To this end, there are algorithm-specific quality measures, such as confidence, lift, support, or error rate, among a lot of others. Besides deciding on the applicability of one single model, quality measures can be used to select the best model if different algorithms were applied in parallel to the same problem. To obtain a reliable estimate on the performance of the model on new data, it is important not to employ the training data on which the model was generated but instead employ test data for model evaluation (e.g., Webb, 2017).

As a final, sixth task, *model application* refers to applying the data of one or more new cases to the model to gain information on these new cases and utilize this information in HR management.

The above-described process maps the dominant approach of *"batch ML"*. Batch ML is based on static data, which emerge with longer time intervals, are finite, and are stored persistently before model generation. The process described above is basically also valid for the approach of *"real-time* (also *online*) *ML"*, while there are some differences. Real-time ML is based on stream data, which emerge continuously in very short time intervals, are infinite, and are analyzed on arrival without persistent storage (see section "Data of HR Machine Learning"). In this case, the continuously arriving small data packages are frequently used first to evaluate an already generated model and second to (re-)train and eventually change the model. Due to this "prequential model evaluation" there is no partition between training and test data, while it is anyway assured that the model is tested on data not used for generating the model.

There are different ways to perform this process, but *explicit* and *embedded ML* constitute two core varieties (Strohmeier & Piazza, 2013). An explicit process involves the performance of all the described process steps by HR using a general ML software. An embedded process implies that a software vendor performs the first five process steps and subsequently embeds the evaluated model into an HR-specific software. HR then performs only the last step of model application – simply by entering application data into the software and using the results. Embedded ML therefore is clearly more convenient in terms of effort and requirements (Strohmeier & Piazza, 2013), yet necessarily also much more opaque in terms of process and results (Burrell, 2016).

Algorithms of HR Machine Learning

Algorithms generally denote a sequence of machine-processable instructions to solve a class of problems. By now, there is a large set of ML algorithms (cf. the entries in Sammut & Webb, 2017). To offer an overview, in the following a rough categorization of ML algorithms is provided. The categorization is based on the three interrelated criteria of the *function* (the general purpose of an algorithm), the *generic procedure* (the general method-type of an algorithm), and the *specific procedure* (the concrete method-type of an algorithm). Figure 2.2 renders core (yet *not* all) functions, generic procedures, and specific procedures of HR ML algorithms.

Regarding the *function*, prediction, classification, anomaly detection, segmentation, and association algorithms constitute interrelated core functions. *Prediction algorithms* create a model that predicts unknown future yet also unknown current states or events. Examples refer to predicting future employee turnover numbers (e.g., Strohmeier & Piazza, 2015) or predicting the current suitability of applicants for vacant jobs (e.g., Chien & Chen, 2008). *Classification algorithms* create a model that classifies cases into different predefined classes. Examples refer to classifying applicants into the classes "job hopper" and "non-job hopper" (e.g., Kosylo et al., 2018) or classifying employees into different ordinal performance classes ranging from "needs improvement" to "outstanding" (e.g., Kirimi & Moturi, 2016). Since classification algorithms predict an otherwise unknown class affiliation of a new case, they also provide the function of prediction. Moreover, since classification algorithms allow for classifying cases into the classes "normal" and "abnormal", they additionally allow for anomaly detection. *Anomaly detection algorithms* create a model that identifies single cases significantly differing from the other cases (e.g., Chandola et al., 2017). Examples refer to detecting employee fraud (e.g., Luell, 2010) or detecting performance anomalies (e.g., Lukashin et al., 2019). Since anomaly detection algorithms classify cases into the classes "normal" and "abnormal" and predict the class of "abnormal" cases, they also show the functions of classification and of prediction. *Segmentation algorithms* (also "cluster algorithms") create a model that allows for grouping cases with similar characteristics into groups (e.g., Berkhin, 2006). Examples refer to creating job families by grouping similar job positions together (e.g., Morgeson et al., 2019) or to detecting clusters of learners with different needs regarding learning paths and content (e.g., Zakrzewska, 2009). By detecting deviating clusters with (very) few participants, segmentation algorithms also allow for anomaly detection. *Association algorithms* create a model that allows the prediction of the significant simultaneous or sequential occurrence of several different characteristics of a case, such as recommending learning content to learners (e.g., Vélez-Langs & Caicedo-Castro, 2019) or typical "click sequences" of applicants on recruiting websites (e.g., Strohmeier & Piazza, 2011). Association algorithms additionally allow for prediction since the known existence of a characteristic allows for the prediction further characteristics of this case. The fact that four out of five core ML functions (also) allow for prediction, thereby explains the alternative term of "predictive analytics".

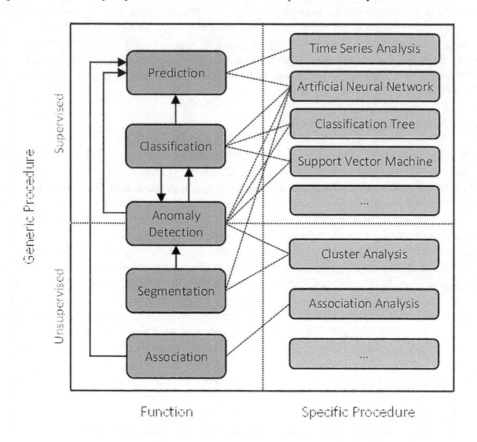

Figure 2.2   Algorithms of HR machine learning (modified from Piazza, 2010)

Regarding the *generic algorithm procedure*, supervised and unsupervised algorithms constitute core categories (e.g., Jordan & Mitchell, 2015). Supervised algorithms learn regularities from known sets of predictor and target data that present the regularity to be learned. "Supervised" thus means that a target is specified and the algorithm is confronted with already known cases. Because of its predictive possibilities, supervised learning regularly represents the more powerful and important category (e.g., Brynjolfsson & Mitchell, 2017). Since the functions of prediction and classification imply the specification of a prediction or classification target and the usage of known pairs of predictor/classifier data and target data, prediction and classification algorithms are supervised algorithms. Since segmentation and association algorithms show no specified target, they are not confronted with known regularities between predictor and targets, and thus are unsupervised algorithms. Since one can use supervised or unsupervised algorithm types, anomaly detection constitutes a hybrid category.

Regarding the *specific algorithm procedure*, times series analysis, artificial neural networks, classification trees, support vector machine, cluster analysis, and association analysis constitute prominent (yet by no means all) categories (e.g., Piazza, 2010). *Time series analysis* designates an algorithm category that analyzes numeric data in timely order to identify regularities, in particular trend and seasonality, to predict future developments (e.g., Keogh, 2017). Time series analysis thus provides the function of prediction. *Artificial neural networks* designate an algorithm category that learns complex quantitative relationships between predictors and targets based on a network of computing units ("artificial neurons"), which are organized in layers. The term "deep learning", which is often erroneously used for ML as a whole, refers to a subset of artificial neural networks that is characterized by numerous ("deep") layers of artificial neurons (e.g., Jordan & Mitchell, 2015). Artificial neural networks allow for prediction and classification, and based on the latter also for anomaly detection. *Classification trees* designate an algorithm category that classifies cases into predefined classes by stepwise identifying predictors for the respective classes (e.g., Fürnkranz, 2017). Classification trees offer the function of classification, therewith including the function of prediction (prediction of a certain class) and anomaly detection (prediction of the class "abnormal"). *Support vector machine* designates an algorithm category that classifies cases into predefined classes by representing known cases as mathematical vectors and searching for hyperplanes that separate different objects, thereby classifying them in different classes. Like classification trees, support vector machines allow for classification, prediction, and anomaly detection. *Cluster analysis* designates an algorithm category that groups cases based on their similarity into groups with similar cases (e.g., Berkhin, 2006). Cluster analysis allows for segmentation and, based on detecting clusters with very few cases, anomaly detection. *Association analysis* designates an algorithm category that searches for sets of characteristics that regularly occur together in each case (e.g., Toivonen, 2017). Association analysis algorithms provide the association function and, based on this, the prediction function.

Data of HR Machine Learning

Data refer to a set of machine-processable binary digits that represent information and are gained by observation, measurement, or recording. For the generation of meaningful models, HR ML crucially depends on suitable input data. While it is often – implicitly – assumed that ML uses secondary input data that already exist, having been generated for other purposes (e.g., Oswald et al., 2020), primary data ascertained explicitly for ML purposes can also be used. Using the structuredness (structured vs. unstructured data) and the motion (static vs. stream data) of data as categorization criteria allows for a simple categorization of input data.

Table 2.1   Data of HR machine learning

		Data Structuredness	
		Structured	Unstructured

Data Motion	**Static**	• Operational HR Data
		  • Payroll
		  • Recruiting
		  • Learning
		  • Performance
		  • …
		• Operational Business Data
		• Open (Public) Data
		• …
			• Employee Documents
			• Application Credentials
			  • Documents
			  • Audios
			  • Videos
			• e-Portfolio Data
			• Learning Objects
			• …

		• Operational HR Data
		  • Time and Attendance Data
		  • Access Data
			• Mails
			• Video Conferences
			• …

		• Gamification Data • …	

	Stream	• Log Data
		  • System Log Data
		  • Learning Log Data
		  • Web Log Data
		• Sensor Data
		  • Mobile Phone Sensors
		  • Wearable Sensors
		  • IoT Sensors
		  • Microchip Sensors
		  • …
		• …
			• Social Media Data
			  • Employer Rating Data
			  • Social Networking Data
			  • (Micro-) Blog Data
			  • Multimedia Sharing Data
			  • …
			• …

Structured data follow a predefined organization into data fields and records, while unstructured data do not show any predefined organization. Static data occur within longer time intervals, are finite, and are of manageable volume, while stream data occur continuously in very short time intervals, are infinite, and, thus, amount to massive volumes (see Table 2.1).

First, *structured static data* constitute an important category of input data (e.g., Piazza, 2010). A major source is the increasing number of different HR system categories ranging from payroll systems to learning management systems with a corresponding larger set of structured data (e.g., Oswald et al., 2020). Since complementing HR-specific data, general business data such as production or sales data related to employees can additionally be used. Open ("public") data, such as labor market data or benchmarking data might constitute a further source of structured static data.

Second, based on methodical advances, *unstructured data* can also be used as input (e.g., Gandomi & Haider, 2015). Text, image, audio, and video data constitute major categories (see CHAPTERS 3 and 4). Since unstructured data regularly represent the prevalent category of existing data, this is an important extension. Examples of unstructured data include employee text documents such as contracts, certificates, or correspondence, stored in document management systems. Moreover, different types of application credentials ranging from text documents to telephone-based interviews also constitute unstructured input data. Similar to this, e-portfolios documenting the qualifications of applicants and employees represent a different type of unstructured data. Finally, learning objects used in digital learning courses also constitute unstructured data.

Third, based on advances in processing power and algorithm development, *stream data* can also be used as an input for HR ML (e.g., Benczúr et al., 2019). In the category of *structured stream data*, access data, which record accesses and leavings, and time management data, which record attendances and absences, can occur as a data stream in larger companies. Moreover, the emerging use of sensors constitutes a further example of structured data streams, with there being a broad set of "sensors" ranging from mobile phones to wearables (e.g., Strohmeier, 2018). Also log data that record the usage of HR systems, the Internet, or learning applications can constitute data streams. In the category of *unstructured stream data*, entries in social media such as employer rating websites, social networking sites, or (micro-) blog sites can constitute data streams (see CHAPTER 5). The categorization of a given data type as "static" or "stream", however, depends on its specific emergence. In particular, HR transaction data might constitute static *or* stream data. For instance, the employee attendance data of smaller corporations might not fulfill the criteria of continuous occurrence in very short time intervals and of massive volumes, and, thus, are static data. Conversely, the employee attendance data of a large global corporation might clearly fulfill these criteria and thus are stream data. Furthermore, stream data can be processed as stream data in real time or as static data in batch. To realize the latter, samples of stream data are taken, persistently stored, and only then analyzed.

In sum, with the possibility to use data of different structuredness and motion, *all* data categories can be used as input for HR ML. Based on the particularities of different input data (sub-)categories, different ML sub-categories such as *text mining* (text data as input; see CHAPTER 3), *process mining* (system log data as input; e.g., Arias et al., 2018), *web mining* (web log data as input; e.g., Strohmeier & Piazza, 2011), *social media mining* (social network-ing data; see CHAPTER 5), and *opinion mining* (employer rating data as input; e.g., Brindha & Santhi, 2012) have emerged.

APPLICATION OF HR MACHINE LEARNING

ML constitutes a core category of AI that can be applied directly in a given domain, yet beyond also constitutes an enabling technology for further AI categories such as computer vision, robotics, or natural language processing (e.g., Jordan & Mitchell, 2015; see CHAPTER 1). This section focuses on *direct* applications of ML in HR and discusses core *potentials* and *challenges*.

Application Potentials of HR Machine Learning

Potentials refer to the abilities to advantageously apply ML in HR; this includes already real-ized current, but also unrealized future, applications. In the following, potentials are briefly discussed on three different levels of abstraction – the general level of mimicking functions of natural intelligence (NI) in HR, the medium level of realizing HR conceptions, and the detail level of realizing concrete HR use cases with ML.

General-level potentials
On the general level of mimicking functions of NI (see CHAPTER 1), ML initially shows the core potential for *learning* and, as an obligatory result of successful learning, *knowing*. The process of using input data and algorithms to generate a model thus can be understood as an artificial learning process and the resulting model as an artificial mapping of knowledge. For instance, ML can be employed for learning and subsequently knowing which criteria differentiate suitable applicants from unsuitable ones. Based on the learning and knowing function, generally tasks related to or based on knowing can be tackled. A prominent managerial task based on knowing is *deciding*. ML can provide knowledge that supports a decision or can even learn to decide based on the data of past human decisions. For instance, ML can learn the criteria that led to the (non-)invitation of applicants. In the same way, knowledge on past solutions of complex problems can be learned to determine an acceptably good solution, thereby *solving* a problem. Moreover, given the close relation of deciding and solving to acting, by automating decisions or solutions ML can also mimic *acting*. For instance, an automated invitation of applicants by an HR system with embedded ML constitutes an action. In sum, while *learning* constitutes its eponymous core function, ML shows the potential of realizing complex sequences of *learning*, *knowing*, *deciding*, *solving*, and *acting* functions in HR.

Conceptional-level potentials
On the medium level of realizing conceptions, with *big HR data (analytics)*, *HR analytics*, and *algorithmic HR decision making* there are three prominent and largely overlapping conceptions directly related to HR ML.

First, as in many domains, *big data (analytics)* is increasingly being discussed in HR (see the review by Garcia-Arroyo & Osca, 2021). Big data are regularly defined by the criteria of large volume, large variety, and high velocity (Laney, 2001). While there is reasonable doubt whether HR reaches the volume-, variety-, and velocity-levels of other domains (Cappelli, 2017), HR increasingly disposes of some unstructured data, which add to data variety and volume, and of some stream data, which add to data velocity and volume (see section "Data of HR Machine Learning" of this chapter and CHAPTERS 3–5). Taken together, these developments can be considered a domain-specific variant of "big data" (Gandomi & Haider, 2015; Strohmeier, 2020b). With the possibility to utilize structured data as well as unstructured and stream data, ML is able to exploit *all* categories of big data. For many sub-categories of big data, such as text data, ML is even the only way of performing a meaningful analysis. Therefore, ML is rightly considered to be an essential facilitator of big HR data analytics (Gandomi & Haider, 2015; Strohmeier, 2020b).

Second, largely overlapping with big HR data (analytics), *HR analytics* constitutes an increasingly discussed concept of transforming HR from an intuition- and experience-based to an information- and evidence-based corporate domain (see the reviews by Ben-Gal, 2019; Margherita, 2021; Marler & Boudreau, 2017; Tursunbayeva et al., 2018). Compared to previous approaches of providing mere descriptive information, the core advancement of HR analytics is regularly seen in its offering of predictive and prescriptive information (e.g., Marler & Boudreau, 2017). Predictive information allows for a proactive HR management that knows, and thus can cope with, risks and opportunities in advance. Prescriptive information is based on predictive information and supports or even automates decisions in HR. For instance, predictive information on the future success of a given HR activity offers prescriptive information on whether or not to conduct this activity. Since prediction is a core function, both information categories of HR analytics are provided and enabled by HR ML (Strohmeier & Piazza, 2010). Therefore, ML is rightly considered to be the core facilitator of HR analytics (e.g., van der Laken, 2018).

Third, largely overlapping with big data (analytics) and HR analytics, *algorithmic HR decision making* (sometimes even *algorithmic HR management*) constitutes a further, currently only just emerging, conception (Strohmeier, 2020a). Algorithmic HR decision making refers to choosing between different alternatives under uncertainty augmented or even automated by algorithms to improve the efficiency and quality of decisions (e.g., Strohmeier, 2020a). Based on the general potentials of augmenting and automating decisions, ML constitutes the core enabling technology of the conception of algorithmic HR decision making as well.

In sum, on a conceptional level, ML must be seen as a trigger and enabler of prominent HR conceptions.

Detail-level potentials

On the detail level of realizing concrete *use cases*, by now there are abundant suggestions in literature (see the reviews by Berhil et al., 2020; Garg et al., 2021; and Strohmeier & Piazza, 2013). While sometimes mere conceptions of use cases are presented, very frequently use cases are concretized by a practical realization of algorithms, models, and sometimes even prototypes of software. Existing use cases cover the entire range of HR tasks, HR data, and ML algorithms. From an *HR task* perspective, there are for instance use cases for recruiting (e.g., Pessach et al., 2020), selection (e.g., Chien & Chen, 2008), retention (e.g., Punnose & Ajit, 2016), performance management (e.g., Kirimi & Moturi, 2016), career management (e.g., Lockamy & Service, 2011), development (e.g., Zakrzewska, 2009), and compensation (e.g., Petruzzellis et al., 2006). From an *HR data* perspective, there are for instance use cases based on structured data (e.g., Jantan et al., 2010), text data (e.g., Jung & Suh, 2019), social media data (e.g., Jere et al., 2017), web-log data (e.g., Strohmeier & Piazza, 2013), and audio and video data (e.g., Fernández-Martínez & Fernández, 2020). From an *ML algorithm* perspective, there are for instance use cases employing supervised ML such as classification trees (e.g., Jantan et al., 2010), artificial neural networks (e.g., Ali Shah et al., 2020), support vector machines (e.g., Liu et al., 2009), and Bayesian networks (e.g., Pessach et al., 2020), as well as use cases employing unsupervised ML such as cluster analysis (e.g., Estrada-Cedeno et al., 2019) and association analysis (e.g., Danping & Jin, 2011). In sum, while existing use cases are of different detailedness and quality, they uncover a very broad and highly differentiated spectrum of concrete application possibilities of ML in HR.

Application Challenges of HR Machine Learning

Application challenges refer to problems of applying ML in HR. In the following, major and interrelated *technical* and *human challenges* are briefly introduced.

Technical challenges

Technical challenges refer to problems in the basic procedural and methodical approach of ML.

First, ML can involve *spuriousness of regularities* (e.g., Calude & Longo, 2017). Using a strictly empirical-inductive approach, ML does not offer explanations for the regularities found. This brings about the possibility of spurious "regularities". For instance, ML might find the regularity that employees who drink alcohol on a regular basis are less effective than employees who do not, while an explanation for this regularity is not offered. A frequent position towards this is that for the purpose of making a prediction the underlying reason for a regularity does not matter; as long as the regularity is stable over time one can use it to make predictions (e.g., Calude & Longo, 2017). In this way, the above regularity could be used for instance in the selection of (anti-alcoholic) applicants. However, a decision on the spuriousness (and thus applicability) of a regularity needs an explanation: If the true explanation is that the physiological effects of alcohol actually reduce the mental and physical performance of humans, the regularity is non-spurious. If, however, the true explanation is that some malicious managers are mistreating their employees, with the parallel yet unrelated consequences of decreased performance and increased alcohol consumption, the regularity is spurious.

Second, ML involves *conservatism of suggestions*. For suggesting future managerial actions ("prescriptive information"), ML regularly needs data on different *alternative managerial actions* (a_1, a_2, a) and *their respective consequences* (c_1, c_2, c). Only based on such data can ML find the type of action that maximizes an intended consequence. For instance, for deciding on a benefit program to improve employee performance, it is necessary to have data on different alternative program designs and their respective performance consequences. Only based on such data can the benefit program design with the best performance consequences be identified. Such data on alternative managerial actions, however, are frequently not available, just because organizations regularly implement just *one* alternative. This evidently excludes the identification of possibly more suitable alternatives. Since these have not been implemented, there is no data available and consequently no possibility for an algorithm to recognize better alternatives. ML thus cannot suggest innovative managerial alternatives that have not already been practiced in the past.

Third, ML can involve *replication of problems*. If input data map unrecognized problems, such as managerial errors, prejudices, or inefficiencies, ML will possibly (learn and) replicate them (e.g., Hagendorff & Wezel, 2019). For instance, when past employee promotion decisions systematically but erroneously preferred technicians for managerial positions, even though non-technicians would be more suited, ML might replicate this error and prefer technicians. An important sub-category of problem replication refers to *discrimination* (see below).

Fourth, ML involves *limitations of accuracy*. In the evaluation phase the accuracy of each ML model is evaluated with quality measures and used only if accepted standards are met (e.g., Webb, 2017). However, "accepted standards" do not imply optimal predictions and subsequent optimal decisions, actions, and solutions. For instance, when using neural networks in applicant pre-selection to predict the classes "suitable applicant" and "unsuitable applicant" an acceptable error rate might be ≤ 5 percent. This means a model is accepted if the share of "false negatives" (applicants that are rejected, even though suitable) and "false positives" (applicants that are invited, even though unsuitable) together do not exceed 5 percent. The prediction of applicant suitability and the subsequent decision on which applicants to invite, thus, are not completely perfect. ML therefore usually cannot provide *optimal* (in the sense of completely error-free) predictions (Brynjolfsson & Mitchell, 2017).

Fifth, ML is confronted with the *unavailability* and *unsuitability of data*. As a first problem, despite the discussion on growing ("big") HR data stocks, the data needed for an envisioned model might not be available, with the consequence that a useful model cannot be generated. The above example of prescriptive information on the design of benefit programs serves as an example. A second and overlapping problem is that data might not be suitable for an envisioned model. This might be the case if data do not show the required veracity due to containing problems such as incorrectness, incompleteness, or biases (e.g., Rubin & Lukoianova, 2014). Moreover, this might be the case if data do not show the needed fit with the respective ML problem. For instance, a model that aims at predicting which applicants will become "good" employees might need other data than just appraisal results to adequately map the complex "good employee" construct (Tambe et al., 2019). Constituting a challenge in its own right, unavailability and unsuitability of input data additionally constitute the reason for the methodical problems of spuriousness, conservativism, replicationism, and inaccuracy, as well as for the ethical-social problems of discrimination and mistreatment. Such problems could be entirely avoided or at least clearly reduced by using "perfect" input data. This uncovers the availability and suitability of input data as being the *core challenge and core bottleneck* of ML in HR (Strohmeier & Piazza, 2013).

Human challenges

Human challenges refer to the ethical, social, and psychological problems of ML regarding the treatment of and the interaction with humans.

First, ML can replicate existing *discrimination of humans* (see CHAPTER 16 and the reviews by Köchling & Wehner, 2020 and Robert et al., 2020). If prejudices in past managerial decisions include inequal treatment, for instance regarding gender, age, or ethnic origin, these prejudices are mapped in the input data and, thus, are potentially replicated by ML (e.g., Barocas & Selbst, 2016). For instance, if female applicants were systematically rejected in pre-selection processes of the past, this pattern might be learned and replicated. Discrimination therefore constitutes an important sub-category of problem replication (see above). There are large efforts to cope with discrimination by ML (see CHAPTER 16).

Second, ML involves a *limited mistreatment*. As uncovered by the "limitation of accuracy", ML usually does not allow for optimal (completely error-free) predictions. However, if ML-based decisions affect humans, the clearly dominant share is treated correctly, while a (very) small share is not. For instance, if an applicant suitability model shows an error rate of 3 percent for the class of "unsuitable applicants", this means that based on the model, 97 percent of rejected applicants are rejected rightly while 3 percent are not ("false negatives"). This evidently represents an unfair treatment of this smaller applicant group. Limited mistreatment therefore is a direct consequence of limited accuracy.

Third, ML is characterized by *opacity of process and results* (Burrell, 2016 and CHAPTER 15). There are three variants of ML opacity (Burrell, 2016): *intentional opacity* occurs in embedded ML when an external software provider does not disclose the data and model underlying the software in order to not reveal their procedures to competitors; *illiterate opacity* results from a widespread lack of ML literacy, not least in the HR domain; and *intrinsic opacity* results from the technical and methodical complexity of algorithms (and resulting models), while algorithm categories differ in their respective level of intrinsic opacity. Opacity is a problem since stakeholders, in particular HR professionals and affected employees, have no information on how an ML result was generated and why a result emerged. Subsumed under the term of "explainable artificial intelligence" ("XAI"), there are large efforts to cope with opacity (see CHAPTER 15).

Fourth, ML can be confronted with the *algorithm aversion* of users (see the review by Burton et al., 2020). Algorithm aversion refers to the reluctance of HR decision makers to use superior but imperfect algorithms (and respectively the models resulting from algorithms and data). Reasons for this reluctance are wrong expectations, a lack of control over decisions, or a lack of incentivization of human users, among others (Burton et al., 2020). This uncovers the augmentation of humans by ML as being challenging, and mere improvements of decision quality are obviously not enough for human acceptance of ML. Moreover, because a lack of human control on decisions is one reason for reluctance, acceptance of automated decisions seems even more difficult. Currently, there are initial suggestions on overcoming algorithm aversion, such as creating algorithm literacy or involving humans in the decision ("human in the loop") (see Burton et al., 2020).

Fifth, ML can imply *violations of privacy* (see the review by Nelson & Olovsson, 2016). Input and application data in HR are frequently personal and confidential data that are ethically, and often also legally, not to be revealed even to the party running the algorithm. For instance, the above example that the regular consumption of alcohol detracts from performance needs truthful data on both individual alcohol consumption and individual performance – personal information that is widely regarded as particularly sensitive. However, since input data can be fully anonymized without restricting the generation and evaluation of models, input data protection can often be ensured by anonymization. If decisions on individuals have to be supported, application data conversely cannot be anonymized. Beyond ethical considerations, data privacy is frequently regulated by nationally differing legal frameworks (see CHAPTER 18). Subsumed under the terms of "privacy by design" and more specifically of "privacy preserving data mining" ("PPDM"), there are large efforts to cope with privacy in ML.

RESEARCH ON HR MACHINE LEARNING

Current research on ML in HR is heterogeneous, patchy, and scattered regarding the disciplines involved, the approaches taken, and the topics investigated. In the following, the current state of, and future implications for, the *disciplines* and *tasks of HR ML research* are discussed.

Disciplines of HR Machine Learning Research

Constituting a multi-disciplinary subject by its very nature, current research on HR ML is scattered over different disciplines. In a rough categorization, *methodical-technical disciplines*, such as applied statistics and computer science, and *managerial-behavioral disciplines*, such as human resource management and industrial and organizational psychology, can be distinguished.

Methodical-technical research started about two decades ago and, in the interim, there has been a larger number of contributions. Aggravating any structured overview, this research does not take place under the common header of "machine learning", but also uses some of its synonyms such as "data mining" or "predictive analytics", or employs diverse algorithm categories or even single algorithms (Strohmeier & Piazza, 2013). Due to disciplinary conventions, such contributions deal with the *development of HR ML*. The objective, generally, is developing technical artifacts of HR ML. These refer particularly to conceptualizing use cases (e.g., Strohmeier & Piazza, 2010), developing algorithms and resulting models for use cases (e.g., Jantan et al., 2010), and sometimes also developing prototypical and even application-ready software for use cases (e.g., Faliagka et al., 2012). Regularly, development of such artifacts constitutes the focus of methodical-technical contributions, while aspects of artifact application, such as relevance, ease of use, or success of the respective artifact in HR, do not constitute core topics in this research (Strohmeier & Piazza, 2013).

Managerial-behavioral research on HR ML started about half a decade ago and there is a smaller but growing set of contributions. However, aggravating any structured overview and neat delineation, this research often does not take place under the header of "machine learning", but uses overlapping concepts such as general "AI" (see the review by Vrontis et al., 2021), "algorithms" (see the review by Cheng & Hackett, 2021), "big data" (see the review by Garcia-Arroyo & Osca, 2021), or "HR analytics" (see the reviews by Ben-Gal, 2019; Margherita, 2021; Marler & Boudreau, 2017; Tursunbayeva et al., 2018). A deeper engagement with this research shows that all these concepts are largely based on ML. A contribution on the ethical challenges of "algorithms" in HR (e.g., Leicht-Deobald et al., 2019), thus, implicitly is also a contribution on the ethical challenges of "ML" in HR. However, while the overlap between the ML concept and the researched concepts is large, it is not absolute. Existing contributions must therefore be checked regularly for their degree of ML relevance. Due to disciplinary conventions, such contributions deal with the *application of ML in HR*, and typically research the potentials (e.g., Tambe et al., 2019), adoption (e.g., Baldegger et al., 2020), acceptance (e.g., van Esch et al., 2019), or challenges (e.g., Leicht-Deobald et al., 2019) of ML. Methodical-technical aspects such as input data, algorithms and models, or more comprehensive use cases and software of HR ML are regularly not considered.

At first glance, this disciplinary division of labor seems to be obvious and appropriate: Methodical-technical research cares for the development of technology while managerial-behavioral research subsequently cares for the application of technology. Both research streams, however, take little to no notice of each other, and so far, interdisciplinary research that integrates both perspectives constitutes an exception (e.g., König et al., 2020). As a consequence, methodical-technical research suffers from "domain distance", while managerial-behavioral research suffers from "technology distance". Methodical-technical researchers regularly lack deep HR domain knowledge. Consequently, methodical-technical research often addresses HR tasks that are imaginary (since not constituting an actual problem of HR practice), trivialized (since oversimplified and thus not supporting HR practice), or solved (since already effectively handled by other methods and thus not in need of further treatment) (Strohmeier & Piazza, 2013). Vice versa, managerial-behavioral researchers regularly lack deep methodical-technical knowledge, and "illiterate opacity" is also a problem in research. ML is frequently not defined, not categorized, and not delineated from further concepts such as overarching AI, algorithms, or "deep learning". Since not (well) understood, researchers frequently treat ML as a "black box", and, depending on their basic attitude, tend to have exaggerated expectations regarding the performance or else exaggerated concerns regarding the harm of ML in HR. Evidently, these respective disciplinary shortcomings undermine the objective of domain- *and* technology-adequate research on HR ML.

Against this backdrop, future research can take two approaches: First, taking a *development-oriented approach*, each disciplinary stream can develop the missing expertise. While eventually promising, it is clear that this approach might turn out to be lengthy and exhausting. Since methodical-technical disciplines regularly lack deep knowledge of their multifarious applications domains, the concept of "*domain-driven*" ML was developed (e.g., Cao, 2010; Strohmeier & Piazza, 2013). Domain-driven ML aims at providing methodical-technical researchers with the necessary domain knowledge by ascertaining domain-specific requirements and constraints from domain experts. Such domain knowledge then allows for offering "actionable" outcomes that meet the expectation of practice (e.g., Cao, 2010). Second, taking a *cooperation-oriented approach*, researchers from both streams can directly cooperate and therewith realize interdisciplinary research (König et al., 2020). As core advantage, such a cooperation combines the domain *and* technology expertise necessary for successful research. Again, however, this requires that researchers in each stream get involved with those in the other stream and respectively learn the terminologies and approaches of the other research stream (König et al., 2020).

Tasks of HR Machine Learning Research

Current research on HR ML uses different research approaches and thus tackles different corresponding tasks. Following methodological considerations, a rough categorization refers to the interrelated tasks of *theoretically explaining, empirically investigating*, and *socio-technically designing* HR ML.

Theoretical explanation of HR machine learning

Theoretical research aims at clarifying general regularities underlying a phenomenon with the basic objective of explaining (and predicting) the phenomenon by means of theory (e.g., Hambrick, 2007). Being a research objective in its own right, theoretical research additionally constitutes the fundament for both empirical and design research.

Following methodological standards, both disciplinary streams should employ theoretical explanations. First, technical-managerial disciplines should employ theoretical explanations of why a suggested ML artifact solves a certain class of HR tasks (e.g., Gregor & Jones, 2007). Despite this standard, methodical-technical research on HR ML, however, is largely atheoretical so far. Following a "proof-of-concept" approach, researchers derive and explain the feasibility of a developed artifact, often not through theory, but through demonstrating it practically by realizing it (Strohmeier & Piazza, 2013). Second, managerial-behavioral disciplines should employ theories for explaining relevant phenomena of HR ML. Despite this standard, managerial-behavioral research is largely atheoretical so far (see e.g. the review of employed theories in Marler & Boudreau, 2017). The few existing theoretical foundations employ well-established micro- and macro-level theories. On the micro level, for instance, the unified theory of acceptance and usage is employed to explain the acceptance of ML based on performance expectancy, effort expectancy, and social influence (e.g., Ochmann & Laumer, 2020). On the macro level, for instance, the resource-based view is employed to explain the success of analytical procedures based on their uniqueness and the value of their results (e.g., Werkhoven, 2017). Current theoretical research on HR ML therefore is in a very early phase. While the phenomenon in need of theory is identified, both the requirements and possibilities to grasp it theoretically are rather untreated.

Against this backdrop, future research has two interrelated tasks: First, research must clarify *requirements*, that is, identify HR ML aspects that require scholarly explanation. To not overlook aspects of HR ML that are relevant yet not covered by existing theories, it is important to start with this (Hambrick, 2007). While this identification constitutes a research task in its own right, examples can be given. A first example refers to the intriguing finding that algorithmic decision making is (slightly) superior to human decision making (see the review by Spengler, 2013), while a second example refers to the finding that decision makers are reluctant to use superior algorithmic models, that is, there is algorithm aversion (see the review by Burton et al., 2020). Both examples evidently refer to interesting and intriguing phenomena that clearly require deeper theoretical understanding and explanation: Understanding the reasons for algorithmic (non-)superiority is essential for any adequate future design and implementation of HR ML; understanding the reasons for decision-maker reluctance is essential for overcoming them and utilizing HR ML at all. In this way, a foreseeably larger set of different relevant HR ML phenomena needs future theoretical treatment. Second, research must clarify *possibilities*, that is, identify and concretize theories suitable for explaining and predicting the respective phenomena. To this end, a larger set of different theories can be evaluated regarding the explanatory contributions they can make. In doing so, particularly theories dealing with *managerial decisions* (e.g., the overview by Peterson, 2017) and *managerial technologies* (e.g., the overview by Dwivedi et al., 2011) are promising. Decision-theoretic approaches are promising, since they offer insights into the existing decision types, the phases of decision making, or the relation of information and decision, as well as the complementarity of humans and ML in decision making. Technology-theoretic approaches are promising, since they deal with aspects such as acceptance, adoption, and success of digital technologies in management, and thus are also directly relevant. Beyond theories of decision making and technology in management, there are of course further theories that could and should be used for founding ML in HR.

Empirical investigation of HR machine learning

Empirical research aims at gaining evidence on HR ML based on experience, and this comprises both quantitative and qualitative empirical approaches.

Following methodological standards, again both disciplinary streams should employ empirical investigations. First, following design research standards, *methodical-technical disciplines* should employ empirical research to evaluate the artifacts developed (e.g., Strohmeier, 2014). Despite this standard, methodical-technical disciplines only infrequently use empirical investigations. As mentioned, researchers frequently follow a "proof-of-concept" approach and demonstrate the feasibility of the suggested artifact by mere realization without empirical evaluations (Strohmeier & Piazza, 2013). Second, managerial-behavioral disciplines should also employ empirical investigations to get descriptive and inferential statistical information on HR ML phenomena. Even though more empirically oriented, managerial-behavioral disciplines so far have not systematically investigated HR ML empirically. Even the better-researched downstream concepts of big HR data analytics and HR analytics have not been well investigated up to now, and there are urgent calls for more empirical work on the subject (e.g., Marler & Boudreau, 2017). As a consequence, there is a systematic lack of empirical knowledge and evidence on HR ML. Even simple descriptive questions such as what share of corporations have already adopted (some kind of) HR ML cannot be sufficiently answered at present. Even less answered are more complex, inferential empirical questions, such as does HR ML actually lead to improved HR decision making.

Against this backdrop, future systematic empirical research on HR ML is necessary to get much needed insights. Initially, methodical-technical disciplines should systematically evaluate their artifacts empirically. It is only based on positive empirical evaluations that ML artifacts can be suggested for practical implementation. Moreover, managerial-behavioral research should systematically empirically investigate the overall phenomenon of HR ML. Since this refers to a large set of different empirical topics, a framework of empirical research on general technology-based HRM can lend a structure and delineate different relevant empirical topics (Strohmeier, 2007). Following the framework, empirical research needs to investigate the contexts, configurations, and consequences of HR ML at the individual and the organizational level. *Contexts* refer to the facilitating or impeding conditions of ML, such as the algorithm literacy of HR professionals on the individual level, or restrictive data privacy legislations on the organizational level. *Configurations* refer to the individual or organizational actors that employ ML, the objectives of these actors regarding ML, the HR activities that are augmented or automated by ML, and the ML technologies that are employed. *Consequences* refer to all desired and undesired, individual and organizational outcomes of ML in HR. Based on the framework, the interactions of contexts, configurations, and consequences also need to be considered. Following these suggestions allows a future systematic empirical investigation and depiction of HR ML. While this evidently implies numerous detailed empirical questions that have yet to be worked out, the overarching empirical core question refers to the *success of HR ML*. The answer to this question will (or at least should) have a significant influence on the future of ML in HR. If general empirical findings on the (slight) superiority of algorithmic decision making (see the overview by Spengler, 2013) can be replicated and confirmed for the HR domain, this provides a strong argument for a broader adoption of ML. In this case, not only a *rational* argument of improving HR's organizational contribution, but also and in particular an *ethical* argument of reducing mistreatment of employees through improved decisions, imply the need to use ML in HR. Conversely, if ML systematically fails to improve HR decision quality, this is a strong argument not to get involved.

Socio-technical design of HR machine learning
Design research refers to solving classes of real-world problems by developing HR ML solutions.

Following methodological standards, again both disciplinary streams should perform design research. First, following design research standards, *methodical technical-disciplines* should employ design research to develop and evaluate ML artifacts that solve practical HR problems (e.g., Hevner et al., 2004). In fact, methodical-technical research deals almost exclusively with the development of artifacts (see the reviews by Berhil et al., 2020; Garg et al., 2021; and Strohmeier & Piazza, 2013). While basically aiming at providing meaningful concrete *use cases* of ML in HR, there are three differently elaborated categories: A first, basic and rather infrequent category refers to mere *conceptions*, which describe yet do not realize a use case (e.g., Strohmeier & Piazza, 2010). A second, more elaborated and very common category refers to *realizations*, which go beyond mere descriptions by implementing algorithms and developing models of a use case (e.g., Pessach et al., 2020). A third, very elaborate yet also very rare category refers to *facilitations*, which go beyond realizations by offering prototypical or even application-ready software for the respective use case (e.g., Faliagka et al., 2012). These use cases basically cover a broader range of HR tasks (with some emphasis on employee selection, performance prediction, and turnover prediction), HR data (with some emphasis on structured static data), and ML algorithms (with clear emphasis on supervised ML). In the meantime, this sums up to a larger number and broader variety of different contributions (see the reviews by Berhil et al., 2020; Garg et al., 2021; Strohmeier & Piazza, 2013). As mentioned, frequently a "proof-of-concept" rather than a fully developed design research approach is chosen. Consequently, both theoretical foundations and empirical evaluations of artifacts are often missing. Moreover, due to the mentioned "domain distance", the use cases provided do not necessarily meet the requirements of the HR domain. This refers in particular to ensuring the domain relevance and success of the use case, the availability of suitable input data, the provision of easy-to-use software for end-users, and the compliance of the use case with ethical and legal standards (Strohmeier & Piazza, 2013). Moreover, use cases are scattered across numerous authors and outlets, and cumulative research that considers and improves earlier approaches on the same or a similar use case is still seldom performed.

Second, also *managerial-behavioral research* should employ design research to offer general solutions to the practical problems of HR (e.g., van Aken, 2005). In clear contrast to methodical-technical research, design research is very limited in managerial-behavioral disciplines (Strohmeier & Piazza, 2013). While there are noteworthy contributions offering use cases (e.g., Campion et al., 2016; Park et al., 2015; Sajjadiani et al., 2019) and recommendations on exploiting the potentials of ML in practical HR (e.g., Oswald et al., 2020; Tambe et al., 2019), design research does not constitute the core focus of managerial-behavioral research.

Against this backdrop, future design research on HR ML should be improved and intensified. Since the respective disciplinary limitations mentioned above are particularly detrimental in design research, an interdisciplinary approach is promising. This allows overcoming the limitations of the so far rather technology-driven use cases, such as lack of domain relevance and practical applicability, and both disciplinary streams would profit from an improved relevance of their scholarly results. Particularly for managerial-behavioral disciplines, design research offers the chance to proactively contribute to the development of ML in HR, instead of reactively awaiting developments in practice and only then researching them *ex post facto*. Moreover, future research would profit from a transition from a mere "proof-of-concept" approach to a fully developed design research approach (e.g., Strohmeier, 2014). Systematically employing founding theories and empirical evaluations will contribute to the quality and applicability of the artifacts developed. In doing so, design research should employ a cumulative approach. Instead of again and again developing new artifacts for the same use case from scratch, new solutions should be based on and improve existing solutions for the respective use case. For instance, employee turnover prediction constitutes a well-established use case of HR ML (see the reviews by Ekawati, 2019 and Zhao et al., 2018; CHAPTER 7) and still there are ample new contributions tackling the topic by offering a new suggestion, which is, however, largely or completely detached from previous suggestions. Evidently, *cumulative* design research, which compares different predicting input data, different algorithms, and different predictive models, shows the potential to improve HR use cases and finally offer solutions that work and thus matter in the real world.

CONCLUSIONS

The ongoing development of ML in the last decades constitutes a much noticed and intriguing phenomenon. As in many other domains, ML shows broad and promising potentials, yet also serious challenges, in the HR domain. Overall, ML offers possibilities to support learning, knowing, deciding, solving, and acting in HR – thereby opening up managerial HR tasks for processing by machines. This might result in profound changes in HR and could even drive its much-cited "digital transformation". Roughly speaking, research on ML in HR so far has been divided between two different research streams that are engaged in technology-driven development issues or else in domain-driven application issues. Given their respective strengths and shortcomings, both are destined to learn from each other and to cooperate in order to manage all the intriguing and challenging issues related to ML in HR.

REFERENCES

Abdallah, Z. S., Du, L., & Webb, G. I. (2017). Data preparation. In C. Sammut & G. I. Webb G. I. (Eds.), *Encyclopedia of machine learning and data mining* (pp.318–327). Springer.

Ali Shah, S. A., Uddin, I., Aziz, F., Ahmad, S., Al-Khasawneh, M. A., & Sharaf, M. (2020). An enhanced deep neural network for predicting workplace absenteeism. *Complexity*, Article 5843932.

Arias, M., Saavedra, R., Marques, M. R., Munoz-Gama, J., & Sepúlveda, M. (2018). Human resource allocation in business process management and process mining. *Management Decision, 56*(2), 376–405.

Azevedo, A. I. R. L., & Santos, M. F. (2008). *KDD, SEMMA and CRISP-DM: A parallel overview.* IADS-DM.

Baldegger, R., Caon, M., & Sadiku, K. (2020). Correlation between entrepreneurial orientation and implementation of AI in human resources management. *Technology Innovation Management Review, 10*(4), 72–79.

Barocas, S., & Selbst, A. D. (2016). Big data's disparate impact. *California Law Review, 104*, 671–732.

Benczúr A. A., Kocsis, L., & Pálovics, R. (2019). Online machine learning algorithms over data streams. In S. Sakr & A. Y. Zomaya (Eds.), *Encyclopedia of big data technologies* (pp. 1199–1207). Springer.

Ben-Gal, H. C. (2019). An ROI-based review of HR analytics: Practical implementation tools. *Personnel Review, 48*(6), 1429–1448.

Berhil, S., Benlahmar, H., & Labani, N. (2020). A review paper on artificial intelligence at the service of human resources management. *Indonesian Journal of Electrical Engineering and Computer Science, 18*(1), 32–40.

Berkhin, P. (2006). A survey of clustering data mining techniques. In J. Kogan, C. Nicholas, & M. Teboulle (Eds.), *Grouping multidimensional data* (pp. 25–71). Springer.

Brindha, G. R., & Santhi, B. (2012). Application of opinion mining technique in talent management. In *2012 International Conference on Management Issues in Emerging Economies (ICMIEE)* (pp. 127–132). IEEE.

Brynjolfsson, E., & Mitchell, T. (2017). What can machine learning do? Workforce implications. *Science, 358*(6370), 1530–1534.

Burrell, J. (2016). How the machine "thinks": Understanding opacity in machine learning algorithms. *Big Data and Society, 3*(1), 1–12.

Burton, J. W., Stein, M. K., & Jensen, T. B. (2020). A systematic review of algorithm aversion in augmented decision making. *Journal of Behavioral Decision Making, 33*(2), 220–239.

Calude, C. S., & Longo, G. (2017). The deluge of spurious correlations in big data. *Foundations of Science, 22*(3), 595–612.

Campion, M. C., Campion, M. A., Campion, E. D., & Reider, M. H. (2016). Initial investigation into computer scoring of candidate essays for personnel selection. *Journal of Applied Psychology, 101*(7), 958–975.

Cao, L. (2010). Domain-driven data mining: Challenges and prospects. *IEEE Transactions on Knowledge and Data Engineering, 22*(6), 755–769.

Cappelli, P. (2017). There's no such thing as big data in HR. *Harvard Business Review.* https://hbr.org/2017/06/theres-no-such-thing-as-big-data-in-hr, accessed January 20, 2021.

Chandola, V., Banerjee, A., & Kumar, V. (2017). Anomaly detection. In C. Sammut & G. I. Webb (Eds.), *Encyclopedia of machine learning and data mining* (pp. 42–56). Springer.

Cheng, M. M., & Hackett, R. D. (2021). A critical review of algorithms in HRM: Definition, theory, and practice. *Human Resource Management Review, 31*(1), Article 100698.

Chien, C. F., & Chen, L. F. (2008). Data mining to improve personnel selection and enhance human capital: A case study in high-technology industry. *Expert Systems with Applications, 34*(1), 280–290.

Danping, Z., & Jin, D. (2011). The data mining of the human resources data warehouse in university based on association rule. *Journal of Computers, 6*(1), 139–146.

Dwivedi, Y. K., Wade, M. R., & Schneeberger, S. L. (Eds.). (2011). *Information systems theory: Explaining and predicting our digital society.* Springer Science & Business Media.

Ekawati, A. D. (2019). Predictive analytics in employee churn: A systematic literature review. *Journal of Management Information and Decision Sciences, 22*(4), 387–397.

Estrada-Cedeno, P., Layedra, F., Castillo-López, G., & Vaca, C. (2019). The good, the bad and the ugly: Workers profiling through clustering analysis. In *2019 Sixth International Conference on eDemocracy and eGovernment (ICEDEG)* (pp. 101–106). IEEE.

Faliagka, E., Ramantas, K., Tsakalidis, A., & Tzimas, G. (2012). Application of machine learning algorithms to an online recruitment system. In *Proceedings of the Seventh International Conference on Internet and Web Applications and Services* (pp. 215–220).

Fernández-Martínez, C., & Fernández, A. (2020). AI and recruiting software: Ethical and legal implications. *Paladyn. Journal of Behavioral Robotics, 11*(1), 199–216.

Fürnkranz, J. (2017). Decision tree. In C. Sammut & G. I. Webb (Eds.), *Encyclopedia of machine learning and data mining* (pp. 330–335). Springer.

Gandomi, A., & Haider, M. (2015). Beyond the hype: Big data concepts, methods, and analytics. *International Journal of Information Management, 35*(2), 137–144.

Garcia-Arroyo, J., & Osca, A. (2021). Big data contributions to human resource management: A systematic review. *The International Journal of Human Resource Management, 32*(20), 4337–4362.

Garg, S., Sinha, S., Kar, A. K., & Mani, M. (2021). A review of machine learning applications in human resource management. *International Journal of Productivity and Performance Management*, volume ahead of print.

Gregor, S., & Jones, D. (2007). The anatomy of a design theory. *Journal of the Association for Information Systems, 8*(5), 312–335.

Hagendorff, T., & Wezel, K. (2019). 15 challenges for AI: Or what AI (currently) can't do. *AI and Society, 35*, 355–365.

Hambrick, D. C. (2007). The field of management's devotion to theory: Too much of a good thing? *Academy of Management Journal, 50*(6), 1346–1352.

Hevner, A. R., March, S. T., Park, J., & Ram, S. (2004). Design science in information systems research. *MIS Quarterly, 28*(1), 75–105.

Jain, N. (2018). Big data and predictive analytics: A facilitator for talent management. In U. M. Munshi & N. Verma (Eds.), *Data science landscape* (pp. 199–204). Springer.

Jantan, H., Hamdan, A. R., & Othman, Z. A. (2009). Managing talent in human resource: A knowledge discovery in database (KDD) approach. *Social and Management Research Journal, 6*(1), 51–61.

Jantan, H., Hamdan, A. R., & Othman, Z. A. (2010). Human talent prediction in HRM using C4.5 classification algorithm. *International Journal on Computer Science and Engineering, 2*(8), 2526–2534.

Jere, S., Jayannavar, L., Ali, A., & Kulkarni, C. (2017, February). Recruitment graph model for hiring unique competencies using social media mining. In *Proceedings of the 9th International Conference on Machine Learning and Computing* (pp. 461–466).

Jordan, M. I., & Mitchell, T. M. (2015). Machine learning: Trends, perspectives, and prospects. *Science, 349*(6245), 255–260.

Jung, Y., & Suh, Y. (2019). Mining the voice of employees: A text mining approach to identifying and analysing job satisfaction factors from online employee reviews. *Decision Support Systems, 123*, Article 113074.

Keogh, E. (2017). Time series. In C. Sammut & G. I. Webb (Eds.), *Encyclopedia of machine learning and data mining* (pp. 1274–1275). Springer.

Kirimi, J. M., & Moturi, C. A. (2016). Application of data mining classification in employee performance prediction. *International Journal of Computer Applications, 146*(7), 28–35.

Köchling, A., & Wehner, M. C. (2020). Discriminated by an algorithm: A systematic review of discrimination and fairness by algorithmic decision-making in the context of HR recruitment and HR development. *Business Research, 13*, 795–848.

König, C. J., Demetriou, A. M., Glock, P., Hiemstra, A. M., Iliescu, D., Ionescu, C., … & Vartholomaios, I. (2020). Some advice for psychologists who want to work with computer scientists on big data. *Personnel Assessment and Decisions, 6*(1), 17–23.

Kosylo, N., Smith, J., Conover, M., Chan, L., Zhang, H., Mei, H., & Cao, R. (2018, August). Artificial intelligence on job-hopping forecasting: AI on job-hopping. In *2018 Portland International Conference on Management of Engineering and Technology (PICMET)* (pp. 1–5). IEEE.

Laney, D. (2001). *3-D data management: Controlling data volume, velocity, and variety.* META Group Research Note.

Leicht-Deobald, U., Busch, T., Schank, C., Weibel, A., Schafheitle, S., Wildhaber, I., & Kasper, G. (2019). The challenges of algorithm-based HR decision-making for personal integrity. *Journal of Business Ethics, 160*(2), 377–392.

Liu, H., Dai, S., & Jiang, H. (2009). Application of rough set and support vector machine in competency assessment. In *Fourth International Conference on Bioinspired Computing, Theories and Applications (BIC-TA '09)* (pp. 1–4).

Lockamy, A., & Service, R. W. (2011). Modelling managerial promotion decisions using Bayesian networks: An exploratory study. *Journal of Management Development, 30,* 381–401.

Luell, J. (2010). *Employee fraud detection under real world conditions* [Doctoral dissertation, University of Zurich].

Lukashin, A., Popov, M., Timofeev, D., & Mikhalev, I. (2019). Employee performance analytics approach based on anomaly detection in user activity. In *Proceedings of the International Scientific Conference on Telecommunications, Computing and Control: TELECCON 2019* (pp. 321–331). Springer Nature.

Margherita, A. (2021). Human resources analytics: A systematization of research topics and directions for future research. *Human Resource Management Review,* in press.

Mariscal, G., Marban, O., & Fernandez, C. (2010). A survey of data mining and knowledge discovery process models and methodologies. *The Knowledge Engineering Review, 25*(2), 137–166.

Marler, J. H., & Boudreau, J. W. (2017). An evidence-based review of HR analytics. *The International Journal of Human Resource Management, 28*(1), 3–26.

Morgeson, F. P., Brannick, M. T., & Levine, E. L. (2019). *Job and work analysis: Methods, research, and applications for human resource management.* Sage Publications.

Nelson, B., & Olovsson, T. (2016, December). Security and privacy for big data: A systematic literature review. In *2016 IEEE International Conference on Big Data* (pp. 3693–3702). IEEE.

Ochmann, J., & Laumer, S. (2020). *AI recruitment: Explaining job seekers' acceptance of automation in human resource management* [Conference presentation]. 15th International Conference on Wirtschaftsinformatik, March 8–11, Potsdam, Germany.

Oswald, F. L., Behrend, T. S., Putka, D. J., & Sinar, E. (2020). Big data in industrial-organizational psychology and human resource management: Forward progress for organizational research and practice. *Annual Review of Organizational Psychology and Organizational Behavior, 7,* 505–533.

Park, G., Schwartz, H. A., Eichstaedt, J. C., Kern, M. L., Kosinski, M., Stillwell, D. J., ... & Seligman, M. E. (2015). Automatic personality assessment through social media language. *Journal of Personality and Social Psychology, 108*(6), 934–952.

Pessach, D., Singer, G., Avrahami, D., Ben-Gal, H. C., Shmueli, E., & Ben-Gal, I. (2020). Employees recruitment: A prescriptive analytics approach via machine learning and mathematical programming. *Decision Support Systems, 134,* Article 113290.

Peterson, M. (2017). *An introduction to decision theory.* Cambridge University Press.

Petruzzellis, S., Licchelli, O., Palmisano, I., Bavaro, V., & Palmisano, C. (2006). Employee profiling in the total reward management. In *International Symposium on Methodologies for Intelligent Systems* (pp. 739–744). Springer.

Piazza, F. (2010). *'Data Mining im Personalmanagement'* (in English: *Data Mining in personell management*). Springer-Gabler.

Punnose, R., & Ajit, P. (2016). Prediction of employee turnover in organizations using machine learning algorithms. *International Journal of Advanced Research in Artificial Intelligence, 5*(9), 22–26.

Robert, L. P., Pierce, C., Marquis, L., Kim, S., & Alahmad, R. (2020). Designing fair AI for managing employees in organizations: A review, critique, and design agenda. *Human–Computer Interaction, 35*(5–6), 545–575.

Rubin, V., & Lukoianova, T. (2014). Veracity roadmap: Is big data objective, truthful and credible? *Advances in Classification Research Online, 24*(1), 4–15.

Sajjadiani, S., Sojourner, A. J., Kammeyer-Mueller, J. D., & Mykerezi, E. (2019). Using machine learning to translate applicant work history into predictors of performance and turnover. *Journal of Applied Psychology, 104*(10), 1207–1225.

Sammut, C., & Webb, G. I. (Eds.) (2017). *Encyclopedia of machine learning and data mining*. Springer.

Spengler, P. M. (2013). Clinical versus mechanical prediction. In J. R. Graham, J. A. Naglieri, & I. B. Weiner (Eds.), *Handbook of psychology: Assessment psychology* (pp. 26–49). John Wiley & Sons.

Strohmeier, S. (2007). Research in e-HRM: Review and implications. *Human Resource Management Review, 17*(1), 19–37.

Strohmeier, S. (2014). Research approaches in e-HRM: Categorisation and analysis. In F. J. Martínez-López (Ed.), *Handbook of strategic e-business management* (pp. 605–632). Springer.

Strohmeier, S. (2018). Smart HRM – a Delphi study on the application and consequences of the internet of things in human resource management. *The International Journal of Human Resource Management*, 1–30.

Strohmeier, S. (2020a). Algorithmic decision making in HRM. In T. Bondarouk & S. Fisher (Eds.), *Encyclopedia of electronic HRM* (pp. 54–60). De Gruyter.

Strohmeier, S. (2020b). Big data in HRM. In T. Bondarouk & S. Fisher (Eds.), *Encyclopedia of electronic HRM* (pp. 259–264). De Gruyter.

Strohmeier, S., & Piazza, F. (2010). Informating HRM: A comparison of data querying and data mining. *International Journal of Business Information Systems, 5*(2), 186–197.

Strohmeier, S., & Piazza, F. (2011). "Web mining" as a novel approach in e-HRM research. In T. V. Bondarouk, H. J. M. Ruël, & J. C. Looise (Eds.), *Electronic HRM in theory and practice* (pp. 41–53). Emerald Group Publishing.

Strohmeier, S., & Piazza, F. (2013). Domain driven data mining in human resource management: A review of current research. *Expert Systems with Applications, 40*(7), 2410–2420.

Strohmeier, S., & Piazza, F. (2015). Artificial intelligence techniques in human resource management – a conceptual exploration. In C. Kahraman & S. Çevik Onar (Eds.), *Intelligent techniques in engineering management* (pp. 149–172). Springer.

Tambe, P., Cappelli, P., & Yakubovich, V. (2019). Artificial intelligence in human resources management: Challenges and a path forward. *California Management Review, 61*(4), 15–42.

Toivonen, H. (2017). Association rule. In C. Sammut & G. I. Webb (Eds.), *Encyclopedia of machine learning and data mining* (pp. 70–71). Springer.

Tursunbayeva, A., Di Lauro, S., & Pagliari, C. (2018). People analytics – a scoping review of conceptual boundaries and value propositions. *International Journal of Information Management, 43*, 224–247.

van Aken, J. E. (2005). Management research as a design science: Articulating the research products of mode 2 knowledge production in management. *British Journal of Management, 16*(1), 19–36.

van der Laken, P. A. (2018). *Data-driven human resource management* [Doctoral dissertation, Tilburgh University].

van Esch, P., Black, J. S., & Ferolie, J. (2019). Marketing AI recruitment: The next phase in job application and selection. *Computers in Human Behavior, 90*, 215–222.

Vélez-Langs, O., & Caicedo-Castro, I. (2019, July). Recommender systems for an enhanced mobile e-learning. In *International Conference on Human–Computer Interaction* (pp. 357–365). Springer.

Vrontis, D., Christofi, M., Pereira, V., Tarba, S., Makrides, A., & Trichina, E. (2021). Artificial intelligence, robotics, advanced technologies and human resource management: A systematic review. *The International Journal of Human Resource Management*, https://doi.org/10.1080/09585192.2020.1871398

Webb, G. I. (2017). Model evaluation. In C. Sammut & G. I. Webb (Eds.), *Encyclopedia of machine learning and data mining* (pp. 844–845). Springer.

Werkhoven, J. (2017). Conceptualizing business value creation through human resource analytics. In *Twenty-Third Americas Conference on Information Systems*.

Zakrzewska, D. (2009). Cluster analysis in personalized e-learning systems. In N. T. Nguyen & E Szczerbicki (Eds.), *Intelligent systems for knowledge management* (pp. 229–250). Springer.

Zhao, Y., Hryniewicki, M. K., Cheng, F., Fu, B., & Zhu, X. (2018). Employee turnover prediction with machine learning: A reliable approach. In *Proceedings of the SAI Intelligent Systems Conference* (pp. 737–758). Springer.

3.   HR machine learning on text data
Felix Gross

INTRODUCTION

For many years, the increasing use of digital technologies has influenced and substantially changed a wide variety of industry sectors and business divisions. Digitalization enables companies to work more efficiently and presents benefits for employers as well as employees. On the other hand, the use of digital technologies results in an immense amount of data. In the environment of a company, for example, this can be customer data, supplier data, or production data, but also employee data in the field of human resources. All these different types of data have in common that they can contain valuable information for a company, which can be identified by viewing, comparing, and analyzing the data stocks. A manual evaluation is not usually practicable, so the knowledge must be provided by other digital technologies such as machine learning, a core category of artificial intelligence (Alpaydin, 2020). Usually, the term *machine learning* is associated with structured data, both in the scientific literature and in practical applications. Such structured data allow for a relatively uncomplicated and efficient recognition and interpretation of patterns in the databases using machine learning algorithms (Fayyad, Piatetsky-Shapiro, & Smyth, 1996). However, the share of this structured data in the total worldwide data stock is comparatively small. Only about 15–20 percent of all data is available in a structured form, whereas the vast majority has no particular structure (Hotho, Nürnberger, & Paaß, 2005).

A core category of such unstructured data is text data. Text data in this context refers to a collection of written texts that are, for example, not stored in a database with fixed schemas. Due to the lack of structure, it is much more difficult to apply standardized algorithms of machine learning to these data. However, by adapting the algorithms and by preparing and transforming the data accordingly, it is possible to analyze unstructured text data, recognize patterns, and, thus, retrieve information and knowledge. Following the term *data mining*, which describes pattern recognition with machine learning algorithms in structured data sets, the application of machine learning algorithms to text data is usually called *text mining* (Mehler & Wolff, 2005). Other terms used synonymously, though less frequently, are *text analytics*, *text data mining*, and *textual data mining* (Hotho, Nürnberger, & Paaß, 2005; Banu & Chitra, 2015). Following the definition of machine learning (see CHAPTER 2), however, in this chapter the term *machine learning on text data* will be used synonymously for the above-mentioned concepts.

Machine learning on text data is not predestined for a specific application context and can basically be applied domain-independently (Aggarwal & Zhai, 2012a). For this reason, it can also be applied to text data in HR. Textual data can be found in numerous business processes in the HR department. Just to name a few examples, applicant documents, employee files, job references, or employee evaluations all contain useful information that can – in principle – be analyzed by machine learning algorithms. The aim of this chapter is to give a systematic overview on this topic. In particular, basic machine learning technologies for text data are presented, the current state of research along with the practical application possibilities of these methods in the HR domain is discussed, and an outlook for future research options and directions is given. The rest of the chapter is structured as follows. The second section deals with the basics of machine learning on text data. Basic terms, the technological basis, typical procedures, algorithms, and objectives are explained. The third section explains the current state of research and discusses practical application scenarios of machine learning on text data in HR. Based on the identified shortcomings, in the fourth section future research possibilities are drawn.

BASICS OF MACHINE LEARNING ON TEXT DATA

Definition of Machine Learning on Text Data

As there is no generally accepted definition for the term *machine learning on text data* or its synonyms, they are defined differently depending on the point of view. The definitions often refer to the field of *knowledge discovery and data mining*, so that machine learning on text data can be characterized as a largely automated process for discovering patterns and, thus, for discovering knowledge in textual data (Aggarwal & Zhai, 2012a; Goetz, Piazza, & Bodendorf, 2019; Mehler & Wolff, 2005).

Due to the similarities with machine learning on structured data, this research area is often regarded as the origin of machine learning on text data (Gupta & Lehal, 2009). However, despite the similar process, machine learning on text data falls back on a more extensive technological basis for data analysis. The necessity of specific preparation of the unstructured data basis for the application of algorithms alone requires the recourse to other research areas such as linguistic methods, for example natural language processing. Since the automated recognition of texts by computer-aided systems in a broader sense was already possible before the emergence of the machine learning research field (Hotho, Nürnberger, & Paaß, 2005), the older research field of information retrieval, which deals with the retrieval and provision of text documents in data stocks, can also be regarded as an origin of machine learning on text data (Mehler & Wolff, 2005). Information retrieval, however, focuses on providing access to information rather than on finding patterns in large text corpora (Aggarwal & Zhai, 2012a). It is undisputed, though, that machine learning on text data is based on different fields of research and is therefore highly interdisciplinary (Aggarwal & Zhai, 2012a). Apart from linguistic methods and information retrieval, the research area also heavily relies on statistical basics and methods of information extraction (Banu & Chitra, 2015).

Process of Machine Learning on Text Data

The process to achieve the overall goal of finding patterns in text data is basically the same as the generic machine learning process for structured data (for a detailed description of this process see CHAPTER 2). Once an understanding of the data has been attained, the data must be suitably prepared, after which they can be subjected to an analysis algorithm and, thus, evaluated in terms of content (Mehler & Wolff, 2005). The data preparation component is, however, particularly important and differs from the standard process. Text data are much noisier than structured data and therefore require proprietary preparation methods. In general, raw text input data first have to be transformed into a structured form so that they can be interpreted by algorithms that are derived from machine learning on structured data (Verma, 2017).

Data Input for Machine Learning on Text Data

The input data for machine learning on text data are usually available in completely different forms. For example, there can be fragments from a database, text, or PDF files, but in the field of web mining, there can also be websites and social media postings (e.g. for sentiment analysis, Chaturvedi et al., 2018). As far as the HR domain is concerned, the spectrum covers all the aforementioned categories and ranges from applicant documents such as résumés, cover letters, and data from professional social networks to job references, employee evaluations, and e-learning documents. Due to their individual characteristics, the respective data sources must be collected differently, for example by using parsing algorithms (e.g. optical character recognition, Smith, 2007) or application programming interfaces (APIs). Each collected fragment, file, or posting then represents a unit in the raw data for the analysis. The different units are called *documents*. The entire collection, in which the patterns should be found, constitutes the *document corpus* (Feinerer, 2008). In most cases, the document corpus consists of a fixed number of documents that are arranged before the analysis; thus the data is static. However, many applications create continuous streams of data (see CHAPTER 2). The pattern recognition task has thus to be performed continuously as well, since new text data come in. The general idea of pattern recognition does not change with this approach; however, text data streams are more challenging to mine (Aggarwal & Zhai, 2012a). No matter whether the documents are collected continuously or a fixed number of documents is available, after collecting the raw data, the actual data preparation must be applied to these documents.

Data Preparation for Machine Learning on Text Data

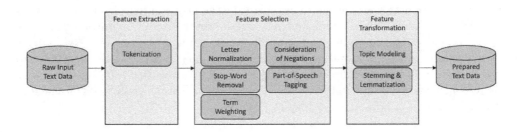

Figure 3.1   Preparation of text data

As mentioned, machine learning on text relies on an extensive number of preparation methods. Data preparation refers to steps to manipulate raw unstructured input data in such a way as to prepare it for the application of machine learning algorithms. The general goal of this process step is to implement a structure within the text documents, which is necessary to conduct analyses with machine learning algorithms (Verma, 2017). Figure 3.1 shows the different categories of preparation methods for text data. Apart from these specific methods, standard data preparation methods such as partitioning, filtering, and so on may be applied to the document corpus.

The proposed order of the different steps is not mandatory and can be altered. Usually though, the first step consists of *tokenization* (Camacho-Collados & Pilehvar, 2018). During this relatively trivial step, the texts in the documents are divided into single units. In general, a unit reflects a single word (in this context called *token* or *feature*) and is extracted by automatically recognizing blank spaces and punctuation marks (Angiani et al., 2016). As a result, each text is thus placed into a multidimensional vector space, in which each different word represents a dimension. This *vector space model* provides the basis for further analysis of a text collection and already gives the texts a basic structure (Uysal & Gunal, 2014).

There are two general approaches to representing the structure of a text. In the *bag-of-words* approach, each individual word in the sequence is considered detached from its position in the text, whereas in the *string-of-words* approach, the sequence of words within the texts is still considered (Aggarwal & Zhai, 2012a). The latter approach therefore conserves more information, but is more complex. The problem in both cases is that each text contains a large number of different words, resulting in an enormous number of dimensions that can no longer be processed meaningfully (Ravi & Ravi, 2015). The essential goal of further data preparation is therefore, in addition to structuring, a reduction of dimensionality to ensure an effective reduction of entropy and complexity (Angiani et al., 2016).

This can be achieved in a simple form by *letter normalization*. For this purpose, all words are transformed into lower case. Since the system then no longer differentiates between uppercase and lowercase letters, several words that were previously treated differently now represent the same dimension. However, this transformation can also increase ambiguity and, therefore, cause information to get lost (Camacho-Collados & Pilehvar, 2018; Denny & Spirling, 2018). In many languages, there is a semantic difference between words, depending on whether they are written in lower case or upper case. Therefore, as with all other methods of text data preparation, it is not possible to make a blanket judgment about whether a method should be applied to the raw data (Aggarwal, 2018). This must be done according to the context of the analysis. Apart from simple letter normalization, words can also be normalized in the sense of unifying words that are written in different ways, for example due to wrong or informal spelling (e.g. cool vs. coooool, 4 u vs. for you). Similarly, emoticons can be transformed to their corresponding sentiment (Angiani et al., 2016).

Part-of-speech tagging enables the automated annotation of words and allocation to their parts of speech. The goal is to assign the correct word type to each word based on its definition and its position in the sentence, depending on the context (Kumar & Ravi, 2016). For example, verbs are further distinguished as to whether they are present in the infinitive or in a conjugated form. In the same way, the predecessors and successors of a word are taken into account in order to be able to deduce the most probable part of speech based on the sentence position (Brill, 1992). In this way, a deeper understanding of the text is possible. Obviously, part-of-speech tagging is thus dependent on the language of the documents. Therefore, for each language a suitable tag set has to be used, in which the data for the recognition of the parts of speech are stored (Schmid, 1999).

Another important operation during data preparation is *stop-word removal*. Stop words include all those words that are very frequently used in a language but which do not provide essential information for the content (Denny & Spirling, 2018). These include, among others, pronouns, conjunctions, prepositions, and articles. They are removed by applying various methods, such as list-based methods (e.g. table look up), which compare the documents with a prepared lexicon containing the corresponding stop words (Kadhim, 2018). Similarly, rule-based cleaning methods can be applied to other terms to remove hyphens, special characters, URLs, hashtags, or mentions, especially when analyzing data from social media sources (Angiani et al., 2016; Denny & Spirling, 2018).

Another major problem in the structuring of text data is the *consideration of negations*. If the words are considered independently of their order in the text, negations may be lost. For example, if an applicant states in his/her cover letter "I have no car", then if the word "car" is considered independently, an algorithm could conclude that the applicant owns a car because the word in question appears in the text. To avoid these misunderstandings, sequences of multiple tokens with the length n, so-called *n-grams*, are often formed as features instead of individual words (Denny & Spirling, 2018). In the above example, two-token sequences would include the combination "no car", which correctly reflects the actual situation. Also, multiword expressions that cannot sensibly be interpreted individually (e.g. human resources) can be considered as single units for better model training (Camacho-Collados & Pilehvar, 2018).

Feature selection can also be achieved with the help of various *weighting and threshold procedures*. These have their origin in information retrieval and are used there to measure similarities between a keyword and the words in the documents to be searched (Salton & Buckley, 1987). This idea can also be applied to determine the similarity between documents and thus measure the importance of features in the documents. The most common method is the frequency-based *TF-IDF* method, which relates the frequency of a term (TF) to the inverse document frequency (IDF). Term frequency refers to the number of times a term appears in a text document. Inverse document frequency measures how specific a term is for the whole document corpora. Thus, a numerical value can be assigned to each individual term (or feature), which measures the significance within the document collection. Features that fall below a specified threshold value are then discarded (Salton & Buckley, 1987).

A somewhat more complex concept for dimension reduction is the so-called *feature transformation*. The basic idea is to combine several semantically similar features in a group on a conceptual level in order to apply the algorithm to the generated groups and not to the (much larger number of) individual features. The new features are defined as a functional representation of the original features (Aggarwal & Zhai, 2012b). Since the groups thus represent topic complexes, this is also referred to as *topic modeling* (Alghamdi & Alfalqi, 2015). Topic modeling during the feature transformation step can be carried out both in supervised form in the sense of classification with predefined classes and in unsupervised form in the sense of clustering, with the latter being the more common variant. Topic modeling can reduce undesirable effects such as synonymy and polysemy, so that semantics can be better taken into account when clustering or classifying documents (Crain et al., 2012). However, through this aggregation, information can get lost. A possibility to avoid this dilemma is therefore to combine the group features that have been created with the original features for use in later analyses (Aggarwal & Zhai, 2012b).

The *stemming* and *lemmatization* step has a similar purpose. In this step, the words in the documents are transformed in such a way that they are traced back to their stem, for example by removing suffixes or unifying singular and plural. For example, the terms "go", "goes", and "going" are all reduced to the word stem "go" in order to further reduce dimensionality (Angiani et al., 2016; Kadhim, 2018). In this case, too, various methods analogous to stop-word removal are common. Usually, stemming and lemmatization do not influence the meaning of the considered terms. However, the methods can sometimes reduce terms with different meanings to the same dimension (Denny & Spirling, 2018). For example, if the words "employer" and "employee" are reduced to the stem "employ", ambiguity may occur.

Tasks of Machine Learning on Text Data

After conducting the data preparation steps, the actual algorithm is applied to the processed text data. Typically, four major groups of tasks can be distinguished. These are clustering as an unsupervised learning method and classification as the supervised counterpart, both derived from machine learning on structured data, as well as text-specific analyses such as information extraction from text data and summarization of text documents. In addition, further sub-areas of the aforementioned tasks can be distinguished (for a detailed overview see Aggarwal, 2018), but these are essentially based on the four groups mentioned and are therefore dealt with within these sections. Because of its great importance and the broad field of research, a separate section is however devoted to sentiment analysis (see Figure 3.2).

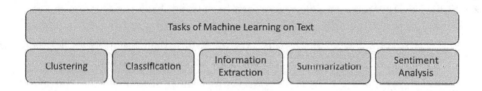

Figure 3.2   *Tasks of machine learning on text data*

Clustering of text data

Clustering refers to the problem of finding similar groups of objects in data stocks (Aggarwal & Zhai, 2012b). The analysis is an unsupervised learning approach and therefore does not necessarily require any dedicated training data (Aggarwal & Zhai, 2012a). Clustering fulfills various purposes in the analysis of text data. On the one hand, grouping makes it easier to find documents with specific content, and on the other hand, clustering also provides a form of content summary of text documents. In addition, clustering can also be used as a preliminary stage to improve results in the context of classification (Aggarwal & Zhai, 2012b). In general, different clustering algorithms can be applied to text data. The goal is to create groups of documents with similar content. Often, procedures derived from machine learning on structured data are used, including *hierarchical* and *partitioning clustering algorithms*. In both cases, a distance function is used to determine the similarity between documents (Aggarwal & Zhai, 2012b). Variants of the algorithms can also be used to cluster streaming text data in real time (Zhong, 2005).

Another approach extends clustering to two levels. In *word- and phrase-based clustering*, clusters are formed within documents at the feature level, which in turn are used to find clusters of documents (Aggarwal & Zhai, 2012b). To find relevant clusters at the feature level, the technique of frequent pattern mining is used. In the context of text data, this means that sets of frequently occurring terms and combinations of terms are formed as clusters. Each cluster is then assigned those documents that contain this term set (Beil, Ester, & Xu, 2002). If the basis is not the bag-of-words but the string-of-words approach, the procedure is referred to as *frequent phrases*, since the sequence of the terms in the documents is observed accordingly (Zamir et al., 1997). If clusters are formed simultaneously on both levels, this is also referred to as *co-clustering*. Since word and document clusters are often closely related, a combination of both levels facilitates the finding of clusters in a document corpus (Dhillon, Mallela, & Modha, 2003).

Most of the methods have in common that they work deterministically. A document is therefore either assigned to a cluster or not. This results in a clear separation between the individual groups. In terms of content, however, this separation is often not correct, since a single document can cover several topics and would therefore have to be assigned to several clusters. For example, in a recruiting process, an unsolicited application may not be assigned to one specific position, but could in principle fit several. Accordingly, the application should be assigned to both (thematically different) groups. *Probabilistic clustering* solves this problem by assigning each document a probability of belonging to a (thematic) cluster (Aggarwal & Zhai, 2012b). This topic modeling approach has already been presented in the context of feature transformation. In contrast to the data preparation step, clusters are not formed on the feature level within the documents for dimension reduction, but the documents themselves are grouped (Crain et al., 2012).

Classification of text data
Text classification enables the possibility to categorize documents into predefined classes and based on existing knowledge. Known correlations between the occurrence of features in the documents and the class affiliation of the documents are used to assign other documents for which the class affiliation is not known to an appropriate class based on their properties. To determine the properties of the documents, again their features are used (Niharika, Latha, & Lavanya, 2012). Text classification is often used when documents are to be filtered, for example for spam detection in e-mails (Niharika, Latha, & Lavanya, 2012) or for ranking suitable and unsuitable candidates in a staff selection process (e.g. Kessler et al., 2009).

Regarding the technical possibilities of text classification, a wide range of methods is available. These are based on the assumption that the text data have been structured within the data preparation step to such an extent that classical machine learning algorithms can be applied to the documents. In principle, almost all classification algorithms can be applied to preprocessed text data (Aggarwal & Zhai, 2012c). This especially includes *neural networks*, which can process very noisy data sets very well, a core advantage in machine learning on text data. For the end user, however, the underlying processes are often difficult to understand (Niharika, Latha, & Lavanya, 2012). *Vector-based classifiers* are also widely used in machine learning on text data, for example support vector machines (SVMs, Niharika, Latha, & Lavanya, 2012). *Decision trees* divide the documents into ever smaller partitions in a hierarchical approach. Each individual partition is characterized by specific properties, which in turn result from the features of the documents assigned to it (Aggarwal, Singh, & Gupta 2018). New documents are then assigned to the partition to which they are most likely to belong for classification purposes (Aggarwal & Zhai, 2012c). *Rule-based classifiers* match word patterns in the documents with the specified classes and their labels. If a certain word pattern occurs, it is assigned to a class with a certain probability. This results in a set of rules that can then be used to automatically assign unknown documents to the respective classes (Aggarwal & Zhai, 2012c).

Methods derived from information retrieval are used to find similarities between documents and can therefore also be used for classification. An unknown document can then be assigned to the one with which it has the greatest similarity or smallest distance, respectively (Irfan et al., 2015; Korde & Mahender, 2012). Similar to clustering, *probability-based forms* are also used for classification. These are characterized by the fact that a document is assigned to predefined classes based on its properties with a certain probability (Aggarwal & Zhai, 2012c).

Information extraction from text data

Another core task of machine learning on text data is the extraction of information from the underlying document corpus (Aggarwal & Zhai, 2012a). In contrast to the methods presented above, information extraction does not primarily aim at classifying documents into specific groups, but rather at extracting the essential information from a set of documents. Nevertheless, it uses comparable algorithms from machine learning (Jiang, 2012). Conversely, information extraction can also serve as a preparatory measure for the enrichment of text data in the context of a clustering or classification task. The extracted information can thus be used both to make it available to the end user and for further processing in computer-based systems (Jiang, 2012). The main difference to information retrieval is that the latter is primarily used to find documents in a document corpus, whereas information extraction is aimed much more specifically at individual information components in the documents themselves (Jiang, 2012).

While in early forms of information extraction manually created rule-based systems were used, information extraction today is based on classical machine learning approaches. As a result, the processes can usually be broken down to simple classification problems (Jiang, 2012). *Named Entity Recognition* (NER) is an essential method. The basic idea of NER is to assign words or groups of words to real-world generic entities. The entities are automatically recognized in text data and assigned to the appropriate category, thus creating a content-related understanding of the text (Jiang, 2012). Typically considered categories are persons, places, and organizations, which can be used in a wide range of applications (Jiang, 2012). For example, in a résumé with information about previous workplaces, the term "London" would be assigned to the generic term "location". In addition, domain-specific types also exist. In the same way, it is also possible to extract certain keywords or phrases from the documents and ultimately determine a thematic assignment (Martinez-Rodriguez, Hogan, & Lopez-Arevalo, 2020). Possible sources of problems with NER are context-dependent different meanings of a word or homonyms (Jiang, 2012). The problem is circumvented by the fact that the context is often known in advance of an analysis, for example when documents on a certain topic or a narrowed category (e.g. résumés) are examined (Chan & Roth, 2010). NER thus follows a similar approach to part-of-speech tagging in data preparation. Since, as mentioned above, the manual creation of patterns for recognition is far too time-consuming, the process is based on automated recognition, for example by means of rules. If a pattern fulfills a condition of any kind in a rule, it can be used to assign a suitable category (e.g. Ciravegna, 2001; Soderland, 1999). In addition, statistical machine-learning approaches also serve as a basis for NER (e.g. Bikel et al., 1997; Isozaki & Kazawa, 2002; Settles, 2004).

While NER mainly aims at single, isolated features, *Relation Extraction* (RE) offers the possibility to investigate the semantic connection of these features (Jiang, 2012). Again, the process is broken down to a classification problem by examining whether two entities can be assigned to a predefined relation. The analysis is mostly limited to relations within a sentence. Again, the above-mentioned methods are used. As a basis for the predefined classes, lexical as well as syntactical relations, for example based on sentence order, can be used (Jiang, 2012). An extension in the sense of covering a wider range of topics is realized by *Open Information Extraction*. Here, the relation types are not defined in advance, but the goal is to extract all possible connections between entities (Banko et al., 2007). Again, learning-based as well as rule-based systems are common (Niklaus et al., 2018).

Summarization of text data

Often there is not only the desire to extract certain information from a text, but to display the essential contents in a compressed form. For this purpose, the method of text summarization is used. Unlike with the other tasks, the feature basis in this variant is not a single word or group of words, but a sentence. The idea here is to extract those sentences of a text that best represent the topic. The focus is thus on an adequate ranking of the sentences and a subsequent selection of a certain number of sentences (Nenkova & McKeown, 2012). This can be useful in a variety of situations, for example to compress cover letters in a recruiting process to the most informative and important aspects.

In order to determine the meaning of each sentence for the text, a wide range of data preparation operations is used, typically including weighting by frequency-based procedures such as TF-IDF or topic modeling (Nenkova & McKeown, 2012). For the consideration of semantic relationships, it is also possible to fall back on corresponding lexicons and libraries. In addition, the sentence length and its position in the document can be included in the evaluation. Under certain circumstances, the extent to which similar sentences occur in other documents of the corpus under consideration is also taken into account. Frequently occurring phrases in several documents can, for example, be an indication of an important component of the topic (Nenkova & McKeown, 2012).

The score of each sentence is then calculated by combining the above input variables. In the last step, a suitable selection of the sentences must then be made. On the one hand, the selection must be based on an optimal representation of the topic or, if necessary, several topics together, and on the other hand, the selection should not exceed a fixed overall length (Nenkova & McKeown, 2012). The context and the target group can also be taken into account when selecting sentences (Prabha, Duraiswamy, and Priyanga, 2014). With respect to the technological basis, the problem of text summarization is also ultimately attributed to a (supervised) classification or (unsupervised) clustering procedure. Also in this case, a variety of the already mentioned methods can be used for text summarization. In a simple observation, sentences are then classified into summary sentences and non-summary sentences (Nenkova & McKeown, 2012).

Sentiment analysis in text data

Sentiment analyses serve to identify the feelings, attitudes, and emotions of a person (Medhat, Hassan, & Korashy, 2014; Patil et al., 2014). These can be carried out using various media forms, whereby the analysis of text data is the most common form. The aim is to infer the author's sentiments or personal views on the underlying topic by using text data. *Opinion mining* constitutes a largely overlapping term that accentuates the aspects of opinions on events, products, or services (Kumar & Harish, 2018). Both variants ultimately rely on the same idea and technological basis.

A major goal is the recognition of subjectivity in texts. In this subjectivity detection, texts are classified according to whether they have an objective or subjective character (Boudad et al., 2018). This can be conducted on a feature, sentence, or document level (Gamal et al., 2019). The classes can also be further subdivided and extended by a polarity, for example into objective, subjectively negative, subjectively positive, and subjectively mixed (Nabil, Aly, & Atiya, 2015). The classification in the context of sentiment detection also aims in a similar direction. Here, texts are classified depending on whether they reflect a positive, negative, or neutral opinion on a topic, a product, or a service (Gamal et al., 2019). The data basis is formed by the features in the documents viewed. Just like information extraction and summarization of text data, sentiment analysis is ultimately a classification or clustering task.

The algorithms can be based on both lexicon-based and purely statistic-based methods (Chaturvedi et al., 2018). Especially for very strong and precisely formulated emotions ("awesome", "the worst"), a classification seems comparatively simple. However, it is problematic that a pure observation of the words is often not sufficient, because negations, sarcasm, and the context have to be considered as well (Ravi & Ravi, 2015). In the HR domain, this is especially true for documents that have to be read "between the lines", for example job references. For this reason, a broad spectrum of natural language processing (NLP) technologies is used in sentiment analysis and, in addition, extensive background knowledge in the thematic domain under consideration is necessary (Chaturvedi et al., 2018). As of today, syntactic NLP technologies are the most common form. Basic variants include, for example, simple *keyword spotting*, which is based on the presence of unambiguous words. More accurate results tend to be obtained by *lexical affinity*, where words are likely to be related to a sentiment based on a lexicon. The assignment of the document to an appropriate category is then based on this (Chaturvedi et al., 2018). Semantic-based sentiment analyses are much rarer. Ideas are usually based on the use of lexicons such as WordNet to determine synonyms and antonyms and thus derive the polarity of certain words in the document corpus (Chaturvedi et al., 2018).

Sentiment analysis is often applied to text sources from the internet, for example in data from social media activities or product reviews (e.g. Boudad et al., 2018). But, as mentioned, sentiment analyses can also be useful in the HR domain, for example to analyze employee feedback. Challenges in sentiment analysis generally arise from the need for optimization for a large number of languages, different polarities within a document or even within a sentence, and the context-dependent polarity of a word. Also, the recognition of irony and sarcasm and the individual writing style of an author can be problematic for a correct classification (Prakash & Dinesh, 2018).

RESEARCH ON MACHINE LEARNING ON HR TEXT DATA

Therewith, a broad technological basis of machine learning on text data can be identified and can therefore also be applied to text data in the HR sector. In research, this area is considered from different perspectives. However, the current state of research in the field of machine learning on HR text data is highly heterogeneous and unbalanced. The following sections give an overview on the extent to which machine learning on HR text data is currently covered and addressed in research.

General Aspects of Research on Machine Learning on HR Text Data

As an interdisciplinary field of research, machine learning on HR text data is located at the interface between methodological-technical research disciplines, which provide the described technological basis for the analysis of text data, and behavior-oriented disciplines such as primarily the domain of human resource management and related research areas such as organizational and occupational psychology. Similar to machine learning on HR data in general, there is a strong imbalance between the methodological-technical and behavioral disciplines in the field of text data analysis. The research focuses primarily on the former. In view of the already mentioned universal applicability of existing machine learning technologies for text data to highly diverse content domains, this does not come as a surprise. The majority of research contributions to machine learning on text in general are concerned with methodological and technical considerations and thus concentrate, for example, on the performance enhancement of algorithms or the application of certain technologies in specific scenarios (e.g. Schouten et al., 2019; Stalin & Suresh, 2018). One of the domains where such technologies have been applied is that of HR, a domain to which some research contributions establish a direct link. In most cases, a concrete use case is considered in this context, in which a certain technology is applied to a content-related scenario from the HR domain. The result is then usually a corresponding concept in the form of a model or, in individual cases, a functional prototype (e.g. Cabrera-Diego, Torres-Moreno, & El Bèze, 2013; Faliagka, Tsakalidis, & Tzimas, 2012; Kessler et al., 2009; Zhang & Wang, 2018). The origin of these contributions, however, is also to be assigned to the methodological-technical disciplines, since behavioral aspects are frequently not explicitly considered. Recently, however, application challenges in particular have increasingly been viewed from a legal perspective, thus also touching upon behavioral and management-oriented research (e.g. Brkan, 2019). This is important for the HR department in that the text data used usually consists of personal data that is subject to strict data protection laws.

Overall, this opens up a central problem. In research, a certain number of applications with a strong technical reference exist, but they only implicitly address the specifics of the human resources area or assume them as given without a theoretical foundation. On the other hand, domain-specific behavioral science research lacks the necessary technical knowledge to understand algorithms, evaluate their effectiveness, and use the resulting possibilities in a targeted way. Therefore, a stronger connection between the two disciplines is necessary. The domain-driven approach, in which methodological-technical research is provided with the necessary domain-specific expertise (Cao, 2010), could be a solution to this problem.

If one considers the division of research into the three task areas discussed in CHAPTER 2, another problem arises in this context, however. The strong concentration on individual application cases results in theoretical research and empirical research taking a back seat. Instead, current research on machine learning on HR text data focuses almost exclusively on design-oriented research. To give an overview on this topic, a rough description of the different use cases as well as some suggestions for future research based on further text data potential are given.

Current State of Research on Machine Learning on HR Text Data

In general, there is a strong imbalance within the individual functional areas of HR management. Personnel selection is the area that by far the most design-oriented research on machine learning on HR text data currently concentrates on. This functional area covers the complete process of providing employees for a company, starting with planning, recruiting, and hiring and ending with the deployment and release of employees (Tichy, Fombrun, & Devanna, 1982). Unsurprisingly, this is the area where countless documents with textual content are handled. The text data potential while recruiting *new employees* is extensive. In addition to the still common personal cover letter, the material that applicants provide to a company usually includes a résumé as well as the applicant's certificates, references, and information. Similarly, the text data potential that *existing employees* produce is substantial. Documents with text content in this case represent employment contracts, (interim) job references, vacation requests, sick leave, and letters of resignation when an employee leaves the company.

Use cases in this context primarily focus on analyzing the résumé of an applicant (e.g. Cabrera-Diego, Torres-Moreno, & El Bèze, 2013; Kessler et al., 2009) and can methodically be assigned to the classification and information extraction task. At first, the aim is to extract the essential information about the applicant. Since résumés usually have a more or less standardized structure, information extraction is easier than with completely unstructured documents. In many cases, the résumés are first broken down into multiple sections, such as personal data, work experience, and educational information (e.g. Garg et al., 2017; Roy, Chowdhary, & Bhatia, 2020; Yu, Guan, & Zhou, 2005; Zu & Wang, 2019). These data can then be searched for and extracted specifically in the relevant sections of the résumé with the help of keyword matching algorithms or additional semantical information stored in dedicated ontologies (e.g. Abdessalem & Amdouni, 2011; Çelik & Elçi, 2012; Mhapasekar, 2017). In this context, the extraction is primarily aimed at the recognition of the skill sets of the applicants (e.g. Schiller, 2019), but other constructs such as personality traits are also common (e.g. Mihuandayani, Utami, & Luthfi, 2018). With the help of such information extraction from résumés, it is then possible in a second step to classify applicants into suitable and unsuitable for a given job advertisement. The documents are compared with prepared training data (Banu & Chitra, 2015). In this context, the annotation of texts and the use of corresponding ontologies play an important role. Methods such as topic modeling can also be successfully applied (Moniz & de Jong, 2014; Schiller, 2019). The aim is to use these criteria to make an initial automated selection of applicants in the context of a job advertisement in order to reduce the time and effort required for manual review by an administrator. Especially in large companies, this results in a considerable savings potential. Additional textual data, such as data from social networks or interviews, can also be used to assess the suitability of an applicant (Bahri et al., 2020; Brandt & Herzberg, 2020; Forsyth & Anglim, 2020). Similarly, in the latter stages of a selection process, machine learning on text data can serve different purposes. For example, additional information about applicants can also be obtained from their written statements during the selection process (Mostafa & Beshir, 2021). Based on this, suggestions can then be identified for questions that can be asked of the applicant during an interview (Qin et al., 2019).

In the same way, there are suggestions to search specifically for applicants with certain characteristics who have deposited their résumés for companies in job portals (e.g. Amdouni, Karaa, & Limam, 2010; Kaczmarek et al., 2010). Information is extracted both from job advertisements on the platforms (e.g. Pater, Szkola, & Kozak, 2019) and from the résumés of the registered applicants (e.g. Ivaschenko & Milutkin, 2019; Schiller, 2019) and analyzed for similarities. This automated matching of résumés and job offers is one of the oldest and most common use cases in the context of machine learning on HR text data (e.g. Bizer et al., 2005; Yan et al., 2019; Yi, Allan, & Croft, 2007). Often the structure of a résumé also allows it to be displayed as an XML document. This is done, for example, in accordance with the HR-XML standard (Dorn & Naz, 2006). Candidates in social networks can also be analyzed in order to draw conclusions about their characteristics and personality on the basis of the postings they have made (Mihuandayani, Utami, & Luthfi, 2018). In some cases, the information from the résumé can also be automatically transferred to the input fields during an online application so that it can be analyzed afterwards as structured data (Farkas et al., 2014). With the help of this information, applicants can also be compared with each other and ranked. Various studies show that such a ranking can achieve good results (e.g. Deshpande et al., 2016; Dixit et al., 2019; Mostafa & Beshir, 2021), especially for frequently vacated positions with simpler activities (Faliagka et al., 2014). For hierarchically higher positions with more complex requirements, however, the accuracy decreases (Faliagka, Tsakalidis, & Tzimas, 2012). In addition to the résumé, occasionally further information on an applicant is used specifically for such a ranking. For example, an investigation could deal with the idea of examining the content of applicants' blog posts. These findings should help to obtain additional information about the author's personality (Oberlander & Nowson, 2006).

Machine learning on text data can also be used profitably in the context of workforce planning. For example, skill sets and performance appraisals can be extracted from employee documents, which can then be used to automatically assign employees to suitable positions in the company (e.g. Bafna, Shirwaikar, & Pramod, 2019; Gonzalez et al., 2012; Nikitinsky, 2016). In a somewhat broader context, research on automated detection of sexism and sexual harassment in the workplace can also be considered. Text data can also provide information in this context. An analysis that deals with the problem shows, for example, that topic modeling and clustering can reveal corresponding clues in text data (Karami et al., 2019).

As mentioned above, however, many of these studies are mostly limited to the pure development of an artifact in conceptual or prototypical form by applying and, if necessary, adapting existing technologies of machine learning to HR text data. The actual technical necessity is usually only justified on a very general level and is not supported by concrete empirical studies. In particular, there is a lack of studies that address the actual relevance of the created artifacts and, thus, their necessity and success for the HR domain. There is also a lack of systematic research on the real-world application of machine learning on HR text data. This is especially astonishing, since, for example, the analysis of résumés by machine learning on text has also become a standard tool in numerous HR information systems (Abed & El-Halees, 2017). In fact, résumé parsing components are included in many e-recruiting software offerings nowadays and represent the application for which machine learning on HR text data is used the most. In this e-recruiting context, so-called chat bots are also increasingly being used as an extension (see CHAPTER 12). Although the evaluation of large quantities of documents is not the primary focus of this activity, the texts entered are used as training data, so that the system can learn based on this information and thus improve itself independently (e.g. Gianvecchio et al., 2011).

Regarding the functional areas of *employee performance* and *development*, text data potential arises primarily from employee assessments and the use of e-learning systems for the internal training of employees. A frequently used instrument being connected to machine learning on text data in this area is again the chat bot, which is intended to provide learners with the relevant knowledge when they have questions (Hristova, 2019). Internal data and data from social networks can also be used to identify development opportunities (e.g. Xu et al., 2017). Numerous publications also deal with information extraction and classification tasks to create performance appraisals based on text documents (e.g. Shami et al., 2015). The other way round, performance appraisals of companies and individuals can also be analyzed themselves (e.g. Palshikar et al., 2017). The results of a performance assessment can then also be used to identify suitable learning materials for the identified development potentials (e.g. Quan et al., 2018).

Similarly, sentiment analyses can be used in this context, especially for the analysis of employee satisfaction in companies. The satisfaction of employees can, for example, again be analyzed on the basis of textual performance appraisals (e.g. Costa & Veloso, 2015; Luo, Zhou, & Shon, 2016) or on the basis of text data retrieved from external platforms (e.g. Luo, Zhou, & Shon, 2016; Moniz & de Jong, 2014). This results in enormous potentials for companies, since employee satisfaction is a key for success. Problems can thus be recognized early, meaning that, for example, forecasts for employee performance and engagement can be created (e.g. Kamtar, Jitkongchuen, & Pacharawongsakda, 2019; Sajjadiani et al., 2019; Xue et al., 2021) and employee turnover analyses conducted (e.g. Gloor et al., 2017; Sokolov et al., 2018). This shows that a domain orientation is advantageous in this case and domain-oriented sentiment analysis clearly surpasses general sentiment analysis in its accuracy. This underlines the importance of focusing future research on machine learning on text data on the domain specifics of the HR sector (Goldberg & Zaman, 2018). Google has experimented with a similar algorithm to identify employees who feel underused, by considering employee reviews, promotions, and pay history (Abed & El-Halees, 2017). As with the approaches in the selection area, in this case research is also nearly exclusively design-oriented. An extension to a theoretical foundation and an empirical verification of the usefulness of the considered application scenarios would therefore be desirable.

Future Potentials in Research on Machine Learning on HR Text Data

As already mentioned, future research potential comes from two main areas. First, from the combination of the technical-methodological discipline and the behavioral discipline at the domain level and, second, from the extension of the current design-oriented focus to other research tasks. However, also within design-oriented research, numerous gaps arise when comparing the current state of research with the potential of textual data. Especially in view of the existing strong focus on staffing, an investigation of the potential applications of machine learning on HR text data in other functional areas of human resource management would seem to be useful.

Yet in the *selection department* also, a discrepancy between the application contexts studied and the text data potential available in this area can be found, and therefore a wide variety of possibilities to enlarge the application spectrum exists. For example, machine learning on text data could be used for requirements planning not only in the context of analyses of the general market situation, but also to automatically analyze internal company e-mails to identify, for example, persistent demand due to bottlenecks caused by a lack of employees in certain departments. Machine learning could also be used to draw conclusions about future staffing needs from the increased integration of marketing instruments for employer brand analysis, for example in social networks (Luo, Zhou, & Shon, 2016). Such external data sources could also be used in the context of recruitment as a basis for analyzing the company's external image or the wishes and expectations of future generations on the job market. In this context, and in view of the shortage of skilled workers, an automated analysis of competitor job advertisements on job exchanges or on their company websites would also be conceivable in order to optimize the company's image and attractiveness for potential applicants. A task that is predestined to do this is information extraction.

As the spread of the technology in software systems shows, applicant selection is undoubtedly the area in human resource management where machine learning on text plays the most important role today. However, the usual classification into suitable and unsuitable applicants could still be significantly refined. On the one hand, further documents apart from the usual partially standardized résumé could be used. With information extraction, job references and certain skills and characteristics of an applicant could also be included in the consideration. On the other hand, sentiment analyses of the style used in detecting employee satisfaction could also be carried out with regard to the personality traits of applicants. This could be based on the cover letter, on written interviews, or on other available documents. That way, the applicants could be classified in advance into the "big five" personality traits (Rothmann & Coetzer, 2003) or their work motivation and honesty could be determined. In this context, machine learning could also use audio data already converted to text data by speech-to-text algorithms as a data basis (Trivedi et al., 2018).

Job references are another important source of information. These could also be used as a document source in machine learning on text data. In this context, a special ontology would be required for the evaluation, since job references are usually always formulated positively and the actual information is rather hidden between the lines. Further data potential arises in the context of employment through contracts. For example, large numbers of individually concluded employment contracts could be analyzed using machine learning methods. From this, information could be extracted that reveals, for example, update or supplementation needs. There is also data potential for comparable document types from the electronic personnel file, such as applications for holidays or sick leave. Letters of termination could also be examined and categorized in large companies with regard to anomalies and the reasons for termination in order to derive improvements for the working atmosphere and improve employee turnover prediction.

As the functional domain of *employee rewards* addresses the monetary and non-monetary remuneration of employees (Tichy, Fombrun, & Devanna, 1982), it offers the least text data potential of all areas and, correspondingly, few application possibilities for machine learning on HR text data. This area is mainly based on numerical data, which can be examined and evaluated by machine learning on structured data (e.g. Strohmeier & Piazza, 2013). A certain potential for machine learning on text data can still be derived. Written performance reviews of employees and supervisors could be used to influence bonus payments based on a classification into positive, neutral, and negative categories. The performance assessment could also be used to compare the fulfillment of previously defined objectives. There is also a potential for evaluation in the settlement of travel expenses. For example, information extraction from documents such as invoices could be used to draw a profile of the employee concerned.

CONCLUSIONS AND GENERAL OUTLOOK

In conclusion, several key aspects of research on machine learning on text data in the HR domain can be identified. Machine learning on text data offers a broad and mature technological basis for automated text analyses, which, due to the existing data potential, also offers numerous application possibilities for the HR domain. In research, however, this potential has so far only been used to a limited extent. Research on machine learning on HR text data currently methodically focuses mainly on single, isolated use cases. These approaches are exemplary proofs of how existing machine learning technologies can be projected onto individual applications in the HR domain. In view of the data potential in the staffing area, it is not surprising that the majority of the investigations are functionally limited to this domain. Occasionally, implementation considerations are also found in the other functional areas of the HR domain, but they are rare.

Another main problem in the use case research context is that methodological-technical and behavioral research are isolated from each other. The intersection is small, so that even those use cases that are related to the HR domain are strongly based on technical disciplines. A consideration of behavioral science or management theory aspects is usually omitted. Another problem is that the added value of a technical solution is not derived theoretically, but is demonstrated in the form of a "proof-of-concept". There is also a lack of empirical studies at both the micro and the macro level. The created artifacts are only sporadically empirically evaluated for their effectiveness. There is also a lack of studies dealing with the actual application of machine learning on HR text data in practice. Ultimately, it cannot be confirmed that the artifacts created in the use cases actually cover a real need. This knowledge would, however, enable more targeted use case research. This would provide appropriate evidence and trigger more focused development that would also benefit the practice.

In the future, research on machine learning on HR text data should therefore focus on two essential aspects. On the one hand, the transfer of previous findings to other functional areas of the HR domain is a logical step. Research should therefore focus on the use and integration of existing technologies in these functional areas. This should, however, be done in any case considering the aforementioned need for an improved theoretical foundation and for a more extensive empirical evaluation.

A similar problem arises in the practical use of the technologies. Software systems are often based on general technologies and apply them to the HR domain without taking into account HR specifics. Exceptions can be found in some dedicated HR software systems, but in many cases, the practical implementation of machine learning on HR text data relies on a misappropriation of software systems that were actually created for a different application context. A proper integration into existing workflows in the HR domain is therefore missing. Future development should therefore focus on integrating machine learning on text data into HR business processes.

Apart from the methodical and technical component, legal and ethical problems of using automated analyses for personal data present a huge challenge for the practical application of machine learning on HR text data. In many countries, but especially in Europe, the use of such technologies is only permitted with the consent of the person concerned (Brkan, 2019). The possible lack of trust in algorithmic decision making contributes to the fact that broad consent, for example among applicants and employees, cannot be expected. Moreover, a final decision must always be taken by a human being and must not be left to the algorithm alone

(Brkan, 2019). This restricts the cost-saving potentials. In some cases, the problem can be circumvented by anonymizing the data, but in many cases this process leads to the analysis being unusable. The examples of extension possibilities shown here must therefore be checked for legal and moral concerns before they are put into practice. This is probably one of the main reasons why machine learning on text data has not yet made the breakthrough in human resource management that one would expect from the data potential. However, this aspect is not text data specific, but more a general problem in the application of artificial intelligence.

REFERENCES

Abdessalem, W. K. B., & Amdouni, S. (2011). E-recruiting support system based on text mining methods. *International Journal of Knowledge and Learning*, *7*(3–4), 220–232.

Abed, A. A., & El-Halees, A. M. (2017). Detecting subjectivity in staff performance appraisals by using text mining: Teachers appraisals of Palestinian government case study. In *2017 Palestinian International Conference on Information and Communication Technology (PICICT)* (pp. 120–125). IEEE.

Aggarwal, A., Singh, J., & Gupta, D. K. (2018). A review of different text categorization techniques. *International Journal of Engineering and Technology*, *7*(3.8), 11–15.

Aggarwal, C. C. (2018). Machine learning for text: An introduction. In *Machine learning for text* (pp. 1–16). Springer.

Aggarwal, C. C., & Zhai, C. (2012a). An introduction to text mining. In C. C. Aggarwal & C. Zhai (Eds.), *Mining text data* (pp. 1–10). Springer.

Aggarwal, C. C., & Zhai, C. (2012b). A survey of text clustering algorithms. In C. C. Aggarwal & C. Zhai (Eds.), *Mining text data* (pp. 77–128). Springer.

Aggarwal, C. C., & Zhai, C. (2012c). A survey of text classification algorithms. In C. C. Aggarwal & C. Zhai (Eds.), *Mining text data* (pp. 163–222). Springer.

Alghamdi, R., & Alfalqi, K. (2015). A survey of topic modeling in text mining. *International Journal of Advanced Computer Science Applications (IJACSA)*, *6*(1), 147–153.

Alpaydin, E. (2020). *Introduction to machine learning*. MIT Press.

Amdouni, S., Karaa, W. B. A., & Limam, M. (2010). E-recruitment and CV structuring. In *Proceedings of the Second Meeting on Statistics and Data Mining* (pp. 96–103).

Angiani, G., Ferrari, L., Fontanini, T., Fornacciari, P., Iotti, E., Magliani, F., & Manicardi, S. (2016). A comparison between preprocessing techniques for sentiment analysis in Twitter. In *KDWeb*.

Bafna, P., Shirwaikar, S., & Pramod, D. (2019). Task recommender system using semantic clustering to identify the right personnel. *VINE Journal of Information and Knowledge Management Systems*, *49*(2), 181–199.

Bahri, S., Adiwisastra, M. F., Alawiyah, T., Purnia, D. S., & Simpony, B. K. (2020). Sentiment analysis for decision support systems of employee. *Journal of Physics: Conference Series*, *1477*, Article 022014.

Banko, M., Cafarella, M. J., Soderland, S., Broadhead, M., & Etzioni, O. (2007). Open information extraction from the web. In *Proceedings of the 20th International Joint Conference on Artificial Intelligence* (pp. 2670–2676).

Banu, G. R., & Chitra, V. K. (2015). A survey of text mining concepts. *International Journal of Innovations in Engineering and Technology*, *5*(2), 121–127.

Beil, F., Ester, M., & Xu, X. (2002). Frequent term-based text clustering. In *Proceedings of the Eighth ACM SIGKDD International Conference on Knowledge Discovery and Data Mining* (pp. 436–442).

Bikel, D. M., Miller, S., Schwartz, R., & Weischedel, R. (1997). Nymble: A high-performance learning name-finder. In *Proceedings of the 5th Conference on Applied Natural Language Processing* (pp. 194–201).

Bizer, C., Heese, R., Mochol, M., Oldakowski, R., Tolksdorf, R., & Eckstein, R. (2005). The impact of semantic web technologies on job recruitment processes. In *Wirtschaftsinformatik Proceedings 2005* (pp. 1367–1381).

Boudad, N., Faizi, R., Thami, R. O. H., & Chiheb, R. (2018). Sentiment analysis in Arabic: A review of the literature. *Ain Shams Engineering Journal, 9*(4), 2479–2490.

Brandt, P. M., & Herzberg, P. Y. (2020). Is a cover letter still needed? Using LIWC to predict application success. *International Journal of Selection and Assessment, 28*(4), 417–429.

Brill, E. (1992). A simple rule-based part of speech tagger. In *ANLC'92: Proceedings of the Third Conference on Applied Natural Language Processing* (pp. 152–155). Association for Computational Linguistics.

Brkan, M. (2019). Do algorithms rule the world? Algorithmic decision-making and data protection in the framework of the GDPR and beyond. *International Journal of Law and Information Technology, 27*(2), 91–121.

Cabrera-Diego, L. A., Torres-Moreno, J. M., & El Bèze, M. (2013). *SegCV: traitement efficace de CV avec analyse et correction d'erreurs* [Conference presentation]. TALN-Récital 2013, 17–21 Juin, Les Sables d'Olonne.

Camacho-Collados, J., & Pilehvar, M. T. (2018). *On the role of text preprocessing in neural network architectures: An evaluation study on text categorization and sentiment analysis.* arXiv preprint arXiv:1707.01780.

Cao, L. (2010). Domain-driven data mining: Challenges and prospects. *IEEE Transactions on Knowledge and Data Engineering, 22*(6), 755–769.

Çelik, D., & Elçi, A. (2012). An ontology-based information extraction approach for résumés. In *Joint International Conference on Pervasive Computing and the Networked World* (pp. 165–179).

Chan, Y. S., & Roth, D. (2010). Exploiting background knowledge for relation extraction. In *Proceedings of the 23rd International Conference on Computational Linguistics (Coling 2010)* (pp. 152–160).

Chaturvedi, I., Cambria, E., Welsch, R. E., & Herrera, F. (2018). Distinguishing between facts and opinions for sentiment analysis: Survey and challenges. *Information Fusion, 44*, 65–77.

Ciravegna, F. (2001). Adaptive information extraction from text by rule induction and generalisation. In *Proceedings of the 17th International Joint Conference on Artificial Intelligence* (Vol. 2, pp. 1251–1256).

Costa, A., & Veloso, A. (2015). Employee analytics through sentiment analysis. In *Proceedings of the 30th Brazilian Symposium on Database* (pp. 101–112).

Crain, S. P., Zhou, K., Yang, S. H., & Zha, H. (2012). Dimensionality reduction and topic modeling: From latent semantic indexing to latent dirichlet allocation and beyond. In C. C. Aggarwal & C. Zhai (Eds.), *Mining text data* (pp. 129–161). Springer.

Denny, M. J., & Spirling, A. (2018). Text preprocessing for unsupervised learning: Why it matters, when it misleads, and what to do about it. *Political Analysis, 26*(2), 168–189.

Deshpande, A., Deshpande, D., Khatri, D., Das, P., Mentor, F., & Khedkar, S. (2016). Proposed system for résumé analytics. *International Journal of Engineering Research and Technology (IJERT), 5*(11), 468–471.

Dhillon, I. S., Mallela, S., & Modha, D. S. (2003). Information-theoretic co-clustering. In *Proceedings of the Ninth ACM SIGKDD International Conference on Knowledge Discovery and Data Mining* (pp. 89 98).

Dixit, V. V., Patel, T., Deshpande, N., & Sonawane, K. (2019). Résumé sorting using artificial intelligence. *International Journal of Research in Engineering, Science and Management, 2*(4), 423–425.

Dorn, J., & Naz, T. (2006). Meta-search in human resource management. *International Journal of Human and Social Sciences, 1*(2), 105–110.

Faliagka, E., Iliadis, L., Karydis, I., Rigou, M., Sioutas, S., Tsakalidis, A., & Tzimas, G. (2014). On-line consistent ranking on e-recruitment: Seeking the truth behind a well-formed CV. *Artificial Intelligence Review, 42*(3), 515–528.

Faliagka, E., Tsakalidis, A., & Tzimas, G. (2012). An integrated e-recruitment system for automated personality mining and applicant ranking. *Internet Research, 22*(5), 551–568.

Farkas, R., Dobó, A., Kurai, Z., Miklós, I., Nagy, Á., Vincze, V., & Zsibrita, J. (2014). Information extraction from Hungarian, English and German CVs for a career portal. In R. Prasath, P. O'Reilly, & T. Kathirvalavakumar (Eds.), *Mining intelligence and knowledge exploration* (pp. 333–341). Springer.

Fayyad, U., Piatetsky-Shapiro, G., & Smyth, P. (1996). From data mining to knowledge discovery in databases. *AI Magazine, 17*(3), 36–53.

Feinerer, I. (2008). *A text mining framework in R and its applications* [Doctoral dissertation, WU Vienna University of Economics and Business].

Forsyth, L., & Anglim, J. (2020). Using text analysis software to detect deception in written short-answer questions in employee selection. *International Journal of Selection and Assessment*, *28*(3), 236–246.

Gamal, D., Alfonse, M., M. El-Horbaty, E.-S., & M. Salem, A.-B. (2019). Analysis of machine learning algorithms for opinion mining in different domains. *Machine Learning and Knowledge Extraction*, *1*(1), 224–234.

Garg, S., Singh, S. S., Mishra, A., & Dey, K. (2017). CVBed: Structuring CVs using word embeddings. In *Proceedings of the Eighth International Joint Conference on Natural Language Processing (Volume 2: Short Papers)* (pp. 349–354).

Gianvecchio, S., Xie, M., Wu, Z., & Wang, H. (2011). Humans and bots in internet chat: Measurement, analysis, and automated classification. *IEEE/ACM Transactions on Networking*, *19*(5), 1557–1571.

Gloor, P. A., Colladon, A. F., Grippa, F., & Giacomelli, G. (2017). Forecasting managerial turnover through e-mail based social network analysis. *Computers in Human Behavior*, *71*, 343–352.

Goetz, R., Piazza, A., & Bodendorf, F. (2019). Hybrider Ansatz zur automatisierten Themen-Klassifizierung von Produktrezensionen. *HMD Praxis der Wirtschaftsinformatik*, *56*(5), 932–946.

Goldberg, D., & Zaman, N. (2018). Text analytics for employee dissatisfaction in human resources management. In *Proceedings of the 24th Americas Conference on Information Systems*.

Gonzalez, T., Santos, P., Orozco, F., Alcaraz, M., Zaldivar, V., De Obeso, A., & Garcia, A. (2012). Adaptive employee profile classification for resource planning tool. In *2012 Annual SRII Global Conference* (pp. 544–553). IEEE.

Gupta, V., & Lehal, G. S. (2009). A survey of text mining techniques and applications. *Journal of Emerging Technologies in Web Intelligence*, *1*(1), 60–76.

Hotho, A., Nürnberger, A., & Paaß, G. (2005). A brief survey of text mining. *Ldv Forum*, *20*(1), 19–62.

Hristova, V. (2019). Advantages and limitations of chat bots in human resources management activities. *Научные горизонты*, *8*(24), 74–80.

Irfan, R., King, C. K., Grages, D., Ewen, S., Khan, S. U., Madani, S. A., … & Tziritas, N. (2015). A survey on text mining in social networks. *The Knowledge Engineering Review*, *30*(2), 157–170.

Isozaki, H., & Kazawa, H. (2002). Efficient support vector classifiers for named entity recognition. In *COLING 2002: Proceedings of the 19th International Conference on Computational Linguistics* (pp. 1–7). ACM.

Ivaschenko, A., & Milutkin, M. (2019). HR decision-making support based on natural language processing. In *Creativity in intelligent technologies and data science* (pp. 152–161). Springer.

Jiang, J. (2012). Information extraction from text. In C. C. Aggarwal & C. Zhai (Eds.), *Mining text data* (pp. 11–41). Springer.

Kaczmarek, T., Zyskowski, D., Walczak, A., & Abramowicz, W. (2010). Information extraction from web pages for the needs of expert finding. *Studies in Logic, Grammar and Rhetoric*, *22*(35), 141–157.

Kadhim, A. I. (2018). An evaluation of preprocessing techniques for text classification. *International Journal of Computer Science and Information Security (IJCSIS)*, *16*(6), 22–32.

Kamtar, P., Jitkongchuen, D., & Pacharawongsakda, E. (2019). Multi-label classification of employee job performance prediction by DISC personality. In *Proceedings of the 2nd International Conference on Computing and Big Data* (pp. 47–52).

Karami, A., Swan, S. C., White, C. N., & Ford, K. (2019). Hidden in plain sight for too long: Using text mining techniques to shine a light on workplace sexism and sexual harassment. *Psychology of Violence*. Advance online publication.

Kessler, R., Béchet, N., Torres-Moreno, J. M., Roche, M., & El-Bèze, M. (2009). Job offer management: How improve the ranking of candidates. In *International Symposium on Methodologies for Intelligent Systems* (pp. 431–441). Springer.

Korde, V., & Mahender, C. N. (2012). Text classification and classifiers: A survey. *International Journal of Artificial Intelligence and Applications*, *3*(2), 85–99.

Kumar, B. S., & Ravi, V. (2016). A survey of the applications of text mining in financial domain. *Knowledge-Based Systems*, *114*, 128–147.

Kumar, H. K., & Harish, B. S. (2018). Classification of short text using various preprocessing techniques: An empirical evaluation. In P. K. Sa, S. Bakshi, I. K. Hatzilygeroudis, M. N. Sahoo (Eds.), *Recent findings in intelligent computing techniques* (pp. 19–30). Springer.

Luo, N., Zhou, Y., & Shon, J. (2016). Employee satisfaction and corporate performance: Mining employee reviews on glassdoor.com. In *Thirty-Seventh International Conference on Information Systems*.

Martinez-Rodriguez, J. L., Hogan, A., & Lopez-Arevalo, I. (2020). Information extraction meets the semantic web: A survey. *Semantic Web, 11*(2), 255–235.

Medhat, W., Hassan, A., & Korashy, H. (2014). Sentiment analysis algorithms and applications: A survey. *Ain Shams Engineering Journal, 5*(4), 1093–1113.

Mehler, A., & Wolff, C. (2005). Einleitung: Perspektiven und Positionen des Text Mining. *Zeitschrift für Computerlinguistik und Sprachtechnologie, 20*(1), 1–18.

Mhapasekar, D. P. (2017). Ontology based information extraction from résumé. In *2017 International Conference on Trends in Electronics and Informatics (ICEI)* (pp. 43–47).

Mihuandayani, M., Utami, E., & Luthfi, E. T. (2018). Profiling analysis based on social media for prospective employees recruitment using SVM and Chi-Square. *Journal of Physics: Conference Series, 1140*, Article 012043.

Moniz, A., & de Jong, F. (2014). Sentiment analysis and the impact of employee satisfaction on firm earnings. In *European Conference on Information Retrieval* (pp. 519–527). Springer.

Mostafa, L., & Beshir, S. (2021). Job candidate rank approach using machine learning techniques. In *Advanced Machine Learning Technologies and Applications: Proceedings of AMLTA 2021* (pp. 225–233). Springer.

Nabil, M., Aly, M., & Atiya, A. F. (2015). Arabic sentiment tweets dataset. In *Proceedings of the 2015 Conference on Empirical Methods in Natural Language Processing* (pp. 2515–2519).

Nenkova, A., & McKeown, K. (2012). A survey of text summarization techniques. In C. C. Aggarwal & C. Zhai (Eds.), *Mining text data* (pp. 43–76). Springer.

Niharika, S., Latha, V. S., & Lavanya, D. R. (2012). A survey on text categorization. *International Journal of Computer Trends and Technology, 3*(1), 39–45.

Nikitinsky, N. S. (2016). Improving talent management with automated competence assessment: Research summary. In *Proceedings of the Scientific-Practical Conference "Research and Development – 2016"* (pp. 73–82). Springer.

Niklaus, C., Cetto, M., Freitas, A., & Handschuh, S. (2018). A survey on open information extraction. In *Proceeding of the 27th International Conference on Computational Linguistics (COLING 2018)* (pp. 3866–3878).

Oberlander, J., & Nowson, S. (2006). Whose thumb is it anyway? Classifying author personality from weblog text. In *Proceedings of the COLING/ACL 2006 Main Conference Poster Sessions* (pp. 627–634).

Palshikar, G. K., Pawar, S., Chourasia, S., & Ramrakhiyani, N. (2017). Mining supervisor evaluation and peer feedback in performance appraisals. In *International Conference on Computational Linguistics and Intelligent Text Processing* (pp. 628–641). Springer.

Pater, R., Szkola, J., & Kozak, M. (2019). A method for measuring detailed demand for workers' competences. *Economics: The Open-Access, Open-Assessment E-Journal, 13*(27), 1–29.

Patil, G., Galande, V., Kekan, V., & Dange, K. (2014). Sentiment analysis using support vector machine. *International Journal of Innovative Research in Computer and Communication Engineering, 2*(1), 2607–2612.

Patil, S., Palshikar, G. K., Srivastava, R., & Das, I. (2012). *Learning to rank résumés*. Technical Report, Tata Research Development and Design Center (TRDDC), Tata Consultancy Services, India.

Prabha, S., Duraiswamy, D. K., & Priyanga, B. (2014). Context-based similarity analysis for document summarization. *International Journal of Advanced Research in Computer Engineering and Technology (IJARCET), 3*(4), 1485–1491.

Prakash, M. K., & Dinesh, G. (2018). A perspective survey on opinion mining tools and techniques. *International Journal of Engineering Science, 8*(3), 16436–16439.

Qin, C., Zhu, H., Zhu, C., Xu, T., Zhuang, F., Ma, C., Zhang, J., & Xiong, H. (2019). Duerquiz: A personalized question recommender system for intelligent job interview. In *Proceedings of the 25th ACM SIGKDD International Conference on Knowledge Discovery and Data Mining* (pp. 2165–2173).

Quan, P., Liu, Y., Zhang, T., Wen, Y., Wu, K., He, H., & Shi, Y. (2018, June). A novel data mining approach towards human resource performance appraisal. In *International Conference on Computational Science* (pp. 476–488). Springer.

Ravi, K., & Ravi, V. (2015). A survey on opinion mining and sentiment analysis: Tasks, approaches and applications. *Knowledge-Based Systems, 89*, 14–46.

Rothmann, S., & Coetzer, E. P. (2003). The big five personality dimensions and job performance. *SA Journal of Industrial Psychology, 29*(1), 68–74.

Roy, P. K., Chowdhary, S. S., & Bhatia, R. (2020). A machine learning approach for automation of résumé recommendation system. *Procedia Computer Science, 167*, 2318–2327.

Sajjadiani, S., Sojourner, A. J., Kammeyer-Mueller, J. D., & Mykerezi, E. (2019). Using machine learning to translate applicant work history into predictors of performance and turnover. *Journal of Applied Psychology, 104*(10), 1207–1225.

Salton, G., & Buckley, C. (1987). *Term weighting approaches in automatic text retrieval.* Technical Report, Department of Computer Science, Cornell University.

Schiller, A. (2019). *Knowledge discovery from CVs: A topic modeling procedure* [Doctoral Dissertation, University of Regensburg].

Schmid, H. (1999). Improvements in part-of-speech tagging with an application to German. In S. Armstrong, K. Church, P. Isabelle, S. Manzi, E. Tzoukermann, & D. Yarowsky (Eds.), *Natural language processing using very large corpora* (pp. 13–25). Springer.

Schouten, K., Frasincar, F., Dekker, R., & Riezebos, M. (2019). Heracles: A framework for developing and evaluating text mining algorithms. *Expert Systems with Applications, 127*, 68–84.

Settles, B. (2004). Biomedical named entity recognition using conditional random fields and rich feature sets. In *Proceedings of the International Joint Workshop on Natural Language Processing in Biomedicine and Its Applications (NLPBA/BioNLP)* (pp. 107–110).

Shami, N. S., Muller, M., Pal, A., Masli, M., & Geyer, W. (2015). Inferring employee engagement from social media. In *Proceedings of the 33rd Annual ACM Conference on Human Factors in Computing Systems* (pp. 3999–4008).

Smith, R. (2007). An overview of the Tesseract OCR engine. In *Ninth International Conference on Document Analysis and Recognition (ICDAR 2007)* (Vol. 2, pp. 629–633). IEEE.

Soderland, S. (1999). Learning information extraction rules for semistructured and free text. *Machine Learning, 34*(1–3), 233–272.

Sokolov, D. N., Selivanovskikh, L. V., Zavyalova, E. K., & Latukha, M. (2018). Why employees leave Russian companies? Analyzing online job reviews using text mining. *Российский журнал менеджмента, 16*(4), 499–512.

Stalin, J., & Suresh, P. (2018). Text categorization and text mining using different types of classifiers. *International Journal of Emerging Technologies in Engineering Research (IJETER), 6*(4), 278–284.

Strohmeier, S., & Piazza, F. (2013). Domain driven data mining in human resource management: A review of current research. *Expert Systems with Applications, 40*(7), 2410–2420.

Tichy, N. M., Fombrun, C. J., & Devanna, M. A. (1982). Strategic human resource management. *Sloan Management Review, Winter 1982*, 47–61.

Trivedi, A., Pant, N., Shah, P., Sonik, S., & Agrawal, S. (2018). Speech to text and text to speech recognition systems – a review. *IOSR Journal of Computer Engineering, 20*(2), 36–43.

Uysal, A. K., & Gunal, S. (2014). The impact of preprocessing on text classification. *Information Processing and Management, 50*(1), 104–112.

Verma, M. (2017). Cluster based ranking index for enhancing recruitment process using text mining and machine learning. *International Journal of Computer Applications, 157*(9), 23–30.

Xu, H., Gu, C., Zhou, H., Kou, S., & Zhang, J. (2017). JCTC: A large job posting corpus for text classification. arXiv preprint arXiv:1705.06123.

Xue, X., Gao, Y., Liu, M., Sun, X., Zhang, W., & Feng, J. (2021). GRU-based capsule network with an improved loss for personnel performance prediction. *Applied Intelligence, 51*, 4730–4743.

Yan, R., Le, R., Song, Y., Zhang, T., Zhang, X., & Zhao, D. (2019). Interview choice reveals your preference on the market: To improve job-résumé matching through profiling memories. In *Proceedings of the 25th ACM SIGKDD International Conference on Knowledge Discovery & Data Mining* (pp. 914–922).

Yi, X., Allan, J., & Croft, W. B. (2007). Matching résumés and jobs based on relevance models. In *Proceedings of the 30th Annual International ACM SIGIR Conference on Research and Development in Information Retrieval* (pp. 809–810).

Yu, K., Guan, G., & Zhou, M. (2005). Résumé information extraction with cascaded hybrid model. In *Proceedings of the 43rd Annual Meeting of the Association for Computational Linguistics (ACL '05)* (pp. 499–506).

Zamir, O., Etzioni, O., Madani, O., & Karp, R. M. (1997). Fast and intuitive clustering of web documents. In *KDD-97 Proceedings* (pp. 287–290).

Zhang, C., & Wang, H. (2018). RésuméVis: A visual analytics system to discover semantic information in semi-structured résumé data. *ACM Transactions on Intelligent Systems and Technology (TIST)*, *10*(1), 1–25.

Zhong, S. (2005). Efficient streaming text clustering. *Neural Networks*, *18*(5–6), 790–798.

Zu, S., & Wang, X. (2019). Résumé information extraction with a novel text block segmentation algorithm. *International Journal on Natural Language Computing (IJNLC)*, *8*(5), 29–48.

4. HR machine learning on audio and video data

Carmen Fernández-Martinez and Alberto Fernández

INTRODUCTION

Lately, we have witnessed a tendency towards the use of Artificial Intelligence (AI) in Human Resources (HR), from candidate background and CV screening to emotion recognition, turnover prediction, and employee attrition (Cappelli et al., 2019). Several authors (see, e.g., Strohmeier & Piazza, 2015; Buzko et al., 2016) have explored in general AI's potential in HR, whereas many others have focused on specific applications. Authors like Kindiroglu et al. (2017), Chandar et al. (2017), and Bavaresco et al. (2020) suggest some uses of Machine Learning (ML) in corporate environments, such as predicting extraversion and leadership from meeting videos or providing onboarding assistance to new employees through AI-powered corporate conversational agents.

While the use of AI in HR is for the time a step behind that in other sectors, its applicability in this field is gaining momentum in areas such as *recruiting, performance assessment, retention, workforce planning,* and control of *attrition* rates. Moreover, it is common to use ML in *talent acquisition, training and learning,* and *administrative* tasks. Other applications of ML audio and video processing in HR include *health monitoring,* computer vision based workforce *activity assessment, candidate/employee sentiment analysis, fraud prevention* in call center/employee calls, call center *performance,* and *personnel monitoring.*

Audio and video data generation and analysis using AI in HR, especially in recruitment, is becoming an active research area spanning several disciplines such as image processing, natural language processing, pattern recognition, computer vision, machine learning, cognitive science, psychology, and physiology. AI/ML is being widely used in video interviewing. As the recruiting process becomes increasingly global, the number of candidates to be interviewed is increasing. Several video interview products and services have emerged and are widely accepted by large multinationals for use in HR. However, this trend raises the moral dilemma of comparing candidates with former datasets with the aim of selecting according to protected attributes for business purposes. For example, companies may benefit from tax discounts for hiring individuals belonging to minorities. More controversial (illegal in most countries) is the case of preselecting candidates according to *protected* characteristics such as race, sex, or sexual orientation. But other data, like ZIP code or prefix could lead to indirect discrimination too, given that they are indirect predictors of belonging to certain races and communities.

In this chapter, we focus on the use of ML techniques for processing audio and video data in HR. We cover the recognition of important features from video and audio data, some of them leading to ethical concerns. Basic and general ML works on video and audio processing are overviewed, along with their specific applications in HR. We also discuss ethical issues and concerns that rise from the use of ML in HR and point out open issues and challenges on this topic.

The rest of the chapter is organized as follows. In the next section we introduce the most important ML techniques used for processing HR audio and video data. In the third section we present specific HR areas in which ML is being applied. The fourth and fifth sections overview the main existing ML techniques used for video and audio processing, including recognition of different features and emotions relevant in HR. Setting out from those bases, in the sixth section we explore how HR applications combine video and audio analysis techniques, focusing on video interview as the main HR application in which video and audio processing ML techniques are currently used. In the seventh section we discuss ethical issues and concerns raised by the use of ML in HR. In the penultimate section we discuss open issues and challenges for the future development of ML for HR video and audio information, before the final section concludes the chapter with a summary and discussion.

ML TECHNIQUES IN AUDIO AND VIDEO PROCESSING

This section briefly describes some of the most common ML techniques for processing audio and video data in HR.

AI tries to build intelligent machines which have autonomous learning capacities. ML is a subfield of AI and includes various techniques (Jordan & Mitchell, 2015). Although there are also methods that can learn during operation (e.g., reinforcement learning), they mostly learn models offline from historical datasets applied in production. For example, a machine could be trained to identify whether or not a picture contains a person by learning a classifier from a training set of positive (with person) and negative (no person) labeled images. Therefore, the size and quality of the training datasets are extremely important for the model's effectiveness. Supervised models rely on labeled (known results) datasets, while unsupervised learning is typically used for organizing new unlabeled data in clusters. Detailed information about HR ML can be found in CHAPTER 2 of this book. Bearing in mind the whole array of ML techniques, algorithms, and trends that exist, it would be advisable to introduce the most common ones currently applied in HR.

Artificial Neural Networks (ANNs) are arguably the most used techniques for audio and video HR processing. They are inspired by biological neural networks, typically organized in layers. Strengths of connections among neurons are adapted through a training process where many (usually thousands) of examples (input–output pairs) are provided. Once the model is learned, it is used with new unknown cases, that is, input cases whose outputs want to be inferred (e.g., for classification purposes).

Several ANN architectures (or configuration patterns) have been provided, as well as learning algorithms. Among them, *Convolutional Neural Networks (CNNs)* and *Recurrent Neural Networks (RNNs)* are widely used for video processing. CNNs are a sort of advanced ANN and are the core of artificial vision models today. They consist of two main parts. First, a convolution step applies a set of different filters (which detect characteristics). This is followed by a subsampling step. These two steps are repeated several times. Finally, a full connected ANN acts as a classifier. By contrast, RNN, LSTM, and GRU cells are popular ANN architectures. Their characteristic trait is that output from previous steps is used for the present state. The main drawbacks are slow computation time and not foreseeing future inputs for current state. LSTMs (or Long Short Term Memory Units) are a kind of RNN that can "remember" information in the long run. Gated Recurrent Units (GRUs) are very similar to LSTMs in that both depend on memory cells. They are used for most speech recognition models based on RNNs.

In addition to the above, *Deep Learning (DL)* (LeCun et al., 2015) is associated with specific ANNs consisting of many (deep) layers. Lately, DL has become a mainstream technology and is frequently used for image processing. A typical DL architecture for image classification consists of several CNN phases followed by a final ANN-based classification step.

Support Vector Machine (SVM) is a linear model for classification (identifying different classes) and regression problems (finding a model to predict something). It is also called Support Vector Classifier. SVMs rely on a representation of classes in a hyperplane in a multi-dimensional space. Then, it is possible to separate the training data into two groups.

Hidden Markov Model (HMM) is an ML technique that models a system as a Markov Process. In this type of modeling, the state of a system is represented as a random variable whose probability distribution only depends on the distribution of the previous state. The parameters of the model are not known (they are "hidden"). HMMs try to infer the hidden parameters from some observable values. HMMs are often seen in modern audiovisual speech recognition and audio recognition systems, for instance to classify musical genres (Pop, Jazz, Classical, etc.).

Logistic Regression is a supervised predictive classification algorithm previously used in the field of statistics. It predicts the probability of a target variable and its belonging to one class out of two. The starting point is a dataset with one or more independent variables. Drawing a parallel with Linear Regression, there is a function behind this algorithm too. It is called the logit function.

k-nearest neighbors (k-NN) is a supervised learning algorithm. This method bases its decision on the values of the k nearest points in the training set. Thus, a distance function needs to be defined. Each input data is typically defined as a vector of features and the Euclidean distance is commonly used. k-NN can be used for classification or regression. When used for classification a voting method is used (e.g., the most common category among the k nearest neighbors), whereas for regression a combination of the k values is used (e.g., the average).

Random Forest is an ensemble learning algorithm used mainly for classification. The method consists in generating several random decision trees (a classification algorithm). The result is supplied by the different decision trees using a voting mechanism. Decision trees are parallel estimators and are ruled by a method called bagging.

AdaBoost is another ensemble algorithm used for both classification and regression problems. In this case, new learners – decision trees – are adapted taking into account the examples that previous learners misclassified. It enables the capture of many non-linear relationships, in contrast to linear and logistic regression, and provides accurate predictions.

Gradient Boosted Decision Tree (GBDT) combines an ensemble of decision trees to generate final predictions. It uses a method called boosting to enhance the results of decision trees, often called weak learners. This method means error minimization: each tree does not spread the errors of the previous one.

When it comes to considering what ML technique to use, we encounter, for example, the opacity of RNNs. Authors like Hemamou et al. (2019) rightly argue that RNNs, more precisely GRUs, are more powerful (allow to find more statistical patterns) than other techniques such as SVMs, logistic regression, or random forest. RNNs are even capable of modeling temporality. As a counterpoint and drawback, they emphasize the opacity of ANNs and RNNs that makes difficult their use in critical applications. Although there are frequently used techniques, like SVM and CNN, most typical ML methods are still being used today, for instance SVM and logistic regression for communication skills in interviews, MultiLayer Perceptron (MLP), a type of ANN that is often called feedforward ANN, for speaker fluency level classification, and so on. We are observing a tendency towards DL models, for example LSTM.

Models for audio and video recognition have been trendy lately. Preliminary findings and results are not always entirely accurate due to the shortage of samples. The accuracy of algorithms is relatively high, though. Concerning DL, access to large amounts of training data is essential for its applicability.

COMMON USE CASES OF HR ML ON AUDIO AND VIDEO

In this section, we explore the main HR areas in which ML on audio and video are being applied. Table 4.1 summarizes the main uses cases and their application to recent HR ML audio and video research projects. As can be observed, ML has diverse applications in the HR field.

UC1: Video Interviewing Software

ML is used throughout all the interviewing process, from question formation for employment interviews (Rupasinghe et al., 2016) to agents in video interviewing (Suen et al., 2020). It is worth mentioning previous personality recognition attempts targeting asynchronous video interviewing (Rasipuram et al., 2016). Existing proprietary interviewing software assessments do not disclose details of the ML/DL models used, on intellectual property grounds. For this reason, we mainly focus on open research projects carried out by research groups that study model prototypes very similar to commercial products. Other relevant works include Bavaresco et al. (2020) and Nawaz and Gomes (2019). They introduce themes such as conversational agents in business and chatbot recruiters.

UC2: Candidate/Employee Sentiment Analysis

Sentiment analysis is crucial in organizations. By means of natural language processing (NLP) and AI techniques, it is possible to create models that give insight into employees' feelings towards their organization. Hemamou et al. (2019) apply DL methods to candidates' body language/non-verbal behavior during interviews. Body language analysis will be essential for better emotion measurement technologies in the future. Thus, models can target more complex patterns beyond facial expression or voice detection. Authors such as Kindiroglu et al. (2017) have explored the potential of sentiment analysis to detect mood and extraversion in employees' meeting videos. These traits could be related to future leadership indirectly.

UC3: Employee Fraud and Misconduct Detection

Audio analysis is extensively used in HR corporate phone call keyword recognition in relation to fraud. For example, financiers' phone calls are analyzed to detect keywords that could imply financial misconduct. It is worth mentioning previous research by Özlan et al. (2019) and Xing et al. (2020) on using various ML algorithms for fraud detection in phone calls. They both studied call behavior patterns, Özlan et al. being specific to call centers. Özlan et al.'s approach based on DL could be applied to monitoring in other corporate areas. Xing et al.'s ideas could be generalized to HR employee fraud in calls.

UC4: Candidate/Employee Skills/Personality Assessment

There are very diverse applications concerning employees' skills and personalities. Chen et al. (2017) analyze online candidates' monologues for personality detection using video and audio; Rasipuram et al. (2016) focus on automatic communication skills prediction; while Preciado-Grijalva and Brena (2018) attempt to automatize foreign language level assessment.

As mentioned in the following sections, skills assessment could lead to ethical challenges. Companies design their recruitment criteria based on a set of features, for example attention to detail, mother tongue, customer orientation. These features are not selected automatically, and most HR managers design their interviews and HR assessment for promotions or employee performance according to their idiosyncrasies or their business guidelines.

UC5: Employee Performance and Industrial Organization

Mumtaz and Habib (2012) use video analytics for quantitative employee performance, that is, based on numerical measures only, whereas Lebedeva et al. (2019), Khan and Habib (2010), Alom et al. (2014), and Luo et al. (2018) present works on employee performance and employee attrition (Alduayj & Rajpoot, 2018). Lebedeva et al. (2019) target two metrics related to employees' location to rate performance. Other computer vision approaches to assess workers' activities followed by Luo et al. (2018) apply to construction workers.

There is a parallel line of research regarding industrial organization and HR organization. Sardis and Varvarigou (2010) target industrial control of workflows. Their research also applies to small and medium-sized enterprises (SMEs), where they registered abnormal alarm events during workflow execution.

UC6: Employee Control

Recent works focus on video surveillance and control of employee presence (Averkov & Kulalov, 2020; Cahyono et al., 2020; Paray et al., 2020), attendance (Mady & Hilles, 2017), and health monitoring (Seo et al., 2015). In particular, Cahyono et al. (2020) compare two main DL architectural methods for face recognition: Openface and FaceNet. The latter is a model developed by Google researchers and has the highest accuracy in face recognition.

UC7: Employee Engagement and Conflict Detection. Onboarding Agents

Nawaz and Gomes (2019) explore the use of chatbots in the recruitment process to check employees' engagement. Chandar et al. (2017) concentrate on conversational agents in other recruitment phases such as onboarding. Predictive tools like KeepCorp[1] search for patterns found in emails and chats with the aim of tracking areas of conflict within the organization. Retorio[2] is a similar tool mainly used for new personnel. It works as a video recruiting and soft skills assessment, the mission of which is to help incoming employees recognize their professional strengths.

Table 4.1 Use cases of ML in HR audio and video data

Application (Use Case)	Topic	Works
UC1: Video Interviewing Software	Question formation for employment interviews	Rupasinghe et al. (2016)
	Asynchronous video interviewing	Suen et al. (2020) Rasipuram et al. (2016)
	Conversational agents	Bavaresco et al. (2020) Nawaz & Gomes (2019)
UC2: Candidate/Employee Sentiment Analysis	Body language and non-verbal behavior during interviews	Hemamou et al. (2019) Kindiroglu et al. (2017)
	Extraversion and mood detection in video meetings	Kindiroglu et al. (2017)
UC3: Employee Fraud and Misconduct Detection	Audio/phone call assessment in call centers and fraud detection in corporate conversations	Özlan et al. (2019) Xing et al. (2020)
UC4: Candidate/Employee Skills/Personality Assessment	Foreign languages level assessment	Preciado-Grijalva & Brena (2018)
	Communication skills prediction	Rasipuram et al. (2016)
	Monologue interviews analysis for personality detection	Chen et al. (2017)
UC5: Employee Performance and Industrial Organization	Employee performance analysis from videos	Mumtaz & Habib (2012) Lebedeva et al. (2019) Khan & Habib (2010) Alom et al. (2014) Luo et al. (2018)
	Employee attrition	Alduayj & Rajpoot (2018)
	Industrial control of workflows	Sardis & Varvarigou (2010)
UC6: Employee Control	Video surveillance and control of employee presence	Averkov & Kulalov (2020) Cahyono et al. (2020) Paray et al. (2020)
	Attendance	Mady & Hilles (2017)
	Health monitoring	Seo et al. (2015)
UC7: Employee Engagement and Conflict Detection. Onboarding Agents	Predictive employee engagement	Nawaz & Gomes (2019)
	Onboarding	Chandar et al. (2017)
	Conflict areas identification	KeepCorp[3], Retorio[4]

VIDEO PROCESSING

Video processing is a live issue in HR. The current state of the art in computer vision and pattern recognition based on DL (Suen et al., 2020) has fostered the creation of proprietary software companies that can successfully recognize human traits and candidate skills characteristics both in video streaming and video/audio recordings. Lately, applications and systems like HireVue, Google Hire, Montage, SparkHire, WePow, and Convey and databases like Affectiva have introduced digital interviews and AI-powered analyses to the recruiting scene. Companies like Human apply ML to better understand humans' feelings, emotions, characteristics, and personality, minimizing human bias. They mainly depend on CNN models and try to identify traits that correlate with corporate expectations of a good prospective employee.

When it comes to the specific case of recruitment, the first steps in job candidates' video processing resemble traditional artificial vision problems. Object detection and face recognition seem to be crucial when handling HR images in the same way as conventional images and video. Previous work in HR video detection is based on surveillance camera streaming processing. DL has been used assiduously regarding intelligent video crowd surveillance (Sreenu

& Durai, 2019; Nawaratne et al., 2019). Recently, other purposes have been proposed such as employee attrition prediction (Alduayj & Rajpoot, 2018). There is indeed a promising future ahead for cognitive technologies and video processing in HR.

Video processing in HR poses similar challenges for data scientists to traditional artificial vision problems, such as those related to video surveillance and facial recognition/cognitive technologies. Indeed, facial recognition is a recurrent topic in video interviewing software.

Regarding ML techniques used in video processing, early works introduced ANNs combined with AdaBoost for face recognition problems. ANNs were used for signal recognition and their application to facial recognition systems was a turning point. Some papers present experimental evidence that k-nearest neighbors (k-NN) is better than Hidden Markov Model (HMM) and Kernel Methods in facial recognition in video sequences (Baviskar, 2013). Others claim that k-NN is less time-consuming than Support Vector Machines (SVMs) and AdaBoost but less accurate (Dhriti & Kaur, 2012). SVM seems to perform better in most cases. Some studies show different performances according to different facial expressions: disgust, fear, and so on (e.g., Dino & Abdulrazzaq, 2019). As time goes by, neural network architectures become deeper (Wang & Deng, 2018). Taigman et al. (2014) made an important contribution in this respect, delivering a deep net, named DeepFace, a world-first when it comes to using a nine-layer CNN. Researchers trained it on the largest facial dataset to date, an identity labeled dataset of four million facial images. It provided a 25 percent error improvement with the dataset *Labeled Faces in the Wild*. It could be of particular interest for HR applications for video analysis, due to the accuracy in detecting very diverse facial characteristics. In comparison with previous methods, DL has the advantage of being trained with extensive datasets to learn the best features to represent the data (Saez-Trigueros et al., 2018). There is a price to be paid for this accuracy. One of the cons of DL models is indeed the need for large datasets. To achieve significant performance, even under conditions of bad lighting or limited technical conditions, robust DL models would need a great volume of datasets gathering information under diverse lighting or technical conditions. The key is not just working with big datasets but working with diverse datasets.

Facial Detection and Facial Feature Extraction

Facial recognition consists of identifying human faces and their features in two-dimensional images. Human faces are three-dimensional and look different dependent on changes in lighting and facial expression. Facial recognition systems perform different steps. The final goal is, most commonly, extracting features in faces. The first step is facial detection. In a later step, facial feature extraction carries out a more in-depth analysis to extract characteristics from the faces, like the location of elements (eyes, mouth), the ratio/distance between features, or more elaborated characteristics as mentioned below (see Figure 4.1).

Facial recognition systems depend on a database of persons of interest that could be matched against facial images. The first step is face detection in videos and images. Most images in HR are still unlike video surveillance, so this task is manageable. The second step involves some adjustments concerning the image's size and grayscale to enable the extraction of features in the third step. Then, the analogic face is processed considering parameters including ratio/distance between eyes, mouth, and other features. This process is known as facial feature extraction and constitutes the third step in facial recognition. The fourth step requires contrasting image vectors with datasets of faces. Emotion recognition analyses are frequently carried out by facial recognition technology used in HR. The state of the art of these systems is so advanced that it is even possible to determine age, sexual orientation, and social skills.

Understanding facial recognition is critical to the development of current video interviewing software. We should acknowledge the extensive body of work in facial recognition that supports recent analyses in HR. Lately, DL methods based on CNN have surpassed traditional

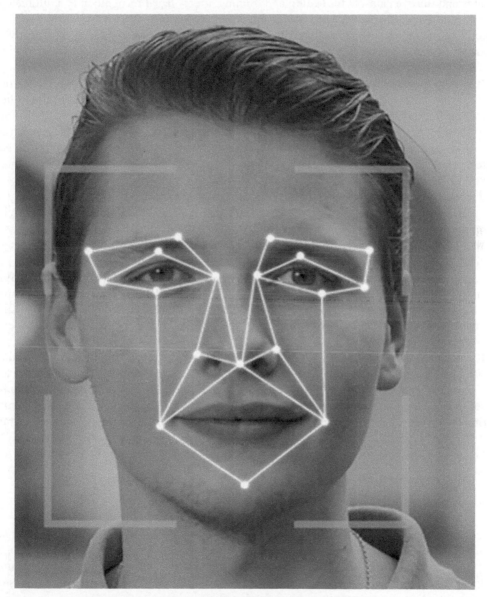

Source:　Pixabay, https://pixabay.com/photos/man-face-facialrecognition-5946820/.

Figure 4.1　*Example of facial detection (outer gray lines) and facial feature extraction (white lines and points)*

accurate ML techniques in this regard. HR ML video data problems are reduced to face/voice/keyword recognition problems, particularly a visual pattern recognition problem. Video interviewing software today faces a tremendous challenge: facial detection. The main difficulties associated with face detection are lighting and those related to the different camera resolutions and shooting angles. There is an actual problem of racial bias and ageism. The shortage of proper and diverse datasets for testing and training affects facial recognition and, ultimately, software in HR departments. Thus, racial and other types of bias come up. In this regard, it is noted that not all AI-powered software used in HR has a racial bias. Here we focus mainly on those using facial recognition technology. The choice of uninformative facial features could foster the endemic problem of algorithmic bias too.

It is worth mentioning relevant research conducted by Viola and Jones (2004) as a starting point for face detection and facial recognition. They presented a rapid method that allows face detection in real time, establishing the foundation for other models in the future. It is known that Viola–Jones performs better with frontal faces. It comprises two phases after converting the image to grayscale: training (which includes stages *training classifiers* and *AdaBoost*) and detection. The most significant detail is the introduction of rectangle and *Haar*-like features for quick detection.

The following list of relevant studies in facial recognition summarizes the main findings in the area. Survey papers in face recognition (Chellappa et al., 1995; Wang et al., 2017) provide summary reports of the early and current studies. The introduction of the Eigenface approach in the early 1990s was very meaningful (Turk & Pentland, 1991). Facial key point has been critical for face recognition and analysis in recent years. Introducing ANN (Le, 2011) as a problem-solving tool eased many research challenges. DL's irruption has drastically simplified long-standing problems in facial recognition (Sun et al., 2014; Parkhi et al., 2015; Schroff et al., 2015; Farfade et al., 2015). DL works well for face point detection (Sun et al., 2013; Wang & Deng, 2018) and face verification (Yang et al., 2015) to the extent of human-level performance (Taigman et al., 2014) or even surpassing it (Lu and Tang, 2015).

Recognition of frontal faces in still images is sensitive to various factors such as lighting, expression, occlusion, and aging (Taigman et al., 2014). There are standard images to test image recognition algorithms, for example the so-called Lena. There are standard datasets for video processing too, such as *Hollywood* and *Hollywood 2*[5] (containing 12 classes of human actions and scenes), *TVHI*, *Wearefamily* (for multiple people recognition) (Eichner & Ferrari, 2010), *UCF50*,[6] *UCF101*[7] (the largest dataset of human actions), and *Moment in Time*[8] (2018 MIT research project that gathers video scenes to produce a dataset for action and event recognition).

Recognition of Controversial Characteristics

According to previous literature related to the recognition of human *gender*, some works are again considered to be important milestones. They introduced rectangle or Haar-like features for rapid face detection and used them for real-time gender and ethnicity classification of videos (Zhao et al., 2003). Walavalkar et al. (2003) used SVM for gender classification, supporting their theories using only audio and video cues.

One of the most controversial characteristics that can be analyzed with video interviewing software is *race*. It is common knowledge that learning algorithms and classifiers were traditionally trained with images of white people and offer different results for diverse races.

Buolamwini and Gebru (2018) highlighted an open debate regarding the inclusion of racial differences in algorithms. Siyao et al. (2014) provided a basic survey concerning race and emphasized the complexities in detecting non-white individuals in night conditions. For race detection, the most frequently used ML algorithms are k-NN, ANN, and AdaBoost.

Models can be trained to detect *physical attractiveness* and beauty. Signals of beauty could be a good proportion of intraocular distance and coherency with eye size. For example, a good ratio of face width/height and a proportional mouth contrasted with the rest of the face would signify beauty. These ideas pose a challenge regarding the legitimacy of measuring attractiveness through data generated by audio and video, especially in countries where data protection law is not applied fully. Even more controversial is the possibility of detecting *sexual orientation* in multimodal analysis. As an illustration of the advances in recognizing sexual orientation, we should point to some recent experiments carried out by Wang and Kosinski (2018).

Companies could follow implicit criteria to recruit according to *age*. It is a matter of detecting the effect of aging on facial features. Analysis of audiovisual data generated in interviews could lead to a direct or indirect preference for employees of a particular age group. Inspection is necessary to avoid direct or indirect discrimination according to all these protected attributes, like age, gender, race, and so on. Levi and Hassner (2015) have proposed using CNN for estimating some controversial characteristics such as age and gender.

Even at the expense of trespassing too far on private data, the state of the art of AI lets companies use this information in the current social and legal environment. It sometimes leads to discrimination based on protected attributes. Applications related to controversial characteristics, such as age, are used regularly in convenience stores to detect underage customers purchasing spirits. For example, Yoti's age prediction system helps staff to screen the necessity of requesting ID cards (Yoti, 2019). The system relies on indicators of age and screens out customers using a ten-year error margin. Besides its use in retail and supermarkets in the UK, its possible application in hiring has been suggested. Recently, Yoti (2019) published a White Paper related to the application of facial recognition technology and age tracking with AI.

Recognition of Emotion Intensities

Recognition of emotion has always been crucial in human–computer interaction, interactive video games, or artificial vision applied to health. As of today, an essential part of video interview analysis is feature extraction and emotion recognition. Affective computing is a field of its own (see CHAPTER 13 for more information). There are also challenges related to emotion recognition such as bias related to gender differences in non-verbal cues. Understanding emotion by contrasting images of candidates with standardized video images used for training and testing could seem controversial, but it is actually the state of the art of emotion recognition in video images.

Authors like Remaida et al. (2020) have worked on surveys on personality traits analyses. Likewise, Mehta et al. (2019) have identified recent trends in DL targeting personality detection. They reviewed different ML techniques for personality detection, emphasizing multimodal analysis, a topical issue in personality computing. Hjelmås and Low (2001) categorize ML algorithms in their face detection survey as either feature-based or image-based and comment on their differences in performance. Ekman, one of the fathers of emotion recognition, categorized a set of human emotions back in the 1950s. These six basic emotions (anger, fear, disgust, happiness, sadness, and surprise) are common to all human beings in relation to expression and understanding (Ekman, 2003). Artificial vision can indeed track emotions, but there is a long way to go to integrate subtle cultural emotions, gender, and corporate differences into software tools for emotion intensities recognition used across different countries. There is no causal link between emotion and facial expression. Abdulsalam et al. (2019) propose algorithms for video-based emotion recognition with outstanding results and recognize the importance of Ekman's work.

AUDIO PROCESSING

Audio analysis is a field that comprises automatic speech recognition (ASR), digital signal processing, and sounds classification, tagging, and generation/synthesis. Today, many companies are experimenting with the extraction of information from audio signals, with popular products being Alexa, Siri, and Google Home, to mention a few (Laskaris, 2019). The goal of audio analysis is primarily extracting information from audio samples, namely audio signals. Sound/audio comes in an unstructured format. So first, there are some preprocessing steps like the sampling or representation of audio data.

Corporate audio processing applications index company calls, recommendations, similarity for audio files, and voice generation for corporate onboarding conversational agents. In our case, it all comes down to a ML problem. One can subdivide any of these problems into three categories: *data preprocessing, feature extraction*, and *training and evaluation*.

Feature extraction is a crucial step and prepares the model for accurate results (Laskaris, 2019). What is remarkable is that MFCCS (Mel Frequency Cepstral Coefficients), a tool presented by Davis and Mermelstein (1980), is still relevant and state of the art today. Audio analysis starts out by extracting mathematically complex MFCCs from speech samples. These MFCCs identify features and serve as a cornerstone to train an ANN and model evaluation. Models are finally evaluated based on additional audio samples (Laskaris, 2019). Key items for audio analysis in HR are the toolboxes to extract audio features (Eyben et al., 2010). The problem of feature extraction goes along with that of noise, which is a problem of greater magnitude than speech recognition. Goecke (2005) shows that for a significant performance improvement it is better to mix audio with additional visual speech information. There are very effective tools for emotion extraction from audio too, like MIRtoolbox (Lartillot, 2020). Moffat et al. (2015) analyzed ten frequently used audio feature extraction toolboxes, according to four of six criteria of the Cranfield Model (Cleverdon & Keen, 1966), for the evaluation of information retrieval systems.

Undoubtedly, speech recognition can be considered the leading category within the audio analysis area. In the beginning, speech recognition was based on Gaussian mixtures and feature coding (Deng et al., 2013). DL has replaced this trend over recent years and is now mainstream.

Next, we focus on the analysis of accent, a particular pattern within speech which could be targeted in HR software. State of the art of audio analysis is so advanced that it allows analyzing some patterns of speech pronunciation. Through accent, we can identify a person's linguistic, social, or cultural background. There have been different computational approaches to analyzing accents. Pedersen and Diederich (2007) investigated speech classification according to accent. A more detailed HR software analysis concentrates on the prosodic features extracted from an employee's speech. Prosody focuses on intonation and is enlightening and informative when it comes to the analysis of a person's speaking style.

Currently, different speech analysis tools are used, but details are not disclosed. There is indeed a need for transparency concerning the tools and datasets used as well as a need for governance and joint efforts within corporate and research spheres for better speech recognition. So, concerning audio, it is widely believed that video interviews seek to target specific characteristics in users, for example their fluency in foreign languages. There is previous work related to this level of assessment. Preciado-Grijalva and Brena (2018) – see UC4 – propose to automate the evaluation of speaker fluency level by implementing ML techniques.

Recognition of Emotions from HR Audio

Speech analysis is as important as image analysis for emotion recognition. Automatic feature extraction is based on a multimodal analysis (both audio and image). The specific analysis of emotion recognition in audio is a topic of interest in corporate environments too, such as in tracking fraudulent calls (see UC3). *Human*,[9] a start-up founded in London in 2016, analyzes subliminal emotions in video-based job applications in order to predict human behavior. *Affectiva*,[10] a start-up targeting human emotions analyses, deals with very diverse applications. Affectiva is one of the most important pieces of emotion recognition software. It analyzes and describes the facial descriptors associated with many speech events – such as laughter, sighs, grunts, and pauses – and organizes audio information in "emotion bearing segments". As an example, "engagement" is implied by the following set of facial gestures: brow raise, brow furrow, nose wrinkle, lip corner depressor, chin raise, lip pucker, lip press, mouth open, lip suck, and smile. Affectiva can identify emotions directly from YouTube videos and from video streaming. It has been primarily focused on video analysis, but it is extending research towards audio/speech analysis. Speech-based products, such as *EMOSpeech*[11] and *Vokaturi*[12] are used frequently nowadays. EMOSpeech allows call centers to analyze all recorded calls. Vokaturi can recognize emotions in the human voice, and it is often integrated into other software products. It should be noted that Vokaturi is based on the world's leading emotion recognition tool, *Praat*.[13]

MULTIMODAL PROCESSING

Multimodal processing is having an enormous impact on HR models. Traditionally, HR applications have been very much focused on video processing. It is noted that combining audio and video allows obtaining more accurate results. One of the most realistic applications of ML in audio and video data in HR is *video interviewing software* (UC1). Digital interviews are being increasingly used by corporations all over the planet and have a real impact on business processes. Video interviewing software's technical peculiarities address various problems that we face in both video and audio analysis. *Google Hire*[14] was one of the leading products but as of September 2020 is no longer available. Most HR products focus on the recruiting phase, whereas others are more oriented to the employee's emotions and well-being. *Montage*,[15] *SparkHire*,[16] and *WePow*[17] fall under the area of interview software or SAAS (Software as a Service). These software products are diversified across different areas and sectors. For example, the customer base of SparkHire is predominantly based in the United States, whereas WePow has a bigger market in Europe and in certain sectors like pharmaceuticals.[18]

Video interview/assessment software measures traits and competencies associated with performance at work. It looks at competencies such as cognitive ability and personality. There are several studies related to personality computing. For these analyses, tools like *HireVue* produce scores considering three dimensions: (i) voice and speech, (ii) visual-face, and (iii) textual. So, they look at voice tone, micro facial expressions, and speech-to-text analysis to extract *sentiment*. In brief, total sentiment is dependent on answer content, facial micro expression, and voice tone.

Figure 4.2 shows the process of candidate information extraction in multimodal analysis combining video, audio, and text. Candidate answers and information gathered by camera and sensors are branched into three different types of analysis: facial expression, voice tone and mood, and responses. Then, video, voice, and keywords sentiment analyses are carried out. All analyses are contrasted with former employees' databases and external datasets. The combination of the various types of sentiment analysis results in a multimodal analysis which is used along with the interview responses to calculate the candidate's score.

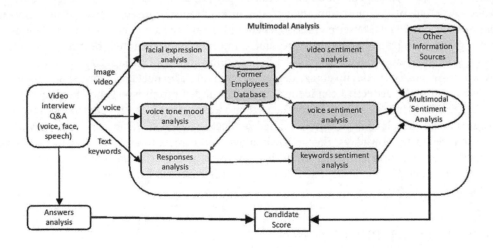

Figure 4.2   Video interview analysis

Another trend is combining audio and video in analyses. Suen et al. (2019) develop an asynchronous video interview (AVI) embedded in a semi-supervised DL model to guess applicants' personality. This is only a visual approach, namely looking at unimodal features in video. Authors acknowledge that applying multimodal features, both image frames and audio, to ML/DL models produces better results when predicting the big five personality traits (extraversion, agreeableness, openness to experience, conscientiousness, neuroticism).

One aspect criticized by researchers is the opacity of the models used, both audio and video, which make their application difficult in critical sectors like healthcare (Hemamou et al., 2019). Neither the applicants nor the recruiters know many details about the intrinsic technical information that influences the final decision. It is known that sensor technology, microphone and camera, take data for every question which are processed according to three groups: voice, face, and speech (keywords). Facial analysis and facial micro expressions are connected to a candidate's personality. These sophisticated connections were introduced a long time ago by the psychologist Paul Ekman (2003).

Abdulsalam et al. (2019) acknowledge this influential milestone in the analysis of facial micro expressions. Tone of voice expresses emotion and personality too. A candidate's speech is analyzed to extract the keywords used and contrasted with former employees' answers. Top employees tend to have similar backgrounds and similar responses.

ETHICAL ASPECTS AND OTHER CONCERNS

ML applications in HR can be suboptimal and their consequences may have ethical and even legal implications (Fernández-Martínez & Fernández, 2020). Some research claims, with evidence, that ML used in this domain is *racially biased*, or *privileges people* based on *gender* or *race*, intentionally or unintentionally (Buolamwini & Gebru, 2018). For many, ML used in HR video and audio is not entirely trustworthy. For sure, bias detection gets complicated due to the *lack of transparency* in algorithms for face and racial recognition. The state of the art in image and audio analysis is so advanced that it could lead to controversy (Das et al., 2018; Buolamwini & Gebru, 2018). The problem of racial bias in AI is not new, just like the problem of detection of mixed race in bad lighting conditions (Siyao et al., 2014). More research is taking place to detect bias. Even so, researchers and users need to be able to identify bias. Authors like Davenport (2018) recommend that technologists explore approaches to remove bias. Our overall aim should be looking for *transparency in ML* and explainable models in HR.

As far as our field of study is concerned, video interview systems carry bias due to the very nature of the technology (e.g., use of historic data from former employees who performed well). Similarly, it may be the case that the recruiting company introduces variables or seeks specific outcomes in HR ML models that also cause bias. Countries have laws and regulations to prevent discrimination by protected attributes (e.g., race and gender) at the workplace. And yet, even while these regulations exist to reduce discrimination, enterprises are given more and more freedom to customize their systems due to privacy issues. The black-box nature of some models does not help to prevent bias.

The idea of *identifying sexual orientation* reminds us of the difficulty level. The cues and sounds in every language vary and some of them are more prone to be considered homosexual by listeners and automatic classifiers. The same applies to gender; for example, males produce a shorter vowel duration than females. Problems could arise not just with the technicalities of the sounds for females, males, and different nationalities; that a company or state can predict the sexual orientation of employees could be potentially dangerous. This is critical when bearing in mind the number of countries that condemn homosexuality.

Some involuntary misclassifications can be generated by the inaccuracy of *data acquisition technology* (e.g., cameras). For example, race detection (or skin color) can be highly affected if the flashlight falls directly on the face or under night conditions. This may create race discrimination without anybody ever knowing it.

In many cases, *candidates are unfamiliar with the technical settings* and/or the specific application used in a video interview, even though they may have been given the option of exploring and testing it beforehand. This may be very important for their performance and for maximizing their success rate. Some gestures, like looking away from the camera, are certainly mistaken for global performance. Self-confidence is compromised due to a distorted image produced by smartphones.

Nowadays, video interviews are constrained to questions and answers. It would be highly recommendable to introduce the *body language* of the candidates into the assessments. Usually, people behave differently in person than in a video call. For example, tracking how many times candidates look away from the camera disadvantages candidates who are natural and spontaneous and not used to maintaining a direct gaze.

OPEN ISSUES AND CHALLENGES

In the next few years, HR will become fully digital. As the sector goes digital, more HR tools will become mainstream. The global pandemic has increased the need for more secure communications, and current and future tools will surely fill this need. Security will be the common denominator of future solutions.

Current research directions of ML methods in HR are related to the miscellaneous information inputs generated in recruitment processes, mainly audio, video, and information from sensors. All this content is generated in a corporate environment, and the intention is for it to be handled more efficiently. Noise extraction seems a traditional problem when it comes to analyzing audio.

One of the main open issues which requires future research work in the context of ML in HR audio and video is whether the models used should be more *explainable*. Video interviewing software faces this challenge. Companies will take on ML in different corporate situations. They will develop areas requiring new ML uses in corporate environments, such as chatbot technology (Nawaz & Gomes, 2019), which will indeed be very convenient. Explainability and transparency are important topics in discussions on the applicability of AI in many domains. If a model is not transparent enough, it cannot be used in crucial sectors. Future initiatives will involve applying those standards of explainability in a wide range of industries. Likewise, models should be transparent rather than being a "black box". Transparent and explainable models are indispensable requirements for a better future ML. XAI (Explainable AI) is a must in crucial sectors ranging from healthcare to security. Banking and insurance should only rely on explainable models too. Companies can be active stakeholders in mitigating bias. Some recent research initiatives involve letting companies and public entities verify their own models to check they do not incorporate bias inherited from past decisions. More information about Explainability of AI in HR can be found in CHAPTER 15.

There is a necessity to work on the *removal of algorithmic bias* and improvement of models. Working on *tools to remove or mitigate bias* is essential and remains an open challenge. One solution would be letting companies check for themselves quantitatively the bias in their algorithms and processes. In the same fashion, *datasets audit* remains an open challenge too. Applying models to different international and miscellaneous scenarios could affect gender, ethnic, disability, and social bias. Thus, the problem becomes more complex in multinational companies that use the same ML system to support the hiring process in different countries (with different laws or social norms).

It is essential to *foster proper auditing* and supervision of these systems by third-party non-profit entities, to avoid manipulative uses (Fernández-Martínez & Fernández, 2020). Most existing systems are slightly opaque and not officially audited. *Governments* should track selection processes if there is an infringement of fundamental employment laws and human rights on a wider scale. In particular, due to the diverse nature of global job markets, an ever-growing number of employees exposed to different approaches to regulation (for instance, some countries reserve some jobs just for their nationals) is expected.

As mentioned earlier, the imprecision of technology due to reduced signal quality may cause unfair candidate evaluation. *Candidates need to be informed* of the technical requirements for a good signal so they can set up an adequate video interview infrastructure (e.g. adequate lighting, good microphone, and a well-positioned camera) that will let them perform well technically. Wearables, such as microphones and augmented reality glasses, and/or cognitive help will be needed in the future to give candidates the opportunity to perform well and overcome their individual handicaps.

As regards future lines of work, ML for multimedia content analysis has a long journey ahead, especially multimodal and fusion technology. In the future, ML models will be more stable and have close to human accuracy. More auditing will be needed due to the fusion of multimedia technologies. External reviewers could have an independent say in the improvement of automated HR processes. The auditing process should watch every step of a model's development. It should check if the *datasets are good and neutral enough* as well as scrutinizing *different model outcomes*. This is an open issue in the ML discipline in general.

Improvement of audio models remains a present line of work that will continue into the future, especially in relation to achieving high-quality *conversions and sampling of voice models*, due to the uniqueness of human voice and speech patterns and differences in intonation, pronunciation, dialect, and so on. We still have much to do in developing good audio datasets and extraction libraries containing HR data.

SUMMARY AND DISCUSSION

This chapter provides an overview of the application of ML on video and audio data in HR. We surveyed existing HR works on both traditional and novel models for all audio and video analysis steps in HR software. Traditional problems in artificial vision, like facial and speech recognition, were a basis for our analysis. We focused on applications at the industrial scale as well as research initiatives, such as video interviewing software and speech analysis in HR calls and corporate conversational agents. Video interview faces a tremendous challenge; video analysis could be divided into complex artificial vision problems that can be improved with advances in ML and better and fair datasets. Unlike many proprietary applications that are being used these days, experimental projects offer an insight and comparatives of the ML techniques used.

The future of ML in HR is presumably going to be very bright. We are at the early stages of what should be a very promising field. Working from home along with travel restrictions due to the Covid 19 pandemic have enhanced the use of video interviewing and HR video software. There are challenges, though, especially concerning audio. It is critical to work on improving audio models and consider vocal differences among international speakers. Likewise, information loss in analog–digital conversion or sampling should be given due consideration.

Videoconferencing platforms will surely have an impact on future advances of ML for video. Undoubtedly, future research will head in that direction and we hope the insights given in this chapter will provide inspiration for further efforts.

According to one survey, 37 percent of organizations deployed AI solutions in some form throughout 2018. This survey[19] also shows that corporate AI grew by over 270 percent from 2014 to 2018. ML related to video interviewing is especially important, since every day more companies are using it. But we also mentioned numerous other promising applications of ML in HR. Many other areas of HR in the near future will potentially use ML video and audio data, such as candidate sourcing, hiring, agent-led video interview, and prediction of employee attrition and future performance.

The ethical implications of using ML in corporate environments still constitutes an open challenge. Some of them apply to several ML applications in other fields, namely non-representative or biased data. Another aspect to be considered is the black-box nature of many ML models. They sometimes seem to be very simple models, leading to an underfitting of the data, or to be too complex, leading to an overfitting of the data. More explainability and transparency when it comes to the application of ML in corporate environments is needed.

ACKNOWLEDGEMENTS

This work has been partially supported by the Spanish Ministry of Science, Innovation and Universities, co-funded by EU FEDER Funds, through project grant InEDGEMobility RTI2018-095390-B- C33 (MCIU/AEI/FEDER, UE).

NOTES

1. https://keencorp.com/
2. https://www.retorio.com/
5. Hollywood-2 Human Actions and Scenes dataset: https://pgram.com/dataset/hollywood-2-human -actions-and-scenes-dataset/
6. https://www.crcv.ucf.edu/data/UCF50.php
7. https://www.crcv.ucf.edu/data/UCF101.php
8. http://moments.csail.mit.edu/
9. https://citysail.co.uk/
10. https://www.affectiva.com/
11. https://emospeech.net
12. https://vokaturi.com
13. https://www.fon.hum.uva.nl/praat/
14. https://googlehire.com
15. https://www.montagetalent.com/
16. https://www.sparkhire.com/
17. https://www.wepow.com/es/
18. https://siftery.com/product-comparison/spark-hire-vs-wepow, accessed January 2021
19. https://www.gartner.com/en/newsroom/press-releases/2019-01-21-gartner-survey-shows-37 -percent-of-organizations-have, accessed November 9, 2021

REFERENCES

Abdulsalam, W. H., Alhamdani, R. S., & Abdullah, M. N. (2019). Facial emotion recognition from videos using deep convolutional neural networks. *International Journal of Machine Learning and Computing*, *9*(1), 14–19.

Alduayj, S. S., & Rajpoot, K. (2018, November 18–19). *Predicting employee attrition using machine learning* [Paper presentation]. 2018 International Conference on Innovations in Information Technology (IIT), Al Ain, United Arab Emirates.

Alom, M. Z., Karim, N. T., Rozario, S. P., Hoque, M. R., Bin, M. R., & Ashraf, S. L. R. (2014). Computer vision based employee activities analysis. *International Journal of Computer and Information Technology*, *3*(5), 942–946.

Averkov, V., & Kulalov, K. (2020, September 7–9). *Video monitoring of personnel in manufacturing equipment activity* [Paper presentation]. 27th Conference of Open Innovations Association, FRUCT, Trento, Italy.

Bavaresco, R. D., Silveira, E., Reis, J., Barbosa, R., Righi, C., Costa, C. R., Antunes, M., Gomes, C., Gattib, M., Vanzin, S., Junior, C., Silva, E., & Moreira, C. (2020). Conversational agents in business: A systematic literature review and future research directions. *Computer Science Review*, *36*(4), Article 100239.

Baviskar, M. (2013). Face tracking and recognition in videos: HMM vs KNN. *International Journal of Advance Research in Computer Science and Management Studies*, *1*(7), 317–327.

Buolamwini, J., & Gebru, T. (2018). Gender shades: Intersectional accuracy disparities in commercial gender classification. In A. S. Friedler & C. Wilson (Eds.), *Proceedings of the 1st Conference on Fairness, Accountability and Transparency* (pp. 77–91). PMLR.

Buzko, I., Dyachenko, Y., Petrova, M., Nenkov, N., Tuleninova, D., & Koeva, K. (2016). Artificial intelligence technologies in human resource development. *Computer Modelling and New Technologies*, *20*(2), 26–29.

Cahyono, F., Wirawan, W., & Rachmadi, R. F. (2020). Face recognition system using Facenet algorithm for employee presence. In *2020 4th International Conference on Vocational Education and Training (ICOVET)* (pp. 57–62). IEEE.

Cappelli, P., Tambe, P., & Yakubovich, V. (2019, April 8). *Artificial intelligence in human resources management: Challenges and a path forward*. SSRN. http://dx.doi.org/10.2139/ssrn.3263878

Chandar, P., Khazaeni, Y., Davis, M., Muller, M., Crasso, M., Liao, Q. V., Shami, N. S., & Geyer, W. (2017). Leveraging conversational systems to assist new hires during onboarding. In R. Bernhaupt, G. Dalvi, A. Joshi, D. K. Balkrishan, J. O'Neill, & M. Winckler (Eds.), *Human–Computer Interaction – INTERACT* (pp. 381–391). Springer.

Chellappa, R., Wilson, C. L., & Sirohey, S. (1995). Human and machine recognition of faces: A survey. *Proceedings of the IEEE*, *83*(5), 705–741.

Chen, L., Zhao, R., Leong, C. W., Lehman, B., Feng, G., & Hoque, M. E. (2017). Automated video interview judgment on a large-sized corpus collected online. In *Proceedings of Seventh International Conference on Affective Computing and Intelligent Interaction (ACII)* (pp. 504–509). https://doi.org/10.1109/ACII40879.2017

Cleverdon, C. W., & Keen, M. (1966). *Aslib Cranfield research project – factors determining the performance of indexing systems; volume 2, test results*. Technical Report, Cranfield University. http://hdl.handle.net/1826/861

Das, A., Dantcheva, A., & Bremond, F. (2018). Mitigating bias in gender, age and ethnicity classification: A multi-task convolution neural network approach. In *Proceedings of the European Conference on Computer Vision (ECCV)*. https://hal.inria.fr/hal-01892103

Davenport, T. H. (2018). *The AI advantage: How to put the AI revolution to work*. MIT Press.

Davis, S., & Mermelstein, P. (1980). Comparison of parametric representations for monosyllabic word recognition in continuously spoken sentences. *IEEE Transactions on Acoustics, Speech, and Signal Processing*, *28*(4), 357–366.

Deng, L., Jinyu, Li, Huang, J-T., Yao, K., Yu, D., Seide, F., Seltzer, M., Zweig, G., He, X., Williams, J., Gong, Y., & Acero, A. (2013). Recent advances in deep learning for speech research at Microsoft. In *IEEE International Conference on Acoustics, Speech, and Signal Processing, ICASSP-88*.

Dhriti, D. I, & Kaur, M. (2012). K-nearest neighbor classification approach for face and fingerprint at feature level fusion. *International Journal of Computer Applications*, *60*(14), 13–17.

Dino, H. I., & Abdulrazzaq, M. B. (2019). Facial expression classification based on SVM, KNN and MLP classifiers. In *International Conference on Advanced Science and Engineering (ICOASE)* (pp. 70–75). IEEE.

Eichner, M., & Ferrari, V. (2010). We are family: Joint pose estimation of multiple persons. In K. Daniilidis, P. Maragos, & N. Paragios (Eds.), *Computer vision – ECCV 2010* (pp. 228–242). Springer.

Ekman, P. (2003). Darwin, deception and facial expression. *Annals of the New York Academy of Sciences*, *1000*(1), 205–221.

Eyben, F., Wöllmer, M., & Schuller, B. (2010). Opensmile: The munich versatile and fast open-source audio feature extractor. In *Proceedings of the 18th ACM International Conference on Multimedia* (pp. 1459–1462). Association for Computing Machinery.

Farfade, S., Saberian, M., & Li, L. (2015). Multi-view face detection using deep convolutional neural networks. In *Proceedings of the 5th ACM on International Conference on Multimedia Retrieval* (pp. 643–650). Association for Computing Machinery.

Fernández-Martínez, C., & Fernández, A. (2020). AI and recruiting software: Ethical and legal implications. *Paladyn. Journal of Behavioral Robotics*, *11*(1), 199–216.

Goecke, R. (2005). Audio-video automatic speech recognition: An example of improved performance through multimodal sensor input. In *Proceedings of the 2005 NICTA-HCSNet Multimodal User Interaction Workshop* (pp. 25–32). Australian Computer Society, Inc.

Hemamou, L., Felhi, G., Martin, J. C., & Clavel, C. (2019). Slices of attention in asynchronous video job interviews. In *8th International Conference on Affective Computing and Intelligent Interaction (ACII)* (pp. 1–7). IEEE.

Hjelmås, E., & Low, B. K. (2001). Face detection: A survey. *Computer Vision and Image Understanding*, *83*(3), 236–274.

Jordan, M. I., & Mitchell, T. M. (2015). Machine learning: Trends, perspectives, and prospects. *Science*, *349*, 255–260.

Khan, M. F., & Habib, H. A. (2010). Video analytics for quantitative employee performance evaluation. *Canadian Journal on Image Processing and Computer Vision*, *1*(1), 9–15.

Kindiroglu, A. A., Akarun, L., & Aran, O. (2017). Multi-domain and multi-task prediction of extraversion and leadership from meeting videos. *EURASIP Journal on Image and Video Processing*, *2017*, Article 77.

Lartillot, O. (2020). *MIRtoolbox*. MATLAB Central File Exchange. https://www.jyu.fi/hytk/fi/laitokset/mutku/en/research/materials/mirtoolbox, accessed November 16, 2020.

Laskaris, N. (2019, November 18). How to apply machine learning and deep learning methods to audio analysis. *Towards Data Science*. https://towardsdatascience.com/how-to-apply-machine-learning-and-deep-learning-methods-to-audio-analysis-615e286fcbbc, accessed November 9, 2021.

Le, T. H. (2011). Applying artificial neural networks for face recognition. *Advances in Artificial Neural Systems*. *2011*, Article 673016. https://doi.org/10.1155/2011/673016

Lebedeva, E., Zubkov, A., Bondarenko, D., Rymarenko, K., Nukhaev, M., & Grishchenko, S. (2019). Evaluation of oil workers' performance based on surveillance video. In *2019 International Multi-Conference on Engineering, Computer and Information Sciences (SIBIRCON)* (pp. 432–435). IEEE.

LeCun, Y., Bengio, Y., & Hinton, G. (2015). Deep learning. *Nature*, *521*, 436–444.

Levi, G., & Hassner, T. (2015). Age and gender classification using convolutional neural networks. In *Proceedings of the IEEE Conference on Computer Vision and Pattern Recognition Workshops* (pp. 34–42). IEEE. https://doi.org/10.1109/CVPR31182.2015

Lu, C., & Tang, X. (2015). Surpassing human-level face verification performance on LFW with gaussian face. In *Proceedings of the Twenty-Ninth AAAI Conference on Artificial Intelligence (AAAI'15)* (pp. 3811–3819). AAAI Press.

Luo, H., Xiong, C., Fang, W., Love, P. E. D., Zhang, B., & Ouyang, X. (2018). Convolutional neural networks: Computer vision-based workforce activity assessment in construction. *Automation in Construction*, *94*, 282–289.

Mady, H. H., & Hilles, S. M. (2017). Efficient real time attendance based on face detection case study "MEDIU Staff". *International Journal on Contemporary Computer Research (IJCCR)*, *1*(2), 21–25.

Mehta, D., Siddiqui, M. F., & Javaid, A. Y. (2019). Recognition of Emotion intensities using machine learning algorithms: A comparative study. *Sensors, 19*(8), Article 1897.

Moffat, D., Ronan, D., & Reiss, J. D. (2015). An evaluation of audio feature extraction toolboxes. In *Proceedings of the 18th International Conference on Digital Audio Effects (DAFx-15)*. https://www.ntnu.edu/dafx15/proceedings.

Mumtaz, M., & Habib, H. A. (2012). Evaluation of activity recognition algorithms for employee performance monitoring. *IJCSI International Journal of Computer Science Issues, 9*(5), 203–210.

Nawaratne, R., Alahakoon, D., De Silva, D., & Yu, X. (2019). Spatiotemporal anomaly detection using deep learning for real-time video surveillance. *IEEE Transactions on Industrial Informatics, 16*(1), 393–402.

Nawaz, N., & Gomes, A. M. (2019). Artificial intelligence chatbots are new recruiters. *IJACSA International Journal of Advanced Computer Science and Applications, 10*(9), 1–5.

Özlan, B., Haznedaroğlu, A., & Arslan, L. M. (2019). Automatic fraud detection in call center conversations. In *2019 27th Signal Processing and Communications Applications Conference (SIU)* (pp. 1–4). IEEE.

Paray, M., Espinosa, S. K. K., Tanquiamco, D., Jandayan, C., & Grace D. P. (2020, June 27). *Analysis and design of employee attendance monitoring using face recognition system for Archempress Fruit Corporation*. SSRN. https://ssrn.com/abstract=3636604

Parkhi, O. M., Vedaldi, A., & Zisserman, A. (2015). Deep face recognition. In *Proceedings of the British Machine Vision Conference (BMVC)* (pp. 41.1–41.12). BMVA Press.

Pedersen, C., & Diederich, J. (2007). Accent classification using support vector machines. In *The 6th IEEE/ACIS International Conference on Computer and Information Science (ICIS 2007)* (pp. 444–449). IEEE.

Preciado-Grijalva, A., & Brena, R. (2018, August 31). *Speaker fluency level classification using machine learning techniques*. ArXiv. arXiv:abs/1808.10556.

Rasipuram, S., Pooja Rao, S. B., & Jayagopi, D. B. (2016). Asynchronous video interviews vs. face-to-face interviews for communication skill measurement: A systematic study. In *Proceedings of the 18th ACM International Conference on Multimodal Interaction* (pp. 370–377). Association for Computing Machinery.

Remaida, A., Abdellaoui, B., Moumen, A., & El Idrissi, Y. E. B. (2020). Personality traits analysis using artificial neural networks: A literature survey. In *2020 1st International Conference on Innovative Research in Applied Science, Engineering and Technology (IRASET)* (pp. 1–6). IEEE.

Rupasinghe, A. T, Gunawardena, N. L, Shujan, S., & Atukorale, D. A. S. (2016). Employee recruitment: Question formation for employment interviews based on facial cue analytics. In *Proceedings of International Conference on Business Management*. https://journals.sjp.ac.lk/index.php/icbm/article/view/2994

Saez-Trigueros, D., Meng, L., & Hartnett, M. (2018, October 31). *Face recognition: From traditional to deep learning methods*. ArXiv. arXiv:abs/1811.00116.

Sardis, E., & Varvarigou, T. (2010). Industrial workflows recognition by computer vision and AI technologies. In *Sixth International Conference on Intelligent Information Hiding and Multimedia Signal Processing* (pp. 587–590). IEEE.

Schroff, F., Kalenichenko, D., & Philbin, J. (2015). FaceNet: A unified embedding for face recognition and clustering. In *IEEE Conference on Computer Vision and Pattern Recognition (CVPR)* (pp. 815–823). IEEE.

Seo, J., Han, S., Lee, S., & Kim, H. (2015). Computer vision techniques for construction safety and health monitoring. *Advanced Engineering Informatics, 29*(12), 239–251.

Siyao, F., Haibo, H., & Zeng-Guang, H. (2014). Learning race from face: A survey. *IEEE Transactions on Pattern Analysis and Machine Intelligence, 36*(12), 2483–2509.

Sreenu, G., & Durai, M. A. (2019). Intelligent video surveillance: A review through deep learning techniques for crowd analysis. *Journal of Big Data, 6*, Article 48.

Strohmeier, S., & Piazza, F. (2015). Artificial intelligence techniques in human resource management – a conceptual exploration. In C. Kahraman & S. Çevik Onar (Eds.), *Intelligent techniques in engineering management* (pp. 149–172). Springer. https://doi.org/10.1007/978-3-319-17906-3_7

Suen, H. Y., Hung, K. E., & Lin, C. L. (2019). TensorFlow-based automatic personality recognition used in asynchronous video interviews. *IEEE Access, 7*, 61018–61023.

Suen, H., Hung, K., & Lin, C. (2020). Intelligent video interview agent used to predict communication skill and perceived personality traits. *Human-centric Computing and Information Sciences*, *10*, Article 3.

Sun, Y., Wang, X., & Tang, X. (2013). Deep convolutional network cascade for facial point detection. In *Proceedings of the IEEE Conference on Computer Vision and Pattern Recognition* (pp. 3476–3483). IEEE.

Sun, Y., Wang, X., & Tang, X. (2014). Deep learning face representation from predicting 10,000 classes. In *Proceedings of the IEEE Conference on Computer Vision and Pattern Recognition* (pp. 1891–1898). IEEE.

Taigman, Y., Yang, M., Ranzato, M., & Wolf, L. (2014). DeepFace: Closing the gap to human-level performance in face verification. In *Proceedings of the IEEE Conference on Computer Vision and Pattern Recognition* (pp. 1701–1708). IEEE.

Turk, M. A., & Pentland, A. P. (1991). Face recognition using eigenfaces. In *IEEE Computer Society Conference on Computer Vision and Pattern Recognition* (pp. 586–591). IEEE.

Viola, P., & Jones, M. J. (2004). Robust real-time face detection. *International Journal of Computer Vision*, *57*, 137–154.

Walavalkar, L., Yeasin, M., Narasimhamurthy, A., & Sharma, R. (2003). Support vector learning for gender classification using audio and visual cues. *International Journal of Pattern Recognition and Artificial Intelligence*, *17*(3), 417–439.

Wang, M., & Deng, W. (2018, August 18). *Deep face recognition: A survey*. ArXiv. abs/1804.06655.

Wang, Y., & Kosinski, M. (2018). Deep neural networks are more accurate than humans at detecting sexual orientation from facial images. *Journal of Personality and Social Psychology*, *114*(2), 246–257.

Wang, Y., See, J., Oh, Y. H., Phan, R. C. W., Rahulamathavan, Y., Ling, H. C., Tan, S. W., & Li, X. (2017). Effective recognition of facial micro-expressions with video motion magnification. *Multimedia Tools and Applications*, *76*, 21665–21690.

Xing, J., Yu, M., Wang, S., Zhang, Y., & Ding, Y. (2020). Automated fraudulent phone call recognition through deep learning. In *2020 International Wireless Communications and Mobile Computing (IWCMC)*. IEEE. https://doi.org/10.1109/IWCMC48107.2020

Yang, S., Luo, P., Loy, C. C., & Tang, X. (2015). From facial parts responses to face detection: A deep learning approach. In *IEEE International Conference on Computer Vision (ICCV)* (pp. 3676–3684). IEEE.

Yoti (2019). *Yoti age scan – public version* [White paper]. https://www.yoti.com/wp-content/uploads/2019/09/Age-Scan-White-Paper-Executive-Summary-December19.pdf, accessed February 23, 2021.

Zhao, W., Chellappa, R., Phillips, P. J., & Rosenfeld, A. (2003). Face recognition: A literature survey. *ACM Computing Surveys*, *35*(4), 399–458.

5. HR machine learning on social media data

Jake T. Harrison and Christopher J. Hartwell

INTRODUCTION

For years, Human Resource (HR) departments have gathered data from various sources to aid in responsibilities such as recruitment and selection, strategic planning, and employee management. However, recent years have seen an incredible increase in the use of digital technology in these functions, largely due to the development of a myriad of software programs, the heightened study of people analytics, and artificial intelligence (AI). Many of today's tech giants such as Apple, Netflix, Amazon, and Google are using these digital technologies to close the gap between tech and culture (Safian, 2017), and others are quickly following.

Those involved in Human Resource Management (HRM) have begun capitalizing on this intersection between digital technology and the individual lives of potential, current, and former employees by utilizing machine learning, a type of AI which aims to convert data inputs into predictions (Agrawal, Gans, & Goldfarb, 2020). While the term AI broadly refers to a computer's capability to act intelligently (Nilsson, 2014), machine learning is specifically concerned with allowing computers to learn (Ayodele, 2010). As noted in CHAPTER 2, a distinction can be made between direct machine learning processes, such as search engine results refinement and email filtering, and AI-based systems that indirectly employ machine learning approaches, such as chatbots. Throughout this chapter, we consider both direct and indirect machine learning as they relate to social media. By "outsourcing" certain HR tasks to AI and using machine learning to quickly and efficiently gather and analyze information, HR personnel can devote more time to higher-level tasks.

Perhaps the richest venue for the HR workforce to acquire digital information input is social media platforms, which have become a staple in our society, particularly with younger generations. Social media content harvested from platforms such as Facebook, Twitter, Instagram, or LinkedIn provides insight into the lives of potential or current employees that could be useful in HRM by illuminating strengths and weaknesses via posts, photos, and connections (Hartwell, 2015). With the use of AI, particularly machine learning, social media platforms can quickly and easily be mined for particular keywords or attitudes that are desirable, thus providing leads for recruiting. As AI becomes more advanced, many people are becoming concerned with practices that have developed; the mining, analysis, and human-like interactions that are displayed fall into a largely unclear ethical gray area, and could become difficult to control (Dietterich & Horvitz, 2015).

In this chapter, we detail the use of social media data in HR functions that are of common interest, such as recruiting and selecting employees, and further explain how machine learning uses social media data. Additionally, we provide insight into the evolving job roles of HR personnel, the ethical implications of using machine learning, and future directions for application and research.

THE USE OF SOCIAL MEDIA DATA IN HR FUNCTIONS

The effectiveness of HRM within an organization is partly based on the amount and quality of information the HR department has. Traditionally, raw information has been harvested from internal sources that are often referred to as the 'digital exhaust' of an organization, including email exchanges, chats, and file transfers (Leonardi & Contractor, 2018). More recently, HR departments have started shifting towards a technology-based approach to HR, which often harvests information from online sources such as social media websites (Johnson & Gueutal, 2011). While privacy risks exist, there is relatively little discouragement towards using social media data in the various HR functions. Rather, it has proven to be remarkably beneficial and often results in a win-win situation for the user and the viewer.

Increasing Popularity and Use

Although many have offered broad definitions, Howard and Parks (2012) have more specifically defined social media as a technology that consists of three parts: (a) the information infrastructure and tools used to produce and distribute content, (b) the content that takes the digital form of personal messages, news, ideas, and cultural products, and (c) the people, organizations, and industries that produce and consume digital content. To further break down the construct, social media can be split into several subcategories. *Social Networking Websites* (SNWs) are the most common type of social media and promote personal human interaction through knowledge sharing between individuals and groups of individuals (Biteable, 2019). Facebook, for example, is the world's most popular SNW and has constantly grown in use since its inception. Currently, it harbors over 2.7 billion active global monthly users (Facebook, 2020). Twitter follows with 68 million (Twitter, 2019) active global monthly users. Emerging as a widely popular professional SNW is LinkedIn, with 62 million active global monthly users in 2020 and a projected 67 million by 2022 (eMarketer, 2020a).

Another type of social media is *Multi-Media Websites* (MMWs), which specialize in the creation, sharing, and viewing of photos and videos (Bump, n.d.). Instagram, for instance, boasts 112 million active global monthly users (eMarketer, 2020b). Other examples include YouTube, TikTok, and Snapchat, which rely on users to create and view content as a way of connecting humans. A notable third type of social media is *Discussion and Blog Websites* (DBWs), which create a venue for dialogue to be exchanged that addresses specific news, interests, or opinions (Foreman, 2020). Quorra, Reddit, and Tumblr are examples. Finally, there are *Review Websites* (RWs), where users can rate and comment on various targets, such as movies (e.g., Rotten Tomatoes), businesses (e.g., Yelp), and even employers (e.g., Indeed, Glassdoor). As social media quickly evolves, the lines have begun to blur between the subcategories, making clear definitions difficult to solidify. For example, multiple SNWs, such as Facebook and LinkedIn, now offer features such as "live video" and "stories" which would traditionally fit into the MMW category. Facebook is an especially interesting case, as it currently includes features that fit into all four subcategories (e.g., ability to recommend and review businesses). In order to help make sense of the social media landscape, Table 5.1 categorizes social media platforms in terms of three characteristics: the type of media used/ supported (video/audio, photos, text), level of interaction (high, medium, low), and platform type (SNW, MMW, DBW, RW).

Table 5.1   *Categorization of social media platforms*

Social media platform	Media type used/supported			Level of interaction	Platform type			
	Video/Audio	*Photos*	*Text*		*SNW*	*MMW*	*DBW*	*RW*
Facebook	○	○	●	High	▪	▫	▫	▫
Twitter	○	○	●	High	▪	▫		
LinkedIn	○	○	●	Medium	▪	▫	▫	
Instagram	○	●	○	High	▫	▪		
TikTok	●	○	○	Medium	▫	▪		
Snapchat	●	○	○	High	▫	▪		
YouTube	●		○	Medium		▪	▫	
Reddit	○	○	●	High			▪	
Indeed			●	Low				▪

Note: The number of social media platforms available worldwide is immense. The list of social media platforms listed in this table is meant to be representative, and not at all exhaustive. *SNW* = Social Networking Website, *MMW* = Multi-Media Website, *DBW* = Discussion and Blog Website, *RW* = Review Website. ● Main media focus, ○ Secondary media focus, ▪ Main platform type, ▫ Secondary platform type.

Aggregated, there are approximately 3.6 billion users worldwide across all SNW platforms, accounting for nearly half (46 percent) of the world's population (Statista, 2020). These enormous numbers provide opportunities for HR departments to access information that is generally freely available online, as well as create content for advertisement purposes. Taking advantage of this phenomenally large and dense access to people data could be a major opportunity for organizations looking for a competitive advantage in the recruitment, selection, and management of their workforce. Each of the subcategories of social media show promise for machine learning integration by HR departments, although SNWs seem to be where the majority of efforts are directed currently.

Unique Information Harvested from Social Media Platforms

The nature of the information available on social media is vastly different from that of the information which could be collected internally. Specifically, social media information provides first-person, naturalistic accounts of user behaviors and opinions that are often unseen in the workplace (Conway & O'Connor, 2016). Further, social media often highlights the more personal dimension of an individual's life, which can provide insight when it comes to that individual's personality, integrity, or work ethic. In the recruiting context, behaviors, values, and competencies that are displayed through group affiliations, friendships, photos, or commentary on social media platforms provide HR staff with a potentially valuable new perspective when determining organizational fit (Stoughton, Thompson, & Meade, 2015). In a management perspective, these same social interactions may shed light on unethical or inappropriate actions of current employees that could be damaging to the organization. Thus, social media is often a major component when companies use cybervetting – the practice of screening online information about a person – during the hiring process (Hartwell & Eggli, 2020).

A distinction has been made between *personal social media platforms* (Facebook, Twitter, etc.), which focus on the personal identity of an individual, and *professional social media platforms* (LinkedIn, ResearchGate, etc.), which focus on the professional identity of an individual

(Hartwell, 2019; Roulin & Bangerter, 2013). Further, research has shown that in the context of human resources, personal social media platforms are typically used to seek out negative information, while professional social media platforms are typically used to seek out positive information (Hartwell & Campion, 2020). Users on LinkedIn are often intentionally *trying* to be discovered by recruiters or other professionals, whereas Facebook users are generally using the platform to focus on family and friends. Therefore, users of personal social media platforms are typically not expecting employers to gather and use that information for work purposes (Mgrditchian, 2015). This may, in fact, contribute to the value of the information, given that, typically, no manipulations have been made by the user to manage employer impressions.

While various HR functions could be affected by the application of machine learning techniques to social media data, we focus on the HR functions likely to be most strongly affected. First is recruitment and selection. Recruitment refers to finding pools of potential applicants to the organization as well as ways to effectively market and advertise job openings that effectively motivate that talent pool to actually apply for the job. Selection is focused on how to determine the best qualified individual(s) for the job out of the applicants that have applied. These functions are often intertwined in practice, and we discuss them together for the sake of clarity and conciseness. The second HR function has to do with managing the current workforce. Part of managing current employees is monitoring job performance and communicating effectively. Doing these things helps to ensure that employees are engaged in their work, are adding value to the organization, and are clear on their roles and job duties.

Recruitment and Selection

The responsibility to recruit new talent and to make employment selection decisions is not new for HR departments. In fact, these duties are at the heart of HR. However, the increasing use of social media has significantly changed the way many firms are performing these functions, and provides another angle of attack that is less traditional in nature.

Organizations succeed or fail based largely upon the people within them. The aim of recruiting in HRM is to attract individuals that have desirable knowledge, skills, and abilities that will benefit the organization. While some highly skilled potential applicants are actively seeking employment (active job seekers), many firms have realized that high-quality talent is often already employed with other companies. These individuals may not be actively seeking new employment, but could be open to the right opportunity if it is brought to their attention (passive job seekers). Thus, the employer could bring added value by actively recruiting high-quality passive job seekers. In addition to the orthodox recruiting methods of pursuing referrals, developing advertising (signs, billboards, etc.), utilizing third-party organizations (employment agencies or placement services), and particular school or company targeting (Marsden, 1994) to find active job seekers, HR managers can now use multiple social media methods to recruit passive job seekers, which may prove to be faster and more effective.

One of these techniques plays off of a traditional marketing approach by creating social media posts or advertisements that outline a job opportunity. Not only can these types of posts be sponsored – meaning that the recruiting firm pays the social media site a fee to display their post or ad to more users over a certain period of time – but they can be targeted, meaning that the ad will display to only desirable segments of the social media site, such as individuals in a certain geographic location, individuals with a certain age range or level of experience, or individuals that have been determined to possess particular traits or skills. These types of targeting activities can be completed via machine learning, which most social media sites already employ. Facebook, for example, has an entire business model that depends on advertising, which is manipulated based upon which users Facebook's algorithms determine to be a worthwhile target (Mcnamee, 2019). Recruiting firms can buy into this system by leveraging Facebook's extensive gathered information to display their job posting to the desired audience. In the language of CHAPTER 2, this represents an embedded machine learning process, where a third-party vendor (e.g., Facebook, LinkedIn) utilizes machine learning processes that can be accessed downstream by the hiring firm.

As well, algorithms have become successful at identifying the presence of individuals' personality traits based on the content they share on SNWs (Song et al., 2020), which is desirable for recruiters. For instance, one recent meta-analytic study on the use of social media to predict personality concluded that the correlations between a user's social media content and the characteristics of openness, conscientiousness, and neuroticism were positive and statistically significant (Azucar, Marengo, & Settanni, 2018). It has been observed that in the context of organizational fit, personality could potentially be more influential than values, due to its stability, ability to predict behavior, and observability (Judge & Kristof-Brown, 2004). Personality predictions made by a social media site's machine learning algorithms (an embedded machine learning process) can allow recruiting companies to present opportunities to individuals that are more likely to be desirable based on their aptitude for the position and organizational fit. The same things can be done using an explicit machine learning process, where the company utilizes its own machine learning capabilities to analyze applicant SNW content. However, most SNWs include language in their user agreements that prohibits or severely limits automated gathering and analysis of their users' data. Finally, there are issues with validity and validation that need to be addressed when measuring personality via SNW content (Bleidorn & Hopwood, 2019; Tay et al., 2020).

When utilizing SNWs to target qualified passive job seekers, organizations are really recruiting and selecting simultaneously. When targeting individuals online that already possess knowledge, skills, abilities, and personality traits (as determined by the AI), the applicant pool that results is largely "pre-screened" against whatever targeted criteria are used. LinkedIn has recently developed assessments that users can take to display certain skills they possess, which are often searched for by recruiters (Jersin, 2019). Additionally, the time that HR managers take to select new employees can be drastically reduced, because the applicants recruited in this manner are more likely to meet minimum job qualifications.

Hiring firms and SNW platforms can work in tandem to utilize machine learning for their mutual benefit in these situations. As a hypothetical example, a company could work with LinkedIn to target potential applicants with a specific skill set, such as a specific degree, current/prior job title, skills listed in their profile, and demonstrated competency of a skill through LinkedIn assessment. When LinkedIn provides a list of users that meet one or more of the company's requested qualifications, the company would then review these users and reach out to those it is interested in pursuing. Based on the users that the company pursues, LinkedIn could use machine learning to analyze those user profiles to better target a second round of prospective applicants (or for similar jobs – with the same company or even a different one – in the future).

Traditional selection procedures rely on active input (applications, interviews, etc.) from an applicant, whereas social media screening methods are passive and asynchronous (Hartwell & Campion, 2020). Many have suggested that social media information could be used in the selection process to measure potentially job-related criteria, such as personality, interpersonal skills, cognitive ability, creativity, leadership, professionalism, person–organization fit, and writing ability (Brown & Vaughn, 2011; Davison et al., 2012; Kluemper, 2013; Van Iddekinge et al., 2016). If social media information provided accurate measures of these or other job-related constructs (there is not enough research yet to know for sure), social media could provide a quick and inexpensive way for organizations to gain this information, rather than using company resources to develop and administer such assessments to applicants. The use of machine learning to gather and analyze the SNW content would also provide a quicker and much more objective approach, though it would require a large initial investment of resources to develop effective algorithms and consistent monitoring to ensure that the algorithms remain relevant, effective, and free from bias.

Monitoring and Communication

Another notable function in HRM is managing the current workforce. One major facet of this function is employee monitoring, which refers to assessing the productivity, capacity, and engagement of employees in an organization. While office roaming (management by walking around [MBWA]; Tucker & Singer, 2015), regular employee interviews, and engagement surveys can provide some insight into the minds of employees, using social media to monitor employees can give additional insights into factors that may be concerning, and which may not be expressed while at work. For example, a certain employee may not feel comfortable voicing a certain concern to the leadership at their place of work, yet will post about that concern on social media. As well, companies that have an internal social media platform of their own can receive engagement there that may not have happened in person. By monitoring social media, HR departments can be made aware of areas for improvement in the lives of employees. In addition, HR departments scan employee SNW content for illegal, unethical, or otherwise undesirable information that has the potential to present a liability for the company, or simply damage the company's reputation. Privacy concerns are often raised with regard to using this method of employee monitoring, which we will discuss in a later section.

In addition to SNWs, RWs are a fruitful area for employers to better understand the engagement of their workforce. Studies using machine learning to analyze and categorize employee feedback on RWs like Glassdoor.com and Indeed.com have demonstrated that this information can provide unique insights into some of the salient factors that relate to job satisfaction and employee engagement, and that could also impact employee retention (Jung & Suh, 2019; Landers, Brusso, & Auer, 2019; Sainju, 2020).

Aside from using social media to determine areas of improvement for employees or discover "red flags," many companies are regularly using social media profiles to disperse information not only to employees, but also to the general public. Surveys of internet users in the United States indicated that 73 percent (AudienceProject, 2020a), 63 percent (AudienceProject, 2020b), and 52 percent (AudienceProject, 2020c) of people in the United States use Facebook, Instagram, and Twitter every day, respectively. Given that a large portion of social media users is represented by the younger generation, those that are entering the workforce or early in their careers are likely to be more active on social media than their older-generation counterparts. Thus, companies who use social media to disseminate information are likely to capture the attention of many of their employees, specifically the younger ones. However, because older individuals are less likely to use social media (Kontos et al., 2010), a company focusing solely on social media for recruitment or disseminating information to employees may face legal challenges associated with age discrimination.

When companies post about initiatives, events, or values on social media, it is not only the general public that views them. Employees of that company will also see the posts, and in turn gain the perspective that the general public has regarding the company. This is often a good way to alert employees and the public at the same time to certain announcements. In an increasingly digital world, many HR managers lack the technology skills and knowledge to keep up with these opportunities for communication (Ellis, 2018). Thus, an area for improvement is presented.

THE USE OF MACHINE LEARNING ON SOCIAL MEDIA DATA

Machine learning relies on good data to develop useful results; closely modeling the oft-cited "garbage in, garbage out" mantra, clear, useful data is imperative for valuable and interpretable results. While data harvested from users' social media behavior is not always perfectly accurate, it can often provide useful insights. As noted in Table 5.1, various social media platforms focus on different forms of media (audio/visual, photos, text), and data gathered and analyzed from these sites will differ based on the type of media available.

The practice of using machine learning to gather and analyze social media data has been realized in many domains. For example, the medical community has outlined ways in which machine learning can be used on social media for dealing with such issues as cancer (De Silva et al., 2018), latent infectious diseases (Lim, Tucker, & Kumara, 2017), schizophrenia (Birnbaum et al., 2017), or suicide risk (Cheng et al., 2017). Similarly, machine learning with social media has many applications in organizations and could provide benefits for HR departments. For example, Jimenez-Marquez et al. (2019) developed a framework that uses machine learning to show what social media users are saying about a certain company. Actions such as these present unique opportunities for clarity within organizations.

Increasing Popularity and Use

Practices often termed as "people analytics," "HR metrics," or "machine learning," all serve the same purpose of digitizing human behavior and subsequently developing useful conclusions (Tavis, 2016). There are many prospective benefits that persuade companies to adopt machine learning practices. For example, pattern recognition and subsequent market prediction – determining trends that mirror consumer behavior and adjusting to meet demand changes – can be done quickly and efficiently via machine learning (Agrawal, Gans, & Goldfarb, 2020; Dhaoui, Webster, & Tan, 2017). Given the massive social media user base and increasingly digital world that we live in, it is no surprise that the two are progressively coming together.

How Machine Learning Is Used with Social Media Data

With a myriad of technologies constantly being developed, new machine learning programs, algorithms, and tactics are consistently hitting the market. In the social media context, these technologies can be used proactively or reactively. In other words, the AI can reach out to and communicate with social media users, or the social media users can initiate an interface with the AI. One popular use of machine learning in the social media sphere revolves around data "scraping," which translates an individual's social media behavior into quantitative data (Chamorro-Premuzic, 2015). This process can be used to pinpoint either desirable or undesirable characteristics in individuals to be used when recruiting or monitoring employees. More specifically, an algorithm can be designed that will search social media platforms for words or phrases that highlight what a certain employer is looking for. Further, machine learning algorithms can learn and continue filtering users in or out with each social media activity. This approach has been found to be useful in assessing organizationally relevant criteria, such as social media user personality (Golbeck, Robles, & Turner, 2011), consumer sentiment (Dhaoui, Webster, & Tan, 2017; Vermeer et al., 2019), cyberbullying (Chavan & Shylaja, 2015), and organizational communication (van Zoonen & Toni, 2016). As an example, Facebook leverages internally built machine learning algorithms to adjust the News Feed, Search, and Advertising functions of the SNW to display the content that the user would like to see, as determined by the model (Hazelwood et al., 2018). Facebook has specifically built these types of models to create the most personalized content possible.

Machine learning algorithms can also be used as emotion-detection tools to identify positive or negative feelings towards a company, product, or individual (Gaind, Syal, & Padgalwar, 2019). This type of information can deliver value in HRM because it provides a snapshot of what real people are saying and feeling without investing in efforts like customer satisfaction surveys, which may be less accurate since the surveyed individual knows that their responses are being analyzed. For example, algorithms can scour social media posts for textual emotion (using exclamation points or all caps), words and phrases with positive or negative valence, emoticon usage, or imagery emotion (photos of people smiling or grimacing) that relates to a company and create conclusions as to whether an individual's perception is positive or negative. By using this approach, HR departments could potentially identify employee or consumer pain points that need attention, or receive confirmation of practices that are having a positive influence in people's lives.

Another notable use of machine learning on social media data revolves around the "chatbot," which is a device that perceives its environment and takes actions to maximize its chance of success in achieving some goal (Kerlyl, Hall, & Bull, 2006). As noted in CHAPTER 2, this is an indirect application of machine learning, wherein deep learning techniques (e.g., recurrent neural network) are utilized to train the chatbot (Sheikh, Tiwari, & Singhal, 2019). These bots have been described as intelligent agents that are able to understand human communication and further interface with human counterparts (Androutsopoulou et al., 2019). With the use of chatbots on social media, a certain user who employs the chatbot can have a conversation with another social media user without physically communicating. Thus, the chatbot uses AI to take the place of the human on one side, yet still gains information from the party on the other side. This may have particular application for a company's internal social networking platform, as the chatbot can gather employee information and answer basic employee questions. Similarly, when potential applicants interact on the company website, chatbots can answer their questions or help them through the application process.

Chatbots are largely used in social media contexts to provide consumer support by "figuring out" what the user's problem is and providing solutions or answering questions. For example, the chatbot algorithm can be designed to understand certain words or phrases and, in turn, display a common solution. However, there are also a number of companies that are deploying chatbots in social media for the purpose of recruiting. Chatbots can be developed to exchange information with job candidates when they are considering a job opportunity, follow up with individuals after they have submitted employment applications, or use calendaring software to schedule interviews with hiring managers (Kulkarni & Che, 2019). Additionally, chatbots can engage by offering social media users survey options that present certain information when the user clicks on a particular answer. For example, a chatbot may ask the question, "Are you looking for a full-time role or a part-time role?" Depending on which option the user chooses, the chatbot will then reply with more information, thus leading the user down a path specific to their inputs. Many social media users prefer this type of information gathering to the traditional methods of phone calls, emails, or pamphlet reading because it is specific, fast, and casual, resulting in a low social commitment.

Although the benefits of using machine learning to digitize social media content are many, this relatively new technology has certain limitations. Along with unintended biases and prejudices, which will be discussed at length later, algorithms simply are not humans. It has been suggested that AI should be used to automate administration rather than attempt to replace human judgment (Kolbjørnsrud, Amico, & Thomas, 2016). Machine learning algorithms are becoming incredibly intelligent – often indistinguishable from real humans – and as mentioned in CHAPTER 1, can mimic many human traits. Yet they lack the very important true feelings, emotions, and understanding that only a human being can display (CampaignUK, 2015).

Another key limitation lies in the fact that technology is not always completely accurate. Although most algorithms account for user errors, certain misspellings or informal/abbreviated text used by social media users may not be accurately deciphered by natural language processing algorithms. Additionally, if a chatbot cannot sufficiently satisfy a user, that user may be transferred to a real person, thus dismissing the purpose of the bot.

There is also a notable obstacle in the interpretation of an algorithm's decision-making. That is, fully understanding retroactively why an algorithm made a decision is often difficult and leads to generalizability issues (Bikmukhametov & Jäschke, 2020; Carvalho, Pereira, & Cardoso, 2019; Molnar, Casalicchio, & Bischl, 2020). For example, an algorithm may determine that a certain individual is not suitable for a position, yet may not be able to clearly justify the rationale used in that decision.

CHANGING JOB FUNCTIONS OF HR AND RECEPTION

One of the classic issues with HRM functions is that HR personnel often find themselves bogged down by the menial management tasks that they are responsible for. Research has shown that managers generally spend over half of their working time performing administrative coordination or control tasks (Kolbjørnsrud, Amico, & Thomas, 2016). As time progresses, more and more companies are crafting HR roles to use strategy and creativity in their job functions, rather than consign intelligent individuals exclusively to administrative tasks, such as approving hours, synthesizing schedules, or filing records. Therefore, AI has proven itself as a valuable "assistant" to HR personnel by automating menial tasks and opening up more time for human employees to perform higher-level tasks.

The process of implementing AI in HR departments can potentially lead to feelings of apprehension and worry among current employees, as well as creating ambiguity for them. Yet the majority of employees do not perceive the introduction of AI as a job threat, but rather as a valuable aid (van Esch & Black, 2019). Further, many managers and employees have begun viewing AI as a "colleague," reducing the likelihood that they will harbor negative attitudes or even act in deviant manner against the AI (Kolbjørnsrud, Amico, & Thomas, 2016). As well, employees generally understand that machine learning techniques can drastically cut down the time they would spend doing certain tasks, and thus provide relief when it comes to their capacity.

PRIVACY/ETHICS ISSUES

The introduction of machine learning methods, particularly in the social media sphere, has brought about many ethical and legal concerns. Many HR departments have hesitated to implement the technology due to the fear of perceived infringement of privacy on the part of the social media user. When making the decision whether to adopt machine learning tactics in HRM, there are several considerations to examine.

First, AI deployed on social media is commonly working when users do not know that it is. In situations such as the chatbot, the user is generally cognizant of the machine learning technology being used. However, when it comes to data scraping and collection, the user is generally unaware that it is taking place because it happens in the "background" so to speak. In other words, machine learning techniques can gather and analyze information on a user without active input from the user. Rather, the algorithms use historical content and behavior to develop conclusions.

Virtually all social media platforms now include information related to informed consent in their usage agreements. Therefore, when users sign up to a social media website, they are essentially giving their consent for the website to collect data. In this regard, legal hoops are jumped through. Companies are legally entitled to collect information for the purpose of performance assessment (Chamorro-Premuzic, 2015). However, usage agreements often disallow mechanical data scraping from outside sources without consent. Therefore, companies who are interested in this method must understand the legal risks that are associated with it. The vast majority of individuals who sign up for a profile do not read the full agreement, including the fine print, before they "sign." Therefore, while consent is given, it is usually given unknowingly. This does, however, contribute to the richness of data collected. If users were completely aware that their behavior was being monitored, there would likely be a reactivity issue in that they would act differently, thus skewing results.

Another concern present in the use of machine learning on social media data, particularly for HRM uses, is that of bias. Machine learning, by nature, is self-reinforcing; any bias that was intentionally or unintentionally coded into the original algorithm can be built upon automatically, thus strengthening the bias (Garcia, 2016). Further, if algorithms are built from historical data, then the potential biases or prejudices of the individuals that produced the historical data can be inherited by the algorithm (Barocas & Selbst, 2016). For example, if a company historically had fewer female employees, then the algorithm could be unintentionally looking for more male employees when it scrapes social media data (Bauer et al., 2020). This was the case for Amazon, who recently scrapped an AI recruiting tool that was unintentionally giving precedence to male applicants over females due to a design error (Dastin, 2018). There is an argument that algorithms, while developed by humans, have less opportunity for bias by nature because they do not have the ability to feel as humans do (CampaignUK, 2015). Thus, once an algorithm is created, new biases such as discrimination will not develop on their own.

However, while AI is growing in intelligence, there are still many technical issues that could render results inaccurate.

While there are few examples of legal cases regarding companies using AI to monitor or evaluate employees using social media, AI-related lawsuits are anticipated to grow rapidly in coming years (Lewis, 2020). Given the lack of legal precedent, additional laws and policies are likely to be enacted that better define the legal and ethical uses of AI and machine learning on social media.

FUTURE RESEARCH DIRECTIONS FOR MACHINE LEARNING ON SOCIAL MEDIA AND HRM

As the age of technology progresses, machine learning will likely continue to develop in relation to processing speed and ability to manage complexity, just as it has in recent years. Given that this technology is relatively new, there is much room for research on the effects of its use in various capacities. The current shortcomings of research in this area lead us to consider a number of possible research topics that would further strengthen our knowledge and perspective.

The first application for future research is in assessing skills, abilities, and work-related personal attributes of applicants and employees. Personality is a construct that is commonly assessed via social media profiles in organizational research and practice, though it is often done using human assessors (Kluemper, Rosen, & Mossholder, 2012; Roulin & Bangerter, 2013). Machine learning has demonstrated significant promise in measuring social media users' personality outside of an organizational setting (Golbeck, Robles, & Turner, 2011; Park et al., 2015; Schwartz et al., 2013). Thus, utilizing machine learning to measure applicant or employee personality based on social media information may add value, and future research should compare the reliability, validity, and utility of assessing the personality of prospective employees using machine learning techniques (Tay et al., 2020). Similar approaches to other work-related constructs in hiring (e.g., cognitive ability, interpersonal skills, aggression) may also prove valuable.

A second area that could be fruitful for future research is the use of machine learning to identify problematic information ("red flags") in the social media content of prospective or current employees. Problematic information such as discriminatory comments, drug use, negative comments about the employer, and sharing of confidential information are all cited as red flags that managers often look for in social media profiles (Hartwell & Campion, 2020). It is plausible that machine learning algorithms could more quickly and accurately detect problematic social media content like this, as compared to human reviewers. However, because AI processes (and machine learning processes by extension) are all *narrow* (see CHAPTER 1), it is likely that multiple different machine learning processes would be needed to identify a broad range of red flags, especially if/when different media types (video, audio, picture, text) are being examined.

A third area that relates to the two previous paragraphs is how machine learning processes can reduce potential discrimination. When an organizational representative examines the social media profiles of current or prospective employees, the representative is often exposed to protected class characteristics, such as age, gender, race, or sexual orientation. Consciously or unconsciously, these attributes may then factor into employment decisions like who is hired, promoted, or fired. This opens the organization up to legal challenges related to discrimination and adverse impact. Utilizing machine learning algorithms to analyze social media data could minimize these legal and ethical concerns, but future research is needed to better understand how to design and monitor machine learning applications to reduce discrimination.

A final potential application that requires future research is the use of machine learning based chatbots in organizations, particularly internal social media platforms. Employees' questions and concerns can use up valuable HR resources, but chatbots have the potential to free up these resources by being the first line of interaction with employees. General questions, such as questions about insurance or retirement plans, could theoretically be managed by chatbots that become increasingly accurate as they interact with more and more employees (Androutsopoulou et al., 2019). However, employees' reactions to these chatbots may be negative, especially if the employees feel like the company is using the bots to reduce human interaction or if the bots are unable to resolve their concerns.

Taken together, the suggested research gap could be addressed by further investigating how AI-based tactics and machine learning algorithms can detect positive and negative indicators on an individual's social media profile, while avoiding discrimination. As well, the overall consequences that are associated with adoption of these technologies would provide practitioners with ammunition for decision-making.

CONCLUSION

As AI becomes more commonly used, more human-like, and more intrusive, the privacy and ethical concerns that it now faces are likely to increase. Yet it is not far-fetched to hypothesize that machine learning techniques will soon become commonplace in HRM due to their benefits and ability to create competitive HR departments. It is important for research to stay ahead of practice to provide much-needed guidance to organizations seeking to implement or improve machine learning techniques to monitor and assess social media information.

Social media use does not appear to be declining at any rate, and has already staked its place in society as a foundational communication channel. The policies of specific social media sites may change, yet AI will almost certainly play a role in how these sites gather, analyze, and monetize data, just as they currently do. Therefore, the task to develop further creative and useful ways that social media data can be utilized falls upon those employing the AI and machine learning. In contrast, the need for human interaction is not likely to disappear entirely. While machine learning will become more popular as it becomes more sophisticated and easy to use, it will likely not replace humans in final decision-making any time soon.

REFERENCES

Agrawal, A., Gans, J., & Goldfarb, A. (2020). How to win with machine learning. *Harvard Business Review*, 98(5), 126–133. https://doi.org/10.3386/w24284

Androutsopoulou, A., Karacapilidis, N., Loukis, E., & Charalabidis, Y. (2019). Transforming the communication between citizens and government through AI-guided chatbots. *Government Information Quarterly*, 36(2), 358–367. https://doi.org/10.1016/j.giq.2018.10.001

AudienceProject. (2020a, September 17). *Frequency of Facebook use in the United States as of 3rd quarter 2020* [Graph]. In Statista. Retrieved September 29, 2020, from https://www.statista.com/statistics/199266/frequency-of-use-among-facebook-users-in-the-united-states/.

AudienceProject. (2020b, September 17). *Frequency of Instagram use in the United States as of 3rd quarter 2020* [Graph]. In Statista. Retrieved September 29, 2020, from https://www.statista.com/statistics/308152/us-instagram-usage-frequency/.

AudienceProject. (2020c, September 17). *Frequency of Twitter use in the United States as of 3rd quarter 2020* [Graph]. In Statista. Retrieved September 29, 2020, from https://www.statista.com/statistics/234245/twitter-usage-frequency-in-the-united-states/.

Ayodele, T. O. (2010). Types of machine learning algorithms. *New Advances in Machine Learning, 3*, 19–48. https://doi.org/10.5772/9385

Azucar, D., Marengo, D., & Settanni, M. (2018). Predicting the Big 5 personality traits from digital footprints on social media: A meta-analysis. *Personality and Individual Differences, 124*, 150–159. https://doi.org/10.1016/j.paid.2017.12.018

Barocas, S., & Selbst, A. D. (2016). Big data's disparate impact. *California Law Review, 104*, 671–732. https://doi.org/10.2139/ssrn.2477899

Bauer, T. N., Truxillo, D. M., Jones, M. P., & Brady, G. (2020). Privacy and cybersecurity challenges, opportunities, and recommendations: Personnel selection in an era of online application systems and big data. In S. E. Woo, L. Tay, & R. W. Proctor (Eds.), *Big data in psychological research* (pp. 393–409). American Psychological Association. https://doi.org/10.1037/0000193-018

Bikmukhametov, T., & Jäschke, J. (2020). Combining machine learning and process engineering physics towards enhanced accuracy and explainability of data-driven models. *Computers and Chemical Engineering, 138*, Article 106834. https://doi.org/10.1016/j.compchemeng.2020.106834

Birnbaum, M. L., Ernala, S. K., Rizvi, A. F., De Choudhury, M., & Kane, J. M. (2017). A collaborative approach to identifying social media markers of schizophrenia by employing machine learning and clinical appraisals. *Journal of Medical Internet Research, 19*, Article e289. https://doi.org/10.2196/jmir.7956

Biteable. (2019, January 6). The 7 different types of social media. Retrieved November 24, 2020, from https://biteable.com/blog/the-7-different-types-of-social-media/.

Bleidorn, W., & Hopwood, C. J. (2019). Using machine learning to advance personality assessment and theory. *Personality and Social Psychology Review, 23*, 190–203. https://doi.org/10.1177/1088868318772990

Brown, V. R., & Vaughn, E. D. (2011). The writing on the (Facebook) wall: The use of social networking sites in hiring decisions. *Journal of Business Psychology, 26*, 219–225. https://doi.org/10.1007/s10869-011-9221-x

Bump, P. (n.d.). The 5 types of social media and pros & cons of each. Retrieved January 6, 2021, from https://blog.hubspot.com/marketing/which-social-networks-should-you-focus-on.

CampaignUK. (2015, July 15). Does social media require a human touch? CampaignUK. Retrieved July 26, 2020, from https://www.campaignlive.co.uk/article/does-social-media-require-human-touch/1355947.

Carvalho, D. V., Pereira, E. M., & Cardoso, J. S. (2019). Machine learning interpretability: A survey on methods and metrics. *Electronics, 8*(8), Article 832.

Chamorro-Premuzic, T. (2015, June 26). 3 emerging alternatives to traditional hiring methods. *Harvard Business Review Digital Articles*, 2–4.

Chavan, V. S., & Shylaja, S. S. (2015). Machine learning approach for detection of cyber-aggressive comments by peers on social media network. In *International Conference on Advances in Computing, Communications and Informatics (ICACCI)* (pp. 2354–2358). IEEE. https://doi.org/10.1109/ICACCI.2015.7275970

Cheng, Q., Li, T. M., Kwok, C., Zhu, T., & Yip, P. S. F. (2017). Assessing suicide risk and emotional distress in Chinese social media: A text mining and machine learning study. *Journal of Medical Internet Research, 19*, Article e276. https://doi.org/10.2196/jmir.6937

Conway, M., & O'Connor, D. (2016). Social media, big data, and mental health: Current advances and ethical implications. *Current Opinion in Psychology, 9*, 77–82. https://doi.org/10.1016/j.copsyc.2016.01.004

Dastin, J. (2018, October 10). Amazon scraps secret AI recruiting tool that showed bias against women. Retrieved October 23, 2020, from https://www.reuters.com/article/us-amazon-com-jobs -automation-insight/amazon-scraps-secret-ai-recruiting-tool-that-showed-bias-against-women -idUSKCN1MK08G.

Davison, H. K., Maraist, H. C., Hamilton, R. H., & Bing, M. N. (2012). To screen or not to screen? Using the internet for selection decisions. *Employee Responsibilities and Rights Journal, 24*, 1–21. https:// doi.org/10.1007/s10672-011-9178-y

De Silva, A., Ranasinghe, W., Bandaragoda, T., Adikari, A., Mills, N., Iddamalgoda, L., Alahakoon, D., Lawrentschuk, N., Persad, R., Osipov, E., Gray, R., & Bolton, D. (2018). Machine learning to support social media empowered patients in cancer care and cancer treatment decisions. *PLoS ONE, 13*(10), Article e0205855. https://doi.org/10.1371/journal.pone.0205855

Dhaoui, C., Webster, C. M., & Tan, L. P. (2017). Social media sentiment analysis: Lexicon versus machine learning. *Journal of Consumer Marketing, 34*, 480–488. https://doi.org/10.1108/JCM-03 -2017-2141

Dietterich, T. G., & Horvitz, E. J. (2015). Rise of concerns about AI: Reflections and directions. *Communications of the ACM, 58*(10), 38–40.

Ellis, R. K. (2018). Employees' digital skills deficits are problematic. *Talent Development, 72*(12), 16–17.

eMarketer. (2020a, January 13). *Number of LinkedIn users in the United States from 2018 to 2022 (in millions)* [Graph]. In Statista. Retrieved September 5, 2020, from https://www.statista.com/statistics/ 194471/number-of-linkedin-users-usa/.

eMarketer. (2020b, January 15). *Number of Instagram users in the United States from 2019 to 2023 (in millions)* [Graph]. In Statista. Retrieved September 5, 2020, from https://www.statista.com/statistics/ 293771/number-of-us-instagram-users/.

Facebook. (2020, July 30). *Number of monthly active Facebook users worldwide as of 2nd quarter 2020 (in millions)* [Graph]. In Statista. Retrieved September 5, 2020, from https://www.statista.com/ statistics/264810/number-of-monthly-active-facebook-users-worldwide/.

Foreman, C. (2020, June 17). 10 types of social media and how each can benefit your business. Hootsuite. Retrieved November 24, 2020, from https://blog.hootsuite.com/types-of-social-media/.

Gaind, B., Syal, V., & Padgalwar, S. (2019, January 19). *Emotion detection and analysis on social media.* arXiv. arXiv:1901.08458

Garcia, M. (2016). Racist in the machine: The disturbing implications of algorithmic bias. *World Policy Journal, 33*(4), 111–117. https://doi.org/10.1215/07402775-3813015

Golbeck, J., Robles, C., & Turner, K. (2011). Predicting personality with social media. In *CHI'11 Extended Abstracts on Human Factors in Computing Systems* (pp. 253–262). Association for Computing Machinery. https://doi.org/10.1145/1979742.1979614

Hartwell, C. J. (2015). *The use of social media in employee selection: Prevalence, content, perceived usefulness, and influence on hiring decisions* [Doctoral dissertation, Purdue University].

Hartwell, C. J. (2019). Social media and e-HRM. In M. Thite (Ed.), *e-HRM: Leveraging digital technology to transform HRM* (pp. 143–159). Routledge.

Hartwell, C. J., & Campion, M. A. (2020). Getting social in selection: How social networking website content is perceived and used in hiring. *International Journal of Selection and Assessment, 28*(1), 1–16.

Hartwell, C. J., & Eggli, R. (2020). Social media screening in employee selection. In T. Bondarouk & S. Fisher (Eds.), *Encyclopedia of electronic HRM* (pp. 220–228). De Gruyter.

Hazelwood, K. et al. (2018). Applied machine learning at Facebook: A datacenter infrastructure perspective. In *2018 IEEE International Symposium on High Performance Computer Architecture (HPCA)* (pp. 620–629). IEEE. https://doi.org/10.1109/HPCA.2018.00059

Howard, P. N., & Parks, M. R. (2012). Social media and political change: Capacity, constraint, and consequence. *Journal of Communication, 62*, 359–362.

Jersin, J. (2019). Announcing skill assessments to help you showcase your skills. Retrieved October 23, 2020, from https://blog.linkedin.com/2019/september/17/announcing-skill-assessments-to-help-you -showcase-your-skills.

Jimenez-Marquez, J. L., Gonzalez-Carrasco, I., Lopez-Cuadrado, J. L., & Ruiz-Mezcua, B. (2019). Towards a big data framework for analyzing social media content. *International Journal of Information Management, 44*, 1–12. http://dx.doi.org/10.1111/j.1460-2466.2012.01626.x

Johnson, R. D., & Gueutal, H. G. (2011). *Transforming HR through technology: The use of E-HR and HRIS in organizations.* Society for Human Resource Management Effective Practice Guidelines Series. Retrieved November 24, 2020, from http://www.shrm.org/about/foundation/products/Documents/HR%20Tech%20EPG-%20Final.pdf.

Judge, T. A., & Kristof-Brown, A. (2004). Personality, interactional psychology, and person–organization fit. In B. Schneider & D. B. Smith (Eds.), *Personality and organizations* (pp. 87–109). Lawrence Erlbaum Associates Publishers.

Jung, Y., & Suh, Y. (2019). Mining the voice of employees: A text mining approach to identifying and analyzing job satisfaction factors from online employee reviews. *Decision Support Systems, 123*, Article 113074. https://doi.org/10.1016/j.dss.2019.113074

Kerlyl, A., Hall, P., & Bull, S. (2006). Bringing chatbots into education: Towards natural language negotiation of open learner models. In *International Conference on Innovative Techniques and Applications of Artificial Intelligence* (pp. 179–192). Springer. https://doi.org/10.1007/978-1-84628-666-7_14

Kluemper, D. H. (2013). Social network screening: Pitfalls, possibilities, and parallels in employment selection. In T. Bondarouk & M. R. Olivas-Lujan (Eds.), *Social media in human resources management* (pp. 1–21). Emerald.

Kluemper, D. H., Rosen, P. A., & Mossholder, K. W. (2012). Social networking websites, personality ratings, and the organizational context: More than meets the eye? *Journal of Applied Social Psychology, 42*, 1143–1172. https://doi.org/10.1111/j.1559-1816.2011.00881.x

Kolbjørnsrud, V., Amico, R., & Thomas, R. J. (2016). How artificial intelligence will redefine management. *Harvard Business Review Digital Articles*, 2–6.

Kontos, E. Z., Emmons, K. M., Puleo, E., & Viswanath, K. (2010). Communication inequalities and public health implications of adult social networking site use in the United States. *Journal of Health Communication, 15*(3), 216–235. http://doi.org/10.1080/10810730.2010.522689

Kulkarni, S. B., & Che, X. (2019). Intelligent software tools for recruiting. *Journal of International Technology and Information Management, 28*(2), 2–16.

Landers, R. N., Brusso, R. C., & Auer, A. M. (2019). Crowdsourcing job satisfaction data: Examining the construct validity of Glassdoor.com ratings. *Personnel Assessment and Decisions, 5*, 45–55. https://doi.org/10.25035/pad.2019.03.006

Leonardi, P., & Contractor, N. (2018). Better people analytics. *Harvard Business Review, 96*(6), 70–81.

Lewis, N. (2020, February 28). AI-related lawsuits are coming. Retrieved October 23, 2020, from https://www.shrm.org/resourcesandtools/hr-topics/technology/pages/ai-lawsuits-are-coming.aspx.

Lim, S., Tucker, C. S., & Kumara, S. (2017). An unsupervised machine learning model for discovering latent infectious diseases using social media data. *Journal of Biomedical Informatics, 66*, 82–94. https://doi.org/10.1016/j.jbi.2016.12.007

Marsden, P. V. (1994). The hiring process: Recruitment methods. *American Behavioral Scientist, 37*(7), 979–991. https://doi.org/10.1177/0002764294037007009

Mcnamee, R. (2019). How to fix social media before it's too late. *Time International (South Pacific Edition), 193*(3), 22–28.

Mgrditchian, G. (2015). Employment and social media privacy: Employer justifications for access to "private" material. *Rutgers Computer and Technology Law Journal, 41*, 108–133.

Molnar, C., Casalicchio, G., & Bischl, B. (2020). *Interpretable machine learning – a brief history, state-of-the-art and challenges.* arXiv. arXiv:2010.09337.

Nilsson, N. J. (2014). *Principles of artificial intelligence.* Morgan Kaufmann. https://doi.org/10.1016/b978-0-934613-10-1.50007-4

Park, G. H., Schwartz, H. A., Eichstaedt, J. C., Kern, M. L., Kosinski, M., Stillwell, D. J., Ungar, L. H., & Seligman, M. E. P. (2015). Automatic personality assessment through social media language. *Journal of Personality and Social Psychology, 108*, 934–952. https://doi.org/10.1037/pspp0000020

Roulin, N., & Bangerter, A. (2013). Social networking websites in personnel selection: A signaling perspective on recruiters' and applicants' perceptions. *Journal of Personnel Psychology, 12*, 143–151. https://doi.org/10.1027/1866-5888/a000094

Safian, R. (2017). When artificial intelligence meets actual life. *Fast Company, 220*, 14.

Sainju, B. (2020). *Job satisfaction and employee turnover determinants in Fortune 50 companies: Insights of employee reviews from Indeed.com* (7985) [Master's thesis, Utah State University]. Digital Commons Database.

Schwartz, H. A., Eichstaedt, J. C., Kern, M. L., Dziurzynski, L., Ramones, S. M., Agrawal, M., Shah, A., Kosinski, M., Stillwell, D., & Ungar, L. H. (2013). Personality, gender, and age in the language of social media: The open-vocabulary approach. *PloS ONE, 8*(9), Article e73791. https://doi.org/10.1371/journal.pone.0073791

Sheikh, S. A., Tiwari, V., & Singhal, S. (2019). Generative model chatbot for human resource using deep learning. In *2019 International Conference on Data Science and Engineering (ICDSE)* (pp. 126–132). IEEE.

Song, Q., Liu, M., Tang, C., & Long, L. F. (2020). Applying principles of big data to the workplace and talent analytics. In S. E. Woo, L. Tay, & R. W. Proctor (Eds.), *Big data in psychological research* (pp. 319–344). American Psychological Association. https://doi.org/10.1037/0000193-015

Statista. (2020, July 15). *Number of social network users worldwide from 2017 to 2025 (in billions)* [Graph]. In Statista. Retrieved 2020, September 5, from https://www.statista.com/statistics/278414/number-of-worldwide-social-network-users/.

Stoughton, J. W., Thompson, L. F., & Meade, A. W. (2015). Examining applicant reactions to the use of social networking websites in pre-employment screening. *Journal of Business and Psychology, 30*(1), 73–88. https://doi.org/10.1007/s10869-013-9333-6

Tavis, A. A. (2016). The transparency paradox at work. *People and Strategy, 39*(4), 8–9.

Tay, L., Woo, S. E., Hickman, L., & Saef, R. M. (2020). Psychometric and validity issues in machine learning approaches to personality assessment: A focus on social media text mining. *European Journal of Personality, 34*(5), 826–844. https://doi.org/10.1002/per.2290

Tucker, A. L., & Singer, S. J. (2015). The effectiveness of management-by-walking-around: A randomized field study. *Production and Operations Management, 24*(2), 253–271.

Twitter (2019, April 23). *Number of monthly active Twitter users in the United States from 1st quarter 2010 to 1st quarter 2019 (in millions)* [Graph]. In Statista. Retrieved September 5, 2020, from https://www.statista.com/statistics/274564/monthly-active-twitter-users-in-the-united-states/.

van Esch, P., & Black, J. S. (2019). Factors that influence new generation candidates to engage with and complete digital, AI-enabled recruiting. *Business Horizons, 62*(6), 729–739. https://doi.org/10.1016/j.bushor.2019.07.004

Van Iddekinge, C. H., Lanivich, S. E., Roth, P. L., & Junco, E. (2016). Social media for selection? Validity and adverse impact potential of a Facebook-based assessment. *Journal of Management, 42*, 1811–1835. https://doi.org/10.1177/0149206313515524

van Zoonen, W., & Toni, G. L. A. (2016). Social media research: The application of supervised machine learning in organizational communication research. *Computers in Human Behavior, 63*, 132–141. https://doi.org/10.1016/j.chb.2016.05.028

Vermeer, S. A., Araujo, T., Bernritter, S. F., & van Noort, G. (2019). Seeing the wood for the trees: How machine learning can help firms in identifying relevant electronic word-of-mouth in social media. *International Journal of Research in Marketing, 36*(3), 492–508. https://doi.org/10.1016/j.ijresmar.2019.01.010

6.   HR machine learning in recruiting

Sven Laumer, Christian Maier, and Tim Weitzel

INTRODUCTION

Recruiting within human resources management (HRM) plays a decisive role in providing a qualified and motivated workforce for an organization (Noe et al., 2017). With the help of recruiting, suitable and skilled employees can be identified, thus providing the company with valuable resources (Wirtky et al., 2016). However, the complexity in this area is continuously increasing (Oehlhorn et al., 2020). Changes due to advancing internationalization, demographic change, the threat of a shortage of skilled workers, and constant technological change create complex business challenges that make recruiting more difficult (Laumer et al., 2010). Nevertheless, the technological change is an opportunity to meet these challenges (Strohmeier, 2009). It provides many opportunities to improve processes as well as to simplify and automate the finding, recruiting, and evaluation of candidates (Eckhardt et al., 2014; Laumer et al., 2015).

One innovative opportunity is artificial intelligence (AI) (Duan et al., 2019; van Esch et al., 2019). This term refers to information technology (IT) that can interpret and learn from large amounts of data. The knowledge gained can be used to achieve goals or complete tasks (Kaplan & Haenlein, 2010). Organizations using these AI-based approaches benefit from better financial and operational performance (McAfee & Brynjolfsson, 2012).

AI can also be used to analyze information about candidates and jobs to make predictions about a candidate's fit for a vacancy (Malinowski et al., 2006; Strohmeier & Piazza, 2015). These approaches automatically extract the candidates' data, provide additional background information, and score the candidates on an objective scoring system, enabling faster comparisons. They can also predict the candidates' future performance using current employees' data and their job performance, resulting in accurate AI-based recommendations supporting recruiters in finding the best match for an open position. Organizations are using these AI-based systems, where different machine learning (ML) algorithms are deployed for diverse recruiting purposes as part of an organization's HRM.

Therefore, this chapter aims to provide an overview of the current state of research on AI, especially ML, in HR recruiting. The focus is on which approaches exist to support recruiting with AI concerning finding, selecting, and evaluating candidates and predicting candidates' fit for a vacancy. A descriptive literature review is used to provide this overview, and its results are presented. In the next section, conceptual foundations are provided, constituting a conceptual matrix for conducting the review. The subsequent sections explain the process of searching for and analyzing the literature and present the literature review results. The chapter concludes with a discussion providing opportunities for future research.

CONCEPTUAL FOUNDATION

HRM uses various practices to effectively acquire and utilize talent in an organization (Jackson et al., 2014; Noe et al., 2020). One of the critical functions is recruiting to meet workforce demands for addressing organizational challenges. Organizations can staff jobs either internally or recruit candidates externally. Internal staffing requires careful coordination of the existing team and changes in open job positions. External recruitment is necessary when open positions cannot be adequately staffed with existing personnel. Potential candidates from outside the organization are attracted, selected, and hired (Maier et al., 2021).

For recruiting, a so-called job profile contains all the relevant criteria to be considered when selecting personnel for a specific job. Typical contents of a job profile are job descriptions and required knowledge, experience, and skills (Münstermann et al., 2010). Organizations support their decision on filling a vacancy by utilizing various selection mechanisms, including job interviews, personality tests, or competence tests. These approaches also include online assessments, such as online games (Laumer et al., 2012). Usually, the focus is on the current skills and capabilities of the applicant. The used selection mechanisms test whether the applicant's skills and requirements match the job's requirement profile (Laumer et al., 2009; Malebye et al., 2015).

Various dimensions express this match, constituting the person–environment fit, with its dimensions including, among others, person–job fit. Selection mechanisms predict this match, focusing on different dimensions (Boon et al., 2011). AI-based approaches used for finding, recruiting, and evaluating candidates can predict this person–environment fit and its different dimensions. Hence, the person–environment fit concept is central for recruiting approaches, which is why we will introduce it in the following. Afterward, we provide a short introduction to AI. This constitutes a conceptual matrix for the literature review to illustrate which AI-based approaches are used to predict person–environment fit dimensions.

Person–Environment Fit

A candidate's fit for a particular job considers various aspects of the working environment (Jansen & Kristof-Brown, 2006). Accordingly, there is no one-dimensional view of this fit. Instead, it consists of and depends on various multidimensional factors. The person–environment (PE) fit includes the person–vocation (PV) fit, the person–job (PJ) fit, the person–organization (PO) fit, the person–person (PP) fit, and the person–team (PT) fit. These individual aspects are interlinked, and their interaction influences an individual's work experience (Jansen & Kristof-Brown, 2006). However, the dimensions within the recruiting process's phases differ in their relevance. They consider different aspects before (pre-hire) and after the hiring decision (post-hire). This work focuses on the pre-hire perspective, that is, the focus is on the recruiting activities (Edwards et al., 2006; Jansen & Kristof-Brown, 2006; Werbel & Gilliland, 1999), such that we explain the general concept of PE fit and its dimensions in the following as a base for our literature review.

The PE fit is a superordinate, general construct that describes an individual's relationship to their environment. Various dimensions concerning vocation, job, organization, and the team constitute this fit (Jansen & Kristof-Brown, 2006), while the fit can also be expressed in terms of multiple characteristics (see Figure 6.1).

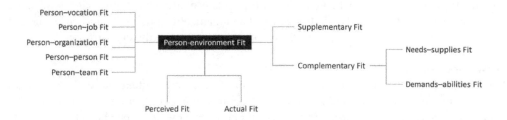

Figure 6.1   *Person–environment fit (Jansen & Kristof-Brown, 2006; Muchinsky & Monahan, 1987)*

The first PE fit characteristic distinguishes between a supplementary fit and a complementary fit (Muchinsky & Monahan, 1987). Supplementary means that a person fits into a context if they have characteristics similar to those of other individuals in the same context. In contrast, complementary fit means that the characteristics of an individual complement or complete the existing context (Muchinsky & Monahan, 1987).

As a second PE fit characteristic, the complementary fit has two additional sub-characteristics: needs–supplies and demands–abilities. A match between needs and supplies occurs when the context's resources match the needs of individuals. A fit between demands and abilities is achieved when an individual can meet the demands of the context (Sekiguchi, 2004).

The third characteristic is the distinction between a perceived fit and an actual fit. Both describe how well an individual fits into a given context. The perceived fit is a subjective interpretation of the fit by an individual. The actual fit represents how the individual and the context fit together objectively (Sekiguchi, 2004).

Person–vocation fit
The PV fit dimension expresses the match between the individual and their vocation. The presumption is that when an individual's general interests match with their job they are more satisfied and perform better (Marcus & Wagner, 2015).

Person–job fit
The PJ fit dimension expresses the match of a person's characteristics with those of a specific job (Edwards, 1991; Ostroff & Zhan, 2012). When selecting a person for a particular job, the candidate who has the required skills and abilities should be hired (Sekiguchi, 2004). PJ fit has a complementary fit dimension. The needs–supplies perspective distinguishes between an individual's needs and the characteristics of a position that could satisfy those needs. For example, an individual's values may contrast with the salary offered and the job itself. The demands–abilities perspective considers prerequisites, such as knowledge, skills, or competences necessary to perform the job. It checks whether candidates provide those.

Person–organization fit
The PO fit dimension can be understood as the match of an individual and an organization (Kristof, 1996). PO fit considers a supplementary fit between an organization's culture and the individual's characteristics and a complementary one between the supply and demand of specific skills and competences. For example, an organization provides financial incentives

demanded by individuals and individuals offer skills and competences demanded by the organization. The PO fit is achieved when either side provides something that the other side demands. A good fit between an individual and an organization positively influences the individual's satisfaction, willingness to perform, and commitment to the organization.

Person–person fit

The PP fit refers to the match of two people within the working context. For example, this can be the match of an applicant and a HR employee, other employees, or a superior and a subordinate (Jansen & Kristof-Brown, 2006). The fit expresses how personal characteristics match the two people (Ostroff & Zhan, 2012).

Person–team fit

The PT fit describes the match of a person with a group of people. It is not only the dyadic relationship, as expressed by the PP fit. It is at least a triadic relationship. Hence, the PT fit describes an individual's fit in a social network consisting of more than two actors (Cooman et al., 2016; Kristof-Brown et al., 2005; St J. Burch & Anderson, 2004).

Artificial Intelligence and Machine Learning

Artificial intelligence (AI) is generally understood as information technologies' (IT) "ability to interpret data correctly, learn from it, and use this knowledge to achieve specific goals or solve tasks" (Haenlein & Kaplan, 2019, p. 5). A distinction can be made between artificial general intelligence (AGI) and narrow artificial intelligence (NAI). AGI, also known as strong AI, is an IT system that can think and act independently, similar to a human being. However, such an AI has so far only existed as an object of fiction. NAI, also called weak AI, refers to a genus of IT systems developed to fulfill a special task (see CHAPTER 1 and CHAPTER 2 for a general introduction to machine learning in HRM). Within a given framework, they support human decision-making or even make autonomous decisions. NAI also includes various subcategories and procedures, whereby machine learning (ML) is the most popular one (Jordan & Mitchell, 2015).

However, there is no clear definition of ML. Bolander (2019, p. 854) defines ML as "any AI algorithm that does not have a static behavior but can learn from experience". Goodfellow (2016), according to Haenlein and Kaplan (2019), characterizes ML algorithms as a set of IT that can extract patterns, also called models, from raw data, turn these into knowledge, and propose decisions based on the models. In general, ML algorithms can be classified into supervised learning, unsupervised learning, and reinforcement learning algorithms (Ayodele, 2010). Supervised learning is the most applied form of ML (LeCun et al., 2015; Ongsulee, 2017), such that it is focused on in this review. Relevant ML algorithms (see Table 6.1 for an overview) include naïve Bayes (NBs), logistic regression (LogRegs), support vector machines (SVMs), k-nearest neighbors (KNNs), decision trees (DTs), and random forests (RFs), as well as artificial neural networks (ANNs) and deep neural networks (DNNs). The algorithms are based on either statistical, instance-based, DT, or neural network models (Gunning & Aha, 2019; Hagras, 2018).

Table 6.1   *Supervised learning machine learning algorithms (based on Rudolph, 2020)*

Category	Algorithm	Definition
Statistical models	Naïve Bayes (NB)	The Bayes Theorem is the base for classification of instances
	Logistic regression (LogReg)	A regression coefficient is assessed to learn a LogReg function that constitutes the LogReg-based ML model
Instance-based models	Support vector machine (SVM)	n-1 dimensional separators are used to separate n-dimensional features into subgroups
	K-nearest neighbors (KNN)	The k most similar data instances are identified to classify unknown instances
Decision tree models	Decision tree (DT)	A DT can be described as IF-THEN rules as it is a graph that has a parental node and several child nodes
	Random forest (RF)	RF models are a set of DTs
Neural network models	Artificial neural network (ANN)	A neural network with one hidden layer
	Deep neural network (DNN)	A neural network with more than one hidden layer

Machine learning using statistical models

Relevant statistical models include ML models based on NB and LogReg. The base for the NB learning is the Bayes Theorem. It assumes that all features are independent of each other and equally important (Forsyth, 2019). Based on the assessment of a regression coefficient a LogReg function is estimated that constitutes the LogReg-based ML model (James et al., 2013).

Machine learning using instance-based models

Relevant examples of instance-based models are KNN- and SVM-based models (Russell & Norvig, 2016). The KNN algorithm classifies unknown instances based on identifying the k most similar data instances in the training set (Domingos, 2012). The similarity is calculated using, for example, the Euclidean distance or Minkowski distance (Russell & Norvig, 2016). SVM-based models use n-1 dimensional separators to divide the n-dimensional feature space into subgroups (James et al., 2013; Russell & Norvig, 2016). Quadratic programming is used to determine the separator (Ayodele, 2010).

Machine learning using decision tree models

A DT is a graph that consists of a parental node and child nodes (Chien & Chen, 2008; Goodfellow, 2016). Heuristic functions, which recursively partition data instances until an overfitting tree is constructed, are used to build a DT (Cho & Ngai, 2003). Every node represents a splitting criterion for one feature, constituting IF-THEN rules described by the parent node and the child node (Goodfellow, 2016). Classifying new instances is done based on the nodes and following the paths (IF-THEN rules) to the nodes (James et al., 2013).

     RF models are a set of DTs. Each DT is built including a subset to generate different DTs. For classification of new instances, each of these trees are used (James et al., 2013).

Machine learning using neural network models

A neural network consists of neurons, activation functions, weights, input and output layer, hidden layer(s), and a learning algorithm. Each layer of a neural network has neurons with input and output links constituting the neural network. Two neurons are linked with a corresponding weight. When the neural network is trained, data is provided into the model using the input layer. In contrast, the output layer forwards the prediction as the neuron's output provided by the neuron's activation function (Russell & Norvig, 2016). Neural networks can be categorized regarding their depth and width. The depth corresponds to the number of hidden layers. The width describes the number of hidden neurons. The number of hidden layers can vary between one and several tens of thousands of layers. The more hidden layers a neural network has, the more complex it is (Russell & Norvig, 2016). Neural networks with one hidden layer are referred to as ANNs, while networks with more than one hidden layer are termed DNNs (Goodfellow, 2016).

Other approaches

Besides the ML approaches, other approaches are also discussed in the literature that can be considered AI and are relevant in the HRM context. These approaches can be subsumed using the term "data mining" (DM), which is according to Aggarwal (2015, p. 1) "the study of collecting, cleaning, processing, analyzing, and gaining useful insights from data". The goal of DM is to collect a large amount of raw data, also known as Big Data (McAfee & Brynjolfsson, 2012), cleanse it, and convert it into a format that can be analyzed using various analysis methods (Wu et al., 2014). For example, matching is used, which refers to comparing two data sources (Burch & Long, 1992), and so-called Boolean Matching is often applied. This means the number of identical terms or keywords that occur in different sources is checked. It corresponds to a simple count of common elements. Also, the term "recommender system" was established by Resnick and Varian (1997) and describes processing user data to configure personalized recommendations that match users' needs (Aggarwal, 2016). There are different forms of recommender systems, including content-based and collaborative-based filtering approaches (Aggarwal, 2016). Their overall objective is to reduce possible information overload by sorting and filtering alternatives concerning individual preferences (Adomavicius et al., 2013). Recommender systems have also been used in the HR context (Freire & Castro, 2021; Laumer et al., 2018).

Summary

The goal of recruiting is to find the most suitable person for a vacant position. "Best" in this context does not mean literally "the best" but "the most suitable" person in terms of the various person–environment fit dimensions, and different dimension characteristics. In this context, it is important to acknowledge that recruiting consists of several tasks. One is staffing (see CHAPTER 7). Another one is diagnostics and selection (see CHAPTER 8). The use of ML in these tasks is described in more detail in the other chapters. In this chapter, the focus is on AI-based approaches, especially ML, that can help recruiters estimate the various person–environment fit dimensions and predict how well a person might perform on a particular job, and not on a specific step of the recruiting process.

METHODOLOGICAL APPROACH: LITERATURE REVIEW

This literature review investigates which AI-based approaches, especially ML, are already documented in the literature and used to predict at least one dimension of the PE fit and its characteristics. The literature review follows the guidelines proposed by vom Brocke et al.

(2009). The focus is on the research outcomes, and it retains a neutral perspective. The results address general and specialized scholars, practitioners, and the general public. The literature review's coverage is representative as it considers only literature from the keyword search. Among these, solely scholarly literature, such as peer-reviewed journal articles and conference papers, are analyzed. There is no restriction regarding time or geographic region.

The following search string was used to search in the Scopus database[1] for relevant articles:

TITLE-ABS-KEY ("Hire" OR "Hiring" AND "AI-based" OR "ai" OR "Artificial Intelligence" AND ("recruiting") OR ("recruitment") OR ("human resources management"))

The final literature search iteration resulted in a total of 421 hits. A first reduction of the hits considered only peer-reviewed articles and proceedings written in English, resulting in 327 papers. After removing duplicates (n = 13), the 319 remaining articles' titles and abstracts were first analyzed to ensure that they fit thematically. Those articles that focus on AI and at least one person–environment fit dimension are included. Papers that did not discuss AI concerning PE fit dimensions are excluded. The forward and backward search using Web of Science and Google Scholar revealed additional relevant articles. In total, the literature review considers a total of 56 studies, summarized in Table 6.2.

The literature is analyzed and synthesized using a concept matrix. First, the analysis assesses what ML approach is used to automate recruiting (based on Rudolph, 2020). Second, it codes the different person–environment fit dimensions and characteristics (based on Kramer, 2020). Third, it focuses on the purpose of identifying candidates, pre-selecting applications, or assessing applicants. Fourth, the underlying data source and the extracted information to predict the person–environment fit dimensions are coded. This approach enables us to describe the status quo of AI and recruiting and indicate future research opportunities.

RESULTS

In total, 56 papers report an AI-based approach that predicts person–environment fit dimensions (see Figure 6.1). Given the general activities in recruiting, nine papers focus on identifying potential candidates, 36 on the pre-selection of candidates based on CVs or additional information, and 15 on further assessing candidates. In the following, the 56 papers (see Table 6.2) are summarized, constituting the HR recruiting ML model (see Figure 6.2). Afterward, some examples of how prior research has applied ML in HR recruiting are described.

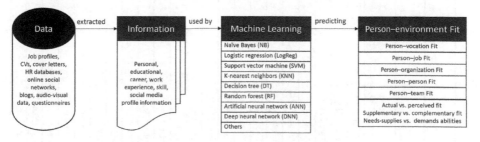

Figure 6.2   The HR recruiting machine learning model

Table 6.2   Papers using machine learning approaches predicting person–environment fit dimensions

Paper	Machine learning algorithm (partly based on Rudolph, 2020)									Person–environment fit (partly based on Kramer, 2020)				
Author(s) (Year of publication)	NB	Log Reg	KNN	DT	SVM	RF	ANN	DNN	Other	PV	PJ	PO	PP	PT
	5	9	8	18	8	9	8	10	19	0	34	8	0	3
Alghamlas & Alabduljabbar (2019)	X		X								X			
Ali Shah et al. (2020)				X	X	X		X						
Almalis et al. (2014)									X		X			
Almalis et al. (2015)									X		X			
Bello et al. (2020)		X									X			
Bian et al. (2019)							X	X			X			
Buranasing (2020)								X			X			
Chen et al. (2016)					X									
Chien & Chen (2008)				X								X		
Cho & Ngai (2003)				X			X				X			
Coll & Fornés (2009)							X							
Dainty et al. (2005)		X												
Escolar-Jimenez et al. (2019)				X					X		X			
Faliagka et al. (2014)				X	X									
Farber et al. (2003)									X		X			
Güçlütürk et al. (2018)								X						
Harris (2017)									X		X			
Harris (2018)				X										
Ivan et al. (2019)		X	X								X			
Jere et al. (2017)														X
Kamaru Zaman et al. (2019)				X					X		X			
Kessler et al. (2008)			X								X			
Kessler et al. (2012)			X								X			
Le et al. (2019)							X				X			

Paper	Machine learning algorithm (partly based on Rudolph, 2020)									Person–environment fit (partly based on Kramer, 2020)				
Author(s) (Year of publication)	NB	Lcg Reg	KNN	DT	SVM	RF	ANN	DNN	Other	PV	PJ	PO	PP	PT
Lee & Ahn (2020)		X									X	X		X
Li et al. (2011)					X									X
Luo et al. (2019)		X		X				X			X			
Mahmoud et al. (2019)				X							X			
Mairesse et al. (2007)	X		X	X	X									
Malinowski et al. (2006)									X		X			
Malinowski et al. (2008)									X					X
Manad et al. (2019)									X			X		
Martin et al. (2018)		X	X	X	X	X		X						
Martinez-Gil et al. (2016)									X		X			
Martinez-Gil et al. (2020)									X		X			
Mehta et al. (2013)									X		X	X		
Min & Emam (2003)				X		X					X			
Nguyen & Gatica-Perez (2016)						X								
Nguyen et al. (2014)						X								
Paoletti et al. (2016)									X		X			
Paparrizos et al. (2011)	X			X							X			
Qin et al. (2018)							X				X			
Qin et al. (2019)				X			X							
Qin et al. (2020)		X		X		X	X				X			
Saat & Singh (2011)				X					X		X	X		
Shen et al. (2018)				X	X						X			
Siraj et al. (2011)									X		X			
Suciu et al. (2019)									X			X		
Sun et al. (2019)			X				X					X		
Ting & Varathan (2018)									X					
Tondji (2018)			X								X			

| Paper | Machine learning algorithm (partly based on Rudolph, 2020) | | | | | | | | | Person–environment fit (partly based on Kramer, 2020) | | | | |
Author(s) (Year of publication)	NB	Log Reg	KNN	DT	SVM	RF	ANN	DNN	Other	PV	PJ	PO	PP	PT
Tung et al. (2005)				X				X						
Verina et al. (2019)									X		X			
Yan et al. (2019)	X	X		X		X		X						
Zaroor et al. (2018)									X		X			
Zhu et al. (2018)	X	X		X	X	X		X			X			

Summary

Considering the different ML algorithms, the identified papers focus on statistical methods in terms of naïve Bayes (N=5), logistic regression (N=9), k-nearest neighbors (N=8), support vector machines (N=8), decision trees (N=18), random forests (N=9), artificial neural networks (N=8), and deep neural networks (N=10). Hence, most use decision trees to apply ML algorithms to either the identification, pre-selection, or assessment of candidates (see Table 6.2). Several papers do not only apply one approach; instead, they test and compare various approaches to identify the most appropriate one for the described problem statement. Nineteen papers do not explicitly focus on ML, as they focus instead on either recommender systems, data mining in general, natural language process, matching, fuzzy logic, graph models, or sentiment analysis.

Concerning the different PE fit dimensions, none of the identified papers focus on PV or PP fit, 34 focus on PJ fit, eight on PO fit, and three on PT fit (see Table 6.2). The papers use data to predict the perceived fit by recruiters and business managers, and to some extent the actual fit using ML algorithms for prospective candidates (e.g., using social media data) and applicants (e.g., using résumés data). In most of the papers analyzed, fit does not mean fit in an aptitude-diagnostic sense. Instead, the papers focus on a perceived fit by either a recruiter or business manager. Still, they are supposed to imitate human decision behavior to predict individuals' subjective assessment of a fit and benefit from automation instead of a better fit. They do not explicitly explain whether they predict a supplementary, complementary, needs–supplies, or demands–abilities fit. Nevertheless, from the general idea described, one can conclude that approaches that focus on identifying people for jobs, pre-selecting candidates concerning a specific job, and assessing candidates concerning the job requirements predict a complementary PJ fit and, in particular, the demands–abilities fit. In contrast, approaches that focus on identifying jobs for people (e.g., job recommender systems) predict a complementary fit and, in particular, the needs–supplies fit. However, other approaches focus on needs–supplies and demands–abilities fits in parallel (e.g., predicting a person's fit for a team; Malinowski et al., 2006; Malinowski et al., 2008).

The data source used to extract information that can be used to predict the various PE fit dimensions using the different ML approaches varies. To get information about jobs and organizations, mainly job profiles are used (e.g., Luo et al., 2019; Qin et al., 2020; Shen et al., 2018; Zhu et al., 2018). Focusing on candidates, some approaches extract information from résumés, others use résumés and cover letters (e.g., Harris, 2018; Kessler et al., 2008; Kessler et al., 2012; Yan et al., 2019; see CHAPTER 3 for an introduction to the use of machine learning on text data). Moreover, approaches are reported that use internal HR databases (e.g., employee profiles; Manad et al., 2019; Yan et al., 2019), social media networks (e.g., LinkedIn, Facebook; Faliagka et al., 2014; Kamaru Zaman et al., 2019; Ting & Varathan, 2018; Tondji, 2018; explained in more detail in CHAPTER 5), blogs, and audio-visual data (e.g., Chen et al., 2016; Nguyen et al., 2014; Nguyen & Gatica-Perez, 2016; see CHAPTER 4 for an introduction to machine learning and audio and video data). Some approaches also apply explicit data collection techniques (e.g., questionnaires; Lee & Ahn, 2020).

The information extracted and used for predicting the various PE fit dimensions includes personal information, educational information, career information, skills, work experience, and characteristics of the social media profile (see Table 6.3).

Table 6.3   Information extracted to be used in HR machine learning

Category	Attributes	References (Examples)
Personal information	Age, gender, race, status, number of kids, candidate's home address, country, salary, Big Five personality traits, Myers-Briggs Type Indicator (MBTI), union membership, and health condition	Chien & Chen (2008); Faliagka et al. (2014); Harris (2018); Jere et al. (2017); Kessler et al. (2008); Mahmoud et al. (2019); Min & Emam (2003); Siraj et al. (2011); Sun et al. (2019); Tondji (2018)
Educational information	Educational background and degree, quality of the academic institution, university type, and student performance	Almalis et al. (2014); Almalis et al. (2015); Bello et al. (2020); Harris (2018); Kessler et al. (2008); Min & Emam (2003)
Career information	Company size, contract details (e.g., full vs. part-time), duration of employment, average number of months in each previous job, job promotions, job title, reasons for leaving current job	Bello et al. (2020); Chien & Chen (2008); Cho & Ngai (2003); Harris (2017, 2018); Paparrizos et al. (2011); Tondji (2018)
Skills	Language, programming	Kamaru Zaman et al. (2019); Kessler et al. (2008); Kessler et al. (2012); Luo et al. (2019); Qin et al. (2020); Yan et al. (2019); Zaroor et al. (2018)
Work experience	Invested time in learning, worked in a team, project experience, awards, research paper publication	Lee & Ahn (2020); Luo et al. (2019); Mahmoud et al. (2019); Manad et al. (2019); Shen et al. (2018); Zhu et al. (2018)
Social media profile	Number of friends, number of likes, number of posts, number of photos in album	Faliagka et al. (2014); Ting & Varathan (2018)

Examples

The following examples from the identified 56 papers illustrate how research has applied ML in HR recruiting.[2]

Identifying potential candidates

Min and Emam (2003) propose a decision tree (DT) model to identify potential candidates by predicting turnover. High turnover intentions indicate potential candidates for a new job. The ML model uses individuals' profiles consisting of various information, for example in their résumé, in addition to the corresponding company size, its legal form, and employee turnover. An validation, based on 422 questionnaires, demonstrates that individuals' characteristics such as duration of employment, membership status in a union, and company size can predict an employee's turnover probability. Those individuals are a potential source for recruiting activities.

Predicting person–job fit based on résumés

Zhu et al. (2018) use a deep neural network (DNN) model to predict a candidate's fit for a job based on the degree of match between a candidate's work experience and the corresponding job requirements. The job requirements are extracted from job postings. The work experience is extracted from résumés using a DNN layer. Subsequently, based on the DNN, the authors estimate the distance between corresponding vector pairs, which, in turn, directly translates to the candidate's fit for a job. In an study based on 15,039 job postings and 12,007 successful applications, their DNN model predicts PJ fit with an accuracy of 0.76.

Predicting person–job fit based on résumés and cover letters
Kessler et al. (2008) use a k-nearest neighbors (KNN) model to extract relevant characteristics from résumés and cover letters, including skills, work experience, salary, and address. They create a vector representation of candidate profiles and job postings to derive the best fitting model for ranking candidates for their fit for a job. The ML algorithm was trained on 25 job postings and 2,916 candidate profiles labeled with their job fit as an output label, revealing an accuracy of 0.64.

Predicting person–job fit based on résumés and an internal HR database
Yan et al. (2019) use a DNN model to predict a candidate's job fit. Data to train the model is extracted from historic interview transcripts, résumés, and job requirements. Hence the DNN model is based on recruiters' latent preferences for candidates. The model was evaluated using a dataset consisting of 78,107 job postings and 87,208 résumés.

Predicting person–job fit based on online social network profiles and blogs
Faliagka et al. (2014) use data from online social network profiles, blogs, and job descriptions for predicting PJ fit. The authors extract several pieces of information from the social media profiles, such as education, work experience, and the average number of months spent per job. Based on individual blog posts, scores for the Big Five personality traits are calculated. From job descriptions, the required professional experience is extracted. Faliagka et al. (2014) use all three data sources as inputs for different ML algorithms, of which the DT algorithm performs best. A study using 100 applications and three job postings labeled by a recruiter with the PJ fit demonstrates that the derived model can predict HR experts' ranking of PJ fit with accuracy levels of between 0.63 and 0.85 depending on the job.

Predicting candidates' person–team fit
Li et al. (2011), Ivan et al. (2019), and Malinowski et al. (2008) aim to predict an individual's team fit. Li et al. (2011) use the Big Five personality traits to predict the potential team fit of individuals using an SVM algorithm. As input, the Big Five personality traits are derived from personality questionnaires completed by candidates and employees labeled with their corresponding department. Based on a study with 310 questionnaires from seven departments, Li et al. (2011) demonstrate that an accuracy of up to 0.96 can be reached when predicting PT fit using SVM. Ivan et al.'s (2019) KNN approach uses individuals' characteristics extracted from social media profiles to predict PT fit, which are used to label individuals as fitting well with the team or not. In a study using 400 profiles, a KNN model predicts PT fit with an accuracy of 0.65. Malinowski et al. (2008) relies on recommender systems and predicts PT fit based on trust assessments between individuals working at an organization. It adapts collaborative filtering to predict the trust relationships between the members of a team and a potential new member.

DISCUSSIONS AND IMPLICATIONS

The literature review reported in this chapter illustrates how research has applied ML in the HR recruiting context. Fifty-six papers are identified using various ML approaches to predict the person–job fit dimension of the person–environment fit, partly based on Kramer (2020) and Rudolph (2020). Given the accuracy of these approaches and the results reported in these papers, the use of AI and especially ML in recruiting can increase the recruiting process's efficiency in terms of costs and time-to-hire. It is indicated that a time reduction of up to 88 percent can be achieved by using AI-based recruiting approaches (Black & van Esch, 2020). At the same time, the quality of decision-making can be enhanced through increased information quality. It can potentially lead to more objectivity in decision-making. AI-based recruiting can enhance candidate pools' size and quality (van Esch et al., 2019 and van Esch & Black, 2019). Similarly, Fernández-Martínez and Fernández (2019) point out that the validity of the decision-making is enhanced through AI-based recruiting, as it is not restricted to a maximum amount of processable information and can also take latent relationships into account. However, most of these approaches focus on efficiency in imitating human behavior to benefit from HR recruiting automation. Still, the focus is on automatically predicting individuals' (e.g., HR employees', business managers') subjective assessment of person–environment fit dimensions. The focus is not on fit in an aptitude-diagnostic sense as a basis for better decision-making.

The majority of the publications analyzed base their claim for the appropriateness of ML for HR recruiting on the fact that their ML model achieves a superior performance regarding various evaluation metrics (e.g., accuracy; as Rudolph, 2020 concluded). In general, good scores in these evaluation metrics correspond to well-trained ML models and AI-based approaches. Still, it cannot be guaranteed that if an ML model scores a good accuracy on one dataset, it would also perform equally well on another (Deng, 2018). Next to these criteria, dataset size, diversity, and quality, which are all hard to evaluate objectively with the information provided in publications, also play a critical role in the generalizability and performance of an AI-based tool (Chalfin et al., 2016; Harris, 2018).

The literature review also reveals that several approaches use discriminatory characteristics such as age, gender, race, and so on (see CHAPTER 16 for a detailed discussion on machine learning and fairness in HRM). Only some approaches set classifiers or use discrimination mitigation methods to address discrimination actively (Hirsch, 2016; Jobin et al., 2019; Schmalenbach & Laumer, 2020). Regarding pre-processing discrimination mitigation methods, extended feature removal, relabeling, or reweighting methods could be implemented to enhance AI-based recruiting tools' fairness (Feldman et al., 2015; Kamiran & Calders, 2012; Schmalenbach & Laumer, 2020). Furthermore, a variety of relevant publications regarding in-processing or post-processing discrimination mitigation methods have already been published. Kamishima et al.'s (2012) in-processing approaches are suitable for the recruiting context. Geyik et al. (2019) provide applicable post-processing discrimination mitigation methods.

Given these results and based on a first analysis by Rudolph (2020) and Kramer (2020), the implications of the literature review for research are five-fold. First, research needs to create an increased interest in ML and HR recruiting. Although the number of publications has been increasing in past years, the research field is still in its infancy, especially as the majority of the papers focus on specific person–environment fit dimensions (e.g., person–job fit, neglecting the person–vocation, person–organization, and person–person fit) or ML algorithms (e.g., decision trees and neural networks). Second, there is a need for the research community to create large, high-quality datasets and to provide these to other researchers. So far, available datasets are limited (Nguyen & Gatica-Perez, 2016). The importance is underscored when considering that a relatively trivial ML algorithm trained on a large, high-quality dataset can perform better than a highly advanced and personalized algorithm trained on a limited dataset (Domingos, 2012; Handelman et al., 2019). Due to the lack of publicly available recruiting data, different ML models cannot be directly compared against each other, as most of the analyzed publications train their models on datasets not open to the rest of the research community. Thus, researchers that aim to enhance a previously published ML approach cannot differentiate whether differences regarding evaluation metric scores are due to a better fitting ML model or only the underlying data. Third, and interrelated with the second point, researchers need to lay a strong focus on testing different ML algorithms against each other to identify the best fitting approach for the issue at hand, as there is no single solution to every task (Goodfellow, 2016). Although many of the analyzed publications already compare different ML algorithms during the evaluation of the model, the comparison often only focuses on a subset of the main ML algorithms. Fourth, addressing fairness and transparency needs to become a central part of model conceptualization and evaluation in the field of AI-based recruiting to fulfill especially legal requirements. Hence, failing to address discrimination in AI-based recruiting leads not only to an unfair and thus discriminatory recruiting, but also to an illegal one (see CHAPTER 16 for a detailed discussion). Fifth, research might shift its focus from applying AI-based approaches to imitate human decision behavior, and hence benefit solely from the automation of HR recruiting, to applying AI-based approaches in an aptitude-diagnostic sense to predict better person–environment fits in order to increase decision quality in HR recruiting.

This literature review has provided a summary of research on the use of ML in HR recruiting, constituting the HR recruiting ML model to guide future research approaches. This model summarizes the status quo but also illustrates that research so far has set some specific foci. In contrast, it also reveals problematic patterns in using discriminatory variables when predicting person–environment fit dimensions. Therefore, future research has various opportunities to focus on ML in HR recruiting to make these activities more efficient, more effective, fair, and discrimination-free. ML provides the base for this, but it still needs to unveil its full potential, as shown by the literature review in this chapter.

NOTES

1. https://www.scopus.com/. Searching Scopus means that we have not limited ourselves to any specific set of journals or conferences. Each journal and conference indexed by Scopus was simultaneously searched.
2. Given the space limitations we selected examples that provide a good overview of how different machine learning approaches are used to predict different PE fit dimensions. The examples were identified by Rudolph (2020) such that this section is based on this work.

REFERENCES

Adomavicius, G., Bockstedt, J. C., Curley, S. P., & Zhang, J. (2013). Do recommender systems manipulate consumer preferences? A study of anchoring effects. *Information Systems Research*, *24*(4), 956–975. https://doi.org/10.1287/isre.2013.0497

Aggarwal, C. C. (2015). *Data mining*. Springer International Publishing.

Aggarwal, C. C. (2016). *Recommender systems*. Springer International Publishing.

Alghamlas, M., & Alabduljabbar, R. (2019). Predicting the suitability of IT students' skills for the recruitment in Saudi labor market. In *2019 2nd International Conference on Computer Applications & Information Security (ICCAIS)* (pp. 1–5). IEEE.

Ali Shah, S. A., Uddin, I., Aziz, F., Ahmad, S., Al-Khasawneh, M. A., & Sharaf, M. (2020). An enhanced deep neural network for predicting workplace absenteeism. *Complexity*, Article 5843932. https://doi .org/10.1155/2020/5843932

Almalis, N. D., Tsihrintzis, G. A., & Karagiannis, N. (2014). A content based approach for recommending personnel for job positions. In *The 5th International Conference on Information, Intelligence, Systems and Applications (IISA)* (pp. 45–49). IEEE.

Almalis, N. D., Tsihrintzis, G. A., Karagiannis, N., & Strati, A. D. (2015). FoDRA – A new content-based job recommendation algorithm for job seeking and recruiting. In *2015 6th International Conference on Information, Intelligence, Systems and Applications (IISA)* (pp. 1–7). https://doc.org/10.1109/IISA .2015.7388018.

Ayodele, T. O. (2010). Types of machine learning algorithms. In Y. Zhang (Ed.), *New advances in machine learning* (pp. 19–48). IntechOpen. https://doi.org/10.5772/9385

Bello, M., Luna, A., Bonilla, E., Hernandez, C., Pedroza, B., & Portilla, A. (2020). A novel profile's selection algorithm using AI. *Applied Computer Science*, *16*(1), 18–32. https://doi.org/10.23743/acs -2020-02

Bian, S., Zhao, W. X., Song, Y., Zhang, T., & Wen, J.-R. (2019). Domain adaptation for person–job fit with transferable deep global match network. In K. Inui, J. Jiang, V. Ng, & X. Wan (Eds.), *Proceedings of the 2019 Conference on Empirical Methods in Natural Language Processing* (pp. 4809–4819). Association for Computational Linguistics. https://doi.org/10.18653/v1/D19-1487

Black, J. S., & van Esch, P. (2020). AI-enabled recruiting: What is it and how should a manager use it? *Business Horizons*, *63*(2), 215–226. https://doi.org/10.1016/j.bushor.2019.12.001

Bolander, T. (2019). What do we loose when machines take the decisions? *Journal of Management and Governance*, *23*(4), 849–867. https://doi.org/10.1007/s10997-019-09493-x

Boon, C., Den Hartog, D. N., Boselie, P., & Paauwe, J. (2011). The relationship between perceptions of HR practices and employee outcomes: Examining the role of person–organisation and person–job fit. *The International Journal of Human Resource Management*, *22*(1), 138–162. https://doi.org/10.1080/ 09585192.2011.538978

Buranasing, A. (2020). Efficiency assessment of undergraduate students based on academic record using deep learning methodology. *International Journal of Information and Education Technology*, *10*(7), 511–515. https://doi.org/10.18178/ijiet.2020.10.7.1416

Burch, J. R., & Long, D. E. (1992). Efficient Boolean function matching. In *International Conference on Computer-Aided Design (ICCAD '92)* (pp. 408–411). IEEE.

Chalfin, A., Danieli, O., Hillis, A., Jelveh, Z., Luca, M., Ludwig, J., & Mullainathan, S. (2016). Productivity and selection of human capital with machine learning. *The American Economic Review*, *106*(5), 124–127.

Chen, L., Feng, G., Martin-Raugh, M., Leong, C. W., Kitchen, C., Yoon, S.-Y., Lehman, B., Kell, H., & Lee, C. M. (2016). Automatic scoring of monologue video interviews using multimodal cues. In *Proceedings of the 18th ACM International Conference on Multimodal Interaction* (pp. 32–36). ACM.

Chien, C.-F., & Chen, L.-F. (2008). Data mining to improve personnel selection and enhance human capital: A case study in high-technology industry. *Expert Systems with Applications*, *34*(1), 280–290. https://doi.org/10.1016/j.eswa.2006.09.003

Cho, V., & Ngai, E. W. T. (2003). Data mining for selection of insurance sales agents. *Expert Systems*, *20*(3), 123–132.

Coll, R., & Fornés, J. (2009). Graphological analysis of handwritten text documents for human resources recruitment. In M. Kamel & A. Campilho (Eds.), *Proceedings of the 10th International Conference on Document Analysis and Recognition* (pp. 1081–1085). Springer.

Cooman, R. de, Vantilborgh, T., Bal, M., & Lub, X. (2016). Creating inclusive teams through perceptions of supplementary and complementary person–team fit. *Group and Organization Management*, *41*(3), 310–342. https://doi.org/10.1177/1059601115586910

Dainty, A. R. J., Cheng, M.-I., & Moore, D. R. (2005). Competency-based model for predicting construction project managers' performance. *Journal of Management in Engineering*, *21*(1), 2–9.

Deng, L. (2018). Artificial intelligence in the rising wave of deep learning: The historical path and future outlook. *IEEE Signal Processing Magazine, 35*(1), 173–180.

Domingos, P. (2012). A few useful things to know about machine learning. *Communications of the ACM, 55*(10), 78–87. https://doi.org/10.1145/2347736.2347755

Duan, Y., Edwards, J. S., & Dwivedi, Y. K. (2019). Artificial intelligence for decision making in the era of Big Data – evolution, challenges and research agenda. *International Journal of Information Management, 48*, 63–71. https://doi.org/10.1016/j.ijinfomgt.2019.01.021

Eckhardt, A., Laumer, S., Maier, C., & Weitzel, T. (2014). The transformation of people, processes, and IT in e-recruiting: Insights from an eight-year case study of a German media corporation. *Employee Relations, 36*(4), 415–431. https://doi.org/10.1108/ER-07-2013-0079

Edwards, J. R. (1991). Person-job fit: A conceptual integration, literature review, and methodological critique. In C. Cooper & I. T. Robertson (Eds.), *International review of industrial and organizational psychology* (pp. 283–357). John Wiley & Sons.

Edwards, J. R., Cable, D. M., Williamson, I. O., Lambert, L. S., & Shipp, A. J. (2006). The phenomenology of fit: Linking the person and environment to the subjective experience of person–environment fit. *Journal of Applied Psychology, 91*(4), 802–827. https://doi.org/10.1037/0021-9010.91.4.802

Escolar-Jimenez, C. C., Matsuzaki, K., & Gustilo, R. C. (2019). Intelligent shortlisting process for job applicants using fuzzy logic-based profiling. *International Journal of Advanced Trends in Computer Science and Engineering, 8*(3), 567–572. https://doi.org/10.30534/ijatcse/2019/36832019

Faliagka, E., Iliadis, L., Karydis, I., Rigou, M., Sioutas, S., Tsakalidis, A., & Tzimas, G. (2014). On-line consistent ranking on e-recruitment: Seeking the truth behind a well-formed CV. *Artificial Intelligence Review, 42*(3), 515–528. https://doi.org/10.1007/s10462-013-9414-y

Färber, F., Weitzel, T., & Keim, T. (2003). An automated recommendation approach to selection in personnel recruitment. In *AMCIS 2003 Proceedings* (pp. 2329–2339).

Feldman, M., Friedler, S. A., Moeller, J., Scheidegger, C., & Venkatasubramanian, S. (2015). Certifying and removing disparate impact. In L. Cao & Z. Chengqi (Eds.), *Proceedings of the 21st ACM SIGKDD International Conference on Knowledge Discovery and Data Mining* (pp. 259–268). ACM.

Fernández-Martínez, M. d. C., & Fernández, A. (2019). AI in recruiting. Multi-agent systems architecture for ethical and legal auditing. In S. Kraus (Ed.), *Proceedings of the Twenty-Eighth International Joint Conference on Artificial Intelligence* (pp. 6428–6429). IJCAI.

Forsyth, D. (2019). *Applied machine learning*. Springer International Publishing.

Freire, M. N., & Castro, L. N. de (2021). e-Recruitment recommender systems: A systematic review. *Knowledge and Information Systems, 63*(1), 1–20. https://doi.org/10.1007/s10115-020-01522-8

Geyik, S. C., Ambler, S., & Kenthapadi, K. (2019). Fairness-aware ranking in search and recommendation systems with application to LinkedIn talent search. In A. Teredesai, V. Kumar, Y. Li, R. Rosales, E. Terzi, & G. Karypis (Eds.), *Proceedings of the 25th ACM SIGKDD International Conference on Knowledge Discovery & Data Mining* (pp. 2221–2231). Association for Computing Machinery.

Goodfellow, I. (Ed.). (2016). *Deep learning*. MIT Press.

Güçlütürk, Y., Guclu, U., Baro, X., Escalante, H. J., Guyon, I., Escalera, S., van Gerven, M. A., & van Lier, R. (2018). Multimodal first impression analysis with deep residual networks. *IEEE Transactions on Affective Computing, 9*(3), 316–329. https://doi.org/10.1109/TAFFC.2017.2751469

Gunning, D., & Aha, D. (2019). DARPA's explainable artificial intelligence (XAI) program. *AI Magazine, 40*(2), 44–58. https://doi.org/10.1609/aimag.v40i2.2850

Haenlein, M., & Kaplan, A. (2019). A brief history of artificial intelligence: On the past, present, and future of artificial intelligence. *California Management Review, 61*(4), 5–14. https://doi.org/10.1177/0008125619864925

Hagras, H. (2018). Toward human-understandable, explainable AI. *Computer, 51*(9), 28–36.

Handelman, G. S., Kok, H. K., Chandra, R. V., Razavi, A. H., Huang, S., Brooks, M., Lee, M. J., & Asadi, H. (2019). Peering into the black box of artificial intelligence: Evaluation metrics of machine learning methods. *American Journal of Roentgenology, 212*(1), 38–43.

Harris, C. G. (2017). Finding the best job applicants for a job posting: A comparison of human resources search strategies. In R. Gottumukkala (Ed.), *Proceedings of the 17th IEEE International Conference on Data Mining Workshops (ICDMW)* (pp. 189–194). IEEE.

Harris, C. G. (2018). Making better job hiring decisions using "human in the loop" techniques. In A. L. Gentile, L. Aroyo, G. Demartini, & C. Welty (Eds.), *Proceedings of the 2nd International Workshop on Augmenting Intelligence with Humans-in-the-Loop* (pp. 16–26). CEUR Workshop Proceedings.

Hirsch, P. B. (2016). The caliphate of numbers. *Journal of Business Strategy*, *37*(6), 51–55. https://doi .org/10.1108/JBS-09-2016-0098

Ivan, I., Budacu, E., & Despa, M. L. (2019). Using profiling to assemble an agile collaborative software development team made up of freelancers. *Procedia Computer Science*, *162*, 562–570. https://doi.org/ 10.1016/j.procs.2019.12.024

Jackson, S.E., Schuler, R. S., Jiang, K. (2014). An aspirational framework for strategic human resource management. *The Academy Management Annals*, *8*(1), 1–56. https://doi.org/ 10.1080/19416520.2014.872335

James, G., Witten, D., Hastie, T., & Tibshirani, R. (2013). *An introduction to statistical learning*. Springer.

Jansen, K. J., & Kristof-Brown, A. (2006). Toward a multidimensional theory of person–environment fit. *Journal of Managerial Issues*, *18*(2), 193–212.

Jere, S., Jayannavar, L., Ali, A., & Kulkarni, C. (2017). Recruitment graph model for hiring unique competencies using social media mining. In *ICMLC 2017: Proceedings of the 9th International Conference on Machine Learning and Computing* (pp. 461–466). https://doi.org/10.1145/3055635 .3056575

Jobin, A., Ienca, M., & Vayena, E. (2019). The global landscape of AI ethics guidelines. *Nature Machine Intelligence*, *1*(9), 389–399. https://doi.org/10.1038/s42256-019-0088-2

Jordan, M. I., & Mitchell, T. M. (2015). Machine learning: Trends, perspectives, and prospects. *Science*, *349*(6245), 255–260. https://doi.org/10.1126/science.aaa8415

Kamaru Zaman, E. A., Ahmad Kamal, A. F., Mohamed, A., Ahmad, A., & Raja Mohd Zamri, R. A. Z. (2019). Staff Employment Platform (StEP) using job profiling analytics. In B. Yap, A. Mohamed, & M. Berry (Eds.), *Soft Computing in Data Science. SCDS 2018* (pp. 387–401). Springer. https://doi.org/ 10.1007/978-981-13-3441-2_30

Kamiran, F., & Calders, T. (2012). Data preprocessing techniques for classification without discrimination. *Knowledge and Information Systems*, *33*(1), 1–33.

Kamishima, T., Akaho, S., Asoh, H., & Sakuma, J. (2012). Fairness-aware classifier with prejudice remover regularizer. In P. A. Flach, D. B. Tijl, & N. Cristianini (Eds.), *Proceedings of the Joint European Conference on Machine Learning and Knowledge Discovery in Databases* (pp. 35–50). Springer.

Kaplan, A. M., & Haenlein, M. (2010). Users of the world, unite! The challenges and opportunities of social media. *Business Horizons*, *53*(1), 59–68. https://doi.org/10.1016/j.bushor.2009.09.003

Kessler, R., Béchet, N., Roche, M., El-Bèze, M., & Torres-Moreno, J. M. (2008). Automatic profiling system for ranking candidates answers in human resources. In R. Meersman, Z. Tari, & P. Herrero (Eds.), *On the Move to Meaningful Internet Systems: OTM 2008 Workshops* (pp. 625–634). Springer.

Kessler, R., Béchet, N., Roche, M., Torres-Moreno, J.-M., & El-Bèze, M. (2012). A hybrid approach to managing job offers and candidates. *Information Processing and Management*, *48*(6), 1124–1135. https://doi.org/10.1016/j.ipm.2012.03.002

Kramer, S. A. (2020). *Künstliche Intelligenz im Recruiting – Eine Literaturanalyse* [Unpublished thesis]. Friedrich-Alexander-Univeristät Erlangen-Nürnberg.

Kristof, A. L. (1996). Person–organization fit: An integrative review of its conceptualizations, measurement, and implications. *Personnel Psychology*, *49*(1), 1–49. https://doi.org/10.1111/j.1744-6570 .1996.tb01790.x

Kristof-Brown, A., Barrick, M. R., & Stevens, C. K. (2005). When opposites attract: A multi-sample demonstration of complementary person–team fit on extraversion. *Journal of Personality*, *73*(4), 935–957. https://doi.org/10.1111/j.1467-6494.2005.00334.x

Laumer, S., Eckhardt, A., & Weitzel, T. (2010). Electronic human resources management in an e-business environment. *Journal of Electronic Commerce Research*, *11*(4), 240–250.

Laumer, S., Eckhardt, A., & Weitzel, T. (2012). Online gaming to find a new job – examining job seekers' intention to use serious games as a self-assessment tool. *Zeitschrift für Personalforschung (ZfP) (German Journal of Research in Human Resource Management)*, *26*(3), 218–240.

Laumer, S., Gubler, F., Maier, C., & Weitzel, T. (2018). Job seekers' acceptance of job recommender systems: Results of an empirical study. In T. Bui (Ed.), *Proceedings of the 51st Hawaii International Conference on System Sciences*. https://doi.org/10.24251/HICSS.2018.491

Laumer, S., Maier, C., & Eckhardt, A. (2015). The impact of business process management and applicant tracking systems on recruiting process performance: An empirical study. *Journal of Business Economics, 85*(4), 421–453. https://doi.org/10.1007/s11573-014-0758-9

Laumer, S., Stetten, A. v., & Eckhardt, A. (2009). E-assessment. *Business and Information Systems Engineering, 1*(3), 263–265.

Le, R., Hu, W., Song, Y., Zhang, T., Zhao, D., & Yan, R. (2019). Towards effective and interpretable person–job fitting. In *CIKM'19: Proceedings of the 28th ACM International Conference on Information and Knowledge Management* (pp. 1883–1892). ACM.

LeCun, Y., Bengio, Y., & Hinton, G. (2015). Deep learning. *Nature, 521*(7553), 436–444. https://doiorg/10.1038/nature14539

Lee, D. S., & Ahn, C. K. (2020). Industrial human resource management optimization based on skills and characteristics. *Computers and Industrial Engineering, 144*, 106–463. https://doi.org/10.1016/j.cie.2020.106463

Li, Y.-M., Lai, C.-Y., & Kao, C.-P. (2011). Building a qualitative recruitment system via SVM with MCDM approach. *Applied Intelligence, 35*(1), 75–88.

Luo, Y., Zhang, H., Wen, Y., & Zhang, X. (2019). RésuméGAN. In *CIKM'19: Proceedings of the 28th ACM International Conference on Information and Knowledge Management* (pp. 1101–1110). Association for Computing Machinery.

Mahmoud, A. A., Al Shawabkeh, T., Salameh, W. A., & Al Amro, I. (2019). Performance predicting in hiring process and performance appraisals using machine learning. In *2019 10th International Conference on Information and Communication Systems, ICICS 2019* (pp. 110–115). https://doi.org/10.1109/IACS.2019.8809154.

Maier, C., Laumer, S., Joseph, D., Mattke, J., & Weitzel, T. (2021). Turnback intention: An analysis of the drivers of IT professionals' intention to return to a former employer. *MIS Quarterly, 45*(4), 1777–1806.

Mairesse, F., Walker, M. A., Mehl, M. R., & Moore, R. K. (2007). Using linguistic cues for the automatic recognition of personality in conversation and text. *Journal of Artificial Intelligence Research, 30*, 457–500.

Malebye, W. P. R., Seeletse, S. M., & Rivera, M. A. (2015). Merit measures and validation in employee evaluation and selection. *Problems and Perspectives in Management, 13*(3), 66–78.

Malinowski, J., Keim, T., Wendt, O., & Weitzel, T. (2006). Matching people and jobs: A bilateral recommendation approach. In *Proceedings of the 39th Annual Hawaii International Conference on System Sciences (HICSS'06)* (pp. 137c–137c). IEEE.

Malinowski, J., Weitzel, T., & Keim, T. (2008). Decision support for team staffing: An automated relational recommendation approach. *Decision Support Systems, 45*(3), 429–447.

Manad, O., Bentounsi, M., & Darmon, P. (2019). Enhancing talent search by integrating and querying big HR data. In *Proceedings – 2018 IEEE International Conference on Big Data, Big Data 2018* (pp. 4095–4100). https://doi.org/10.1109/BigData.2018.8622275

Marcus, B., & Wagner, U. (2015). What do you want to be? Criterion-related validity of attained vocational aspirations versus inventoried person–vocation fit. *Journal of Business and Psychology, 30*(1), 51–62. https://doi.org/10.1007/s10869-013-9330-9

Martín, I., Mariello, A., Battiti, R., & Hernández, J. A. (2018). Salary prediction in the IT job market with few high-dimensional samples: A Spanish case study. *International Journal of Computational Intelligence Systems, 11*(1), 1192–1209.

Martinez-Gil, J., Paoletti, A. L., & Pichler, M. (2020). A novel approach for learning how to automatically match job offers and candidate profiles. *Information Systems Frontiers, 22*, 1265–1274. https://doi.org/10.1007/s10796-019-09929-7

Martinez-Gil, J., Paoletti, A. L., & Schewe, K.-D. (2016). A smart approach for matching, learning and querying information from the human resources domain. In M. Ivanović, B. Thalheim, B. Catania, K.-D. Schewe, M. Kirikova, P. Šaloun, A. Dahanayake, T. Cerquitelli, E. Baralis, & P. Michiardi (Eds.), *New trends in databases and information systems* (pp. 157–167). Springer.

McAfee, A., & Brynjolfsson, E. (2012). Big data: The management revolution. *Harvard Business Review*, *90*(10), 60–68.

Mehta, S., Pimplikar, R., Singh, A., Varshney, L. R., & Visweswariah, K. (2013). Efficient multifaceted screening of job applicants. In *ACM International Conference Proceeding Series* (pp. 661–671). https://doi.org/10.1145/2452376.2452453

Min, H., & Emam, A. (2003). Developing the profiles of truck drivers for their successful recruitment and retention. *International Journal of Physical Distribution and Logistics Management*, *33*(2), 149–162. https://doi.org/10.1108/09600030310469153

Muchinsky, P. M., & Monahan, C. J. (1987). What is person–environment congruence? Supplementary versus complementary models of fit. *Journal of Vocational Behavior*, *31*(3), 268–277. https://doi.org/10.1016/0001-8791(87)90043-1

Münstermann, B., Stetten, A. v., Laumer, S., & Eckhardt, A. (2010). The performance impact of business process standardization: HR case study insights. *Management Research Review*, *33*(9), 924–939. https://doi.org/10.1108/01409171011070332

Nguyen, L. S., Frauendorfer, D., Mast, M. S., & Gatica-Perez, D. (2014). Hire me: Computational inference of hirability in employment interviews based on nonverbal behavior. *IEEE Transactions on Multimedia*, *16*(4), 1018–1031.

Nguyen, L. S., & Gatica-Perez, D. (2016). Hirability in the wild: Analysis of online conversational video résumés. *IEEE Transactions on Multimedia*, *18*(7), 1422–1437. https://doi.org/10.1109/TMM.2016.2557058

Noe, R. A., Hollenbeck, J. R., Gerhart, B. A., & Wright, P. M. (2017). *Fundamentals of human resource management* (7th ed.). McGraw-Hill Education.

Noe, R. A., Hollenbeck, J. R., Gerhart, B. A., & Wright, P. M. (2020). *Fundamentals of human resource management* (8th ed.). McGraw-Hill Education.

Oehlhorn, C. E., Maier, C., Laumer, S., & Weitzel, T. (2020). Human resource management and its impact on strategic business–IT alignment: A literature review and avenues for future research. *The Journal of Strategic Information Systems*, *29*(4), Article 101641. https://doi.org/10.1016/j.jsis.2020.101641

Ongsulee, P. (2017). Artificial intelligence, machine learning and deep learning. In *Proceedings of the 15th International Conference on ICT and Knowledge Engineering* (pp. 1–6). IEEE.

Ostroff, C., & Zhan, Y. (2012). *Person–environment fit in the selection process*. Oxford University Press.

Paoletti, A. L., Martinez-Gil, J., & Schewe, K.-D. (2016). Top-k matching queries for filter-based profile matching in knowledge bases. In S. Hartmann & H. Ma (Eds.), *Database and Expert Systems Applications* (pp. 295–302). Springer.

Paparrizos, I., Cambazoglu, B. B., & Gionis, A. (2011). Machine learned job recommendation. In B. Mobasher (Ed.), *Proceedings of the Fifth ACM Conference on Recommender Systems* (pp. 325–328). ACM.

Qin, C., Zhu, H., Xu, T., Zhu, C., Jiang, L., Chen, E., & Xiong, H. (2018). Enhancing person–job fit for talent recruitment. In *SIGIR'18: The 41st International ACM SIGIR Conference on Research and Development in Information Retrieval* (pp. 25–34). Association for Computing Machinery.

Qin, C., Zhu, H., Xu, T., Zhu, C., Ma, C., Chen, E., & Xiong, H. (2020). An enhanced neural network approach to person–job fit in talent recruitment. *ACM Transactions on Information Systems*, *38*(2), 1–33. https://doi.org/10.1145/3376927

Qin, C., Zhu, H., Zhu, C., Xu, T., Zhuang, F., Ma, C., Zhang, J., & Xiong, H. (2019). DuerQuiz: A personalized question recommender system for intelligent job interview. In A. Teredesai, V. Kumar, Y. Li, R. Rosales, E. Terzi, & G. Karypis (Eds.), *Proceedings of the 25th ACM SIGKDD International Conference on Knowledge Discovery and Data Mining* (pp. 2165–2173). Association for Computing Machinery.

Resnick, P., & Varian, H. R. (1997). Recommender systems. *Communications of the ACM*, *40*(3), 56–58.

Rudolph, M. D. (2020). *Artificial intelligence in recruiting: A literature review on the usage of artificial intelligence technologies, its ethical implications and the resulting chances and risks* [Unpublished thesis]. Friedrich-Alexander-Univeristät Erlangen-Nürnberg.

Russell, S. J., & Norvig, P. (2016). *Artificial intelligence: A modern approach*. Pearson.

Saat, N. M., & Singh, D. (2011). Assessing suitability of candidates for selection using candidates' profiling report. In *Proceedings of the 2011 International Conference on Electrical Engineering and Informatics* (pp. 1–6). https://doi.org/0.1109/ICEEI.2011.6021594

Schmalenbach, K., & Laumer, S. (2020). Does data-driven recruitment lead to less discrimination? – A technical perspective. In N. Gronau, M. Heine, K. Poustcchi, & H. Krasnova (Eds.), *WI2020 Zentrale Tracks* (pp. 1649–1664). GITO.

Sekiguchi, T. (2004). Person–organization fit and person–job fit in employee selection: A review of the literature. *Osaka keidai ronshu, 54*(6), 179–196.

Shen, D., Zhu, H., Zhu, C., Xu, T., Ma, C., & Xiong, H. (2018). A joint learning approach to intelligent job interview assessment. In J. Lang (Ed.), *Proceedings of the 27th International Joint Conference on Artificial Intelligence* (pp. 3542–3548). AAAI Press.

Siraj, F., Mustafa, N., Haris, M. F., Yusof, S. R. M., Salahuddin, M. A., & Hasan, M. R. (2011). Pre-selection of recruitment candidates using case based reasoning. In *Proceedings – CIMSim 2011: 3rd International Conference on Computational Intelligence, Modelling and Simulation* (pp. 84–90). https://doi.org/10.1109/CIMSim.2011.24.

St J. Burch, G., & Anderson, N. (2004). Measuring person–team fit: Development and validation of the team selection inventory. *Journal of Managerial Psychology, 19*(4), 406–426. https://doi.org/10.1108/02683940410537954

Strohmeier, S. (2009). Concepts of e-HRM consequences: A categorisation, review and suggestion. *The International Journal of Human Resource Management, 20*(3), 528–543. https://doi.org/10.1080/09585190802707292

Strohmeier, S., & Piazza, F. (2015). Artificial intelligence techniques in human resource management – a conceptual exploration. In C. Kahraman & S. Çevik Onar (Eds.), *Intelligent techniques in engineering management* (pp. 149–172). Springer.

Suciu, G., Pasat, A., & Vasilescu, C. (2019). Novel artificial intelligence technologies for enhanced recruitment campaigns using social media. In I. Roceanu (Ed.), *The 15th International Conference eLearning and Software for Education* (Vol. 3, pp. 232–239). Carol I National Defence University Publishing House.

Sun, Y., Zhuang, F., Zhu, H., Song, X., He, Q., & Xiong, H. (2019). The impact of person–organization fit on talent management. In A. Teredesai, V. Kumar, Y. Li, R. Rosales, E. Terzi, & G. Karypis (Eds.), *Proceedings of the 25th ACM SIGKDD International Conference on Knowledge Discovery and Data Mining* (pp. 1625–1633). Association for Computing Machinery.

Ting, T. L., & Varathan, K. D. (2018). Job recommendation using Facebook personality scores. *Malaysian Journal of Computer Science, 31*(4), 311–331. https://doi.org/10.22452/mjcs.vol31no4.5

Tondji, L. N. (2018). *Web recommender system for job seeking and recruiting.* AIMS. https://doi.org/10.13140/RG.2.2.26177.61286

Tung, K.-Y., Huang, I.-C., Chen, S.-L., & Shih, C.-T. (2005). Mining the Generation Xers' job attitudes by artificial neural network and decision tree – empirical evidence in Taiwan. *Expert Systems with Applications, 29*(4), 783–794. https://doi.org/10.1016/j.eswa.2005.06.012

van Esch, P., & Black, J. S. (2019). Factors that influence new generation candidates to engage with and complete digital, AI-enabled recruiting. *Business Horizons, 62*(6), 729–739. https://doi.org/10.1016/j.bushor.2019.07.004

van Esch, P., Black, J. S., & Ferolie, J. (2019). Marketing AI recruitment: The next phase in job application and selection. *Computers in Human Behavior, 90*, 215–222. https://doi.org/10.1016/j.chb.2018.09.009

Verina, W., Fauzi, M., Nasari, F., Tanjung, D. H., & Iriani, J. (2019). Decision support system for employee recruitment using multifactor evaluation process. In *2018 6th International Conference on Cyber and IT Service Management, CITSM 2018* (Citsm) (pp. 2018–2021). https://doi.org/10.1109/CITSM.2018.8674277

Vom Brocke, J., Simons, A., Niehaves, B., Niehaves, B., & Reimer, K. (2009). Reconstructing the giant: On the importance of rigour in documenting the literature search process. In *ECIS 2009 Proceedings, 161*. https://aisel.aisnet.org/ecis2009/161.

Werbel, J. D., & Gilliland, S. W. (1999). Person–environment fit in the selection process. In *Research in human resources management* (pp. 209–243). Elsevier Science/JAI Press.

Wirtky, T., Laumer, S., Eckhardt, A., & Weitzel, T. (2016). On the untapped value of e-HRM: A literature review. *Communications of the Association for Information Systems, 38*, 20–83. http://doi.org/10.17705/1CAIS.03802

Wu, X., Zhu, X., Wu, G.-Q., & Ding, W. (2014). Data mining with big data. *IEEE Transactions on Knowledge and Data Engineering, 26*(1), 97–107. https://doi.org/10.1109/TKDE.2013.109

Yan, R., Le, R., Song, Y., Zhang, T., Zhang, X., & Zhao, D. (2019). Interview choice reveals your preference on the market. In A. Teredesai, V. Kumar, Y. Li, R. Rosales, E. Terzi, & G. Karypis (Eds.), *Proceedings of the 25th ACM SIGKDD International Conference on Knowledge Discovery and Data Mining* (pp. 914–922). Association for Computing Machinery.

Zaroor, A., Maree, M., & Sabha, M. (2018). JRC: A job post and résumé classification system for online recruitment. In *Proceedings – International Conference on Tools with Artificial Intelligence, ICTAI* (pp. 780–787). https://doi.org/10.1109/ICTAI.2017.00123

Zhu, C., Zhu, H., Xiong, H., Ma, C., Xie, F., Ding, P., & Li, P. (2018). Person–job fit: Adapting the right talent for the right job with joint representation learning. *ACM Transactions on Management Information Systems, 9*(3), 1–17. https://doi.org/10.1145/3234465

7. Machine learning in HR staffing

Florian J. Meier and Sven Laumer

INTRODUCTION

People working in organizations are critical for their success (Beechler & Woodward, 2009; Grant, 1996). Human resources (HR), including people and their knowledge, skills, and motivation, are essential for a firm to establish and maintain its competitive advantage (Barney, 1991; Wright et al., 1994). In practice, executives and HR managers focus on effectively managing, motivating, attracting, and keeping their employees at the organization (Wright & McMahan, 2011). In daily business and strategic foresight, it is necessary to have the right amount of people working in different parts of the organization to meet rapidly changing requirements (Bechet & Walker, 1993). Hence, executives need to calculate and foresee the current and future staffing needs. In this context, we define the term HR staffing as the provision of employees to meet the staffing needs of an organization in an optimal and cost-saving manner.

Staffing the right amount of people is a complicated task that includes predicting the required number of current and future employees. As organizations are subject to employee attrition, they need to hire employees to meet replacement requirements for those that have left. Furthermore, organizations are subject to economic changes, resulting in the need to grow the workforce or the necessity to release employees from occupations. This challenge is made greater by interfirm competition for employees with particular skills (Y. Liu et al., 2020).

There are various approaches to predicting organizational employee requirements (O'Brien-Pallas et al., 2001). Early prediction models commonly comprise a qualitative approach, relying on managerial experience or static deterministic mathematical models that lack historical data to test their validity. However, there are uncertainties in real-life scenarios when it comes to predicting employee requirements, and this has led to a call for more advanced methods that account for stochastic factors (Safarishahrbijari, 2018).

One of these advanced methodological approaches involves the use of machine learning (ML) algorithms that promise to increasingly support executives with the calculation and prediction of HR staffing metrics (L. Liu et al., 2020). These algorithms use various data sources to foresee the number of employees in an organization, considering absenteeism (Lima et al., 2020), hiring (Pessach et al., 2020), and attrition (Zhao et al., 2018). The algorithmically generated predictions help human resources management (HRM) work more efficiently, which results in cost savings through less spontaneous personnel recruitment.

With this chapter, we aim at supporting HRM in organizations to obtain these fundamental HR staffing predictions using ML. However, there are various ML algorithms for supporting HRM and HR staffing (de Oliveira, 2019), focusing on different metrics that are relevant for predicting HR staffing requirements (Ekawati, 2019). This chapter provides a structured literature analysis for the application of ML in HR staffing, based on the recommendations of Vom Brocke et al. (2009, 2015) and Webster and Watson (2002) for conducting a structured literature analysis. More specifically, we aim at exploring the data sources necessary for good

HR staffing predictions along with the best-fitting ML algorithms for supporting HRM in their staffing tasks, and at identifying shortcomings in the state-of-the-art research in order to derive a future research agenda.

In this chapter we focus on supervised ML algorithms, which are commonly used for classification problems (Osisanwo et al., 2017), and mostly used in the HRM domain (Ekawati, 2019) to process data in order to improve HR predictions (Molnar, 2020). This chapter summarizes the current state of research on ML in HR staffing.

The remainder of this chapter is structured as follows: The next section provides a theoretical background on HR staffing and ML. The subsequent section sets out the structured literature review as our methodological approach. This is followed by a section that presents the results of the literature review in a concept matrix. The chapter concludes with a discussion and possibilities for future research.

THEORETICAL BACKGROUND

HRM is, among other things, responsible for planning and resourcing HR according to organizational needs (Noe et al., 2007; Wirtky et al., 2016). These needs depend on the organizational environment and are subject to fluctuations (Noe et al., 2007). HRM has to cope with staff assimilation, staff turnover, and staff acquisition (Abdel-Hamid, 1989). To meet short-term demands alongside the more long-term ones, HRM needs to allocate resources on a frequent basis to ensure the workforce can deal with organizational requirements at all times (Oehlhorn et al., 2020).

Organizations can fill vacancies as well as new jobs either externally by advertising outside of the company and recruiting from the external labor market or internally by reallocating existing personnel. External recruitment is essential if the HRM cannot fill open vacancies with personnel from inside the organization. Tasks for external recruitment include the attraction of candidates through various advertisement practices, along with the selection and hiring of suitable candidates through using various HRM activities (Todd et al., 1995), making it a costly process (Abdel-Hamid, 1989). However, certain aspects of the recruitment process, such as posting job advertisements or processing incoming applications, can be standardized to save costs (Laumer et al., 2015; Muenstermann et al., 2010). Other aspects need proactive attention, for example reaching out to potential candidates and screening applications, which require close integration with the organization's network (Wirtky et al., 2016).

The Concept of HR Staffing

HR staffing is a critical function in HRM that organizations must perform highly effectively and efficiently. The concept of HR staffing comprises the allocating of individuals to open vacancies (Al-Bdareen & Khasawneh, 2019; Judge & Ferris, 1992). This allocation involves an earlier process of identifying the number of employees needed in the organization and planning for shortages due to absenteeism (Jensen & McIntosh, 2007). Furthermore, planned or expected hires and employee attrition need to be taken into account (Rowley & Purcell, 2001) to predict total recruitment requirements and meet the gross employee requirements of an organization.

In the remainder of this chapter, we define the net number of needed employees as net employee requirements (NER), that is, the workforce demands to enable the organization to operate normally. This number of employees is not to be equated with the gross number of needed employees, the gross employee requirements (GER), as absenteeism needs to be taken into account. Hence, we define the demand of employees needed to cope with absenteeism (Breaugh, 1981) as reserve employee requirements (RER). The addition of the RER to the NER finally forms the total number of employees in an organization, the GER (see Figure 7.1).

Our concept of HR staffing furthermore consists of calculating the future number of employees in the organization. For this calculation, we need the headcount of the current employees. To finally predict the future number of employees, we add expected hires (EH) to the current number of employees and subtract the prediction of employee attrition (EA). Hence, the future number of employees is the current number of employees plus EH and minus EA. In Figure 7.1, we expect the number for EH to be smaller than that for EA, which results in fewer predicted future employees than the current workforce.

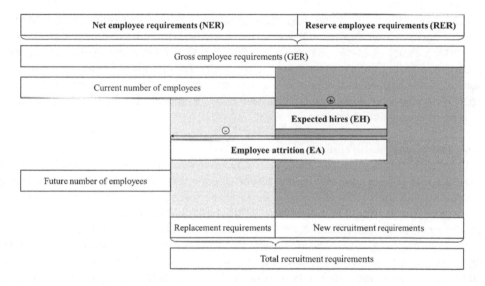

Figure 7.1   HR staffing model

The prediction of the future number of employees provides the opportunity to calculate additional necessary HR staffing metrics. In more detail, replacement requirements can be predicted from this model. Based on the future number of employees, the replacement requirements are the number of employees to reach the number of the currently employed workforce. Please note that this number is zero if EH is bigger than EA and no replacement is needed. Furthermore, knowing the GER and the replacement requirements, we can foresee new recruitment requirements. This foresight is based on the assumption that the GER are equal to the future number of employees plus replacement and new recruitment requirements. Henceforth, the replacement and new recruitment requirements define the total number of recruitments needed.

Our HR staffing model in Figure 7.1 demonstrates the possibility to calculate GER and recruitment requirements based on the prediction of our four HR staffing categories: NER, RER, EH, and EA. Please note that this model assumes positive recruitment requirements. If we predict a higher headcount for the future number of employees than our GER, negative recruitment requirements result. To cope with these negative requirements, organizations could implement measures connected with staff redundancies that are not this chapter's direct focus.

Net employee requirements
We define NER as the organization's HR demand for a specific period of time, depending on different variables. For instance, the number of needed employees in specific industries, for example healthcare, retail, and travel, varies according to the following variables: day of the week, holiday, month of the year, and weather (Au-Yeung et al., 2009; Batal et al., 2001; Wargon et al., 2009). These variables modify the theoretical number of needed employees for a given time period.

While overstaffing constitutes a waste of financial resources (Zlotnik et al., 2015), the results of understaffing departments are severe, including declining customer care (Kennedy et al., 2008), financial losses (Bayley et al., 2005), ethical dilemmas (Moskop et al., 2009), and adverse service outcomes (Bernstein et al., 2009). These negative results are particularly observed in the healthcare industry, but can be generalized to other industries (Mani et al., 2015). Organizations need to predict NER with a high degree of accuracy to reduce the adverse effects of over- and understaffing.

Reserve employee requirements
Employee absenteeism is a form of withdrawal behavior apart from turnover, resulting in staffing bottlenecks (Muchinsky, 1977). These bottlenecks result in high costs for organizations and loss in productivity. Absenteeism is caused by personal (e.g., anxiety, commitment, satisfaction, personality) and organizational (e.g., shift work, flextime) factors. Using these factors, executives can predict individual-level absenteeism (Avey et al., 2006). There are two ways to cope with employee absenteeism: First, organizations can hire and staff more employees than theoretically needed by NER. Second, organizations can staff temporarily open jobs with external service providers. Both options result in higher costs for the organization. However, with RER, we focus on limiting over-hiring because of the possibility to predict absenteeism and employ enough HR to achieve a high amount of productivity and decrease the chance of employee understaffing situations.

Expected hires
Hiring new employees has a massive impact on an organization's performance (Donovan et al., 2014). However, hiring is complicated, time-consuming, and a challenge (Hunt, 2007). In fact, the hiring process itself consists of various steps that include, among other things, the development of a hiring strategy, sourcing channels, candidate selection, and communication practices (Breaugh, 2008; Breaugh & Starke, 2000).

Despite the complexity, HRM seeks to predict recruitment success (Pessach et al., 2020), to reduce the adverse financial effects of spontaneous hires (Abdel-Hamid, 1989). Furthermore, predicting EH enhances the planning reliability for HRM. The prediction of EH relies on modern algorithms and techniques capable of processing large amounts of data, to cope with the complex structure of hiring. However, hiring data is needed for the prediction that includes the success of job advertisements (Pessach et al., 2020) and the number of available candidates on the market (Lei et al., 2009). The availability of this data and algorithms that can process it makes it possible to predict recruitment success and EH.

Employee attrition

Employee attrition, or churn, is the term used to describe the voluntarily departure of employees from an organization, a process that often results in adverse effects (L. Liu et al., 2020). These effects include disruptions, customer dissatisfaction, and higher costs due to recruiting and training efforts (Subramony & Holtom, 2012). The average cost of an employee leaving an organization is approximately 1.5 times the employee's annual salary. For IT service providers, the churn rate is as high as 12–15 percent (Saradhi & Palshikar, 2011).

Factors leading to employees leaving the company include, for example, distrust (Burnes, 2006), age, years in the organization, work–life balance, relationship satisfaction, environment satisfaction, job involvement, job level, total years spent working, and income (Frye et al., 2018). Executives can thus use these factors to reduce attrition with countermeasures and recruit employees at an early stage, that is, before existing employees leave.

Machine Learning

"Machine learning is a set of methods that computers use to make and improve predictions [of] behaviors based on data" (Molnar, 2020, p. 13). We can understand data as experience, that is, past information available to the learner, which usually takes the form of electronic data collected and made available for predictions and analysis. Furthermore, data can be in the form of digitized human-labeled datasets or other types of information generated via interaction with humans and the overall environment (Mohri et al., 2018). Hence, there is no restriction on where the data used in ML datasets come from. However, in all cases, the data's quality and volume is crucial for ML success.

The applicability of ML methods is manifold. For instance, ML methods are able to process natural language in speech and text form, graphics, numerical data, and complex forms of biological data. Hence, ML is theoretically and practically applicable in all HRM disciplines (Garg et al., 2021). However, we focus on ML methods in HR staffing, which limits the possible data range to HR data, surveys, environmental data, open data, CVs, advertisements, questionnaires, and interviews (see Figure 7.2).

ML methods and their algorithms can broadly be classified into supervised learning, unsupervised learning, and reinforcement learning (Kotsiantis et al., 2007). Supervised learning is the most common in classification problems because of its ability to identify the data classification system (Osisanwo et al., 2017). This review focuses on supervised ML algorithms, as they make up about 70 percent of all ML methods (LeCun et al., 2015; Ongsulee, 2017) and are the algorithms most commonly used in HRM (Garg et al., 2021).

The goal of ML in HR staffing is to predict and foresee specific staffing metrics which perform best in the field of HRM. However, several algorithms are available for this prediction, making it difficult for executives to identify the right method at a particular time. We choose a selection of eight well-performing algorithms in the HR domain to have a broad body of relevant literature with applicability to practice. These eight algorithms include the neural network models artificial neural network (ANN) and deep neural network (DNN), the decision tree models decision tree (DT) and random forest (RF), the instance-based models K-nearest neighbors (KNN) and support vector machine (SVM), statistical models including logistic regression (LogReg) and naïve Bayes (NB), and others (O). For detailed descriptions of the named algorithms, see CHAPTER 2 and CHAPTER 6.

METHODOLOGICAL APPROACH

This review aims to provide an overview of documented ML algorithms in HR staffing. We focus on the different categories of HR staffing and the aforementioned ML algorithms. To achieve this, we employ a literature review methodologically guided by the recommendations of Vom Brocke et al. (2009, 2015).

To start, we defined two inclusion criteria (Vom Brocke et al., 2015): First, we only looked at literature with a focus on ML in HR staffing that reveals the underlying algorithms and data used. Furthermore, we used only scholarly literature in the English language for this review, that is, peer-reviewed journal articles and conference papers. There was no restriction regarding time or geographic region and no restriction to a specific set of journals or conferences. We specifically refrained from excluding literature published at conferences, as they are an accepted means to exchange new findings rapidly.

Next, we used the following search string for searching the exhaustive online database Scopus:

> TITLE-ABS-KEY (("staff" OR "staffing" OR "personnel" OR "absentee prediction" OR "churn" OR "turnover" OR "attrition" OR "turnover" OR "retention" OR "recruitment prediction" OR "recruiting prediction" OR ("hire" OR "hiring" AND "prediction" OR "forecast") OR "absenteeism" OR "absentee" OR "absence") AND ("ai-based" OR "ai" OR "artificial intelligence" OR "machine learning") AND ("human resources management" OR "hrm" OR "human resources" OR "human resource" OR "workplace"))

The Scopus search with the given search string yielded 635 papers. As mentioned, we excluded papers that are not peer-reviewed and not written in English, resulting in 504 papers. After removing eight duplicates, we further analyzed the body of literature by reviewing titles and abstracts for a thematical fit to any of our HR staffing categories and the application of ML algorithms. This analysis further excluded 439 papers, resulting in 57 papers. The forward and backward search, proposed by Webster and Watson (2002), using Google Scholar revealed additional (N=8) relevant articles. Finally, we considered 65 sources in the review, which we present in Table 7.1.

Following the approach in Webster and Watson (2002), we then used a concept matrix to analyze and synthesize the literature in more detail. Note that some articles revealed more than one finding and belong to more than one category (see Table 7.1). We assigned relevant articles to the HR staffing categories (NER, RER, EH, and EA) and brought forth the different ML algorithms used in the specific category. Hence, we matched the ML algorithms with HR staffing categories to provide a state-of-the-art analysis of ML in HR staffing. Furthermore, we assigned the identified articles to the four different outlets they originated in and clustered them by purpose.

The matrix was finally used to synthesize our findings from a literature review. The focus is on the research outcomes, and the review retains a neutral perspective. This literature review is representative, as only literature yielded from the paper search is considered.

RESULTS

The results of this chapter are addressed to general and specialized scholars, practitioners, and the overall public. Our literature review yielded 65 sources, which are presented in Table 7.1. In the remainder of this section, we summarize the findings of this literature review, which form the HR staffing ML model (see Figure 7.2), and present various examples of how research has applied ML methods and algorithms in the HR staffing categories.

Literature Review Summary

Considering the concept matrix presented in Table 7.1, the identified papers focus on ML algorithms in terms of ANN (N=6), DNN (N=5), DT (N=23), KNN (N=12), LogReg (N=19), NB (N=15), RF (N=22), SVM (N=22), and others (O) (N=38). Most researchers focus on DTs to apply ML in predicting their NER and conduct foresights for EA. However, RF- and SVM-methods also get great attention in helping HRM with attrition and RER. Moreover, 38 papers in total use other ML methods and algorithms, such as the meta-algorithm AdaBoost (Rätsch et al., 2001), and variations of DTs like Gradient Boosting (Friedman, 2002).

To the largest extent (N=55), the analyzed papers originate in technical journals and conferences from scientific and computer-related fields, including computer science, ML and artificial intelligence, or statistics. Fewer are from management-oriented areas (N=4), from healthcare-related fields (N=4), or human resources (N=2). However, the overall objective differs across the papers. The majority of the identified research papers (N=44) focus on proof-of-concept works, creating models and artifacts to display the possibility of predictions with ML in HR staffing. The second-largest amount (N=27) of papers compare different ML algorithms in HR staffing for quality criteria such as accuracy, precision, and recall of the predictions, for example Zhao et al. (2018). Note that authors often focused on both proofing the concept and comparing ML algorithms. Only four papers make use of case studies, and another four define whole kernel theories and test their results accordingly.

Most research conducted analyzes EA, with 46 pieces in this literature review doing this. Table 7.1 further shows that ten papers focus on RER and seven on NER, while only two investigate EH. No author explores more than one HR staffing category with ML methods. In the following, we summarize the applicability of ML in the four HR staffing categories:

Machine learning in net employee requirements
The NER category results state that only two authors (Vollmer et al., 2021; Zlotnik et al., 2015) use the aforementioned eight supervised ML algorithms. Vollmer et al. (2021) compare forecasting methods to predict hospital emergency department demand for the next one, three, or seven days. The authors aim at dynamically staffing employees based on the predictions obtained. However, by comparing linear methods to the two ML approaches RF and Gradient Boosting, the authors conclude that the latter are equal or even inferior to the linear models. However, Vollmer et al. (2021) testify that ML approaches improve the diversity of model

Table 7.1   Reviewed literature

Paper	Algorithm/Method									Staffing category				Outlet				Objective			
Author(s) (Year of publication)	ANN	DNN	DT	KNN	LogReg	NB	RF	SVM	OI	NER	RER	EH	EA	T2	H3	M4	HR5	AC6	CS7	TD8	POC9
Σ = 65	6	5	23	12	19	15	22	22	38	7	10	2	46	55	4	4	2	27	4	4	44
Alam et al. (2018)			x	x		x	x	x	x				x	x				x			x
Alao & Adeyemo (2013)			x										x	x						x	
Alduayj & Rajpoot (2019)				x		x	x	x					x	x				x			
Ali Shah et al. (2020)		x	x				x	x			x			x				x			x
Ameer et al. (2020)			x		x		x						x	x							x
Anh et al. (2020)					x		x						x	x				x			
Bhartiya et al. (2019)			x	x		x	x	x					x	x				x			
Bindra et al. (2019)				x									x	x				x			
Cahyani & Budiharto (2017)								x					x	x							x
Chang (2020)									x				x	x				x			x
de Jesus et al. (2018)			x										x	x				x			
de Oliveira (2019)					x	x	x	x	x		x			x				x			
de Oliveira et al. (2019)						x	x	x	x		x			x				x			
Du & Li (2015)									x	x				x							x
Elacio et al. (2020)			x										x	x							x
Fallucchi et al. (2020)						x							x	x				x			
Fan et al. (2012)	x												x	x					x		
Frierson & Si (2018)					x				x				x	x				x			x
Frye et al. (2018)				x	x		x						x	x				x			x
Gabrani & Kwatra (2018)			x				x		x				x	x							x
Gaur et al (2019)									x				x	x							x
Gurvich et al (2010)										x						x				x	
Hebbar et al. (2018)					x		x	x					x	x							x

Paper Author(s) (Year of publication)	Algorithm/Method									Staffing category				Outlet				Objective			
	ANN	DNN	DT	KNN	LogReg	NB	RF	SVM	OI	NER	RER	EH	EA	T2	H3	M4	HR5	AC6	CS7	TD8	POC9
Hegde & Poornalatha (2021)					x						x			x							x
Hu et al. (2007)									x	x				x							x
Islam et al. (2018)							x						x	x							x
Jain & Nayyar (2018)									x				x			x					x
Jain et al. (2021)			x						x				x	x				x			
Kang et al. (2021)			x		x								x				x				x
Khan & Hayat Khan (2019)					x								x	x				x			x
Khera & Divya (2018)			x		x			x	x				x	x				x			
L. Liu et al. (2020)				x			x						x	x							x
Leandro et al. (2019)				x				x	x		x			x							x
Lei et al. (2009)	x											x									x
Lima et al. (2020)		x						x	x		x			x							x
Lin et al. (2018)									x	x				x							x
Ma et al. (2020)	x	x						x	x				x	x					x		x
Madane & Chitre (2020)	x			x		x	x						x	x							
McNair (2015)						x			x		x				x						
Moyo et al. (2018)			x		x	x							x				x	x			x
Ozdemir et al. (2020)				x	x	x	x	x	x				x	x				x			
Pessach et al. (2020)								x	x			x				x				x	
Ray & Sanyal (2019)					x	x			x				x	x							x
Ribes et al. (2017)						x	x	x	x				x	x					x		x
Rista et al. (2020)			x			x		x	x		x			x				x			x
Schuetz & Larson (2019)										x					x						
Sehgal et al. (2019)									x				x	x				x			x
Sexton et al. (2005)	x												x	x							x
Shankar et al (2018)			x	x	x		x	x					x	x				x			
Singer & Cohen (2020)						x			x		x			x							x

Paper	Algorithm/Method									Staffing category				Outlet				Objective			
Author(s) (Year of publication)	ANN	DNN	DT	KNN	LogReg	NB	RF	SVM	O1	NER	RER	EH	EA	T2	H3	M4	HR5	AC6	CS7	TD8	POC9
Srivastava & Nair (2017)			x						x				x	x				x			x
Tewari et al. (2020)								x	x				x	x				x			x
Tharani & Raj (2020)		x											x	x				x			x
Vasa & Masrani (2019)			x		x		x		x				x	x				x			
Vollmer et al. (2021)			x						x	x					x						x
Wahid et al. (2019)			x				x		x		x			x				x			x
Y. Liu et al. (2020)									x				x			x					x
Yadav et al. (2018)			x		x		x	x	x				x	x							x
Yiğit & Shourabizadeh (2017)			x	x	x	x	x						x	x				x			x
Yunmeng & Chengyi (2019)				x					x				x	x							
Zhao et al. (2018)	x		x	x	x		x	x	x				x	x				x			x
Zhenkui Jin et al. (2020)									x				x	x							x
Zhu et al. (2017)									x				x	x							x
Ziwei jin et al. (2020)		x					x						x	x					x		x
Zlotnik et al. (2015)			x					x		x					x						x

Notes: 1 = Others; 2 = Technical; 3 = Health; 4 = Management; 5 = Human resources; 6 = Algorithm comparison; 7 = Case study; 8 = Theory defining; 9 = Proof-of-concept.

predictions to increase robustness, which is superior to linear models. Zlotnik et al. (2015) make allocation predictions in a time horizon of 2 to 24 weeks in a nursing environment. The authors use a derived DT and SVM approach to allocate staff dynamically. However, no comparison to linear models is made. Based on the lack of papers in the NER category, it can be said that research into the applicability of ML in NER is very limited. However, authors in this area report significant cost savings by dynamically allocating staff (Lin et al., 2018; Schuetz & Larson, 2019).

Machine learning in reserve employee requirements
In the RER category, the authors reported different results for the best-performing algorithm. Ali Shah et al. (2020) report that DNN with 90.6 percent precision outperforms RF with 82.4 percent, DT with 82.8 percent, and SVM with 84.3 percent for predicting workplace absenteeism in terms of accuracy. The authors conclude that ML models can be applied effectively to predict employee absenteeism behavior at an early stage thus giving time to put in place countermeasures. However, Hebbar et al. (2018) testify a performance of 90 percent in terms of accuracy for SVM, 90 percent for RF, and 88 percent for LogReg, with no comparison with a neural network algorithm being provided. Rista et al. (2020) report efficacy of 99.9 percent for RF and 88.9 percent for LogReg. The performance of ML algorithms in RER largely depends on the data they work with. The number of features and entries of data cause performance differentiations, limiting the choice of the applicable algorithm to use. For instance, with a low number of data entries, DT and SVM often outperform DNN (Ali Shah et al., 2020). Hence, no statement regarding the "best" algorithm can be made. However, all authors report improvements for the usage of ML algorithms to predict RER.

Machine learning in expected hires
In the EH category, Lei et al. (2009) use an ANN and Pessach et al. (2020) use a variable-order Bayesian network to predict prospective new employees and hiring success. Lei et al. (2009) provide a model to forecast the growth of national science and technology talents. The authors use an ANN with eight hidden layers and numbers of researchers in China from 1991 to 2003 as data input. A derivation of this prediction could be put into a different context, such as predicting the number of talents in a certain industry. However, the authors give no detailed information about the richness of the data used. Pessach et al. (2020) predict job advertisement success using large-scale recruitment records (see section "Predicting recruitment success and optimizing recruitment itself" for detailed information). The recruitment records are processed with a Bayesian network that allows interpretability of the results and high accuracy to predict recruitment success considering turnovers at the pre-hire stage. Combining these two papers' work could yield a forecast on the number of available employees (Lei et al., 2009) and a forecast for the success of trying to hire such a prospective new employee (Pessach et al., 2020). Henceforth, an organization could predict EH with the support of these two papers. However, the research work carried out in this field is scant and further investigation to develop ML in EH is needed.

Machine learning in employee attrition
Turning to EA, the authors disagree whether LogReg, RF, or DT is superior. For instance, Frye et al. (2018) state that LogReg delivers the highest performance, while Yadav et al. (2018) say that it is RF that works best. Reasons for this disagreement are manifold. For instance, Frye et

al. (2018) testify that LogReg reduced the dimensionality of their 99 feature input dataset best, which resulted in a superior trained model compared to RF and KNN and hence in the highest accuracy with 74 percent for the prediction of an employee leaving the organization. By contrast, Yadav et al. (2018) report RF, with an accuracy of 98.6 percent, to be superior to LogReg with 78.8 percent. Furthermore, SVM with 95.2 percent and DT with 97.6 percent outperform LogReg in this article. Interestingly, Yadav et al. (2018) base their predictions solely on a data source by IBM (McKinley Stacker, 2015) with 11 features, while Frye et al. (2018) further add HR open data from the U.S. Office of Personnel Management and the Bureau of Labor Statistics to reach their 99 feature input dataset. Apparently, the merging of these additional data sources provides a higher dimensionality but decreases the predictions' accuracy.

Data sources and HR staffing ML model
The analyzed papers make use of various data sources, including HR stock data (Khan & Hayat Khan, 2019; L. Liu et al., 2020; Moyo et al., 2018; Rista et al., 2020; Zhao et al., 2018; Zhu et al., 2017) which is often enriched by surveys, questionnaires, and interviews. We can find enriched HR stock data in publicly available datasets (Alao & Adeyemo, 2013; Bhartiya et al., 2019; Frye et al., 2018; Gabrani & Kwatra, 2018; Hebbar et al., 2018; Ozdemir et al., 2020; Yadav et al., 2018), such as the IBM HR dataset (McKinley Stacker, 2015). Other authors use job advertisements (Pessach et al., 2020), environmental data (Ali Shah et al., 2020), and synthetic data (Vasa & Masrani, 2019).

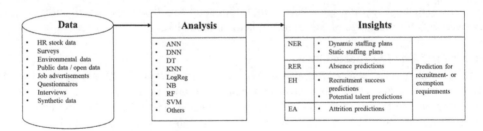

Figure 7.2   HR staffing ML model

Figure 7.2 displays a derived data-mining model that corresponds to the findings in Table 7.1. The authors process one or multiple forms of data with one or multiple ML algorithms to gain insights into desired fields. These fields are manifold, including all four HR staffing categories, and consequently provide sufficient predictions for the HR staffing model (see Figure 7.1).

Examples of Machine Learning in HR Staffing

In the following, we present examples for the application of ML algorithms in the four HR staffing categories. Note that only a small sample of the numerous applications of ML in HR staffing is provided.

Predicting workload for staffing plan development
We often observe the application of data-driven models to HR staffing in call centers (see Bassamboo & Zeevi, 2009) and the healthcare industry (see Zlotnik et al., 2015). Irrespective of the method for prediction, call center staffing relies on historical call observations, such as inbound calls (Liao et al., 2012), call arrival times, and call abandonment (Atlason et al., 2008). The methods are simulations based on making approximations for real-world scenarios, taking historical data into account to predict employee workloads, and then developing staffing plans and shifts accordingly.

To extend existing approaches, Lin et al. (2018) propose a model to quantify short-term traffic prediction with two neural network algorithms to make staffing plans to reduce average waiting times at country borders during holidays and on weekdays. The algorithms process short-term traffic volume data with 900 observations. The authors compare their approach with two state-of-the-art traffic prediction models (Guo et al., 2014; Zhang et al., 2014) with a focus on generating prediction intervals with high reliability and sharpness. The authors extend existing models from various industries (like call centers) to go beyond the limitation of one-time calculations and reuse pretrained models with new data entries to further enhance ML models. This approach guides possibilities to consider strategies based on historical data and extend their predictions to other data foresights.

Predicting employee absenteeism even before employee recruitment
Ali Shah et al. (2020) propose a DNN to predict employees' punctuality in their workplace. At the time of hiring, there is no indication whether a candidate will be punctual and put in the necessary effort required to do the job successfully. Hence, absenteeism from the workplace is a costly problem for various organizations, and firing new employees may be costlier than dealing with absenteeism. The proposed DNN uses the UCI Machine Learning repository with 20 features and a sample size of N=740. The data specifies employee behavior towards workplace punctuality at a Brazilian courier company. Features include, among others, reason for absence, season, age, distance from residence to work, social attributes (smoking, drinker), some physical attributes, work-related attributes (e.g., hit target and service time), and a binary value considering the absenteeism category, being either between 0 to 5 hours or more than 5 hours of absenteeism, to categorize the data. After standardization to cope with the different data ranges, the proposed DNN uses six hidden layers with varying counts of hyperparameters chosen by random search for optimization.

The authors mention the "data-hungry" characteristic of DNN technologies. With an input size of N=740 and the observed performance of 97.5 percent in terms of precision, improvements for larger data sizes can be made. Organizations willing to utilize a DNN may consider data size as a factor in choosing this algorithm in their ML approach. Ali Shah et al. (2020) mention a higher efficacy of DT and SVM for smaller data samples in comparison to neural networks.

Predicting recruitment success and optimizing recruitment itself
The proposed model from Pessach et al. (2020) aims to serve two goals: First, to predict the recruitment success at the level of a single job placement. Second, to provide a global recruitment optimization scheme for an organization. For predicting the recruitment success, the authors use a variation of NB, named variable-order Bayesian network, on large-scale (N>700,000) recruitment records of employees. The records include 164 features, such as

age, gender, marital status, nationality, education, grades, test scores, and details about the job positions. The Bayesian network identifies context-based patterns in the data which are used to support organizations in achieving recruitment success. This is shown in the probability of success in aligning a candidate to a position. Hereby, the authors test different ML approaches for interpretability and accuracy, concluding that the Bayesian network is interpretable with high accuracy (71.9 percent), while others (e.g., RF, SVM, and NB) lack either interpretability or accuracy. Furthermore, turnover scenarios at a pre-hire stage are taken into account, giving recommendations about the recruiting success for HRM.

For the global optimization scheme, the authors aim at satisfying three requirements: (1) minimizing the need for required workforce and therefore for recruiting employees, (2) maximizing recruitment success, and (3) enhancing diversity. The authors provide a mathematical model based on the recruitment success prediction to optimize HRM on the three requirements. This model incorporates the following features: set of candidates, set of positions, binary qualification, success prediction, and number of open jobs. Finally, the model provides a global optimization scheme by considering a multi-stakeholder environment with multisided balance and process diversity. Using a mathematical model, decision support for HRM is provided to improve the work of the recruiters.

Predicting which employee will leave next and why
It is a complex task to fill vacant job positions in organizations when talents are rare. Binding high potentials to organizations is desirable. Hence, various authors, for example Zhao et al. (2018) and Zhu et al. (2017), analyze employees to predict turnovers in order to derive early countermeasures. The predictions are often based on features including satisfaction levels, workload attributes, and salaries (Yadav et al., 2018), and different ML algorithms can be applied for the analysis. However, the real-world scenario is more complex, and the available datasets often do not incorporate higher structures that accurately reflect reality.

Y. Liu et al. (2020) enhance existing predictions with interfirm competition based on online profiles from employees (N=89,943) and organizations (N=3,467) generated from 2000 to 2014. This takes features like skill-, product-, and labor overlaps into consideration. Moreover, the consideration of interfirm competition forms a human capital flow as employees move between organizations and gives insights into industrial homophily. For predicting employee attrition, the authors use the basic economic metrics of an organization (e.g., revenue and number of employees), product overlap metrics (e.g., cosine similarity between two organizations' business summaries), and human capital overlap metrics (e.g., cosine similarity between two firms' skill summaries). These metrics, among others, are analyzed with the ML methods KNN, LogReg, and SVM. Their predictions vary based on the selected features, as the proposed ML methods differ between their feature sets of economic, product, and human capital metrics. However, the analysis underpins the complexity of employee attrition and further calls for research to further explore causes of considerable attrition.

DISCUSSION AND IMPLICATIONS

Our literature review on ML in HR staffing sheds light on different methods to support HRM. In particular, we investigated research on four HR staffing categories and the different ML algorithms that authors applied in forecasting metrics in each category. In total we examined

65 papers that fit into the concept matrix presented in Table 7.1, illustrating the applicability of ML in supporting executives in the HR domain. Interestingly, the area of focus differs highly between the papers, resulting in EA getting the most and EH the lowest attention.

We investigated eight different ML algorithms suitable for supervised learning in HR. The increased use of these algorithms was also reported by Ekawati (2019), who focused her work on EA. The distribution of the different algorithms across the concept matrix suggests that RF, DT, and SVM have the highest applicability in HR staffing. However, in terms of performance, the results vary between the authors (Ali Shah et al., 2020; Y. Liu et al., 2020; Vasa & Masrani, 2019). This performance difference is related to the number of features processed by the ML algorithm and the input data size (Ali Shah et al., 2020). Furthermore, Zhao et al. (2018) state that the accuracy of ML algorithms depends on the organizational sizes to which they are applied. Henceforth, there is not a single go-to algorithm for the application of ML in HR staffing, but different aspects regarding data availability and sources need consideration.

The reviewed authors make use of different data sources for their analysis. However, a large number utilize the IBM HR dataset for the EA category (Alduayj & Rajpoot, 2019; Bhartiya et al., 2019; Hebbar et al., 2018; Khan & Hayat Khan, 2019; Wahid et al., 2019). In predicting EA, various factors are significant (Burnes, 2006; Frye et al., 2018) which are not considered by the IBM dataset, for example distrust and relationship satisfaction as well as interfirm competition (Y. Liu et al., 2020). Using a common dataset for training and testing ML methods further raises the question of the transferability of the results and models to other organizational contexts (Tan et al., 2018). Hence, one problem of the reviewed approaches is that they rely mostly on one publicly available dataset which might not consider specific aspects of the context the developed and trained ML models will be used in.

Environmental data usage gives new opportunities for researchers and practitioners to further enhance the ML results. The researchers identified in this chapter often rely on HR data, but complex data is needed for precise and close-to-reality predictions. Predictions for HR staffing might not only rely on data from Human Resources Information Systems (HRIS), but also from other organizational IS. For example, predicting workload as a basis for HR staffing might require the use of sales data. Hence, it is important to integrate HR data with other data sources in an organization or with available external data. Luckily, the availability of live data like weather forecasts, economic perspectives, and public events is rising, providing the opportunity for enhanced predictions in HR staffing (Vollmer et al., 2021).

Despite the beneficial results from applying ML in HR staffing, there are concerns regarding the ethical aspects of the usage of data-driven approaches in HRM (Newell & Marabelli, 2015). Only a few authors in this research area are concerned with ethics, for example Moyo et al. (2018), Pessach et al. (2020), and Zlotnik et al. (2015). However, predictions on attrition, recruitment, and staffing have a powerful impact on employees. The predictions identified in this research make use of discriminatory attributes, including age, gender (Pessach et al., 2020), and ethnicity. Historical data is based on the decisions of humans, which incorporate bias. Hiring decisions are often subjective (Cable & Judge, 1997), and the data resulting from these decisions may carry, even if unintentionally, discriminatory behavior. Algorithms working with this historic data perpetuate the contained discrimination and could even enhance it. Hence, sensitivity is essential when working with ML in HR, and the impact of data-driven methodologies in HR has not yet been adequately researched (Gal et al., 2017, 2020).

Future research agendas may shift from a primarily proof-of-concept based approach to a user-centered one, focusing on the targeted clients. Furthermore, there is a lack of participation in outlets from the fields of human resources and management, leaving a question mark over the impact of ML in HR staffing on employees from an organizational and socio-technical perspective. Additionally, the authors' elaborated concepts need to be contrasted with live scenarios to define the applicability further. Possible research questions could be as follows: How do ML applications in HRM need to be designed to increase the quality of work and workers' well-being? How do ML applications impact employees at organizations? What are the different results obtained for HR staffing tasks by using experts, traditional methods, and ML algorithms? How do employees in HRM react to ML-based staffing recommendations?

The outcomes of this study are beneficial for practitioners and researchers alike. Practitioners can explore various approaches for supporting HR staffing with ML, while researchers can further develop existing approaches to enhance accuracy and applicability. Furthermore, this research has four conclusions. First, there is a need for more research on the application of ML in HR staffing, especially in NER, RER, and EH, as EA revealed the highest count of published research. Second, available datasets in all four HR staffing categories are lacking. The almost exclusive usage of the IBM dataset reveals that more datasets are needed in research to further explore the four categories. Generally, the lack of datasets is a known problem in HRM (Nguyen & Gatica-Perez, 2016). Research needs to incorporate data from various kinds of sources to address real-world staffing scenarios. Third, the performance of various algorithms needs to be explored in more detail and with a broader scope, as authors only utilized subsets of the main ML methods. Thirty-eight papers made use of ML approaches other than the ones mentioned, questioning the most suitable ones to use in the four HR categories. The need for greater research is reinforced by the fact that the ML industry is fast-moving with the systematic development of new algorithms occurring at a considerable pace (Jordan & Mitchell, 2015). Forth, ethical concerns remain a challenge for data-driven HR and ML. This challenge is not limited to HR staffing but extends to society in general. Further exploration of the chances of managing HR with an ML approach needs to consider discrimination and ethical aspects.

This chapter has highlighted the possible utilization of ML for dynamic HR staffing. Further research needs to consider the various approaches presented in this chapter and reweigh the importance of data generation and live data. Another challenge is empirically exploring the consequences of executives applying ML in HR staffing, as well as exploring ethical concerns regarding the usage of ML on employees. Organizations can benefit highly from utilizing data-driven approaches in their HRM, but need to pay due regard to the potential downsides regarding their greatest asset – their employees.

REFERENCES

Abdel-Hamid, T. K. (1989). A study of staff turnover, acquisition, and assimilation and their impact on software development cost and schedule. *Journal of Management Information Systems, 6*(1), 21–40.

Alam, M. M., Mohiuddin, K., Islam, M. K., Hassan, M., Hoque, M. A.-U., & Allayear, S. M. (2018). A machine learning approach to analyze and reduce features to a significant number for employee's turn over prediction model. In *Science and Information Conference* (pp. 142–159). Springer.

Alao, D., & Adeyemo, A. B. (2013). Analyzing employee attrition using decision tree algorithms. *Computing, Information Systems, Development Informatics and Allied Research Journal, 4*(1), 17–28.

Al-Bdareen, R., & Khasawneh, H. (2019). Human resources staffing process and its impact on job involvement: Irbid District Electricity Company as a case study. *Problems and Perspectives in Management, 17*(2), 254–266.

Alduayj, S. S., & Rajpoot, K. (2019). Predicting employee attrition using machine learning. In *Proceedings of the 2018 13th International Conference on Innovations in Information Technology, IIT 2018* (pp. 93–98). https://doi.org/10.1109/INNOVATIONS.2018.8605976

Ali Shah, S. A., Uddin, I., Aziz, F., Ahmad, S., Al-Khasawneh, M. A., & Sharaf, M. (2020). An enhanced deep neural network for predicting workplace absenteeism. *Complexity*, Article 5843932. https://doi.org/10.1155/2020/5843932

Ameer, M., Rahul, S. P., & Manne, S. (2020). Human resource analytics using power bi visualization tool. In *Proceedings of the International Conference on Intelligent Computing and Control Systems, ICICCS 2020* (pp. 1184–1189). https://doi.org/10.1109/ICICCS48265.2020.9120897

Anh, N. T. N., Tu, N. D., Solanki, V. K., Giang, N. L., Thu, V. H., Son, L. N., Loc, N. D., & Nam, V. T. (2020). Integrating employee value model with churn prediction. *International Journal of Sensors, Wireless Communications and Control*, *10*(4), 484–493.

Atlason, J., Epelman, M. A., & Henderson, S. G. (2008). Optimizing call center staffing using simulation and analytic center cutting-plane methods. *Management Science*, *54*(2), 295–309.

Au-Yeung, S. W. M., Harder, U., McCoy, E. J., & Knottenbelt, W. J. (2009). Predicting patient arrivals to an accident and emergency department. *Emergency Medicine Journal*, *26*(4), 241–244.

Avey, J. B., Patera, J. L., & West, B. J. (2006). The implications of positive psychological capital on employee absenteeism. *Journal of Leadership and Organizational Studies*, *13*(2), 42–60.

Barney, J. (1991). Firm resources and sustained competitive advantage. *Journal of Management*, *17*(1), 99–120. https://doi.org/10.1177/014920639101700108

Bassamboo, A., & Zeevi, A. (2009). On a data-driven method for staffing large call centers. *Operations Research*, *57*(3), 714–726.

Batal, H., Tench, J., McMillan, S., Adams, J., & Mehler, P. S. (2001). Predicting patient visits to an urgent care clinic using calendar variables. *Academic Emergency Medicine*, *8*(1), 48–53.

Bayley, M. D., Schwartz, J. S., Shofer, F. S., Weiner, M., Sites, F. D., Traber, K. B., & Hollander, J. E. (2005). The financial burden of emergency department congestion and hospital crowding for chest pain patients awaiting admission. *Annals of Emergency Medicine*, *45*(2), 110–117.

Bechet, T. P., & Walker, J. W. (1993). Aligning staffing with business strategy. *Human Resource Planning*, *16*(2), 1–16.

Beechler, S., & Woodward, I. C. (2009). The global "war for talent". *Journal of International Management*, *15*(3), 273–285. https://doi.org/1h0.1016/j.intman.2009.01.002

Bernstein, S. L., Aronsky, D., Duseja, R., Epstein, S., Handel, D., Hwang, U., McCarthy, M., John McConnell, K., Pines, J. M., … & Rathlev, N. (2009). The effect of emergency department crowding on clinically oriented outcomes. *Academic Emergency Medicine*, *16*(1), 1–10.

Bhartiya, N., Jannu, S., Shukla, P., & Chapaneri, R. (2019). Employee attrition prediction using classification models. In *2019 IEEE 5th International Conference for Convergence in Technology (I2CT)* (pp. 1–6). IEEE.

Bindra, H., Sehgal, K., & Jain, R. (2019). Optimisation of C5. 0 using association rules and prediction of employee attrition. In *International Conference on Innovative Computing and Communications* (pp. 21–29). Springer.

Breaugh, J. A. (1981). Predicting absenteeism from prior absenteeism and work attitudes. *Journal of Applied Psychology*, *66*(5), Article 555.

Breaugh, J. A. (2008). Employee recruitment: Current knowledge and important areas for future research. *Human Resource Management Review*, *18*(3), 103–118.

Breaugh, J. A., & Starke, M. (2000). Research on employee recruitment: So many studies, so many remaining questions. *Journal of Management*, *26*(3), 405–434.

Burnes, P. T. (2006). Voluntary employee turnover: Why IT professionals leave. *IT Professional*, *8*(3), 46–48.

Cable, D. M., & Judge, T. A. (1997). Interviewers' perceptions of person–organization fit and organizational selection decisions. *Journal of Applied Psychology*, *82*(4), 546–561.

Cahyani, A. D., & Budiharto, W. (2017). Modeling intelligent human resources systems (IRHS) using big data and support vector machine (SVM). In *Proceedings of the 9th International Conference on Machine Learning and Computing* (pp. 137–140). ACM. https://doi.org/10.1145/3055635.3056660

Chang, K. (2020). Artificial intelligence in personnel management: The development of APM model. *The Bottom Line*, *33*(4), 377–388. https://doi.org/10.1108/bl-08-2020-0055

de Jesus, A. C. C., Júnior, M. E. G. D., & Brandao, W. C. (2018). Exploiting LinkedIn to predict employee resignation likelihood. In *Proceedings of the 33rd Annual ACM Symposium on Applied Computing* (pp. 1764–1771). ACM.

de Oliveira, E. L. (2019). Machine learning techniques applied to predict the performance of contact centers operators. In *2019 14th Iberian Conference on Information Systems and Technologies (CISTI)* (pp. 1–4). IEEE.

de Oliveira, E. L., Torres, J. M., Moreira, R. S., & de Lima, R. A. F. (2019). Absenteeism prediction in call center using machine learning algorithms. In *World Conference on Information Systems and Technologies* (pp. 958–968). Springer.

Donovan, J. J., Dwight, S. A., & Schneider, D. (2014). The impact of applicant faking on selection measures, hiring decisions, and employee performance. *Journal of Business and Psychology*, *29*(3), 479–493.

Du, W., & Li, S. (2015). Application of Markov model in human resource supply forecasting in enterprises. In *2015 International Conference on Computational Science and Engineering* (pp. 151–156). Atlantis Press. https://doi.org/10.2991/iccse-15.2015.26

Ekawati, A. D. (2019). Predictive analytics in employee churn: A systematic literature review. *Journal of Management Information and Decision Sciences*, *22*(4), 387–397.

Elacio, A., Lacatan, L., Vinluan, A., & Balazon, F. (2020). Machine learning integration of Herzberg's theory using C4.5 algorithm. *International Journal of Advanced Trends in Computer Science and Engineering*, *9*, 57–63. https://doi.org/10.30534/ijatcse/2020/1191.12020

Fallucchi, F., Coladangelo, M., Giuliano, R., & William De Luca, E. (2020). Predicting employee attrition using machine learning techniques. *Computers*, *9*(4), Article 86.

Fan, C.-Y., Fan, P.-S., Chan, T.-Y., & Chang, S.-H. (2012). Using hybrid data mining and machine learning clustering analysis to predict the turnover rate for technology professionals. *Expert Systems with Applications*, *39*(10), 8844–8851. https://doi.org/10.1016/j.eswa.2012.02.005

Friedman, J. H. (2002). Stochastic gradient boosting. *Computational Statistics and Data Analysis*, *38*(4), 367–378.

Frierson, J., & Si, D. (2018). Who's next: Evaluating attrition with machine learning algorithms and survival analysis. In F. Chin, C. Chen, L. Khan, K. Lee, & L. J. Zhang (Eds.), *International Conference on Big Data* (pp. 251–259). Springer.

Frye, A., Boomhower, C., Smith, M., Vitovsky, L., & Fabricant, S. (2018). Employee attrition: What makes an employee quit? *SMU Data Science Review*, *1*(1), Article 9.

Gabrani, G., & Kwatra, A. (2018). Machine learning based predictive model for risk assessment of employee attrition. In *Computational Science and Its Applications – ICCSA 2018* (pp. 189–201). Springer. https://doi.org/10.1007/978-3-319-95171-3_16

Gal, U., Jensen, T. B., & Stein, M.-K. (2017). People analytics in the age of big data: An agenda for IS research. In *ICIS 2017: Transforming Society with Digital Innovation*. http://aisel.aisnet.org/cgi/viewcontent.cgi?article=1000&context=icis2017

Gal, U., Jensen, T. B., & Stein, M.-K. (2020). Breaking the vicious cycle of algorithmic management: A virtue ethics approach to people analytics. *Information and Organization*, *30*(2), Article 100301. https://doi.org/10.1016/j.infoandorg.2020.100301

Garg, S., Sinha, S., Kar, A. K., & Mani, M. (2021). A review of machine learning applications in human resource management. *International Journal of Productivity and Performance Management*, volume ahead of print. https://doi.org/10.1108/IJPPM-08-2020-0427

Gaur, B., Shukla, V. K., & Verma, A. (2019). Strengthening people analytics through wearable IoT device for real-time data collection. In *2019 International Conference on Automation, Computational and Technology Management (ICACTM)* (pp. 555–560). IEEE.

Grant, R. M. (1996). Prospering in dynamically-competitive environments: Organizational capability as knowledge integration. *Organization Science*, *7*(4), 375–387. https://doi.org/10.1287/orsc.7.4.375

Guo, J., Huang, W., & Williams, B. M. (2014). Adaptive Kalman filter approach for stochastic short-term traffic flow rate prediction and uncertainty quantification. *Transportation Research Part C: Emerging Technologies*, *43*, 50–64.

Gurvich, I., Luedtke, J., & Tezcan, T. (2010). Staffing call centers with uncertain demand forecasts: A chance-constrained optimization approach. *Management Science*, *56*(7), 1093–1115I.

Hebbar, A. R., Patil, S. H., Rajeshwari, S. B., & Saqquaf, S. S. M. (2018). Comparison of machine learning techniques to predict the attrition rate of the employees. In *2018 3rd IEEE International Conference on Recent Trends in Electronics, Information & Communication Technology (RTEICT)* (pp. 934–938). IEEE.

Hegde, A., & Poornalatha, G. (2021). Human resource working prediction based on logistic regression. In N. N. Chiplunkar & T. Fukao (Eds.), *Advances in artificial intelligence and data engineering* (pp. 299–306). Springer.

Hu, J., Ray, B. K., & Singh, M. (2007). Statistical methods for automated generation of service engagement staffing plans. *IBM Journal of Research and Development, 51*(3.4), 281–293.

Hunt, S. T. (2007). *Hiring success: The art and science of staffing assessment and employee selection.* John Wiley & Sons.

Islam, M. K., Alam, M. M., Islam, M. B., Mohiuddin, K., Das, A. K., & Kaonain, M. S. (2018). An adaptive feature dimensionality reduction technique based on random forest on employee turnover prediction model. In M. Singh, V. Tyagi, P. K. Gupta, J. Flusser, T. Ören, & V. R. Sonawane (Eds.), *International conference on advances in computing and data sciences* (pp. 269–278). Springer.

Jain, N., Tomar, A., & Jana, P. K. (2021). A novel scheme for employee churn problem using multi-attribute decision making approach and machine learning. *Journal of Intelligent Information Systems, 56,* 279–302. https://doi.org/10.1007/s10844-020-00614-9

Jain, R., & Nayyar, A. (2018). Predicting employee attrition using Xgboost machine learning approach. In *2018 International Conference on System Modeling and Advancement in Research Trends (SMART)* (pp. 113–120). IEEE.

Jensen, S., & McIntosh, J. (2007). Absenteeism in the workplace: Results from Danish sample survey data. *Empirical Economics, 32*(1), 125–139.

Jin, Ziwei, Shang, J., Zhu, Q., Ling, C., Xie, W., & Qiang, B. (2020). RFRSF: Employee turnover prediction based on random forests and survival analysis. In *International Conference on Web Information Systems Engineering* (pp. 503–515). Springer.

Jin, Zhenkui, Zhen, L., & Shen, J. (2020). Prediction model of employee flow based on semi-Markov chain and its application analysis. In *2020 IEEE 5th Information Technology and Mechatronics Engineering Conference (ITOEC)* (pp. 1829–1833). IEEE.

Jordan, M. I., & Mitchell, T. M. (2015). Machine learning: Trends, perspectives, and prospects. *American Association for the Advancement of Science, 349*(6245), 255–260. https://doi.org/10.1126/science.aaa8415

Judge, T. A., & Ferris, G. R. (1992). The elusive criterion of fit in human resources staffing decisions. *Human Resource Planning, 15*(4), 47–48.

Kang, I. G., Croft, B., & Bichelmeyer, B. A. (2021). Predictors of turnover intention in U.S. federal government workforce: Machine learning evidence that perceived comprehensive HR practices predict turnover intention. *Public Personnel Management, 50*(4), 538–558. https://doi.org/10.1177/0091026020977562

Kennedy, M., MacBean, C. E., Brand, C., Sundararajan, V., & McD Taylor, D. (2008). Leaving the emergency department without being seen. *Emergency Medicine Australasia, 20*(4), 306–313.

Khan, E. A., & Hayat Khan, S. M. (2019). Factors affecting employee attrition and predictive modelling using IBM HR data. *Journal of Computational and Theoretical Nanoscience, 16*(8), 3379–3383.

Khera, S. N., & Divya (2018). Predictive modelling of employee turnover in Indian IT industry using machine learning techniques. *Vision, 23*(1), 12–21.

Kotsiantis, S. B., Zaharakis, I., & Pintelas, P. (2007). Supervised machine learning: a review of classification techniques. *Emerging Artificial Intelligence Applications in Computer Engineering, 160*(1), 3–24.

Laumer, S., Maier, C., & Eckhardt, A. (2015). The impact of business process management and applicant tracking systems on recruiting process performance: An empirical study. *Journal of Business Economics, 85*(4), 421–453.

Leandro, C., Ramos, R., & Moro, S. (2019). Anticipating the duration of public administration employees' future absences. *Public Administration Issue, 6,* 23–40. https://doi.org/10.17323/1999-5431-2019-0-6-23-40

LeCun, Y., Bengio, Y., & Hinton, G. (2015). Deep learning. *Nature, 521*(7553), 436–444. https://doi.org/10.1038/nature14539

Lei, G., Feng, D., Chunxin, W., Dongkai, Z., & Yong, Z. (2009). Strategic planning for scientific and technological human resource based on BP neural network. In *2009 Fifth International Conference on Natural Computation* (pp. 311–315). IEEE.

Liao, S., Koole, G., Van Delft, C., & Jouini, O. (2012). Staffing a call center with uncertain non-stationary arrival rate and flexibility. *OR Spectrum, 34*(3), 691–721.

Lima, E., Vieira, T., & de Barros Costa, E. (2020). Evaluating deep models for absenteeism prediction of public security agents. *Applied Soft Computing, 91*, Article 106236. https://doi.org/10.1016/j.asoc.2020.106236

Lin, L., Handley, J. C., Gu, Y., Zhu, L., Wen, X., & Sadek, A. W. (2018). Quantifying uncertainty in short-term traffic prediction and its application to optimal staffing plan development. *Transportation Research Part C: Emerging Technologies, 92*, 323–348.

Liu, L., Akkineni, S., Story, P., & Davis, C. (2020). Using HR analytics to support managerial decisions: A case study. In *ACMSE 2020 – Proceedings of the 2020 ACM Southeast Conference* (pp. 168–175). Association for Computing Machinery. https://doi.org/10.1145/3374135.3385281

Liu, Y., Pant, G., & Sheng, O. R. L. (2020). Predicting labor market competition: Leveraging interfirm network and employee skills. *Information Systems Research, 31*(4), 1443–1466. https://doi.org/10.1287/isre.2020.0954

Ma, Z., Li, R., Li, T., Zhu, R., Jiang, R., Yang, J., Tang, M., & Zheng, M. (2020). A data-driven risk measurement model of software developer turnover. *Soft Computing, 24*(2), 825–842.

Madane, S., & Chitre, D. (2020). A survey of employee and customer churn prediction methodologies. *Advances in Mathematics: Scientific Journal, 9*(6), 3955–3962. https://doi.org/10.37418/amsj.9.6.76

Mani, V., Kesavan, S., & Swaminathan, J. M. (2015). Estimating the impact of understaffing on sales and profitability in retail stores. *Production and Operations Management, 24*(2), 201–218.

McKinley Stacker, I. V. (2015). *IBM Waston Analytics. Sample data: HR employee attrition and performance* [Data file].

McNair, D. S. (2015). Enhancing nursing staffing forecasting with safety stock over lead time modeling. *Nursing Administration Quarterly, 39*(4), 291–296.

Mohri, M., Rostamizadeh, A., & Talwalkar, A. (2018). *Foundations of machine learning*. MIT Press.

Molnar, C. (2020). *Interpretable machine learning*. Leanpub.

Moskop, J. C., Sklar, D. P., Geiderman, J. M., Schears, R. M., & Bookman, K. J. (2009). Emergency department crowding, Part 1 – concept, causes, and moral consequences. *Annals of Emergency Medicine, 53*(5), 605–611.

Moyo, S., Doan, T. N., Yun, J. A., & Tshuma, N. (2018). Application of machine learning models in predicting length of stay among healthcare workers in underserved communities in South Africa. *Human Resources for Health, 16*(1), Article 68. https://doi.org/10.1186/s12960-018-0329-1

Muchinsky, P. M. (1977). Employee absenteeism: A review of the literature. *Journal of Vocational Behavior, 10*(3), 316–340.

Muenstermann, B., von Stetten, A., Laumer, S., & Eckhardt, A. (2010). The performance impact of business process standardization: HR case study insights. *Management Research Review, 33*(9), 924–939. https://doi.org/10.1108/01409171011070332

Newell, S., & Marabelli, M. (2015). Strategic opportunities (and challenges) of algorithmic decision-making: A call for action on the long-term societal effects of "datification". *The Journal of Strategic Information Systems, 24*(1), 3–14. https://doi.org/10.1016/j.jsis.2015.02.001

Nguyen, L. S., & Gatica-Perez, D. (2016). Hirability in the wild: Analysis of online conversational video resumes. *IEEE Transactions on Multimedia, 18*(7), 1422–1437.

Noe, R. A., Hollenbeck, J. R., Gerhart, B. A., & Wright, P. M. (2007). *Fundamentals of human resource management*. McGraw-Hill.

O'Brien-Pallas, L., Baumann, A., Donner, G., Murphy, G. T., Lochhaas-Gerlach, J., & Luba, M. (2001). Forecasting models for human resources in health care. *Journal of Advanced Nursing, 33*(1), 120–129.

Oehlhorn, C. E., Maier, C., Laumer, S., & Weitzel, T. (2020). Human resource management and its impact on strategic business–IT alignment: A literature review and avenues for future research. *Journal of Strategic Information Systems, 29*(4), Article 101641. https://doi.org/10.1016/j.jsis.2020.101641

Ongsulee, P. (2017). Artificial intelligence, machine learning and deep learning. In *2017 15th International Conference on ICT and Knowledge Engineering (ICT&KE)* (pp. 1–6). IEEE.

Osisanwo, F. Y., Akinsola, J. E. T., Awodele, O., Hinmikaiye, J. O., Olakanmi, O., & Akinjobi, J. (2017). Supervised machine learning algorithms: Classification and comparison. *International Journal of Computer Trends and Technology (IJCTT)*, *48*(3), 128–138.

Ozdemir, F., Coskun, M., Gezer, C., & Gungor, V. C. (2020). Assessing employee attrition using classifications algorithms. In *Proceedings of the 2020 the 4th International Conference on Information System and Data Mining* (pp. 118–122). ACM.

Pessach, D., Singer, G., Avrahami, D., Chalutz Ben-Gal, H., Shmueli, E., & Ben-Gal, I. (2020). Employees recruitment: A prescriptive analytics approach via machine learning and mathematical programming. *Decision Support Systems*, *134*, Article 113290. https://doi.org/10.1016/j.dss.2020.113290

Rätsch, G., Onoda, T., & Müller, K.-R. (2001). Soft margins for AdaBoost. *Machine Learning*, *42*(3), 287–320.

Ray, A. N., & Sanyal, J. (2019). Machine learning based attrition prediction. In *2019 Global Conference for Advancement in Technology (GCAT)* (pp. 1–4). IEEE. https://doi.org/10.1109/GCAT47503.2019.8978285

Ribes, E., Touahri, K., & Perthame, B. (2017, July 17). *Employee turnover prediction and retention policies design: A case study*. ArXiv. ArXiv:1707.01377

Rista, A., Ajdari, J., & Zenuni, X. (2020). Predicting and analyzing absenteeism at workplace using machine learning algorithms. In *43rd International Convention 2020* (pp. 485–490). IEEE.

Rowley, G., & Purcell, K. (2001). "As cooks go, she went": Is labour churn inevitable? *International Journal of Hospitality Management*, *20*(2), 163–185.

Safarishahrbijari, A. (2018). Workforce forecasting models: A systematic review. *Journal of Forecasting*, *37*(7), 739–753.

Saradhi, V. V., & Palshikar, G. K. (2011). Employee churn prediction. *Expert Systems with Applications*, *38*(3), 199–2006. https://doi.org/10.1016/j.eswa.2010.07.134

Schuetz, G., & Larson, J. (2019). How to grow your workforce through staff optimization. *Nurse Leader*, *17*(4), 344–346.

Sehgal, K., Bindra, H., Batra, A., & Jain, R. (2019). Prediction of employee attrition using GWO and PSO optimised models of C5. 0 used with association rules and analysis of optimisers. In H. Saini, R. Sayal, A. Govardhan, & R. Buyya (Eds.), *Innovations in computer science and engineering* (pp. 1–8). Springer.

Sexton, R. S., McMurtrey, S., Michalopoulos, J. O., & Smith, A. M. (2005). Employee turnover: A neural network solution. *Computers and Operations Research*, *32*(10), 2635–2651. https://doi.org/10.1016/j.cor.2004.06.022

Shankar, R. S., Rajanikanth, J., Sivaramaraju, V. V, & Murthy, K. (2018). Prediction of employee attrition using datamining. In *2018 IEEE International Conference on System, Computation, Automation and Networking (Icscan)* (pp. 1–8). IEEE.

Singer, G., & Cohen, I. (2020). An objective-based entropy approach for interpretable decision tree models in support of human resource management: The case of absenteeism at work. *Entropy*, *22*(8), Article 821. https://doi.org/10.3390/E22080821

Srivastava, D. K., & Nair, P. (2017). Employee attrition analysis using predictive techniques. In *International Conference on Information and Communication Technology for Intelligent Systems* (pp. 293–300). Springer.

Subramony, M., & Holtom, B. C. (2012). The long-term influence of service employee attrition on customer outcomes and profits. *Journal of Service Research*, *15*(4), 460–473.

Tan, C., Sun, F., Kong, T., Zhang, W., Yang, C., & Liu, C. (2018). A survey on deep transfer learning. In V. Kurková, Y. Manolopoulos, B. Hammer, L. Iliadis, & I. Maglogiannis (Eds.), *International Conference on Artificial Neural Networks* (pp. 270–279). Springer.

Tewari, K., Vandita, S., & Jain, S. (2020). Predictive analysis of absenteeism in MNCs using machine learning algorithm. In *Proceedings of ICRIC 2019* (pp. 3–14). Springer.

Tharani, S. K. M., & Raj, S. N. V. (2020). Predicting employee turnover intention in IT&ITeS industry using machine learning algorithms. In *2020 Fourth International Conference on I-SMAC (IoT in Social, Mobile, Analytics and Cloud)(I-SMAC)* (pp. 508–513). IEEE.

Todd, P. A., McKeen, J. D., & Gallupe, R. B. (1995). The evolution of IS job skills: A content analysis of IS job advertisements from 1970 to 1990. *MIS Quarterly*, *19*(1), 1–27. https://doi.org/10.2307/249709

Vasa, J., & Masrani, K. (2019). Foreseeing employee attritions using diverse data mining strategies. *International Journal of Recent Technology and Engineering (IJRTE)*, 8(3), 620–626.

Vollmer, M. A. C., Glampson, B., Mellan, T., Mishra, S., Mercuri, L., Costello, C., Klaber, R., Cooke, G., Flaxman, S., & Bhatt, S. (2021). A unified machine learning approach to time series forecasting applied to demand at emergency departments. *BMC Emergency Medicine*, 21(1), Article 9. https://doi .org/10.1186/s12873-020-00395-y

Vom Brocke, J., Simons, A., Niehaves, Bjoern, Niehaves, Bjorn, Reimer, K., Plattfaut, R., & Cleven, A. (2009). Reconstructing the giant: On the importance of rigour in documenting the literature search process. In *ECIS 2009 Proceedings*. https://aisel.aisnet.org/ecis2009/161

Vom Brocke, J., Simons, A., Riemer, K., Niehaves, B., Plattfaut, R., & Cleven, A. (2015). Standing on the shoulders of giants: Challenges and recommendations of literature search in information systems research. *Communications of the Association for Information Systems*, 37(1), Article 9.

Wahid, Z., Satter, A. K. M. Z., Al Imran, A., & Bhuiyan, T. (2019). Predicting absenteeism at work using tree-based learners. In *Proceedings of the 3rd International Conference on Machine Learning and Soft Computing* (pp. 7–11). ACM.

Wargon, M., Guidet, B., Hoang, T. D., & Hejblum, G. (2009). A systematic review of models for forecasting the number of emergency department visits. *Emergency Medicine Journal*, 26(6), 395–399.

Webster, J., & Watson, R. T. (2002). Analyzing the past to prepare for the future: Writing a literature review. *MIS Quarterly*, 26(2), xiii–xxiii.

Wirtky, T., Laumer, S., Eckhardt, A., & Weitzel, T. (2016). On the untapped value of e-HRM: A literature review. *Communications of the Association for Information Systems*, 38, 20–83. https://doi.org/ 10.17705/1CAIS.03802

Wright, P. M., & McMahan, G. C. (2011). Exploring human capital: Putting "human" back into strategic human resource management. *Human Resource Management Journal*, 21(2), 93–104. https://doi.org/ 10.1111/j.1748-8583.2010.00165.x

Wright, P. M., McMahan, G. C., & McWilliams, A. (1994). Human resources and sustained competitive advantage: A resource-based perspective. *The International Journal of Human Resource Management*, 5(2), 301–326. https://doi.org/10.1080/09585199400000020

Yadav, S., Jain, A., & Singh, D. (2018). Early prediction of employee attrition using data mining techniques. In *2018 IEEE 8th International Advance Computing Conference (IACC)* (pp. 349–354). IEEE. https://doi.org/10.1109/IADCC.2018.8692137

Yiğit, I. O., & Shourabizadeh, H. (2017). An approach for predicting employee churn by using data mining. In *IDAP 2017 – International Artificial Intelligence and Data Processing Symposium* (pp. 1–4). https://doi.org/10.1109/IDAP.2017.8090324

Yunmeng, Z., & Chengyi, Z. (2019). The application of the decision tree algorithm based on k-means in employee turnover prediction. *Journal of Physics: Conference Series*, 1325, Article 012123. https:// doi.org/10.1088/1742-6596/1325/1/012123

Zhang, Yanru, Zhang, Yunlong, & Haghani, A. (2014). A hybrid short-term traffic flow forecasting method based on spectral analysis and statistical volatility model. *Transportation Research Part C: Emerging Technologies*, 43, 65–78.

Zhao, Y., Hryniewicki, M. K., Cheng, F., Fu, B., & Zhu, X. (2018). Employee turnover prediction with machine learning: A reliable approach. In K. Arai, S. Kapoor, & R. Bhatia (Eds.), *Intelligent systems and applications* (pp. 737–758). Springer. https://doi.org/10.1007/978-3-030-01057-7

Zhu, X., Seaver, W., Sawhney, R., Ji, S., Holt, B., Sanil, G. B., & Upreti, G. (2017). Employee turnover forecasting for human resource management based on time series analysis. *Journal of Applied Statistics*, 44(8), 1421–1440. https://doi.org/10.1080/02664763.2016.1214242

Zlotnik, A., Gallardo-Antolín, A., Cuchí Alfaro, M., Pérez Pérez, M. C., & Montero Martínez, J. M. (2015). Emergency department visit forecasting and dynamic nursing staff allocation using machine learning techniques with readily available open-source software. *Computers, Informatics, Nursing: CIN*, 33(8), 368–377.

8. Machine learning in personnel selection

Cornelius J. König and Markus Langer

INTRODUCTION

New approaches to personnel selection based on artificial intelligence (AI) including its subfield machine learning (ML) offer much promise for the field: "We can deal with a large amount of unstructured, quickly incoming data to allow valid and fair personnel selection decisions." These represent an attractive proposition for human resource (HR) professionals who are responsible for making hiring decisions as many HR departments have to balance the interests of their organization with the fast-paced nature of work. HR professionals often have to fill open positions quickly with the most suitable of a potentially large number of applicants. For example, when the European Union advertises a new vacancy through its European Personnel Selection Office (EPSO), it is not uncommon for EPSO to receive tens of thousands of applications (Christensen, 2015). Even if EPSO might be an extreme case, any organization that has to cope with large numbers of applicants would welcome tools that help to automatically select the "right" candidates, or at least distinguish the most viable candidates from the less suitable ones, ideally in an objective way. These are some of the most common expectations regarding AI and ML in personnel selection.

This chapter first describes the current state of affairs in the field of personnel selection and introduces ML approaches to readers in a non-technical way. The chapter then reviews the empirical research that has looked at the potentials of ML approaches in a selection context as well as research that has looked at the challenges and disadvantages of such approaches. In particular, we stress that using ML approaches does not necessarily reduce biases in personnel selection and that AI-based personnel selection could lead to negative reactions among applicants and users as well as alter HR managers' everyday work processes. The final part of the chapter discusses future research needs for this area.

SOME BACKGROUND INFORMATION

A Short Description of the State of Affairs in the Field of Personnel Selection

Personnel selection can be described as a crucial but difficult part of HR management. Personnel selection is crucial because selecting the wrong person for a job can have many negative effects for organizational performance. By calculating the monetary value of personnel selection, readers interested in the financial side of HR are able to see how quickly an investment in a good personnel selection system pays off (Cascio & Boudreau, 2008). At the same time, personnel selection is difficult because despite more than 100 years of research, there is still no silver bullet when it comes to hiring the right person and errors are still expected. As such, there seems to be quite some room for improvement in hiring decisions, particularly in relation to non-cognitive traits such as personality and motivation. For example, even the personality construct with the best predictive validity, conscientiousness, only correlates with job performance at $r \approx 0.20$ or maybe 0.25 (and this is only after meta-analytical corrections, Barrick et al., 2001).

Research has tirelessly explored why the predictive validities of typical personnel selection methods are not higher. One reason is that applicants have an inherent incentive to present themselves as better than they are (Bangerter et al., 2012). This might lead to misrepresentation or even fraud in résumés (e.g., Henle et al., 2019), to faking in personality inventories (e.g., Birkeland et al., 2006) and situational judgment tests (e.g., Peeters & Lievens, 2005), and to impression management in interviews (e.g., Ingold et al., 2015) and Assessment Centers (ACs; e.g., McFarland et al., 2003). A second reason is that many personnel selection methods require human decisions, making them prone to human biases. For example, some HR professionals might have prejudices against immigrant applicants and thus evaluate them differently than non-immigrant applicants (Horverak et al., 2013). Another example that highlights human biases in selection is ACs. Observing candidates in ACs is a demanding task, as probably all HR professionals with AC experience know. Although writing notes may help to alleviate the cognitive burden (Kolk et al., 2002), observing each and every aspect of applicant behavior is still an enormous task. Interviews, for example, are full of verbal, nonverbal, and paraverbal information (with paraverbal information being the way things are said), and assessing all these nuances is impossible. As another example, if organizations use electronic versions of situational judgment tests, the time that applicants take to formulate their responses might contribute to the validity of those tests, but this information is usually lost in traditional personnel selection where assessors will only look at the applicants' final responses. Thus, there seems to lie vast untapped potential in data that currently slips through our fingers (Oswald et al., 2020).

Even though an error-free world, where all personnel selection decisions lead to the perfect choice, is unrealistic, an HR manager can still strive for a world in which personnel selection decisions are better. It is realistic, and feasible, to make less biased personnel selection decisions such that they are based on more objective, reliable, and valid data. Such decisions can be made while still being economically sound and efficient, and fair to all applicants. The question is thus whether new approaches developed by computer and data scientists (in particular in the area of AI and ML) can help in coming closer to this ideal world.

What ML Approaches Can Do

ML can generally be understood as a subfield of AI. A functional definition of AI was proposed by Strohmeier (see CHAPTER 1): "AI designates the set of digital technologies that mimic certain functions of NI [natural intelligence], such as perceiving, learning, knowing, or reasoning, to augment or automate human tasks, which conventionally require such functions of NI to be performed" (p. 2). Furthermore, he categorizes the field of AI into several subfields, with ML being one of them, and describes ML as employing "existing data to 'learn' knowledge inherent in these data and map this knowledge in a model" (p. 4). For this learning and mapping, it is necessary to train ML algorithms with data that enables the algorithms to detect patterns in the data that relate to criteria of interest and that optimize prediction or classification. Although it would go far beyond the scope of this chapter to describe ML in detail (for an introduction see CHAPTER 2; see also, e.g., Putka et al., 2018, and Theobald, 2017), it is likely helpful to explain how ML approaches can be used in the field of personnel selection more generally.

How ML approaches work in the personnel selection field

Let us use the following example. Imagine an organization had invited 500 applicants to respond to an asynchronous interview in which they presented applicants with eight interview questions (e.g., "Tell me about your strengths and weaknesses") and applicants recorded short videos with their responses (see Langer et al., 2017). All these interviews were then scored by HR managers who gave an overall hirability rating of between 0 and 10.

The HR department now wonders how to extract meaningful information out of the videos because they do not want to manually score the next 500 responses. If they give this task to data scientists, they will likely conclude that analyzing those videos for predicting the hirability of applicants is a prototypical situation where ML approaches should be used. This is because this dataset of applicant videos is an example of "large, noisy, multimodal, and high-dimensional field data" (König et al., 2020, p. 19). They are large because a typical uncompressed color video file consists of 14 megabytes per second (which means 4.2 gigabytes per 5 minutes of video); they are noisy because, for instance, the background of the videos is not standardized and there might be actual noise in the data (e.g., background noises; technical issues during recording); they are multimodal because they include visual, verbal, paraverbal, and nonverbal information; and they are high-dimensional because they can be described from low levels such as pixels to high levels such as inferred behavior (e.g., a smile).

Data scientists will likely try to link the videos to the hirability ratings in an optimal way. "Optimal way" means that they will try to achieve the best possible prediction accuracy, and to do so they have to (a) pre-process the data, (b) extract and (c) engineer features, and (d) train and test a variety of ML approaches. Pre-processing is one of the most labor-intensive steps in ML. This means converting the data into forms that can be used by algorithms, cleaning the data, normalizing data, or controlling for noise in the data. Consider the example of video interviews: The video of every participant will look different because it is recorded with different hardware, with differing internet bandwidth, in front of a different physical background, with different background noise, and in different lighting conditions. These differences are challenging if we want to extract useful information from the video and audio stream of applicant recordings. If we, for instance, want to use the content of applicant responses, steps to go through would include extracting the audio signal, using speech-to-text methods to automatically transcribe the audio signal, checking for inconsistencies and errors in transcription, and preparing the resulting text data (e.g., stemming [i.e., reducing different forms from a word to a common stem]).

Feature extraction means to reduce the number of variables ("features") that will be used to build the ML model. In our example, this could mean to extract single words from the interview and use those words in prediction. However, it could be more informative to use combinations of two, three, or more words as features. In such cases we quickly arrive at points where datasets become too large and sparse to be practically useful in algorithms (e.g., because it would take too much time to process them). In such cases, feature extraction can also mean condensing the data (e.g., using principal component analysis) to make it more usable within algorithms. Closely associated with feature extraction is feature engineering, where developers of algorithms can use different ways to create ("to engineer") new features from existing ones (e.g., in the case of the video interview, it might be an idea to include the word count or word complexity as new features).

Once the feature extraction and engineering process is finished, it is possible to start testing different kinds of algorithms for prediction or classification. Those algorithms can range from linear and logistic regression to single decision trees, ensemble methods (e.g., random forests), and deep neural networks, knowing that each method has its own advantages, disadvantages, and boundary conditions. Each kind of algorithm then requires an iterative optimization process to find the best combination and weighting of features as well as to tune parameters in the ML models (e.g., parameters that penalize for the number of features included in the model). To find the most promising algorithm, data scientists randomly divide the sample into a training set and a test set (which is sometimes called cross-validation). In the simplest case, 70 percent of the sample might be used to develop the algorithm and 30 percent to test (or to validate) it. The overall goal here is to prevent overfitting and to make the algorithm as generalizable to new data as possible.

Although the focus of such ML approaches will be on optimizing prediction accuracy, it is also possible to take other target criteria into account, for instance optimizing not only for predictive accuracy but also for preventing biases (Raghavan et al., 2020). Furthermore, explainability and human understandability of algorithms has been introduced as another important success criterion of AI and ML (David, 2018). In fact, there has been a recent boom in trying to balance prediction accuracy and explainability of algorithms (see CHAPTER 15). On the one hand, this could mean using transparent ML approaches (e.g., linear regression as compared to deep neural networks) or that algorithms are not allowed to contain complex interactions with nonlinear effects (Lipton, 2018). On the other hand, this could mean that in cases where less transparent algorithms are applied, post-hoc methods to increase interpretability or explainability are used (e.g., methods to try to explain prediction outcomes; Arrieta et al., 2020). Furthermore, the decision on which features to use for the algorithm could be grounded on theoretical arguments, making them more comprehensible (e.g., smiling is included because prior research argues that smiling is relevant in job interviews).

Our previous application examples from applied personnel selection focused on the evaluation of interview recordings, but it is important to keep in mind that approaches from AI and ML can easily be used in other applications. It could be motivation letters, videos from applicants waiting to be let into the interview room, and even applicants' handwriting (see Joshi et al., 2015). In particular, we refer the interested reader to CHAPTER 6 on HR Machine Learning in Recruiting and CHAPTER 7 on HR Machine Learning on Staffing for more details about how ML can be used for predicting person–environment fit.

Other applications of ML approaches
AI approaches are not only used for analyzing data obtained from applicants; they are often also part of the technology used in a selection process. For example, if virtual characters are used to present interview questions (see Chollet et al., 2019; Langer et al., 2018), ML approaches help characters to adapt and respond to applicants (e.g., by analyzing applicants' emotional states). Furthermore, ML might also be used to detect faking and impression management (see Calanna et al., 2020, but see also Auer, 2018). AI can also be used to optimize the combination of information from various personnel selection methods or the combination of single items in personnel selection approaches (Putka et al., 2018). Especially in cases of low n/k ratios (i.e., number of applicants/number of predictors), ML approaches can have advantages over classical statistical methods of data combination (Putka et al., 2018).

A RESEARCH REVIEW

Emphasizing a caveat seems appropriate before we review the research in this particular field. Most HR practitioners and researchers have been trained to understand personnel selection studies conducted by industrial/organizational psychologists or management scholars. Thus, they are primarily used to studies in which, for instance, certain features of a test are manipulated (e.g., Krumm et al., 2015) and meta-analytical studies that summarize, for example, the predictive validity of ACs versus general mental ability tests (Sackett et al., 2017). As such, most HR practitioners and researchers will likely not be familiar with research conducted by computer scientists (König et al., 2020; Oswald et al., 2020). Three differences between the two academic fields are particularly relevant here. First, computer scientists are often mainly interested in proof-of-concept studies. Thus, they care more about whether it is possible to link certain input data to a criterion and less about whether the data were collected under realistic, real-life conditions (see for instance Naim et al., 2018, or further studies as reviewed in CHAPTER 6). Second, the main focus of ML is prediction, which means studies from computer science with a focus on ML investigating personnel selection issues will likely include information on how well it was possible to predict an outcome and on what kind of algorithm ended up being the one with the highest predictive accuracy, but less likely to include theoretical foundation for why to include various predictors in a prediction model. Third, personnel selection might just be a "use case" for computer scientists, among many other use cases, and therefore they might not pay too much attention to standards that researchers from the personnel selection field uphold (e.g., psychometric properties of scales; König et al., 2020).

The following review is based on our long and extensive work in this area, which started with our involvement in the TARDIS project (e.g., Anderson et al., 2013), where the first author sat on the advisory board. For writing this chapter, we complemented our database of studies by searching for additional studies in the Scopus database.[1] Our focus was on studies that use ML for making personnel selection decisions, and although we searched for studies about the selection of external and of internal candidates (e.g., for a promotion), all the studies we found were about external candidates.

Research Showing the Potential of ML Approaches for Personnel Selection

Previous research showing the potential of ML largely focused on text data (see CHAPTER 3). For several computer scientists (and some psychologists), it seems a worthwhile challenge to predict personality test scores from texts and spoken language in videos, which falls under the broad area termed Natural Language Processing (NLP). NLP, which "aims at mimicking the language-based communication of humans" (CHAPTER 1, p. 5), goes beyond just counting words, by statistically taking the context and co-occurrences of words and word patterns into account (see CHAPTER 12; see also, e.g., Turney & Pantel, 2010). With NLP, text can be a useful source to infer personality (Tskhay & Rule, 2014; see also Boyd & Pennebaker, 2017). In particular, researchers have tried to predict personality traits on the basis of information from Facebook and other digital footprints (Azucar et al., 2018; Bleidorn & Hopwood, 2019).

We are aware of only two studies that have used NLP to analyze written material as part of a personnel selection process: Campion et al. (2016) and Sajjadiani et al. (2019). Campion et al. obtained around 40,000 accomplishment records, described as 200-word mini-essays in which applicants describe their accomplishments regarding one of six specific competences such as leadership, written by applicants to a large public employer in the United States. All accomplishment records had previously been scored by three raters. With the help of NLP, Campion et al. constructed automatically scored ratings that correlated mostly in the 0.60 to 0.65 range with the averaged human ratings in a test sample.

Sajjadiani et al. (2019) obtained online application data of prospective school teaching positions in Minnesota that contained information about the applicants' work experience, their history of tenure and turnover, and attributions of turnover history. They used ML approaches to estimate work experience relevance and to categorize the turnover history attributions. Sajjadiani et al. found that the "avoiding bad jobs" category of the turnover history attributions negatively predicted teachers' performance and was positively linked to involuntary turnover. They also found that the work experience relevance measure positively predicted some performance measures and was negatively related to voluntary turnover.

Whereas NLP just uses verbal material, other researchers focused on other modalities (audio and visual) or on combining data from different modalities (see CHAPTER 4; see also Mehta et al., 2020). This stream of research finds similar results; indeed, audio files can be used to predict personality (e.g., Mohammadi & Vinciarelli, 2012) and so can video files (e.g., Aran & Gatica-Perez, 2013), and it is therefore not surprising that this is also possible if modalities are combined (e.g., Pianesi et al., 2008; Zhang et al., 2016). Furthermore, constructs other than personality can be predicted by such data, particularly communication skills (e.g., Rasipuram & Jayagopi, 2018, 2019; Suen et al., 2020). This is not surprising given that ML approaches do not have any restrictions on outcome variables. Since ML methods are usually good at detecting patterns in data, this makes it likely that there will be at least a certain degree of prediction accuracy for any outcome that is at least remotely related to the data.

Some researchers have tried to directly link multimedia data to hirability scores and interview scores. Escalante et al. (2020) describes a dataset of 10,000 short YouTube clips (with an average length of 15 seconds) where each clip was annotated with a hirability score (scores were achieved by paying around 2,500 MTurkers – people working for Amazon's Mechanical Turk platform). Different ML approaches were then used to predict the hirability scores using audio and visual information. Naim et al. (2018) tried to link automated analyses of interviews with interview performance. In this study, 69 students participated in two short mock interviews with one professional career counsellor (which they counted as 138 interviews). These interviews were video-taped and transcribed and then rated by nine MTurkers regarding the overall interview performance (as well as some other ratings). Naim et al. used an algorithm-based evaluation of the interviews based on facial, prosodic (speech), and lexical (words) features. They found that the prosodic and the lexical features were particularly important for predicting the overall interview rating.

Admittedly, without evidence for predictive validity, this stream of research will likely not convince many personnel selection researchers and practitioners: Do these ML approaches lead to scores that predict job performance, organizational citizenship behavior, and turnover in practice? Unfortunately, there is only scarce research providing responses to those questions. It is even more unfortunate that providers of AI-based solutions for personnel selection do not offer any convincing openly available information on the validity of their tools (Raghavan et al., 2020). Furthermore, previous research often only predicts personality scores, and personality scores themselves are weak predictors of job performance (e.g., Salgado & Táuriz, 2014). This means that the indirect link between, for example, Facebook likes and performance via personality scores is even weaker (mathematically, it means that a weak correlation between Facebook likes and conscientiousness needs to be multiplied with the weak correlation between conscientiousness and performance). The only exception (apart from the aforementioned study by Sajjadiani et al., 2019) we know of is one small unpublished study by Schmid Mast et al. (2017; see also Nguyen et al., 2014). The authors invited applicants to an interview for a real job (to work as a research assistant recruiting people to participate in studies). The interview was automatically scored based on nonverbal cues obtained with a camera and a microphone. These scores were indeed related to the performance of the research assistants (measured as the number of people the research assistants convinced to sign up for studies). Although this finding is encouraging, the small sample size ($N = 54$) likely makes the results unstable. Clearly, the field would benefit from studies investigating validity evidence with further job performance indicators and with actual employees in organizations.

Research Showing the Challenges of ML Approaches for Personnel Selection

Despite the potential of ML approaches for personnel selection, there is also evidence about their (potential) downsides. Although a considerable number of studies have focused on biases in algorithms, the negative effects on applicants and on users is another downside worth noting. These challenges will be reviewed in the next section.

Replication of biases

Although some people assume that ML approaches work bias-free, this is clearly a wrong assumption as ML approaches can replicate, reinforce, and perpetuate biases (Veale & Binns, 2017). One famous example is Amazon's attempt to use a personnel selection tool for automatic selection of applicants (Dastin, 2018). However, in due time Amazon realized that because of their historically and primarily male applicant population, their tool also favored male applicants in personnel selection. It is especially interesting to see that Amazon reportedly tried to diminish this bias (e.g., using more diverse data, retraining, and adjusting algorithms), but ultimately decided to abandon their AI tool for personnel selection. Potential unfair bias is also an issue for providers of AI systems in practice (see also CHAPTER 16). This is especially true because some providers of AI-based solutions market their solutions as less biased than the traditional means in personnel selection (i.e., human ratings). Raghavan et al. (2020) reviewed information that some of the biggest providers of AI solutions in personnel selection offer on their websites about their AI solutions (e.g., HireVue, Pymetrics) and found that most of the providers were aware of the issue of potential biasing issues in their AI solutions. Some of the providers emphasized that they take measures against bias (e.g., actively removing features from datasets, constantly testing for adverse impact against minorities), but did not go deeper into detail.

There are several reasons for how unfair bias is introduced into ML-based applications. Most likely, datasets are not representative and include skewed data (Zerilli et al., 2019). This is basically what happened in the case of Amazon. Second, the training data can reflect human biases. If an algorithm was optimized for a biased criterion, the algorithm will also be biased (O'Neil, 2016). Specifically, if minority applicants previously received systematically lower ratings or if they performed significantly worse than majority applicants, ML algorithms will pick up on this information and use the majority status as a "signal" reflective of what distinguishes the more from the less suitable applicants. Removing identifying information from applicant data might mitigate this issue to a certain degree, but since ML approaches are good at detecting patterns in data, it is still likely that they would pick up on information that points to the minority status of applicants. For instance, the number and kinds of words used in responses, voice features in interviews, and previous employers in résumés can all reveal a person's gender, race, age, or origin. Solutions to this issue are far from trivial as removing features that are potentially correlated with sensitive applicant information (as done by several providers of AI solutions for personnel selection; Raghavan et al., 2020) can render ML approaches useless as virtually no information might be left (Goodman & Flaxman, 2017).

An issue that should make the problem of potential unfair biases in selection even more salient is the extent to which such systems might be applied in the future. If one human errs, it can affect applicants in one organization. For example, if one HR manager does not like redhaired men, their organization will likely not employ any redhaired men – but redhaired men might still have a fair chance in other organizations. However, if an ML system provides biased outputs, this can affect all selection processes based on this system (Langer, König, & Busch, 2021).

We want to end this section on a more hopeful note regarding the elimination of unfair bias in ML-based personnel selection. If providers take every effort to constantly check for potential bias, and if they do their best to provide a representative set of training data, good criterion data, and update ML-based selection tools in case contexts and demands for employees change, it might be possible to make personnel selection less biased. However, as the list of conditionals in the previous sentence indicates, this is far from a trivial task and requires a lot of human work (e.g., humans as data curators, humans monitoring systems for potential biases, humans updating systems).

Predominantly negative effects on applicants – their reactions and their behavior
To date, evidence suggests that applicants dislike being evaluated by automated systems based on AI and ML. In comparison to being evaluated by humans, applicants describe lower interpersonal justice and lower social presence, lower perceived controllability, stronger privacy concerns, and lower trust (Acikgoz et al., 2020; Gonzalez et al., 2019; Kanning et al., 2019; Langer, König, & Papathanasiou, 2019; Langer, König, & Scheuss, 2019; Lee, 2018; Newman et al., 2020). However, people perceive personnel selection using AI systems as being more consistent and potentially more objective than human selection decisions (Langer, König, Sanchez, et al., 2020; Lee, 2018; Newby-Clark et al., 2000). Although there is also research showing no differences in fairness perceptions between human and AI ratings (Suen et al., 2019), organizations who are already struggling to attract applications should be warned that using such AI-based tools might further reduce the applicant pool. As the aforementioned studies were not conducted with actual applicants or in actual selection settings, and because familiarity with selection tools can always affect people's reactions, future research investigating whether applicants can have more favorable reactions to automated personnel selection processes if AI-based systems continue to spread (Gonzalez et al., 2019) is needed.

For classical personnel selection approaches, providing applicants with information and explanations was found to be a promising strategy in improving applicant reactions (Truxillo et al., 2009). However, in the case of AI for personnel selection, this might not be the case. Langer et al. (2018) found that providing applicants with information regarding automated job interviews increased the perceived transparency of the process but at the same time decreased the perceived organizational attractiveness of the hiring organization. In a second study, Langer, Baum, et al. (2021) found that providing people with information regarding what kind of information will be used in automated job interviews can have detrimental effects on applicant reactions, whereas providing information regarding why respective information is used has more potential to improve applicant reactions. However, providing people with no information at all was not found to be especially problematic, thus posing the question of what kind of information would be most beneficial to applicant reactions. Similarly, results obtained by Newman et al. (2020) indicate that information and explanation might have unexpected negative effects for the acceptance of AI-based personnel selection situations. Further research indicates that providing no information might not be detrimental since people might not expect information when being confronted with AI-based decisions (Schlicker et al., 2021).

Aside from perceptions of AI-based selection, the use of AI might also affect applicant behavior. Langer, König, and Hemsing (2020) found that applicants who believed that their answers to an asynchronous interview (i.e., recorded video answer to interview questions presented as text on screens) were analyzed automatically by a computer (vs. manually by a human rater) gave shorter answers and reported using less impression management. One possible reason for this latter effect could be that people believe that a computer can better detect impression management than humans. Furthermore, users have less experience of being evaluated by automated systems, which could mean they might behave differently compared to when they anticipate another human being responsible for evaluating their answers.

Potentially negative effects on users

Users' perceptions of AI-based systems have received less attention than the reactions of affected people, but we can infer negative perceptions from the general decision-making literature. Research on holistic versus mechanical decision making found that hiring managers do not seem to like relying on systems that reduce their opportunity to show their own skills and expertise (Highhouse, 2008; Nolan et al., 2016). Furthermore, further research from the area of decision making has implied that there are conditions under which users discount advice from automated systems, even when people see that systems make better decisions than themselves (Burton et al., 2020). This discounting of algorithmic advice has been called "algorithm aversion" (Dietvorst et al., 2015). We should note however that there are certain conditions in which people are more likely to rely on algorithmic advice rather than human advice (Logg et al., 2019).

There are already some studies looking at the reactions of users of AI-based systems in HRM. In Feldkamp et al. (2020), participants took the role of a hiring manager and received a preselection of applicants selected either by a human colleague or an automated system. This preselection either had an equal distribution of male and female applicants or showed more male applicants. Findings show that the kind of advisor (human vs. system) matters more to people's reactions than the actual unfair bias in the preselection. Specifically, participants perceived the algorithmic preselection generally as less fair. However, similar to applicants' perception of AI-based systems, users also perceived it to be more consistent and objective than the human preselection but as offering less voice in the process. There is further research indicating that the use of ML approaches might lead to feelings of less control and maybe even feelings of dehumanization (Kellogg et al., 2020). In particular, results by Schlicker et al. (2021) indicate that people who delegate their decisions to automated systems will perceive having less control over these outcomes and might consequently feel less responsible in cases where people complain about outcomes. In another example of research on the side of the decision maker, Langer, König, and Busch (2021) used a work characteristics frame to show that different versions of automated systems supporting decisions in personnel selection can lead to different user reactions. They introduced participants to systems providing advice in personnel selection tasks. Those systems either provided advice before participants received the raw applicant information or provided advice after participants made their first decision for one of the applicants. They found that people are more satisfied with their decisions and showed a stronger increase in self-efficacy in the case of advice following a first initial decision. They conclude that certain work characteristics (e.g., decision autonomy, feedback, the amount of information processing) differ with different implementations of automated systems, suggesting a need to further investigate these influences in future work.

FUTURE RESEARCH

As this review of research into ML approaches to personnel selection has shown so far, there are many exciting opportunities for future research because our knowledge is still fairly limited. If more researchers and practitioners from the HR field engage in this line of research, they can bring their domain knowledge into the research, the methodological rigor that the field values, and hopefully their connections to field samples. Studying ML approaches in the field will surely boost the impact of this research as most previous studies are proof-of-concept papers with students or participants from crowdsourcing platforms. In the remaining part of this chapter, we will outline several particularly promising areas for future research.

The Need for (Predictive) Validity Research

Similar to classical personnel selection research, the most important but potentially most challenging area for future research is validity research. If there is no evidence that a system can predict job performance, no organization will be interested in investing any money in it. Even if organizations consider the preliminary evidence obtained so far as convincing, they should be aware that it will be difficult to defend the use of existing systems in court. From a data science point of view, producing predictive validity evidence should not be that difficult: It does not matter if the variable one wants to predict is a hirability rating or a job performance rating.

The challenges for getting predictive validity research lie elsewhere. Let us start with the following rather simple scenario. An organization regularly hires a large number of people for a specific job from a highly consistent applicant pool (e.g., not much variation in applicant skills over time), say 600 new sales agents per year. In the course of year 1, all applicants go through a selection procedure that includes a video self-presentation, which is, however, not used for selection purposes. After six months (i.e., partly in year 2), supervisors rate the job performance of these 600 sales agents. The rest of year 2 can then be used to develop an automatic scoring system for the self-presentation videos, for example by using the data of 400 sales agents for training the algorithm and the data of the remaining sales agents for testing it. This should produce convincing predictive validity, with one caveat: It remains unknown in this scenario whether the algorithm also predicts job performance in a different organization.

Let us now extend this scenario. The organization in the previous example that developed the automatic scoring of the self-presentation videos now plans to sell this system to another organization. However, the applicant pools of the second organization will differ significantly.

For instance, they might come from a different region (where applicants speak a different dialect) and they might be more ethnically diverse (which means more variety in facial features such as the shape of the eyes). All this could affect the ML algorithm such that if it was not trained with the new dialect, it might or might not be able to adequately evaluate applicants who speak it. But because the ML algorithm remains a black box (see also CHAPTER 15), and if we do not understand the internal processes of the algorithm that produce its outputs, we cannot convincingly build the argument that the same algorithm will work for applicants in another organization. Thus, it is necessary to ensure that the predictive validity results generalize to the other organizations. In the United States, such validity evidence is legally required by the Uniform Guidelines (Equal Employment Opportunity Commission et al., 1978).

In addition to predictive validity, other aspects of the output of the algorithm also need to be examined. In particular, research needs to assess subgroup differences, because many personnel selection instruments produce gender and racial differences (Ployhart & Holtz, 2008). As well, research could try to establish the construct validity of the variables. More generally speaking, classical psychometric standards also apply to the use of ML in selection (Jacobucci & Grimm, 2020). A lack of reliability of the included measures in ML systems will undermine the usefulness of those approaches without offering any evidence on its effectiveness.

Furthermore, predictive validity might be reduced if applicants know how to outwit automatic scoring systems, which might be called "faking" (e.g., Melchers et al., 2020) or "gaming the system" (e.g., Bambauer & Zarsky, 2018). Previous research has shown that by providing an individual with hints on how a personnel selection procedure is scored can affect faking levels (König et al., 2017), and signaling theory (Bangerter et al., 2012) predicts that applicants have a strong incentive to outwit such systems. For instance, if applicants become aware that system evaluations tend to favor people who talk more loudly, it might be logical that people will try to speak louder. Similarly, if people have an intuition into what kinds of words a system based on NLP associates with job suitability, people might try to adapt their résumés in a way that might enhance their résumé evaluations. It is even imaginable that they might try to game a system by using strategies that are not outwardly obvious (e.g., applicants using white font in self-developed résumés to add words they think could increase their evaluation).

The Need for Research on Human–AI Collaboration

Not even companies who try to sell ML approaches for personnel selection propose that their product should become the only selection procedure in a selection process (Raghavan et al., 2020). A multiple-hurdle approach in which ML approaches are used for screening and other procedures are used either in addition or in a later hurdle is the most likely scenario for incorporating ML approaches into personnel selection systems. However, even within the screening stage, fully automated selection through AI might not be legally defensible (e.g., the General Data Protection Regulation of the European Union includes regulation against completely automated processing and profiling of humans; see also CHAPTER 18). Thus, human decision makers will remain a vital part of the selection process. This could indicate that HR practitioners have to integrate information from the ML approach with other information and their own evaluation. In cases of such augmentation scenarios (i.e., where humans and systems jointly contribute to a decision task, Raisch & Krakowski, 2021), many questions arise. For instance, how to design the joint human–AI decision process is yet to be determined. One option could be that a system provides humans with advice that humans can then use as an additional source of information. Another option would be that humans initially evaluate applicant information and then get advice from a system as additional information (van Dongen & van Maanen, 2013). In this case, the system could even be used for questioning the human's evaluation in an attempt to improve the human decision maker's reasoning about their decision, thus potentially improving decision quality (e.g., Guerlain et al., 1999). Yet another potentially more time-efficient option would be to put the human in the decision loop, meaning that they only monitor systems decisions and either approve each of the decisions or only intervene as soon as they realize that there is an error.

The previous examples mainly describe ideas regarding "when" to receive advice from a system and the "how" (e.g., as advice or as feedback) of human–system collaboration for selection processes. It remains to be tested which information from the ML approach should be presented (e.g., how much detail, graphical representations, technical detail). In addition, long-term effects need to be studied. It is likely that users of such systems will learn from interacting with those systems over time. If the experience is positive, users might over-trust systems, which could mean they will overly rely on a system's processes and outputs (Parasuraman & Manzey, 2010; Parasuraman & Riley, 1997). This could lead to situations where human decision makers utilize biased or weak recommendations by the system without realizing that the system advice might have been suboptimal. If the experience is negative, users might lose trust in the system, which could eventually lead to under-trust even in situations where the system has been improved by developers. In such systems, users might needlessly engage in controlling and monitoring behavior, undermining the efficiency gains of system use.

Finally, with the implementation of automated systems in selection processes, there will likely also be the need for employee training (Oswald et al., 2020). Given that AI has only started to play a role in the education of the HRM profession, the current generation of HR professionals is likely not especially literate in the use of AI-based systems and thus would benefit from training that explains the capabilities and limitations of such systems. However, except for more generic online trainings on the foundations of ML, we know of no such training for the use of AI for management purposes.

The Need for More Reaction Research

Future research may also want to consider other stakeholder reactions to ML approaches. Whereas previous research mostly examined applicant reactions (e.g., Acikgoz et al., 2020; Kanning et al., 2019; Langer et al., 2018; Mirowska, 2020; Newman et al., 2020) and user reactions (e.g., Langer, König, & Busch, 2021), researchers need to pay attention to the reactions of other stakeholders such as decision makers in organizations, unions, and works councils, developers of software, and so on (see also CHAPTER 15 and Langer, Oster, et al., 2021). In particular, understanding ML approaches and convincingly communicating the advantages and caveats of such approaches might require more detailed knowledge than decision makers in organizations typically have (Oswald et al., 2020).

The Need for Research on Other Technologies

So far, research has typically worked with data that arise as a by-product during selection procedures (e.g., accomplishment records, Campion et al., 2016; videos sent by applicants in asynchronous interviews, Langer, König, & Hemsing, 2020). It might be worthwhile to extend these datasets by using data from alternative and new sources. In particular, such new data could come from using sensors like wearables (for an overview see Langer, Schmid Mast, et al., 2019). For example, if a desirable characteristic of an air traffic controller is the ability to cope in high-stress situations (Pecena et al., 2013), it should be possible to measure air traffic controller applicants' stress levels in roleplays by using wearables that measure variables such as skin conductance, heart rate, and blood pressure. Such wearable data could supplement (or even replace) human ratings of applicants' stress resistance.

SUMMARY

Undoubtedly, ML approaches will become more and more important for the field of personnel selection. The field of personnel selection will not do itself any favors by ignoring this trend or by pointing to the non-existence of convincing evidence that ML approaches work in practice – two reactions we have repeatedly heard in the past. Instead, we hope that the selection field can build on the existing findings as summarized in Table 8.1 and engage in more research that will provide evidence for the validity of ML approaches to selection, explore the human–AI interface, and examine the reactions of users, applicants, and other stakeholders. We predict (without any algorithm!) that this will be, on average, a rewarding experience.

Table 8.1   Current status of the field

Aspect	Main question	Our evaluation	Sources
General idea	Does it make sense for HR management to try to use ML approaches to extract meaningful information from verbal, audio, and visual traces that applicants leave during a personnel selection process?	Yes. There is general support for this idea because many studies have shown that such ML approaches can, in principle, work	e.g., Escalante et al. (2020); Naim et al. (2018)
Real-life validity	Can field research provide HR managers with evidence that these ML approaches work in practice?	Not yet. Even in the two field studies scores were not used for selection decisions.	Campion et al. (2016); Sajjadiani et al. (2019)
Biases	Can HR managers be sure that biases in ML approaches for personnel selection contain only minimal biases against, for instance, women?	Not yet. The field has become aware of this challenge, but convincing solutions and systematic investigation are still missing.	e.g., Raghavan et al. (2020); Veale & Bins (2017)
Applicant reactions	Should HR managers worry about negative reactions by applicants?	Yes. Although applicants might perceive such ML approaches as consistent and objective, they generally do not seem to like being evaluated by a machine.	e.g., Langer, König, & Papathanasiou (2019); Lee (2018)
User reactions	Should top managers worry about the negative reactions of HR managers who use ML approaches for personnel selection?	Likely. The limited research so far suggests there are at least some negative reactions, although positive reactions (e.g., due to work design improvements) are also possible.	e.g., Langer, König, & Busch (2021)

NOTE

1. Using the search string: TITLE-ABS("artificial intelligence" OR "machine learning" OR "intelligent system" OR automated OR automation OR algorithm* OR "decision support system" OR "expert system*" OR {computer-based} OR {computer-assisted}) AND TITLE-ABS-KEY(participants OR {subjects} OR {experiment} OR {experiments} OR "field study" OR "laboratory study" OR employee OR applicants) AND ALL (decision OR decide OR advi*) AND TITLE-ABS-KEY (management OR manager OR managerial OR organization OR workplace OR job OR employee OR advisor* OR {individuals}) AND TITLE-ABS-KEY (react* OR accept* OR perceive* OR perception OR satis* OR belief OR fairness)

REFERENCES

Acikgoz, Y., Davison, K. H., Compagnone, M., & Laske, M. (2020). Justice perceptions of artificial intelligence in selection. *International Journal of Selection and Assessment*, *28*(4), 399–416. https://doi.org/10.1111/ijsa.12306

Anderson, K., André, E., Baur, T., Bernardini, S., Chollet, M., Chryssafidou, E., Damian, I., Ennis, C., Egges, A., Gebhard, P., Jones, H., Ochs, M., Pelachaud, C., Porayska-Pomsta, K., Rizzo, P., & Sabouret, N. (2013). The TARDIS framework: Intelligent virtual agents for social coaching in job interviews. In D. Reidsma, H. Katayose, & A. Nijholt, *ACE 2013: Advances in Computer Entertainment* (pp. 476–491). Springer. https://doi.org/10.1007/978-3-319-03161-3_35

Aran, O., & Gatica-Perez, D. (2013). Cross-domain personality prediction: From video blogs to small group meetings. In *Proceedings of the 15th ACM on International Conference on Multimodal Interaction* (pp. 127–130). ACM. https://doi.org/10.1145/2522848.2522858

Arrieta, A. B., Díaz-Rodríguez, N., Del Ser, J., Bennetot, A., Tabik, S., Barbado, A., Garcia, S., Gil-Lopez, S., Molina, D., Benjamins, R., Chatila, R., & Herrera, F. (2020). Explainable artificial intelligence (XAI): Concepts, taxonomies, opportunities and challenges toward responsible AI. *Information Fusion*, *58*, 82–115. https://doi.org/10.1016/j.inffus.2019.12.012

Auer, E. M. L. (2018). Detecting deceptive impression management behaviors in interviews using natural language processing [Master thesis, Old Dominion University]. Old Dominion University Digital Commons. https://digitalcommons.odu.edu/psychology_etds/70

Azucar, D., Marengo, D., & Settanni, M. (2018). Predicting the Big 5 personality traits from digital footprints on social media: A meta-analysis. *Personality and Individual Differences*, *124*(1), 150–159. https://doi.org/10.1016/j.paid.2017.12.018

Bambauer, J. R., & Zarsky, T. (2018). The algorithm game. *Notre Dame Law Review*, *94*, 1–48.

Bangerter, A., Roulin, N., & König, C. J. (2012). Personnel selection as a signaling game. *Journal of Applied Psychology*, *97*(4), 719–738. https://doi.org/10.1037/a0026078

Barrick, M. R., Mount, M. K., & Judge, T. A. (2001). Personality and performance at the beginning of the new millennium: What do we know and where do we go next? *International Journal of Selection and Assessment*, *9*(1), 9–30. https://doi.org/10.1111/1468-2389.00160

Birkeland, S. A., Manson, T. M., Kisamore, J. L., Brannick, M. T., & Smith, M. A. (2006). A meta-analytic investigation of job applicant faking on personality measures. *International Journal of Selection and Assessment*, *14*(4), 317–335. https://doi.org/10.1111/j.1468-2389.2006.00354.x

Bleidorn, W., & Hopwood, C. J. (2019). Using machine learning to advance personality assessment and theory. *Personality and Social Psychology Review*, *23*(2), 190–203. https://doi.org/10.1177/1088868318772990

Boyd, R. L., & Pennebaker, J. W. (2017). Language-based personality: A new approach to personality in a digital world. *Current Opinion in Behavioral Sciences*, *18*, 63–68. https://doi.org/10.1016/j.cobeha.2017.07.017

Burton, J. W., Stein, M.-K., & Jensen, T. B. (2020). A systematic review of algorithm aversion in augmented decision making. *Journal of Behavioral Decision Making*, *33*(2), 220–239. https://doi.org/10.1002/bdm.2155

Calanna, P., Lauriola, M., Saggino, A., Tommasi, M., & Furlan, S. (2020). Using a supervised machine learning algorithm for detecting faking good in a personality self-report. *International Journal of Selection and Assessment*, *28*(2), 176–185. https://doi.org/10.1111/ijsa.12279

Campion, M. C., Campion, M. A., Campion, E. D., & Reider, M. H. (2016). Initial investigation into computer scoring of candidate essays for personnel selection. *Journal of Applied Psychology*, *101*(7), 958–975. https://doi.org/10.1037/apl0000108

Cascio, W. F., & Boudreau, J. W. (2008). *Investing in people: Financial impact of human resource initiatives*. Pearson.

Chollet, M., Ochs, M., & Pelachaud, C. (2019). A methodology for the automatic extraction and generation of non-verbal signals sequences conveying interpersonal attitudes. *IEEE Transactions on Affective Computing*, *10*(4), 585–598. https://doi.org/10.1109/TAFFC.2017.2753777

Christensen, J. (2015). Recruitment and expertise in the European Commission. *West European Politics*, *38*(3), 649–678. https://doi.org/10.1080/01402382.2014.982353

Dastin, J. (2018, October 10). Amazon scraps secret AI recruiting tool that showed bias against women. https://www.reuters.com/article/us-amazon-com-jobs-automation-insight/amazon-scraps-secret-ai-recruiting-tool-that-showed-bias-against-women-idUSKCN1MK08G, accessed January 20, 2021.

David, C. B. (2018). Learning from artificial intelligence's previous awakenings: The history of expert systems. *AI Magazine*, *39*(3), 3–15. https://doi.org/10.1609/aimag.v39i3.2809

Dietvorst, B. J., Simmons, J. P., & Massey, C. (2015). Algorithm aversion: People erroneously avoid algorithms after seeing them err. *Journal of Experimental Psychology: General*, *144*(1), 114–126. https://doi.org/10.1037/xge0000033

Equal Employment Opportunity Commission, Civil Service Commission, Department of Labor, & Department of Justice. (1978). *Uniform guidelines on employee selection procedures*. Federal Register, *43*, 38290–39315.

Escalante, H. J., Kaya, H., Salah, A. A., Escalera, S., Güçlütürk, Y., Güçlü, U., Baró, X., Guyon, I., Jacques, J. C. S., Madadi, M., Ayache, S., Viegas, E., Gürpınar, F., Wicaksana, A. S., Liem, C. C. S., van Gerven, M. A. J., & van Lier, R. (2020). Modeling, recognizing, and explaining apparent personality from videos. *IEEE Transactions on Affective Computing*, advance online publication. https://doi.org/10.1109/TAFFC.2020.2973984

Feldkamp, T., Langer, M., König, C. J., & Wies, L. (2020, April). *A question of morality: Is there a double standard when it comes to algorithms?* [Poster presentation]. Annual Conference of the Society for Industrial and Organizational Psychology (SIOP), Austin, TX.

Gonzalez, M. F., Capman, J. F., Oswald, F. I., Theys, E. R., & Tomczak, D. L. (2019). "Where's the I-O?": Artificial intelligence and machine learning in talent management systems. *Personnel Assessment and Decisions*, *5*(3), 33–44. https://doi.org/10.25035/pad.2019.03.005

Goodman, B., & Flaxman, S. (2017). European Union regulations on algorithmic decision-making and a "right to explanation". *AI Magazine*, *38*(3), 50–57. https://doi.org/10.1609/aimag.v38i3.2741

Guerlain, S. A., Smith, P. J., Obradovich, J. H., Rudmann, S., Strohm, P., Smith, J. W., Svirbely, J., & Sachs, L. (1999). Interactive critiquing as a form of decision support: An empirical evaluation. *Human Factors*, *41*(1), 72–89. https://doi.org/10.1518/0018720099779577363

Henle, C. A., Dineen, B. R., & Duffy, M. K. (2019). Assessing intentional résumé deception: Development and nomological network of a résumé fraud measure. *Journal of Business and Psychology*, *34*(1), 87–106. https://doi.org/10.1007/s10869-017-9527-4

Highhouse, S. (2008). Stubborn reliance on intuition and subjectivity in employee selection. *Industrial and Organizational Psychology: Perspectives on Science and Practice*, *1*(3), 333 – 342. https://doi.org/10.1111/j.1754-9434.2008.00058.x

Horverak, J. G., Bye, H. H., Sandal, G. M., & Pallesen, S. (2013). Managers' evaluations of immigrant job applicants: The influence of acculturation strategy on perceived person–organization fit (P–O fit) and hiring outcome. *Journal of Cross-Cultural Psychology*, *44*(1), 46–60. https://doi.org/10.1177/0022022111430256

Ingold, P. V., Kleinmann, M., König, C. J., & Melchers, K. G. (2015). Shall we continue or stop disapproving of self-presentation? Evidence on impression management and faking in a selection context and their relation to job performance. *European Journal of Work and Organizational Psychology*, *24*(3), 420–432. https://doi.org/10.1080/1359432x.2014.915215

Jacobucci, R., & Grimm, K. J. (2020). Machine learning and psychological research: The unexplored effect of measurement. *Perspectives on Psychological Science*, *15*(3), 809–816. https://doi.org/10 .1177/1745691620902467

Joshi, P., Agarwal, A., Dhavale, A., Suryavanshi, R., & Kodolikar, S. (2015). Handwriting analysis for detection of personality traits using machine learning approach. *International Journal of Computer Applications*, *130*(15), 40–45. https://doi.org/10.5120/ijca2015907189

Kanning, U. P., Kraul, L.-F., & Litz, R. Z. (2019). Einstellungen zu digitalen Methoden der Personalauswahl [Attitudes towards digital methods for personnel selection]. *Journal of Business and Media Psychology*, *10*(1), 57–71.

Kellogg, K. C., Valentine, M. A., & Christin, A. (2020). Algorithms at work: The new contested terrain of control. *Academy of Management Annals*, *14*(1), 366–410. https://doi.org/10.5465/annals.2018 .0174

Kolk, N. J., Born, M. P., Van Der Flier, H., & Olman, J. M. (2002). Assessment center procedures: Cognitive load during the observation phase. *International Journal of Selection and Assessment*, *10*(4), 271–278. https://doi.org/10.1111/1468-2389.00217

König, C. J., Demetriou, A. M., Glock, P., Hiemstra, A. M. F., Iliescu, D., Ionescu, C., Langer, M., Liem, C. C. S., Linnenbürger, A., Siegel, R., & Vartholomaios, I. (2020). Some advice for psychologists who want to work with computer scientists on big data. *Personnel Assessment and Decisions*, *6*(1), 17–23. https://doi.org/10.25035/pad.2020.01.002

König, C. J., Jansen, A., & Lüscher Mathieu, P. (2017). What if applicants knew how personality tests are scored? A minimal intervention study. *Journal of Personnel Psychology*, *16*(4), 206–210. https:// doi.org/10.1027/1866-5888/a000183

Krumm, S., Lievens, F., Hüffmeier, J., Lipnevich, A. A., Bendels, H., & Hertel, G. (2015). How "situational" is judgment in situational judgment tests? *Journal of Applied Psychology*, *100*(2), 399–416. https://doi.org/10.1037/a0037674

Langer, M., Baum, K., Hähne, V., König, C. J., Oster, D., & Speith, T. (2021). Spare me the details: How the type of information about automated interviews influences applicant reactions. *International Journal of Selection and Assessment*, *29*(2), 154–169. https://doi.org/10.1111/ijsa.12325

Langer, M., König, C. J., & Busch, V. (2021). Changing the means of management decisions: Effects of automated decision-support systems on personnel selection tasks. *Journal of Business and Psychology*, *36*(5), 751–769. https://doi.org/10.1007/s10869-020-09711-6

Langer, M., König, C. J., & Fitili, A. (2018). Information as a double-edged sword: The role of computer experience and information on applicant reactions towards novel technologies for personnel selection. *Computers in Human Behavior*, *81*, 19–30. https://doi.org/10.1016/j.chb.2017.11.036

Langer, M., König, C. J., & Hemsing, V. (2020). Is anybody listening? The impact of automatically evaluated job interviews on impression management and applicant reactions. *Journal of Managerial Psychology*, *35*(4), 271–284. https://doi.org/10.1108/JMP-03-2019-0156

Langer, M., König, C. J., & Krause, K. (2017). Examining digital interviews for personnel selection: Applicant reactions and interviewer ratings. *International Journal of Selection and Assessment*, *25*(4), 371–382. https://doi.org/10.1111/ijsa.12191

Langer, M., König, C. J., & Papathanasiou, M. (2019). Highly automated job interviews: Acceptance under the influence of stakes. *International Journal of Selection and Assessment*, *27*(3), 217–234. https://doi.org/10.1111/ijsa.12246

Langer, M., König, C. J., Sanchez, D. R.-P., & Samadi, S. (2020). Highly automated interviews: Applicant reactions and the organizational context. *Journal of Managerial Psychology*, *35*(4), 301–314. https://doi.org/10.1108/JMP-03-2018-0402

Langer, M., König, C. J., & Scheuss, A. I. (2019). Love the way you lie: Hiring managers' impression management in company presentation videos. *Journal of Personnel Psychology*, *18*(2), 84–94. https:// doi.org/10.1027/1866-5888/a000225

Langer, M., Oster, D., Speith, T., Kästner, L., Baum, K., Hermanns, H., Schmidt, E., & Sesing, A. (2021). What do we want from explainable artificial intelligence (XAI)? A stakeholder perspective on XAI and a conceptual model guiding interdisciplinary XAI research. *Artificial Intelligence*, *296*, Article 103473. https://doi.org/10.1016/j.artint.2021.103473

Langer, M., Schmid Mast, M., Meyer, B., Maass, W., & König, C. J. (2019). Research in the era of sensing technologies and wearables. In R. Landers (Ed.), *The Cambridge handbook of technology and employee behavior* (pp. 806–835). Cambridge University Press.

Lee, M. K. (2018). Understanding perception of algorithmic decisions: Fairness, trust, and emotion in response to algorithmic management. *Big Data and Society, 5*(1). https://doi.org/10.1177/2053951718756684

Lipton, Z. C. (2018). The mythos of model interpretability. *Communication of the ACM, 61*(10), 36–43. https://doi.org/10.1145/3233231

Logg, J. M., Minson, J. A., & Moore, D. A. (2019). Algorithm appreciation: People prefer algorithmic to human judgment. *Organizational Behavior and Human Decision Processes, 151*, 90–103. https://doi.org/10.1016/j.obhdp.2018.12.005

McFarland, L. A., Ryan, A. M., & Kriska, S. D. (2003). Impression management use and effectiveness across assessment methods. *Journal of Management, 29*(5), 641–661. https://doi.org/10.1016/S0149-2063_03_00030-8

Mehta, Y., Majumder, N., Gelbukh, A., & Cambria, E. (2020). Recent trends in deep learning based personality detection. *Artificial Intelligence Review, 53*(4), 2313–2339. https://doi.org/10.1007/s10462-019-09770-z

Melchers, K. G., Roulin, N., & Buehl, A.-K. (2020). A review of applicant faking in selection interviews. *International Journal of Selection and Assessment, 28*(2), 123–142. https://doi.org/10.1111/ijsa.12280

Mirowska, A. (2020). AI evaluation in selection: Effects on application and pursuit intentions. *Journal of Personnel Psychology, 19*(3), 142–149. https://doi.org/10.1027/1866-5888/a000258

Mohammadi, G., & Vinciarelli, A. (2012). Automatic personality perception: Prediction of trait attribution based on prosodic features. *IEEE Transactions on Affective Computing, 3*(3), 273–284. https://doi.org/10.1109/T-AFFC.2012.5

Naim, I., Tanveer, M. I., Gildea, D., & Hoque, M. E. (2018). Automated analysis and prediction of job interview performance. *IEEE Transactions on Affective Computing, 9*(2), 191–204. https://doi.org/10.1109/TAFFC.2016.2614299

Newby-Clark, I. R., Ross, M., Buehler, R., Koehler, D. J., & Griffin, D. (2000). People focus on optimistic scenarios and disregard pessimistic scenarios while predicting task completion times. *Journal of Experimental Psychology: Applied, 6*, 171–182. https://doi.org/10.1037/1076-898X.6.3.171

Newman, D. T., Fast, N. J., & Harmon, D. J. (2020). When eliminating bias isn't fair: Algorithmic reductionism and procedural justice in human resource decisions. *Organizational Behavior and Human Decision Processes, 160*, 149–167. https://doi.org/10.1016/j.obhdp.2020.03.008

Nguyen, L. S., Frauendorfer, D., Schmid Mast, M., & Gatica-Perez, D. (2014). Hire me: Computational inference of hirability in employment interviews based on nonverbal behavior. *IEEE Transactions on Multimedia, 16*(4), 1018–1031. https://doi.org/10.1109/TMM.2014.2307169

Nolan, K. P., Carter, N. T., & Dalal, D. K. (2016). Threat of technological unemployment: Are hiring managers discounted for using standardized employee selection practices? *Personnel Assessment and Decisions, 2*(1), 30–47. https://doi.org/10.25035/pad.2016.004

O'Neil, C. (2016). *Weapons of math destruction: How big data increases inequality and threatens democracy.* Crown Publishing Group.

Oswald, F. L., Behrend, T. S., Putka, D. J., & Sinar, E. (2020). Big data in industrial-organizational psychology and human resource management: Forward progress for organizational research and practice. *Annual Review of Organizational Psychology and Organizational Behavior, 7*, 505–533. https://doi.org/10.1146/annurev-orgpsych-032117-104553

Parasuraman, R., & Manzey, D. H. (2010). Complacency and bias in human use of automation: An attentional integration. *Human Factors, 52*(3), 381–410. https://doi.org/10.1177/0018720810376055

Parasuraman, R., & Riley, V. (1997). Humans and automation: Use, misuse, disuse, abuse. *Human Factors, 39*(2), 230–253. https://doi.org/10.1518/001872097778543886

Pecena, Y., Keye, D., Conzelmann, K., Grasshoff, D., Maschke, P., Heintz, A., & Eißfeldt, H. (2013). Predictive validity of a selection procedure for air traffic controller trainees. *Aviation Psychology and Applied Human Factors, 3*(1), 19–27. https://doi.org/10.1027/2192-0923/a000039

Peeters, H., & Lievens, F. (2005). Situational judgment tests and their predictiveness of college students' success: The influence of faking. *Educational and Psychological Measurement, 65*(1), 70–89. https://doi.org/10.1177/0013164404268672

Pianesi, F., Mana, N., Cappelletti, A., Lepri, B., & Zancanaro, M. (2008). Multimodal recognition of personality traits in social interactions. In *Proceedings of the 10th International Conference on Multimodal Interfaces* (pp. 53–60). ACM. https://doi.org/10.1145/1452392.1452404

Ployhart, R. E., & Holtz, B. C. (2008). The diversity-validity dilemma: Strategies for reducing racioethnic and sex subgroup differences and adverse impact in selection. *Personnel Psychology*, *61*(1), 153–172. https://doi.org/10.1111/j.1744-6570.2008.00109.x

Putka, D. J., Beatty, A. S., & Reeder, M. C. (2018). Modern prediction methods: New perspectives on a common problem. *Organizational Research Methods*, *21*(3), 689–732. https://doi.org/10.1177/1094428117697041

Raghavan, M., Barocas, S., Kleinberg, J., & Levy, K. (2020). Mitigating bias in algorithmic hiring: Evaluating claims and practices. In M. Hildebrandt & C. Castillo (Eds.), *Proceedings of the ACM Conference on Fairness, Accountability, and Transparency (FAT*'20)* (pp. 469–481). ACM. https://doi.org/10.2139/ssrn.3408010

Raisch, S., & Krakowski, S. (2021). Artificial intelligence and management: The automation–augmentation paradox. *Academy of Management Review*, *46*(1), 192–210. https://doi.org/10.5465/2018.0072

Rasipuram, S., & Jayagopi, D. B. (2018). Automatic assessment of communication skill in interview-based interactions. *Multimedia Tools and Applications*, *77*(14), 18709–18739. https://doi.org/10.1007/s11042-018-5654-9

Rasipuram, S., & Jayagopi, D. B. (2019). A comprehensive evaluation of audio-visual behavior in various modes of interviews in the wild. In *Proceedings of the 12th ACM International Conference on Pervasive Technologies Related to Assistive Environments* (pp. 94–100). ACM. https://doi.org/10.1145/3316782.3321528

Sackett, P. R., Shewach, O. R., & Keiser, H. N. (2017). Assessment centers versus cognitive ability tests: Challenging the conventional wisdom on criterion-related validity. *Journal of Applied Psychology*, *102*(10), 1435–1447. https://doi.org/10.1037/apl0000236

Sajjadiani, S., Sojourner, A. J., Kammeyer-Mueller, J. D., & Mykerezi, E. (2019). Using machine learning to translate applicant work history into predictors of performance and turnover. *Journal of Applied Psychology*, *104*(10), 1207–1225. https://doi.org/10.1037/apl0000405

Salgado, J. F., & Táuriz, G. (2014). The Five-Factor Model, forced-choice personality inventories and performance: A comprehensive meta-analysis of academic and occupational validity studies. *European Journal of Work and Organizational Psychology*, *23*(1), 3–30. https://doi.org/10.1080/1359432X.2012.716198

Schlicker, N., Langer, M., Ötting, S. K., Baum, K., König, C. J., & Wallach, D. (2021). What to expect from opening up "black boxes"? Comparing perceptions of justice between humans and automated agents. Computers in Human Behavior, 122, 106837. https://doi.org/10.1016/j.chb.2021.106837.

Schmid Mast, M., Frauendorfer, D., Gatica-Perez, D., Choudhury, T., & Odobez, J.-M. (2017). *A step towards automatic applicant selection: Predicting job performance based on applicant nonverbal interview behavior* [Unpublished manuscript]. Université de Lausanne, Switzerland.

Suen, H.-Y., Chen, M. Y.-C., & Lu, S.-H. (2019). Does the use of synchrony and artificial intelligence in video interviews affect interview ratings and applicant attitudes? *Computers in Human Behavior*, *98*, 93–101. https://doi.org/10.1016/j.chb.2019.04.012

Suen, H.-Y., Hung, K.-E., & Lin, C.-L. (2020). Intelligent video interview agent used to predict communication skill and perceived personality traits. *Human-centric Computing and Information Sciences*, *10*(1), Article 3. https://doi.org/10.1186/s13673-020-0208-3

Theobald, O. (2017). *Machine learning for absolute beginners* (2nd ed.). Scatterplot Press.

Truxillo, D. M., Bodner, T. E., Bertolino, M., Bauer, T. N., & Yonce, C. A. (2009). Effects of explanations on applicant reactions: A meta-analytic review. *International Journal of Selection and Assessment*, *17*(4), 346–361. https://doi.org/10.1111/j.1468-2389.2009.00478.x

Tskhay, K. O., & Rule, N. O. (2014). Perceptions of personality in text-based media and OSN: A meta-analysis. *Journal of Research in Personality*, *49*(1), 25–30. https://doi.org/10.1016/j.jrp.2013.12.004

Turney, P. D., & Pantel, P. (2010). From frequency to meaning: Vector space models of semantics. *Journal of Artificial Intelligence Research*, *37*, 141–188. https://doi.org/10.1613/jair.2934

van Dongen, K., & van Maanen, P.-P. (2013). A framework for explaining reliance on decision aids. *International Journal of Human-Computer Studies, 71*(4), 410–424. https://doi.org/10.1016/j.ijhcs.2012.10.018

Veale, M., & Binns, R. (2017). Fairer machine learning in the real world: Mitigating discrimination without collecting sensitive data. *Big Data and Society, 4*(2). https://doi.org/10.1177/2053951717743530

Zerilli, J., Knott, A., Maclaurin, J., & Gavaghan, C. (2019). Transparency in algorithmic and human decision-making: Is there a double standard? *Philosophy and Technology, 32*(4), 661–683. https://doi.org/10.1007/s13347-018-0330-6

Zhang, C.-L., Zhang, H., Wei, X.-S., & Wu, J. (2016). Deep bimodal regression for apparent personality analysis. In G. Hua & H. Jégou (Eds.), *Computer Vision – ECCV 2016 Workshops* (pp. 311–324). Springer. https://doi.org/10.1007/978-3-319-49409-8_25

PART I.2

FURTHER APPLICATIONS OF ARTIFICIAL INTELLIGENCE IN HUMAN RESOURCES

9. HR knowledge representation and reasoning
Jorge Martinez-Gil

INTRODUCTION

In the human resources industry, one of the most important aspects is usually the management of the right personnel to carry out the operational, tactical, and strategic aspects of the activity that organizations carry out. Therefore, it seems clear that choosing and hiring the right people from the wide and heterogeneous range of candidates that is usually available might be of vital importance for the future success of the organizations that need them. This usually means that a process that could perform a proper brokerage between employers and potential workers could be of high interest for a number of organizations. But human resources processes do not end there, since after recruitment, a period of monitoring and management of the employees begins in order to obtain the best possible performance aligned with the interests of the organizations for which they work.

Advances in both basic and applied research in fields such as knowledge representation and automated reasoning open up a wide range of possibilities for the human resources industry to automate and optimize most of its processes. For instance, knowledge representation is a discipline that tries to study how to represent the information necessary for a computational system to solve complex tasks in a way analogous to how a person would do it. For this reason, this discipline is of fundamental importance for producing new results in the field of human resources. Moreover, this discipline complements perfectly that of automated reasoning, which seeks to enable computers to reason autonomously. Reasoning is understood as the ability to issue a conclusion from a set of ideas or concepts known in advance.

In the context of this work, we focus mainly on the automation of recruitment processes. These processes are the ones that attract the most attention from both academia and industry because they are scientifically and technically challenging and are the ones that the market demands. This is not to say that other processes are not interesting. For example, the ability to reason about which training courses are the most beneficial for the employees that the organization already has can result in improvements in the quality of life and comfort of the employees (Martinez-Gil & Freudenthaler, 2019). However, most of these processes are purely administrative, have a medium or low technical complexity, and do not represent a competitive activity to achieve a certain accomplishment. Therefore, science and industry allocate a large part of their resources to solutions with the ability to recruit people with the most suitable profiles.

Throughout this work, we will adopt an eminently technical approach. In fact, we focus on knowledge representation approaches providing a formal specification of a knowledge domain using knowledge bases in the form of ontologies or simply ontologies to represent entities, properties, relations, and the underlying rules of that domain. The requirements of the knowledge modeling have to be formally specified. A notation has to follow a logical specification using propositional expressions and symbolical structures, such as tree-like structures, concepts, operations, and axioms. Moreover, the constructs must be interpretable as propositions, and they should clearly reflect the domain theory.

To do that, most researchers and practitioners consider Description Logics (DL), which are logics serving primarily as formal description of concepts and roles. These logics were created from the attempts to formalize semantic networks and frame-based systems. Semantically they are founded on predicate logic, but their language is formed so that it would be enough for practical modeling purposes and so that the logic would have good computational properties such as decidability.

The other fundamental piece is the structured representation of the information, as well as the curated sources to which we can go to obtain it. The reason is that from the knowledge represented on these knowledge bases, it is possible to answer questions and, through reasoning, acquire new knowledge. These knowledge bases are generated according to ontologies and collect structured knowledge of a specific domain. In this way, there are knowledge bases such as Wordnet,[1] which represents concepts that are similar to others on a semantic level (synonyms), or concepts that are contained in other concepts. It is important to remark that the use of ontologies as knowledge models is very convenient since it brings several advantages. Some of the more obvious ones focus on, but are not limited to, the field of recruitment systems. Let us enumerate the advantages of using ontologies from a scientific point of view:

- It avoids the problem of semantic heterogeneity since both the employer and the candidate are obliged to use a shared vocabulary that ensures consistency.
- It allows the validation of the information presented since it is possible to determine if inconsistencies are found in the data provided by both the employer and the potential employee.
- It allows for automatic processing by a computer. Although recently the techniques for processing natural language have improved a lot, they are still unable to understand the meaning of going beyond what is written.
- It allows making inferences to find out information that was expressed implicitly, but not explicitly. Through some reasoning mechanisms, this kind of implicit information can emerge.
- It facilitates interoperability between different databases and information systems, as long as all the information represented refers to ontologies or knowledge models that are public.
- It facilitates the design and execution of a large number of queries that are not possible with traditional processes. For example, it is possible to consult programmers who know object-oriented programming and the query can return people with knowledge of Java, C++, and so on, or musicians who can play string instruments and the query can return people with knowledge of the guitar, violin, harp, and so on.

Apart from the purely scientific and technological benefits that ontologies bring, there are also practical and measurable advantages for the industry that can be objectively measured in the form of Key Performance Indicators (KPIs). For example, it is widely agreed that automatic matching algorithms between job and candidate profiles are able to provide a technology of high impact for organizations with hiring needs (Bizer et al., 2005). Therefore, the contribution of this work focuses on offering an overview of the state of the art as well as the future challenges related to the use of knowledge representation techniques in the form of ontologies by the human resources industry.

The rest of this chapter is structured as follows: In the second section we introduce the state of the art regarding the use of knowledge representation and reasoning in the domain of human resources. In the third section we introduce our contribution. In the fourth section we offer an overview of the future challenges that need to be faced. Finally, we remark on the major conclusions that can be extracted from this work.

STATE OF THE ART

As one of the most important processes in the world of human resources, there have been many attempts to automate and optimize recruitment processes. This process, until now, has usually consisted of manual and individual evaluation of each of the candidates who have been interested in the job offer. This often represents a great waste of resources in terms of time, money, and effort and is subject to numerous human errors. As a result, a scenario often occurs that is not optimal for either the organization seeking to hire or the candidate seeking to be hired. Therefore, such recruitment processes are the ideal candidates to be digitized and optimized (Martinez-Gil, 2014).

For example, given a job offer that describes the requirements necessary to perform the job, the problem that a human resources expert has to solve is to identify the best candidate among all those who have applied for the job (Colucci et al., 2003). Therefore, it makes sense to have decision support tools that help identify for the human resources experts the applications that have the most words in common with the initially published offer (Mochol et al., 2007). It is obvious that the method has some disadvantages, but those disadvantages lose their importance because the candidates will be contacted one by one to gather additional information before making a decision. Therefore, although the method may seem simple at first, and it is easy to find situations in which it would fail, it is no less true that the method usually works well in a reasonable majority of cases and is, therefore, one of the most widely used in the human resources industry.

This is the major reason why, in general, problems of this kind have been usually based in classical methods, for example keyword search methods used across documents representing job offers or applicant profiles with keywords characterizing the open position or job seeker, respectively. In recent years, there have also been solutions based on machine and deep learning (Boselli et al., 2017). Solutions of this kind are dominant in research today. The truth is that the results that these techniques usually achieve are good (Pessach et al., 2020). However, these methods are usually considered to be black-box models, that is, it is possible to provide some input and get some output, but it is not usually possible for a person to understand what has happened during the process, mainly because models with tens of thousands of nodes and interconnections between them are difficult to interpret by humans.

For this reason, some scientists and practitioners have focused on the issue of handling structured data in both private and public organizations, and the ontology-based solutions to deal with it is a recurring topic in the literature. In the specific case of human resource data, the proposed solutions are mainly related to the extraction of information from candidates' profiles and ontology-based information extraction systems for matching résumés to job openings.

Some of the most popular techniques for performing automated reasoning are classical logics and calculi, fuzzy logics, Bayesian inference, and description logics. In this chapter, we focus on the last of these, since the OWL-2 standard (Grau et al., 2008) has made it one of the most popular approaches in the domain of modern information systems. Moreover, we do it through the conceptualization and linking of entities using ontologies. This brings basic advantages over other statistically based methods.

One of the reasons for that is that ontological methods can successfully replace methods based on keyword search. For example, there is no need to convert the raw data, that is, the texts of job offers or applicant profiles, into a structured form to be able to apply the automated matching (Faliagka et al., 2014). On the other hand, the classical methods require hard coding of similarity between key notions into the underlying feature space, which is error-prone and hard to maintain given changes and extensions that occur because the job market is a very flexible field, where job titles, skill and education concepts, and general terminology are subject to permanent change.

Knowledge bases in the form of ontologies have been used in the field of knowledge representation for decades. The rationale behind this approach is to take a fraction of first-order logic for which implication is decidable. The most common form adopted is to focus on unary and binary predicates known as concepts and roles and to permit a limited set of constructors for them (Cali et al., 2004b). Then the terminological layer (TBox) is defined by axioms usually expressing implication between concepts. In addition, an assertional layer (ABox) is defined by instances of the TBox satisfying the axioms. The different description logics differ mainly by their expressiveness. A prominent representative of the family of description logics is $SROIQ(D)$, which establishes the formal basis of the web ontology language OWL-2 (Grau et al., 2008), and is one of the more expressive description logics.

Moreover, $SROIQ(D)$ is a great facilitator of reasoning, that is, extracting logical consequences from a set of asserted facts or axioms (Cali et al., 2004a). The notion of reasoning generalizes the concept of inference, by providing a richer set of mechanisms to work with. It is necessary to use a formal specification in order to be able to perform automated reasoning on ontologies. By reasoning, it is possible to make explicit facts that are not already explicitly expressed in the ontology. Some of the facts that can be automatically derived by means of a reasoner could be (Martinez-Gil, 2015):

* Determine the satisfiability of a concept so that a given concept description is not contradictory;
* Determine the subsumption of concepts so that a given concept subsumes another concept;
* Determine the consistency of ABox for TBox so that individuals in ABox might not violate descriptions and axioms stated in the TBox;
* Determine if any given individual is an instance of a concept;
* Determine all individuals that are instances of a concept;
* Determine all concepts which the individual belongs to, with special interest for the most specific ones.

All these operations can be performed at the document level, making it easier to obtain valuable knowledge for decision-making. This ability to bring out knowledge that was implicit is undoubtedly the great advantage of this type of approach and contrasts sharply with the classical statistical techniques that fail to apply logic in the same way that people do.

Description Logics and Reasoning

In general, a description logic is a fragment of first-order logic restricted to unary and binary predicate symbols (concepts and roles) that are subject to definitions exploiting intersection (conjunction), union (disjunction), and negation as well as universal and existential restrictions for the roles (Cali et al., 2004a). The key idea is to support terminological knowledge through theories that consist of subsumption statements (i.e. implication) for concept terms. The main differences between the various description logics concern their expressiveness, that is, which constructs are supported in the language for concept terms. The key idea is to ensure that subsumption will always remain decidable because in this way it is possible to add definitions for named concepts and to infer all implied subsumption relations.

Most of the existing approaches rely on the description logic $SROIQ(D)$, which is the formal description logic underlying the web ontology language OWL-2. As such it has received a lot of attention, and many implementations exist that can be used. It already supports role chains, nominals to refer to individual values, inverse roles, qualified cardinality restrictions, and datatypes. This way of modeling knowledge is used to define in detail recruitment concepts, in particular those appearing in commonly used taxonomies. For instance, an aggregate skill (programming language, version, experience, context, complexity) could give rise to a concept "aggregate skill" with five roles associating the facets "programming language", "version", and so on with it. Alternatively, "version" might be associated with "programming language", in which case role concatenation would be required for the definition of the aggregate skill. All these alternatives will lead to mapping rules from aggregate descriptions to subsumption and equivalence axioms.

$SROIQ(D)$ could further be used as the syntactical basis for the development of the tools. For this first "blow-up" operators are defined that remove roles and substitute them with subconcepts, that is, additional subsumption axioms. For instance, for an aggregate skill with "programming language" and "experience" we may introduce "programming language with one year's experience", "programming language with two years' experience", and so on, that is, instead of exploiting the roles we would use a (theoretically infinite) collection of subconcepts. In this way, a profile in the knowledge base could again be defined by a filter in the lattice resulting from the blow-up operators. This is needed to make the knowledge base concepts and their instances usable by matching queries. Second, this can be used to re-transform such definitions of profiles into high-level aggregate-based definitions.

Moreover, it is necessary to remark that reasoning algorithms are an inseparable part of any ontology or description logics. In fact, without reasoners, an ontology would be merely a data model, where it is left to the users to define which concept an individual belongs to. Any implementation of an ontology has at its core an implementation of reasoning algorithms.

The reasoners that we refer to in this chapter are grounded in the decidability of subsumption. If we start from a defined concept, that is, axioms *subs(C,exp)* and *subs(exp,C)* for a concept name C and a concept term *exp*, the task of the reasoner is to infer all valid subsumption relations *subs(C,D)* and *subs(D,C)* for other concept names D in the TBox. In other words, the concept will be "properly placed" within the subsumption hierarchy of the TBox. The task of the reasoner is to infer for a given individual an all valid relationship *inst(a,D)* for concepts D in the TBox, that is, the individual will be "properly classified" into the ABox.

Using $SROIQ(D)$ allows working with the reasoning algorithms for concepts and instances of this description logic, and the solutions usually exploit existing implementations of these algorithms. As reasoning algorithms use the given subsumption axioms to derive complete descriptions for named concepts, the solutions intend to extend this completion to the aggregate concepts that are added on top of the description logic. This leads to extended aggregate definitions exploiting the fact that the tools developed enable re-transformations into aggregate-based descriptions. Moreover, the extensions do not alter the expressiveness of the ontology, so the extensions to the algorithms are only needed for reasons of complexity. Therefore, the complexity of the direct classification including the use of aggregates and the indirect way using only the underlying descriptions and the transformation and re-transformation tools are usually aspects to consider.

Knowledge Sources

On the other hand, it is well known that most ontology-based systems suffer from the so-called knowledge acquisition bottleneck, which is to say it is difficult to model the knowledge relevant for the domain in question. Therefore, this kind of development is known to be a hard and time-consuming task. However, solutions of this kind need to use knowledge sources to perform their operations. Fortunately, today there are many sources of knowledge that can be used by the human resources industry. Below, we offer a small overview.

- DISCO, which stands for European DIctionary of Skills and COmpetences, is an online thesaurus that currently covers more than 100,000 skills and competence terms and approximately 36,000 example phrases. This thesaurus is available in many European languages, and it is one of the largest collections of its kind in the education and labor market.
- ISCED, that stands for International Standard Classification of Education, is a statistical instrument that increases the international comparability of qualifications. The structures of education systems vary between countries and can therefore be compared only with difficulty in many cases. ISCED helps educational researchers and educational policymakers compare, analyze, and enhance the education systems in the OECD area.
- ESCO is a classification schema for European Skills, Competences, Qualifications, and Occupations developed in a number of different languages. ESCO aims to identify those skills, competences, qualifications, and occupations that are of high relevance for the European labor market as well as for education and training activities.

It is also possible to use other ontologies that, although smaller, are a very rich source of information oriented to much more specific domains. A very clear example is, among others, the ACM Computing Classification System,[2] which is a hierarchical ontology that could be used in specific domains related to computing.

Systems

Most of the systems implement some kind of feature vectors, weighted means, keyword-based search, assessment based on recall and precision. In case of non-suitable highly ranked profiles, human expertise can be used to correct inaccuracies. The problem with these techniques is that they are not suited for dealing with incomplete information usually present in scenarios of this kind. In fact, information about profiles is not always complete, not only because some information is unavailable, but also because either the employer or the applicant considers some details irrelevant. Trying to force to the use of an interface for entering profiles, with long and tedious forms to be filled in, is the solution most often adopted for this problem.

Here, we will talk about existing systems. The customers who use systems of this kind are, on the one hand, recruiters and job portals, either for their own use or to provide access for their customers as well as human resources managers in personnel-seeking companies, and, on the other hand, job seekers, unemployed persons, change-oriented persons, and persons who want to start their own business because of their expertise.

The matching between job openings and job applications has been extensively addressed in the literature. The most important research question is to see if a more realistic technology could be built (Maree et al., 2019). In this context, the big industrial players do not usually publish details about their systems, but some examples of systems or at least prototypes can be found in the literature. For example, Färber et al. (2003) presented an automated recommendation approach for the selection of employees; Seta et al. (2005) proposed an ontological model for the evaluation of IT skills; and García-Sánchez et al. (2006) proposed an additional ontology-based intelligent system for e-recruitment. Besides these, Malinowski et al. (2006) considered a bilateral approach for automated matching. At the same time, Radevski and Trichet (2006) introduced two novel ontology-based decision support systems. Some years after, Ramli et al. (2010) proposed a new decision support system with improved functionality. Faliagka et al. (2012) built a system for recruiting and ranking job applicants in online recruitment systems, with the objective to automate the pre-screening procedure. Senthil Kumaran and Sankar (2013) have developed an automated system for intelligent screening of candidates for recruitment using ontology matching techniques. Poch et al. (2014) have designed a new ranking tool for the human resources industry. Finally, Alamro et al. (2018) have recently presented a conceptual model based on an ontology for Enterprise e-Recruitment and Sandanayake et al. (2018) have proposed a novel ranking tool for ordering the results of the matching.

Interpretability, Fairness, and Bias Avoidance

In recent times, the human resources industry has begun to pay close attention to combating practices that promote discrimination against candidates on grounds beyond those that are strictly professional (Thielsch et al., 2012). The fight against these corporate biases is currently based on protocols that have been manually compiled, and whose implementation is at the discretion of recruiters. Most of the suggested actions are related to the way in which job offers should be prepared, that is, using gender-neutral titles, being careful with the choice of personal pronouns, and so on.

In this context, the industry has also begun to realize that one of the advantages with greater potential is that working with ontologies is gender relevant because some groups of people are in a disadvantaged position with respect to labor market participation and showing their skills and competences acquired through non-formal and informal learning over the life-course. For example, when women leave the labor market due to childbirth and childcare, they run more risks than men with respect to atrophy of their human capital even though they acquire new skills and competences during this time. Therefore, when women enter the second stage of their labor market career, they run a greater risk than men of being at a disadvantage. The use of ontologies usually brings a number of advantages in relation to gender-relevant aspects. They:

- Support gender equality through a gender-neutral recruitment process by using new technologies for ranking of candidates based on information retrieved from CVs irrespective of the person's gender, ethnicity, and so on. Besides this, years of experience can be additionally associated with a particular skill to further include information on the level of experience and performance for specific skills.
- Support gender equality through taking into account gender-neutral terminology used in the recruitment process. Terminology is crucial with regard to gender equality, not only with regard to the existing legal regulations for occupation names that have to be applied in job advertisements and in the recruiting process, but also with regard to the expression of job titles, skills and competence descriptions, and so on and the overall skills profiling of candidates.
- Support gender equality through shifting the focus to a competence orientation: ontologies support gender equality in recruiting by shifting the focus from more occupations and qualification requirements to acquired skills and competences (no matter if they have been acquired formally, non-formally, or informally). By following a more user-centric viewpoint and placing a stronger focus on the best matching of competences, solutions of this kind contribute to a more competence orientation in recruiting and thus to better and equal opportunities for job candidates irrespective of the person's gender, ethnicity, and so on.

Using ontologies facilitates a common umbrella for recruitment knowledge bases that can be exploited with matching, querying engines, and knowledge extraction tools. All the inputs, that is, curricula vitae and job offer descriptions, will be represented by gender-neutral formulations, as is the case with their representation in the knowledge base. As a result, software solutions are able to mediate between the domain-specific view of the recruiting experts, the capabilities of the underlying description logic, and the needs of the matching algorithms. Therefore, gender-neutral recruitment can also be supported through the knowledge-based approach to the problem of accurate mediation between open employment offers and suitable candidates.

In addition, it is widely assumed that in order for these kinds of systems to gain a wider acceptance among the public, it would be necessary to implement capabilities to deliver good explanations of their results to the people that use them. This information should be provided clearly and concisely so that there is no space for any kind of misunderstanding. In this context, it should be noted that ontology-based solutions have clear advantages over most other approaches, both in terms of interpretability (i.e. how a model makes the decisions it does) and in terms of explainability (i.e. why a given model makes that decision). Although it is true that some of the existing techniques in the field of machine learning have high degrees of interpretability, research based on architectures of a neural nature has a large gap to fill in this regard.

USE OF ONTOLOGIES IN THE HUMAN RESOURCES INDUSTRY

Most of the existing approaches focus on a knowledge-based approach centered on a solution that captures the terminology used for recruitment as well as assertional profiles for job and candidate descriptions. Such a knowledge base requires the definition of an ontology, that is, both a language that can be used to define the terminological concepts and their dependencies as well as the assertional profiles, and efficient classification algorithms (Martinez-Gil et al., 2016a). Most of the solutions try to exploit the capabilities offered by description logics to capture the terminology used in recruitment applications, but existing frameworks such as DISCO, ISCED, ESCO, and so on that are meant to capture skill concepts only support taxonomies or tree-like structures.

Formally, concepts are interpreted as subsets of a domain and roles as binary relations over the domain, and all constructors are equipped with precise set-theoric semantics. The most common constructors include Boolean operators on concepts and quantification over roles. Other constructors that can be considered important include more general forms of quantification, number restrictions, which allow one to state limits on the number of connections that an individual may have via a certain role, and constructors on roles, such as intersection, concatenation, and inverse. The main difference to databases is focused on decidability of implication, that is, automatic classification.

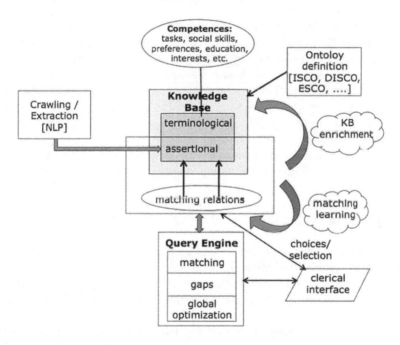

Figure 9.1   *Description of a human resource management system making use of techniques based on knowledge representation*

Figure 9.1 shows us an example of a typical solution for the human resources industry making use of ontologies. The three most popular approaches include capabilities for matching, querying, and learning (Martinez-Gil et al., 2016b). However, as we have already mentioned, no rich ontologies for recruitment purposes exist currently. This means that, to date, only taxonomies are supported (no roles, no fine-tuned descriptions, no classification, but fixed hierarchies), and there is no support for complex structures (needed for tasks, fine-tuned skills, personal characteristics, etc.), nor for making inferences, and so on. The limitations of taxonomies, in general, become obvious as soon as one tries to describe a specific relation between two concepts: "Microsoft" is not only "related" to "SQL Server", it is the "creator of" this certain software product. Therefore, it is necessary to extend the use of two concepts ("Creator" and "Software Product") and the property "creator of", which is the inverse of "created by", to reflect real relations between concepts.

Most of the approaches try to implement some kind of knowledge base capturing the terminology used for recruitment, such that all job and candidate descriptions can be represented by assertional profiles in an adequate knowledge base. As indicated above, matching can be based on likeliness measures defined on filters in knowledge bases. The advantage of these approaches is the flexibility in the matching relations and the perspective that automatic concept classification can be supported by knowledge base technology, that is, the maintenance of terminology will be greatly eased. On the other hand, however, an ontology-based approach requires the definition of an ontology, that is, both a language that can be used to define the terminological concepts and their dependencies as well as the assertional profiles, and efficient classification algorithms.

To the best of our knowledge, no satisfactory set-up of a knowledge base for job recruitment exists. This means that existing frameworks that are meant to capture skill concepts do not fully exploit the opportunities offered by ontologies and their underlying description logics (Gómez-Pérez et al., 2007). Currently, these frameworks only support taxonomies, that is, they merely exploit concept subsumption in ontologies, whereas roles that can be used to fine-tune the description are not supported. Therefore, scientists and practitioners are currently looking for ways to fully exploit the capabilities by means of the widely used ontology language OWL-2 (Martinez-Gil et al., 2018b). The goal is to capture the terminology used in recruitment applications, for example to associate the years of experience with a particular skill such as programming with a particular programming language or assessing marketing studies with a particular tool.

Filter-Based Matching

One of the most common approaches for matching between job offers and potential candidates often uses ontologies, which in addition to storage also facilitates the automated reasoning and classification as we have already seen. In this way, new terminology can be easily integrated and defined in terms of existing concepts and notions without affecting previous matching relationships.

The idea consists of exploiting the underlying lattice structure of the knowledge bases, that is, the partial order of concepts representing competences. For example, a skill such as Java knowledge is much more detailed than programming knowledge. Therefore, profiles are defined through filters, that is, knowledge of C implies knowledge of programming as well.

Filter-based matching benefits from partially ordered sets. The idea is simple: Given two filters F1 and F2 (representing a job opening and a candidate profile respectively), it is possible to calculate the matching value as follows:

$$m(F1, F2) = \frac{\#(F1 \cap F2)}{\#F2}$$

That is, the matching value can be calculated simply by counting the elements that both filters have in common in relation to one of the two filters (depending on whether the evaluation is done from the viewpoint of the employer or the potential employee). Previous research based on the use of DISCO has shown that the results that can be achieved are quite good (Paoletti et al., 2016).

Moreover, it appears natural to approach other requirements that arise in semantic matching on the grounds of such matching measures. Possible extensions result from defining more matching measures using weighted averages, for example if profiles are to be split into an essential part capturing indispensable skills and less important skills. Similarly, defining partial orders on the grounds of several matching measures that are taken in a predefined order seems also possible. Furthermore, it is also possible to capture over-qualification by applying the same measures to the dual notion of ideal, that is, downward closed, non-empty sets of concepts. Then we would look for maximality for the filter-based measures and minimality for the ideal-based ones.

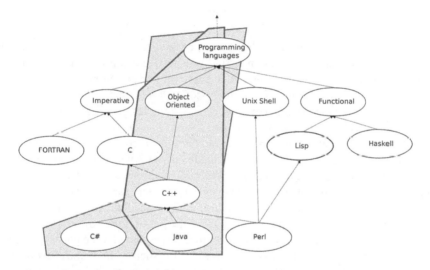

Figure 9.2   *Ontology of programming languages whereby two filters have been applied to assess the degree of matching between Java and C#*

Figure 9.2 shows us a clear example of filter-based matching. Let us assume that a given company is looking for a talented programmer with knowledge of Java, and we have a great candidate who already has experience in C#. In a traditional automated matching process, that candidate would be automatically discarded, since that candidate does not have the skill that the company is looking for. With filter-based matching, things work in a different manner: both filters are applied over the same ontology, and it can be noted that the candidate has already experience in a programming language with three predecessors in common with Java (thanks to the partial order representation of the skills and competences). Thus, while we cannot assign the total score to the candidate, it would also be extremely unfair to assign nothing. So this type of matching would give the candidate 3/4 of the estimated score.

In addition, defining matching relations only on filters in lattices is in accordance with a lot of previous research in the human resources domain that results in skill taxonomies. However, such approaches would only exploit a small fragment of the knowledge base, as only the concepts in the TBox would be considered, whereas the roles would be neglected (Paoletti et al., 2015). To benefit from the way profiles are represented, the idea is to define transformations of the TBox through operators that can eliminate roles and instead extend the knowledge base with new subconcepts. We call such operators "blow-ups" because the elimination of a single role leads to the emergence of many new concepts, even theoretically an infinite number. Nonetheless, the filters should remain finite. The key idea is that if a role links a concept A with a concept B, then each instance b of B (in any ABox) defines a subconcept of A. The order on the instances of B gives rise to subsumption between the so-defined subconcepts of A. Inflating a knowledge base, that is, the TBox, in such a way, allows the filter-based matching measures to remain unchanged, but nonetheless the knowledge represented by the roles will be taken into account.

Queries

One of the most desirable features in the domain of human resources is the possibility of formulating queries in order to, for example, find prospective candidates. In fact, in the context of human resource management systems, the possibility of executing queries effectively and efficiently is of great importance (Ilyas et al., 2004). Fortunately, there is a lot of research related to databases that can be adapted to work with knowledge bases. In this context, the two most popular types of queries are top-k queries and skyline queries.

For the top-k queries, we have to take into account that a query produces an answer set that is totally ordered (Straccia et al., 2009). From the result of such a query, one is left with the best k results. So, while performing the sorting and cutting operations is relatively simple, the great challenge is to optimize the efficiency of the queries in very large databases, which requires very well-designed data structures and rewriting techniques that allow the calculation of the best k elements without computing one by one all the possibilities. Similarly, skyline queries look for all maximal elements in an answer set that it is assumed to be partially ordered.

With respect to the knowledge base queries, in particular in the human resources domain, the most usual approach is to find the best k (with k=1 in most cases) matches for a given profile (either a CV or a job offer). This is usually called top-k querying and is the subject of intense research today. Although top-k queries have already been extensively explored in the context of databases (usually in the specific context of the relational model), there is still not much literature in the context of knowledge bases. Nevertheless, some of the results obtained for the relational model can be adapted to work with knowledge bases (Paoletti el al., 2016), in particular the focus on a single relation as the driver for the querying.

It should also be noted that skyline queries play a fundamental role in what is known as gap analysis. Gap analysis consists of identifying minimally enlarged filters that are capable of improving the results of matching. In other words, they are capable of exploiting a partial order on filters for queries. The enlargement requires data structures that support neighborhoods. Providing systems with good capabilities for gap analysis usually means skyline queries play a fundamental role in supporting good e-recruitment systems.

Knowledge Base Enrichment

Most of the time, solutions work for a single given matching relation on the ABox of a knowledge base. As this is a binary relation, Formal Concept Analysis (FCA) can be applied to generate a concept lattice, the elements of which are pairs of matching sets of profiles corresponding to sets of CVs and job offers, respectively (Looser et al., 2013).

As subsumption on the TBox is reflected by subset relationships on the ABox, this concept lattice may give rise to new concepts in the TBox. This basic idea can then be extended in several ways. First, the coupling with the theory of matching as established. That is, if the relationship on the ABox stems from one matching according to the theory instead of being given manually, the question is under which circumstances new concepts in the TBox will arise (Rácz et al., 2018). In other words, the question is whether the computation of matchings and TBox enrichment by means of FCA are inverse to each other. The case of TBox enrichment with more than one matching relation is also interesting. In this case the effects of unions, intersections, and differences need to be further studied. In fact, this can be extended to an investigation of stability conditions for the TBox enrichment under updates of the ABox. Finally, the question is how the basic FCA approach can be modified by turning binary relations into ternary or higher-order relations reflecting the dependence of the matching from other factors such as the source of the assessment, the validity, and so on. All these approaches to TBox enrichment using FCA might lead to solid results in the near future (Ma et al., 2018).

Database Technology

The challenge is not only to deal with empirical matchings (i.e. given by a human expert) but also to investigate the feedback to the matching theory and the integration of this theory with empirical evidence. This can be applied to both the enrichment of the knowledge base and the fine-tuning of the matching relations. In this context, if we ignore the knowledge bases' ability to make inferences, we can assure that these types of solutions have many things in common with a database. For example, there is a schema, that is, the concepts and roles in the TBox, and a pool of instances, that is, the ABox, so most advances in the field of databases are also applicable to knowledge bases.

In the case of top-k and skyline queries, both types of queries are very important in matching systems where the (partial) order is needed. In the particular case of the simultaneous use of several matching measures, a partial order may result. Therefore, there is a great challenge in adopting solutions that come from the field of databases so that they can be adapted to the knowledge bases. A clear example is the use of rings and spiders that were quite popular in the network database era and that have regained prominence in the object-oriented database field. This kind of data structure usually performs very well when it comes to facilitating queries that exploit hierarchical data structuring. In addition, indexes based on partial fractions are often used.

Last, but not least, when exploring query optimization, it is also natural to think of solutions for global matching in relation to some given criteria. This usually leads to a partial order. Therefore, questions concerning the efficiency of the database technology will be always important in this context.

FUTURE CHALLENGES

Although all these issues are the subject of intense research by both industry and academia, there are still many gaps to be addressed as future challenges. Without prejudice to challenges with a much more managerial focus, the literature recurrently identifies the improvement of methods that promote more accurate but also faster and more transparent methods. Here is a small description of the challenges that must be solved in order to continue advancing in the development of solutions for human resources management.

Future Managerial Research

In the set of processes of a managerial nature for human resources management, there are still a multitude of challenges to be faced. Throughout this work, we have focused on the matching of candidates and job offers, that is, the attraction of new talent. However, there are many other aspects that deserve investigation, for example talent development and talent retention. Regarding the development aspect, future work is required in terms of knowing the strengths of employees in an objective manner, so that they can be fully leveraged in the pursuit of the organization's strategic and tactical objectives. As for the retention aspect, we need to be constantly updated about market trends, or else we run the risk that our employees will be attracted to other organizations. Nevertheless, it seems clear that ontology-based knowledge representation methods are highly transparent, so they seem to have a clear advantage over black-box methods that often cannot clearly and reliably communicate the outcome of their processes. Therefore, a key aspect for the industry to adopt these systems is interpretability and explainability. In fact, there are some preliminary works that try to establish some criteria on how e-recruitment systems should deliver explanations (Martinez-Gil, 2015).

In the future, it should be possible to manage the corresponding profiles by means of the capabilities resulting from the research. The systems should ensure that these profiles capture all desirable parts such as skills, education, experiences, tasks, personal characteristics, and preferences. Thus, it will be necessary to first design and implement new interfaces to the querying and matching tools developed elsewhere, being as the quality and efficiency of the matching is the major concern of such solutions. This can involve also the design and implementation of user interfaces of existing knowledge extraction tools, such that the knowledge base (more precisely the ABox) can be filled automatically from these tools. The extraction technology itself needs also to be improved. Unfortunately, most solutions of this kind are restricted to the academic field, and it is necessary to make a greater effort to integrate these results in projects of an industrial nature.

Future Technical Research

Regarding the scientific-technical aspects, there are still many details to be addressed so that the systems can reach their full potential. Let us look at some examples.

Dealing with automatically built knowledge bases

One of the major factors that is making the proliferation of systems of this kind difficult is that knowledge is currently often stored in ontologies that are at present manually built (which are costly in terms of resource consumption in the form of time, money, and effort). Therefore, in order to spark the adoption of these solutions, one important challenge would be to develop a methodology for the evaluation of ontologies that have been automatically built. In the next few years, we hope to see results in this direction. For example, the use of graph embeddings to predict new nodes and relationships is currently under intense research. Because of this research, we will be able to obtain knowledge bases built automatically, so we must work on methodologies that can objectively measure aspects such as accuracy, naturalness, usefulness, augmentation of existing knowledge, and so on.

Improving the efficiency of exploitation methods

Another challenge would be to develop strategies for improving the efficiency of knowledge exploitation methods. Most of the methods that work with ontologies have great computational costs. For example, there is currently intense research into reasoners that can deal with ontologies on a large scale, but current solutions require large investments in equipment, which often make them inaccessible to most researchers and companies. To date, great progress has been made. However, the industry cannot afford slow waiting times that inevitably lead to rather poor user experiences. It is a great challenge for the future to ensure that the techniques of exploiting ontology-based models present response times similar to, for example, those of other approaches based on natural language processing or information retrieval.

Automatize the maintenance of the knowledge bases

Also as part of future work, it could be interesting to develop ways to automatically manage the maintenance of the knowledge bases in the form of ontologies. The combination of the knowledge bases with the inference engines is referred to as Knowledge-Based Systems. The idea is to build a system that represents knowledge with uncertainty through a set of rules so that they are given a certainty factor. The aim is to reduce the problem of incompleteness existing in the knowledge bases, as this is one of the problems that most limits the exploitation of these solutions. To carry out this task, it is assumed that the introduction of ontological information about each of the entities facilitates the creation of new entities in the knowledge base. To date, great progress has been made. It is a great challenge for the future to ensure that the techniques of exploiting ontology-based models present good accuracy as well as good response times.

CONCLUSIONS

In this chapter, we have seen how knowledge representation techniques are often used to optimize recruitment processes in a wide range of organizations. We have seen how the digitalization and optimization of such processes bring a number of advantages including cost, time, and effort reduction compared to classical techniques from the human resources domain. From a purely scientific point of view, we have also seen how the possibility of going beyond traditional syntactic matching opens a great field of opportunities for the research of new techniques and even business models. Besides this, we have seen how, nowadays, the process of matching CVs (candidate profiles) and job offers (job profiles) is usually done using some kind of knowledge base that might define a domain-specific ontology capturing skills, experiences, tasks, and so on as well as classification algorithms for terminological and assertional knowledge defined in the ontology.

In addition, such systems can also be interesting for organizations dedicated to teaching or training to overcome unemployment. For example, tools designed under this approach can be used to study which are the skills and competencies that can help an individual to find a job with the lowest possible cost in terms of resources and time (Martinez-Gil et al., 2018a). In addition, new processes can be designed to find suitable candidates for hard-to-fill jobs. The truth is that being able to avoid the semantic gap that may exist between requirements needed and requirements offered usually results in many advantages that are beginning to be discovered today.

As future work, there are still many details that need to be studied. For example, it is not entirely clear that knowledge-based technology can lead to decisions that are strictly objective. That is, this type of technology can be very useful when working with easily verifiable credentials such as certifications or knowledge of programming languages, but it does not answer important aspects such as determining whether a candidate is suitable for teamwork. In addition, the research community is well aware of the so-called "aversion algorithm", which is where people are more likely to lose confidence in computer models that fail sometimes (however small the number of times they fail). Therefore, it is more or less assumed that although these kinds of technologies can help and improve many processes, they cannot eradicate the need for human intervention in the hiring process.

Moreover, another process where knowledge representation technology can help is in assigning existing workers to projects or roles where their performance should be more favorable. Currently, organizations have large pools of talent, but in most cases this talent is not well organized. For example, when an organization wants to start a new project, it requires a great deal of manual effort to identify the people who will work on the project. This task, when done manually, is costly and prone to not being fully optimized. However, a slight adaptation of existing techniques could go a long way in helping to get the most out of the talent at our disposal.

ACKNOWLEDGMENTS

We would like to thank the anonymous reviewers for their help towards improving this work. This research work has been partially supported by the Austrian Ministry for Transport, Innovation and Technology, the Federal Ministry of Science, Research and Economy, and the Province of Upper Austria in the framework of the COMET center SCCH.

NOTES

1. https://wordnet.princeton.edu/.
2. https://dl.acm.org/ccs.

REFERENCES

Alamro, S., Dogan, H., Cetinkaya, D., & Jiang, N. (2018). Problem-oriented conceptual model and ontology for enterprise e-recruitment. In *Proceedings of the 20th International Conference on Enterprise Information Systems ICEIS* (pp. 280–289). https://doi.org/10.5220/0006702902800289

Bizer, C., Heese, R., Mochol, M., Oldakowski, R., Tolksdorf, R., & Eckstein, R. (2005). The impact of semantic web technologies on job recruitment processes. In *Wirtschaftsinformatik* (pp. 1367–1381). Physica.

Boselli, R., Cesarini, M., Mercorio, F., & Mezzanzanica, M. (2017). Using machine learning for labour market intelligence. In *Joint European Conference on Machine Learning and Knowledge Discovery in Databases* (pp. 330–342). Springer International Publishing.

Cali, A., Calvanese, D., Colucci, S., Di Noia, T., & Donini, F. M. (2004a). A description logic based approach for matching user profiles. In V. Haarslev & R. Moller (Eds.), *International Workshop on Description Logics*. CEUR Workshop Proceedings.

Cali, A., Calvanese, D., Colucci, S., Di Noia, T., & Donini, F. M. (2004b). A logic-based approach for matching user profiles. In *Knowledge-based intelligent information and engineering systems* (pp. 187–195). Springer.

Colucci, S., Di Noia, T., Di Sciascio, E., Donini, F. M., Mongiello, M., & Mottola, M. (2003). A formal approach to ontology-based semantic match of skills descriptions. *Journal of Universal Computer Science, 9*(12), 1437–1454.

Faliagka, E., Iliadis, L., Karydis, I., Rigou, M., Sioutas, S., Tsakalidis, A., & Tzimas, G. (2014). On-line consistent ranking on e-recruitment: Seeking the truth behind a well-formed CV. *Artificial Intelligence Review, 42*(3), 515–528.

Faliagka, E., Tsakalidis, A., & Tzimas, G. (2012). An integrated e-recruitment system for automated personality mining and applicant ranking. *Internet Research, 22*(5), 551–568.

Färber, F., Weitzel, T., & Keim, T. (2003). An automated recommendation approach to selection in personnel recruitment. In *AMCIS 2003 Proceedings*. AMCIS.

García-Sánchez, F., Martínez-Béjar, R., Contreras, L., Fernández-Breis, J. T., & Castellanos-Nieves, D. (2006). An ontology-based intelligent system for recruitment. *Expert Systems with Applications, 31*(2), 248–263.

Gómez-Pérez, A., Ramírez, J., & Villazón-Terrazas, B. (2007). An ontology for modelling human resources management based on standards. In *International Conference on Knowledge-Based and Intelligent Information and Engineering Systems* (pp. 534–541). Springer.

Grau, B. C., Horrocks, I., Motik, B., Parsia, B., Patel-Schneider, P., & Sattler, U. (2008). OWL 2: The next step for OWL. *Journal of Web Semantics, 6*(4), 309–322.

Ilyas, I. F., Aref, W. G., & Elmagarmid, A. K. (2004). Supporting top-k join queries in relational databases. *The VLDB Journal, 13*(3), 207–221.

Looser, D., Ma, H., & Schewe, K. D. (2013). Using formal concept analysis for ontology maintenance in human resource recruitment. In *Proceedings of the Ninth Asia-Pacific Conference on Conceptual Modelling* (pp. 61–68). ACM.

Ma, H., Hartmann, S., & Vechsamutvaree, P. (2018). Towards FCA-facilitated ontology-supported recruitment systems. *Enterprise Modelling and Information Systems Architectures (EMISAJ), 13*, 182–189.

Malinowski, J., Keim, T., Wendt, O., & Weitzel, T. (2006). Matching people and jobs: A bilateral recommendation approach. In *Proceedings of the 39th Annual Hawaii International Conference on System Sciences (HICSS'06)* (pp. 137c–137c). IEEE.

Maree, M., Kmail, A.B., & Belkhatir, M. (2019). Analysis and shortcomings of e-recruitment systems: Towards a semantics-based approach addressing knowledge incompleteness and limited domain coverage. *Journal of Information Science, 45*(6), 713–735.

Martinez-Gil, J. (2014). An overview of knowledge management techniques for e-recruitment. *Journal of Information and Knowledge Management, 13*(2), Article 1450014. https://doi.org/10.1142/S0219649214500142

Martinez-Gil, J. (2015). Automated knowledge base management: A survey. *Computer Science Review, 18*, 1–9.

Martinez-Gil, J., & Freudenthaler, B. (2019). Optimal selection of training courses for unemployed people based on stable marriage model. In *iiWAS 2019* (pp. 260–266). ACM. https://doi.org/10.1145/3366030.3366063

Martinez-Gil, J., Freudenthaler, B., & Natschläger, T. (2018a). Recommendation of job offers using random forests and support vector machines. In *Proceedings of the Workshops of the EDBT/ICDT 2018 Joint Conference (EDBT/ICDT 2018)*. CEUR Workshop Proceedings.

Martinez-Gil, J., Paoletti, A. L., Rácz, G., Sali, A., & Schewe, K. D. (2018b). Accurate and efficient profile matching in knowledge bases. *Data and Knowledge Engineering, 117*, 195–215.

Martinez-Gil, J., Paoletti, L., Rácz, G., Sali, A., & Schewe, K. D. (2016a). Maintenance of profile matchings in knowledge bases. In *International Conference on Model and Data Engineering* (pp. 132–141). Springer International Publishing.

Martinez-Gil, J., Paoletti, A. L., & Schewe, K. D. (2016b). A smart approach for matching, learning and querying information from the human resources domain. In *East European Conference on Advances in Databases and Information Systems* (pp. 157–167). Springer International Publishing.

Mochol, M., Wache, H., & Nixon, L. (2007). Improving the accuracy of job search with semantic techniques. In *International Conference on Business Information Systems* (pp. 301–313). Springer International Publishing.

Paoletti, A. L., Martinez-Gil, J., & Schewe, K. D. (2015). Extending knowledge-based profile matching in the human resources domain. In *Database and expert systems applications* (pp. 21–35). Springer International Publishing.

Paoletti, A. L., Martinez-Gil, J., & Schewe, K. D. (2016). Top-k matching queries for filter-based profile matching in knowledge bases. In *Database and expert systems applications* (pp. 295–302). Springer International Publishing.

Pessach, D., Singer, G., Avrahami, D., Ben-Gal, H. C., Shmueli, E., & Ben-Gal, I. (2020). Employees recruitment: A prescriptive analytics approach via machine learning and mathematical programming. *Decision Support Systems, 134*, Article 113290. https://doi.org/10.1016/j.dss.2020.113290

Poch, M., Bel Rafecas, N., Espeja, S., & Navio, F. (2014). Ranking job offers for candidates: Learning hidden knowledge from big data. In N. Calzolari, K. Choukri, T. Declerck, H. Loftsson, B. Maegaard, J. Mariani, A. Moreno, J. Odijk, & S. Piperidis (Eds.), *Proceedings of the Ninth International Conference on Language Resources and Evaluation (LREC-2014)* (pp. 2076–2082). European Language Resources Association

Rácz, G., Sali, A., & Schewe, K. D. (2018). Refining semantic matching for job recruitment: An application of formal concept analysis. In *International Symposium on Foundations of Information and Knowledge Systems* (pp. 322–339). Springer International Publishing.

Radevski, V., & Trichet, F. (2006). Ontology-based systems dedicated to human resources management: An application in e-recruitment. In *OTM Confederated International Conferences "On the Move to Meaningful Internet Systems"* (pp. 1068–1077). Springer International Publishing.

Ramli, R., Noah, S. A., & Yusof, M. M. (2010). Ontological-based model for human resource decision support system (HRDSS). In *OTM Confederated International Conferences "On the Move to Meaningful Internet Systems"* (pp. 585–594). Springer International Publishing.

Sandanayake, T. C., Limesha, G. A. I., Madhumali, T. S. S., Mihirani, W. P. I., & Peiris, M. S. A. (2018). Automated CV analyzing and ranking tool to select candidates for job positions. In *Proceedings of the 6th International Conference on Information Technology: IoT and Smart City* (pp. 13–18). https://doi .org/10.1145/3301551.3301579

Senthil Kumaran, V., & Sankar, A. (2013). Towards an automated system for intelligent screening of candidates for recruitment using ontology mapping (EXPERT). *International Journal of Metadata, Semantics and Ontologies, 8*(1), 56–64.

Seta, K., Ikeda, M., Hirata, K., Hayashi, Y., & Kuriyama, K. (2005). A human resource model and evidence based evaluation – ontology for IT skill standards. In *ICCE* (pp. 388–395). IEEE.

Straccia, U., Tinelli, E., Colucci, S., Di Noia, T., & Di Sciascio, E. (2009). A system for retrieving top-k candidates to job positions. In *Proceedings of the 22nd International Workshop on Description Logics (DL 2009)*. CEUR Workshop Proceedings.

Thielsch, M. T., Träumer, L., & Pytlik, L. (2012). E-recruiting and fairness: The applicant's point of view. *Information Technology and Management, 13*(2), 59–67.

10. HR robotic process automation

Peter Fettke and Stefan Strohmeier

INTRODUCTION

The automation of business processes in general and the automation of Human Resources (HR) processes in particular have been major and recurring topics for many decades. With the advent of Robotic Process Automation (RPA) during the last half decade, this discussion has gained an important new impetus. RPA envisions *substituting, assisting*, or *innovating* a process step typically performed by a human with an intelligent machine called a *robot* (also *bot* or *intelligent agent*) (Czarnecki & Fettke, 2021; Enríquez et al., 2020; Syed et al., 2020). This idea has gained rapid practical recognition, and according to market predictions RPA is one of the fastest-growing segments of the enterprise software market (e.g., Gartner, 2020).

Today, a growing number of suggestions are also being put forward on ways to apply RPA in HR (e.g., Cloudpay, 2021; Kryon, 2020; Papageorgiou, 2018; PeopleDoc, 2020). On the one hand, RPA aims at performing processes autonomously. On the other hand, it is safe to say that many process steps will not be automated at all because it is simply not possible, desirable, or efficient. However, the exact dividing line between these two extremes is often not that sharply defined and strongly depends on the characteristics of the particular field of automation. For example, many so-called dirty, dangerous, and demeaning jobs can be fulfilled by robots. Workers who perform professional, desk, managerial, or administrative work can be – at least in part – substituted by robots. However, there is still no mature understanding of how automation in general and RPA in particular work precisely.

One explanation for this shortcoming is that the term RPA is not uniformly used in research and practice. For example, narrow definitions restrict RPA just to simple routine work and define RPA "as a licensed software tool to integrate any application via the user interface to automate routine, predictable tasks using structured digital data" (Gartner, 2020, n.p.). However, the understanding of RPA is not consistent. In academia, RPA is much more broadly defined. In particular, more intelligent RPA solutions are included and more sophisticated techniques from the field of artificial intelligence (AI) are subsumed under this term, thereby making RPA a new emerging field of applied AI (Agostinelli et al., 2019; Chakraborti et al., 2020; Viehhauser, 2020). Against this background, a deeper academic analysis is needed, and it is time to consolidate the academic substance of the topic of HR RPA (Cabello et al., 2020).

The current chapter thus aims at such an analysis by addressing the following questions in three subsequent sections:

- What are the basics of RPA?
- Which HR RPA application potentials exist?
- Which HR RPA research problems are open?

BASICS OF ROBOTIC PROCESS AUTOMATION IN HR

Conceptual Foundations of RPA

In research and engineering, a term is often simultaneously used to denote a class of *problems*, a class of *solution methods* that work well on the problem, and the *field* that studies these particular problems and solution methods. The same is true for RPA. Although it is convenient to use a single name for different things, it is at the same time essential to keep the understandings conceptually separate (Czarnecki & Fettke, 2021). In particular:

- RPA as a *problem*: Typically, there is a task to be fulfilled, or a business problem to be solved. A task can be accomplished entirely manually, manually with the help of a robot, or completely autonomously by the robot. RPA as a problem focuses on particular types of automation problems in HR processes.
- RPA as a *solution*: There are typical solution methods that are used to solve the RPA problem. The current class of solution methods is determined by the offerings of current RPA vendors. Besides these mature solutions, there are many ideas for next-generation "intelligent" or "cognitive" RPA solutions that are under research and development.

In the following, RPA as a problem and solution is described in more detail.

RPA as a Problem

Overview

Often the automation of business processes is understood as a kind of "greenfield approach": All business processes and necessary digital applications are developed from scratch with no limitations and restrictions imposed by prior work and prior digital applications. In contrast, RPA originates from the fact that it is much more realistic to assume that many digital applications are already implemented for automating HR processes. However, the already running applications are operated by humans. Against that background, RPA is based on a "brownfield approach" and asks the question: *How can the operation of the already implemented applications be further automated?* The following three aspects are of importance to answer the question from the perspective of RPA.

Problem aspect I: homogeneous user-interface for humans and robots

First, RPA relies on the premise that *humans and robots use the same interface* for operating the applications (e.g., van der Aalst et al., 2018; Fettke & Loos, 2019). This idea seems at first counterintuitive, but it is one historical origin of RPA. Hence, a deeper elaboration of this characteristic is necessary. Typically, a digital application has different types of interfaces. One main distinction can be made between interfaces that are preliminarily designed for humans on the one hand, and, on the other hand, interfaces for machines, for instance network communication, data storage, or connections to external devices. In the context of RPA, the interfaces that are preliminarily designed for humans are of major importance:

- Keyboard: The operator strikes the keys of the keyboard to input some characters, numbers, or other signs into the computer.

- Mouse: The operator uses the mouse to change the focus of the input window of the graphical user interface.
- Microphone: The microphone is used to grasp audio inputs from the environment, namely speech and noise.
- Display devices: The display of a computer visualizes windows, graphics, and texts.

The design of such user interfaces is of major importance and there are large research communities that deal with the effective and efficient design of such interfaces, for instance the field of human–computer interaction.

However, practice shows that there are many situations in which humans are not satisfied in operating digital applications through these standard interfaces. Typical situations are (Houy et al., 2019):

- Routine work or standard workflows: Often using an application involves some routine usage patterns; for instance, first open a file, change some data, recalculate and visualize the results, save and forward the results to some colleague.
- Poorly designed user interfaces: Although interfaces should be designed for perfectly matching the requirements and capabilities of humans, reality often shows that it is not the case; for instance, the user interface is too complicated, making it difficult to identify the correct menu button. The pre-designed application workflow might be designed with some other objectives in mind; for instance, novice or occasional users have different needs than power users.
- Cross-application workflows: Sometimes several applications are used in a standard workflow at the workplace; for instance, first open the time and attendance management system and extract some data which must be changed in the payroll system.
- Integration of some particular applications: Sometimes another application is used since it offers better functionality for a particular task; for instance, the visualization function of a spreadsheet is typically better, but not well integrated in the standard HR information system.
- Conversion of data: Similar to cross-application, it is sometimes necessary not only to exchange data from one application to another but also to convert the data; for instance, the currency of payroll results must be recalculated.
- Structuring data: Data is already digitalized but only in an unstructured or inappropriate form; for instance, the data of an application must first be manually extracted from an electronic mail and transferred manually to the applicant tracking system.

In many instances, these situations might often be solved by an appropriate design of the application software installed at a workplace. However, it is clear that in reality this is often not the case and it would be impossible to change or expand the underlying application software. The main reasons for such restrictions and limitations are:

- Organizations use standard software which is not customized or customizable for the particular user needs.
- Although the developer of the standard software might accept that the desired functions might be necessary for particular users, it is not reasonable to integrate them because these functions are too specific to the particular user's needs and there is no demand for such functions in the broader market.

- Even if some individual software applications are used, it may be much too costly to change the software or it might take too long to wait for a new product release.
- The demands for particular functions might only exist at some user workplaces and cannot be easily implemented in a more general form. Hence, once again it might be questionable as to whether it is worth integrating a more powerful user interface.
- Cross-application and integration needs: The realization might sometimes be impossible because it relies on cross-organizational demand and integration of several applications. Hence, it does not make sense to develop and integrate the needed functions into one particular application.

These sketched application scenarios are the practical starting point for developing RPA systems which are able to mimic and imitate the behavior of a human operator of an application. The original idea for such techniques is old and originated from different fields of technology, namely:

- *Screen scraping*: These techniques originate from extracting data from the memory of a computer terminal and are nowadays used to extract information from a bitmap displayed on a computer screen.
- *Macro recording*: Several steps of a complex operation of an application are automatically recorded and can be executed several times after recording within a single user step.
- *Systems scripting*: A high-level systems scripting language can be used to execute a complex set of system commands automatically in one single user step.

In the meantime, these technologies are being developed further in a more application-oriented direction. Hence, it is possible that end-users with less application knowledge can use such techniques for the automation of the operation of typical business applications.

Problem aspect II: real-world application of AI
Second, RPA problems are strongly *intertwined with typical problems of* applied *AI*. Ironically, RPA has historically no or just minor connections to the field of AI. In the past the application of AI in the field was very limited. However, this situation has changed dramatically in recent years. Nowadays the development of general services of AI is maturing, hence, not only simple RPA problems can be addressed but much more demanding business problems. Against that background, the wide spectrum of RPA problems can be narrowed down to two extreme poles, namely simple RPA problems and cognitive RPA problems (e.g., Houy et al., 2019; Czarnecki & Fettke, 2021):

- *Simple* RPA problems: Simple RPA addresses routine tasks; the RPA system only follows simple rules; different application scenarios are available. The market offerings are stable. Simple RPA can be implemented in a short time frame with low costs. Market offerings are mature.
- *Cognitive* RPA problems: Cognitive RPA addresses non-routine tasks which require deep cognitive capabilities for problem solving, for instance cognitive functions for business understanding, language understanding, speech generation, decision making, anomaly detection, process predictions, identification of critical events, and many more.

It is clear that the two categories of simple RPA problems and cognitive RPA problems provides only a first approximation of two extreme forms. In laboratory application settings, such an analytical distinction often makes sense. However, applications in the field support a much broader spectrum of typical work performed by humans and cannot often be sharply separated into these two problem categories. It is more natural to understand field applications as a more heterogeneous environment in which a human worker has to fulfill tasks which have different complexities and heterogeneous cognitive demands. The fulfillment of these requirements is accomplished by applied AI.

Problem aspect III: need for business process management
Third, it has become clear that RPA problems are often interlinked in a more complex way. Against this background, it is necessary to better understand the problem structure from the perspective of *business process management*. To put it differently, tasks in field applications for solving problems are not isolated from each other but constitute a complex net of different interrelationships. Hence, in the context of RPA, it is strongly recommended that RPA problems are understood not as the automation of single, isolated tasks but as the management of complex work situations in organizations (Mendling et al., 2018).

To sum up, RPA as a problem consists of three different but strongly interconnected aspects:

1. An RPA problem deals with the automation of the operation of an already implemented digital application in which robots use interfaces originally designed for humans.
2. The solution to the RPA problem typically relies on the cognitive abilities of a human. Hence, techniques from the field of applied AI are necessary to solve the problem adequately.
3. Automation is not understood as a single task, but as a complex network of different business processes which are interconnected to form a complex business system. Hence, some kind of business process management is necessary for an effective and efficient overall solution to a business problem.

Characteristics of RPA Problems
To better understand a particular kind of RPA problem, the RPA problem can be described from three different aspects (Czarnecki & Fettke, 2021; Martínez-Rojas et al., 2020):

1. *Objective of the RPA problem*: An RPA problem can be characterized by the overall objective of the intended RPA solution. Typically, three different approaches are used:
   a. Replace humans: The RPA problem can be described in terms of replacing the job of a human worker. The aim of the robot is to take over the work of a human worker.
   b. Assist humans: The RPA problem can best be described as the assistance of a human worker. The navigation system of a car does not replace a real human ("co-pilot") but assists the driver.
   c. Innovate business processes: The RPA system developed neither replaces nor assists a human worker. Instead, it provides the technique for an innovative step in a business process; for instance, a drone allows the delivery of small packages in a totally new way compared to known technologies.
2. *Complexity of the RPA problem*: For fulfilling the defined objective, typically an action must be taken. Such an action can be very simple, for instance just clicking a button, or very complex, for instance deciding which applicants should be selected for a job invitation. In computer science, well-accepted concepts for defining the complexity of a problem exist, namely the number of computational steps or the amount of memory needed for

solving the problem. Although these complexity considerations are of major importance for determining the complexity of an RPA problem, it is safe to say that an RPA problem is often not well structured or precisely defined. Nevertheless, input, output, and behavior are important factors that constitute an RPA problem:

- *Input* needed for problem solving: Typically, an action can only be performed when a particular condition is fulfilled. These conditions can be explicitly defined.
- *Output* produced by problem solving: An action results in a condition that can be described. This result can be viewed as some kind of output condition.
- *Behavior* for problem solving: The robot behavior for problem solving can be described in detail.

3. *Performance measure:* While problem complexity focuses on the difficulty of the problem, a performance measure describes how the quality of a potential solution to the problem could be estimated (Russell & Norvig, 2021). Typically, a solution to an RPA problem can be evaluated from different angles, for instance costs per action, time needed, error rate, and many more. These performance measures can be defined or just intuitively given for a particular RPA problem.

RPA as a Solution

Overview on RPA systems

The core of an RPA solution is an *RPA system* comprising one or more robots which is typically complemented by an appropriate *management or development* approach (Czarnecki & Fettke, 2021). The general management and development approach for an RPA solution is on a coarse level very similar to other IT technology management methods and development approaches. On a more detailed level, these approaches are very specific to the RPA problem addressed. Hence, in the following, only the RPA system is focused on in more detail.

To understand an RPA system, typically its inner components and its environment has to be distinguished. In its *environment*, three different types of modules can be differentiated (Czarnecki & Fettke, 2021; Enríquez et al., 2020):

1. One or many activities or an operational flow of business activities: Typically, an RPA system has an interface to one particular business task, a more complex business process, operational flows, or some other kind of business activity.
2. One or many application systems: These application systems are operated by the RPA system.
3. One or many humans: These humans can be fully replaced, partially replaced, or just assisted by the RPA system.

The *interior of an RPA system* is decomposed into different sub-modules:

- *Core modules* providing the main functionality of the RPA system: These core modules enable the RPA system to grasp its environment, analyze the received data, process the data, and produce some output. The RPA core system can be implemented multiple times. Some users of RPA report that they have already deployed hundreds or even thousands of different RPA robots. Hence, an RPA system may consist of many robots, each working autonomously.

- *Managing modules* providing functionality for development and maintenance: Typically, different management methods for user interaction, learning, security, administration, and monitoring are supplied by an RPA system.

AI techniques in RPA systems

Since techniques from the field of AI are typically applied for the development of the core modules, these techniques are focused on next in more detail.

Knowledge representation. The knowledge for performing different tasks must be encoded by some representation formalism (Gao et al., 2019). Typical examples are rule-based approaches, for instance:

IF [condition] THEN [command].

Such rules can be explicitly coded and represented inside an RPA system. Although AI technologies offer several sophisticated techniques, current RPA systems often use just simple rule-based approaches for knowledge representation.

Behavior recording and rule mining. The aforementioned rules must be formulated explicitly to be useful in controlling a robot. This can be done manually by some (end) user, or it can be done automatically. For doing this, some mining techniques are typically used. In the simple form, the RPA systems use some kind of "macro recorder". However, such simple techniques do not allow the generalization of observed behavior. Hence, more sophisticated techniques are used by some systems. Learning rules in the context of RPA is described in more detail by Gao et al. (2019).

Decision mining, decision automation, and automated planning. In a business process, several decisions have to be made. The spectrum ranges from very simple (send a job contract by mail or e-mail) to complex decisions (which applicant should be selected for the position to be filled). Several techniques are used to automate such decisions in an RPA robot. Techniques from rule mining, decision mining, and process mining are used for that task. Automated planning provides a different approach to defining the behavior of an RPA robot (Leno et al., 2021).

Document analysis and processing. Techniques for optical character recognition are well known. However, in business processes, paper documents are often handled, for instance invoices, contracts, job ads, application documents, and so on. Such documents often do not consist of long texts, instead consisting of semi-structured data, typically containing information in tables or figures, for instance different invoice items. To extract information from such business documents, specialized techniques from the field of machine learning are available, for instance end-to-end information extraction or improved understanding of tables (Houy et al., 2019). Typically, humans do not have difficulties identifying a paper document as an invoice, delivery note, account statement, and so on. Improved optical character recognition and image processing techniques can detect and classify a scanned image as an instance of a particular business document type; for instance, invoice data about address, customer, or amount can be extracted by key-value-pairs.

Natural language processing, multi-modal dialog systems, and human–computer interaction. The processing of written or oral language is an important sub-field of AI which has many applications in RPA (Chakraborti et al., 2020). Hence, several RPA platforms integrate functionalities for natural language processing, for instance speech recognition and synthesis for a natural interface between a human and machine. More sophisticated approaches are based on personal assistance. For example, making a reservation at a hairdresser or a restaurant is often done by a phone call. Such dialogues can be automated by robots with natural-language interfaces. One prominent application area is that of so-called chatbots, an important sub-category of a multi-modal dialog system. These chatbots can be understood as RPA robots that just focus on the interaction between a human and a machine. Application scenarios for chatbots in HR are discussed in CHAPTER 12 of this volume.

Model-based, low- or no-code software development. Additionally, sometimes the feature of low-code or even no-code usage of RPA solutions is mentioned. This means that no sophisticated programming is needed. At best, the RPA robot is allowed to observe once, or a couple of times, how the work is done by a human, and by observing how humans conduct the work, the RPA robot learns to perform it autonomously by itself.

Further technologies. Recent developments show that many more core techniques from the field of AI will be integrated into an RPA system, namely:

1. Computer vision: The use of camera and other techniques can enhance the data which can be used by an RPA robot (see CHAPTER 4).
2. Multiagent systems: Classical RPA robots are built to fulfill one task, although in the context of RPA the use of several RPA robots is typical.
3. Machine learning: It could be of great use if an RPA robot can learn the steps which are necessary to perform a task on its own (see CHAPTER 2).
4. Physical robotics: The use of physical robots in business processes is already standard in many manufacturing scenarios and should be integrated in RPA scenarios (see CHAPTER 1).

Categorization of RPA systems

Against the backdrop of an application in HR, different categories of RPA robots are imaginable. In the following, core categories are briefly introduced.

A first categorization criterion refers to the interaction of robots with humans (e.g., Taulli, 2020). So-called *unattended robots* aim at a full "end-to-end" automation, where bots are enabled to execute entire HR processes on their own without any interaction with humans. Unattended robots can be used for large-scale "back-office" processes. Unattended robots work according to a predefined schedule or are triggered by events in the process flow (e.g., Taulli, 2020). *Attended robots* in contrast interact with humans. Attended robots function as virtual assistants that help employees with their tasks within the process. Attended robots are triggered by the user or by user actions such as making a call or receiving a request and then take over certain "back-office" or "front-office" tasks. Robots and humans thus work as a "team" (e.g., Taulli, 2020). Both types can therefore evidently be employed in Human Resource Management (HRM). A particular application of attended robots in HR is realizing (applicant, employee, and manager) self-service approaches. The robot then does not (or at least not only) interact with an HR professional, but instead (or additionally) interacts with an applicant, employee, or line manager involved in an HR process, supporting them in completing tasks.

A second categorization criterion refers to *decision making* by robots. As long as operative processes, such as transferring data from one application to another, do not need explicit decisions, they can be automated by non-decision-making robots. As HR processes frequently include low- and high-stake decisions, however, there are decision-making robots. Low-stake decisions, in particular decisions over things, can be fully automated by using such robots. High-stake decisions, in particular over humans, with larger impacts on these humans, can, however, be used within attended RPA to support the final decision of a human RPA user as required by different legal systems (for instance by the General Data Protection Regulation [GDPR] in the EU; see CHAPTER 19) and as managerially suitable. Again, both types are relevant for HRM.

A third categorization criterion restricted to attended robots refers to the *usage of natural language by robots*, where robots with or without natural language processing can be distinguished (e.g., Rizk et al., 2020). Robots without natural language processing use conventional means of user interfaces for interaction with users. Robots with natural language processing can be used to mimic human dialog patterns, therewith easing the human–robot interaction and making interaction more attractive. In particular, when using attended robots for self-service, for instance for informing interested applicants of existing vacancies, the usage of natural language can constitute an interesting alternative (Rizk et al., 2020). RPA robots that employ natural language processing evidently overlap with "conversational agents" or "chatbots" (see CHAPTER 12).

A fourth categorization criterion, again restricted to attended robots, refers to *personalization of robots*, where non-personalized and personalized robots can be distinguished (e.g., Feine et al., 2019). Personalization refers to concealing the robot as a virtual person with different social cues such as gender, age, gestures, or facial expressions. Since humans react socially to such personalizations, this could be used for instance in self-service RPA in recruiting.

A fifth and related categorization criterion, once again restricted to attended robots, refers to *incorporation of emotions into robots*, where non-emotionalized and emotionalized robots can be distinguished (e.g., Saxena et al., 2020). As emotionalized robots aim at discovering emotions in humans and, vice versa, simulating emotions, this is only possible if humans are "in the loop", and therefore makes sense for attended RPA only. Like and beyond personalization, emotionalization of robots can be used to deepen and intensify interaction with human process participants such as applicants (e.g., Saxena et al., 2020). Emotionalized robots therefore constitute an application of affective computing (see CHAPTER 13).

Understanding of algorithms in RPA systems

One final remark on the understanding of an RPA system: In many situations it is natural to understand an RPA system as an implementation of an *algorithm* starting with some kind of input, some kind of processing, and, finally, generating some kind of output. This understanding might make perfect sense for many applications. However, the mentioned characteristics of RPA systems clearly show that the interaction between the robot and the human can often be better understood as a *reactive* computational process in which the robot interacts with the environment *continuously* and *not deterministically*. In such an RPA system, the behavior in at least three different phases must be understood: (1) warming-up phase: the RPA system is switched on and enters its normal operating mode; (2) running phase: the RPA system reacts to some stimulus received from its environment; (3) cooling-down phase: the normal operating mode of the RPA system is abandoned, and the system is switched off.

In other words, there are many scenarios in which an RPA system is better understood as a *reactive process* and not as a transformation of input data into output data. This difference has major theoretical implications for the understanding of *algorithmic* decision making and management. In such a scenario, the *global state* of an RPA system and its digital environment is not fully known; instead, *local states* are available for understanding the RPA problem (Fettke & Reisig, 2021).

APPLICATION OF ROBOTIC PROCESS AUTOMATION IN HR

Application Potentials of HR RPA

Potentials refer to realized current and imaginable future applications of RPA in HRM. In the following, potentials are briefly discussed on three different levels of abstraction – the general level of mimicking functions of natural intelligence (NI) in HR, the medium level of realizing HR conceptions, and the detail level of realizing actual use cases of RPA in HR.

General-level potentials

On the general level of mimicking functions of NI (see CHAPTER 1), RPA robots initially show the potential of mimicking human *action*, given that performing operational HR processes, such as ascertaining or transferring HR data, doubtlessly constitute purposeful activities. Moreover, as performing the necessary sequence of tasks is based on propositional and procedural knowledge, *knowing* is a preceding and prerequisite function that RPA bases its action upon. As this knowledge is gained by machine learning (e.g., Chakraborti et al., 2020), *learning* constitutes a third related function. If the HR processes that are automated include decisions, such as deciding on the invitation for job interviews (e.g., Chichester & Giffen, 2019), RPA also mimics *deciding*. Finally, if an attended RPA application also involves communications between a robot and employees, applicants, or line managers, for instance when performing a job interview (e.g., Nørskov & Ulhøi, 2020), *communicating* and *perceiving* are mimicked NI functions as well. Finally, if robots include affective computing, such as emotion recognition based on video (e.g., Saxena et al., 2020; Ng et al., 2021), RPA also mimics *empathizing*. Acting therefore constitutes the basic NI function mimicked by HR RPA, while the mimicking of further NI functions depends on the actual design of a given HR RPA application.

Conceptional-level potentials

On the medium level of realizing HR conceptions, RPA shows potential to support and realize different previously discussed HR conceptions. In the following, the widespread conceptional trisection into *operational*, *relational*, and *transformational* applications of digital technologies (e.g., Snell et al., 1995), and subsequently the currently emerging concept of *algorithmic management* (e.g., Feshchenko, 2021), are briefly discussed as HR conceptions with evident relations to RPA.

Regarding the trisection into operational, relational, and transformational technology applications in HR, it is initially evident that RPA shows broad potentials for *operational HRM*. Even though operational HR processes were automated for several decades (e.g., Strohmeier, 2007), they frequently could not be *fully* automated. Thus, despite an advanced first phase of automation of operational HR processes, there are operational automation gaps that need to be tediously filled by humans at great expense. Transferring HR data between two different, incompatible operational HR applications constitutes a simple example. In this way, RPA constitutes literally the "missing link" for completing the automation of operational HR processes – without effortful, lengthy, and costly changes of established legacy systems and processes. Moreover, self-service RPA with direct contact to stakeholders additionally shows the potential to address *relational HRM* (e.g., Malik et al., 2020). Relational processes initiate, manage, and sustain relationships with the stakeholders of HR, such as line managers, applicants, and, of course, employees. As an example process, the onboarding of new employees includes beyond operational tasks clearly relational aspects such as welcoming an employee, introducing her/him to her/his workplace and team, and so on – therewith starting a relationship with this employee. In this way, HR robots that communicate and interact with humans show the potential to realize "AI-mediated social exchange" (e.g., Malik et al., 2020; Ma & Brown, 2020).

Switching to a second conception, if self-service RPA not only includes communication and interaction but also decisions on stakeholders, it shows the potential for realizing the currently just emerging concept of *algorithmic management* in HR (see the review by Feshchenko, 2021). By handing over diverse HR processes to robots, at least the operative management of HR is performed by robots (e.g., Malik et al., 2020). As robots constitute a specific category of algorithms, it is possible and appropriate to speak of *algorithmic HRM*.

In sum, on a conceptual level, RPA shows potentials for *operational*, *relational*, and, if employed intensively, even *algorithmic* HRM.

Use case level potentials
Regarding the detail level of individual use cases, there is a large set of suggestions from practice (e.g., Deloitte, 2018; Kryon, 2020; UIPath, 2021) that is gradually being complemented by suggestions from research (e.g., Cartiş & Suciu, 2019; Garimella & Paruchuri, 2015; Rizk et al., 2020; Suen et al., 2020). These use cases suggestions, however, show differing degrees of elaboration and range from the mere naming of an HR use case (e.g., Taulli, 2020) to the full-fledged elaboration of an HR robot prototype (e.g., Garimella & Paruchuri, 2015).

Suggestions of use cases are spread over all operational HR functions and refer to recruiting (e.g., Garimella & Paruchuri, 2015), selection (e.g., Nørskov & Ulhøi, 2020), compensation (e.g., Papageorgiou, 2018), learning (e.g., Kryon, 2020), performance management (e.g., Balasundaram & Venkatagiri, 2020), and HR reporting (e.g., BluePrism, 2020), among others. Beyond automating the internal execution of HR processes, it is emphasized that RPA is particularly well suited for automating external execution of HR processes by shared service centers (SSC) or business process outsourcing (BPO) providers (e.g., BluePrism, 2020; Hallikainen et al., 2018). Beyond rather simple processes, such as transferring data from one HR system to another (e.g., Taulli, 2020), use cases also refer to rather complex processes such as conducting job interviews (e.g., Nørskov & Ulhøi, 2020), offboarding employees (e.g., PeopleDoc, 2020), or identifying the career aspirations of employees (e.g., Malik et al., 2020).

Suggested HR use cases often refer to unattended ("back-office") RPA, such as the weekly creation of an HR report (e.g., Taulli, 2020), aiming at a full end-to-end automation of the process. However, given the relational character of numerous HR processes involving interaction with stakeholders, attended and attended self-service RPA use cases are also discussed. Regarding the latter, use cases map the interaction with core HR stakeholder categories, such as (conducting job interviews with) *applicants* (e.g., Nørskov & Ulhøi, 2020), (scheduling performance management interviews with) *line managers* (e.g., Balasundaram & Venkatagiri, 2020), or (answering the questions of) *employees* (e.g., UIPath, 2021). Moreover, as attended RPA implies interactions with HR stakeholders, there are different use cases that include natural language processing, with examples referring to conversational robots that answer general employee questions (e.g., UIPath, 2021), interview applicants (e.g., Carțiș & Suciu, 2019), inform employees about their travel preapprovals (Rizk et al., 2020), or even coach and mentor employees (e.g., Zel & Kongar, 2020; Satam et al., 2020). In particular, the latter use cases highlight the fluent boundaries between RPA and natural language processing (see CHAPTER 12), between automation and conversation robots respectively. Automation robots frequently need to additionally converse with stakeholders, while conversation robots frequently need to additionally automate certain process steps.

Moreover, even though there is certain doubt as to whether HR robots can and should make decisions, there are use cases that include HR decision making. Such decisions range from minor "low-stake" decisions, such as approval or refusal of business travel (e.g., Papageorgiou, 2018), to more important "high-stake" decisions, such as the (non-)invitation of applicants to job interviews (e.g., Chichester & Giffen, 2019). However, it remains often unclear whether such decisions are based on rules predefined by humans or rules learned by ML algorithms of RPA.

As characteristic for and intended by RPA, the vast majority of use cases refer to *software* robots. However, blurring the boundaries between RPA and robotics, there are a few use case suggestions with embodied (i.e., physical humanoid) robots, in particular for conducting job interviews (e.g., Inoue et al., 2020; Nørskov & Ulhøi, 2020) – therewith expanding the objectives of physical robots beyond the mere "physical manipulation" of the world (see CHAPTER 1). These constitute examples of a humanoid personalization of robots. In the same vein, these emotionalize RPA by at least expressing some emotions such as interest and attention.

While use cases of unattended HR RPA, such as the creation of an HR report or the transfer of data from one HR system to another, refer to simple RPA problems, the above examples of decision making, communication, and emotionalization show that there are also use cases which clearly address cognitive RPA problems in HR.

In sum, while of different quality and level of elaboration, there is now a large set of use case suggestions uncovering very broad and differentiated application potentials of RPA in HR. These not only refer to simple operational processes, but also to more complex relational processes including interactions with and decisions on human HR stakeholders. It therefore comes as no surprise that the overall application potential of RPA in HR is considered to be very good, and that HR is judged to be among the "best candidates" (Ivančić et al., 2019) for RPA. Against this backdrop, RPA shows the potential to trigger a massive second phase of automation of HRM, and thus ushers in an "algorithmic management" of HR.

Application Challenges of HR RPA

Application challenges refer to the potential problems of applying RPA in HR. In the following, major *technical* and *human challenges* are briefly introduced.

Technical challenges
Technical challenges refer to the conceptual, methodical, and procedural problems of applying RPA in HR.

First, HR RPA is prone to *process exceptions* (e.g., Santos et al., 2019; Syed et al., 2020). Exceptions refer to unforeseen deviations from the automated process. For instance, a recruiting robot can be trained to perform the handling of unsolicited applications (extracting and entering applicant data, creating and sending an acknowledgment of receipt, etc.). If unsolicited applications of the past, which were used to program or train the robot, stemmed exclusively from *one* applicant, the robot would not be able to handle an unsolicited application of a dual career couple with *two* applicants and *two* applications within *one* application letter. This can lead to the termination of the process, or worse, an incorrect execution of the process that messes up the data of both applicants. Thus, the handling of exceptions by robots that eliminates the need for costly human intervention is one of the challenges of future RPA applications (Syed et al., 2020).

Second and related, HR RPA is prone to *technical and managerial process changes* (e.g., Santos et al., 2019; Syed et al., 2020). Technical changes refer to modifications of back-end systems or further robots that the robot interacts with. For instance, an update of an ERP system, which changes the screen and data fields for inputting applicant data, might cause the termination of an automated applicant data ascertainment process. Managerial changes refer to modifications of business rules. For instance, changing recruiting rules by accepting applicants without a university degree for management positions will not prevent the robot from executing the previous rules and automatically rejecting those applying for management positions that do not have a university degree. Both cases thus need the adaption of the robot to the respective technical or managerial change. Depending on the frequency of such changes, the ongoing maintenance of RPA robots might turn out effortful and costly, thus counteracting the intended efficiency gains (e.g., Santos et al., 2019). Thus, the development of self-adapting robots that recognize and react to changes of their environment constitutes a further future challenge (e.g., Wewerka & Reichert, 2020).

Third, HR RPA might induce *error propagation* (e.g., Santos et al., 2019; Syed et al., 2020). As with any automation project, the automation of errors by RPA robots will not only increase the speed with which errors are created but will also make the errors systematic, therewith significantly increasing the damage. For instance, if human recruiters did not inform the works council about new job postings for reasons of time pressure, even though there is a legal obligation to do so, and if a robot is trained on the respective process performance data, the robot will systematically ignore this right of the works council in every execution of the process.

Human challenges

Human challenges refer to the ethical, social, and/or psychological problems of applying RPA in HR.

First, HR RPA might induce *job losses* for HR professionals (e.g., Santos et al., 2019; Wewerka & Reichert, 2020). As RPA promises to bring about a second wave of advanced automation, it will reduce the amount of work available to HR professionals going forward. As a rough estimate, it is suggested that in terms of productivity one RPA robot is equivalent to about nine human full-time equivalents (FTEs) (Papageorgiou, 2018), which uncovers the huge rationalization potentials of RPA in HR. Of course, as already happened in earlier automation phases in HR, this could again be used to "liberate" HR professionals and free them up for more "value-adding" activities. Beyond operational benefits such as reducing the costs, time lengths, and errors of HR processes, a better use of human potentials might actually constitute a core reason for adopting RPA (e.g., Syed et al., 2020). However, given the large automation potentials, the question arises as to whether these value-adding activities can occupy HR professionals sufficiently to fully cover the spare time created by RPA (e.g., Wewerka & Reichert, 2020).

Second, HR RPA might induce a *dehumanization of HR* (e.g., Zel & Kongar, 2020). To the extent to which attended ("front-office") HR processes are also automated, attributes of these processes that are valued by human HR process participants, such as appreciation, warmth, or closeness, might be lost. For instance, from a merely technical perspective, the process of expressing recognition for an employee's outstanding contribution could be fully automated by using an RPA (chat-) robot. From a managerial perspective, however, there are obvious reasons why the human line manager of the employee should perform this recognition task. In contrast, however, a degree of "dehumanization" of certain HR processes due to the use of robots can sometimes even be seen as an advantage, as for instance when it reduces human bias in selection (e.g., Chichester & Giffen, 2019). Thus, depending on the actual HR process and the corresponding HR robot, "dehumanization" might represent a challenge in one situation but an opportunity in another.

Third and related, HR RPA is likely to induce *acceptance issues* (e.g., Syed & Wynn, 2020), where such affect both the process-owner side and the process-participant side. On the process-owner side, acceptance refers to the need for senior HR management to be able to trust the robots to execute the respective HR processes quickly, efficiently, and without error. Since robots take control over a significant amount of the process, RPA performance is vital for acceptance by HR process owners (e.g., Syed & Wynn, 2020). Even more critical is the acceptance of RPA by HR process participants. A core group consists of the HR professionals that are responsible for the process steps that are to be automated by RPA robots. This group is confronted with deep changes, be it switching to more "value-adding" HR tasks, switching to robot implementation, maintenance, and control tasks ("HR bot manager"), or, in the worst case, being made redundant and having to leave the company (e.g., Syed & Wynn, 2020). In the case of attended RPA, further participants of HR processes, in essence employees, applicants, and line managers, need to accept the interactions with robots and the results generated by them (e.g., Malik et al., 2020). Also for this group, the actual performance of the robot constitutes a crucial precondition for their acceptance, not to mention their perceived integrity and benevolence (Syed & Wynn, 2020).

RESEARCH ON HR ROBOTIC PROCESS AUTOMATION

Current Research

As RPA constitutes a rather new development, being around for less than a decade, and as in this time it has mainly been driven by practice, general research on RPA is only now just emerging (see, e.g., the reviews by Ivančić et al., 2019; Syed et al., 2020; Wewerka & Reichert, 2020). It therefore comes as no surprise that domain-specific research on HR RPA is very scarce and restricted to a small number of relevant contributions.

First, there are a few *conceptual introductions* into HR RPA that present the concept of RPA, discuss its application possibilities including expected advantages (Papageorgiou, 2018; Nawaz, 2019; Zel & Kongar, 2020), or describe general implementation procedures (Balasundaram & Venkatagiri, 2020). While these contributions usually broadly refer to general HR processes, there are also contributions focusing on a specific HR process such as conducting job interviews (Nørskov & Ulhøi, 2020).

Second, there are a few *cases studies* on HR RPA realizations that refer to utilizing RPA in payroll outsourcing (Anagnoste, 2018; Hallikainen et al., 2018), in onboarding (Šimek & Šperka, 2019), or for a set of different HR processes (Balasundaram & Venkatagiri, 2020; Malik et al., 2020). Hence, some first insights on the experiences of pioneering corporations are available, ranging from describing benefits such as "significant cost savings through a reduced HR headcount" (Malik et al., 2020, p. 15), to highlighting issues such as "problems occurred because the robot worked much faster than humans and did not wait for the responses from the applications" (Hallikainen et al., 2018, p. 46).

Third, there are a few studies that *develop prototypes* of HR RPA robots. These support the processes of recruiting (Garimella & Paruchuri, 2015; Mhaske et al., 2019), selection (Carţiş & Suciu, 2019; Suen et al., 2020), employee travel approval (Rizk et al., 2020), or employee contract management (Parchande et al., 2019). The respective design processes and the resulting robots illustrate and substantiate large overlaps of RPA with natural language processing if RPA robots also communicate with human process participants (e.g., Carţiş & Suciu, 2019; Rizk et al., 2020; see CHAPTER 12), as well as with machine learning if RPA robots also make decisions, such as granting or refusing travel approvals (e.g., Parchande et al., 2019), or if robots predict characteristics of human process participants, such as the personality traits of applicants (e.g., Suen et al., 2020) (see CHAPTERS 2–8).

Fourth, given the very nascent state of HR RPA, it is not surprising that systematic *empirical studies* on the adoption and consequences of HR RPA are missing. Two brief descriptive studies include estimations of the future possibilities (Karuna & Sushma, 2019) and future plans (Saukkonen et al., 2019) for adopting HR RPA, hinting at rather positive expectations of respondents.

In sum, research on HR RPA has just started and offers few initial and patchy insights. Additionally, relevant research to date has mostly been conducted outside the HR discipline, and frequently gives the impression that HR processes are selected rather randomly and mainly for illustrative purposes. The topic is just starting to touch the discipline of HR (cf. the case study of Malik et al., 2020).

Future Research

Regarding future research, the above delineation hints at a broad set of relevant topics. Already, there is a large set of general open research questions that have been compiled by existing general RPA contributions (e.g., Czarnecki & Fettke, 2021; Syed et al., 2020; van der Aalst et al., 2018). However, inasmuch as these questions are of a rather technical nature, such as improving the scalability of RPA robots (e.g., Syed et al., 2020), these are relevant but not necessarily HR-specific topics. HR-specific research topics thus group around specific *applications* of RPA in the *HR domain*. The manifold issues related to the domain-specific application can be systematized with a simple framework that distinguishes the interrelated areas of the *context, configuration*, and *consequences* of an HR RPA application (Strohmeier, 2007).

First, researching the *context* implies determining organizational characteristics that either further or hinder an HR RPA application – therewith addressing the overarching question of *"What kinds of context are (not) suitable for HR RPA?"*. General research already lists diverse characteristics for RPA such as frequent execution, transparency, maturity of existing processes, a large share of human-based tasks in these processes, the involvement of different backend systems in these processes, or the high data quality of these systems (e.g., Santos et al., 2019; Syed et al., 2020). Future research needs to concretize these characteristics by elaborating on the domain-specific suitability of RPA in HR. While this of course also refers to unattended RPA, core domain issues arise in particular for attended and self-service RPA, such as which stakeholders are suitable (e.g., only active employees or also retirees with little computer literacy), which types of emotional situations are suitable (e.g., only consensual processes or also processes with conflict potential such as disciplinary action), and should RPA draw decisions and, if so, which types of decisions are suitable (e.g., no decisions, only minor "everyday" decisions, or also major decisions such as hiring or promotion). Systematic knowledge on contextual conditions (un-)suitable for RPA can then be used for adoption decisions in practice.

Second, researching the *configuration* implies determining suitable technical, task, and human elements of an HR RPA application (Strohmeier, 2007) – therewith addressing the overarching question of *"How should HR RPA (not) be designed?"*. *Technical elements* refer to the adequate technical design of HR robots. Again, this implies numerous issues of detail, and again core domain issues particularly refer to robots for attended RPA. For instance: (How) should a robot interact with stakeholders (e.g., through screens, e-mails, or by written or spoken language)? (How) should a robot be personalized (e.g., not at all, as a human, or as a humanoid fantasy creature)? (How) should a robot be emotionalized (e.g., should a robot understand and react to stakeholder emotions, and beyond express its emotions such as empathy or joy)? (See, e.g., Feine et al., 2019.) *Task elements* refer to the adequate design of the planning, implementation, application, and maintenance of RPA. Again, general research offers initial insights such as incorporating RPA in the overall automation strategy, considering all stakeholders in planning and implementation, caring for compliance with legal regulations, or systematically documenting the bot knowledge (cf. the review of Syed et al., 2020). It is thus necessary to concretize such issues for HR, by clarifying what is needed for legal compliance (e.g., does an RPA-based granting of vacations to employees constitute a "decision" in the sense of the EU GDPR, or not?), how acceptance of current HR professionals can be ensured, and whether, and if so how, stakeholders that interact with robots should be trained, among many others. Closely related, *human elements* refer to determining the minimum number and qualification of humans needed to perform the above RPA-related tasks adequately. An overarching core question is who should "own" an HR robot and, thus, bear the overall responsibility for the above tasks? For example, given the technical complexity of RPA, should it be handed over to technical departments, or should HR as the applying domain take over responsibility? In the same way, the specific responsibilities and requirements of humans need to be investigated. In sum, researching the configuration of an HR RPA application goes beyond mere technical issues of robot design by also incorporating related tasks and humans. Systematic knowledge on HR RPA configurations with fitting technical, task, and human elements can be used for RPA design decisions in practice.

Third, researching *consequences* implies determining the phenomena that accompany or follow an HR RPA application – therewith addressing the overarching question of *"What are the desired and undesired outcomes of HR RPA?"*. This initially refers to general outcomes. Regarding desired general outcomes, research should for instance evaluate the improvements promised by RPA such as increased efficiency, cost-effectiveness, and speed of HR process executions (e.g., Syed et al., 2020). Regarding undesired general outcomes, research should evaluate anticipated problems such as job losses and acceptance issues among human process performers (e.g., Syed et al., 2020). Beyond general consequences, design-dependent consequences particularly need to be better researched and understood, especially the design-dependent consequences of *attended and self-service* robots. Corresponding with the different design possibilities as delineated above, this refers to a broader set of questions. Illustrated by the design option to personalize robots, the comparative consequences of personalized versus non-personalized robots need to be researched. Regarding desired consequences, this refers for instance to researching whether personalized robots are better accepted than non-personalized ones by human process participants. Regarding undesired consequences, this refers for instance to researching whether personalized robots raise too high expectations, that is, expectation of human-level performance across *all* tasks ("strong AI") (e.g., Malik et al., 2020). In this way, the consequences of different design possibilities of robots are in need of systematic research. Against the backdrop of wanting to achieve desired consequences of HR RPA while avoiding undesired ones, systematic knowledge on the consequences of HR robots can be used to support adoption decisions, but beyond that also design decisions.

In sum, knowledge on *which types of HR RPA configurations yield which types of consequences in which types of contexts* is needed to uncover the possibilities as well as the limitations of RPA in HRM.

CONCLUSIONS

AI software robots will possibly usher in a massive second phase of automation in HRM. Regarding this, making a distinction between back-office and front-office processes is useful and necessary. HR back-office processes, particularly if unattended, are relatively simple to automate; they do not – at least not mandatorily – need a large set of "intelligent" or "cognitive" components, and there is already an established group of vendors providing software for realizing RPA in such processes. Given the general advantages of automation and the suitability of many HR processes for this type of automation, a broader realization of RPA for HR back-office processes in the nearer future is therefore probable. Contrarily, HR front-office processes are more complex and challenging to automate, are often in need of different intelligent components, and software vendors have just started to realize such intelligent components (rather than already providing them). Given that a lot of value-adding processes in HR necessitate the inclusion of human stakeholders, the automation of such processes is however not only more challenging, but also more rewarding. Core future issues of HR RPA practice and research will thus relate to attended self-service RPA rather than to mere back-office RPA. Evidently, attended self-service RPA will require a set of different "intelligent" components from different AI fields (e.g., Agostinelli et al., 2019; Chakraborti et al., 2020; Viehhauser, 2020), therewith blurring the boundaries between RPA and natural language processing (see Chapter 12) as well as between RPA and machine learning (Chapters 2–8) and, even, between RPA and affective computing (Chapter 13). The advent of RPA in HR thus once again, and with vehemence, raises the questions of how far we *can* push ("technical feasibility") and of how far we *should* push ("managerial desirability") the automation of HR – and therefore of whether and to what extent an *algorithmic management* of HR should be realized.

REFERENCES

Agostinelli, S., Marrella, A., & Mecella, M. (2019). Research challenges for intelligent robotic process automation. In *International Conference on Business Process Management* (pp. 12–18). Springer International Publishing.

Anagnoste, S. (2018). Robotic automation process – the operating system for the digital enterprise. *Proceedings of the International Conference on Business Excellence*, *12*(1), 54–69. https://doi.org/10 .2478/picbe-2018-0007

Balasundaram, S., & Venkatagiri, S. (2020). A structured approach to implementing robotic process automation in HR. *Journal of Physics: Conference Series*, *1427*(1), Article 012008. https://doi.org/10 .1088/1742-6596/1427/1/012008

BluePrism. (2020). *Human resource automation* [White Paper]. BlueprismCloud. https://www .blueprism.com/uploads/resources/white-papers/Human-Resources-Automation-Starter-Kit-Ebook .pdf, accessed May 12, 2021.

Cabello, R., Escalona, M. J., & Enríquez, J. G. (2020). Beyond the hype: RPA horizon for robot–human interaction. In A. Asatiani, J. M. García, N. Helander, & A. Jiménez-Ramírez (Eds.), *Business Process Management: Blockchain and Robotic Process Automation Forum* (pp. 185–199). Springer International Publishing. https://doi.org/10.1007/978-3-030-58779-6_13

Carţiş, A. I., & Suciu, D. M. (2019). Chatbots as a job candidate evaluation tool. In C. Debruyne, H. Panetto, W. Guédria, P. Bollen, I. Ciuciu, G. Karabatis, R. Meersman (Eds.), *On the Move to Meaningful Internet Systems: OTM 2019 Workshops* (pp. 189–193). Springer International Publishing.

Chakraborti, T., Isahagian, V., Khalaf, R., Khazaeni, Y., Muthusamy, V., Rizk, Y., & Unuvar, M. (2020). From robotic process automation to intelligent process automation – emerging trends. In A. Asatiani, J. M. García, N. Helander, A. Jiménez-Ramírez, A. Koschmider, J. Mendling, … & H. A. Reijers (Eds.), *Business Process Management: Blockchain and Robotic Process Automation Forum* (pp. 215–228). Springer International Publishing.

Chichester, M. A., Jr., & Giffen, J. R. (2019). Recruiting in the robot age: Examining potential EEO implications in optimizing recruiting through the use of artificial intelligence. *The Computer and Internet Lawyer*, *98*(6), 34–37.

Cloudpay. (2021). *RPA in global payroll* [White Paper]. Cloudpay. https://www.cloudpay.net/ cloudpaper/how-rpa-is-improving-global-payroll, accessed May 12, 2021.

Czarnecki, C., & Fettke, P. (2021). Robotic process automation: Positioning, structuring, and framing of the work. In C. Czarnecki & P. Fettke (Eds.), *Robotic process automation* (pp. 1–15). De Gruyter.

Deloitte. (2018). *Robotics and cognitive automation in HR* [White Paper]. Deloitte. https://www2 .deloitte.com/content/dam/Deloitte/us/Documents/process-and-operations/us-cons-robotics-and -cognitive-automation-in-hr.pdf, accessed May 12, 2021.

Enríquez, J. G., Jiménez-Ramírez, A., Domínguez-Mayo, F. J., & Garcia-Garcia, J. A. (2020). Robotic process automation: A scientific and industrial systematic mapping study. *IEEE Access*, *8*, 39113–39129.

Feine, J., Gnewuch, U., Morana, S., & Maedche, A. (2019). A taxonomy of social cues for conversational agents. *International Journal of Human-Computer Studies*, *132*, 138–161.

Feshchenko, P. (2021). *Algorithmic leadership and algorithmic management: A systematic literature review* [Master's thesis, Jyväskylä University]. https://jyx.jyu.fi/bitstream/handle/123456789/73759/ 1/URN%3ANBN%3Afi%3Ajyu-202101221224.pdf, accessed May 12, 2021.

Fettke, P., & Loos, P. (2019). Structuring information systems in the era of robotic process automation. In K. Bergener, M. Räckers, & A. Stein (Eds.), *The art of structuring* (pp. 191–201). Springer International Publishing.

Fettke, P., & Reisig, W. (2021). Modelling service-oriented systems and cloud services with Heraklit. In C. Zirpins, I. Paraskakis, V. Andrikopoulos, N. Kratzke, C. Pahl, N. E. Ioini, … & P. Plebani (Eds.), *Advances in Service-Oriented and Cloud Computing. ESOCC 2020. Communications in Computer and Information Science* (pp. 77–89). Springer International Publishing. https://doi.org/10.1007/978 -3-030-71906-7_7

Gao, J., Zelst, S. V., Lu, X., & Aalst, W. (2019). Automated robotic process automation: A self-learning approach. In H. Panetto, C. Debruyne, M. Hepp, D. Lewis, C. A. Ardagna, & R. Meersman (Eds.),

On the Move to Meaningful Internet Systems: OTM 2019 Conferences (pp. 95–112). Springer International Publishing. https://doi.org/10.1007/978-3-030-33246-4_6

Garimella, U., & Paruchuri, P. (2015). (HR)^2: An agent for helping HR with recruitment. *International Journal of Agent Technologies and Systems (IJATS)*, 7(3), 67–85.

Gartner (2020). *Magic quadrant for robotic process automation.* https://www.uipath.com/de/company/rpa-analyst-reports/gartner-magic-quadrant-robotic-process-automation, accessed May 12, 2021.

Hallikainen, P., Bekkhus, R., & Pan, S. L. (2018). How OpusCapita used internal RPA capabilities to offer services to clients. *MIS Quarterly Executive*, 17(1), Article 4. https://aisel.aisnet.org/misqe/vol17/iss1/4

Houy, C., Hamberg, M., & Fettke, P., (2019). Robotic process automation in public administrations. In M. Räckers, S. Halsbenning, D. Rätz, D. Richter, & E. Schweighofer (Eds.), *Digitalisierung von Staat und Verwaltung* (pp. 62–74). Bonn Gesellschaft für Informatik e.V. https://dl.gi.de/bitstream/handle/20.500.12116/20517/ftvi2019_5.pdf?sequence=1&isAllowed=y, accessed May 12, 2021.

Inoue, K., Hara, K., Lala, D., Yamamoto, K., Nakamura, S., Takanashi, K., & Kawahara, T. (2020). Job interviewer android with elaborate follow-up question generation. In *Proceedings of the 2020 International Conference on Multimodal Interaction* (pp. 324–332). ACM. https://doi.org/10.1145/3382507.3418839

Ivančić, L., Vugec, D. S., & Vukšić, V. B. (2019). Robotic process automation: Systematic literature review. In C. D. Ciccio, R. Gabryelczyk, L. García-Bañuelos, T. Hernaus, R. Hull, M. I. Štemberger, A. Kő, & M. Staples (Eds.), *International Conference on Business Process Management* (pp. 280–295). Springer International Publishing.

Karuna, M., & Sushma, S. (2019). Implementation and appraising of modernity of robotic process automation (RPA) in HRM – a case study at Micron EMS TECH PVT LTD. *Emperor Journal of Applied Scientific Research*, 1(6), 16–24.

Kryon (2020). *RPA use cases: Human resources.* https://www.kryonsystems.com/Documents/Kryon-RPA-HR-Use-Cases.pdf, accessed May 12, 2021.

Leno, V., Polyvyanyy, A., Dumas, M., Rosa, M. L., & Maggi, F. (2021). Robotic process mining: Vision and challenges. *Business and Information Systems Engineering*, 3(63), 301–314.

Ma, X., & Brown, T. W. (2020). *AI-mediated exchange theory.* arXiv preprint arXiv:2003.02093.

Malik, A., Budhwar, P., Patel, C., & Srikanth, N. R. (2020). May the bots be with you! Delivering HR cost-effectiveness and individualised employee experiences in an MNE. *The International Journal of Human Resource Management*, 1–31. https://doi.org/10.1080/09585192.2020.1859582

Martínez-Rojas, A., Barba, I., & Enríquez, J. G. (2020). *Towards a taxonomy of cognitive RPA components.* In A. Asatiani, J. M. García, N. Helander, A. Jiménez-Ramírez, A. Koschmider, J. Mendling, … & H. A. Reijers (Eds.), *Business Process Management: Blockchain and Robotic Process Automation Forum* (pp. 161–175). Springer International Publishing. https://doi.org/10.1007/978-3-030-58779-6_11

Mendling, J., Decker, G., Hull, R., Reijers, H. A., & Weber, I. (2018). How do machine learning, robotic process automation, and blockchains affect the human factor in business process management? *Communications of the Association for Information Systems*, 43(1), 297–320.

Mhaske, H., Kulkarni, S., Menon, V., Nikam, P., & Niras, B. (2019). Development of PrimeBot as an assistant to HR in recruitment process using RPA. *International Journal of Engineering Research and Technology*, 8, 97–99.

Nawaz, D. N. (2019). Robotic process automation for recruitment process. *International Journal of Advanced Research in Engineering and Technology*, 10(2), 608–611.

Ng, K. K., Chen, C. H., Lee, C. K. M., Jiao, J. R., & Yang, Z. X. (2021). A systematic literature review on intelligent automation: Aligning concepts from theory, practice, and future perspectives. *Advanced Engineering Informatics*, 47, Article 101246.

Nørskov, S., & Ulhøi, J. P. (2020). The use of robots in job interviews. In T. Bondarouk & S. Fisher (Eds.), *Encyclopedia of electronic HRM* (pp. 208–213). De Gruyter. https://doi.org/10.1515/9783110633702-032

Papageorgiou, D. (2018). Transforming the HR function through robotic process automation. *Benefits Quarterly*, 34(2), 27–30.

Parchande, S., Shahane, A., & Dhore, M. (2019). Contractual employee management system using machine learning and robotic process automation. In *2019 5th International Conference on*

Computing, Communication, Control and Automation (ICCUBEA) (pp. 1–5). IEEE. https://doi.org/10 .1109/ICCUBEA47591.2019.9128818

PeopleDoc. (2020). *The key to strategic HR: Process automation.* https://www.people-doc.com/hubfs/ 2019/UK19/UK19-PDFs/process-ebook-UK.pdf, accessed May 12, 2021.

Rizk, Y., Isahagian, V., Boag, S., Khazaeni, Y., Unuvar, M., Muthusamy, V., & Khalaf, R. (2020). A conversational digital assistant for intelligent process automation. In A. Asatiani, J. M. García, N. Helander, A. Jiménez-Ramírez, A. Koschmider, J. Mendling, … & H. A. Reijers (Eds.), *Business Process Management: Blockchain and Robotic Process Automation Forum* (pp. 85–100). Springer International Publishing.

Russell, S., & Norvig, P. (2021). *Artificial intelligence: A modern approach* (4th ed.). Pearson.

Santos, F., Pereira, R., & Vasconcelos, J. B. (2019). Toward robotic process automation implementation: An end-to-end perspective. *Business Process Management Journal, 26*(2), 405–420.

Satam, S., Nimje, T., Shetty, S., & Kurle, S. (2020). Review on mentoring chatbot. *Journal of Physical Sciences, Engineering and Technology, 12*(1), 147–150.

Saukkonen, J., Kreus, P., Obermayer, N., Ruiz, Ó. R., & Haaranen, M. (2019). AI, RPA, ML and other emerging technologies: Anticipating adoption in the HRM field. In P. Griffiths & M. N. Kabir (Eds.), *Proceedings of the European Conference on the Impact of Artificial Intelligence and Robotics ECIAIR 2019* (pp. 287–296). Theseus. http://urn.fi/URN:NBN:fi-fe2019112043357

Saxena, S., Tripathi, S., & Tsb, S. (2020). Deep robot–human interaction with facial emotion recognition using gated recurrent units and robotic process automation. In A. J. Tallón-Ballesteros & C.-H. Chen (Eds.), *Machine Learning and Artificial Intelligence: Proceedings of MLIS 2020* (pp. 115–126). IOS Press. https://doi.org/10.3233/FAIA200773

Šimek, D., & Šperka, R. (2019). How robot/human orchestration can help in an HR-department: A case study from a pilot implementation. *Organizacija, 52*(3), 204–217.

Snell, S. A., Pedigo, P. R., & Krawiec, G. M. (1995). Managing the impact of information technology on human resource management. In G. R. Ferris, S. D. Rosen, & D. T. Barnum (Eds.), *Handbook of human resource management* (pp. 159–174). Blackwell Publishers.

Strohmeier, S. (2007). Research in e-HRM: Review and implications. *Human Resource Management Review, 17*(1), 19–37.

Suen, H.-Y., Hung, K.-E., & Lin, C.-L. (2020). Intelligent video interview agent used to predict communication skill and perceived personality traits. *Human-centric Computing and Information Sciences, 10*(1), Article 3.

Syed, R., Suriadi, S., Adams, M., Bandara, W., Leemans, S. J., Ouyang, C., … & Reijers, H. A. (2020). Robotic process automation: Contemporary themes and challenges. *Computers in Industry, 115*, Article 103162.

Syed, R., & Wynn, M. T. (2020). How to trust a bot: An RPA user perspective. In A. Asatiani, J. M. García, A. Jiménez-Ramírez, N. Helander, A. Koschmider, J. Mendling, … & H. A. Reijers (Eds.), *Business Process Management: Blockchain and Robotic Process Automation Forum* (pp. 147–160). Springer International Publishing.

Taulli, T. (2020). *The robotic process automation handbook: A guide to implementing RPA systems.* Apress.

UIPath. (2021). *Robotic process automation (RPA) and human resources.* https://dfe.org.pl/wp-content/ uploads/2019/02/RPA-for-HR_Creating-a-More-Human-Workplace.pdf, accessed May 12, 2021.

van der Aalst, W. M. P., Bichler, M., & Heinzl, A. (2018). Robotic process automation. *Business Information Systems Engineering, 60*(4), 269–272.

Viehhauser, J. (2020). Is robotic process automation becoming intelligent? Early evidence of influences of artificial intelligence on robotic process automation. In A. Asatiani, J. M. García, A. Jiménez-Ramírez, N. Helander, A. Koschmider, J. Mendling, … & H. A. Reijers (Eds.), *Business Process Management: Blockchain and Robotic Process Automation Forum* (pp. 101–115). Springer International Publishing.

Wewerka, J., & Reichert, M. (2020). *Robotic process automation – a systematic literature review and assessment framework.* arXiv preprint arXiv:2012.11951.

Zel, S., & Kongar, E. (2020). Transforming digital employee experience with artificial intelligence. In *2020 IEEE/ITU International Conference on Artificial Intelligence for Good (AI4G)* (pp. 176–179). IEEE. https://doi.org/10.1109/AI4G50087.2020.9311088

11. HR evolutionary computing
Lena Wolbeck and Charlotte Köhler

INTRODUCTION

Human resource management includes a variety of planning tasks that are particularly central to industries such as call centers, health care, construction, manufacturing, and logistics. The optimal matching of employees to the company and the tasks to be performed represents a competitive advantage (Weller, 2016) – especially in industries where personnel costs account for a large share of operating costs. Following Warner (1976), there are three essential decision problems within human resource management (HRM): *staffing, scheduling*, and *rescheduling*. Decisions on these can occur at different frequencies and over different time spans during a year, as exemplified in Figure 11.1. Staffing decisions – hiring the number of employees needed – are usually taken long term and are strategic; they do not occur at regular intervals but take place on demand. The operational level comprises the assignment of tasks to persons in a duty roster, which is referred to as scheduling. While fixed working hours are specified in some areas, scheduling is of great importance, especially in areas with shift work where decisions have to be taken at regular intervals. Irregular absences of employees – for example, due to illness – require the spontaneous replanning of schedules, which is known as rescheduling.

Finding optimal solutions for staffing, scheduling, and rescheduling is challenging because the underlying decision problems are very complex as they often contain multiple or even conflicting objectives and a variety of constraints and preferences that have to be considered (Wolbeck et al., 2020). In practice, these problems are often solved by hand based on intuitive decision making and familiar patterns rather than automated decision support. Furthermore, each decision problem has very individual, specific characteristics and therefore developed information systems are hardly transferable. Manual planning, however, requires a lot of work and effort and is often far from the optimal solution. The improvement in technology and integration of information systems is therefore promising for human resources (HR): Planning software enables simple planning, the consideration of several objectives, and at the same time flexible replanning. The Australian start-up *Deputy*, for example, offers a scheduling service that is widely used by various providers in health care and catering, as well as by well-known companies such as Amazon, Google, and Uber, and has raised more than $100 million from investors in its early years, underlining the need for intelligent solutions in these industries.[1]

Although decision support systems can bring benefits to all areas of HR, (re-)scheduling is of particular interest in the literature. On the one hand, this could be due to the fact that staffing takes place less frequently and is often a bureaucratic task, thus benefiting less from algorithmic scheduling. On the other hand, scheduling is a challenging decision problem, but it can be easily translated into mathematical formulations due to its structured nature, and thus allows specific solution approaches.

A well-known example of this is nurse rostering: In an environment where skilled workers are scarce anyway, it must be ensured that all shifts are staffed at minimal cost. Since patient care must be ensured, even if a nurse is absent at short notice, a replacement must be found and the duty roster must be redrawn. At the same time, nurses work strenuous day and night shifts so that at least nurses' preferences – for example, to facilitate sleep patterns – should be taken into account. Legal work and break schedule rules make it difficult to create a feasible roster. We will follow the *Nurse Rostering Problem (NRP)* and revisit it throughout the chapter.

To relieve manual scheduling, planning software ideally relies on solution methods that can handle the complexity of the underlying scheduling problem and are fast enough for practical use. Many of these methods are based on a metaheuristic, which is a powerful algorithm to approximate solutions for complex optimization problems. In recent years, especially meta-heuristics belonging to *evolutionary computing* that are inspired by biological evolution are mentioned along with the problem of human resource scheduling, since they are simple yet flexible and can be applied to a variety of problems (Abraham et al., 2006; Eiben & Smith, 2015b).

In this chapter we want to give an overview of the current and future use of evolutionary computing in HR. We show that evolutionary computing is flexible due to the fitness function used and, thus, particularly suitable for problems in HR, where complex and often multi-criteria optimization problems have to be solved, which in addition can often change dynamically at short notice. The chapter is organized as follows. In the second section we explain the basic concepts of evolutionary computing. The third section discusses the eligibility of evolutionary concepts for solving HR decision problems. Various applications using evolutionary processes are described in the fourth section. Finally, we conclude the chapter with a summary and an outlook on future research directions.

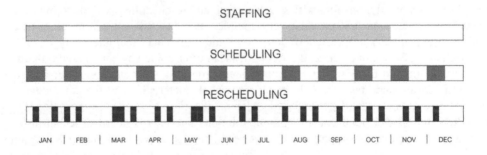

Figure 11.1   Exemplary occurrence of staffing, scheduling, and rescheduling in human resources in one year

BRIEF OVERVIEW ON EVOLUTIONARY COMPUTING

Evolutionary computing represents a major concept spanning several algorithms in computer science. Within the next section we give a brief overview to understand the principles of evolutionary computing and its inspiration from evolution. Then, we introduce the scheme of an evolutionary algorithm. The last section describes the genetic operators on which an evolutionary algorithm is built.

Terminology and Inspiration from Evolution

Algorithms with intelligent information processing can be assigned to the partially overlapping areas of *artificial intelligence* and *computational intelligence* (Kramer, 2009). While artificial intelligence is used to learn intelligent behavior, computational intelligence imitates intelligence that is already present in complex systems. Computational intelligence comprises concepts which are inspired by nature: For example, neural networks mimic the flow of information in the brain, fuzzy logic is based on the imprecise decision making of human beings, and evolutionary computing – which is the focus of this chapter – draws its inspiration from evolution.

Evolutionary concepts are powerful tools developed for solving complex optimization problems. However, the concept of evolutionary algorithms can be adopted in the field of machine learning. In the meantime, the term evolutionary computing has been ambiguously assigned to computational intelligence and machine learning as part of artificial intelligence (see Duch, 2007; Goldberg & Holland, 1988). In this chapter we explain the application of evolutionary computing in terms of solving complex mathematical optimization problems; for a detailed classification of evolutionary computing in the superordinate concept of artificial intelligence, we additionally refer the reader to CHAPTER 1 of this handbook.

To better understand the ideas and principles of evolutionary computing, we give a brief excursus on evolution, the discovery of which goes back to Darwin (1859). *Evolution* describes the change of characteristics of a population over generations by variation and selection. A *population* comprises all the individuals of one species. An *individual* refers to a single being and individuals can reproduce among themselves. Since resources for populations are limited, such as habitat or nourishment, a population as a whole remains stable in size. Some *offspring* have a greater chance of surviving (and thus passing on their genes and characteristics to the next generation) than others, which is known as *natural selection*. By *recombining* the genetic information of *parents* – a crossover of the information stored in the genes – a new genetically unique offspring can be created. Which characteristics are passed on is precisely defined; nevertheless, rare errors, so-called *mutations*, can occur during this transfer. In the end, recombination and mutation can give an offspring an advantage over the rest of the individuals in the population. If this is the case, these mutations are *selected* in the sense of natural selection and contribute to a change in the characteristics of a population. Probably the most famous example of this is the Darwin finch, in which descendants could open up new food sources through altered beak forms. Evolution is the most powerful invention of nature to create superior solutions and therefore it is no surprise that it is used as an inspiration for finding solutions for complex problems in computer science. Within the next section we present how computer science uses Darwin's observations.

Evolutionary Algorithms

Evolutionary algorithms comprises a group of algorithms divided into four classes that all mimic ideas from biological evolution – each algorithm being a complex metaheuristic itself. The classes are *Evolutionary Programming, Evolutionary Strategies, Genetic Programming,* and *Genetic Algorithms*. Although the four algorithm classes share general design principles, small differences can be distinguished; we refer the reader to Abraham et al. (2006) for a detailed understanding of the similarities and differences. While the classification for evolutionary algorithms that we follow here is suggested for evolutionary computing (for example Eiben & Smith, 2015b; Oduguwa et al., 2005), the use of these terms in the literature may not always be as distinct. Publication numbers in Web of Science show that almost 90,000 publications use the term "genetic algorithms"; the second most frequently described term in the literature is "evolutionary algorithms" with just over 10,000 publications using this term.[2] It must be remembered that the field of research of evolutionary computing and its algorithms dates back many decades (Kramer, 2009). Thus, it can be assumed that the definition and use of these terms was also subject to a temporal development as well as a mixing of this terminology and solution methods over time. For that reason, Michalewicz and Fogel (2013) even suggest not using this terminology to differentiate between different algorithms of evolutionary computing any more.

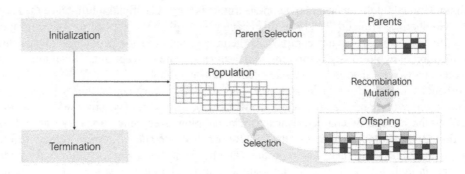

Figure 11.2   Scheme of an evolutionary algorithm based on Eiben and Smith (2015b)

Based on the learning process of evolution, evolutionary algorithms modify an initial population of individuals over generations using genetic operators (Beasley & Chu, 1996), with succeeding populations converging towards an optimum. Like any metaheuristic, an evolutionary algorithm cannot guarantee that an optimal solution will be found (Dréo et al., 2006). The process of an evolutionary algorithm is sketched in Figure 11.2. In the beginning, the respective algorithm is initialized and a first population is formed. An iteration then consists of three steps: First, the parents of the defined population are selected that are to be considered for the propagation. Second, these are recombined with each other to generate offspring. Third, from these offspring, the most promising ones are selected and used as a starting population for the next iteration. The process of forming successive generations is repeated until a termination criterion is met, for example a maximum runtime or a maximum number of generations. Each generation corresponds to an iteration of the algorithm, where at the beginning, from a population with μ individuals, the parents are selected to generate λ offspring (Abraham et al., 2006). The genetic operators of parent selection, recombination, mutation, and selection are described in detail in the section "multi-criteria optimization".

Using the example of the nurse rostering problem, this could work as follows. The first population of rosters is considered in the algorithm, for example rosters that have already been created manually in the past. Then some rosters that have certain characteristics that are desired are chosen as parents. For example, a roster might be especially fair for nurse 1, and another especially fair for nurse 2, but never for both. These rosters could then represent suitable candidates as parents for the next step. By recombining these, new rosters are created, each of which has some of the characteristics of the previous ones, for example some of the shifts of nurse 1 and some of the shifts of nurse 2. From these new solutions, rosters are selected that have desirable characteristics, such as single fairness or a combined consideration of fairness. The process is repeated until a termination criterion is met.

There are only two major design decisions that have to be taken when applying an evolutionary algorithm. First, the representation of the solution space and, second, the evaluation of the solution. This simplicity of this conceptual design is a great advantage of an evolutionary algorithm (Michalewicz & Fogel, 2013). Another advantage of evolutionary algorithms is that a large number of individuals can be considered simultaneously, thus making it possible to find several global optima at the same time. Based on a *fitness function*, an evolutionary algorithm assesses the quality of the solutions – the fitness. Accordingly, the choice of a suitable fitness function is of great importance if the problem itself does not specify one.

Genetic Operators

Although changes in a population in terms of biological evolution can be observed, the influences of nature that have contributed to them are complex and not always obvious. A major challenge is therefore transferring evolutionary concepts to an algorithm, which is done through *genetic operators*. The choice and design of the genetic operators is of particular importance, which is why we give a brief explanation of them in the following. We present genetic operators for the selection of individuals for recombination (*parent selection*) and for survival (*selection*) as well as for variation, more precisely *recombination* and *mutation*.

Parent selection. To decide which parents to choose for an iteration, a roulette wheel selection is often used in which each individual is assigned a selection probability based on its fitness (Dréo et al., 2006): The size of the sector for an individual thus correlates positively with the fitness level, where fitter individuals have a higher probability of being selected. Another commonly used method of parent selection is tournament selection. Here a "tournament" between individuals is simulated: Two disjoint groups of k randomly selected individuals are formed, from which the individual with the best fitness is selected and chosen as parent. This method is often used because it is easy to implement (Dréo et al., 2006).

Recombination. Starting from usually two parent individuals, which were previously selected for reproduction, at least one offspring is produced. The recombination of the characteristics of the parents can be implemented in very different ways. According to Weicker (2015), there are three strategies for recombination. First, combining operators serve to recombine the properties of the parents. Each variable assignment corresponds to a randomly chosen characteristic of a parent. For example, parent individuals (1-2-3-4) and (5-6-7-8) could result in offspring (1-6-7-4). Next, interpolating operators produce offspring. Thus, descendants get a mixture of the characteristics of the parents. Following the example introduced, a possible outcome for an offspring could be (3-4-5-6). Finally, extrapolating operators use the characteristics of the parents to make predictions about the variable-assignment of the offspring and the resulting solution-quality. Thus, completely new individuals – independent of the parents – can be created using these procedures. In the introduced example, the offspring may be (0-2-7-10).

Mutation. With the help of mutation an individual is changed – it mutates. Usually, a mutation represents a minimal change of one parent individual, so that for example only a few variable values change or the modification of the values is small in each case. The mutation rates are usually very low, so that the mutation has a less important role than recombination within an evolutionary algorithm (Goldberg & Holland, 1988). According to Holland (1975), the mutation can be generalized in the following form: Each decision variable can be subjected to a mutation, using a random procedure to select those that actually mutate. Each variable is treated independently and changed according to its probability of mutation. The mutation supports recombination by enumerating the different characteristics of the individuals (Holland, 1975). One strategy for an incremental mutation is, for example, the permuting mutation, which exchanges two numbers of a permutation (Weicker, 2015). For example, the individual (1-2-3-4) becomes (1-4-3-2). If this method is applied to an individual represented by different permutations, an exchange of numbers within a permutation (as already described) or between permutations can occur. The following example illustrates how it works: individual (1-2-3, 4-5-6) mutates to (4-2-3, 1-5-6).

Selection. At the end of an iteration the individuals for the next generation must be determined from the offspring and previous population (parents). The best individuals are selected and form the next population. This corresponds to "survival of the fittest" according to Darwin (Whitley, 2001). However, selection can be interpreted and implemented in different ways (for more details, see Dréo et al., 2006). One possibility is generational replacement, where the number of parent individuals is simply replaced by the same number of offspring ($\mu = \lambda$). This selection mechanism can be implemented with very little effort; if λ is (significantly) larger than μ, only $|\mu|$ individuals of the offspring are considered. Another possibility is the steady state replacement. Here the fitness of the offspring is also taken into account, so that, for example, fitter offspring are more likely to be included in the next population or only the worst parents are replaced. Another selection option is elitism, where the fittest individuals are selected from the parents as well as from the offspring; this is often used for local exploitation of the solution space.

Although it is often not possible to foresee which strategies are best for the problem, the general design decisions for all evolutionary algorithms are similar. This section serves to provide a brief introduction to the concepts of evolutionary algorithms to better understand their use for solving decision problems in HR in the following sections. For a detailed understanding, we refer the reader to Bäck (1996), Abraham et al. (2006) and Dréo et al. (2006).

ELIGIBILITY OF EVOLUTIONARY COMPUTING FOR DECISION PROBLEMS IN HUMAN RESOURCE MANAGEMENT

There are many reasons for, as well as advantages of, using evolutionary algorithms to solve decision problems. On the one hand, strategies based on evolutionary processes benefit from their easy comprehensibility and can be applied flexibly to different problems (Rousseau et al., 2002). On the other hand, because of their characteristics, there are decision problems that are ideally suited to be solved using evolutionary computing.

To emphasize the flexibility and variability of an evolutionary algorithm, we would like to give some examples of applications that have nothing in common with decision problems in HRM. Using a genetic algorithm, David et al. (2013) develop a computer chess program that learns from human behavior stored in a database, further improves by evolution, and is as good as other comparable programs. Similar is the use of genetic operators to solve puzzles (Sholomon et al., 2014) and Sudokus (Sato et al., 2013). In aerospace engineering, Hornby et al. (2011), for example, use an evolutionary algorithm for designing hardware for the NASA Space Technology 5. These examples represent only a very small application area of evolutionary computing, but their diversity already implies that there is a wide range.

If a solution method is easily transferable and can be applied to a large number of problem instances or even optimization problems, this is particularly advantageous in an area with many different decision problems. As HR is such an area, often algorithms based on evolutionary processes are favored. The high complexity of decision problems in HR increasingly necessitates the use of decision support systems. When an exact solution is not possible or takes too much time, heuristic or metaheuristic approaches such as evolutionary computing are often applied. The section "complex decision problems" addresses this aspect. Following Abraham et al. (2006), evolutionary algorithms can adapt to dynamic changes or requirements, which we discuss in the section "dynamic changes in HR". Furthermore, both multi-criteria optimization and varying objective functions can easily be considered by exchanging the fitness function without affecting the functionality of the algorithm, as the last section explains in more detail. Thus, evolutionary computing enables decision support systems to be flexible, which underlines its eligibility for use in HRM.

Complex Decision Problems

There are a variety of decision-making issues in HR, most of which directly affect a company's employees. These issues correspond to complex optimization problems that are currently often solved manually in practice, although automated planning could save a lot of time. The complexity results from the numerous constraints that have to be fulfilled, and therefore an exact solution is rarely possible in a reasonable time. Many of these decision problems even belong to the class of NP-hard problems comprising the computationally most challenging problems to solve (Lenstra & Kan, 1981). Heuristic approaches that aim to approximate an optimal solution, ideally requiring a shorter computational time, seem to be good methods for solving complex optimization problems. This is because, in practice, a feasible solution of good quality computed in a shorter time is far more helpful than an optimal solution whose proof of optimality requires several hours or even days. The risk of an iterative solution approach, which – to put it simply – jumps from one solution to the next better one, getting stuck in a local optimum does not appear with metaheuristics such as evolutionary computing (Dréo et al., 2006). As Eiben and Smith (2015b) state, evolutionary algorithms provide a suitable and robust approach to solve complex problems as their flexibility promotes further development, thus increasing the performance more and more.

Nevertheless, some aspects should be carefully examined during the design and implementation of evolutionary concepts in algorithms, because they have a significant impact on performance. After a few generations, for example, selection may cause the population to drift in a certain direction that does not lead to a satisfactory solution (Whitley, 1994). This is called *premature convergence* as the population is converging towards a suboptimal solution. Such a convergence occurs especially if the population size that has been chosen is rather small. A mutation operator can help by randomly changing the genetic information of the offspring, thereby increasing genetic diversity. Slowik and Kwasnicka (2020) summarize further mechanisms by which premature convergence can be addressed, such as allowing for subpopulations exchanging individuals. In doing this, the population is separated on several islands to get subpopulations but regularly an exchange of individuals is allowed (Whitley et al., 1999). Dréo et al. (2006) also point to this problem when using an approximated fitness function. Thus, it is very likely that premature convergence in a suboptimal direction may occur. Then, it is particularly important to decide on the timing of the fitness function's refinement.

Dynamic Changes in HR

Since evolutionary algorithms are very flexible, there are only a few adjustments needed when applying an algorithm to another decision problem and its instances (Rousseau et al., 2002). Decision problems in HR can vary greatly between companies as well as within a company; for example, different industries have different requirements or countries have different legal regulations on working hours and break times. In the case of a scheduling problem, for example, there may be (new) employees who require modified constraints for their employment. Likewise, (new) customers may demand an adjustment of the planning. Accordingly, it is important that a solution method for solving decision problems in HR is easily adaptable to changes of circumstances. Due to its flexibility, evolutionary computing offers great potential to deal with a wide variety of – often individual – requirements.

The involvement of decision makers, and, thus, their individual preferences during the solution process, is often desired since HRM affects people directly and it is not always possible to model all real circumstances and decision criteria like a gut feeling. Inoue et al. (2003), for example, present an interactive decision support system for nurse rostering based on an evolutionary algorithm, in which the head nurse can manually evaluate and adjust the rosters. Such an interaction with the algorithm may prevent premature convergence because, for example, in this situation the algorithm can learn and adapt its fitness function.

Another changing aspect in today's world is the increasing ecological pressure on companies and the far-reaching change towards a participating workforce. Following the idea of sustainable HRM, the needs of employees are becoming increasingly important and, thus, decision makers should take this trend into account both in their decisions and in the methods and practices used (Macke & Genari, 2019). According to Bush (2020), the most common definition of sustainable HRM corresponds to what Aust et al. (2020) calls Triple Bottom Line HRM, which simultaneously pursues economic, environmental, and social purposes. In addition to illustrating the changing requirements for a solution approach, this idea leads us to multi-criteria optimization.

Multi-criteria Optimization

Decision problems in the field of HR are often multi-criteria because a solution's quality is determined by more than one criterion. Driven by requirements from practice, an evolutionary algorithm is used in Cai and Li (2000) to schedule staff while minimizing total costs, maximizing the surplus of staff, and minimizing the variation within staff surplus over time. There are many other examples like Yannibelli and Amandi (2013) and Toroslu and Arslanoglu (2007) which emphasize the relevance of multiple objectives within HRM.

The definition of an objective function – in evolutionary terms the fitness function – is a problem-specific part of evolutionary optimization (Eiben & Smith, 2015a). Within an evolutionary algorithm, a fitness value is assigned to each individual. This value is crucial both for parent selection and for the selection of the "surviving" individuals for the next generation. According to Dréo et al. (2006), the performance of an evolutionary algorithm can only be as good as the suitability of the fitness function. The function should be constructed considering a stringent inclination towards good or optimal values. Besides, the evaluation of fitness should not take up too much computing power, so that it does not slow down the process, which is why a simple function is preferred over a complex one. If necessary, an approximation should be applied to save computing time (Dréo et al., 2006). However, the nature of evolutionary algorithms allows another advantage that can be used in the evaluation, which is parallel computing. A parallel evaluation of several individuals is an advantage of an evolutionary algorithm compared to other optimization techniques such as tabu search, which evaluates solutions one after the other (Abraham et al., 2006). Defining an appropriate fitness function to evaluate individuals is a challenging and important task. In the end, it is often not a single value but a ranked order of multiple values that is decisive in the evaluation of individuals. In nurse rostering, for example, nowadays they aim at cost minimization, fairness maximization, or other objectives, or even a combination of several, which are modeled in the fitness function. The design of the fitness function is not restricted as long as the function can be applied to the individuals.

EVOLUTIONARY COMPUTING APPLIED IN HR

In this section, we examine the literature on the application of evolutionary computing to HR. We present a keyword-based literature search to identify the major application areas. Based on this, we discuss concepts in the respective application areas.

Overview on Recent Literature

As observed by Dréo et al. (2006), the publication of Goldberg (1989) has led to a significant increase in interest in the research area of evolutionary computing, which is very clearly reflected in the increasing number of publications since then. To get an overview of the relevance of evolutionary computing in the field of HR, we identified literature from the past 20 years in these areas. First, we conducted a search using Web of Science for literature considering evolutionary computing by applying the search string: *TOPIC: (evolutionary computing OR evolutionary algorithm OR genetic algorithm OR genetic programming OR evolution* strateg*)*. In total, this allowed us to identify nearly 10,000 publications. In a second step, we investigated how widespread literature in the application domain HR is. The following search string *TOPIC: (human resources OR staff* OR staff schedule* OR personnel OR roster*)* returned more than 300,000 hits, and even narrowing the search terms to just the title still yields 35,000 results. In Figure 11.3a, we plotted the accumulated number of publications found (y-axis) by year of publication (x-axis). For both areas we see an increasing number of publications over the years.

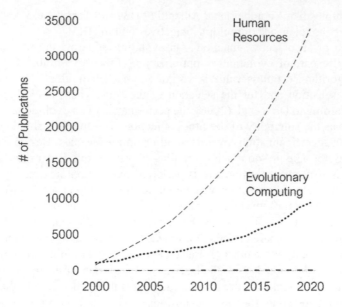

Figure 11.3a

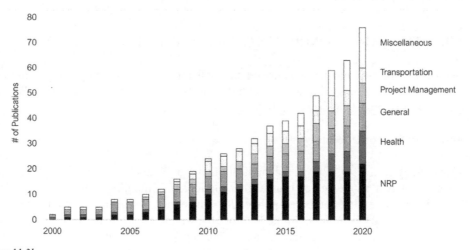

Figure 11.3b

Figure 11.3   *Cumulative number of publications in the last 20 years: (a) areas of human resources and evolutionary computing; (b) application areas of evolutionary computing in human resources*

In a next step, we combined the two search strands to understand how large the intersection of literature interested in both fields is. The search yielded 76 publications by 2020; thus, the intersection of the two research areas is very small despite the very high number of publications in each area. In Figure 11.3b, we have plotted the accumulated number of publications per year. Here we also see a steadily increasing number of publications. In addition, we have examined the 76 papers for the field of application – as can be seen from the different categories within the bars. Most of the literature considers the well-known *NRP*. Another large part considers *Health* problems in a more general sense than the NRP. Some of the literature does not refer to a specific application area (*General*) but presents general solution concepts that would then have to be adapted for different application areas. Another part deals with HR in a *Project Management* context as well as *Transportation*. Under *Miscellaneous* we summarize here further application areas, the more refined subdivision of which would have led to too many categories. It should be emphasized that although *NRP* has always made up a large part of the literature over the years, it seems to have gained less relevance. On the other hand, the increase in *Health*, especially in 2020, is greater than in the other areas. *Miscellaneous* has also seen a significant increase – this could be an indication that recent literature is exploiting new areas of application. Please note that this rough keyword search is only intended to give a brief but not necessarily complete overview on literature and the application area of interest. In the following section we identify and discuss some examples from relevant literature in the areas in detail.

Application Areas

In the following, we will present typical application areas for HR in conjunction with evolutionary computing. We briefly describe the characteristics of the application areas, give the reader an introduction to literature in these areas, and determine the suitability of evolutionary computing concepts for these areas. Doing this, we do not cover the categories *General* and *Miscellaneous* as these would go beyond the scope of this chapter.

Nurse Rostering Problem. The NRP is the most common application example of evolutionary computing. A NRP refers to the optimization problem of generating a roster for nursing staff. In principle, the shifts to be assigned to nurses are specified (or determined in an earlier step) for a known set of nurses. Thus, the task is to assign nurses to shifts, or vice versa, to cover demand, while ensuring that costs are minimized (Cheang et al., 2003; Burke et al., 2004). In doing this, the decision maker – for example the head nurse – has to consider various requirements and rostering rules, which increase problem complexity. These are divided into hard constraints and soft constraints. Hard constraints are those that must be fulfilled mandatorily, for example covering the demand with different shift types that take into consideration individual staff availabilities, working time regulations, and skill levels. Soft constraints are those that are desirable to fulfill in to order to increase roster quality, which may involve the consideration of things like the fulfillment of preferences or requests, an equal distribution of workload, or a combination of these. There are many publications that address the general improvement of nurse rosters through the use of evolutionary computation; approaches can be found in Aickelin and Dowsland (2004), Aickelin and White (2004), Aickelin et al. (2009), Bai et al. (2010), Beddoe and Petrovic (2006), Duenas et al. (2009), Huang et al. (2014), Inoue et al. (2003), Jan et al. (2000), Leksakul and Phetsawat (2014), Lin et al. (2015), Maass et al. (2017), Maenhout and Vanhoucke (2011), Moz and Pato (2007), Ohki (2012), Pato and Moz (2008), Tsai and Li (2009), and Zhou et al. (2012). Additionally, we want to highlight a few publications that give specific insights into the use of evolutionary strategies for problem-specific issues. Jan et al. (2000) design a fitness solution to increase fairness among all nurses by calculating a fitness value for each nurse individually. The overall fitness function objective is then to maximize the average as well as minimize the variance of the individual fitness values. Inoue et al. (2003) propose a learning fitness function based on an assessment by the decision maker, which therefore enables a human–machine interaction that can benefit from the previous experience of decision makers. Some publications focus on rescheduling using evolutionary computing, such as Maass et al. (2017), who attempt to incorporate scheduling uncertainties and nurse absences into scheduling from the beginning. Moz and Pato (2007) define their fitness function in such a way that in the case of rescheduling, the new roster deviates as little as possible from the original roster and thus disrupts ongoing operations as little as possible.

As a complex decision problem in a dynamically changing environment with diverging objectives, the NRP – as a special case of scheduling problems – has all the properties which warrant the use of evolutionary computing. In particular, the circumstances of a rescheduling problem indicate an even better suitability of evolutionary algorithms, because a fast solution is needed, flexible planning to ensure patient care is required, and at the same time multiple objectives have to be considered.

Health. Many publications apply evolutionary algorithms in the health domain. In contrast to the NRP, the application is broader and comprises, for example, available resources such as rooms and medical staff, as well as patients, therapies, and unplanned emergencies. Part of the literature focuses on solutions, especially for scheduling physicians (Puente et al., 2009), laboratory personnel (Boyd & Savory, 2001), or several different qualified groups in emergency settings (Artime Ríos et al., 2019, 2020; Apornak et al., 2021). In addition to scheduling of medical staff, there are many use cases in the field of health care for which evolutionary concepts are used. For example, Roland et al. (2010) look at an operating theater scheduling problem while simultaneously scheduling the personnel needed. Outside of hospitals, physicians are often needed in emergency situations for disaster relief. As part of humanitarian logistics, disaster relief aims at providing immediate help in response to a catastrophe (Kovács & Spens, 2007). The major tasks in disaster relief consider facility planning, logistics such as routing, and repair problems (Zheng et al., 2015). In addition, however, personnel resource deployment must also be planned so that integrated problems also involve a combination of logistics and HR. Here, planning problems contain not only one but several challenging problems that have to be solved simultaneously. Another special feature of disaster relief is the demand for high flexibility (given the unpredictable nature of catastrophes in terms of type and occurrence) and that solutions must be provided quickly; approaches relying on evolutionary computing can be found in Saadatseresht et al. (2009), Reina et al. (2013), and Chang et al. (2014).

Based on the approaches discussed, the characteristics of the application areas for a suitability with evolutionary algorithms can be derived here again: Staff scheduling problems are complex and often need to be extended by further scheduling problems like room planning and route planning. Especially in the area of emergencies and catastrophes, solution approaches must be adaptable in order to be able to quickly meet unforeseen challenges.

Project Management. An important HR task is the organization of projects that require personnel resources. In project management, the division of projects into sub-projects and individual activities, along with their prioritization, is an important decision problem. Usually, a project scheduling problem refers to assigning project activities with different attributes, such as start or end time and required skills, to a set of employees. Projects are managed in many settings and therefore this application is very diverse. The foremost objective in most project scheduling problems is to minimize project duration; see, for example, Jáskowski and Sobotka (2006), where the project duration is translated into a fitness function. However, part of the literature considers the suitability of evolutionary computing when there is more than one objective, which we would like to highlight in the following. In addition to project duration, Yannibelli and Amandi (2013) look at project effectiveness as a second objective. Another widely used criterion besides minimizing duration is cost minimization, as used as a fitness function in Wen and Lin (2008). For software development projects, the authors use adaptable weights – depending on the generation and solution time – to handle the trade-off between exploration and exploitation of the solution space. Park et al. (2015) also examine software projects and include various practically relevant objective criteria in their fitness function such as balancing the allocation of tasks to developers and minimizing their multi-tasking time. According to a survey of developers and managers conducted by the authors, practical objectives are just as important to them as a minimum duration of a project.

The ability of evolutionary computing to react to dynamic changes or interact with the solution method is exploited in Yannibelli and Amandi (2013) and Xiao et al. (2009). Allowing the decision maker to select the most appropriate solution from several project schedules facilitates the acceptance of the method in practice, as it enables human–machine interaction (Yannibelli & Amandi, 2013). Similarly, Xiao et al. (2009) introduce a "value-based" HR scheduling approach in which a comprehensive value function is used to evaluate project schedules and enables decision makers to incorporate various priorities and preferences when dealing with several projects.

Due to the diverse nature of HR project management decision problems, evolutionary algorithms is a suitable method to solve these. Furthermore, one can benefit from the flexibility in designing and changing the fitness function and the promising option of involving the decision maker in the solution process.

Transportation. A large number of publications consider evolutionary algorithms in the area of transportation, providing mobility for cities and municipalities. Airfreight, airlines, road, and rail are the most commonly covered areas within the transportation industry. Within these, crew rostering is the decision problem where evolutionary algorithms are most often used – in particular airline crew rostering. For airlines, crew rostering is a complex problem in which the solution directly affects employees and operations; it refers to the assignment of flight segments – sometimes already combined as pairings – to aircrews. Moreover, a trade-off between the interests of both the air carrier and the aircrew makes the problem even harder to solve. Lučić and Teodorović (2007) therefore use a tripartite objective function, which is easily adopted as a fitness function by the implemented evolutionary algorithm. They consider different balance measures to fairly distribute the workload between crew members. Similarly, Jeng et al. (2008) exploit the capabilities of an evolutionary algorithm to solve multi-criteria optimization problems. In both approaches, the objectives used can be easily exchanged and adapted to different preferences without affecting the functionality of the solution method – strengthening the transferability of the evolutionary algorithms. Further examples for airline crew rostering solution approaches based on evolutionary computing are Souai and Teghem (2009) and El Moudani et al. (2001). A related problem is bus driver rostering, for which evolutionary algorithms are equally well suited due to its complexity and multi-criteria objective. There are some examples in the literature, such as Respicio et al. (2013), who show that a slightly adapted bi-objective evolutionary algorithm yields good results in short time.

Another area using evolutionary strategies for crew scheduling is the underground metro system, as in Elizondo et al. (2010) for example.

Decision problems in the transportation industry are characterized by a high complexity and mostly by a multi-criteria optimization. As pointed out, evolutionary algorithms are very well suited for integrating various objective criteria within the fitness function – which in turn validates their application for HR decision problems in transportation.

FUTURE TRENDS AND CONCLUSION

In this chapter, we have reviewed and discussed the use of evolutionary computing for solving HR decision problems. For this purpose, we first described the procedure and the components of evolutionary algorithms to the reader. Evolutionary computing has its origin in the application of solution methods for complex optimization problems. Here, compared to other solution methods, they excel in finding particularly good solutions where there are dynamic changes as well as when multiple objective functions have to be considered – which both apply to many areas in HR. We have shown that research interest in both HR and evolutionary computing is increasing. However, the overlap of the two in the literature is still limited. Nowadays, evolutionary computing concepts are central in some fields, such as NRP, Health, Project Management, and Transportation. For each of these application areas we have highlighted the suitability of evolutionary algorithms.

While this chapter mainly focuses on the application of evolutionary computing to classical optimization problems like the creation of rosters, it certainly offers valuable insights into evolutionary computing in HR. In the future, however, solution methods will become more and more data-driven and the focus will no longer be only on finding a solution but rather on knowledge discovery and prediction. The availability of data has been limited in the past, especially in the HR area, due to data protection, legal requirements, and manual planning. With increasing digitization, data needed to solve decision problems will be available in a structured form and in large quantities. Although evolutionary computing has hardly been used for data-driven decisions in HR, there is already interest in using evolutionary algorithms for machine learning (Mirjalili et al., 2020).

Continued efforts are needed to shift the focus of HR decisions from costs to long-term employee satisfaction and thus individual preferences (Wolbeck et al., 2020). Even though scheduling has attracted the most interest so far in the literature, the consideration of fairness and employee preferences does not only serve the short-term satisfaction of the employees within a roster; rather, the long-term satisfaction of the employees can be achieved, which in turn has a positive effect on staffing. Less fluctuation due to dissatisfaction also means fewer new, complex hiring processes and a reduced need to recruit new employees. This is particularly important for areas where the next generation of workers is scarce, such as nursing.

Evolutionary computing is based on an analogy with nature. The concept of a fitness function and iterations based on generations is therefore often understandable even without specific knowledge in computer science. This enables the application of evolutionary algorithms in a closer exchange between machine and humans. Some recent research literature, for example, deals with the transformation of linguistic expressions translated into a genetic algorithm (see Herrera et al., 2001; Pei et al., 2009). Further research could usefully enable direct feedback from employees to be incorporated into decision making and enable white-box solution finding.

NOTES

1. https://techcrunch.com/2018/11/28/australian-scheduling-software-company-deputy-brings-in-81m-amid-rapid-growth/, retrieved October 22, 2020.
2. Web of Science, Search for each term in the field TITLE, 10/02/2021.

REFERENCES

Abraham, A., Nedjah, N., & de Macedo Mourelle, L. (2006). Evolutionary computation: From genetic algorithms to genetic programming. In N. Nedjah, L. de Macedo Mourelle, & A. Abraham (Eds.), *Genetic systems programming. studies in computational intelligence* (Vol. 13, pp. 1–20). Springer. https://doi.org/10.1007/3-540-32498-4_1

Aickelin, U., Burke, E. K., & Li, J. (2009). An evolutionary squeaky wheel optimization approach to personnel scheduling. *IEEE Transactions on Evolutionary Computation, 13*(2), 433–443. https//doi.org/10.1109/TEVC.2008.2004262

Aickelin, U., & Dowsland, K. A. (2004). An indirect genetic algorithm for a nurse-scheduling problem. *Computers and Operations Research, 31*(5), 761–778. https://doi.org/10.1016/S0305-0548(03)00034-0

Aickelin, U., & White, P. (2004). Building better nurse scheduling algorithms. *Annals of Operations Research, 128*(1–4), 159–177. https//doi.org/10.1023/B:ANOR.0000019103.31340.a6

Apornak, A., Raissi, S., Keramati, A., & Khalili-Damghani, K. (2021). Human resources optimization in hospital emergency using the genetic algorithm approach. *International Journal of Healthcare Management, 14*(4), 1441–1448. https://doi.org/10.1080/20479700.2020.1763236

Artime Ríos, E., Sánchez Lasheras, F., Suárez Sánchez, A., Iglesias-Rodriguez, F., & Segui Crespo, M. (2019). Prediction of computer vision syndrome in health personnel by means of genetic algorithms and binary regression trees. *Sensors, 19*(12), Article 2800. https://doi.org/10.3390/s19122800

Artime Ríos, E., Suárez Sánchez, A., Sánchez Lasheras, F., & Segui Crespo, M. (2020). Genetic algorithm based on support vector machines for computer vision syndrome classification in health personnel. *Neural Computing and Applications, 32*(5), 1239–1248. https://doi.org/10.1007/s00521-018-3581-3

Aust, I., Matthews, B., & Muller-Camen, M. (2020). Common good HRM: A paradigm shift in sustainable HRM? *Human Resource Management Review, 30*(3), Article 100705. https//doi.org/10.1016/j.hrmr.2019.100705

Bäck, T. (1996). *Evolutionary algorithms in theory and practice: Evolution strategies, evolutionary programming, genetic algorithms*. Oxford University Press.

Bai, R., Burke, E. K., Kendall, G., Li, J., & McCollum, B. (2010). A hybrid evolutionary approach to the nurse rostering problem. *IEEE Transactions on Evolutionary Computation, 14*(4), 580–590. https://doi.org/10.1109/TEVC.2009.2033583

Beasley, J. E., & Chu, P. C. (1996). A genetic algorithm for the set covering problem. *European Journal of Operational Research, 94*(2), 392–404. https://doi.org/10.1016/0377-2217(95)00159-X

Beddoe, G. R., & Petrovic, S. (2006). Selecting and weighting features using a genetic algorithm in a case-based reasoning approach to personnel rostering. *European Journal of Operational Research, 175*(2), 649–671. https://doi.org/10.1016/j.ejor.2004.12.028

Boyd, J. C., & Savory, J. (2001). Genetic algorithm for scheduling of laboratory personnel. *Clinical Chemistry, 47*(1), 118–123.

Burke, E. K., De Causmaecker, P., Vanden Berghe, G., & Van Landeghem, H. (2004). The state of the art of nurse rostering. *Journal of Scheduling, 7*(6), 441–499. https://doi.org/10.1023/B:JOSH.0000046076.75950.0b

Bush, J. T. (2020). Win-win-lose? Sustainable HRM and the promotion of unsustainable employee outcomes. *Human Resource Management Review, 30*(3), Article 100676. https://doi.org/10.1016/j .hrmr.2018.11.004

Cai, X., & Li, K. (2000). A genetic algorithm for scheduling staff of mixed skills under multi-criteria. *European Journal of Operational Research, 125*(2), 359–369. https://doi.org/10.1016/S0377 -2217(99)00391-4

Chang, F.-S., Wu, J.-S., Lee, C.-N., & Shen, H.-C. (2014). Greedy-search-based multi-objective genetic algorithm for emergency logistics scheduling. *Expert Systems with Applications, 41*(6), 2947–2956. https://doi.org/10.1016/j.eswa.2013.10.026

Cheang, B., Li, H., Lim, A., & Rodrigues, B. (2003). Nurse rostering problems – a bibliographic survey. *European Journal of Operational Research, 151*(3), 447–460. https://doi.org/10.1016/S0377 -2217(03)00021-3

Darwin, C. (1859). *On the origin of species by means of natural selection*. John Murray.

David, O. E., van den Herik, H. J., Koppel, M., & Netanyahu, N. S. (2013). Genetic algorithms for evolving computer chess programs. *IEEE Transactions on Evolutionary Computation, 18*(5), 779–789. https://doi.org/10.1109/TEVC.2013.2285111

Dréo, J., Pétrowski, A., Siarry, P., & Taillard, E. (2006). *Metaheuristics for hard optimization: Methods and case studies*. Springer. https://doi.org/10.1007/3-540-30966-7

Duch, W. (2007). What is computational intelligence and where is it going? In W. Duch & J. Mańdziuk (Eds.), *Challenges for computational intelligence* (pp. 1–13). Springer. https://doi.org/10.1007/978-3 -540-71984-71

Duenas, A., Tutuncu, G. Y., & Chilcott, J. B. (2009). A genetic algorithm approach to the nurse scheduling problem with fuzzy preferences. *IMA Journal of Management Mathematics, 20*(4), 369–383. https://doi.org/10.1093/imaman/dpn033

Eiben, A. E., & Smith, J. E. (2015a). From evolutionary computation to the evolution of things. *Nature, 521*, 476–482. https://doi.org/10.1038/nature14544

Eiben, A. E., & Smith, J. E. (2015b). *Introduction to evolutionary computing*. Springer. https://doi.org/ 10.1007/978-3-662-44874-8

El Moudani, W., Cosenza, C. a. N., de Coligny, M., & Mora-Camino, F. (2001). A bi-criterion approach for the airlines crew rostering problem. In E. Zitzlet, K. Deb, L. Thiele, C. a. C. Coello, & D. Corne (Eds.), *Evolutionary Multi-Criterion Optimization, Proceedings* (pp. 486–500). Springer.

Elizondo, R., Parada, V., Pradenas, L., & Artigues, C. (2010). An evolutionary and constructive approach to a crew scheduling problem in underground passenger transport. *Journal of Heuristics, 16*(4), 575–591. https://doi.org/10.1007/s10732-009-9102-x

Goldberg, D. E. (1989). *Genetic algorithms in search, optimization, and machine learning*. Addison Wesley.

Goldberg, D. E., & Holland, J. H. (1988). Genetic algorithms and machine learning. *Machine Learning, 3*, 95–99. https://doi.org/10.1023/A:1022602019183

Herrera, F., Lopez, E., Mendana, C., & Rodriguez, M. A. (2001). A linguistic decision model for personnel management solved with a linguistic biobjective genetic algorithm. *Fuzzy Sets and Systems, 118*(1), 47–64. https://doi.org/10.1016/S0165-0114(98)00373-X

Holland, J. H. (1975). *Adaption in natural and artificial systems*. University of Michigan Press.

Hornby, G. S., Lohn, J. D., & Linden, D. S. (2011). Computer-automated evolution of an x-band antenna for NASA's Space Technology 5 mission. *Evolutionary Computation, 19*(1), 1–23. https://doi.org/10 .1162/EVCOa00005

Huang, H., Lin, W., Lin, Z., Hao, Z., & Lim, A. (2014). An evolutionary algorithm based on constraint set partitioning for nurse rostering problems. *Neural Computing and Applications, 25*(3–4), 703–715. https://doi.org/10.1007/s00521-013-1536-2

Inoue, T., Furuhashi, T., Maeda, H., & Takaba, M. (2003). A proposal of combined method of evolutionary algorithm and heuristics for nurse scheduling support system. *IEEE Transactions on Industrial Electronics, 50*(5), 833–838. https://doi.org/10.1109/TIE.2003.817498

Jan, A., Yamamoto, M., & Ohuchi, A. (2000). Evolutionary algorithms for nurse scheduling problem. In *Proceedings of the 2000 Congress on Evolutionary Computation. CEC00(Cat. No.00TH8512)* (pp. 196–203). IEEE. https://doi.org/10.1109/CEC.2000.870295

Jaśkowski, P., & Sobotka, A. (2006). Scheduling construction projects using evolutionary algorithm. *Journal of Construction Engineering and Management, 132*(8), 861–870. https://doi.org/10.1061/(ASCE)0733-9364(2006)132:8(861)

Jeng, C.-R., Liu, T.-K., & Chang, Y.-H. (2008). Short-haul airline crew rostering by using inequality-based multiobjective genetic algorithm. *Transportation Research Record, 2052*(1), 37–45. https://doi.org/10.3141/2052-05

Kovács, G., & Spens, K. M. (2007). Humanitarian logistics in disaster relief operations. *International Journal of Physical Distribution and Logistics Management, 37*(2), 99–114. https://doi.org/10.1108/09600030710734820

Kramer, O. (2009). *Computational intelligence: Eine Einführung.* Springer. https://doi.org/10.1007/978-3-540-79739-5

Leksakul, K., & Phetsawat, S. (2014). Nurse scheduling using genetic algorithm. *Mathematical Problems in Engineering, 2014*, Article 246543. https://doi.org/10.1155/2014/246543

Lenstra, J. K., & Kan, A. R. (1981). Complexity of vehicle routing and scheduling problems. *Networks, 11*(2), 221–227. https://doi.org/10.1002/net.3230110211

Lin, C.-C., Kang, J.-R., Chiang, D.-J., & Chen, C.-L. (2015). Nurse scheduling with joint normalized shift and day-off preference satisfaction using a genetic algorithm with immigrant scheme. *International Journal of Distributed Sensor Networks, 11*(7). https://doi.org/10.1155/2015/595419

Lučić, P., & Teodorović, D. (2007). Metaheuristics approach to the aircrew rostering problem. *Annals of Operations Research, 155*(1), 311–338. https://doi.org/10.1007/s10479-007-0216-y

Maass, K. L., Liu, B., Daskin, M. S., Duck, M., Wang, Z., Mwenesi, R., & Schapiro, H. (2017). Incorporating nurse absenteeism into staffing with demand uncertainty. *Health Care Management Science, 20*(1), 141–155. https://doi.org/10.1007/s10729-015-9345-z

Macke, J., & Genari, D. (2019). Systematic literature review on sustainable human resource management. *Journal of Cleaner Production, 208*, 806–815. https://doi.org/10.1016/j.jclepro.2018.10.091

Maenhout, B., & Vanhoucke, M. (2011). An evolutionary approach for the nurse rostering problem. *Computers and Operations Research, 38*(10), 1400–1411. https://doi.org/10.1016/j.cor.2010.12.012

Michalewicz, Z., & Fogel, D. B. (2013). *How to solve it: Modern heuristics.* Springer. https://doi.org/10.1007/978-3-662-07807-5

Mirjalili, S., Faris, H., & Aljarah, I. (2020). Introduction to evolutionary machine learning techniques. In S. Mirjalili, H. Faris, & I. Aljarah (Eds.), *Evolutionary machine learning techniques* (pp. 1–7). Springer.

Moz, M., & Pato, M. V. (2007). A genetic algorithm approach to a nurse rerostering problem. *Computers and Operations Research, 34*(3), 667–691. https://doi.org/10.1016/j.cor.2005.03.019

Oduguwa, V., Tiwari, A., & Roy, R. (2005). Evolutionary computing in manufacturing industry: An overview of recent applications. *Applied Soft Computing, 5*(3), 281–299. https://doi.org/10.1016/j.asoc.2004.08.003

Ohki, M. (2012). Nurse scheduling by cooperative GA with effective mutation operator. *IEICE Transactions on Information and Systems, E95D*(7), 1830–1838. https://doi.org/10.1587/transinf.E95.D.1830

Park, J., Seo, D., Hong, G., Shin, D., Hwa, J., & Bae, D.-H. (2015). Human resource allocation in software project with practical considerations. *International Journal of Software Engineering and Knowledge Engineering, 25*(1), 5–26. https//doi.org/10.1142/S021819401540001X

Pato, M. V., & Moz, M. (2008). Solving a bi-objective nurse rerostering problem by using a utopic pareto genetic heuristic. *Journal of Heuristics, 14*(4), 359–374. https://doi.org/10.1007/s10732-007-9040-4

Pei, Z., Xu, Y., Ruan, D., & Qin, K. (2009). Extracting complex linguistic data summaries from personnel database via simple linguistic aggregations. *Information Sciences, 179*(14), 2325–2332. https://doi.org/10.1016/j.ins.2008.12.018

Puente, J., Gomez, A., Fernandez, I., & Priore, P. (2009). Medical doctor rostering problem in a hospital emergency department by means of genetic algorithms. *Computers and Industrial Engineering, 56*(4), 1232–1242. https://doi.org/10.1016/j.cie.2008.07.016

Reina, D., Marin, S. T., Bessis, N., Barrero, F., & Asimakopoulou, E. (2013). An evolutionary computation approach for optimizing connectivity in disaster response scenarios. *Applied Soft Computing, 13*(2), 833–845. https://doi.org/10.1016/j.asoc.2012.10.024

Respicio, A., Moz, M., & Pato, M. V. (2013). Enhanced genetic algorithms for a bi-objective bus driver rostering problem: A computational study. *International Transactions in Operational Research, 20*(4), 443–470. https://doi.org/10.1111/itor.12013

Roland, B., Di Martinelly, C., Riane, F., & Pochet, Y. (2010). Scheduling an operating theatre under human resource constraints. *Computers and Industrial Engineering, 58*(2), 212–220. https://doi.org/10.1016/j.cie.2009.01.005

Rousseau, L.-M., Pesant, G., & Gendreau, M. (2002). A general approach to the physician rostering problem. *Annals of Operations Research, 115*, 193–205. https://doi.org/10.1023/A:1021153305410

Saadatseresht, M., Mansourian, A., & Taleai, M. (2009). Evacuation planning using multiobjective evolutionary optimization approach. *European Journal of Operational Research, 198*(1), 305–314. https://doi.org/10.1016/j.ejor.2008.07.032

Sato, Y., Hasegawa, N., & Sato, M. (2013). Acceleration of genetic algorithms for Sudoku solution on many-core processors. In S. Tsutsui & P. Collet (Eds.), *Massively parallel evolutionary computation on GPGPUs* (pp. 421–444). Springer.

Sholomon, D., David, O. E., & Netanyahu, N. S. (2014). Genetic algorithm-based solver for very large multiple jigsaw puzzles of unknown dimensions and piece orientation. In *Proceedings of the ACM Genetic and Evolutionary Computation Conference (GECCO)* (pp. 1191–1198). ACM. https://doi.org/10.1145/2576768.2598289

Slowik, A., & Kwasnicka, H. (2020). Evolutionary algorithms and their applications to engineering problems. *Neural Computing and Applications, 32*, 12363–12379. https://doi.org/10.1007/s00521-020-04832-8

Souai, N., & Teghem, J. (2009). Genetic algorithm based approach for the integrated airline crew-pairing and rostering problem. *European Journal of Operational Research, 199*(3), 674–683. https://doi.org/10.1016/j.ejor.2007.10.065

Toroslu, I. H., & Arslanoglu, Y. (2007). Genetic algorithm for the personnel assignment problem with multiple objectives. *Information Sciences, 177*(3), 787–803. https://doi.org/10.1016/j.ins.2006.07.032

Tsai, C.-C., & Li, S. H. A. (2009). A two-stage modeling with genetic algorithms for the nurse scheduling problem. *Expert Systems with Applications, 36*(5), 9506–9512. https://doi.org/10.1016/j.eswa.2008.11.049

Warner, D. M. (1976). Scheduling nursing personnel according to nursing preference: A mathematical programming approach. *Operations Research, 24*(5), 842–856. https://doi.org/10.1287/opre.24.5.842

Weicker, K. (2015). *Evolutionäre Algorithmen*. Springer Vieweg. https://doi.org/10.1007/978-3-8351-9203-4

Weller, I. (2016). Human resources. In M. Augier & D. J. Teece (Eds.), *The Palgrave encyclopedia of strategic management* (pp. 1–5). Palgrave Macmillan. https://doi.org/10.1057/978-1-349-94848-2485-1

Wen, F., & Lin, C.-M. (2008). Multistage human resource allocation for software development by multiobjective genetic algorithm. *The Open Applied Mathematics Journal, 2*(1), 95–103. https://doi.org/10.2174/1874114200802010095

Whitley, D. (1994). A genetic algorithm tutorial. *Statistics and Computing, 4*(2), 65–85. https://doi.org/10.1007/BF00175354

Whitley, D. (2001). An overview of evolutionary algorithms: Practical issues and common pitfalls. *Information and Software Technology, 43*(14), 817–831. https://doi.org/10.1016/S0950-5849(01)00188-4

Whitley, D., Rana, S., & Heckendorn, R. B. (1999). The island model genetic algorithm: On separability, population size and convergence. *Journal of Computing and Information Technology, 7*(1), 33–47.

Wolbeck, L., Kliewer, N., & Marques, I. (2020). Fair shift change penalization scheme for nurse rescheduling problems. *European Journal of Operational Research, 284*(3), 1121–1135. https://doi.org/10.1016/j.ejor.2020.01.042

Xiao, J., Wang, Q., Li, M., Yang, Q., Xie, L., & Liu, D. (2009). Value-based multiple soft-ware projects scheduling with genetic algorithm. In Q. Wang, V. Garousi, R. Madachy, & D. Pfahl (Eds.), *Trustworthy software development processes* (pp. 50–62). Springer. https//doi.org/10.1007/978-3-642-01680-67

Yannibelli, V., & Amandi, A. (2013). Project scheduling: A multi-objective evolutionary algorithm that optimizes the effectiveness of human resources and the project makespan. *Engineering Optimization, 45*(1), 45–65. https://doi.org/10.1080/0305215X.2012.658782

Zheng, Y.-J., Chen, S.-Y., & Ling, H.-F. (2015). Evolutionary optimization for disaster relief operations: A survey. *Applied Soft Computing, 27*, 553–566. https://doi.org/10.1016/j.asoc.2014.09.041

Zhou, J., Fan, Y., & Zeng, H. (2012). A nurse scheduling approach based on set pair analysis. *International Journal of Industrial Engineering: Theory Applications and Practice, 19*(9), 359–368.

12. HR natural language processing – conceptual overview and state of the art on conversational agents in human resources management

Sven Laumer and Stefan Morana

INTRODUCTION

Gartner (2020) predicts that by 2022, 70 percent of all interactions between organizations and customers will involve conversational agents. Conversational agents, also referred to as chatbots and digital assistants, are software-based systems designed to interact with humans using natural language in the form of a conversational user interface (Dale, 2016; Maedche et al., 2019; McTear et al., 2016). They are driving a significant paradigm shift in people's interaction with the digital world. Key drivers in this development are the speech-based digital assistants of the "Big Four", namely Apple (Siri), Amazon (Alexa), Google (Assistant), and Microsoft (Cortana), followed by countless text-based conversational agents ("chatbots") for specific functions (Dale, 2016). In addition to classic application areas such as news, entertainment, and, above all, smart home control, conversational agents are also used in a business context (Bavaresco et al., 2020). One important application area is human resources management (HRM) (Sheth, 2018).

The application of conversational agents in HRM follows similar design principles as in other contexts (Nawaz & Mary, 2019). On the one hand there is the individual who has a particular question or concern that is expressed in the dialog. On the other hand there is the conversational agent that is deployed as a combination of different services. First, it has an interface implemented either as a text-based interface (e.g., Facebook Messenger), a voice-based interface (e.g., Amazon's Alexa), or both. Second, there are data- or knowledge bases that provide the information used to answer the individual's questions. Third, there is the service that provides the logic used to answer the individual's question using the data or knowledge available.

These design principles indicate that conversational agents are developed to support the communication between an individual and a provided service. Hence, as HRM provides various services to individuals, it is a classical application area for conversational agents. From workforce planning activities, in which, for example, business managers submit a proposal for an open position and discuss it with HR managers, through sourcing activities, in which job seekers might chat with recruiters about various topics, to administrative or development services, in which employees interact with HR employees, different communication relationships can be supported by conversational agents. Multiple organizations have implemented such conversational agents and report positive experiences (von Wolff et al., 2019). For example, Siemens has deployed Carl, an HR chatbot that supports Siemens's HR services. After its deployment, HR service quality perception increased. The number of employee support requests declined, such that HR employees could focus more on strategic than administrative tasks (IBM, 2019). In parallel, research started to focus on conversational agents in general, and their application in HRM in particular (Listikova et al., 2020).

Natural language processing capabilities in conversational agents in general and in conversational agents in the HR context is an emerging research field. Nevertheless, there are already many reports of studies on conversational agents in HRM. This chapter aims to provide an overview of the status quo and discuss research opportunities in this area. Based on our findings, we develop a general HR conversational agent model to guide future research in this specific application area.

The chapter proceeds as follows. The next section provides an overview of the general HRM services, natural language processing, and conversational agents. The subsequent section explains the literature review approach applied in this chapter. Afterwards, the results are presented and discussed to finalize our general HR conversational agent model guiding future research opportunities.

CONCEPTUAL FOUNDATIONS

Human Resources Management

Human resources management (HRM) aims to create a competitive advantage through the strategic development of a qualified and motivated workforce (Baron et al., 1988). A workforce must be made available in the required quantity, with the necessary quality, and at the right time, as well as for the required duration, at the respective deployment location. This ensures that the operational processes of service creation and utilization can be carried out (Noe et al., 2020).

Therefore, HRM comprises all operational, tactical, and strategic processes and services that provide and manage qualified and motivated people. It includes not only employee-related services but also the associated administrative ones. Administrative HRM services include labor compliance, HR controlling, payroll management, and personnel record keeping. Employee-related services can be further distinguished between workforce planning services, internal and external staffing, employee motivation, and employee development. Workforce planning involves determining how many employees and what skills are required. Jobs and their requirements are analyzed, and plans are made for what skills and capabilities are needed in the future. Staffing entails obtaining the human resources necessary for fulfilling the identified requirements by internal or external staffing activities and selecting the best candidates for vacancies. Developing employees focuses on performance management, training, and other development activities to manage the creation of skills and capabilities. Motivation comprises those services required to support compensation management and talent management, and to maintain a positive work environment in general (Oehlhorn et al., 2020; Wirtky et al., 2016).

Hence, HRM services are provided to external individuals (HR to Applicants (HR2A)) in terms of sourcing services, or to internal ones (HR2E: HR to Employees, also known as Business to Employees (B2E)) in terms of sourcing, development, motivation, or administration. HRM also provides services to managers (HR2B: HR to business, also known as Business to Business (B2B)) in terms of administration, including controlling or planning (Wirtky et al., 2016). The core of HRM services is a human–human relationship that is constituted by communication and information exchange supported by information technology (or information systems) (Eckhardt et al., 2014; Laumer et al., 2009; Strohmeier, 2007). These communication relationships of the various HR2A, HR2E, or HR2B services are the focus of conversational agents that can be used to transform the HRM service delivery model (e.g., speed of request handling), to automate routine HRM services (e.g., screening candidates, scheduling interviews, and managing the recruiting life cycle for candidates and hiring managers), and to increase the accessibility of HRM services (e.g., conversational agents allow the HR team to provide instant, accurate responses to common queries). These opportunities for conversational agents for the various HRM services are the focus of the chapter.

Figure 12.1 visualizes the five key activities of HRM (i.e., administration, planning, sourcing, developing, and motivating), their interdependencies, as well as the three respective groups (i.e., applicants, employees, and managers) receiving HRM services. It also illustrates that we grouped the different HRM services according to their target groups in terms of HRM services provided to applicants (HR2A), employees (HR2E), and managers (HR2B). This model will guide our literature analysis about conversational agents in HRM.

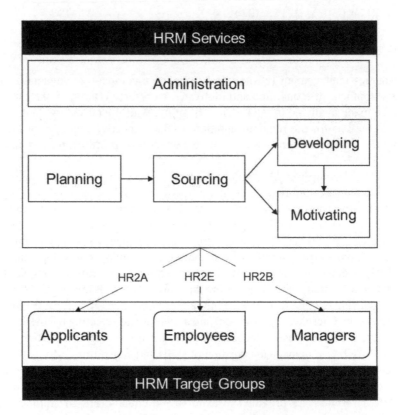

Figure 12.1   HRM services provided to applicants (HR2A), employees (HR2E), and managers (HR2B)

Natural Language Interfaces and Conversational Agents

The idea of interacting with computers through natural language has existed since the early 1960s (Weizenbaum, 1966). Still, recent advances in artificial intelligence (AI), such as deep neural networks, speech recognition, and natural language processing (NLP), have driven the renewed interest in conversational interfaces in research and practice (Gnewuch et al., 2017; McTear, 2017). Conversational interfaces enable users to interact with systems using natural language in the form of text or speech in a conversational form (Araujo, 2018; McTear, 2017). In contrast to command-line interfaces with a fixed set of commands and phrases, conversational interfaces flexibly utilize natural language with a great variety of potential expressions (McTear, 2017). In addition, the so-called agent-based interaction style of systems with conversational interfaces is similar to human–human communication, where both actors (i.e., the human and the conversational agent) contribute to the ongoing conversations (Knijnenburg & Willemsen, 2016; McTear, 2017).

Conversational agents utilize conversational interfaces and can be classified according to two dimensions, their primary communication mode (i.e. speech or text-based interfaces) and the context in which they are used (i.e. general or domain-specific) (Gnewuch et al., 2017). Speech-based conversational agents are commonly referred to as (smart) personal assistants. Prominent examples are Alexa, Siri, and Cortana (Maedche et al., 2019). Text-based conversational agents are commonly referred to as chatbots and used for various application areas, such as customer service or health care (Araujo, 2018; Dale, 2016). In addition, there are embodied conversational agents (Cassell et al., 2000; Nunamaker et al., 2011) that provide a visual representation to the user in addition to the text-based and speech-based interaction mode.

The conversational interfaces of conversational agents comprise five principal components: (1) speech recognition, (2) spoken language understanding, (3) dialog management, (4) response generation, and (5) text-to-speech synthesis (McTear et al., 2016, p. 21). In the following, we briefly explain these components and illustrate how they work using the example of a speech-based conversational agent for managing employees' vacations.

As a first component, "speech recognition" converts the recorded voice of the user to machine-interpretable text. The automatic conversion from spoken language to written text has been of interest for research for decades and is still of high interest (e.g., Chiu et al., 2017; Park et al., 2019; Reddy, 1976). Considering the illustrative example, the employee says the following message to the conversational agent for leave management: "How many vacation days do I have left?"

The second component, "spoken language understanding", is a key element of conversational agents because it is responsible for the natural language processing (NLP). NLP comprises a range of computational techniques for the automatic analysis of human language as well as for the purpose of understanding, representing, and producing human language (Cambria & White, 2014; Hirschberg & Manning, 2015). In general, NLP comprises various tasks such as information extraction, information retrieval, machine translation, natural language interfaces, opinion mining, question answering, text summarization, and topic modeling (Cambria & White, 2014; Chowdhury, 2003). In order to analyze natural language in the form of written text, several consecutive tasks are required, namely, tokenization, sentence splitting, part-of-speech tagging, morphological analysis, named entity recognition, syntactic parsing, coreference resolution, and addition analyses (for an overview see Hirschberg & Manning, 2015; Manning et al., 2014). The recent advances in AI in general and NLP specifically have resulted in a shift from pattern-matching or rule-based algorithms used by early conversational agents towards conversational agents using machine learning approaches for improved conversational abilities (Gnewuch et al., 2017; Knijnenburg & Willemsen, 2016; McTear, 2017). In our illustrative example, the outcome of the second component is the identification of the key words "vacation days" and "left" as well as recognizing the intent "remaining vacation days" that serves as input for the next component.

The third component, "dialog management", implements the conversational agents' specific functionalities and dialogs, such as the provision of customer service or supporting employees in HR processes. Thereby, the dialog management component could be extended to communicate with external systems, depending on the specific use case (McTear, 2002). For example, in the case of the illustrative conversational agent for vacation management, there should be an interface to the HRM system to query the remaining vacation days for the identified user. In our example, the information that the user has 11 vacation days left could be queried. Moreover, the dialog management component includes the implementation of the various dialogs for all available intents (e.g., "remaining vacation days" or "request vacation") that the respective conversational agent is able to process. In addition to implementing more complex dialogs with multiple sentences, the dialog management can also include components that provide replies to less complex questions, for example: "What is the postal address of the HR department?" (e.g., Microsoft QnA Maker[1]). In this case, there is no need to implement the dialogs, but instead pairs of questions and answers need to be provided that are then processed by a machine learning algorithm, resulting in a ready-to-use component for the conversational agent.

The fourth component, "response generation", is usually combined with the third component and prepares the corresponding reply to the user request, based on the implemented dialogs. In our illustrative example, the response would be the written text "You have 11 vacation days left in this year".

Lastly, the fifth component, "text-to-speech synthesis", generates spoken language from the text-based reply of the fourth component. Research is investigating the creation of spoken language, and recent developments in AI provide more advanced speech synthesis (e.g., Bińkowski et al., 2019; Prenger et al., 2019). The speech-based output of the fifth component in our illustrative example would be the spoken reply "You have 11 vacation days left in this year" by the conversational agent. Please note, components 1 (speech recognition) and 5 (text-to-speech synthesis) are only present for speech-based conversational agents. In contrast, text-based conversational agents do not need to convert speech to text and vice versa.

In addition to these rather technical aspects, there are social aspects of conversational agents that need to be considered (Araujo, 2018; Feine et al., 2019). When interacting with other humans, we automatically perceive, interpret, and respond to social cues from them, such as smiling or gestures (Burgoon et al., 2010). According to the Computers are Social Actors (CASA) paradigm, users respond in the same way to the social cues of technology, such as conversational agents, as if they were exhibited by another human being (Nass et al., 1994; Nass & Moon, 2000). Therefore, it does not matter how rudimentary these social cues are (e.g., having a name, avatar, using natural language for interaction), since users recognize the technology unconsciously as a relevant social actor and ascribe human attributes to it, resulting in an increased perception of social presence of this technology (Nass & Moon, 2000). Short et al. define social presence as "the degree of salience of the other person in a mediated communication and the consequent salience of their interpersonal interactions" (1976, p. 65), and it has been used in many studies to assess the effect of social cues on the user's perception of the technology (Appel et al., 2012; Araujo, 2018; Hess et al., 2009; Qiu & Benbasat, 2009).

METHOD

We conducted a systematic and descriptive review of existing research on the usage of conversational interfaces and conversational agents in the context of HRM (vom Brocke et al., 2015). Our review identifies existing research outcomes and central issues in this domain (Cooper, 1988). We did not aim to be fully exhaustive, but present a representative sample of research for interested scholars and practitioners to show the state of the art and outline future research opportunities (Cooper, 1988). Before performing the search, we agreed on the following inclusion criteria: the publication must be peer-reviewed and written in English as well as the publication must address HRM and conversational agents or conversational interfaces. We excluded papers that deal with the application of NLP in general in an HRM context.

We used the following search string:

(chatbot OR "chat bot" OR nlp OR "Natural Language Processing" OR "Conversational Agent" OR "Conversational Interface") AND (recruit* OR hr OR hrm OR "human resources")

We searched the two databases, Scopus and Web of Science. We adapted the search string to the specific requirements of the databases. Thereby, we searched within the title, abstract, and author keywords. The initial hits were screened and included in our sample if fitting our inclusion criteria. Subsequently, we performed a forward and backward search to extend our sample. In total, we identified 50 publications in the two databases. Table 12.1 summarizes the results from our search phase.

Table 12.1   *Descriptive results of the literature search phases*

	Total
Initial hits	412
Meet inclusion criteria	34
Forward search	9
Backward search	7
Publications included in sample	50
Publications on NLP in HRM in general	24
Publications on conversational agents in HRM	26

Next, we analyzed the publications and identified the (1) field of application, (2) target group, and (3) utilized technology for each paper. For the fields of application and target groups, we used the conceptualization depicted in Figure 12.1. The technology was coded freely and consolidated subsequently.

Note, the assignment was not mutually exclusive. Some papers address multiple fields of application and more than one target group. The coding was done independently by two researchers and subsequently discussed to reach a consensus. In the following sections we present the descriptive results from the analysis, describe the current state of research on conversational agents in HRM, and outline future research opportunities.

RESULTS: TOWARDS A MODEL OF CONVERSATIONAL AGENTS IN HUMAN RESOURCES MANAGEMENT

The literature review results reveal in general that there are two types of papers published concerning the use of NLP, conversational agents, and HRM (see Table 12.2 for a detailed overview). First, there are articles that deal with NLP in general, where most of these papers focus on automatically extracting information from CVs for further processing in recruiting, that is, using the extracted data to match with job requirements. In total, we identified 24 papers that deal with the general application of NLP in HRM. Second, there are articles, 26 in total, that focus on conversational agents and their use in HRM in particular. Considering the different HRM functions, two articles focus on administration, none on planning, the majority (N=16) on sourcing, six on development, and four on motivation. Regarding the target group, 14 papers focus on HR to applicants, eight on HR to employees, and two on HR to management. Regarding the different technologies combined to deploy HR conversational agents, Table 12.2 indicates that most papers focus on chatbot technologies or NLP.

Table 12.2   Literature review results

NLP in general	24
Field of application	Administration: 2
	Planning: 0
	Sourcing: 16
	Development: 6
	Motivation: 3
Target group	Applicant: 14
	Employee: 8
	Management: 2
Technology	Conversational agent/chatbots: 5
	Embodied conversational agents: 2
	NLP: 4
	Data/text mining: 1
	Machine learning: 1
	Deep learning: 1
	Naïve Bayes: 1
	Reinforcement algorithms: 1

In the following, we will provide a summary of the papers dealing with NLP in general. Then, we present a comprehensive overview of those papers focusing on conversational agents in HRM to develop our model of conversational agents in HRM.

Research on NLP and HRM in General

Our literature review identifies 24 papers that focus on applying NLP in an HRM context in general. Our search process identified them, as we considered the terms NLP and HRM; however, they do not focus on conversational agents in particular. These papers discuss the use of NLP in general and how it can support HRM tasks and activities. NLP can be used to extract information from job postings to get an overview of the particular professionals' knowledge profiles organizations are searching for (Valdez-Almada et al., 2017). It can also extract information from job descriptions and CVs (Deng et al., 2018). For example, prototypes of CV parsers are reported (Chwastek, 2017; Mittal et al., 2020) to apply NLP in combination with other technologies (e.g., machine learning) to automatically extract information from CVs with high accuracy (Deepak et al., 2020). The extracted information can be further analyzed in the recruiting process (Chen et al., 2018; Guo et al., 2016; Suciu et al., 2018). It is matched with automatically extracted information from job descriptions to identify the most suitable applicants for a vacancy (Chandola et al., 2015; González-Eras & Aguilar, 2019; Kmail et al., 2015; Sayfullina et al., 2018; Tiwari et al., 2019). These prototypes are discussed to support recruiters' CV screening activities (Amin et al., 2019). Using NLP in the recruiting context provides benefits in terms of costs, time, and efforts compared to traditional recruiting methods (Maree et al., 2019). Besides the recruiting context, NLP is also considered in prototypes for work assignments (Bafna et al., 2019; Mo et al., 2020).

These papers focus on applying NLP in an HRM context in general. Most prototypes and studies reported in the literature focus on the recruiting context. It is shown how NLP can be used to parse text documents (CVs, job postings, job descriptions) to extract information automatically that can then be further analyzed, for example to match requirements of a job with candidates' skills and capabilities. NLP is also the foundation for conversational agents. Still, it can also be used as part of other types of information systems.

Research on NLP, Conversational Agents, and HRM

Considering research on NLP, conversational agents, and HRM, the identified studies focus on different **HRM services**, whereas the majority focuses on the *recruiting* context.

In general, conversational agents establish new channels for communication between organizations and job seekers. These channels include using conversational agents in screening candidates, scheduling interviews, and managing the recruiting life cycle for candidates and hiring managers (Sheth, 2018). In the literature, various *use cases and prototypes* are reported. Some prototypes focus on automating the end-to-end recruiting process (e.g., Sheth, 2018), whereas others focus on specific tasks. One application area is to support candidates in preparing their CV and application to the organization (Drozda et al., 2019). The conversational agent is designed to enable candidates to ask questions about the application process as well as submit an application and CV that align with the organization's requirements.

One of the next steps after an application is the job interview. In this context, the use of conversational agents within a *job interview* is discussed. It is tested whether a conversational agent can conduct a job interview instead of a human recruiter (Yakkundi et al., 2019). It is argued that conversational agents can automate a job interview as they will conduct interviews and generate reports (Kessler et al., 2012). Based on these automated reports, candidates will be shortlisted (Carțiș & Suciu, 2020). Some papers focus on the technical design to extract data from candidate statements (Sheikh et al., 2019). Others, however, focus on providing a dialog to reveal candidates' *technical skills* (e.g., Kasundi & Ganegoda, 2019). Conversational agents are also implemented to discover candidates' *personalities* (Jayaratne & Jayatilleke, 2020; Wei et al., 2017). Some papers also focus on administrative support for conducting job interviews (Abishek Rajkumar et al., 2019).

Moreover, conversational agents are used for providing applicants the opportunity to *train for job interviews* (e.g., Callejas et al., 2014; Chollet et al., 2013). Conversational agents are embedded in serious games, and applicants interact with a virtual recruiter to train for specific job interview questions. The conversational agent provides feedback on the answers provided. The results indicate that the implemented model conveys expected social attitudes. In this context, multimodal behaviors and contextual information are focused on, and models are provided to enable specificities in a virtual recruiter's behavior (Chollet et al., 2013). Hence, the focus is on delivering various actions for a virtual recruiter that adapts to different training contexts and responds to the characteristics of the trainee. Another use case in this context focuses on training applicants for an English job interview (Sarosa et al., 2018).

Only a limited number of studies investigate *candidates' expectations and preferences* on the conversational agent design (Schildknecht et al., 2018; Zhou et al., 2019). In this context, the anthropomorphic design (Ochmann et al., 2020) and the gender of conversational agents is discussed to ensure acceptance by conversational agent users (McDonnell & Baxter, 2019).

Six papers focus on use cases and prototypes for employee ***development***. One application area that is discussed is onboarding (Chandar et al., 2017). After a candidate is hired, they are socialized within the organization and a conversational agent can support this process. It enables the new employee to ask questions and get quick answers about the organization. Besides evaluating the accuracy of conversational agents supporting new employees (Chandar et al., 2017), there is also a discussion on whether this support enables better job satisfaction and retention (Chandar et al., 2017). Moreover, conversational agents focus on employee development activities, such as *training* or new work assignments. It is illustrated how conversational agents can be used in general to support employee development (Listikova et al., 2020), and how they can be used to assign work in a crowdworking or microtask context (Mavridis et al., 2019). Another application area is *health support* in an organization (Anuradha et al., 2019). Studies indicate that conversational agents can motivate employees to adopt healthier behaviors at work (Kamita et al., 2019).

The three papers in the employee ***motivation*** context focus on employee health (Anuradha et al., 2019; Kamita et al., 2019) or employee productivity support (Mavridis et al., 2019). Again, these papers report *use cases and prototypes* for conversational agents in HRM.

The two papers on ***administration*** focus on question–answer *use cases and prototypes* to support tasks like payroll management, leaves, and vacations, or those concerning illnesses (Anuradha et al., 2019; Singh et al., 2018).

Besides these general HRM services, the papers also distinguish between the different **potential users of conversational agents**. Possible user groups include applicants, that is, people outside the organization interested in a job; employees, that is, people working in an organization; and managers, that is, people responsible for management tasks, including personnel management.

Fourteen papers focus on conversational agents supporting ***HR to applicant*** interaction. Besides general support for searching for a job, conversational agents, as reported in the literature, support CV and application generation (Drozda et al., 2019), support job interviews (Carțiș & Suciu, 2020; Yakkundi et al., 2019; Zhou et al., 2019), conduct job interviews (Garimella & Paruchuri, 2015; Jayaratne & Jayatilleke, 2020; Zhou et al., 2019), evaluate job interviews (Carțiș & Suciu, 2020), and train job seekers for job interviews (Callejas et al., 2014; Chollet et al., 2013; Sarosa et al., 2018).

Eight papers focus on ***HR to employee*** communication. These papers include use cases and prototypes for onboarding support (Chandar et al., 2017), health support (Wei et al., 2017), knowledge management (Singh et al., 2018), work task assignment (Abishek Rajkumar et al., 2019; Mavridis et al., 2019), the digital workplace (von Wolff et al., 2019), leaves and vacation management (Anuradha et al., 2019), and meeting management (Abishek Rajkumar et al., 2019).

Only two papers focus on ***HR to management*** communication. These papers focus on systems recommending candidates to managers based on their technical skills and personality. Therefore, they are part of the recruiting context and support hiring managers throughout the recruiting life cycle (Kasundi & Ganegoda, 2019; Sheth, 2018).

Concerning the **technology** used to deploy conversational agents in HRM, the identified papers report various studies and prototypes that utilize different technologies. The papers identified focus on technologies such as chatbots (Drozda et al., 2019; McDonnell & Baxter, 2019; Sheth, 2018; Yakkundi et al., 2019; Zhou et al., 2019), embodied conversational agents (Callejas et al., 2014; Chollet et al., 2013), NLP (Abishek Rajkumar et al., 2019; Carţiş & Suciu, 2020; Jayaratne & Jayatilleke, 2020; Kuksenok & Praß, 2019), data mining in general (Schildknecht et al., 2018), machine learning (Listikova et al., 2020; von Wolff et al., 2019), deep learning (Drozda et al., 2019), naïve Bayes (Mavridis et al., 2019), and reinforcement algorithms (Mavridis et al., 2019). Hence, various technologies and combinations of them are deployed to provide conversational agents in an HRM context.

DISCUSSION AND IMPLICATION

The utilization of NLP and especially conversational agents in HRM is an emerging field of research which could open up opportunities to automate HRM services to applicants, employees, and managers. Our literature review uncovered 50 papers of potential interest, among which we identified papers that deal with the application of NLP in HRM in general and papers that focus on the use of conversational agents in HRM (see Table 12.2 for an overview). Our literature review illustrates that NLP is the foundation for providing digital HRM services. Various HRM services rely on text documents. The majority of these documents are semi-structured or even unstructured. NLP can be used to extract information from these documents to enable automated processing of digital HRM services.

Moreover, our review indicates that conversational agents can support digital HRM services applying NLP and other technologies (see Table 12.2 for an overview) by automating the communication between HRM service providers and individuals requesting these services. We divide conversational agents in HRM into three types: HR to applicants, HR to employees, and HR to management. These conversational agents enable individuals to request different HRM services (see Figure 12.2 for an overview of those reported in the literature) or ask specific HRM-related questions. Conversational agents automatically provide the service or the answer to the question. Hence, individuals are the users of these conversational agents that support the HRM service provision quality, as is documented by the studies identified in the literature. These relationships between HRM services, individuals, NLP, and conversational agents, as revealed when analyzing the identified literature, form the basis of our HR conversational agent model (see Figure 12.2).

As the foundation for HRM services, NLP has mainly been applied in the sourcing context. NLP techniques have been prototyped and tested to extract information from documents used in the recruiting process (e.g., CVs, job descriptions) to automate the matching of candidates with jobs. Some approaches have focused on work assignments as well. Nevertheless, recruiting is not the only HRM service that is document-driven, and NLP can be applied to many other HRM contexts. Future research could focus on NLP to automate other document-driven services (applying for leave etc.) by discovering use cases, providing prototypes of NLP-based applications for these services, and analyzing the benefits of NLP-based automation of HRM services for organizations and individuals.

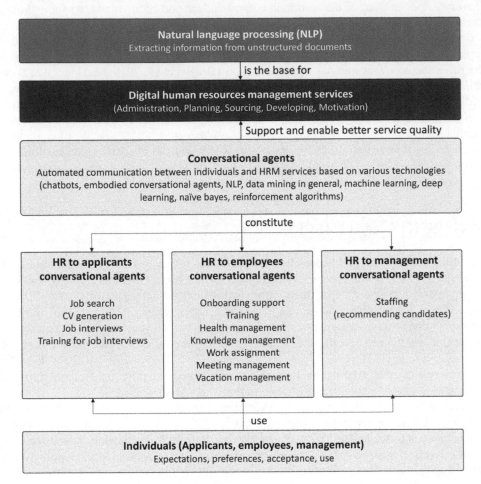

Figure 12.2   HR conversational agent model

Moreover, research on NLP in HRM in general has neglected an individual perspective so far. It is not revealed how individuals deal with automatically extracted information, whether they trust them, and if they use them for their tasks without question. Hence, future research could also focus on the interplay between NLP and human-based HRM services and their various overlaps.

Our literature analysis revealed three types of HR conversational agents. The literature reports use cases and prototypes for HR to applicant, employee, and management conversational agents. Nevertheless, the analysis also reveals that research has mainly focused on HR to applicant use cases and prototypes. In contrast, only a few papers considered HR to employees and, especially, HR to management ones. These contexts also consist of various communication relationships between individuals and HRM service providers, constituting opportunities for conversational agents to automate this conversation and service provision. Hence, future research could focus on analyzing use cases, developing prototypes, and revealing the benefits of conversational agents for these HRM services. Some papers have discussed these general ideas by providing an overview of potential services. Still, the literature does not analyze them in detail. To further increase HRM service provision quality, it is necessary to focus on applying NLP and other technologies to automate and optimize HRM service communication.

Moreover, our literature review indicates that most papers have focused on the recruiting context, while some have concentrated on development, motivation, and administration when considering the different HRM services. In contrast, none has focused on planning. Hence, future research could especially discover use cases, develop prototypes, and analyze their effects for these neglected HRM services. Our review reveals an extended focus on sourcing services and HR to applicant conversational agents and that there are many opportunities for research to focus on the other services or user groups.

In this context, it is important to mention that in their proof-of-concept most papers report prototypes of using NLP in HRM, carried out in rather artificial settings. Only a few papers report results of studies in which they tested NLP in HRM in real-life situations and whether they achieve what they claim to achieve when proposing the prototype and the proof-of-concept. Nevertheless, in developing their prototype, the identified papers focus on specific HR use cases, such that their design considers HR-specific requirements when applying NLP to HRM services. Hence, the literature so far provides – with the discussed limitation of focusing mainly on the sourcing services – HR-specific use cases and prototypes of applying NLP in this context. Nevertheless, future research is required that focuses on the business value provided by these prototypes for the various HRM services discussed.

A third opportunity for future research consists of looking at the use of conversational agents in HRM from the perspective of individuals who need to interact with them. The majority of the papers report use cases or prototypes. In contrast, only a few focus on whether conversational agents are accepted and used by individuals to communicate with HRM service providers. These papers focus on the expectations and preferences of individuals when using conversational agents in HRM. If individuals resist digital HRM services, conversational agents in HRM will not provide the expected benefits in terms of automation, lower costs, lower efforts, and so on. Hence, it is essential to reveal how individuals behave in relation to conversational agents in HRM and whether specific design characteristics would foster acceptance and (long-term) usage. Moreover, it is important to investigate the role of conversational agents' social cues on the user's perception of the conversational agents as responsible and trustworthy social actors in digital HRM services. In this context, it is important not only to focus on general NLP and conversational acceptance and use, but also to reveal characteristics that might be especially relevant in the HRM context (e.g., privacy) and understand how the design of a conversational agents impacts them (Ochmann et al., 2020). For example, it might be important to consider how NLP and conversational agents are perceived in relation to direct and indirect discrimination (Laumer & Schmalenbach, 2020), and whether their design and implementation is free of discrimination and how this impacts individuals' perceptions and behaviors.

In summary, our literature review describes research on using conversational agents in HRM, and on the basis of this review an HR conversational agent model is derived. It illustrates how NLP is applied in an HRM context in general and for deploying conversational agents in particular. NLP forms the foundation of digital HRM services, and conversational agents support these services by automating the communication between individuals and HRM service providers. We classified three types of conversational agents used in HRM. We also show that research has set a specific focus on resourcing services, and especially on external recruiting. However, NLP and conversational agents also provide the opportunity to improve other HRM services. We therefore call for research that extends the knowledge base by focusing on the use of NLP and conversational agents in different HRM services and, furthermore, on the acceptance of NLP and conversational agents in HRM from the perspective of the individuals that have to interact with such agents.

NOTE

1.   https://www.qnamaker.ai/.

REFERENCES

Abishek Rajkumar, S., Raghavan, A., Sathish, A. S., & Rajkumar, V. S. (2019). Use of artificial intelligence and automation of interview process using the chat bot. *International Journal of Innovative Technology and Exploring Engineering*, 8(10S), 192–196. https://doi.org/10.35940/ijitee.J1034 .08810S19

Amin, S., Jayakar, N., Sunny, S., Babu, P., Kiruthika, M., & Gurja, A. (2019). Web application for screening resume. In *2019 International Conference on Nascent Technologies in Engineering (ICNTE 2019)* (pp. 1–7). IEEE.

Anuradha, C., Priya, N., Sangeetha, S., & Kavitha, G. (2019). AI NLP chatbot for HR and employee support. *International Journal of Innovative Technology and Exploring Engineering*, 8(9S3), 580–582. https://doi.org/10.35940/ijitee.I3115.0789S319

Appel, J., Von Der Pütten, A., Krämer, N. C., & Gratch, J. (2012). Does humanity matter? Analyzing the importance of social cues and perceived agency of a computer system for the emergence of social reactions during human–computer interaction. *Advances in Human-Computer Interaction*, *2012*, Article 324694. https://doi.org/10.1155/2012/324694

Araujo, T. (2018). Living up to the chatbot hype: The influence of anthropomorphic design cues and communicative agency framing on conversational agent and company perceptions. *Computers in Human Behavior*, 85, 183–189. https://doi.org/10.1016/j.chb.2018.03.051

Bafna, P., Shirwaikar, S., & Pramod, D. (2019). Task recommender system using semantic clustering to identify the right personnel. *VINE Journal of Information and Knowledge Management Systems*, 49(2), 181–199. https://doi.org/10.1108/VJIKMS-08-2018-0068

Baron, J. N., Jennings, P. D., & Dobbin, F. R. (1988). Mission control? The development of personnel systems in U.S. industry. *American Sociological Review*, 53(4), 497–514. https://doi.org/10.2307/ 2095845

Bavaresco, R., Silveira, D., Reis, E., Barbosa, J., Righi, R., Costa, C., Antunes, R., Gomes, M., Gatti, C., Vanzin, M., Junior, S. C., Silva, E., & Moreira, C. (2020). Conversational agents in business: A systematic literature review and future research directions. *Computer Science Review*, *36*, Article 100239. https://doi.org/10.1016/j.cosrev.2020.100239

Bińkowski, M., Donahue, J., Dieleman, S., Clark, A., Elsen, E., Casagrande, N., Cobo, L. C., & Simonyan, K. (2019). *High fidelity speech synthesis with adversarial networks*. arXiv. http://arxiv .org/abs/1909.11646

Burgoon, J. K., Guerrero, L. K., & Flody, K. (2010). *Nonverbal communication*. Routledge.

Callejas, Z., Ravenet, B., Ochs, M., & Pelachaud, C. (2014). A model to generate adaptive multimodal job interviews with a virtual recruiter. In N. Calzolari, K. Choukri, T. Declerck, H. Loftsson, B.

Maegaard, J. Mariani, A. Moreno, J. Odijk, & S. Piperidis (Eds.), *Proceedings of the 9th International Conference on Language Resources and Evaluation, LREC 2014* (pp. 3615–3619). ACL.

Cambria, E., & White, B. (2014). Jumping NLP curves: A review of natural language processing research. *IEEE Computational Intelligence Magazine, 9*(2), 48–57. https://doi.org/10.1109/MCI.2014.2307227

Cartiş, A.-I., & Suciu, D. M. (2020). Chatbots as a job candidate evaluation tool. In *On the Move to Meaningful Internet Systems: OTM 2019 Workshops* (pp. 189–193). Springer. https://doi.org/10.1007/978-3-030-40907-4_19

Cassell, J., Sullivan, J., Prevost, S., & Churchill, E. (2000). *Embodied conversational agents.* MIT Press.

Chandar, P., Khazaeni, Y., Davis, M., Muller, M., Crasso, M., Liao, Q. V., Shami, N. S., & Geyer, W. (2017). Leveraging conversational systems to assists new hires during onboarding. In R. Bernhaupt, G. Dalvi, A. Joshi, D. K. Balkrishan, J. O'Neill, & M. Winckler (Eds.), *Human–Computer Interaction – INTERACT 2017* (pp. 381–391). https://doi.org/10.1007/978-3-319-67684-5_23

Chandola, D., Garg, A., Maurya, A., & Kushwaha, A. (2015). Online resume parsing system using text analytics. *Journal of Multi Disciplinary Engineering Technologies, 9*(1), 1–5.

Chen, J., Zhang, C., & Niu, Z. (2018). A two-step resume information extraction algorithm. *Mathematical Problems in Engineering, 2018*, Article 5761287. https://doi.org/10.1155/2018/5761287

Chiu, C.-C., Sainath, T. N., Wu, Y., Prabhavalkar, R., Nguyen, P., Chen, Z., Kannan, A., Weiss, R. J., Rao, K., Gonina, E., Jaitly, N., Li, B., Chorowski, J., & Bacchiani, M. (2017). *State-of-the-art speech recognition with sequence-to-sequence models.* arXiv. http://arxiv.org/abs/1712.01769

Chollet, M., Ochs, M., Clavel, C., & Pelachaud, C. (2013). A multimodal corpus approach to the design of virtual recruiters. In *2013 Humaine Association Conference on Affective Computing and Intelligent Interaction* (pp. 19–24). https://doi.org/10.1109/ACII.2013.10

Chowdhury, G. G. (2003). Natural language processing. *Annual Review of Information Science and Technology, 37*(1), 51–89. https://doi.org/10.1002/aris.1440370103

Chwastek, R. (2017). Cognitive systems in human resources. In *International Conference on Behavioral, Economic, Socio-Cultural Computing (BESC)* (pp. 1–4). IEEE. https://doi.org/10.1109/BESC.2017.8256384

Cooper, H. M. (1988). Organizing knowledge syntheses: A taxonomy of literature reviews. *Knowledge in Society, 1*(1), 104–126. https://doi.org/10.1007/BF03177550

Dale, R. (2016). The return of the chatbots. *Natural Language Engineering, 22*(5), 811–817. https://doi.org/10.1017/S1351324916000243

Deepak, G., Teja, V., & Santhanavijayan, A. (2020). A novel firefly driven scheme for resume parsing and matching based on entity linking paradigm. *Journal of Discrete Mathematical Sciences and Cryptography, 23*(1), 157–165. https://doi.org/10.1080/09720529.2020.1721879

Deng, Y., Lei, H., Li, X., & Lin, Y. (2018). An improved deep neural network model for job matching. In *2018 International Conference on Artificial Intelligence and Big Data (ICAIBD)* (pp. 106–112). IEEE. https://doi.org/10.1109/ICAIBD.2018.8396176

Drozda, P., Talun, A., & Bukowski, L. (2019). Emplobot – design of the system. In *Proceedings of the 28th International Workshop on Concurrency, Specification and Programming* (pp. 1–4).

Eckhardt, A., Laumer, S., Maier, C., & Weitzel, T. (2014). The transformation of people, processes, and IT in e-recruiting. *Employee Relations, 36*(4), 415–431. https://doi.org/10.1108/ER-07-2013-0079

Feine, J., Gnewuch, U., Morana, S., & Maedche, A. (2019). A Taxonomy of social cues for conversational agents. *International Journal of Human-Computer Studies, 132*, 138–161. https://doi.org/10.1016/j.ijhcs.2019.07.009

Garimella, U., & Paruchuri, P. (2015). (HR)^2: An agent for helping HR with recruitment. *International Journal of Agent Technologies and Systems, 7*(3), 67–85. https://doi.org/10.4018/IJATS.2015070104

Gartner. (2020). Top CX trends for CIOs to watch. https://www.gartner.com/smarterwithgartner/top-cx-trends-for-cios-to-watch/, accessed November 21, 2021.

Gnewuch, U., Morana, S., & Maedche, A. (2017). Towards designing cooperative and social conversational agents for customer service. In *Proceedings of the 38th International Conference on Information Systems (ICIS)* (pp. 1–13). AIScL.

González-Eras, A., & Aguilar, J. (2019). Determination of professional competencies using an alignment algorithm of academic profiles and job advertisements, based on competence thesauri and similarity measures. *International Journal of Artificial Intelligence in Education, 29*(4), 536–567. https://doi .org/10.1007/s40593-019-00185-z

Guo, S., Alamudun, F., & Hammond, T. (2016). RésuMatcher: A personalized résumé–job matching system. *Expert Systems with Applications, 60*, 169–182. https://doi.org/10.1016/j.eswa.2016.04.013

Hess, T., Fuller, M., & Campbell, D. (2009). Designing interfaces with social presence: Using vividness and extraversion to create social recommendation agents. *Journal of the Association for Information Systems, 10*(12), 889–919.

Hirschberg, J., & Manning, C. D. (2015). Advances in natural language processing. *Science, 349*(6245), 261–266. https://doi.org/10.1126/science.aaa8685

IBM. (2019). *Siemens AG – Watson AI.* https://www.ibm.com/case-studies/siemens-ag-watson-ai, accessed November 12, 2021.

Jayaratne, M., & Jayatilleke, B. (2020). Predicting personality using answers to open-ended interview questions. *IEEE Access, 8*, 115345–115355. https://doi.org/10.1109/ACCESS.2020.3004002

Kamita, T., Ito, T., Matsumoto, A., Munakata, T., & Inoue, T. (2019). A chatbot system for mental healthcare based on SAT counseling method. *Mobile Information Systems, 2019*, Article 9517321. https://doi.org/10.1155/2019/9517321

Kasundi, J., & Ganegoda, G. U. (2019). Candidate recruitment based on automatic answer evaluation using WordNet. In *2019 International Research Conference on Smart Computing and Systems Engineering (SCSE)* (pp. 29–37). https://doi.org/10.23919/SCSE.2019.8842773

Kessler, R., Béchet, N., Roche, M., Torres-Moreno, J.-M., & El-Bèze, M. (2012). A hybrid approach to managing job offers and candidates. *Information Processing and Management, 48*(6), 1124–1135. https://doi.org/10.1016/j.ipm.2012.03.002

Kmail, A. B., Maree, M., Belkhatir, M., & Alhashmi, S. M. (2015). An automatic online recruitment system based on exploiting multiple semantic resources and concept-relatedness measures. In *IEEE 27th International Conference on Tools with Artificial Intelligence (ICTAI)* (pp. 620–627). IEEE. https://doi.org/10.1109/ICTAI.2015.95

Knijnenburg, B. P., & Willemsen, M. C. (2016). Inferring capabilities of intelligent agents from their external traits. *ACM Transactions on Interactive Intelligent Systems, 6*(4), Article 8. https://doi.org/ 10.1145/2963106

Kuksenok, K., & Praß, N. (2019). *Transparency in maintenance of recruitment chatbots.* arXiv. http:// arxiv.org/abs/1905.03640

Laumer, S., & Schmalenbach, K. (2020). Does data-driven recruitment lead to less discrimination? – A technical perspective. In *Proceedings of the 15th International Conference on Wirtschaftsinformatik.* https://doi.org/10.30844/wi_2020_q2-schmalenbach

Laumer, S., von Stetten, A., & Eckhardt, A. (2009). E-assessment. *Business and Information Systems Engineering, 1*(3), 263–265. https://doi.org/10.1007/s12599-009-0051-6

Listikova, A. V., Egorov, E. E., Lebedeva, T. E., Bulganina, S. V., & Prokhorova, M. P. (2020). Research of the best practices of artificial intelligence in the formation and development of personnel. In E. Popkova (Eds.), *Growth poles of the global economy: Emergence, changes and future perspectives. Lecture notes in networks and systems* (Vol. 73, pp. 1345–1352). Springer. https://doi.org/10.1007/ 978-3-030-15160-7_137

Maedche, A., Legner, C., Benlian, A., Berger, B., Gimpel, H., Hess, T., Hinz, O., Morana, S., & Söllner, M. (2019). AI-based digital assistants: Opportunities, threats, and research perspectives. *Business and Information Systems Engineering, 61*(4), 535–544. https://doi.org/10.1007/s12599-019-00600-8

Manning, C. D., Surdeanu, M., Bauer, J., Finkel, J., Bethard, S. J., & McClosky, D. (2014). The Stanford CoreNLP natural language processing toolkit. In *Proceedings of 52nd Annual Meeting of the Association for Computational Linguistics: System Demonstrations* (pp. 55–60). ACL. https://doi .org/10.3115/v1/P14-5010

Maree, M., Kmail, A. B., & Belkhatir, M. (2019). Analysis and shortcomings of e-recruitment systems: Towards a semantics-based approach addressing knowledge incompleteness and limited domain coverage. *Journal of Information Science, 45*(6), 713–735. https://doi.org/10.1177/0165551518811449

Mavridis, P., Huang, O., Qiu, S., Gadiraju, U., & Bozzon, A. (2019). Chatterbox: Conversational interfaces for microtask crowdsourcing. In *Proceedings of the 27th ACM Conference on User Modeling, Adaptation and Personalization* (pp. 243–251). ACM. https://doi.org/10.1145/3320435.3320439

McDonnell, M., & Baxter, D. (2019). Chatbots and gender stereotyping. *Interacting with Computers*, *31*(2), 116–121. https://doi.org/10.1093/iwc/iwz007

McTear, M. F. (2002). Spoken dialogue technology: Enabling the conversational user interface. *ACM Computing Surveys*, *34*(1), 90–169. https://doi.org/10.1145/505282.505285

McTear, M. F. (2017). The rise of the conversational interface: A new kid on the block? In J. Quesada, F.-J. Martín Mateos, & T. López Soto (Eds.), *Future and emerging trends in language technology. Machine learning and big data. FETLT 2016. Lecture notes in computer science* (Vol. 10341, pp. 38–49). Springer. https://doi.org/10.1007/978-3-319-69365-1_3

McTear, M. F., Callejas, Z., & Griol, D. (2016). Introducing the conversational interface. In *The conversational interface: Talking to smart devices* (pp. 1–7). Springer International Publishing. https://doi.org/10.1007/978-3-319-32967-3

Mittal, V., Mehta, P., Relan, D., & Gabrani, G. (2020). Methodology for resume parsing and job domain prediction. *Journal of Statistics and Management Systems*, *23*(7), 1265–1274. https://doi.org/10.1080/09720510.2020.1799583

Mo, Y., Zhao, D., Du, J., Syal, M., Aziz, A., & Li, H. (2020). Automated staff assignment for building maintenance using natural language processing. *Automation in Construction*, *113*, Article 103150. https://doi.org/10.1016/j.autcon.2020.103150

Nass, C., & Moon, Y. (2000). Machines and mindlessness: Social responses to computers. *Journal of Social Issues*, *56*(1), 81–103.

Nass, C., Steuer, J., & Tauber, E. R. (1994). Computers are social actors. In *Conference Companion on Human Factors in Computing Systems – CHI '94* (pp. 72–78). ACM. https://doi.org/10.1145/259963.260288

Nawaz, N., & Mary, A. (2019). Artificial intelligence chatbots are new recruiters. *International Journal of Advanced Computer Science and Applications*, *10*(9), 1–5. https://doi.org/10.14569/IJACSA.2019.0100901

Noe, R. A., Hollenbeck, J. R., Gerhart, B., & Wright, P. M. (2020). *Fundamentals of human resource management*. McGraw-Hill Education.

Nunamaker, J. F., Derrick, D. C., Elkins, A. C., Burgoon, J. K., & Patton, M. W. (2011). Embodied conversational agent-based kiosk for automated interviewing. *Journal of Management Information Systems*, *28*(1), 17–48. https://doi.org/10.2753/MIS0742-1222280102

Ochmann, J., Michels, L., Zilker, S., Tiefenbeck, V., & Laumer, S. (2020). The influence of algorithm aversion and anthropomorphic agent design on the acceptance of AI-based job recommendations. In *Proceedings of the 41st International Conference on Information Systems (ICIS)*.

Oehlhorn, C. E., Maier, C., Laumer, S., & Weitzel, T. (2020). Human resource management and its impact on strategic business–IT alignment: A literature review and avenues for future research. *The Journal of Strategic Information Systems*, *29*(4), Article 101641. https://doi.org/10.1016/j.jsis.2020.101641

Park, D. S., Chan, W., Zhang, Y., Chiu, C.-C., Zoph, B., Cubuk, E. D., & Le, Q. V. (2019). SpecAugment: A simple data augmentation method for automatic speech recognition. In *Proc. Interspeech 2019* (pp. 2613–2617). https://doi.org/10.21437/Interspeech.2019-2680

Prenger, R., Valle, R., & Catanzaro, B. (2019). Waveglow: A flow-based generative network for speech synthesis. In *ICASSP 2019 – 2019 IEEE International Conference on Acoustics, Speech and Signal Processing (ICASSP)* (pp. 3617–3621). IEEE. https://doi.org/10.1109/ICASSP.2019.8683143

Qiu, L., & Benbasat, I. (2009). Evaluating anthropomorphic product recommendation agents: A social relationship perspective to designing information systems. *Journal of Management Information Systems*, *25*(4), 145–182. https://doi.org/10.2753/MIS0742-1222250405

Reddy, D. R. (1976). Speech recognition by machine: A review. *Proceedings of the IEEE*, *64*(4), 501–531. https://doi.org/10.1109/PROC.1976.10158

Sarosa, M., Junus, M., Hoesny, M. U., Sari, Z., & Fatnuriyah, M. (2018). Classification technique of interviewer-bot result using Naïve Bayes and phrase reinforcement algorithms. *International Journal of Emerging Technologies in Learning (IJET)*, *13*(2). https://doi.org/10.3991/ijet.v13i02.7173

Sayfullina, L., Malmi, E., Liao, Y., & Jung, A. (2018). Domain adaptation for resume classification using convolutional neural networks. In W. M. P. van der Aalst, D. I. Ignatov, M. Khachay, S. O. Kuznetsov, V. Lempitsky, I. A. Lomazova, N. Loukachevitch, A. Napoli, A. Panchenko, P. M. Pardalos, A. V.

Savchenko, & S. Wasserman (Eds.), *6th International Conference, AIST 2017* (pp. 82–93). Springer International Publishing. https://doi.org/10.1007/978-3-319-73013-4_8

Schildknecht, L., Eiber, J., & Böhm, S. (2018). Motivators and barriers of chatbot usage in recruiting: An empirical study on the job candidates' perspective in Germany. *Journal of E-Technology, 9*(4), 109–123. https://doi.org/10.6025/jet/2018/9/4/109-123

Sheikh, S. A., Tiwari, V., & Singhal, S. (2019). Generative model chatbot for human resource using deep learning. In *2019 International Conference on Data Science and Engineering (ICDSE)* (pp. 126–132). IEEE. https://doi.org/10.1109/ICDSE47409.2019.8971795

Sheth, B. (2018). Chat bots are the new HR managers. *Strategic HR Review, 17*(3), 162–163. https://doi.org/10.1108/SHR-03-2018-0024

Short, J., Williams, E., & Christie, B. (1976). *The social psychology of telecommunications*. Wiley.

Singh, M., Agarwal, P., Chaudhary, A., Shroff, G., Khurana, P., Patidar, M., Bisht, V., Bansal, R., Sachan, P., & Kumar, R. (2018). KNADIA: Enterprise KNowledge Assisted DIAlogue systems using deep learning. In *2018 IEEE 34th International Conference on Data Engineering (ICDE)* (pp. 1423–1434). IEEE. https://doi.org/10.1109/ICDE.2018.00161

Strohmeier, S. (2007). Research in e-HRM: Review and implications. *Human Resource Management Review, 17*(1), 19–37. https://doi.org/10.1016/j.hrmr.2006.11.002

Suciu, G., Pasat, A., & Rogojanu, I. (2018). SoMeDi: Successful internship programs matching job offers with candidates skills. In *Proceedings of the 13th International Conference on Virtual Learning, ICVL 2018* (pp. 415–420). Bucharest University Press.

Tiwari, A., Vaghela, S., Nagar, R., & Desai, M. (2019). Applicant tracking and scoring system. *International Research Journal of Engineering and Technology, 6*(4), 320–324. www.irjet.net

Valdez-Almada, R., Rodriguez-Elias, O. M., Rose-Gomez, C. E., Velazquez-Mendoza, M. D. J., & Gonzalez-Lopez, S. (2017). Natural language processing and text mining to identify knowledge profiles for software engineering positions: Generating knowledge profiles from resumes. In *5th International Conference in Software Engineering Research and Innovation (CONISOFT) Natural* (pp. 97–106). IEEE. https://doi.org/10.1109/CONISOFT.2017.00019

vom Brocke, J., Simons, A., Riemer, K., Niehaves, B., Plattfaut, R., & Cleven, A. (2015). Standing on the shoulders of giants: Challenges and recommendations of literature search in information systems research. *Communications of the Association for Information Systems, 37*(9), 205–224. https://doi.org/10.17705/1CAIS.03709

von Wolff, R. M., Masuch, K., Hobert, S., & Schumann, M. (2019). What do you need today? – An empirical systematization of application areas for chatbots at digital workplaces. In *25th Americas Conference on Information Systems, AMCIS 2019* (pp. 1–10). AIS eLibrary.

Wei, H., Zhang, F., Yuan, N. J., Cao, C., Fu, H., Xie, X., Rui, Y., & Ma, W.-Y. (2017). Beyond the words: Predicting user personality from heterogeneous information. In *Proceedings of the Tenth ACM International Conference on Web Search and Data Mining – WSDM '17* (pp. 305–314). ACM. https://doi.org/10.1145/3018661.3018717

Weizenbaum, J. (1966). ELIZA – a computer program for the study of natural language communication between man and machine. *Communications of the ACM, 9*(1), 36–45. https://doi.org/10.5100/jje.2.3_1

Wirtky, T., Laumer, S., Eckhardt, A., & Weitzel, T. (2016). On the untapped value of e-HRM: A literature review. *Communications of the Association for Information Systems, 38*(1), 20–83. https://doi.org/10.17705/1CAIS.03802

Yakkundi, S., Vanjare, A., Wavhal, V., & Patankar, S. (2019). Interactive interview chatbot. *International Research Journal of Engineering and Technology, 6*(4), 2746–2748. www.irjet.net

Zhou, M. X., Wang, C., Mark, G., Yang, H., & Xu, K. (2019). Building real-world chatbot interviewers: Lessons from a wizard-of-oz field study. In *Joint Proceedings of the ACM IUI 2019 Workshops* (pp. 1–6). CEUR Workshop Proceedings.

13. HR affective computing

William J. Becker, Sarah E. Tuskey, and Constant D. Beugré

INTRODUCTION

Affective computing, which is a noteworthy field within the sphere of artificial intelligence, interprets, analyzes, and reproduces human emotional expressions. More specifically, affective computing involves two separate computer technologies – emotion recognition and emotion expression – that may operate independently or in concert. Both of these applications are experiencing rapid growth and advances due to corresponding developments in the underlying hardware and software. The rise of wearable technology will almost certainly accelerate the expansion of affective computing systems in real-world applications. Some of these technologies are already creeping into use in consumer and organizational applications.

In this chapter, we will explore how affective computing can be applied in organizational settings, particularly in the field of human resource management, to improve and potentially revolutionize a few processes within the employee life cycle. To that end, we will first introduce the reader to the current state and likely future of affective computing. We then explore several areas within human resources where affective computing might be employed. More specifically, we discuss applications in personnel selection, human resource training, and performance management. These are not meant to be exhaustive, but rather a few of the most promising ways that affective computing technologies can be applied in the very near future.

REVIEW OF CURRENT STATE OF AFFECTIVE COMPUTING TECHNOLOGY

Affective computing refers broadly to the use of computers and other technologies to sense and/or produce authentic human emotional expressions (Picard, 2003). We begin by delineating each of the individual elements within the sphere of affective computing. For each, we define the scope, review the technological capabilities and research findings to date, and outline likely future advances in the near term. We begin with sensing emotion expressions by humans in organizational settings and then move to simulation of authentic emotion expressions by machines.

Sensing Emotions

The human brain has evolved with sophisticated automatic processing to read and interpret the emotional expressions of other human beings. While this has proven difficult to replicate with computer systems, significant progress has been made in dissecting and sensing the different modalities of emotion expression, such as speech and visual cues, with the ability to develop integrated emotion sensing systems on the horizon. For the purposes of this chapter, we will first explore audible-based measures and then visual measures.

Speech processing. Our spoken language is the most observable and readily analyzed mode of human emotion communication. A number of text analysis tools have been developed that assess the affective tone and meaning of words. These methods typically use a lexical approach at the word level using emotion word dictionaries or more complex rules-based linguistic approaches with or without dictionaries to infer emotion from patterns of words (Agrawal & An, 2012). For a more in-depth treatment of machine learning and text analysis, see CHAPTER 3 of this book. These programs are becoming increasing sophisticated and advances in speech to text software means real-time processing of human speech will continue to see improvements.

Of course, language is only one aspect of emotion expression, and likely the least informative for complex and low-intensity emotional expressions that characterize emotions in organizations. Computer interfaces that derive emotion in speech using prosody, pitch, intensity, speaking rate, vocal quality, and other characteristics have been developed (Vogt, André, & Wagner, 2008). Computer systems have been able to recognize a range of emotions in speech at a rate of 70 percent or better (Alu, Zoltan, & Stoica, 2017). The most promising of these employ deep learning convolutional neural networks. One useful tool that is currently available is OliverAPI (https://behavioralsignals.com/oliver/), a software developed by Behavioral Signals, which analyzes tone of voice, word choice, and engagement to formulate emotional reactions, such as empathy (Giannakopoulos et al., 2019). Of course, natural conversations with complex emotions pose a much more difficult problem. Still, this technology continues to advance and represents a much more nuanced window into human emotion speech than the words spoken. For more information about audio analysis methods, see CHAPTER 4, while CHAPTER 12 explores natural language processing in greater depth.

Facial expressions and body language. It is readily apparent that what we say conveys only a fraction of the emotions that we feel and express to others. The groundbreaking research by Ekman (Ekman & Oster, 1979) into universal human facial expressions is but one example of the richness of human body language. Once again, the human brain has specifically evolved to perform automatic and rapid facial monitoring and evaluation in the fusiform face gyrus. Automated facial analysis using computers is developing rapidly. In general, these systems extract vectors related to facial features and map these vectors onto specific emotions (Wang et al., 2018). Current facial expression recognition systems can sense emotions with over 90 percent accuracy in laboratory conditions, but struggle in real-world, dynamic situations where the accuracy drops below 50 percent (Samadiani et al., 2019). It currently performs best for well-lit frontal aspects with limited head movement, but continues to improve rapidly as technology and facial expression libraries mature.

Emotion expression is not limited to the face, however. Body gestures and movement also provide important and dynamic cues that convey emotion. Recognizing emotion in the body is significantly more difficult than facial expression due to more moving parts and the larger degrees of freedom. The most promising computer methodologies for analyzing body movement employ 3-D models of the human body and track its dynamic movement over time to infer emotion based on libraries of motion patterns (Arunnehru & Geetha, 2017). These systems are largely in their infancy, but promise to advance rapidly (Shen, Cheng, Hu, & Dong, 2019; Stathopoulou & Tsihirintzis, 2011).

Physiological emotion monitoring. The experience of emotion creates physiological reactions in the body. Thus far, we have focused on using technology to assess the emotional expressions observed in others. However, affective computing in organizational settings is also concerned with gauging the emotions being experienced and expressed by a focal employee who may be actively engaged in the process. Wearable technology with increasingly capable physiological measures could be used to provide an additional window into the emotion states of an individual. Smart watches and exercise bands can provide real-time measurements of heart rate, galvanic skin response, EKG, and blood oxygen saturation, to name just a few measurements that are currently available and could be used to assess emotional states in the wearer (Kutt et al., 2018). Using a variety of measures, physiology-based methods showed 70 to 80 percent accuracy for determining emotional arousal and valence (Jerritta, Murugappan, Nagarajan, & Wan, 2011) and off-the-shelf wearable devices showed similar capability to medical grade sensors (Ragot et al., 2017).

Multimodal emotion sensing systems. To date, most of these emotion sensing systems have been developed and tested separately. Much like the human brain, multimodal emotion recognition systems that combine all the measures discussed above would provide the capability to accurately detect even subtle and complex emotional expressions (He et al., 2020). Efforts to develop such systems have suggested that combining measures greatly increases the performance of automatic emotion recognition systems (Castellano, Kessous, & Caridakis, 2008). It would seem that the largest challenge in creating these systems lies in the development of software and algorithms to combine and model the multimodal data.

Despite this and other challenges, efforts to develop these multimodal corpus systems are emerging. One current system that employs multimodal sensing to assess emotions is Affectiva (https://www.affectiva.com/), a software developed by the MIT Media Lab. Affectiva uses a standard webcam to identify emotions such as anger, contempt, disgust, fear, joy, sadness, and surprise (McDuff et al., 2013). Speech detection is also integrated in Affectiva. Affectiva is also able to detect how something is said and the frequency at which it is said. These features make it a promising and powerful tool for reading the emotions of people in natural situations that could be employed in organizations right now.

Producing Emotions

While the technological problems facing automatic sensing of human emotions are relatively tractable, the realistic production of emotional expressions by computers faces more significant challenges that will take longer to overcome, particularly in practical applications. Much of this stems from the acuity of the human brain for attending to and interpreting natural human expressions and the difficulty of reproducing this in a natural way with computers. Despite this, some progress is being made, and at some point computers will be able to produce realistic emotion expression in a way that would be useful for a number of human resources applications.

Emotional speech synthesis. While synthetic speech has become more intelligible, it still lacks a naturalness that is capable of conveying emotional expressivity (Kuligowska, Kisielewicz, & Włodarz, 2018; Schröder, 2001). Thus far, efforts to accomplish this have relied on rules-based format synthesis which employs computer-generated speech or diphone concatenation that uses recordings of human voices to splice together synthetic speech. Neither of these methods is likely to be capable of generating the types of dynamic and natural conversations that would be needed for most of the affective computing applications that we discuss in this chapter. Nonetheless, newer methods of speech synthesis that employ deep learning and training show some promise (Ning et al., 2019). Undoubtedly, these problems will be overcome at some point, yielding systems capable of producing emotional voices that can be applied to situations that occur in organizations.

Facial emotion expression synthesis and body language. The dynamic generation of realistic 3-D facial expressions is in its relative infancy. Current systems are limited to talking avatars with a limited number of basic emotion expressions that can be produced through rule-based systems (Raouzaiou, Tsapatsoulis, Karpouzis, & Kollias, 2002). More recent efforts that render photorealistic facial expressions of target emotions from a single photograph show more promise for the level of naturalness that would be most conducive to the human applications we anticipate (Zhou & Shi, 2017). The synthesis of lifelike emotional body language is not likely to be realizable in the foreseeable future. However, there has been some work in this regard in the field of robotics (Marmpena, Lim, & Dahl, 2018). Nonetheless, we limit our discussion here to capabilities that are likely to be available for organizational applications in the next ten years.

AFFECTIVE COMPUTING AND HUMAN RESOURCE MANAGEMENT

While affective computing remains largely a laboratory research activity, workplace applications have been envisioned (Richardson, 2020). The technology is advancing at such a rapid rate that practical applications in the workplace will emerge sooner rather than later. Human resource management is one area where affective computing offers a myriad of promising potential applications. In this section of this chapter, we will discuss a number of these potential applications in greater detail as they pertain to selection, training and development, and talent management.

Selection

Despite vast empirical literature on selection practice, there are a number of ways that affective computing might be employed to improve the validity and reliability of current selection methods, address outstanding issues in selection research, and provide new capabilities that do not currently exist. Here we examine some of the most widely used personnel selection instruments: interviews, assessment exercises, and situational judgment tests.

Interviews. One obvious area where affective computing could be brought to bear would be in selection interviews. An interview is a selection procedure that relies on both the verbal responses and nonverbal behaviors of potential job candidates to predict future job performance (McDaniel, Whetzel, Schmidt, & Maurer, 1994). Nonverbal behavior, particularly, lends itself to affective computing, as it is perceived both visually and aurally. While interviews are among the most commonly employed selection tools in practice, low predictive validity and questionable reliability of interviewers plague this selection practice (Judge, Cable, & Higgins, 2000; Ryan & Ployhart, 2014). The areas that primarily affect the validity and reliability of interviews include interviewee impression management and faking, as well as interviewer bias and capability. These, along with the ways in which affective computing technology can be utilized to mitigate these concerns, are discussed in more depth below.

Affective computing methods could use multiple analyses to observe and sense candidate emotional expression during the interview. One way this might be useful would be to identify employees who might suffer from interview anxiety and perform poorly in interviews despite possessing the requisite skills that the organization is looking for. Affective computing may soon have the ability to provide real-time information on candidate emotions to the interviewer. In this case, the interviewer could be made aware of the candidate's anxiety and attempt to put them at ease before proceeding with the interview.

Observing candidate emotions, particularly subtle emotional expressions, would help to identify candidates who are engaging in excessive impression management. Impression management is the attempt to manage or control the projected images during a social interaction (McFarland et al., 2005). This would be helpful because first impressions often are a disproportionate factor in interview scores (Stewart, Darnold, Barrick, & Dustin, 2008). As these technologies improve, they may also prove capable of detecting candidate deception during interviews. Again, if this information were provided in real time, the interviewer could avoid certain types of bias and even follow up with addition questions when potential deception is suspected.

Affective computing methods also have great potential in identifying interviewee faking behaviors. Faking behavior is "an intentional distortion or a falsification of responses on measures in order to create a specific impression or provide the best answer" (Levashina & Campion, 2006, p. 300). This includes a number of behaviors, such as overstating or fabricating skills, abilities, or experiences; not mentioning or attempting to hide deficiencies in skills, abilities, or experiences; and, finally, deceptive or insincere ingratiation towards the interviewer or the organization (Levashina & Campion, 2007; Buehl & Melchers, 2017). Matching the timeline of candidate emotions with structured interviews could also provide valuable insight into the values, attitudes, and interests of the candidate and how these align with the requirements of the positions and the needs of the organization. Whereas job seekers might attempt to engage in faking behaviors, their emotional reactions when the job is described to them might tell a different story. For example, when team processes are discussed, one candidate might show positive reactions while another might show uncertainty or negative emotions. Overall, these methods would provide a roadmap of the candidate's emotional responses that would provide a useful window into their emotional stability and self-regulation abilities.

Affective computing in interviews need not be limited to candidates. Interviewers contribute as much if not more to the poor predictive validity of selection interviews (Ryan & Ployhart, 2014). These technologies could just as easily be used to observe and track interviewer emotional expressions and responses during the interview. For instance, in their multimodal interview judgment system research, Nguyen, Frauendorfer, Mast, and Gatica-Perez (2014) found that while applicant audio cues were predictive of hirability, interviewer visual cues were also predictive. In the aggregate, organizations could use this to objectively quantify the performance of interviewers across multiple interviews. The training of interviewers has been demonstrated to result in more reliable ratings (Dipboye & Gaugler, 1993), ultimately improving their capability and creating awareness of bias. Individuals who struggle with their own emotions could be provided with additional training, or be removed from interviewing. Real-time feedback to interviewers has even more potential to improve interviews. With guidance and practice, interviewers could respond to prompts that their emotional expressions are moving in an unhelpful direction and take corrective action to move the interview in a more constructive direction. As the technology matures, it might even be possible that an interview tool could use the emotions of both parties to provide verbal prompts to the interviewer that would direct the conversation in effective ways.

The shortcomings of interviewers could actually be overcome with affective computing systems capable of producing emotionally appropriate and consistent interactions across all interviewees. With the growing prevalence of online interviews, particularly for screening, currently available technology has the potential to be adapted to produce an online interviewer whose emotional expressions could be carefully scripted and controlled. Eventually, it might even be possible to develop animatronic interviewers who could monitor and interact with candidates in lifelike and adaptable ways that could eliminate interviewer bias while also providing adaptable assessments of candidates.

Assessment center exercises and situational judgment tests. Both assessment center exercises and situational judgment tests (SJTs) have shown relatively strong predictive validity in more complex jobs (Ryan & Ployhart, 2014). Advances in technology have made it easier to incorporate these methods without resorting to off-site centers or third-party providers, because relatively robust exercises and simulations can be conducted in-house or even online. Adding affective computing to these methods offers several advantages. An assessment center consists of a "… standardized evaluation of behavior based on multiple inputs" (Rupp et al., 2015, p. 1250). Assessment centers consist of both behavioral and simulation exercises, including managerial simulation exercises, leaderless group discussion, role-play, case analysis, and oral presentations (Hoffman et al., 2015). Assessment exercises are generally designed to evaluate specific knowledge, skills, and abilities. By adding emotion, these methods could not only measure how skilled a candidate is at a task, but also how much they enjoy or dislike the task. This would seem to be a much better predictor of their long-term engagement and performance on such a task. This has the potential to greatly expand our ability to assess "other characteristics" which have often been ill-defined but seem to be most strongly associated with in-role performance.

Along these lines, affective computing and observing candidate emotions during these exercises provides a window into several abilities and other characteristics that have proved difficult to quantify with traditional methods. Emotional intelligence and interpersonal skills stand out and are frequently sought after by organizations. By observing candidate emotions during task-oriented exercises and interactive simulations (more on these in the training section), these methods could provide object measures of each of the emotional intelligence domains as well as interpersonal skills that are not really possible through any other available selection method.

Similarly, SJTs where candidates are presented with work-related situations and behavior or knowledge response is assessed, have proven to be some of the most valid selection methods for assessing social skills and ethical decision making (Christian, Edwards, & Bradley, 2010; McDaniel, Hartman, Whetzel, & Grubb, 2007). Adding candidate emotional responses to these methods would have similar benefits to those described above. In additional, adding emotions to SJTs would provide a means for detecting social desirability and deception in candidate responses. Candidate emotions might also be used to detect and account for racial and gender subgroup differences (Ryan & Ployhart, 2014) and thereby reduce any bias that may be inherent in some SJTs.

Training and Development

Affective computing has already been applied to improving electronic learning (Lin et al., 2010). Because affective computing can combine multiple modes of emotion analysis, such as speech, facial expressions, and body language, its application can be extended to new avenues of human resources management training. As discussed previously, affective computing can produce systems that can detect emotions in humans and also express authentic human emotions using video or robotic simulations. These machines are useful in helping to enhance skills that require the combination of emotional states and cognitions. Indeed, adding computer vision for affect recognition leads to the adaptation of behavior that could improve the quality of learning (Ivanova, 2013). Hence, affective computing could lead to training in human resources management in at least three areas: 1) leadership development, 2) emotional intelligence, and 3) diversity and inclusion.

Affective computing and leadership training and development. In the domain of leadership development, organizational scholars contend that emotional intelligence is a critical component of effective leadership (Mayer & Salovey, 1990; Goleman, 1995). Hence, affective computing could become a useful training tool. Training programs using artificial emotional intelligence could involve machines mimicking real-life scenarios where employee or managers would react while their emotions are recorded and analyzed. Participants could interact with computers or directly with fellow humans while their emotional reactions are being recorded.

Leadership training using affective computing would be extremely beneficial for developing leadership skills that are extremely difficult to learn by instruction or self-reflection. One such shortcoming in many leaders is false consensus, the belief that others perceive and respond to the world in the same way that we do (Martinko & Gardner, 1987). Leader simulations could be done in an iterative fashion using affective computing emotion expression systems to simulate a subordinate who is programmed to respond consistent with systematic variance of different individual difference variables such as personality traits and social and work identities. Over time, leaders could learn to appreciate and recognize clues in how employees respond and adapt their communication, feedback, and influence strategies in more dynamic and effective ways.

Real-life applications could also include hiring interviews, counseling situations, performance reviews, or situations involving promotion decisions. For example, computer-assisted performance appraisal could record both the leader's and employee's emotional expressions and reactions. Trainers could then review these interactions to highlight effective and counterproductive elements. These kinds of objective coaching experiences have been shown to be more effective at developing leadership skills (Ladegard & Gjerde, 2014).

Affective computing and training in emotional intelligence. Emotional intelligence is widely regarded to be extremely important for organizational success and yet is widely lacking at all levels of organizations (Kotsou et al., 2019; Goleman, 1995). Affective computing can serve as a tool for organizations to provide practical, skill-based training in emotional intelligence. To this end, emotional self-awareness is a cornerstone of emotional intelligence and a skill that many individuals in organizations lack (Jordan & Ashkanasy, 2006). As mentioned previously, emotion recognition tools could allow organizations to collect an array of emotional reactions from their employees and use them for training purposes to help employees increase their awareness of how their emotions impact their effectiveness. Managers and employees could engage in self-training by using emotion-enhanced computer devices. Automatic face analysis (AFA) software could provide real-time indicators of employee emotions, such as frustration, so that they could be aware of their emotions and respond in adaptive ways. The benefit of such an approach is particularly relevant in the age of COVID-19, where remote working is becoming the norm.

Of course, emotional intelligence also requires that employees not only recognize their emotions but are able to also regulate them appropriately (Grandey, 2000). As discussed previously, affective computing systems could be used to actively monitor a number of everyday interactions and provide real-time indicators to employees of when their emotions are inconsistent with display rules and recommended deep acting tactics for regulating their emotions. A wealth of research has shown that individuals are often able to successfully employ emotion regulation strategies when prompted (Grandey & Melloy, 2017).

In a more training-oriented perspective, affective computing could be used to provide interactive emotional intelligence training. Employees at all levels in the organization could engage in dynamic computer simulations where they are presented with unpredictable emotionally charged interactions. These sessions could be interrupted at any point to provide immediate and detailed feedback as well as allowing participants to rewind and modify their approach to the situation. While emotional intelligence training efforts to date have shown modest improvements, they suggest that practice and feedback are key to developing these skills (Mattingly & Kraiger, 2019). As such, it seems that a training program based on affective computing technology offers a means of improving the relationship management skills which are the most challenging aspect of emotional intelligence to develop.

Affective computing and diversity training. Diversity training is more than important in today's environment where concerns for social justice and inequality are becoming important issues that organizations must address. Years of diversity training have proven only marginally successful (Bezrukova, Spell, Perry, & Jehn, 2016). To successfully train employees in diversity, organizations must ensure that they understand the emotions that employees experience as they interact with individuals from various and different backgrounds. Research in neuroscience has highlighted the neural foundations of in-group and out-group bias (Van Bavel, Packer, & Cunningham, 2008; Moreira, Van Bavel, & Teizer, 2017). It has also demonstrated that perceiving someone to be a member of an out-group elicits some emotional reactions, such as fear and anxiety (Van Bavel, Packer, & Cunningham, 2008). Hence, affective computing could help to record the emotional reactions that individuals experience as they interact with dissimilar others.

Training using emotional artificial intelligence tools could be situational, scripted, or more interactive. Trainees may be engaged in situations where they directly interact with dissimilar others while their emotional reactions are being recorded by a computer. Using AFA software could allow the detection of specific emotions that participants are experiencing. For example, scenarios involving "inappropriate" comments about one's in-group could be expressed by a computer to test participants' emotional reactions. Similarly, participants could be engaged in conversation with in-group and out-group members while their emotional reactions are being recorded. Computers may record emotional reactions to the words and tones of similar and dissimilar others and analyze them. Results could help to determine whether people react differently to words or speech patterns from similar compared to dissimilar others. As these examples illustrate, affective computing offers several applications in human resource management. Hence, it could be a useful tool in the toolkit of managers.

Talent Management

Employee well-being. Poor health and well-being results in reduced availability and pro-ductivity among even typically high-performing employees. A number of recent studies have begun to explore the use of affective computing to actively monitor the emotions and well-being of employees in the workplace (Lee, 2019). Other researchers have tested a system to monitor employees for stress and depression (Lee, Lam, & Chiu, 2019). These efforts show that this is an area of great promise for the use of affective computing technology, which can be used to identify employees who are at risk of poor well-being and burnout early on, and at a stage when the situation can be addressed before it results in reduced productivity or absenteeism.

    Performance management. Affective computing also has a variety of applications within the sphere of performance monitoring and improvement. Performance appraisal systems have long struggled to objectively measure employee performance in a way that connects performance to organizational outcomes while also improving the performance of individual employees (Schleicher et al., 2018). The ability to perceive emotions in employees, custom-ers, clients, and leaders in real-world organizational situations would allow human resource professionals to develop systems to record and catalog emotional expressions to track perfor-mance metrics for individuals and relate them to organizational outcomes.

    Researchers have already tested an affective computing system for detecting flow states in employees (Lee, 2020). Flow at work results in periods of ultra-high performance and effi-ciency and is associated with concentration in the work activity, work enjoyment, and intrinsic work motivation (Bakker, 2005). In another study, researchers used affective computing to monitor employee productivity (Verma, Verma, & Dixit, 2020). While collecting this type of information may present some concerns, the assumption here is that this technology would be utilized in a transparent way to help individuals understand and improve their performance. To that end, we will discuss some specific ways that affective computing might be used in customer service contexts and then how it might be used to improve interpersonal interactions within organizations.

    Customer service. Managing the emotions of customer service employees has been a topic of a wealth of human resources research that includes subjects such as emotional labor, emotional intelligence, and display rules, to name just a few. While this research has yielded a number of interesting insights, it has relied almost entirely on survey research. Affective computing technology provides the ability to extend both research and practice in this area by providing real-time measures of emotions in customer service employees. One recent study used artificial intelligence to monitor stress in customer service agents (Bromuri, Henkel, Iren, & Urovi, 2021).

    Initially, this would provide HR professionals access to how employees express emotions to customers over the course of daily interactions. Unlike previous methods, affective computing technology would not be limited to traditional customer service settings such as call centers. With a few well-placed cameras and microphones, it could be employed in settings such as retail stores, restaurants, and hospitals, to name just a few. This would greatly expand our knowledge of how emotional intelligence and emotional labor play out in dynamic real-world service interactions. The objective nature of affective computing technology could provide reliable time-averaged measures of service employee performance in a variety of situations and circumstances. In situations where display rules exist or are developed, employee compliance with these rules could also be quantified and included in performance assessments.

This discrete data could be analyzed against the wealth of customer satisfaction survey data to identify emotional expressions and patterns of expressions that are particularly effective or ineffective in the eyes of customers. More interestingly, affective computing could also be used to monitor real-time customer emotions. This could provide a more accurate view of customer service employee performance by placing equal or greater emphasis on customer reactions over employee displays. This richer data could also help to develop more nuanced and advantageous emotion display rules and guidance for employees. The customer emotion data could also be used to provide a more balanced picture of employee emotional performance in discrete customer interactions. For example, a wait staff member who displayed a negative emotion to a particularly belligerent diner would be rated differently to one who displayed the same emotion to a happy diner. This would allow supervisors to provide timely and specific feedback on service encounters that went well and poorly, which is key for performance improvement (DeNisi & Murphy, 2017).

In the not so distant future, affective computing devices could provide real-time, in-situ information feedback to service employees regarding their own emotional displays and the emotional responses of their customers. This information could be discreetly provided via wearable technology so that it would be invisible to the customer even during face-to-face interactions. Self and other emotional awareness are key components of emotional intelligence that are extremely important for the management of emotions at work (Ashkanasy & Daus, 2002). Simply providing this information has significant potential to improve employee performance. However, affective computing technology could go even further by incorporating improved display rule algorithms. It could also provide coaching and prompts to help employees manage their emotions and those of their customers. Such a system could drastically reduce the cognitive and emotional load on customer service employees while improving their performance and customer satisfaction.

In a more revolutionary vein, affective computing sensing and expression technology could be employed to develop automated service agent chatbots. Prototypes of these systems have already been proposed and examined in academic settings for text-based interactions (Ghandeharioun, McDuff, Czerwinski, & Rowan, 2019). Customer service call centers have high emotional demands but only pay low wages, and the result is often reduced well-being, high turnover, and low customer satisfaction (Grandey & Sayre, 2019). Emotionally intelligent chatbot service agents could be programed to respond appropriately and empathetically to customers, no matter how irate or disrespectful, with natural voice responses that could even be tailored to the specific local dialect of the customer. This technology could eliminate the need for human agents in all but the most unusual or demanding circumstance, in which case the call could be turned over to a more senior agent to resolve after the customer had vented and their concerns had been recorded and analyzed.

Intra-organizational interpersonal interactions and leadership. These improvements of performance appraisal and management should not be limited to service jobs because emotions and interpersonal skills play a key role in most modern organizations (Ashkanasy & Daus, 2002). The technologies described above could be employed in a myriad of situations within organizations, such as team interactions and meetings, mentoring sessions, annual reviews, counseling sessions, exit interviews, and numerous other interactions between employees and coworkers or supervisors. By improving emotional awareness and regulation, this technology could improve working relationships and effectiveness throughout an organization and increase employee engagement, motivation, and both in-role and extra-role performance.

One of the most interesting, yet difficult to investigate phenomena in organizations is emotional contagion, whereby the emotions of a few employees can spread rapidly and unconsciously throughout a workgroup or organization (Barsade, Coutifaris, & Pillemer, 2018). Affective computing provides an unprecedented means to observe and track the transmission of emotions between individuals through discrete interpersonal interactions. Finally, we could better understand what factors can predict how and why different emotions spread within organizations. This is important because different emotions have unique effects on organizational outcomes such as attitudes and decision making which directly affect performance. Human resource scholars and practitioners could then develop methods to encourage beneficial emotional contagion while limiting the spread of detrimental emotions.

Probably the most impactful application of affective computing would be to improve the emotional intelligence capabilities of leaders at all levels of organizations (Antonakis, Ashkanasy, & Dasborough, 2009). Emotion data could be used to evaluate leadership performance in ways that have not previously been possible. Good leaders could be identified early thus ending the unfortunate tendency to promote individuals to leadership positions who demonstrate excellent task performance but poor interpersonal skills. The data could also be used to provide specific feedback to individual employees on how to improve their leadership skills, and in particular situations where they need to adapt their leadership style and behaviors.

Affective computing emotion data could also be used to investigate and reduce the troubling phenomenon of abusive supervision that is all too prevalent in organizations (Tepper, 2007). Thus far, this research has relied almost entirely on employee perceptions of abusive leader behaviors (Mackey, Frieder, Brees, & Martinko, 2017). By assessing both leader and follower emotions, it would be possible to objectively assess the congruence of perceptions of abusive supervision and actual leader behaviors and emotion expressions. It may be that some of the mixed findings in the empirical literature might be due to inaccurate perceptions of leader emotion expressions (Tepper, Simon, & Park, 2017). In addition, to improving leader performance through the methods discussed in the previous paragraph, inaccurate perceptions by employees could be addressed by identifying the conditions that lead to these misperceptions. Misperception could be reduced by improving the situational awareness of leaders and followers.

CHALLENGES OF AFFECTIVE COMPUTING IN HUMAN RESOURCES

For all its promise, the use of affective computing technology in organizations is not without a number of potential challenges and ethical concerns. First, while most of these systems have performed quite well at emotion detection and expression in laboratory settings, there are concerns over their methodological reliability and validity in dynamic, real-world settings (Beringer et al., 2019). There is already growing concern over using these types of technologies in human resources situations where the rights and livelihood of employees may be negatively impacted by decision systems that haven't been rigorously tested and validated (Buolamwini & Gebru, 2018; Rhue, 2019). Amazon recently stopped using its AI recruitment system after it proved to be biased against female applicants (Dastin, 2018).

Artificial intelligence and affective computing also raise a number of privacy issues (Tucker, 2019). The use of cameras for video recording the workplace and public spaces is growing rapidly. The COVID pandemic has also drastically increased the reliance on videoconferencing technology. While employees might willingly become comfortable with the technology and waive their privacy concerns, some of the applications we have discussed would involve retail, medical, and educational settings where non-employees would potentially be monitored, evaluated, and recorded by these systems. Strict guidelines for these situations would be needed to protect individuals' rights to privacy, particularly where protected information might be involved.

Another concern that would have to be addressed in the design and implementation of this technology is the adverse impact on any subgroups within the workforce or population in general. While much of human emotional experience and expression is universal, there can also be subtle cultural differences between subgroups based on factors such as culture, gender, and age (Keltner, Sauter, Tracy, & Cowen, 2019). Therefore, it might be possible for affective computing systems to evaluate some individuals inaccurately or "prefer" some forms of emotional expression over others. Care would need to be taken, particularly when these systems are initially deployed. Multimodal systems would be less susceptible to these differences. In addition, the artificial intelligence baked into affective computing technology can be designed to adaptively learn on the fly. Especially over time, these systems could assemble a personalized profile of emotional expression for each employee that would transcend any subgroup differences.

One group that would certainly be revealed and disadvantaged by affective computing systems would be psychopaths. There has been growing evidence regarding the prevalence and negative impacts of psychopaths in the workplace (Boddy & Taplin, 2016; Dutton, 2012). Psychopaths are masters of emotional deception and manipulation, but affective computing systems may have the potential to detect this deception and see through misbehavior, quickly and reliably. Some have argued that it is unethical to discriminate against psychopathy (Lindebaum & Zundel, 2013). It is our position that leveraging this technology to identify affective manipulation and misbehavior is not discriminatory. However, this further illustrates the importance of strict guidelines and close monitoring in utilizing this type of technology in organizational settings.

FUTURE RESEARCH ON AFFECTIVE COMPUTING IN HUMAN RESOURCES

Basic research into the technology and software underlying affective computing systems will certainly continue to advance at a rapid rate. In order for these systems to be applied effectively and ethically in human resources management applications, we believe that it will be essential for researchers in business and psychology to take notice and get involved in interdisciplinary research to properly test and validate these systems before they come into widespread use. One such area of promise is the use of qualitative, not just quantitative, research to better understand the potential for bias associated with affective computing and how to actively prevent it in the workplace. While developers of affective computing technology are increasingly looking to the social sciences in their experimentation of affective computing (Irving & Askell, 2019), leveraging qualitative social research approaches can unlock a better understanding of the impacts of this technology, but also serve as a foundation for future empirical research (Sloane & Moss, 2019).

Another evident area for future research is the use of this technology in the field. Given the recent emergence of this technology, much of the related research has occurred in laboratory settings. However, the importance of social context in measuring and displaying human emotional (and subsequently behavioral) responses cannot be overstated. Take, for example, the expression of a smile. A smile can be used to express positive emotions, but there are a myriad of reasons why someone may smile. For instance, smiles can be a response to when we are feeling scared or uncomfortable, or even when a person is in pain (Ambadar, Cohn, & Reed, 2009). Distinguishing between these types of smiles relies heavily on the context in which they are displayed. In order to be employed responsibly, these laboratory systems must be vigorously validated in field settings.

Finally, while context is incredibly important, researchers must also consider the individual differences, such as culture or personality, associated with the display of emotion and not rely on a single mode for interpretation. In their review of more than a thousand studies, Barrett and her colleagues (2019) found that many expressions of emotion are not as universal as previously thought and that inferring emotion from only facial expressions is imprecise at best. Among their conclusions, they point to the many factors, including verbal and physical cues, humans rely on when making emotional assessments. Future research in affective computing should then move heavily to a multimodal approach, leveraging multiple technological sources (i.e. videos, biometrics, and if possible, electroencephalography (EEGs)) in advancing the efficacy of assessing and replicating human emotion in the workplace.

CONCLUSION

Technology that senses emotion expressions by humans, as well as the capability to simulate authentic human emotional expressions, has tremendous potential to influence, and have impacts within, organizational settings. The purpose of this chapter was to provide an overview of affective computing and some of the ways in which it will be incorporated into human resource practices that govern organizational life. From selection practices, to training and development, to performance management, affective computing has a myriad of promising applications. Given that concerns plague current selection practices, affective computing may be a resource that not only improves the validity and reliability of existing selection practices, but addresses outstanding issues in research, as well as brings in new capabilities that extend existing practices. Performance management systems with the ability to record and catalog the emotional expressions of employees and leaders in real-world organizational settings through affective computing have the potential to not only track performance metrics for individuals, but also make important connections to core organizational outcomes. Finally, through combining multiple modes of emotion analysis, affective computing can be extended to advance leadership development, emotional intelligence, and diversity and inclusion within human resources training. Despite this tremendous impact, the implications of this technology are not without ethical concerns. Privacy concerns, as well as the mitigation of adverse impacts to individuals based on cultural differences, highlight the importance of strict guidelines and monitoring in the use of affective computing in organizations.

REFERENCES

Agrawal, A., & An, A. (2012). Unsupervised emotion detection from text using semantic and syntactic relations. In *2012 IEEE/WIC/ACM International Conferences on Web Intelligence and Intelligent Agent Technology* (pp. 346–353). IEEE.

Alu, D. A. S. C., Zoltan, E., & Stoica, I. C. (2017). Voice based emotion recognition with convolutional neural networks for companion robots. *Science and Technology, 20*, 222–240.

Ambadar, Z., Cohn, J. F., & Reed, L. I. (2009). All smiles are not created equal: Morphology and timing of smiles perceived as amused, polite, and embarrassed/nervous. *Journal of Nonverbal Behavior, 33*(1), 17–34.

Antonakis, J., Ashkanasy, N. M., & Dasborough, M. T. (2009). Does leadership need emotional intelligence? *Leadership Quarterly, 20*, 247–261.

Arunnehru, J., & Geetha, M. K. (2017). Automatic human emotion recognition in surveillance video. In N. Dey & V. Santhi (Eds.), *Intelligent techniques in signal processing for multimedia security* (pp. 321–342). Studies in Computational Intelligence (Vol. 660). Springer International Publishing.

Ashkanasy, N. M., & Daus, C. S. (2002). Emotion in the workplace: The new challenge for managers. *Academy of Management Perspectives, 16*(1), 76–86.

Bakker, A. B. (2005). Flow among music teachers and their students: The crossover of peak experiences. *Journal of Vocational Behavior, 66*(1), 26–44.

Barrett, L. F., Adolphs, R., Marsella, S., Martinez, A. M., & Pollak, S. D. (2019). Emotional expressions reconsidered: Challenges to inferring emotion from human facial movements. *Psychological Science in the Public Interest, 20*(1), 1–68.

Barsade, S. G., Coutifaris, C. G., & Pillemer, J. (2018). Emotional contagion in organizational life. *Research in Organizational Behavior, 38*, 137–151.

Beringer, M., Spohn, F., Hildebrandt, A., Wacker, J., & Recio, G. (2019). Reliability and validity of machine vision for the assessment of facial expressions. *Cognitive Systems Research, 56*, 119–132.

Bezrukova, K., Spell, C. S., Perry, J. L., & Jehn, K. A. (2016). A meta-analytical integration of over 40 years of research on diversity training evaluation. *Psychological Bulletin, 142*, 1227–1274.

Boddy, C. R., & Taplin, R. (2016). The influence of corporate psychopaths on job satisfaction and its determinants. *International Journal of Manpower, 37*, 965–988.

Bromuri, S., Henkel, A. P., Iren, D., & Urovi, V. (2021). Using AI to predict service agent stress from emotion patterns in service interactions. *Journal of Service Management, 32*(4), 581–611. doi.org/10.1108/JOSM-06-2019-0163

Buehl, A. K., & Melchers, K. G. (2017). Individual difference variables and the occurrence and effectiveness of faking behavior in interviews. *Frontiers in Psychology, 8*, Article 686.

Buolamwini, J., & Gebru, T. (2018). Gender shades: Intersectional accuracy disparities in commercial gender classification. In *Proceedings of Machine Learning Research* (pp. 1–15). http://hdl.handle.net/1721.1/114068

Castellano, G., Kessous, L., & Caridakis, G. (2008). Emotion recognition through multiple modalities: Face, body gesture, speech. In C. Peter & R. Beale (Eds.), *Affect and emotion in human-computer interaction* (pp. 92–103). Springer.

Christian, M. S., Edwards, B. D., & Bradley, J. C. (2010). Situational judgment tests: Constructs assessed and a meta-analysis of their criterion-related validities. *Personnel Psychology, 63*, 83–117.

Dastin, J. (2018, October 10). Amazon scraps secret AI recruiting tool that showed bias against women. *Reuters*. https://www.reuters.com/article/us-amazon-com-jobs-automation-insight-idUSKCN1MK08G, downloaded February 18, 2021.

DeNisi, A. S., & Murphy, K. R. (2017). Performance appraisal and performance management: 100 years of progress. *Journal of Applied Psychology, 102*, 421–433.

Dipboye, R. L., & Gaugler, B. B. (1993). Cognitive and behavioral processes in the selection interview. In N. Schmitt & W. C. Borman (Eds.), *Personnel selection in organizations* (pp. 135–170). Jossey-Bass.

Dutton, K. (2012). *The wisdom of psychopaths: Lessons in life from saints, spies and serial killers.* Random House.

Ekman, P., & Oster, H. (1979). Facial expressions of emotion. *Annual Review of Psychology, 30*(1), 527–554.

Ghandeharioun, A., McDuff, D., Czerwinski, M., & Rowan, K. (2019, September). Towards understanding emotional intelligence for behavior change chatbots. In *8th International Conference on Affective Computing and Intelligent Interaction (ACII)* (pp. 8–14). IEEE.

Giannakopoulos, T., Dimopoulos, S., Pantazopoulos, G., Chatziagapi, A., Sgouropoulos, D., Katsamanis, A., … & Narayanan, S. (2019, September). Using Oliver API for emotion-aware movie content characterization. In *International Conference on Content-Based Multimedia Indexing (CBMI)* (pp. 1–4). IEEE.

Goleman, D. (1995). *Emotional intelligence: Why it can matter more than IQ*. Bloomsbury Publishing.

Grandey, A. A. (2000). Emotional regulation in the workplace: A new way to conceptualize emotional labor. *Journal of Occupational Health Psychology, 5*(1), 95–110.

Grandey, A. A., & Melloy, R. C. (2017). The state of the heart: Emotional labor as emotion regulation reviewed and revised. *Journal of Occupational Health Psychology, 22*, 407–422.

Grandey, A. A., & Sayre, G. M. (2019). Emotional labor: Regulating emotions for a wage. *Current Directions in Psychological Science, 28*, 131–137.

He, Z., Li, Z., Yang, F., Wang, L., Li, J., Zhou, C., & Pan, J. (2020). Advances in multimodal emotion recognition based on brain–computer interfaces. *Brain Sciences, 10*, 687–706.

Hoffman, B. J., Kennedy, C. L., LoPilato, A. C., Monahan, E. L., & Lance, C. E. (2015). A review of the content, criterion-related, and construct-related validity of assessment center exercises. *Journal of Applied Psychology, 100*(4), 1143–1168.

Irving, G., & Askell, A. (2019). AI safety needs social scientists. *Distill, 4*(2). https://doi.org/10.23915/distill.00014

Ivanova, M. (2013). Researching affective computing techniques for intelligent tutoring systems. In *Proceedings of the International Conference on Interactive Collaborative Learning* (pp. 611–617). IEEE. https://doi.org/10.1109/ICL.2013.6644661

Jerritta, S., Murugappan, M., Nagarajan, R., & Wan, K. (2011). Physiological signals based human emotion recognition: A review. In *2011 IEEE 7th International Colloquium on Signal Processing and its Applications* (pp. 410–415). IEEE.

Jordan, P. J., & Ashkanasy, N. M. (2006). Emotional intelligence, emotional self-awareness, and team effectiveness. In V. U. Druskat, F. Sala, & G. J. Mount (Eds.), *The impact of emotional intelligence on individual and group performance* (pp. 145–163). Lawrence Erlbaum Associates.

Judge, T. A., Cable, D. M., & Higgins, C. A. (2000). The employment interview: A review of recent research and recommendations for future research. *Human Resource Management Review, 10*(4), 383–406.

Keltner, D., Sauter, D., Tracy, J., & Cowen, A. (2019). Emotional expression: Advances in basic emotion theory. *Journal of Nonverbal Behavior, 43*, 133–160.

Kotsou, I., Mikolajczak, M., Heeren, A., Grégoire, J., & Leys, C. (2019). Improving emotional intelligence: A systematic review of existing work and future challenges. *Emotion Review, 11*, 151–165.

Kuligowska, K., Kisielewicz, P., & Włodarz, A. (2018). Speech synthesis systems: Disadvantages and limitations. *International Journal of Engineering and Technology, 7*, 234–239.

Kutt, K., Nalepa, G. J., Giżycka, B., Jemiolo, P., & Adamczyk, M. (2018). Bandreader – a mobile application for data acquisition from wearable devices in affective computing experiments. In *2018 11th International Conference on Human System Interaction (HSI)* (pp. 42–48). IEEE.

Ladegard, G., & Gjerde, S. (2014). Leadership coaching, leader role-efficacy, and trust in subordinates. A mixed methods study assessing leadership coaching as a leadership development tool. *The Leadership Quarterly, 25*(4), 631–646.

Lee, J., Lam, M., & Chiu, C. (2019). Clara: Design of a new system for passive sensing of depression, stress and anxiety in the workplace. In *International Symposium on Pervasive Computing Paradigms for Mental Health* (pp. 12–28). Springer International Publishing.

Lee, M. (2020). *Detecting affective flow states of knowledge workers using physiological sensors*. arXiv preprint arXiv:2006.10635.

Lee, M.-F. (2019). Working place monitoring emotion by affective computing model. In *International Conference on Frontier Computing* (pp. 51–54). Springer.

Levashina, J., & Campion, M. A. (2006). A model of faking likelihood in the employment interview. *International Journal of Selection and Assessment, 14*(4), 299–316.

Levashina, J., & Campion, M. A. (2007). Measuring faking in the employment interview: Development and validation of an interview faking behavior scale. *Journal of Applied Psychology*, *92*(6), 1638–1656.

Lin, H., Pan, F., Wang, Y., Lv, S., & Sun, S. (2010). Affective computing in E-learning. In M. Jakobovic (Ed.), *E-learning* (pp. 117–128). InTech. https://doi.org/10.5772/7780

Lindebaum, D., & Zundel, M. (2013). Not quite a revolution: Scrutinizing organizational neuroscience in leadership studies. *Human Relations*, *66*(6), 857–877.

Mackey, J. D., Frieder, R. E., Brees, J. R., & Martinko, M. J. (2017). Abusive supervision: A meta-analysis and empirical review. *Journal of Management*, *43*(6), 1940–1965.

Marmpena, M., Lim, A., & Dahl, T. S. (2018). How does the robot feel? Perception of valence and arousal in emotional body language. *Journal of Behavioral Robotics*, *9*(1), 168–182.

Martinko, M. J., & Gardner, W. L. (1987). The leader/member attribution process. *Academy of Management Review*, *12*(2), 235–249.

Mattingly, V., & Kraiger, K. (2019). Can emotional intelligence be trained? A meta-analytical investigation. *Human Resource Management Review*, *29*(2), 140–155.

Mayer, J., & Salovey, P. (1990). Emotional intelligence. *Imagination, Cognition and Personality*, *9*(3), 185–211. https://doi.org/10.2190/DUGG-P24E-52WK-6CDG

McDaniel, M. A., Hartman, N. S., Whetzel, D. L., & Grubb III, W. L. (2007). Situational judgment tests, response instructions, and validity: A meta-analysis. *Personnel Psychology*, *60*(1), 63–91.

McDaniel, M. A., Whetzel, D. L., Schmidt, F. L., & Maurer, S. D. (1994). The validity of employment interviews: A comprehensive review and meta-analysis. *Journal of Applied Psychology*, *79*(4), 599–616.

McDuff, D., Kaliouby, R., Senechal, T., Amr, M., Cohn, J., & Picard, R. (2013). Affectiva-MIT facial expression dataset (AM-FED): Naturalistic and spontaneous facial expressions collected "in-the-wild". In *Proceedings of the IEEE Conference on Computer Vision and Pattern Recognition Workshops* (pp. 881–888). IEEE.

McFarland, L. A., Yun, G., Harold, C. M., Viera Jr., L., & Moore, L. G. (2005). An examination of impression management use and effectiveness across assessment center exercises: The role of competency demands. *Personnel Psychology*, *58*(4), 949–980.

Moreira, J. F. G., Van Bavel, J. J. , & Telzer, E. H. (2017). The neural development of "us and them". *Social Cognitive and Affective Neuroscience*, *12*(2), 184–196.

Nguyen, L. S., Frauendorfer, D., Mast, M. S., & Gatica-Perez, D. (2014). Hire me: Computational inference of hirability in employment interviews based on nonverbal behavior. *IEEE Transactions on Multimedia*, *16*(4), 1018–1031.

Ning, Y., He, S., Wu, Z., Xing, C., & Zhang, L. J. (2019). A review of deep learning based speech synthesis. *Applied Sciences*, *9*(19), Article 4050.

Picard, R. W. (2003). Affective computing: Challenges. *International Journal of Human-Computer Studies*, *59*(1–2), 55–64.

Ragot, M., Martin, N., Em, S., Pallamin, N., & Diverrez, J. M. (2017). Emotion recognition using physiological signals: Laboratory vs. wearable sensors. In *International Conference on Applied Human Factors and Ergonomics* (pp. 15–22). Springer International Publishing.

Raouzaiou, A., Tsapatsoulis, N., Karpouzis, K., & Kollias, S. (2002). Parameterized facial expression synthesis based on MPEG-4. *EURASIP Journal on Advances in Signal Processing*, *2002*, Article 521048. https://doi.org/10.1155/S1110865702206149

Rhue, L. (2019). *Anchored to bias: How AI-human scoring can induce and reduce bias due to the anchoring effect*. SSRN. http://dx.doi.org/10.2139/ssrn.3492129

Richardson, S. (2020). Affective computing in the modern workplace. *Business Information Review*, *37*, 78–85.

Rupp, D. E., Hoffman, B. J., Bischof, D., Byham, W., Collins, L., Gibbons, A., & Jackson, D. J. (2015). Guidelines and ethical considerations for assessment center operations. *Journal of Management*, *41*(4), 1244–1273.

Ryan, A. M., & Ployhart, R. E. (2014). A century of selection. *Annual Review of Psychology*, *65*, 693–717.

Samadiani, N., Huang, G., Cai, B., Luo, W., Chi, C. H., Xiang, Y., & He, J. (2019). A review on automatic facial expression recognition systems assisted by multimodal sensor data. *Sensors*, *19*, 1863–1890.

Schleicher, D. J., Baumann, H. M., Sullivan, D. W., Levy, P. E., Hargrove, D. C., & Barros-Rivera, B. A. (2018). Putting the system into performance management systems: A review and agenda for performance management research. *Journal of Management, 44*(6), 2209–2245.

Schröder, M. (2001). Emotional speech synthesis: A review. In *Eurospeech 2001* (pp. 561–564).

Shen, Z., Cheng, J., Hu, X., & Dong, Q. (2019). Emotion recognition based on multi-view body gestures. In *IEEE International Conference on Image Processing* (pp. 3317–3321). IEEE.

Sloane, M., & Moss, E. (2019). AI's social sciences deficit. *Nature Machine Intelligence, 1*(8), 330–331.

Stathopoulou, I. O., & Tsihrintzis, G. A. (2011). Emotion recognition from body movements and gestures. In G. A. Tsihrintzis, M. Virvou, L. C. Jain, & R. J. Howlett (eds) *Intelligent interactive multimedia systems and services* (pp. 295–303). Springer.

Stewart, G. L., Darnold, T., Barrick, M. R., & Dustin, S. D. (2008). Exploring the handshake in employment interviews. *Journal of Applied Psychology, 93*, 1139–1146.

Tepper, B. J. (2007). Abusive supervision in work organizations: Review, synthesis, and research agenda. *Journal of Management, 33*(3), 261–289.

Tepper, B. J., Simon, L., & Park, H. M. (2017). Abusive supervision. *Annual Review of Organizational Psychology and Organizational Behavior, 4*, 123–152.

Tucker, C. (2019). Privacy, algorithms, and artificial intelligence. In A. Agrawal, J. Gans, & A. Goldfarb (Eds.), *The economics of artificial intelligence: An agenda* (pp. 423–437). University of Chicago Press.

Van Bavel, J. J., Packer, D. J., & Cunningham, W. A. (2008). The neural substrates of in-group bias: A functional magnetic resonance imaging investigation. *Psychological Science, 19*(11), 1131–1139.

Verma, H., Verma, G., & Dixit, S. (2020). Hybrid deep learning model for emotion recognition using facial expressions: Channelizing employee productivity. *TEST Engineering and Management, 82*, 8224–8226.

Vogt, T., André, E., & Wagner, J. (2008). Automatic recognition of emotions from speech: A review of the literature and recommendations for practical realisation. In C. Peter & R. Beale (Eds.), *Affect and emotion in human-computer interaction* (pp. 75–91). Springer.

Wang, N., Gao, X., Tao, D., Yang, H., & Li, X. (2018). Facial feature point detection: A comprehensive survey. *Neurocomputing, 275*, 50–65.

Zhou, Y., & Shi, B. E. (2017). Photorealistic facial expression synthesis by the conditional difference adversarial autoencoder. In *2017 Seventh International Conference on Affective Computing and Intelligent Interaction (ACII)* (pp. 370–376). IEEE.

PART II

CONSEQUENCES OF ARTIFICIAL INTELLIGENCE IN HUMAN RESOURCES

14. Consequences of artificial intelligence in human resource management

Maarten Renkema

INTRODUCTION

Human Resource Management (HRM) refers to all activities that organizations perform to effectively manage their employees (Wright & McMahan, 1992). In performing HRM activities, organizations seek to achieve competitive advantages through the strategic utilization of their workforce. Although HRM is about managing people, technologies are increasingly used to do this in a more effective and efficient way. Whereas the field of HRM may have initially been hesitant to adopt new techniques, nowadays the use of technologies is growing. This is unsurprising given the enormous amount of employee data that is currently available; data that serves as input for these smart technologies. Thereby, Artificial Intelligence (AI) can potentially be used to help make better decisions, reduce routine work, and eventually create economic value. Various developments and examples show how HRM can adopt AI (Jia et al., 2018; Strohmeier & Piazza, 2015) and use these digital technologies to work *smarter* (Bondarouk et al., 2017). AI technologies are rapidly advancing and the application in HRM has seen many developments since its uptake in the mid-2010s. In fact, the Society of Human Resource Management (SHRM) has identified AI as one of the most important technology trends in recent years (Zielinski, 2020).

As this book illustrates, contributions in the fields of AI and HRM take many different perspectives and offer various insights. However, to date, empirical research that has examined the outcomes of using AI in HRM and its consequences for both (HR) managers and employees is scarce. In this chapter we continue from earlier explorations of the use of AI (Strohmeier & Piazza, 2015) and present an overview of recent developments in terms of specific *consequences*. Specifically, we provide an outline of the effects of using AI for both HRM activities and stakeholders, thereby responding to calls for more research about the consequences of AI in HRM (Malik et al., 2020). Here, consequences of AI in HRM are defined as the results and/or effects of using Artificial Intelligence in the domain of Human Resource Management. This speaks to the implications that AI has for HRM activities and the effects this has on (HR) managers and employees. Therefore, we develop and describe an organizing framework including components and dimensions of the effects of AI, provide examples from existing research, and discuss implications for future research. In addressing the consequences of AI in HRM, we draw on both advantages and disadvantages and discuss both intended and unintended consequences. We do so by addressing the following questions: What are the consequences of the application of AI in HRM? How can these consequences be categorized? And what implications can be derived from current research?

This chapter is structured as follows: We first clarify and categorize the above-mentioned consequences of AI in HRM by adopting a multidimensional perspective. Based on this classification we sketch an overview of recent developments of AI in HRM and develop future research directions. Lastly, we discuss the general implications of our framework.

ARTIFICIAL INTELLIGENCE IN HRM

Artificial Intelligence as a field of research was born in the 1950s – at a conference at Dartmouth College (see Haenlein & Kaplan, 2019). AI refers to digital technologies that mimic functions of natural intelligence, such as sensing and learning, to augment or automate human tasks (see CHAPTER 1). As several of the chapters in this book have shown, there are many ways to categorize AI in HR. This is particularly important for analyzing the consequences of the adoption of AI in the HRM domain because it can be expected that consequences are dependent on these specific categories. In general, AI draws on the availability of (large) datasets, data-based predictions (algorithms), and the capacity to learn and improve (Kaplan & Haenlein, 2019). AI has many application areas and can be used for several purposes that mimic natural intelligence: automated reasoning, robotics, knowledge representation, language processing, and machine learning (see CHAPTERS 2–7).

Being relatively late in adopting and studying AI technology, the HRM literature lacks an integrative structure for studying the consequences of AI. To advance the field, this chapter explores the links between HRM and AI and develops a multidimensional organizing framework, which highlights how HRM and AI are linked at different organizational levels of analysis.

AN ORGANIZING FRAMEWORK FOR THE RESEARCH ON CONSEQUENCES OF AI IN HRM

While the body of literature on AI in HRM is growing, and various studies have aimed at examining its effects, the applications of AI are diverse and for that reason the studies into consequences have been specific and disparate. Earlier studies have highlighted how AI techniques can be applied in HRM (Jia et al., 2018; Lawler & Elliot, 1996; Renkema, forthcoming; Strohmeier & Piazza, 2015). However, to our knowledge, there are no existing attempts to uncover the variety and complexity of *specific consequences* of AI in HRM. Therefore, to develop this field of research, we provide an organizing framework that addresses these consequences and captures its multidimensional nature. This framework should help to establish a common understanding of the components and dimensions of such consequences. There are multiple ways to categorize consequences; here we do so by exploring the types of consequences and the types of research to study these consequences. They help to structure and gain a better understanding of the research about consequences, because AI potentially affects both HRM practice and the academic research into these practices (e.g. Cheng & Hackett, 2019; Minbaeva, 2021; Strohmeier, 2007). They enable the illustration of the wide variety of effects that AI (potentially) has on HRM practice and research and facilitate getting an overview of the sheer heterogeneity of AI consequences in HRM. Table 14.1 shows a framework for the categorization of the consequences of using AI in HRM.[1]

Table 14.1   *An organizing framework for the research on consequences of AI in HRM*

Components	Dimensions	Sub-dimensions				
Types of consequence	*Level of analysis*	Organization (macro)		Team (meso)		Individual (micro)
	HRM practice	Hiring	Job design	Performance	Development	...
	HRM stakeholder	HR professional		Senior & line manager		Employees & applicants
	AI area	Machine learning		Natural language programming	Robotics	...
	Desirability	Desired			Undesired	
	Transformation	Transformational			Non-transformational	
Research types	*Theory base*	Theoretical			Non-theoretical	
	Methodological approach	Conceptual		Non-experimental		Experimental

The framework consists of two main components. The first component ("types of consequences") identifies the different kinds of AI consequences in HRM and includes dimensions that can be used to categorize current and future research on the consequences of AI in HRM. The second component ("research types") classifies research approaches for studying AI consequences and includes dimensions that are useful to categorize types of research in current studies and identifies approaches for studying consequences in the future.

In each of these components several dimensions and sub-dimensions are employed as criteria to categorize consequences. In the following sections, we provide reasoning, and where possible, empirical support for our categorization and highlight why these components and (sub-)dimensions are important to consider when analyzing the consequences of AI in HRM. Next, we highlight several main findings, derive implications from these findings, and offer future considerations. In doing so, we can achieve our goal of developing an organizing framework for the *consequences* of AI in HRM. Unlike a full-fledged systematic literature review, we describe initial insights and highlight examples of recent and instructive studies to develop a categorization of consequences of AI in HRM with several distinct dimensions and sub-dimensions.

TYPES OF CONSEQUENCES OF AI IN HRM

Before we can analyze the types of consequences of AI in HRM, we need to specify what HRM practice itself entails. HRM involves all organizational activities performed to effectively manage employees (Wright & McMahan, 1992), and the HR function is defined as "... all managerial actions carried out at any level regarding the organisation of work and the entry, development and exit of people in the organisation so that their competencies are used at their best in order to achieve corporate objectives" (Valverde, 2001, p. 19).

The HRM literature distinguishes between HRM professionals and HRM activities, the difference being that HRM professionals are people working in an HR department and that HRM practices are activities performed in organizations (Björkman et al., 2014). The first body of work is focused on the HRM professional and the roles that HR functions fulfill within organizations (Ulrich & Brockbank, 2005), whereas the second studies to what extent and how HRM systems and practices are related to organizational outcomes (Boselie et al., 2005). Therefore, both these two fields are integrated into our framework, distinguishing between consequences for HRM practices and consequences for HRM stakeholders. Furthermore, HRM is an inherently multilevel phenomenon that integrates multiple organizational levels of analysis (Renkema et al., 2017), and therefore our organizing framework classifies AI consequences among the different organizational levels. Lastly, our framework includes the distinction between desired and undesired consequences, given that on the one hand AI can be helpful for improving effectiveness in HRM (e.g. Malik et al., 2021), but on the other there are less desirable outcomes such as increased bias and organizational control (Kellogg et al., 2020; Leicht-Deobald et al., 2019).

In combination, various AI application areas pose a variety of desired and undesired consequences for the HRM practice; they affect the role of various HRM stakeholders and the ways in which HRM activities are performed at various organizational levels of analysis. Some of these developments are transformational, whereas other might merely change or add to current HR activities.

Categorization by Organizational Level

The level of analysis forms an important dimension of AI consequences for HRM. The proposed framework divides consequences of AI in HRM into different organizational levels of analysis. Hence, the consequences of applying AI within the HRM domain should be categorized with respect to the organizational level at which these consequences emerge, that is, the overall organization, the team level, and the individual level. While some studies are focused on organization-level consequences such as organizational functioning and/or performance, other studies examine consequences and outcomes at the individual level. In other words, AI influences the ways in which organizations develop and apply HRM, and how AI-mediated HRM practices affect and are experienced by employees and their respective teams/units.

Individual-level consequences are consequences that arise from the impacts AI has on the micro level. Here we refer to consequences such as employee or applicant experiences of AI. These experiences and reactions are important because employees are directly affected when using AI and their perceptions of HRM affect their work outcomes.

Several of these reactions have been studied in recent years. Findings from a case study organization that introduced AI into the talent acquisition function reveal that employees who used this AI technology were positive about its effects, indicating that it was easy to use, robust, and productive (Niehueser & Boak, 2020). Furthermore, the use of AI contributes to the complete digitalization of recruitment (Van Esch et al., 2019). At the same time, however, research also indicates that higher levels of automation impair the acceptance of automated job interviews (Langer et al., 2020).

Recent review studies show that employees' fairness perceptions and trust in AI are relevant consequences that should be taken into account (Glikson & Woolley, 2020; Köchling & Wehner, 2020; Ötting & Maier, 2018). For example, Lee (2018) found that performance evaluations made by an algorithm are less likely to be perceived as fair and trustworthy. Additionally, findings concerning the use of a robot-mediated interview show that face-to-face interviews are perceived as fairer (Nørskov et al., 2020). By contrast, research among applicants undergoing AI-based video interviews shows that there were no significant differences in applicants' perceptions of fairness of human decisions compared to fairness of AI-based decisions (Suen et al., 2019). Lee (2018) also discovered that participants indicated that algorithms perform better at scheduling than managers and that they were equally fair and trustworthy. When employees do not trust AI, they will interact with AI-based systems in a different way than envisioned, which will then influence their work outcomes (Parker & Grote, 2020). Hence, because evidence suggests that at the individual-employee level trust in AI and perceived fairness play important roles (Glikson & Woolley, 2020; Köchling & Wehner, 2020), these consequences should be considered when designing and implementing HRM activities which involve the use of AI.

Another consequence is that the use of AI in HRM affords a more personalized and individualized employee experience of HR practices (Malik et al., 2021), which has been described as the situation in which managers negotiate agreements about work arrangements with individual employees (Bal & Dorenbosch, 2015). An AI-powered bot or software application can recommend a personalized HRM experience in terms of training or induction without human involvement – leading to more customized HRM activities at the individual level. This illustrates that employees experience HRM activities through AI-based systems, instead of through human interactions (Malik et al., 2021).

In sum, research focused on AI consequences at the individual level seems to show that employee perceptions of AI usage matter. The use of AI in HRM does not yet appear to be generally accepted and trusted among employees and their perceptions could pose a challenge for further application. Nevertheless, current research is still in its infancy and is mainly focused on employee hiring. Further explorations are needed to gain a more fine-grained understanding of the attitudes of individuals regarding AI.

Team-level consequences are consequences that arise from the effects AI has on groups of employees within the same working unit. Whereas individual-level consequences are about employees' individual experiences, the team level takes into account the context in which employees work. The team level is important to consider because AI would afford the creation of novel interactions and networks between actors within organizations. Therefore, the team level refers to the relational consequences of AI application, such as team composition and interactions. Initial research reveals that algorithms can help in making more informed decisions about team composition and can support the fair evaluation of team outcomes (Andrejczuk, 2018; Garg et al., 2021). However, these consequences at the team level are mostly unexamined in relation to AI and HRM.

Another team-level consequence for HRM, related to relations and interactions between employees, is an increased human–robot interaction (Libert et al., 2020). This results from the fact that teams not only consist of people, but there are teams composed of both humans *and* robots, so-called human–robot teams (De Visser et al., 2020). Some studies have focused on the relational consequences resulting from teams that are composed of both humans and AI-powered robots. Early evidence suggests that having a robot on the work team could have a negative effect on team processes (Savela et al., 2021). Hence, a relevant consequence of AI in HRM at the team level is that AI enables the creation of hybrid teams comprising humans and robots, which is an interesting topic for further research.

Much of the current research is about *consequences at the organizational level*, or in other words, how AI affects the operations and performance of organizations. Early findings from an in-depth case study show that AI bots can help to improve HR cost-effectiveness while at the same time offering a personalized employee experience (Malik et al., 2021). As such, one expected effect of AI in HRM would be a trend towards less standardized HR policies and practices across organizations, since organizations could apply customization for their employees by offering them personalized activities and benefits. In addition, research about

HR optimization in hospital emergency departments shows that AI can help to improve planning and decrease relevant costs (Apornak et al., 2021). Also, the application of AI in recruitment leads to more efficiency and quality gains for both organizations and candidates (Upadhyay & Khandelwal, 2018), although its use can also cause conflicts about the fairness and (perceived) accuracy of these systems (Van den Broek et al., 2019).

In summary, findings about the consequences of AI at the organizational level provide some support for efficiency gains. These studies show that it is important to consider organizational effectiveness and performance as an important consequence dimension of AI in HRM. The research about AI-powered HRM effectiveness is in its early stages, with clear gaps to be filled, and therefore more research is needed to further explore this topic. For example, future research could examine if and how AI affects the level of standardization of HRM policies, and whether the use of AI will be positively related to organizational effectiveness.

Further, not only can consequences be categorized at different levels – some effects emerge at the organizational level (e.g. increased HR effectiveness), whereas others are manifest at the individual level (e.g. employee attitudes about AI) – but they can also be expected to be multilevel in nature (Renkema, forthcoming). It is important to further explore effects which emerge at the organizational level but are not confined to that level. AI-based HRM practices at the organizational level impact individual perceptions and behaviors, which in turn influence team- and firm-level performance outcomes. At the same time individuals' attitudes, behaviors, and use of AI technologies could influence the inner workings of AI technologies, as employees are the "data providers" of these self-learning systems (see section "Employees and applicants"), and thereby influence the way they are managed. Therefore, cross-level effects emerging between the organization-wide adoption of AI and individual-level perceptions of AI is an important topic to further explore. Given that HRM is a multilevel phenomenon, scholars studying the effects of AI would be advised to take a multilevel HRM approach (Kozlowski & Klein, 2000; Renkema et al., 2017).

Categorization by HRM Policy Area

Analyzing the impact of AI for HRM requires a classification by HRM policy domain, because the consequences will likely be dependent on the HRM activity to which AI is applied (Garg et al., 2021; Jia et al., 2018; Renkema, forthcoming; Strohmeier & Piazza, 2015). The application of AI can help organizations make sure that, through HRM activities, employees possess the abilities, motivation, and opportunities to perform their job. Therefore, building on earlier work, we provide a brief overview of the *consequences* of using AI in some of the most prominent HRM practices and highlight possibilities for future research.

In general, organizations deploy AI-powered applications in HRM activities such as hiring and scheduling. A distinction should be made regarding the level of involvement of human actors: (1) they perform these activities with support from AI or (2) no human actors are involved anymore meaning that the algorithm fully manages employees. In other words, HRM activities can be augmented or automated by AI (Raisch & Krakowski, 2020; Strohmeier & Piazza, 2015). Regarding the former, organizations use AI to automate the screening of applicants (Raisch & Krakowski, 2020) or for predicting and preventing employee turnover by making timely adjustments to employee compensation (Cheng & Hackett, 2019). This way, AI augments human actors in their HR decision-making. Concerning the latter, studies argue that some HRM activities can be completely performed by algorithms. Taking this one step further, ten different levels of automation of HRM can be identified, from (1) humans take all decisions and perform all actions to (10) an automated system decides autonomously, with different variants of human–computer interaction in between (see Langer et al., 2020; Parasuraman et al., 2000). In sum, consequences of AI usage in HRM are also likely to be dependent upon the degree of automation of the different HRM activities.

Employee hiring (and firing)

Raisch and Krakowski (2020) highlighted that AI can help increase the number of potential candidates, make pre-selections, and evaluate applicants during job interviews. In fact, review studies indicated that employee hiring is an area where data-techniques and algorithms are commonly applied (Cheng & Hackett, 2019; Strohmeier & Piazza, 2013), a consequence being that hiring practices are often partly or fully conducted by machines (e.g. Langer et al., 2020). Johnson et al. (2021) describe how AI can be applied to talent acquisition, supporting different elements of e-recruitment and e-selection, and Upadhyay and Khandelwal (2018) explored the consequences of AI for employee hiring in the recruitment sector. Nevertheless, several challenges appear when organizations apply AI, and many of these have consequences for recruitment and personnel selection (Tambe et al., 2019; Woods et al., 2020). As indicated earlier, one of the consequences of using hiring algorithms is a debate on how to use AI in practice to ensure both effectiveness and fairness (Van den Broek et al., 2019; Köchling & Wehner, 2020; Ötting & Maier, 2018). A discussion about fairness and effectiveness may be even more significant when algorithms are used for the replacement of workers and for firing decisions (Kellogg et al., 2020). In sum, research findings indicate that recruitment and selection processes will become increasingly automated as a consequence of AI adoption. Future research could further study to what extent HRM stakeholders interact with these systems, and how they do so.

Job design

Job design is also likely to be affected by AI usage. In fact, focusing on job design is vital to grasp the organizational consequences of automation and algorithms (Parker & Grote, 2020). Parker and Grote (2020) argue that we should focus on how jobs are changing rather than on jobs disappearing (Frey & Osborne, 2017). They stress that particular tasks are becoming automated, and as a consequence more intense human–robot collaboration will take place.

Alternatively, employees will have fewer tasks and responsibilities due to AI, as algorithms take decisions. A consequence would be that transparency of decision-making would be at risk and employees may lose touch with their work (Goodman & Flaxman, 2017). Employees who perform mostly routinized tasks are at risk of becoming distanced from the decision-making and losing track of the information processes that are foundational to these decisions (Bader & Kaiser, 2019). Scenarios regarding the dark side of automation highlight that jobs may deteriorate into simple repetitive tasks, also called digital Taylorism (Degryse, 2016).

Summarizing, job design may be significantly impacted by AI, enhancing or diminishing the tasks of workers. Despite ongoing discussions, empirical research is relatively limited and more studies should be conducted on the impact of AI on jobs – see also CHAPTER 15 of this book.

Performance management

AI entails several consequences related to performance management. AI-based systems can predict future employee performance by learning from past job evaluations; instant feedback can improve assessment time, and employees get access to multiple sources of feedback instead of just getting feedback from their managers. As such, AI can be deployed to explain the factors that separate top performers from their colleagues (Eubanks, 2018) and make suggestions on how managers can enhance employee effectiveness (Tambe et al., 2019). In addition, managers can be supported in their performance appraisals by real-time data about employee performance, which could make the performance evaluation more accurate (Drent et al., forthcoming). As feedback is vital for motivation (Hackman & Oldham, 1976), the availability of more feedback that is better timed could improve job performance. On the other hand, organizations may also decide to adopt algorithmic performance management based on rating systems, which reduces employee control (Duggan et al., 2020) and diminishes oversight by managers, which is important to guarantee the quality of performance management (Rosenblat & Stark, 2016). Research indicates that use of personal data for these AI systems may reduce employee motivation (Garg et al., 2021), and job evaluations by algorithms are perceived as less fair and trustworthy (Lee, 2018). This warrants more research into the direct consequences of AI usage in performance management.

In brief, robust results about the consequences of AI for performance management practices are scarce. Some studies indicate that AI may contribute to better performance management; however, the advantages, drawbacks, and effects of using AI in performance management should be further studied.

Training and development

Although the consequences of applying AI in training and development have not been studied extensively, Cheng and Hackett (2019) provide some indications of how algorithms can be used. For example, when AI is trained on workforce data, employees can get more personalized advice about which courses to enroll for. Also, Tambe et al. (2019) point out that machine learning algorithms give advice to employees about the most effective training programs. Evidence from a case study suggests that AI can recommend different learning pathways for different employee roles (Malik et al., 2021). AI also reduces routine tasks, such as scheduling training sessions and conducting surveys, making the role of the HR professional more strategic (Maity, 2019). Nevertheless, further empirical evidence of these claims is limited and more research into the consequences of using AI as recommendation systems for training programs would be welcome.

Compensation

The domain of compensation is not regularly a topic of research. Although Cheng and Hackett (2019) discuss some practical examples of algorithms usage for compensation, empirical research into the consequences of AI application in compensation is lacking (see also Strohmeier & Piazza, 2013) and therefore consequences are difficult to evaluate. The attempts to reduce staff turnover by using a predictive algorithm that indicates when to adjust compensation (Cheng & Hackett, 2019) could inspire more researchers to critically study the effects of such systems, for instance by examining the effectiveness of such systems or by studying the experiences of employees (e.g. fairness perceptions and trust).

Workforce planning

AI seems well suited to performing workforce planning and scheduling tasks. In earlier studies, planning stood out as the main domain for algorithm application (Strohmeier & Piazza, 2015). In addition, workforce planning was the topic of around a third of the articles about HRM algorithms in practitioner publications (Cheng & Hackett, 2019). In the platform economy, workforce planning is usually entirely automated (Meijerink & Keegan, 2019), as AI makes decisions about the number of required workers and assigns workers to activities (Rosenblat & Stark, 2016). Empirical research suggests that people perceive that human managers would be outperformed by algorithms in terms of scheduling (Lee, 2018). In sum, while robust findings may still be absent, research seems to suggest that AI may contribute to a higher effectiveness of workforce planning and scheduling.

HRM systems

We have briefly highlighted the usage of AI in distinct HRM areas, and provided an overview of the consequences of doing so. AI poses salient consequences for these distinct domains. However, what seems absent is research into HRM systems, that is, the integration between HRM practices. For HRM research to advance, we also need to consider that it is important that AI-powered practices are aligned both horizontally (between practices) and vertically (with the strategy of a company) (Schleicher et al., 2018). For example, Tambe et al. (2019) describe how hiring and performance management can be combined using AI: applicant characteristics can be associated with future job performance (management) to select better candidates. Future research could further examine these links between HRM policy areas.

Categorization by HRM stakeholders

As described in the section above, AI can be applied in many different HRM policy areas and is used to improve the effectiveness of HR systems and applications. Subsequently, AI may also affect the roles of HRM stakeholders. Therefore, the following section provides an overview of the functional consequences of using AI for the three most important groups of HRM actors: (1) HRM professionals, (2) senior and line managers, and (3) employees and applicants.

HR department/HR managers

Central HRM stakeholders are HRM managers and the personnel working in HR departments. An important dimension of the consequences of AI in HRM is how AI affects the work of HRM staff. Hence, this category focuses on the role of HRM professionals who work in the HR department, rather than the HRM policies and practices that organizations design and implement. Although we are still at the beginnings of AI developments in HRM, an emerging body of research is focused on the (changing) role of HR managers in the era of smart technologies.

An evolving field of research is focused on the skills that HRM professionals require. Some studies indicate that HR practitioners need to develop new competences (e.g. Nankervis et al., 2021), such as domain competence, data science competence, enterprise architecture expertise, operational IT capabilities, and digital curiosity to deal with AI HRM applications (Malik et al., 2020; Tarafdar et al., 2019). Others argue that HR practitioners do not necessarily have to learn data science skills, because AI can help them without having to understand the inner workings of the algorithms. For example, Pessach et al. (2020) show that a mathematical model based on machine learning can help HR recruiters improve hiring and placement decisions. They add that the proposed methodology can be used by HR professionals without having a deep knowledge of machine learning and can be implemented as a support tool. In this sense, it would be more valuable for HRM professionals to assist workers to collaborate with robots, as a more fine-grained understanding is needed about how HRM can support human–robot collaborations and how this affects the role of HRM professionals (Libert et al., 2020).

The skills required will also partly depend on the actual usage of AI-based systems by HRM specialists. Similar to applicants' reluctance towards AI-based recruitment, HRM professionals could also be reluctant to use AI in their work, which is often referred to as *algorithm aversion* (Dietvorst et al., 2018). Especially in terms of augmentation, AI supports HR decision-making, which means that HRM professionals must accept and use these tools for them to have an effect. Hence, the consequences of AI also depend on the adoption by HRM professionals. Some studies indicate that HR professionals were positive about using AI in talent acquisition (Niehueser & Boak, 2020). Others suggest that implementing and using AI in recruitment leads to debates about how to use AI to ensure fairness and to what extent users should be able to overrule AI recommendations (Van den Broek et al., 2019). In fact, research shows that aversion to algorithms can be reduced by allowing users to modify and control the algorithm (Dietvorst et al., 2018). These insights provide a starting point for more studies about the interaction between HRM stakeholders and AI to understand how HRM professionals' work is affected by AI. It would be valuable to study the interaction between HRM and AI and examine which factors affect the acceptance and use of AI-based systems by HRM stakeholders. These insights could be further developed to enable organizations to successfully implement AI.

Lastly, as work becomes automated, the skills needed for the tasks that remain become vital, which suggests that it will be crucial to hire, motivate, and manage talented workers. Doing so represents a critical success factor for HRM stakeholders when introducing smart technologies such as AI (Makridakis, 2017).

To sum up, so far research on AI in HRM seems to suggest that important changes can be expected to the role of HRM professionals. However, current research provides an inconclusive picture about what that role will look like and which responsibilities and skills HRM professionals need to acquire. A key area for future research should be the investigation of the changing tasks and responsibilities of HRM staff and the skills they need to add value to their organizations. In particular, studies could examine to what extent, and how, AI is adopted by HRM stakeholders and how HR activities are redistributed among the different HRM stakeholders. Mapping the skills and competences needed for this transition would be a further interesting topic for future research.

Senior and line managers

Key reasons for adopting AI in HRM are the automation and augmentation of HR-related management decisions. Hence, AI can fully automate decisions or provide senior and line managers with data, information, and decision-support systems to allow them to perform better at their HR tasks (Drent et al., forthcoming). For example, AI can automate CV screening (automation) and recommend the best candidates for an open job position (augmentation).

This way, managers are supported by AI with tools that improve their abilities to perform their HR tasks.

In the case of full automation of management tasks, also called algorithmic management, the role of managers will significantly change. Instead of performing HR tasks and managing employees directly, managers operate and supervise AI systems. For example, they ensure that the AI systems are designed and operated in a fair way (Robert et al., 2020). Employee–supervisor relationships are expected to change as a consequence of AI, given that algorithmic management automates several HRM activities that line managers usually perform (Duggan et al., 2020). As a consequence, line managers get other responsibilities in performing HRM practices. More drastically, disintermediation, through the removal of management responsibilities, is facilitated by algorithmic management (Kellogg et al., 2020). Instead of managers performing traditional management and HR tasks, software algorithms assume managerial functions such as conducting oversight, governance, and control practices over workers (Lee et al., 2015).

To our knowledge, empirical research examining the changing role of managers as consequence of AI is rare (see Drent et al., forthcoming). Therefore, future research should address this issue, for example by examining how managers themselves respond to the use of AI systems. In addition, it would be valuable to study how employee–manager relations are changing due to the adoption of AI.

Employees and applicants
The third group of key HRM stakeholders are employees and applicants. They are core stakeholders of HRM because they are targeted by HRM activities (e.g. recruitment and performance management) and/or actively co-create HR value (Meijerink et al., 2016). Employees and applicants are likely to experience significant changes in how HRM activities are performed, and how and by whom HR services are delivered. This affects their perceptions and reactions to AI HRM, which has been outlined in the section *individual-level consequences*. Therefore, in addition to those consequences, this section briefly discusses some consequences for their functional (HR) role.

First, employees and applicants have an important (inactive) role as they are the main source of HR data; they are the "providers" of the raw materials, the data that is used to create, develop, and improve AI algorithms. The data that are inserted into HR algorithms, such as keystrokes, emails, facial recognition, and performance indicators (Angrave et al., 2016), are "supplied" by employees and applicants, which raises the question of data ownership (Kellogg et al., 2020). In some cases, workers can still choose whether or not to provide these data and take part in AI-based HRM activities (e.g. using a chatbot for recruitment), whereas in other cases this might not be a choice (e.g. Uber drivers).

A second consequence is that employees are more directly responsible for the operational execution of HRM activities as they directly use HR services powered by AI. For example, employees select training programs or career moves based on recommendations made by algorithms instead of by their (HR) managers (Tambe et al., 2019). Next to that, employees could directly use real-time performance feedback to improve their work and use insights about AI recruitment to prepare for job interviews. Nevertheless, workers may also resist the use of algorithmic systems by rejecting recommendations or even by tricking the system (Kellogg et al., 2020).

Third, when organizations use algorithmic management, the role of employees and applicants shifts significantly. In that case, algorithms are partly or fully responsible for HRM activities (e.g. Duggan et al., 2020). Kellogg et al. (2020) provide an excellent overview of how algorithms can shift control from employees to employers, whereby employees might lose autonomy and dignity but may also decide to resist.

Categorization by AI Technology Application Area

The conceptual exploration of consequences of AI in HRM also requires an examination of the technological application areas of AI. Therefore, AI technology application areas refers to the possible AI-based instruments and techniques that HR actors can use to perform HRM activities (see CHAPTERS 2–13). Regarding AI application areas, it is relevant to distinguish the consequences of different AI subfields, that is, among others, machine learning (ML), natural language processing (NLP), computer vision (CV), and robotics (Russell & Norvig, 1995). The research into ML has a different focus than that into NLP and CV, which in turn is different from the focus in robotics research (i.e. ML enables NLP and CV and support robotics – see CHAPTER 1).

Collaborating with a new robotic colleague poses other challenges beyond working with a new ML-based software system. For example, research into ML algorithms has led to questions about whether algorithms are accurate and fair (Van den Broek et al., 2019), studies about chatbots and virtual assistants have highlighted the enhanced cost-effectiveness (Malik et al., 2021), and research into "HR robotics" has raised doubts about whether applicants want to interact with a robot during job interviews (Nørskov et al., 2020). Hence, the consequences of AI are dependent upon the types of AI applications that are used (see CHAPTER 1). Similar to categorizing research into data mining methods and HRM application domains (Strohmeier & Piazza, 2013), research on the consequences of AI in HRM should consider both the different AI technologies and their HRM application areas. The consequences of AI for HRM practices may vary based on the AI technologies used, and the (long-term) effects and effectiveness of applying such technologies to perform HRM may be different for each HRM practice. Therefore, future studies should find out whether and how these different AI technologies lead to alternative outcomes.

A full exploration of consequence areas would involve the analysis of the distinct consequences of the before-mentioned AI technologies, which is beyond the scope of this chapter. Nevertheless, research into the direct consequences of AI should benefit from earlier explorations such as those performed by Jia et al. (2018) and Strohmeier and Piazza (2015). Both these review studies link specific AI applications (e.g. neural networks, text mining, voice/face recognition) to HRM policy areas. Most fundamentally, the distinct AI techniques can be classified as to whether they lead to automation or augmentation of HR tasks (Strohmeier & Piazza, 2015; Zuboff, 1985). Even though some studies have been focused on the consequences of specific technology areas (e.g. ML in Garg et al., 2021), a systematic categorization of the consequences of distinct AI techniques would be valuable for further research. Such categorization could help to uncover the effects and consequences of different AI technologies.

Categorization by Desirability

Consequences of AI can also be broadly categorized as desirable or undesirable. Desirable consequences are those consequences that are intended and valued, whereas undesirable consequences are the unwelcome effects of applying AI. As is often the case with novel technologies, there is a lively debate about the consequences of AI for humans. Optimists point at the positive results for both businesses and employees, whereas critics discuss the potentially damaging (side) effects.

Desired consequences

Many desired or positive consequences have been discussed in the literature. AI should be able to help increase the efficiency and/or effectiveness of HRM (Garg et al., 2021). For example, AI could make HRM processes more efficient and fairer, enable a better person–job fit, and enhance employee retention and development (Trombin et al., 2018). Furthermore, AI can help HR professionals to spend their time more effectively and in a more meaningful way. For example, AI reduces time per interview and helps to answer questions, thereby allowing HR professionals to focus their attention on the selected candidates and improving the candidate experience (Lee et al., 2018). Automated text processing can also improve the screening process during recruitment and thereby reduce costs and effort (Cheng & Hackett, 2019). To date, there is not much scientific empirical evidence available for these claims, but a study at a strategic recruitment company that introduced AI offers initial support for the improvement of speed and efficiency of work processes as a consequence of AI (Niehueser & Boak, 2020).

Undesired consequences

Several undesired consequences have been mentioned in the recent literature. In fact, when using AI-based systems, the HRM function faces several ethical, managerial, and social consequences. Although not intended to provide a complete overview of these consequences, four relevant issues are discussed below.

Many studies refer to the undesirability of bias that is imbued in algorithms. Because these algorithms are trained using past data, they can be inherently *discriminatory* or *biased* as this can be built into the ML systems (Köchling & Wehner, 2020; Tambe et al., 2019, see also CHAPTER 16). The AI applications may be biased or imprecise through training with existing data (Fernández & Fernández, 2019). For example, Amazon scrapped its AI recruiting tool because it showed a bias towards women.[2] The risk is that these types of AI systems replicate historical trends, such as the tendencies to hire fewer woman or people with a certain demographic background. Hence, AI systems can contain significant biases, which are sometimes downplayed by decision-makers (Leicht-Deobald et al., 2019). Kellogg et al. (2020) describe that training data for algorithms can be biased because the used data can represent actions and activities that incur discrimination and bias (e.g. no females are hired), and/or the data can represent a biased sample of the population (e.g. no females in the data).

A related issue is the *explainability* of AI, or the extent to which managers and employees understand and can describe the decision-making process (see CHAPTER 15). Part of the explainability is that employees understand the criteria and data used for decisions (Tambe et al., 2019). ML algorithms are characterized by the opacity that is inherent in the way they function (Burrell, 2016). Sometimes this is also referred to as a *black box*, which makes decision-makers feel uncomfortable as they do not fully comprehend the basis of the suggested solutions (Cheng & Hackett, 2019). This then leads to serious consequences in terms of justifying HR decisions to employees and applicants.

Third, algorithmic management risks influence the balance between personal integrity and compliance and there is a risk of tipping that balance over to more compliance (Leicht-Deobald et al., 2019). Decision-making processes are sometimes opaque and should therefore be used with caution, particularly when applying them for hiring and firing of employees. Job candidates do not necessary like to use an AI-based application system (Van Esch et al., 2019). Additionally, employees at some point may resist algorithmic management or start gaming the system (Möhlmann & Zalmanson, 2017). Next to that, employees may also challenge collaborating with AI. For instance, oncologists resisted the use of algorithms to identify cancer cases (Tambe et al., 2019). Hence, an (undesirable) consequence of adopting AI in HRM is the increased resistance of workers to being managed by or to using AI applications.

Last, if workers perceive sufficient levels of *autonomy* and *meaningfulness*, their resistance may be reduced. Parker and Grote (2020) argued that the ways in which organizations design and use AI determines whether employees' autonomy is increased or decreased. A well-designed and used AI system can enable more autonomy through decentralized decision-making, whereas AI can also be used to break jobs down into dull and repetitive tasks (Parker & Grote, 2020) and increase surveillance and organizational control over workers (Kellogg et al., 2020). Some scholars argue that an undesirable consequence would be the simplification of tasks, resulting in jobs with simple repetitive tasks, also called digital Taylorism (Degryse, 2016). This way, employees who are involved in routine jobs get distanced from decision-making, which results in the inability to access information and knowledge resources that are used for making decisions (Bader & Kaiser, 2019). These job simplifications may eventually damage performance. For example, Angrave et al. (2016) discuss a case of the usage of an algorithms-based workforce planning system in retail stores that reduced staffing levels to lower costs but did not consider labor quality, which is needed for profitability (Ton, 2009). There are reports showing that human workers even pretend to be AI to ensure investments.[3]

In sum, these themes indicate that the application of AI in HRM poses broader consequences beyond just changes in HRM activities and the roles of HRM stakeholders. Undesirable consequences must also be considered, including issues such as ethics, lawfulness, and data privacy (Malik et al., 2020). There are legal barriers to the use of AI in recruitment, as European privacy law (GDPR) states that people have the right not to be subject to a decision based solely on automated means.[4] Various efforts have been taken to ensure that algorithms comply with the rules of fairness, accountability, and transparency (Kellogg et al., 2020). These themes provide multiple avenues for future research into the "dark side" of AI in HRM, to examine undesirable consequences.

Transformational and Non-transformational Consequences in HRM

Based on the categorization and discussion above, the question arises: What will be the transformational consequences of the overall changes to the HRM function and the role that HRM plays in stimulating effectiveness and performance? While some of the consequences of AI will be more incremental in nature, others have the potential to transform the HRM function, referring to changes in the character, structure, and fundamental processes of organizations (Loebbecke & Picot, 2015). Hence, transformational changes of the HRM function entail the overall changes of the role that HRM activities and stakeholders play in executing practices and supporting organizational performance (e.g. Barney & Wright, 1998; Strohmeier, 2007). Therefore, our organizing framework distinguishes between transformational and non-transformational consequences, where transformational consequences are related to fundamental changes to HRM activities and the HRM function (e.g. algorithmic management and gig work), and non-transformational consequences refer to changes to HRM practices within the same structure and processes (e.g. adoption of an AI tool in recruitment).

Building on a long tradition of interfaces between technology and HRM (e.g. Bondarouk et al., 2017), the rise of advanced technologies, such as big data, analytics, and AI, is expected to have important implications for the nature, structure, and conditions of work (Meijerink et al., 2021). Nevertheless, for now, the question of whether AI will transform the HRM function remains largely unanswered. Although early findings indicate that the HRM function and the way in which HRM activities are performed and contribute to performance are subject to change, these developments in AI are yet to materialize in HRM practice and research, at least not to the extent that we can conclude that the identified consequences for HRM practice are already becoming reality, let alone common practice.

Moreover, as discussed in the introduction to this book (CHAPTER 1), the field of AI has gone through several seasons, and we currently seem to be witnessing a summer. Nevertheless, some developments indicate that a new winter is coming. There are signs that despite the great promises, and dystopian predictions, businesses are having a hard time benefiting from their AI investments.[5] A reason for this so-called *bounded automation* is that capital investments and the maintenance costs of investing in AI are higher than labor costs, which leads to an economic calculation that it is not worthwhile investing in AI (Fleming, 2019). For HRM researchers this means we should also consider whether AI investments are economically viable and will have the consequences that are predicted.

RESEARCH TYPES OF AI CONSEQUENCES FOR HRM

The second main component of our organizing framework involves the consequences AI has for research types that (HRM) academics adopt. There are several consequences for HRM academics because of the growing adoption of AI technologies. It affects the types of studies HRM scholars conduct, the use of theory, and the methodologies these studies use.

Categorization by Theory Base

The first dimension of the research types is the theory base of AI HRM research, which presents the consequences for HRM academics studying AI in HRM. The current research on algorithms in HRM tends to be theory-poor, as was found by a recent systematic review by Cheng and Hackett (2019). It is important to make a distinction between (1) research about the use of AI by organizations and individuals (i.e. AI as a research object), and (2) researchers who themselves use AI systems as a research instrument (i.e. AI as a research instrument). Hence, the use of AI in HRM has consequences for practitioners using those systems to perform HRM activities, for researchers studying those applications, and for researchers using AI tools themselves. Where the HRM research deals with the *research object* of data-driven HR, Cheng and Hackett (2019) also concluded that most of the *research projects* using algorithms in HR are data-driven, rather than testing theoretical causal relationships. Research on algorithmic HRM is either descriptive or predictive and therefore not theory-driven and theory testing, as there are often no a priori assumptions in this literature (Cheng & Hackett, 2019). For example, Colomo-Palacios et al. (2014) studied how competency gaps can be predicted by Artificial Neural Networks, explicitly using statistical models and data-mining algorithms to predict future observations (Shmueli, 2010). This would also imply that the research on consequences lacks a theoretical basis to explore and explain the effects of AI on the earlier discussed HRM outcomes.

These insights indicate that there is space for theoretical developments in this field and that future HRM researchers should assess whether current major theories are still relevant. They could develop new theories on the intersection between AI and HRM. Some argue that HRM theories and underlying assumptions and theories should be challenged and revisited (Minbaeva, 2021). There are multiple suggestions on how to do so. Some theories are mostly focused on the individual-employee level. For example, Krämer et al. (2012) stated that research suggests that human–human interaction theories (e.g. social exchange theory) could also be applied to individuals' experiences of human–robot interactions. This idea of social interactions with robots has been further developed into AI-facilitated social exchanges (Ma & Brown, 2020) and employees' perceptions thereof (Malik et al., 2021). Others have taken a justice perspective (Nørskov et al., 2020) or even examined the human–robot psychological contract in which relationships form between human and robot (Bankins & Formosa, 2020).

Further, recent studies have highlighted the challenge of AI acceptance (e.g. Van Esch et al., 2019), and as a consequence, for HRM academics, theories on technology acceptance (e.g. Venkatesh et al., 2003) and social robot acceptance (Wirtz et al., 2018) may be useful to further explore the consequences of AI in HRM. As employees and HRM stakeholders work more closely with machines, these models could help in understanding the consequences of collaboration with AI systems (Fernandes & Oliveira, 2021). Thereby, the field can expand theory on AI usage, for example by modeling the consequences and effects of AI (Glikson & Woolley, 2020).

Given the different definitions, conceptualizations, and applications of AI, one could argue that the field of AI and HRM could benefit from further theoretical development. Although the field of AI and HRM is developing, there is a clear need for an expansion of existing HR theory and the development and integration of novel theoretical perspectives.

Categorization by Methodological Approach

The second dimension of the research types consequences is the methodological approach adopted to study the effects of AI in HRM. A systematic analysis of methodologies would include a quantified overview of the methods used in current research, but this is beyond the scope of this chapter. Instead, we highlight three of the methodological approaches used in recent publications. The first category is the *conceptual (review) study* regarding the application of AI in HRM (e.g. Jia et al., 2018; Strohmeier & Piazza, 2015); the second category is the *non-experimental* design – such as case studies (e.g. Malik et al., 2021; Van den Broek et al., 2019) and survey research (e.g. Nankervis et al., 2021); and the third category is the *experimental* design (e.g. Langer et al., 2020). The quasi-experimental design seems to be absent in the research into AI and HRM (see CHAPTER 19).

Next to several *conceptual review studies* about the application of AI in HRM (e.g. Jia et al., 2018; Strohmeier & Piazza, 2015), common *non-experimental approaches* such as case studies (e.g. Malik et al., 2021; Van den Broek et al., 2019) and larger surveys are currently adopted to examine the consequences of AI. Some of the survey studies are more descriptive; for example, the study by Nankervis et al. (2021) reports how HR professionals perceive smart technologies, while publications reporting empirical tests concerning theoretical relationships seem scarce. One example of survey research is the paper by Van Esch and Black (2019), who studied participants' perceptions on AI recruitment. Given the novelty of the field, exploratory case studies mainly uncover how organizational and HRM processes are affected by AI (e.g. Malik et al., 2021; Van den Broek et al., 2019). These case studies, along with observations and interviews, can be used for gaining contextualized and in-depth understandings of the implementation and use of AI in HRM. To study how AI-powered systems work in practice, HRM researchers can further use the case study approach with in-depth observations and interviews to analyze what and how consequences take shape, which factors influence the use of and collaboration with AI, how the use in turn influences the AI systems, and how adoption comes about and/or resistance is formed.

In addition, *experimental research designs* are also adopted to study the effects of AI adoption in HRM. For instance, experiments and vignette studies have been conducted to study responses to robotic job interviews (Nørskov et al., 2020), and how applicants would respond to automated job interviews (Langer et al., 2020). More of these experimental studies are discussed in CHAPTER 19 on "Research Design".

Finally, there are examples of mixed-methods approaches. For instance, Nankervis et al. (2021) studied HR professionals' perception of the fourth industrial revolution using focus groups followed by an online survey of senior HR practitioners. In sum, next to developing new theoretical concepts and models, future AI HRM researchers can also benefit from adopting novel methodological approaches that enable them to get insights into the applications of – and consequences of adopting – AI in HRM.

IMPLICATIONS AND DISCUSSION

The HRM function is confronted with a growing number of smart technologies that disrupt its activities. Especially the application of AI in HRM poses unique challenges. When AI is applied in conducting HRM activities, this affects the way in which HRM policies and practices are designed and implemented. The analysis in this chapter shows that doing so could entail a wide variety of consequences, including consequences for HRM practices and stakeholders; consequences that depend on the AI technologies used and that could vary in terms of desirability; and long-term transformational consequences. Eventually, these developments may disrupt HRM and require a transformation of the HR function and HRM research (Minbaeva, 2021). Nevertheless, empirical research into the consequences is still limited and the existing studies into these consequences are scattered across many fields of applications, policy areas, and levels of analysis. To further integrate the conceptual and empirical work, this chapter offers a multidimensional organizing framework that categorizes these consequences into dimensions and sub-dimensions. Based on the framework we identified five important general implications.

First, the influence of AI in HRM is growing, and it is not a question of whether HRM will need to adapt but of how it should adapt. As this and other chapters have shown, HRM activities and the role of HRM professionals will significantly change when the adoption of AI becomes more widespread. The consequences of these changes will be a transformation of the role of HRM, with responsibilities and competences needing to adapt – for example through increased interaction with AI systems and a need to acquire data-related skills (Tarafdar et al., 2019).

Second, we have shown that consequences are manifold, and therefore it is important for both practitioners and academics to be as specific as possible about the type(s) of consequences that are relevant. Although we have outlined the different dimensions separately with the idea of categorizing the different components and highlighting current (empirical) work, they also need to be considered holistically. For example, AI can have positive consequences at an organizational level (increased effectiveness), but negative effects at an individual level (decreased trust). Or AI systems can be used to augment decision-making by HR professionals in recruitment but automate the work of line managers in relation to performance management.

Third, there seems to be some optimism about the use of AI in HRM. However, it is important to consider both positive and negative consequences. In this chapter, we have outlined several (potential) desired and undesired effects and highlighted ethical consequences. As has been discussed in terms of work design (Parker & Grote, 2020), the application of AI will not hinge on the technology but will largely depend on how it is designed and used.

Fourth, the application of AI in HRM poses several challenges that need to be addressed before the consequences will materialize. Some of these challenges are categorized by Tambe et al. (2019): complexity of HR outcomes, restrictions of (available) datasets, ethical considerations, and employee responses to AI. HR outcomes are complex, because it is unclear what constitutes good performance. Next to the necessity to explicate these phenomena, there are also restrictions in terms of data availability, privacy concerns, and employee opposition that pose severe challenges to applying AI in HRM. As we have witnessed with the slow adoption of analytics technology (Angrave et al., 2016), these challenges need to be addressed to avoid AI becoming another HR technology failure.

Last, when evaluating the consequences of AI it is crucial to consider the component of *time*. Some of the framework's dimensions include descriptions of how HRM *could* change, which would then need to *happen* before there are relevant consequences. In other words, a substantial number of the publications about the effects of AI on HRM are conceptual studies. As empirical studies are emerging, we can establish which consequences materialize and which suggested consequences can be alleviated or disregarded.

It would be valuable to conduct a systematic literature review to identify further consequences and implications based on more empirical findings. A comprehensive review of this kind could also add new dimensions to our framework, as this framework may not be all-encompassing, neither now nor in the future.

CONCLUSION

The increasing use of AI in organizations has important consequences for many aspects of HRM. Although there is a growing literature on the application and use of AI in HRM, research integrating consequences for different HRM practices, stakeholders, and organizational levels is relatively scarce. To advance our knowledge about these consequences, this chapter maps out the various components and dimensions of AI for HRM and highlights example research studies that examine these consequences. The multidimensional organizing framework integrates two main components of the effect of AI in HRM: "types of consequences" and "research types" for studying AI consequences in HRM. Through these components we have identified consequences for the HRM practice and consequences for HRM academics. Using the framework we have highlighted some of the most recent studies on the effects of AI. In combination, these contributions show that AI can be disruptive for the HRM practice: many activities can be augmented and automated by AI, with consequences for multiple stakeholders. At the same time, HRM researchers and practitioners are relatively late adopters of the new technology and thereby run the risk of continuing to lag behind. To close the gap, this chapter highlights several avenues for future research based on the framework and the most recent findings. Given the increasing interest in the field, more publications can be expected within the next few years, and we hope our framework can help in conducting studies that inform about the effects of AI in HRM.

ACKNOWLEDGMENTS

I want to thank the editor, Stefan Strohmeier, as well as an anonymous reviewer and Tanya Bondarouk for their support and feedback.

NOTES

1. It is important to note that these components and dimensions are (1) not mutually exclusive and (2) not exhaustive. First, consequences may be categorized into several dimensions – for example, a study into machine learning recruitment tools may be categorized into types of AI technology, policy areas, and HRM stakeholders. Second, more (sub-)dimensions and categories are possible – such as HR strategies and philosophies.
2. https://www.reuters.com/article/us-amazon-com-jobs-automation-insight/amazon-scraps-secret-ai-recruiting-tool-that-showed-bias-against-women-idUSKCN1MK08G.
3. https://www.ft.com/content/21b19010-3e9f-11e9-b896-fe36ec32aece.
4. https://ec.europa.eu/info/law/law-topic/data-protection/reform/rights-citizens/my-rights/can-i-be-subject-automated-individual-decision-making-including-profiling_en.
5. https://www.economist.com/technology-quarterly/2020/06/11/businesses-are-finding-ai-hard-to-adopt.

REFERENCES

Andrejczuk, E. D. (2018). *Artificial intelligence methods to support people management in organisations* [Doctoral dissertation, Universitat Autònoma de Barcelona]. https://digital.csic.es/bitstream/10261/197543/1/Artificial_intelligence.pdf, accessed September 23, 2020.

Angrave, D., Charlwood, A., Kirkpatrick, I., Lawrence, M., & Stuart, M. (2016). HR and analytics: Why HR is set to fail the big data challenge. *Human Resource Management Journal, 26*(1), 1–11.

Apornak, A., Raissi, S., Keramati, A., & Khalili-Damghani, K. (2021). Optimizing human resource cost of an emergency hospital using multi-objective Bat algorithm. *International Journal of Healthcare Management, 14*(3), 873–879. https://doi.org/10.1080/20479700.2019.1707415

Bader, V., & Kaiser, S. (2019). Algorithmic decision-making? The user interface and its role for human involvement in decisions supported by artificial intelligence. *Organization, 26*(5), 655–672.

Bal, P. M., & Dorenbosch, L. (2015). Age-related differences in the relations between individualised HRM and organisational performance: A large-scale employer survey. *Human Resource Management Journal, 25*(1), 41–61.

Bankins, S., & Formosa, P. (2020). When AI meets PC: Exploring the implications of workplace social robots and a human-robot psychological contract. *European Journal of Work and Organizational Psychology, 29*(2), 215–229.

Barney, J. B., & Wright, P. M. (1998). On becoming a strategic partner: The role of human resources in gaining competitive advantage. *Human Resource Management, 37*(1), 31–46.

Björkman, I., Ehrnrooth, M., Mäkelä, K., Smale, A., & Sumelius, J. (2014). From HRM practices to the practice of HRM: Setting a research agenda. *Journal of Organizational Effectiveness: People and Performance, 1*(2), 122–140.

Bondarouk, T., Ruël, H. J., & Parry, E. (2017). *Electronic HRM in the smart era.* Emerald Publishing.

Boselie, P., Dietz, G., & Boon, C. (2005). Commonalities and contradictions in HRM and performance research. *Human Resource Management Journal, 15*(3), 67–94.

Burrell, J. (2016). How the machine "thinks": Understanding opacity in machine learning algorithms. *Big Data and Society, 3*(1), 1–12.

Cheng, M. M., & Hackett, R. D. (2019). A critical review of algorithms in HRM: Definition, theory, and practice. *Human Resource Management Review.* Advance Online Publication. https://doi.org/10.1016/j.hrmr.2019.100698

Colomo-Palacios, R., González-Carrasco, I., López-Cuadrado, J. L., Trigo, A., & Varajao, J. E. (2014). I-Competere: Using applied intelligence in search of competency gaps in software project managers. *Information Systems Frontiers, 16*(4), 607–625. https://doi.org/10.1007/s10796-012-9369-6

De Visser, E. J., Peeters, M. M., Jung, M. F., Kohn, S., Shaw, T. H., Pak, R., & Neerincx, M. A. (2020). Towards a theory of longitudinal trust calibration in human–robot teams. *International Journal of Social Robotics, 12*(2), 459–478.

Degryse, C. (2016). *Digitalisation of the economy and its impact on labour markets* (ETUI Research Paper – Working Paper 2016.02). European Trade Union Institute. https://papers.ssrn.com/sol3/papers.cfm?abstract_id=2730550

Dietvorst, B. J., Simmons, J. P., & Massey, C. (2018). Overcoming algorithm aversion: People will use imperfect algorithms if they can (even slightly) modify them. *Management Science, 64*(3), 1155–1170.

Drent, E., Renkema, M., & Bos-Nehles, A.C. (forthcoming). Reconceptualizing the role of the line manager in the age of artificial intelligence. In K. Townsend, A. C. Bos-Nehles, & K. Jiang (Eds.), *Handbook of line-managers.*

Duggan, J., Sherman, U., Carbery, R., & McDonnell, A. (2020). Algorithmic management and app-work in the gig economy: A research agenda for employment relations and HRM. *Human Resource Management Journal, 30*(1), 114–132.

Eubanks, B. (2018). *Artificial intelligence for HR: Use AI to support and develop a successful workforce.* Kogan Page.

Fernandes, T., & Oliveira, E. (2021). Understanding consumers' acceptance of automated technologies in service encounters: Drivers of digital voice assistants adoption. *Journal of Business Research, 122*, 180–191.

Fernández, C., & Fernández, A. (2019). Ethical and legal implications of AI recruiting software. *ERCIM NEWS, 116*, 22–23. https://ercim-news.ercim.eu/images/stories/EN116/EN116-web.pdf#page=22, accessed November 21, 2021.

Fleming, P. (2019). Robots and organization studies: Why robots might not want to steal your job. *Organization Studies, 40*(1), 23–38.

Frey, C. B., & Osborne, M. A. (2017). The future of employment: How susceptible are jobs to computerisation? *Technological Forecasting and Social Change, 114*, 254–280.

Garg, S., Sinha, S., Kar, A. K., & Mani, M. (2021). A review of machine learning applications in human resource management. *International Journal of Productivity and Performance Management*, ahead of print. https://doi.org/10.1108/IJPPM-08-2020-0427

Glikson, E., & Woolley, A. W. (2020). Human trust in artificial intelligence: Review of empirical research. *Academy of Management Annals, 14*(2), 627–660.

Goodman, B., & Flaxman, S. (2017). European Union regulations on algorithmic decision-making and a "right to explanation". *AI Magazine, 38*(3), 50–57.

Hackman, J. R., & Oldham, G. R. (1976). Motivation through the design of work: Test of a theory. *Organizational Behavior and Human Performance, 16*(2), 250–279.

Haenlein, M., & Kaplan, A. (2019). A brief history of artificial intelligence: On the past, present, and future of artificial intelligence. *California Management Review, 61*(4), 5–14.

Jia, Q., Guo, Y., Li, R., Li, Y., & Chen, Y. (2018). A conceptual artificial intelligence application framework in human resource management. In *Proceedings of the 18th International Conference on Electronic Business* (pp. 106–114). ICEB.

Johnson, R. D., Stone, D. L., & Lukaszewski, K. M. (2021). The benefits of eHRM and AI for talent acquisition. *Journal of Tourism Futures, 7*(1), 40–52. https://doi.org/10.1108/JTF-02-2020-0013

Kaplan, A., & Haenlein, M. (2019). Siri, Siri, in my hand: Who's the fairest in the land? On the inter-pretations, illustrations, and implications of artificial intelligence. *Business Horizons, 62*(1), 15–25.

Kellogg, K. C., Valentine, M. A., & Christin, A. (2020). Algorithms at work: The new contested terrain of control. *Academy of Management Annals, 14*(1), 366–410.

Köchling, A., & Wehner, M. C. (2020). Discriminated by an algorithm: A systematic review of dis-crimination and fairness by algorithmic decision-making in the context of HR recruitment and HR development. *Business Research, 13*, 795–848.

Kozlowski, S. W., & Klein, K. J. (2000). A multilevel approach to theory and research in organizations: Contextual, temporal, and emergent processes. In K. J. Klein & S. W. Kozlowski (Eds.), *Multilevel theory, research, and methods in organizations: Foundations, extensions, and new directions* (pp. 3–90). Jossey-Bass.

Krämer, N. C., von der Pütten, A., & Eimler, S. (2012). Human-agent and human-robot interaction theory: Similarities to and differences from human-human interaction. In M. Zacarias & J. V. de Oliveira (Eds.), *Human-computer interaction: The agency perspective* (pp. 215–240). Springer.

Langer, M., König, C. J., & Hemsing, V. (2020). Is anybody listening? The impact of automatically evaluated job interviews on impression management and applicant reactions. *Journal of Managerial Psychology, 35*(4), 271–284.

Lawler, J. J., & Elliot, R. (1996). Artificial intelligence in HRM: An experimental study of an expert system. *Journal of Management, 22*(1), 85–111.

Lee, H., Lee, S., & Tarpey, M. (2018). *CAHRS partners' implementation of artificial intelligence* [White paper]. Cornell University.

Lee, M. K. (2018). Understanding perception of algorithmic decisions: Fairness, trust, and emotion in response to algorithmic management. *Big Data and Society, 5*(1), https://doi.org/10.1177/2053951718756684

Lee, M. K., Kusbit, D., Metsky, E., & Dabbish, L. (2015). Working with machines: The impact of algorithmic and data-driven management on human workers. In *Proceedings of the 33rd Annual ACM Conference on Human Factors in Computing Systems* (pp. 1603–1612). ACM. https://doi.org/10.1145/2702123.2702548

Leicht-Deobald, U., Busch, T., Schank, C., Weibel, A., Schafheitle, S., Wildhaber, I., & Kasper, G. (2019). The challenges of algorithm-based HR decision-making for personal integrity. *Journal of Business Ethics, 160*(2), 377–392.

Libert, K., Mosconi, E., & Cadieux, N. (2020). Human-machine interaction and human resource man-agement perspective for collaborative robotics implementation and adoption. In *Proceedings of the 53rd Hawaii International Conference on System Sciences* (pp. 533–542). https://doi.org/10.24251/HICSS.2020.066

Loebbecke, C., & Picot, A. (2015). Reflections on societal and business model transformation arising from digitization and big data analytics: A research agenda. *The Journal of Strategic Information Systems, 24*(3), 149–157. https://doi.org/https://doi.org/10.1016/j.jsis.2015.08.002

Ma, X., & Brown, T. W. (2020). *AI-mediated exchange theory*. arXiv. arXiv:2003.02093

Maity, S. (2019). Identifying opportunities for artificial intelligence in the evolution of training and development practices. *Journal of Management Development, 38*(8), 651–663.

Makridakis, S. (2017). The forthcoming artificial intelligence (AI) revolution: Its impact on society and firms. *Futures, 90*, 46–60.

Malik, A., Budhwar, P., Patel, C., & Srikanth, N. R. (2021). May the bots be with you! Delivering HR cost-effectiveness and individualised employee experiences in an MNE. *The International Journal of Human Resource Management*, 1–31. https://doi.org/10.1080/09585192.2020.1859582

Malik, A., Budhwar, P., & Srikanth, N. R. (2020). Gig economy, 4IR and artificial intelligence: Rethinking strategic HRM. In K. Payal, A. Anirudh, & B. Pawan (Eds.), *Human and technological resource management (HTRM): New insights into Revolution 4.0* (pp. 75–88). Emerald Publishing.

Meijerink, J., Boons, M., Keegan, A., & Marler, J. (2021). Algorithmic human resource management: Synthesizing developments and cross-disciplinary insights on digital HRM. *The International Journal of Human Resource Management*, 32(12), 2545–2562. https://doi.org/10.1080/09585192.2021.1925326

Meijerink, J., Bondarouk, T., & Lepak, D. P. (2016). Employees as active consumers of HRM: Linking employees' HRM competences with their perceptions of HRM service value. *Human Resource Management*, 55(2), 219–240.

Meijerink, J., & Keegan, A. (2019). Conceptualizing human resource management in the gig economy. *Journal of Managerial Psychology*, 34(4), 214–232.

Minbaeva, D. (2021). Disrupted HR? *Human Resource Management Review*, 31(4), Article 100820 Advance online publication. https://doi.org/10.1016/j.hrmr.2020.100820

Möhlmann, M., & Zalmanson, L. (2017). Hands on the wheel: Navigating algorithmic management and Uber drivers' autonomy. In *Proceedings of the International Conference on Information Systems (ICIS 2017)*. https://aisel.aisnet.org/icis2017/DigitalPlatforms/Presentations/3/, accessed November 21, 2021.

Nankervis, A., Connell, J., Cameron, R., Montague, A., & Prikshat, V. (2021). "Are we there yet?" Australian HR professionals and the Fourth Industrial Revolution. *Asia Pacific Journal of Human Resources*, 59(1), 3–19.

Niehueser, W., & Boak, G. (2020). Introducing artificial intelligence into a human resources function. *Industrial and Commercial Training*, 52(2), 121–130.

Nørskov, S., Damholdt, M. F., Ulhøi, J. P., Jensen, M. B., Ess, C., & Seibt, J. (2020). Applicant fairness perceptions of a robot-mediated job interview: A video vignette-based experimental survey. *Frontiers in Robotics and AI*, 7, Article 586263. https://doi.org/10.3389/frobt.2020.586263

Ötting, S. K., & Maier, G. W. (2018). The importance of procedural justice in human–machine interactions: Intelligent systems as new decision agents in organizations. *Computers in Human Behavior*, 89, 27–39.

Parasuraman, R., Sheridan, T. B., & Wickens, C. D. (2000). A model for types and levels of human interaction with automation. *IEEE Transactions on Systems, Man, and Cybernetics – Part A: Systems and Humans*, 30(3), 286–297.

Parker, S., & Grote, G. (2020). Automation, algorithms, and beyond: Why work design matters more than ever in a digital world. *Applied Psychology*, 1–45.

Pessach, D., Singer, G., Avrahami, D., Ben-Gal, H. C., Shmueli, E., & Ben-Gal, I. (2020). Employees recruitment: A prescriptive analytics approach via machine learning and mathematical programming. *Decision Support Systems*, 134, Article 113290. https://doi.org/10.1016/j.dss.2020.113290

Raisch, S., & Krakowski, S. (2020). Artificial intelligence and management: The automation–augmentation paradox. *Academy of Management Review*, 46(1), 192–210.

Renkema, M. (forthcoming). AI, digitalisation and HRM: Foundations, extensions and new directions on ai, digitalisation and HRM. In M. Santana & R. Valle-Cabrera (Eds.), *New directions in future of work*. Emerald Publishing.

Renkema, M., Meijerink, J., & Bondarouk, T. (2017). Advancing multilevel thinking in human resource management research: Applications and guidelines. *Human Resource Management Review*, 27(3), 397–415.

Robert, L. P., Pierce, C., Marquis, L., Kim, S., & Alahmad, R. (2020). Designing fair AI for managing employees in organizations: A review, critique, and design agenda. *Human–Computer Interaction*, 35(5–6), 545–575.

Rosenblat, A., & Stark, L. (2016). Algorithmic labor and information asymmetries: A case study of Uber's drivers. *International Journal of Communication*, 10(27), 3758–3784.

Russell, S., & Norvig, P. (1995). *Artificial intelligence: A modern approach* (2nd ed.). Prentice Hall.

Savela, N., Kaakinen, M., Ellonen, N., & Oksanen, A. (2021). Sharing a work team with robots: The negative effect of robot co-workers on in-group identification with the work team. *Computers in Human Behavior, 115*, 106585. https://doi.org/10.1016/j.chb.2020.106585

Schleicher, D. J., Baumann, H. M., Sullivan, D. W., Levy, P. E., Hargrove, D. C., & Barros-Rivera, B. A. (2018). Putting the system into performance management systems: A review and agenda for performance management research. *Journal of Management, 44*(6), 2209–2245.

Shmueli, G. (2010). To explain or to predict? *Statistical Science, 25*(3), 289–310. https://doi.org/10 .1214/10-STS330

Strohmeier, S. (2007). Research in e-HRM: Review and implications. *Human Resource Management Review, 17*(1), 19–37.

Strohmeier, S., & Piazza, F. (2013). Domain driven data mining in human resource management: A review of current research. *Expert Systems with Applications, 40*(7), 2410–2420.

Strohmeier, S., & Piazza, F. (2015). Artificial intelligence techniques in human resource management – a conceptual exploration. In C. Kahraman & S. Çevik Onar (Eds.), *Intelligent techniques in engineering management* (pp. 149–172). Springer.

Suen, H.-Y., Chen, M. Y.-C., & Lu, S.-H. (2019). Does the use of synchrony and artificial intelligence in video interviews affect interview ratings and applicant attitudes? *Computers in Human Behavior, 98*, 93–101.

Tambe, P., Cappelli, P., & Yakubovich, V. (2019). Artificial intelligence in human resources management: Challenges and a path forward. *California Management Review, 61*(4), 15–42.

Tarafdar, M., Beath, C. M., & Ross, J. W. (2019). Using AI to enhance business operations. *MIT Sloan Management Review, 60*(4), 37–44.

Ton, Z. (2009). *The effect of labor on profitability: The role of quality* (Harvard Business School Working Paper 09-040). Harvard Business School.

Trombin, M., Musso, M., Pinna, R., & De Marco, M. (2018). *The unbiased hiring? A critical analysis of artificial intelligence in e-HRM: The case of Pymetrics* [Paper presentation]. The 7th International e-HRM Conference, Milan, Italy.

Ulrich, D., & Brockbank, W. (2005). *The HR value proposition.* Harvard Business Press.

Upadhyay, A. K., & Khandelwal, K. (2018). Applying artificial intelligence: Implications for recruitment. *Strategic HR Review, 17*(5), 255–258.

Valverde, M. (2001). *Mapping the HRM function: An exploratory study of responsibilities and agents in the managing of people* [Doctoral dissertation, Universitat Rovira i Virgili, Reus].

Van den Broek, E., Sergeeva, A., & Huysman, M. (2019). Hiring algorithms: An ethnography of fairness in practice. In *Proceedings of ICIS 2019.* https://aisel.aisnet.org/icis2019/future_of_work/future _work/6, accessed January 28, 2021.

Van Esch, P., & Black, J. S. (2019). Factors that influence new generation candidates to engage with and complete digital, AI-enabled recruiting. *Business Horizons, 62*(6), 729–739.

Van Esch, P., Black, J. S., & Ferolie, J. (2019). Marketing AI recruitment: The next phase in job application and selection. *Computers in Human Behavior, 90*, 215–222.

Venkatesh, V., Morris, M. G., Davis, G. B., & Davis, F. D. (2003). User acceptance of information technology: Toward a unified view. *MIS Quarterly, 27*(3), 425–478.

Wirtz, J., Patterson, P. G., Kunz, W. H., Gruber, T., Lu, V. N., Paluch, S., & Martins, A. (2018). Brave new world: Service robots in the frontline. *Journal of Service Management, 29*(5), 907–931.

Woods, S. A., Ahmed, S., Nikolaou, I., Costa, A. C., & Anderson, N. R. (2020). Personnel selection in the digital age: A review of validity and applicant reactions, and future research challenges. *European Journal of Work and Organizational Psychology, 29*(1), 64–77.

Wright, P. M., & McMahan, G. C. (1992). Theoretical perspectives for strategic human resource management. *Journal of Management, 18*(2), 295–320.

Zielinski, D. (2020, January 2). *What to expect: 2020 HR tech trends.* https://www.shrm.org/ resourcesandtools/hr-topics/technology/pages/2020-hr-tech-trends.aspx, accessed January 20, 2021.

Zuboff, S. (1985). Automate/informate: The two faces of intelligent technology. *Organizational Dynamics, 14*(2), 5–18.

PART III

NORMATIVE ISSUES OF ARTIFICIAL INTELLIGENCE IN HUMAN RESOURCES

15. Explainability of artificial intelligence in human resources

Markus Langer and Cornelius J. König

INTRODUCTION

In the field of Human Resource Management (HRM), there is an emerging use of methods from the area of Artificial Intelligence (AI) (Cheng & Hackett, 2019). In this chapter, we take a functional perspective on AI and use the term to refer to "machines performing cognitive functions usually associated with human minds, such as learning, interacting, and problem solving" (Nilsson, 1971; from Raisch & Krakowski, 2021, p. 192). AI-based systems support HR managers in scheduling, performance management, hiring, and firing decisions. In this regard, AI-based systems produce outcomes that affect the fate of human beings in and outside of organizations (Wesche & Sonderegger, 2019). AI-based systems thus contribute to decisions in ethically sensitive, high-stake management contexts.

In such contexts, understanding the rationale behind AI-based decisions is central (Schnackenberg & Tomlinson, 2016). For instance, this means understanding which inputs AI-based systems use, why they use those inputs, and which processes lead to outputs, as well as understanding the reasons for specific outputs. From the perspective of decision-makers (e.g., HR managers), understanding AI-based systems, their processes, and outputs is assumed to be associated with a more adequate, efficient, and effective use of such systems (Höddinghaus et al., 2021; Hoff & Bashir, 2015). A better understanding of AI is often linked to more adequate trust in systems and to a better justification for using AI-based recommendations (Hoff & Bashir, 2015). From the perspective of people affected by AI-based decisions, understanding relates to justice perceptions of AI-based processes and outputs (Schlicker et al., 2021).

However, understanding AI-based processes and outputs is far from trivial. In fact, research, practice, and policy repeatedly emphasize the opacity of AI-based systems (Ananny & Crawford, 2018; Burrell, 2016; Jobin et al., 2019). This means that (1) the inputs used in AI-based systems remain inaccessible or unintelligible, (2) internal processes of AI-based systems (e.g., relations between inputs and outputs) remain hidden, and (3) there is no explanation or justification for the outputs of systems (Burrell, 2016; Langer & König, 2021). Reasons for AI opacity are manifold and lie within the systems themselves (e.g., the systems rely on a massive number of preprocessed predictors and/or on modern machine learning approaches that can be opaque even to their developers), are associated with developers (e.g., lack of domain knowledge that would help to assess what kinds of insights users need when interacting with systems), and are associated with the people using or affected by the systems (i.e., rudimentary algorithmic literacy) (Burrell, 2016).

In this chapter, we (1) argue that the understandability of AI-based systems and their outputs is crucial for the successful future implementation of AI in HRM, and (2) introduce research that can be subsumed under the term eXplainable Artificial Intelligence (XAI) and attempts to increase AI understandability and emphasize its importance for the future of AI in HRM. This chapter is structured as follows: First, we introduce what constitutes the research field of XAI and why it is important to HRM. We then highlight issues of AI opacity in HRM that motivate research into applications of XAI in HRM. Afterwards, we introduce proposed solutions to increase AI understandability and challenges that may limit the utility of previous work on XAI for HRM. We conclude with suggestions on how to advance XAI research to become more applied and useful for HRM.

WHAT IS XAI?

XAI has its roots in earlier manifestations of AI-based systems for decision-making. Research on the use of expert systems to augment or automate decision-making (i.e., the main manifestation of AI-based systems in the 1980s and 90s; Lawler & Elliot, 1996) found that humans demand more than numeric outputs or final classification suggestions when working with expert systems (e.g., Dhaliwal & Benbasat, 1996). For effective decision-support and to be better able to justify decisions referring to AI-based outputs, experts and laypeople alike want to understand how AI-based systems arrive at their outputs before using those systems for their own decisions. Today, XAI is a quickly evolving multidisciplinary field informed by research from the fields of computer science, philosophy, law, and psychology, to name but a few (see Abdul et al., 2018 for a more detailed overview of fields involved). Its main goal can be roughly summarized as increasing the understandability of AI to enable humans to better understand AI-based processes and outputs (Adadi & Berrada, 2018; Páez, 2019). In recent years, this goal has mainly focused on AI systems based on machine learning or deep learning approaches.

Accompanying the current hype surrounding the use of AI-based systems, the importance of and attention to XAI research has increased dramatically over recent years (Arrieta et al., 2020). There are at least three reasons for this. First, the most promising new AI approaches that fuel systems in practice are often also the ones that are the least understandable for humans (e.g., deep learning approaches) (Burrell, 2016). Second, whereas AI-based systems for low-stakes decisions (e.g., which music to listen to) might not require detailed understanding of AI-based recommendations, understanding AI-based processes and outputs becomes crucial as soon as they augment or automate decisions where ethical and moral questions arise, where the decisions are used to determine the fate of human beings, and, more generally, where the stakes of AI-based decisions become higher (Arrieta et al., 2020). The number of such situations is steadily increasing, ranging from medical to judicial to managerial decisions, thus affecting the lives of an increasing number of people (Jobin et al., 2019; Wesche & Sonderegger, 2019). Third, whereas in the past it was predominantly computer scientists who worked with AI-based systems, the variety of people using AI-based systems in decision-making has steadily grown (Brock, 2018). Thus, even people who have never participated in training on how AI-systems are developed or on how those systems work are increasingly required to use them for their everyday work (Oswald et al., 2020). Making AI-based systems more understandable for those with low algorithmic literacy thus seems to be important if we are to use AI-based systems in a variety of areas of everyday work.

All of this implies an increasingly important role of AI-based systems in practice and also suggests that an increasing number of people want to understand AI-based decisions. On the one hand, there are people who use AI-based systems as decision-support who want to understand the rationale behind AI-based outputs and recommendations. In HRM, this group of people consists of HR managers or general managers who use systems for decision-making. On the other hand, there are people who are affected by AI-based decisions who want to understand the rationale behind AI-based decisions (Arrieta et al., 2020). In HRM, this group of people consists of employees and applicants whose daily work (e.g., through scheduling, task assignment; Schlicker et al., 2021) or future (e.g., through performance reviews and personnel selection decisions; Cheng & Hackett, 2019) is affected by AI-based decisions.

Why Is XAI Important for HRM?

There are many application contexts of AI-based systems in HR, with one of the pioneering contexts being personnel selection, where AI-based systems are used for résumé screening or in job interview analysis (Langer et al., 2021). Additionally, organizations use AI-based systems in scheduling and performance management (Cheng & Hackett, 2019). There are even ideas to use AI-based systems to predict turnover, with implications for retention management (Sajjadiani et al., 2019).

Irrespective of the specific application context, understandability is crucial for the implementation of AI-based systems in HRM. There are at least three main theoretical perspectives highlighting the importance of AI understandability for HRM: a trust perspective, a justice perspective, and a work design perspective (more on the topic of desired outcomes of XAI can be found in the section "Additional Desirable Outcomes"). From a trust perspective (Lee & See, 2004), HR managers might not be able to assess the trustworthiness of AI-based systems without an understanding of AI-based processes and outputs, and might not know when and to what extent to trust systems' outputs. This can lead to issues of underreliance (e.g., not using systems even though this would enhance efficiency) but also of overreliance (e.g., not questioning whether an output might be erroneous) (Parasuraman & Riley, 1997). For instance, HR managers might not utilize AI-based recommendations in a personnel selection context if they do not understand the rationale of those recommendations leading to implementing systems that are never fully used (Gill, 1995). Alternatively, without understanding, HR managers might blindly rely on outputs even if AI-based systems are likely to work less than perfectly (e.g., recommending less suited candidates, providing biased selection outcomes; Dastin, 2018; Langer et al., 2021).

From a justice perspective, understandability of AI-based systems directly relates to informational justice perceptions, and indirectly to people's potential to assess procedural and distributive justice in HRM processes (Schlicker et al., 2021). For instance, imagine an AI-based performance management system used for employees' annual performance reviews. Without an understanding of why the system arrived at its outputs, transparently communicating to the employees the reasons for the outputs as well as providing ways to improve in future will be difficult, thus potentially reducing the employee's informational justice perceptions (Schlicker et al., 2021). Consequently, employees will also be less able to question whether those outputs resulted from unbiased evaluations and are less able to complain against performance evaluation processes (Kellogg et al., 2020).

From a work design perspective (Hackman & Oldham, 1976; Morgeson et al., 2012), understandability of AI-based systems likely has important implications with regard to decision autonomy and perceived responsibility for work outputs. For instance, if applicants file complaints and lawsuits against HR managers' decisions in personnel selection, the respective manager will be held accountable for their decision. However, if the manager just followed system recommendations they do not understand, thus giving up parts of their decision autonomy by letting the system decide on their behalf, they might not feel responsible for the respective decisions (Schlicker et al., 2021). Instead, they might believe that the system developer or the upper management who decided to implement the system should be held accountable – an issue that is known as a potential accountability gap when using AI-based systems in applied settings (Martin, 2019).

AI Opacity

Unfortunately, understanding AI-based processes and outputs is far from trivial as many current AI-based systems suffer from the issues of system-based opacity (Burrell, 2016). There are several factors that contribute to this. Consider the use of an AI-based system for the automatic evaluation of job interviews (Langer & König, 2021). The first issue contributing to opacity is that AI-based systems that support information processing and decision-making can consist of a combination of systems (Burrell, 2016). In the example case, those subsystems may contribute to the gathering, analysis, and evaluation of interviews. There might be a subsystem extracting nonverbal (e.g., facial recognition software) and content-related information from interview videos (Raghavan et al., 2020). Then there is another subsystem that might be trained, based on previous applicant information, to distinguish the most suitable applicants from the less suitable. Understanding the decision logic of the second system does not necessarily mean understanding what kinds of applicant information were extracted from the first subsystem (Langer & König, 2021).

Furthermore, AI-based systems usually analyze a large number and variety of predictors in order to arrive at their outputs. Imagine an empty spreadsheet with rows and columns, and try to fill out this imagined spreadsheet using the following examples. In the case of a video interview recording, every word that applicants use can serve as a potential feature (or predictor) to determine their suitability for a job. Additionally, every frame of a video produces additional features to use for prediction (Liem et al., 2018). Every frame is segregated into its pixels, making every pixel another feature for the prediction of applicants' suitability. Finally, every second of audio data provides additional applicant information, for instance about applicants' speech rate or jitter. Aside from the fact that you may first need to study linguistics to understand what jitter means, this adds additional features to the data frame, further enhancing the dimensionality of the input data. Now imagine that interactions between some of the features in the data frame might provide additional useful information in order to predict applicants' suitability for a job – this could again add a large number of new features to our imagined (or at this point unimaginable) spreadsheet; the nature and number of features used in intelligent systems can evade human cognition capabilities (Arrieta et al., 2020).

However, we as humans do not need to feel too bad about our cognitive shortcomings because with increasing dimensionality, computers can also become over inundated. This is why it is common for data not to enter the final prediction model within AI-based systems in their raw format, but instead be preprocessed first (Liem et al., 2018). Preprocessing can be done using principal component analysis, which results in dimensions or factors combining raw information. Such factors might combine words, pixels, and vocal information while making no intuitive sense to humans, thus further increasing the opacity of AI-based systems.

Until now, we have mostly been talking about data and preprocessing steps – we have yet to talk about algorithms used to analyze data and that help to derive conclusions from data. Some algorithms allow humans to easily understand their decision logic (see Arrieta et al., 2020, for an overview). For instance, it is straightforward to follow a decision tree and its branches to realize what steps the tree-classifier took to arrive at its outputs (e.g., classifications). However, in combination with large dimensionality and preprocessing of features, processes within those algorithms to arrive at their outputs also evade human understanding (Arrieta et al., 2020; Burrell, 2016). With other classes of algorithms, this issue amplifies. In more sophisticated algorithms (e.g., random forest as an ensemble method using many single decision trees), many single training models contribute to an output, making it more difficult to understand what has led to the respective output. Furthermore, one of the most commonly cited classes of opaque algorithms is that of artificial neural networks (ANNs; Arrieta et al., 2020; Felzmann et al., 2019). Heavily simplified, developers of such ANNs determine their initial structure and then feed them with training data (Langer & König, 2021). The ANN algorithm then detects patterns in the data, and adjusts the weights associated with input variables in order to be better capable to classify or predict target variables. This happens without human programming being involved, making ANNs opaque even to their developers (Arrieta et al., 2020). Furthermore, ANNs use internal representations of data that do not readily translate to human semantics and to human ways of problem solving (Burrell, 2016). This means that even if a human could peek into the "decision-making" of an ANN, the decision processes and the representation of information might not contribute to increasing understanding (Ananny & Crawford, 2018; Langer & König, 2021).

XAI Methods to Reduce Opacity and Increase Understandability and Their Shortcomings

The main output of the (still predominantly) computer science XAI research is a variety of technical solutions to address system-based opacity (Arrieta et al., 2020; Guidotti et al., 2019; Sokol & Flach, 2020). We subsume technical solutions that try to address system-based opacity and increase AI understandability under the term "XAI methods". The literature on XAI methods is vast, the technical details require deeper computer science understanding, and delving deeper into this research is beyond the scope of this chapter (see Arrieta et al., 2020; Guidotti et al., 2019 for an overview on those methods), thus the following overview should only be viewed as an introduction to this topic. We will introduce these example methods and then describe the general shortcomings of current XAI methods.

The two classes of XAI methods
Broadly speaking, the two big classes of solutions to system-based opacity can be subsumed under the terms "transparency-by-design" and "post-hoc interpretability and explainability methods" (Guidotti et al., 2019; Lipton, 2018). Transparency-by-design means to implement AI solutions using (to a certain degree) transparent models and features for prediction and classification. Transparency-by-design therefore relates to the actual transparency of an algorithmic model used in AI-based systems. It can be subdivided into simulatability, decomposability, and algorithmic transparency, with the degree of transparency decreasing respectively (Arrieta et al., 2020; Lipton, 2018). Simulatability refers to models whose entire logic is transparent to people, decomposability refers to models where single components (e.g., inputs,

parameters, calculations) are transparent, and algorithmic transparency refers to models where at least the underlying algorithm is transparent (e.g., understanding that linear regression describes linear relations). As an example, imagine an AI-based system is using a decision tree in order to classify applicants into those who are suitable and those who are less suitable for a job. A simulatable tree would indicate that the tree only uses features that are readily interpretable to humans and that consist of a manageable size of branches that would allow humans to understand all decisions that lead to a classification. A decomposable tree increases in size to become unmanageable by humans but the features it uses to classify applicants might still be understandable. An algorithmically transparent tree would additionally include features or combinations of features that are non-interpretable to human stakeholders but still leaves the underlying decision logic understandable (i.e., the general decision logic underlying decision trees). Overall, transparency-by-design aims to increase AI understandability by using AI approaches that keep the complexity of their algorithmic processes at a level manageable to humans.

Post-hoc interpretability and explainability methods play a crucial role when there is low or virtually no model transparency. Those methods generally try to use available information (e.g., inputs, outputs) and mathematical models to provide additional information and explanations to increase understandability of system processes and outputs (see Arrietta et al., 2020, p. 89, for a graphical overview on post-hoc interpretability and explainability methods). There is a large variety of such methods. For instance, text explanations try to generate text to explain the functioning of a system or the rationale behind the outputs of a system (e.g., "this applicant was rejected because they did not respond to question 2"). Visual explanations try to provide graphical information that helps to better understand a system's decision logic. For example, this could mean highlighting sections in video interviews that were especially influential regarding applicants' final AI-based evaluation. As another example, local explanations attempt to come up with an explanation for a single output or a subset of possible outputs (in contrast to global explanations that try to understand the general decision rules of a model) (Arrieta et al., 2020). This could mean using information from applicants similar to the applicant in question to derive information regarding what would have happened if an applicant had provided slightly different information in their application form. Explanations by example would provide further data examples that relate to the output of a system. For instance, this could mean that in addition to the recommendation regarding an applicant (e.g., "this applicant received 8 out of 10 points"), other applicants together with their input information could be presented that are representative for a given recommendation (i.e., for the category "8 out of 10 points"). This could help to identify the patterns a system uses for arriving at a recommendation. Explanations by simplification build a simpler new model based on available information (e.g., inputs and outputs) regarding the respective opaque model whose processes and outputs need explanation. The goal is to keep the performance and functions of the opaque model using a more transparent and understandable one. Finally, feature relevance explanations attempt to calculate relevance scores that provide information regarding how important a respective feature was for a given output (Arrieta et al., 2020).

Shortcomings of XAI methods
One of the most serious issues of XAI research is that there is a lack of evidence on the actual effects of using XAI methods in real-world applications and with human stakeholders involved (Doshi-Velez & Kim, 2017). One of the issues here is that XAI research is still mostly driven

by computer science that develops XAI methods as technical solutions but without testing them with actual human stakeholders. There are, however, some notable exceptions of studies investigating the effects of XAI methods on humans confronted with AI-based systems (e.g., Binns et al., 2018; Ribeiro et al., 2016). For instance, Ribeiro et al. (2016) showed that XAI methods enable human participants to better determine the performance of different AI-based systems, to suggest ways to improve the performance of AI-based systems, and to evaluate why they should trust an AI-based system's outputs. However, those notable exceptions also remain restricted to online or laboratory settings and to low-stake tasks (e.g., music recommendations) where emerging results might not be transferrable to high-stake (HRM) contexts.

Furthermore, commonly mentioned trade-offs associated with XAI methods might become especially important in HRM contexts. For instance, there is a transparency–performance trade-off (Sokol & Flach, 2020). This means in the case of transparency-by-design that using highly transparent AI-based systems can lead to lower performance (e.g., predictive accuracy) compared to when using more complex and thus potentially more opaque AI-based systems (Sokol & Flach, 2020). In applied settings it might therefore be necessary to investigate how much performance users are willing to trade for more transparency and understandability, as, for instance, perceived trustworthiness of systems depends on both performance and understandability (Höddinghaus et al., 2021). Another trade-off affects AI efficiency. Adding XAI methods to AI-based systems can lead to less efficient interactions with AI-based systems, as users need to process additional information (Dhaliwal & Benbasat, 1996).

As another trade-off example of using XAI methods in applied settings, consider that explanations provided by XAI methods might differ in their degree of detail. Whereas highly detailed explanations may provide a rich picture of the rationale of a system's outputs, highly detailed explanations might be discounted (Lombrozo, 2007) or people might react negatively to very detailed information (Langer et al., 2018). In contrast, whereas explanations emphasizing only the most important features contributing to an output might be perceived as useful and efficient, they may not accurately reflect the actual decision process of a system thus undermining people's insight into AI-based decision processes (Sokol & Flach, 2020). Whereas the consequences of such trade-offs are abstract within the context of proof-of-concept studies in computer science, they might lead to serious issues in HRM contexts. Choosing the wrong level of information detail provided by XAI methods could, for instance, lead to users not adequately integrating AI-based outputs in their decision-making processes, could detrimentally affect justice perceptions, or could result in litigation by people affected by AI-based decisions because they were not convinced by the explanation provided for those decisions.

Furthermore, the goal of XAI methods is eventually to increase stakeholder understanding of AI-based processes and outputs (Páez, 2019). However, to what extent existing XAI methods contribute to increasing AI understandability remains disputable. For instance, certain XAI methods use more transparent algorithms as proxies for less transparent ones (Arrieta et al., 2020). However, this implies that a user needs to understand another algorithmic process and its outputs, which might still be challenging for non-experts (Oswald et al., 2020). Recent research thus suggested moving towards more human-centric and theoretically grounded XAI methods, for instance paying attention to the way humans construct explanations as means to increase understanding (Keil, 2006; Lombrozo, 2011). In line with this, researchers have argued that XAI methods should become more contrastive, selective, and social in order to more likely enhance understanding (Miller, 2019; Mittelstadt et al., 2019). In the context of HRM, "contrastive" could mean that explanations in the form of "Why applicant

A was recommended and not applicant B" could be especially helpful to increase the understandability of AI-based systems. "Selective" means that XAI methods need to implement ways to select the most meaningful explanations given a particular recipient. For instance, it is more relevant for understanding if an AI-based system provides information to an HR decision-maker that this person does not already know. "Social" means that it could be fruitful to make XAI methods interactive between system and recipient, providing humans with the possibility to ask follow-up questions and systems with opportunities to tailor explanations to the respective recipient. However, there is still a long way to go for XAI methods to meet those goals. For instance, how can systems infer what users already know in order to tailor provided information? How to implement systems that can provide a useful response to the wide variety of possible follow-up questions that arise when being confronted with an AI-based decision? How can we know whether a system is actually providing information that refers to underlying reasons for its outputs and not just information that sounds reasonable but is actually not the main reason for its outputs?

As a final challenge with XAI methods, note that there are concerns that it might never be possible to make the decision processes of opaque AI approaches understandable to human beings. For instance, it might not be possible to fully translate internal representations of information in complex machine learning models into semantics that humans understand (Ananny & Crawford, 2018; Burrell, 2016). Consequently, there might be limits to what can be achieved with technical solutions to system-based opacity.

CHALLENGES FOR XAI IN HRM

Coming up with new XAI methods is a burgeoning area of research in computer science (Sokol & Flach, 2020). With the growing use of AI-based systems in HRM, it is highly likely that XAI research and XAI methods will become important for the successful implementation of AI-based systems in HRM. On the one hand, this is because an increasing number of HR managers will need to integrate AI outputs into their decision-making and will need to justify and defend decisions based on AI outputs. On the other hand, this is because people affected by AI-based decisions will demand explanations and better understanding of those decisions that affect their lives in and outside of organizations.

Although the aforementioned methods to reduce system-based opacity and increase AI understandability might prove to be helpful in implementing AI-based systems in applied settings such as HRM, we have also emphasized that there is still a strong need for advancements in XAI research for it to be useful in such contexts. In fact, there are several challenges and shortcomings of current XAI research that need to be addressed by future research. In order to highlight important areas for future work it is possible to follow the model proposed in Figure 15.1. In line with our previous focus on AI understandability, this model assumes that XAI methods should contribute to stakeholders' understanding of AI-based systems, and that this degree of understanding will affect other desired outcomes in relation to AI-based systems (e.g., trust, perceived justice, acceptance, perceived responsibility). Furthermore, contextual differences affect the relationships between XAI methods, understanding, and desired outcomes. The central concepts in this model (XAI methods, stakeholder understanding, desirable outcomes, and the context in which an AI-system operates) can be used to emphasize the topics where more research in XAI is needed for it to become useful in applied settings such as

HRM. We have already discussed the challenges for XAI methods in the previous section, thus the following paragraphs refer to challenges in XAI research relating to stakeholder understanding, additional desirable outcomes, and the context in which the AI-system operates.

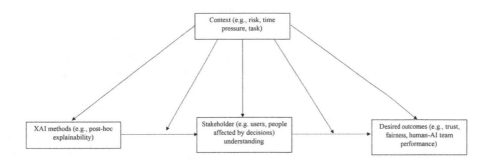

Figure 15.1   The relation of XAI methods, understanding, and outcomes

Stakeholder Understanding

Although questions around what an understanding of AI-based systems actually means and how it can be measured remain (Páez, 2019), research agrees that stakeholders' understanding of AI is a central goal of XAI research. Since understanding of AI-based systems strongly depends on the person confronted with an AI-based system, researchers realize that individual differences need to be considered in designing valuable XAI methods (Arrieta et al., 2020). For instance, users' background knowledge in AI and previous experience with the use of AI-based systems will affect how they react to AI-based systems and how they interact with those systems (Oswald et al., 2020). Similar things are true when using XAI methods in AI-based systems. This means that people with a strong background in computer science or people already experienced with a system in question might react differently to information provided through XAI methods than laypeople. Consequently, the same kind of information or the same level of detail might lead to different degrees of understanding for expert system developers, for HR managers who already have a history of working with a system, and for novice HR managers.

However, XAI methods rarely consider individual differences. This means that XAI methods might predominantly still be perceived as one-size-fits-all approaches not designed to tailor their outputs to stakeholders in question. Thus, every attempt to better consider stakeholders' background knowledge, goals, and interests within XAI methods would represent a valuable addition to existing methods (Sokol & Flach, 2020). For instance, one could imagine XAI methods that determine how much experience a user has with a given system, or XAI methods that infer from interactions with the user what the user already knows about a problem (Corona et al., 2019). Yet it seems extremely challenging to tailor XAI methods to individual users with their specific background, experience, interests, and goals that might additionally vary by context (Ananny & Crawford, 2018).

Another challenge for stakeholder understanding is that users and affected people in HRM will predominantly only have a rudimentary understanding of AI-based processes and outputs (Oswald et al., 2020). This contributes to a lack of understanding of AI-based systems beyond system-based opacity (Burrell, 2016). Thus, solutions to stakeholder understanding cannot be restricted to adding XAI methods to AI-based systems but rather there has to be better training for users and affected people in order to build a solid basis on top of which a better understanding of AI-based processes and outputs can be built.

Similarly, those implementing technical solutions to make AI-based systems more understandable to a variety of stakeholders are computer scientists with a possible lack of domain understanding of the final application context of the systems they develop. For instance, developers with little insight in relation to the respective application scenarios will likely consider it challenging that they have to anticipate what kind of additional information they should extract from a system that will affect HR managers' trust and employees' justice perceptions, or to predict what kind of information is needed to enable HR managers to make informed decisions. It will require a decent amount of user experience research or collaboration with domain experts before technical XAI solutions are readily useful for stakeholders in their respective application domain.

Additional Desirable Outcomes

The primary outcome of XAI methods is an increased understanding of AI-based systems (Páez, 2019). However, as we have already foreshadowed in the section on why XAI is important in HRM, there are many additional important outcomes downstream of this process that require attention in XAI research (Adadi & Berrada, 2018; Sokol & Flach, 2020). Common topics for both users and people affected by AI-based decisions might be uncertainty reduction and increasing controllability of AI-based processes (Kellogg et al., 2020). For users, this might crystallize in a more adequate, efficient, and effective use of AI-based systems. For instance, being able to better understand system outputs can lead to more suitable levels of trust which can translate to better performance of the human–AI team outcomes (Hoff & Bashir, 2015; Langer et al., 2021). Specifically, understanding the rationale behind a system's output can enable users to question if it is appropriate to trust the output in a given context (Ribeiro et al., 2016). Additionally, better understanding can result in being able to better justify AI-based decisions. In other words, if a user knows the most important reasons for a system's output, they might also be better able to rely on those outputs with a good conscience and to communicate decisions based on those outputs to affected people or to their supervisors.

For people affected by AI-based decisions, decreasing uncertainty through understanding might show through changes in fairness and justice perceptions (Lind & van den Bos, 2002). Specifically, justice is a central variable for people affected by decisions in HRM. It affects people's job satisfaction, motivation, job performance, and litigation intentions (Cohen-Carash & Spector, 2001). If an AI-based decision is relayed through no more than numeric information, affected people might not perceive strong informational justice. In contrast, adding information, explanations, and justification for AI-based decisions might increase perceived informational justice (but see Schlicker et al., 2021, who found no effect of an explanation on information justice perceptions in an AI-based decision scenario). In cases where affected people understand the reasons behind a decision, they might even be more likely to accept even unfavorable outcomes (Truxillo et al., 2009). Additionally, better understanding of decision processes might lead to more favorable perceptions of procedural justice as people are better able to identify if a process was unbiased and consistent for all people (Lind & van den Bos, 2002). Furthermore, better understanding might lead to affected people believing that they are better able to control AI-based decisions in the future as they learn what they could have done differently in order to affect the outcome, which could translate to higher acceptance of AI-based decision processes (Kellogg et al., 2020).

These are just some possible desirable outcomes in relation to XAI in HRM, and future research needs to comprehensively identify other downstream outcomes of AI understandability and potential trade-offs between those outcomes. For instance, increasing understanding of AI-based decisions can lead to stronger perceived justice but at the same time to less acceptance of such systems (Langer et al., 2018). Furthermore, understandability can lead to unintended outcomes. For example, Lee et al. (2019) increased understandability of a resource allocation algorithm, which led to two unpredicted side effects. First, as participants were better able to understand how the system allocated resources, they were better able to game the system in order to receive the resources they valued the most. Second, better insight and understanding of AI-based processes led people to believe that the final resource allocation was just the best possible solution. This might indicate that communicating the internal processes of AI-based decisions leads people to believe that AI-based processes are highly complex, leading to solutions that could not have been done better through human intervention (Langer & König, 2021). If this is the case, better understanding might reduce people's intention to question system outputs (Schlicker et al., 2021).

Additionally, future research needs to investigate relations between understanding and further desired outcomes (Langer et al., 2021). For instance, Schlicker et al. (2021) showed that explanations can lead to a better understanding of AI-based decisions, although this did not translate to justice perceptions in people affected by AI-based decisions. They argue that people might not even expect explanations by AI-based systems in contrast to cases where humans make decisions. Thus, it remains unclear if and under what conditions a better understanding of AI-based decisions actually translates to further desired outcomes and if results from research in traditional human-based decision scenarios (e.g., from organizational justice literature; Shaw et al., 2003; Truxillo et al., 2009) will be transferable to research on AI-based decisions. Additional research questions might be: Does better understanding of AI-based systems really contribute to human–AI team performance? How does understanding affect justice perceptions? How does understandability relate to controllability and potential gameability of AI-based systems?

Contextual Influences

In HRM, AI-based systems operate within strong contextual boundaries. Those contexts determine which XAI methods might be useful, the degree of (necessary) understanding in a given context, and the importance of different desired outcomes. For instance, some XAI methods might be more appropriate in low time pressure and/or high-risk contexts (i.e., XAI methods providing detailed descriptions of the rationale behind a decision), whereas XAI methods that emphasize the most important features for system outputs might be more appropriate in daily routines, as they balance efficiency goals with a certain degree of understanding of an outcome.

As we talk about the use of AI-based systems in organizational contexts, it is necessary to consider that not only users and people affected by AI-based decisions are involved in issues surrounding the use of AI in HRM. Specifically, organizations using AI-based systems might have their own interests in regard to XAI (Felzmann et al., 2019). They might want to intentionally keep certain aspects of AI-based systems opaque to users or people affected by AI-based decisions (Burrell, 2016). Making AI-based systems completely transparent would, for instance, make it easier for competitors to copy systems and could make it easier for applicants to game AI-based personnel selection (Langer & König, 2021). In general, this means that organizations might treat XAI methods and understandability of AI-based systems strategically (Burrell, 2016; Felzmann et al., 2019) and might actively decide when to reveal what information about AI-based systems or when to put effort in increasing AI understandability versus when to intentionally keep opacity high.

RESEARCH FOR APPLIED XAI IN HRM

In summary, the challenges regarding XAI methods and XAI research indicate that there is a strong need for XAI research in applied settings. The field of HRM is one where this applied research can be conducted to contribute to the advancement of XAI research. To holistically address XAI in HRM, it is crucial to investigate challenges surrounding XAI with respect to the various stakeholders involved in organizational settings. Furthermore, AI-based systems are used for HRM tasks as varied as scheduling and personnel selection, taking place within contexts that range from being low stakes to being high stakes and that are often dynamically changing. Thus, HRM offers fruitful contexts to investigate the effects of XAI methods in an applied setting. Furthermore, XAI research is inherently interdisciplinary and HR settings offer a playground for people from disciplines as varied as computer science, law, philosophy, management, and psychology to come together to advance XAI research.

XAI and Stakeholders

Most XAI research has looked at users' perspective or the perspective of people affected by AI-based decisions. For future research in applied settings, it will be necessary to consider all relevant stakeholders (Arrieta et al., 2020; Langer & König, 2021). In the case of HRM, additional stakeholders are organizations deploying the systems in question, as well as those regulating entities within (e.g., employee representatives) and outside of organizations (e.g., policy makers). All of them have a different perspective on AI opacity and understandability and have different interests and goals in regard to those issues. For instance, organizations deploying AI-based systems will want those systems to be accepted by the people who are meant to use the systems. Additionally, organizations will need to make sure that AI-based systems follow legal requirements such as the European General Data Protection Regulation (GDPR), which includes paragraphs on the use of AI-based systems when those systems automatically evaluate human beings (see Goodman & Flaxman, 2017). Whereas there is still ongoing debate about what kind of explanations and information in AI-based decision-making the GDPR actually demands, organizations need to consider ways to increase AI understandability if they want to prepare for a future where a right to an explanation becomes more concrete. For regulators involved in discussions about AI-based decision-making in HRM, investigating if organizations adhere to such standards as the GDPR is crucial. For them, it might be additionally important to be able to check if AI-based decisions in organizations follow not only legal, but also ethical standards. There has been a recent upsurge in ethical guidelines for the use of AI in applied settings, and most of them include calls for transparency, explainability, and understandability of AI-based decisions (Jobin et al., 2019). Following those ethical guidelines is not legally binding, but researchers have argued that they will impact organizations' decisions on the use of AI, as ethical guidelines can affect strategical decisions about AI-based decision-making (Jobin et al., 2019). For instance, if organizations claim to ensure human-centric development in the use of AI in HRM, they will need to follow such ethical guidelines as the "Ethic Guidelines for Trustworthy AI[1]" set up by the European Commission as a way to market this ideal to their employees, to people affected by AI decisions, and to policy makers.

XAI and AI Opacity

With the broader view on stakeholders, there also needs to be a broader view on reasons for AI opacity. Previous XAI research has predominantly tried to address issues of system-based opacity by developing various XAI methods. However, reasons for opacity stemming from people being confronted with AI-based systems and decisions or arising from the use of AI-based systems within applied settings have received considerably less attention (Burrell, 2016; Oswald et al., 2020). This means that independently of solutions for system-based opacity, there remain challenges for AI understandability that lie outside of the respective AI-based system. In HRM, current staff (e.g., HR managers) might not be trained in adequately using AI-based systems as decision-support (Cheng & Hackett, 2019; Oswald et al., 2020). They might have no understanding around which criteria differentiate good from bad AI-based systems (e.g., adequate training data), what inputs a respective AI-based system uses, how AI-based systems arrive at their outputs, and how to evaluate if they should follow or reject an AI-based recommendation. For such users, XAI methods might only be helpful if they consider the respective users' background knowledge and, as we have argued before, this is still a long way away. Thus, it might be necessary to educate and train HR staff to be better able to adequately use AI-based recommendations in decision-making (Langer & König, 2021). However, we are not aware of any research testing such training for the use of AI-based systems in management.

Another reason for opacity lies in organizations developing and implementing AI-based systems (Burrell, 2016). Whereas AI-based system users, people affected by AI-based systems, and legal regulations call for a better understanding of AI-based decisions, organizations developing and implementing AI-based systems might be less enthusiastic about the goals of XAI research (Ananny & Crawford, 2018; Felzmann et al., 2019). This is because they might want to control understandability of AI-based systems as every piece of information that helps in understanding AI-based decisions also helps competitors to potentially get insights into intellectual property. Additionally, providing too much detailed information about AI-based decisions might make the use of AI-based systems useless. For instance, consider an AI-based system for personnel selection (see also CHAPTER 8). Telling people what the rationale behind the system's evaluation of applicants is will help applicants adapt their behavior to receive better AI-based evaluations. Similar things might be true in AI-based systems for performance management in organizations, where employees could behave in a way that increases their chances of receiving a better performance evaluation. These are all examples for situations where organizations might intentionally want to maintain opacity of AI-based systems. Future research therefore needs to consider issues of opacity resulting from a respective AI-based system, people confronted with those AI-based systems, and stakeholders potentially motivated to maintain AI-based systems opacity (Langer & König, 2021).

XAI in Context

XAI research has not found its way into applied settings yet. In HRM, XAI methods could be implemented within AI-based systems for various tasks within different contexts, thus investigating the effects of using XAI methods. For example, in AI-based personnel selection, different XAI methods could be used to provide information about recommendations for and against certain applicants. It might be possible to evaluate the usefulness of general information about the decision logic of AI-based systems, ignoring the specific characteristics of individual applicants. This would mean introducing decision-makers to the way an AI-based system arrives at its predictions or classification outputs (Dhaliwal & Benbasat, 1996). It might also be possible to explain the rationale behind individual recommendations using various XAI methods (e.g., what were the most important characteristics of this applicant leading to a certain decision? What distinguished this applicant from an applicant who received a lower evaluation?). In addition to trying different XAI methods, research could investigate the influence of varying contexts on people confronted with AI-based decisions. For example, will better understandability through XAI methods affect human perceptions in lower-stakes decision tasks (e.g., hiring interns versus hiring trainees)? As Schlicker et al.'s (2021) results indicate, people might not even expect detailed information in everyday decisions such as scheduling. However, information and explanations might be more crucial in decision situations that have a stronger impact on people (e.g., in personnel selection) or when the risks involved are higher (e.g., in promotion decisions).

XAI and Interdisciplinarity

To date, XAI research is still mainly driven by computer science. This might be due to the fact that in the past the actual use of AI-based systems has seldom ventured beyond the proof-of-concept stage in computer science papers. However, as AI-based systems now dramatically change the ways and means of humans decision-making in organizations, it is necessary to address XAI from more than just the engineering perspective (Langer et al., 2021). Clearly, computer science will continue to be the main field offering technical solutions to AI understandability. Computer scientists will come up with more interactive, user-friendly, and human-centric XAI methods that can be tested in applied settings. In this regard, it is essential to investigate how XAI methods affect human stakeholders. This is where work from psychology scholars becomes crucial (König et al., 2020). Designing experimental studies investigating the effects of XAI methods on individuals and teams, examining how XAI methods contribute to understanding, defining important outcome variables and testing the effects of XAI methods and understandability on those outcome variables, and considering potential negative side effects of XAI methods on people's use and perception of AI-based systems are just some of the contributions psychology has to offer applied XAI research. Management scholars could take a macro perspective on XAI and investigate how organizations handle legal requirements, ethical guidelines, and concerns about intellectual property in strategic decisions about (X)AI in organizations (Schnackenberg & Tomlinson, 2016). Relatedly, the field of law can assess the articles and paragraphs included in legal regulations such as the GDRP as well as their implementation in organizations in order to make it clearer to what extent AI-based decisions should be made intelligible to people affected by those decisions (Goodman & Flaxman, 2017). Furthermore, philosophy scholars could provide insights on the concept of understandability in regard to AI-based systems and help with conceptual and terminological clarity in regard to the field of XAI, where there is, in spite of several attempts to provide such clarity, still ongoing confusion about the use of terms such as explanations, interpretability, transparency, or understandability in regard to AI (Arrieta et al., 2020).

CONCLUSION

The extent to which AI-based systems are used in HRM is steadily increasing (Cheng & Hackett, 2019; Wesche & Sonderegger, 2019). However, not only is the number of situations where people rely on AI-based decisions or are affected by AI-based decisions rising, but the importance of situations that involve AI-based decision-making is also growing (Mittelstadt et al., 2019). In such situations, people are greatly concerned about whether AI-based decisions are valid and fair. However, without a better understanding of AI-based systems' processes and outputs, what people are left with to rely on are frequently just numeric outputs or classification recommendations by AI-based systems. This is not enough for high-stakes decision situations, and XAI research is working on solutions to address AI opacity and to increase AI understandability. We thus argue that XAI research offers crucial components for a successful implementation of AI-based systems in HRM. However, so far, XAI research has remained a side note in research concerning the use of AI in management (see for instance Oswald et al., 2020). If we want to foster human-centric use of AI systems in management, management research and associated fields (e.g., industrial and organizational psychology) need to become involved in a research field that we might want to call AXAI: "Applied eXplainable Artificial Intelligence".

NOTE

1. https://digital-strategy.ec.europa.eu/en/library/ethics-guidelines-trustworthy-ai, accessed November 9, 2021.

REFERENCES

Abdul, A., Vermeulen, J., Wang, D., Lim, B. Y., & Kankanhalli, M. (2018). Trends and trajectories for explainable, accountable and intelligible systems: An HCI research agenda. In *Proceedings of the CHI Conference on Human Factors in Computing Systems* (pp. 1–18). ACM. https://doi.org/10.1145/3173574.3174156
Adadi, A., & Berrada, M. (2018). Peeking inside the black-box: A survey on explainable artificial intelligence (XAI). *IEEE Access, 6*, 52138–52160. https://doi.org/10.1109/ACCESS.2018.2870052

Ananny, M., & Crawford, K. (2018). Seeing without knowing: Limitations of the transparency ideal and its application to algorithmic accountability. *New Media and Society, 20*(3), 973–989. https://doi.org/10.1177/1461444816676645

Arrieta, A. B., Díaz-Rodríguez, N., Del Ser, J., Bennetot, A., Tabik, S., Barbado, A., Garcia, S., Gil-Lopez, S., Molina, D., Benjamins, R., Chatila, R., & Herrera, F. (2020). Explainable artificial intelligence (XAI): Concepts, taxonomies, opportunities and challenges toward responsible AI. *Information Fusion, 58*, 82–115. https://doi.org/10.1016/j.inffus.2019.12.012

Binns, R., Van Kleek, M., Veale, M., Lyngs, U., Zhao, J., & Shadbolt, N. (2018). "It's reducing a human being to a percentage"; Perceptions of justice in algorithmic decisions. In *Proceedings of the 2018 CHI Conference on Human Factors in Computing Systems* (pp. 1–14). ACM. https://doi.org/10.1145/3173574.3173951

Brock, D. C. (2018). Learning from artificial intelligence's previous awakenings: The history of expert systems. *AI Magazine, 39*(3), 3–15. https://doi.org/10.1609/aimag.v39i3.2809

Burrell, J. (2016). How the machine "thinks": Understanding opacity in machine learning algorithms. *Big Data and Society, 3*(1). https://doi.org/10.1177/2053951715622512

Cheng, M. M., & Hackett, R. D. (2019). A critical review of algorithms in HRM: Definition, theory, and practice. *Human Resource Management Review*, Advance Online Publication. https://doi.org/10.1016/j.hrmr.2019.100698

Cohen-Carash, Y., & Spector, P. E. (2001). The role of justice in organizations: A meta-analysis. *Organizational Behavior and Human Decision Processes, 86*(2), 278–321. https://doi.org/10.1006/obhd.2001.2958

Corona, R., Alaniz, S., & Akata, Z. (2019, November 19). *Modeling conceptual understanding in image reference games*. ArXiv:1910.04872. http://arxiv.org/abs/1910.04872

Dastin, J. (2018). Amazon scraps secret AI recruiting tool that showed bias against women. Reuters.com. https://www.reuters.com/article/us-amazon-com-jobs-automation-insight/amazon-scraps-secret-ai-recruiting-tool-that-showed-bias-against-women-idUSKCN1MK08G, accessed December 15, 2020.

Dhaliwal, J. S., & Benbasat, I. (1996). The use and effects of knowledge-based system explanations: Theoretical foundations and a framework for empirical valuation. *Information Systems Research, 7*(3), 342–362. https://doi.org/10.1287/isre.7.3.342

Doshi-Velez, F., & Kim, B. (2017, March 2). *Towards a rigorous science of interpretable machine learning*. ArXiv:1702.08608. http://arxiv.org/abs/1702.08608

Felzmann, H., Villaronga, E. F., Lutz, C., & Tamò-Larrieux, A. (2019). Transparency you can trust: Transparency requirements for artificial intelligence between legal norms and contextual concerns. *Big Data and Society, 6*(1). https://doi.org/10.1177/2053951719860542

Gill, T. G. (1995). Early expert systems: Where are they now? *MIS Quarterly, 19*(1), 51–81. https://doi.org/10.2307/249711

Goodman, B., & Flaxman, S. (2017). European Union regulations on algorithmic decision-making and a "right to explanation". *AI Magazine, 38*(3), 50–57. https://doi.org/10.1609/aimag.v38i3.2741

Guidotti, R., Monreale, A., Ruggieri, S., Turini, F., Giannotti, F., & Pedreschi, D. (2019). A survey of methods for explaining black box models. *ACM Computing Surveys, 51*(5), 1–42. https://doi.org/10.1145/3236009

Hackman, J. R., & Oldham, G. R. (1976). Motivation through the design of work: Test of a theory. *Organizational Behavior and Human Performance, 16*(2), 250–279. https://doi.org/10.1016/0030-5073(76)90016-7

Höddinghaus, M., Sondern, D., & Hertel, G. (2021). The automation of leadership functions: Would people trust decision algorithms? *Computers in Human Behavior, 116*, Article 106635. https://doi.org/10.1016/j.chb.2020.106635

Hoff, K. A., & Bashir, M. (2015). Trust in automation: Integrating empirical evidence on factors that influence trust. *Human Factors, 57*(3), 407–434. https://doi.org/10.1177/0018720814547570

Jobin, A., Ienca, M., & Vayena, E. (2019). The global landscape of AI ethics guidelines. *Nature Machine Intelligence, 1*(9), 389–399. https://doi.org/10.1038/s42256-019-0088-2

Keil, F. C. (2006). Explanation and understanding. *Annual Review of Psychology, 57*(1), 227–254. https://doi.org/10.1146/annurev.psych.57.102904.190100

Kellogg, K. C., Valentine, M. A., & Christin, A. (2020). Algorithms at work: The new contested terrain of control. *Academy of Management Annals, 14*(1), 366–410. https://doi.org/10.5465/annals.2018.0174

König, C., Demetriou, A., Glock, P., Hiemstra, A., Iliescu, D., Ionescu, C., Langer, M., Liem, C., Linnenbürger, A., Siegel, R., & Vartholomaios, I. (2020). Some advice for psychologists who want to work with computer scientists on big data. *Personnel Assessment and Decisions, 6*(1), Article 2. https://doi.org/10.25035/pad.2020.01.002

Langer, M., & König, C. J. (2021). Introducing a multi-stakeholder perspective on opacity, transparency and strategies to reduce opacity in algorithm-based human resource management. *Human Resource Management Review*. Advance online publication.

Langer, M., König, C. J., & Busch, V. (2021). Changing the means of managerial work: Effects of automated decision-support systems on personnel selection tasks. *Journal of Business and Psychology, 36*, 751–769. https://doi.org/10.1007/s10869-020-09711-6

Langer, M., König, C. J., & Fitili, A. (2018). Information as a double-edged sword: The role of computer experience and information on applicant reactions towards novel technologies for personnel selection. *Computers in Human Behavior, 81*, 19–30. https://doi.org/10.1016/j.chb.2017.11.036

Lawler, J. J., & Elliot, R. (1996). Artificial intelligence in HRM: An experimental study of an expert system. *Journal of Management, 22*(1), 85–111. https://doi.org/10.1177/014920639602200104

Lee, J. D., & See, K. A. (2004). Trust in automation: Designing for appropriate reliance. *Human Factors, 46*(1), 50–80. https://doi.org/10.1518/hfes.46.1.50.30392

Lee, M. K., Jain, A., Cha, H. J., Ojha, S., & Kusbit, D. (2019). Procedural justice in algorithmic fairness: Leveraging transparency and outcome control for fair algorithmic mediation. *Proceedings of the ACM on Human-Computer Interaction, 3*(CSCW), 1–26. https://doi.org/10.1145/3359284

Liem, C. C. S., Langer, M., Demetriou, A., Hiemstra, A. M. F., Sukma Wicaksana, A., Born, M. Ph., & König, C. J. (2018). Psychology meets machine learning: Interdisciplinary perspectives on algorithmic job candidate screening. In H. J. Escalante, S. Escalera, I. Guyon, X. Baró, Y. Güçlütürk, U. Güçlü, & M. van Gerven (Eds.), *Explainable and interpretable models in computer vision and machine learning* (pp. 197–253). Springer International Publishing. https://doi.org/10.1007/978-3-319-98131-4_9

Lind, E. A., & van den Bos, K. (2002). When fairness works: Toward a general theory of uncertainty management. *Research in Organizational Behavior, 24*, 181–223. https://doi.org/10.1016/S0191-3085(02)24006-X

Lipton, Z. C. (2018). The mythos of model interpretability. *Communications of the ACM, 61*(10), 36–43. https://doi.org/10.1145/3233231

Lombrozo, T. (2007). Simplicity and probability in causal explanation. *Cognitive Psychology, 55*, 232–257. https://doi.org/10.1016/j.cogpsych.2006.09.006

Lombrozo, T. (2011). The instrumental value of explanations. *Philosophy Compass, 6*(8), 539–551. https://doi.org/10.1111/j.1747-9991.2011.00413.x

Martin, K. (2019). Ethical implications and accountability of algorithms. *Journal of Business Ethics, 160*(4), 835–850. https://doi.org/10.1007/s10551-018-3921-3

Miller, T. (2019). Explanation in artificial intelligence: Insights from the social sciences. *Artificial Intelligence, 267*, 1–38. https://doi.org/10.1016/j.artint.2018.07.007

Mittelstadt, B. D., Russell, C., & Wachter, S. (2019). Explaining explanations in AI. In *Proceedings of the 2019 FAT* Conference on Fairness, Accountability, and Transparency* (pp. 279–288). ACM. https://doi.org/10.1145/3287560.3287574

Morgeson, F. P., Garzsa, A. S., & Campion, M. A. (2012). Work design. In E. B. Weiner, N. W. Schmitt, & S. Highhouse (Eds.), *Handbook of psychology* (pp. 525–559). Wiley. https://doi.org/10.1002/9781118133880.hop212020

Nilsson, N. J. (1971). *Problem-solving methods in artificial intelligence*. McGraw-Hill.

Oswald, F. L., Behrend, T. S., Putka, D. J., & Sinar, E. (2020). Big data in industrial-organizational psychology and human resource management: Forward progress for organizational research and practice. *Annual Review of Organizational Psychology and Organizational Behavior, 7*(1), 505–533. https://doi.org/10.1146/annurev-orgpsych-032117-104553

Páez, A. (2019). The pragmatic turn in explainable artificial intelligence (XAI). *Minds and Machines, 29*(3), 441–459. https://doi.org/10.1007/s11023-019-09502-w

Parasuraman, R., & Riley, V. (1997). Humans and automation: Use, misuse, disuse, abuse. *Human Factors*, *39*(2), 230–253. https://doi.org/10.1518/001872097778543886

Raghavan, M., Barocas, S., Kleinberg, J., & Levy, K. (2020). Mitigating bias in algorithmic hiring: Evaluating claims and practices. In *Proceedings of the 2020 FAT* Conference on Fairness, Accountability, and Transparency* (pp. 469–481). ACM. https://doi.org/10.1145/3351095.3372828

Raisch, S., & Krakowski, S. (2021). Artificial intelligence and management: The automation–augmentation paradox. *Academy of Management Review*, *46*(1). https://doi.org/10.5465/amr.2018.0072

Ribeiro, M. T., Singh, S., & Guestrin, C. (2016, August 9). *"Why should I trust you?": Explaining the predictions of any classifier*. ArXiv:1602.04938. http://arxiv.org/abs/1602.04938

Sajjadiani, S., Sojourner, A. J., Kammeyer-Mueller, J. D., & Mykerezi, E. (2019). Using machine learning to translate applicant work history into predictors of performance and turnover. *Journal of Applied Psychology*, *104*(10), 1207–1225. https://doi.org/10.1037/apl0000405

Schlicker, N., Langer, M., Ötting, S. K., König, C. J., Baum, K., & Wallach, D. (2021). What to expect from opening "black boxes"? Comparing perceptions of justice between human and automated agents. *Computers in Human Behavior*, *122*, Article 106837. https://doi.org/10.1016/j.chb.2021.106837

Schnackenberg, A. K., & Tomlinson, E. C. (2016). Organizational transparency: A new perspective on managing trust in organization–stakeholder relationships. *Journal of Management*, *42*(7), 1784–1810. https://doi.org/10.1177/0149206314525202

Shaw, J. C., Wild, E., & Colquitt, J. A. (2003). To justify or excuse?: A meta-analytic review of the effects of explanations. *Journal of Applied Psychology*, *88*(3), 444–458. https://doi.org/10.1037/0021-9010.88.3.444

Sokol, K., & Flach, P. (2020). Explainability fact sheets: A framework for systematic assessment of explainable approaches. In *Proceedings of the 2020 Conference on Fairness, Accountability, and Transparency* (pp. 56–67). ACM. https://doi.org/10.1145/3351095.3372870

Truxillo, D. M., Bodner, T. E., Bertolino, M., Bauer, T. N., & Yonce, C. A. (2009). Effects of explanations on applicant reactions: A meta-analytic review. *International Journal of Selection and Assessment*, *17*, 346–361. https://doi.org/10.1111/j.1468-2389.2009.00478.x

Wesche, J. S., & Sonderegger, A. (2019). When computers take the lead: The automation of leadership. *Computers in Human Behavior*, *101*, 197–209. https://doi.org/10.1016/j.chb.2019.07.027

16. Fairness of artificial intelligence in human resources – held to a higher standard?

Sandra L. Fisher and Garret N. Howardson

INTRODUCTION

The fairness of decisions made about human resource management (HRM) issues in organizations has been a concern of both research and practice for decades (Colquitt et al., 2001; Gilliland, 1993; McCarthy et al., 2017). Research has consistently demonstrated that decisions in HRM (e.g., hiring, compensation, performance evaluation, discipline) that are perceived as unfair have negative effects for both individuals and organizations. Individual employees experience lower levels of satisfaction with their jobs, lower commitment to the organization, and reduced trust when they perceive unfair decisions have been made about themselves or others (Colquitt et al., 2001; McCarthy et al., 2017). Organizations may then see decreases in their reputation as an employer, productivity losses among employees, and higher employee turnover.

Many organizations see the use of decision tools that use artificial intelligence (AI) and the corresponding machine learning (ML) algorithms[1] as a way to improve their HR decision-making processes and outcomes (Gonzalez et al., 2019). Following Strohmeier (2020), we define algorithmic decision making in the context of AI and HR as "employing computer-based HR decision algorithms for drawing or supporting HR decisions" (p. 54). Knowing that humans have biases and make errors in HR decisions ranging from selection to discipline to negotiations, AI and the related algorithms are viewed as a way to make consistent decisions based on concrete data. Algorithmic decisions have other advantages in that they can be made more quickly, freeing HR staff and managers from time-consuming tasks such as reviewing job application materials (Gonzalez et al., 2019). These benefits notwithstanding, new technologies often have unintended consequences for organizational processes (Orlikowski, 1992), as may be the case with AI and algorithmic decision making (Kellogg et al., 2020).

Evidence is accumulating that AI-based decision making can also be perceived as unfair (Köchling & Wehner, 2020; Newman et al., 2020). Biases that provide a distinct advantage or disadvantage to members of certain groups have been identified in some selection algorithms, such as the one reported by Amazon that evaluated female applicants as less qualified (Black & van Esch, 2020). These biases are also present in decision-making algorithms affecting daily life outside of the employment context (e.g., the Apple credit card). Although there are clearly concerns with the fairness of AI-based decision making, it appears that people may actually be holding these tools to a higher standard than human decision making (Dietvorst et al., 2015; Zerilli et al., 2019). Consider the example of self-driving cars. Human-operated motor vehicles are associated with over 1 million deaths per year globally (World Health Organization, 2020). In 2017, there were over 35,000 deaths from motor vehicle accidents in the United States and over 25,000 deaths in the European Union (Eurostat, 2017; National Highway Traffic Safety

Administration, n.d.). However, a single 2018 death associated with a test of a self-driving car in Arizona was considered to be a major setback for implementation of the technology. This seems to be an example of how "the errors that we tolerate in humans become less tolerable when machines make them" (Dietvorst et al., 2015, p. 115), a phenomenon that we argue is also observable in HR decision making. A human error that results in an unfair HR decision about hiring or promotion may somehow be more acceptable than an algorithm misclassifying a person in the same situation.

In this chapter, we explore different perspectives on fairness and how they apply to HR decisions made by humans and by algorithms, focusing on perceptual definitions of fairness. We examine the emerging literature on fairness of HR processes and decisions supported by algorithms and AI. We review theories and models used to evaluate and predict the fairness of HR decisions and compare those to how fairness has been addressed in the AI literature to better understand why people might react differently to HR decisions made by humans and those made by AI supported tools. We identify decision-maker intentionality as a critical feature of fairness from the social exchange perspective and examine how intentionality, autonomy, and social context play important roles in judgment of fairness in decisions supported by algorithms. Before describing in more depth the concept of fairness in organizational decision making, it is helpful to first clarify how we conceptualize fairness.

What Is Fairness?

The question of what is fair or unfair in a general, abstract sense likely belongs to the field of ethics or moral philosophy. Much has been written about fairness from this general philosophical perspective, and faithfully summarizing such ideas is well beyond the scope of the current chapter. Nevertheless, for the philosophically inclined reader, our goal here is better described as epistemological, or trying to understand how we can ever know what it means for something to be fair (e.g., Plotkin, 1993).

A moral philosophical perspective might emphasize equity and receiving an appropriate amount of some reward given a particular amount of effort; an epistemological perspective, on the other hand, might strive to understand how we can know at all what is appropriate, particularly when a given amount of rewards-for-effort might be acceptable in one situation but not in another. Our emphasis here is on the latter, arguing that to know whether something is fair in a particular situation requires understanding the situation itself in great detail, and whether those people involved consider the situation and its resolution (or lack thereof) appropriate (i.e., whether people perceive the situation as fair).

While few if any situations are universally appropriate or fair to all parties involved, we can use psychological theory and empirical research to surmise whether a particular situation will, in general, be viewed as fair or appropriate to a particular party. For the remainder of this chapter, we thus restrict our discussion of fairness to questions of how researchers and practitioners can know whether particular individuals view AI use in HR as fair and appropriate.

FAIRNESS IN ORGANIZATIONAL DECISION MAKING

There have been decades of research on fairness in organizational decision making in the fields of industrial-organizational psychology, human resource management, and organizational behavior. Much of this research examines fairness perceptions formed by individuals (such as job applicants or employees) about decisions that various organizational representatives have made about them. This research has been described extensively elsewhere (e.g., Colquitt et al., 2001; Colquitt et al., 2013; McCarthy et al., 2017; Rupp et al., 2014) and in the context of AI decision making (Robert et al., 2020), therefore we will not review it in detail but rather identify some key themes and theoretical perspectives present in this research stream.

While people generally have an intuitive sense of what is fair and what is unfair in decision making within HRM or in other areas of life, these terms are defined in different ways in different academic traditions and for different practical applications, even within the field of HRM (i.e., there is no universal definition of fairness). One point of difference is the use of standardized, mathematical conceptions of fairness compared to individual perceptions of fairness. Definitions of discriminatory hiring decisions are one example of this difference. Many people would consider discriminatory hiring decisions to be unfair when someone is hired or not hired based on race, sex, or religion. Group-level cases of discrimination can be defined mathematically, using the four-fifths rule as described in U.S. employment law to demonstrate initial evidence of adverse impact. Many studies examining fairness of algorithmic decisions in HR have taken this mathematical, bias-oriented viewpoint (Köchling & Wehner, 2020; Raghavan et al., 2020). However, individual cases of discrimination cannot be defined mathematically and are based on perception and an evaluation of the overall situation, considering how an individual was treated. In the existing literature on algorithmic decision making in HR, the perceptual perspective on fairness has been examined less frequently than the more objective, mathematical perspective (Köchling & Wehner, 2020). Thus, we adopt the perceptual fairness viewpoint in this chapter, noting the largely epistemological perspective taken by the field of industrial-organizational psychology that "Fairness is a social rather than a psychometric concept. Its definition depends on what one considers to be fair" (The Society for Industrial and Organizational Psychology, 2018, p. 22).

General Fairness Theories

Organizational Justice. One approach to the study of fairness in organizations is through the lens of organizational justice. This line of research has focused on different types of justice, or the rules people use to decide if a decision or event is fair (Colquitt et al., 2001; Colquitt et al., 2013; Gilliland, 1993). The literature has largely converged on four different types of justice: distributive, procedural, interpersonal, and informational. Distributive justice focuses on the outcomes of decisions about valued resources in organizations such as selection, pay, and promotion. Procedural justice focuses more on the process or procedures used to reach the decision. Informational justice narrows in on the information that people receive about decisions that are made, and the extent to which this information can explain "why procedures were used in a certain way or why outcomes were distributed in a certain fashion" (Colquitt et al., 2001, p. 427). Interpersonal justice addresses the extent to which the actors involved in making a decision treated the focal person with respect. These four types of justice are empirically distinct and show different patterns of relationships with important outcome variables in the literature (Colquitt et al., 2001; Colquitt et al., 2013). This literature has examined HR decision making in organizations broadly rather than focusing on one type of decision (in contrast, below we discuss literature that focuses on selection decisions). For example, the Colquitt et al. (2001) meta-analysis included papers that dealt with individual justice perceptions in HR topics including employee discipline, performance appraisal, layoffs, promotions, pay, negotiations, drug screening, and electronic control systems.

This model of organizational justice is based on a set of criteria set forth by Leventhal (1980), who argued that for decisions to be considered fair, they should be based on decision rules that have the following characteristics: a) applied consistently over time and across people, b) free from bias, meaning that the decision is made without self-interest or preconceptions about people, c) based on accurate information and informed opinion, d) include a mechanism for correcting errors or oversights in the decision process, e) represent and consider the opinions of various groups affected by the decision, and f) conform to standards of ethics or morality "accepted by that individual" (Leventhal, 1980, p. 33). While these are intended to be general rules that apply across people, the individual judgments regarding any one decision could vary based on individual characteristics (e.g., personal standards of ethics). The HR research based on these rules has focused on systematic efforts to improve fairness perceptions across people, such as making decisions more consistent and gathering accurate information for making decisions.

The AI literature (e.g., Robert et al., 2020) has been addressing some of these concepts, with some studies explicitly using the terminology of organizational justice theory and others doing so more implicitly. The focus has been on distributive justice outcomes, with some attention paid to procedural justice and less to interpersonal and informational. For example, in their experimental study on perceptions of fairness in workplace decision making, Ötting and Maier's (2018) vignette-based study found that the decision maker (human team leader, humanoid robot, or intelligent computer system) did not matter in terms of perceptions of procedural justice. Kaibel et al. (2019) examined aspects of procedural and interpersonal justice in two related experiments comparing perceptions about human and algorithmic decision makers. They found mixed results, such that one experiment showed higher perceived fairness for human decision makers and the other showed no difference in perceived procedural fairness between humans and algorithms. We can question the relevance of interpersonal justice with an AI-based decision agent, as this type of justice generally refers to the interactions between two people. Early research on this topic as reviewed by Glikson and Woolley (2020) suggests that AI agents such as chatbots can meet some of the criteria of interpersonal justice, such as treating people with "politeness, dignity, and respect" when "executing procedures or determining outcomes" (Colquitt et al., 2001, p. 427), particularly when they take on human attributes (Kim & Duhachek, 2020).

Social Exchange Perspective. Another view of organizational justice is based on the social exchange perspective (Colquitt et al., 2013; Rupp et al., 2014). Instead of focusing on the policies, procedures, or rules of how a decision is made, this perspective highlights the actor(s) involved in making the decision. A key question becomes, who is responsible for an act of injustice? The resulting attitudes and behavioral reactions are then targeted toward the party at fault, typically the supervisor or the organization as a whole (Rupp et al., 2014). If the decision maker acts in a just manner, then social exchange processes suggest that the individual will respond with positive reactions such as organizational citizenship behaviors, commitment, and trust. The focus of the responsible party and the individual reactions should match, such that supervisor-focused justice results in supervisor-oriented outcomes such as leader–member exchange (LMX), and organization-focused justice results in organization-oriented outcomes such as commitment (Colquitt et al., 2013). For social exchange processes to truly develop, a relatively long time frame is required. As such, the social exchange perspective may be more relevant to justice perceptions of employees that can unfold over multiple decisions in performance management, feedback, and labor relations processes rather than the short-term viewpoint of the typical applicant in a selection scenario (Colquitt et al., 2013; Rupp et al., 2014).

Fairness theory (Folger & Cropanzano, 2001) similarly looks at decision fairness in the context of attribution to different actors, with interest in the process of making accountability judgments or assigning blame. This approach to fairness in HR decisions examines if there is someone who should be held accountable for the unfair decision. Fairness theory requires that there is a negative event that could be considered unfair, that the actions leading to the negative event were discretionary (i.e., the actions were intentional), and that the event violates some kind of moral code. The person who was negatively affected by the event would then use counterfactual thinking to decide when to assign blame. For example, they might imagine what alternative actions the decision maker could have taken. If there were no other feasible options, the actions may be considered as not being under the control of the actor, and therefore this person cannot be blamed.

Conclusions on General Justice and Fairness Theories. The organizational justice and fairness approaches discussed above are complementary. The types of justice approach (Gilliland, 1993; Colquitt et al., 2001) focuses on the "what/how" component of justice perceptions and offers specific rules through which organizations may improve fairness perceptions about its HR processes. The social exchange and fairness theory approaches (Folger & Cropanzano, 2001; Rupp et al., 2014) focus more on the "who/when" component of fairness judgments, thinking about who is responsible for an unfair decision or when they may be absolved from blame, such as when they could not have acted differently. These social exchange and fairness theory perspectives strive to account for situations where no particular individual deserves blame, such as when circumstances are beyond an individual's control. In such cases, holding an individual accountable for events that were beyond their control would, regardless of the specific rule in question, be inappropriate or unfair. Thus, fairness is about more than simply following specific rules for justice, but also considers broader perceptions about the application of decision rules given a specific set of circumstances (Colquitt & Rodell, 2015; Colquitt & Zipay, 2015; Carmody, 2015). Fairness has more recently been defined as "a global perception of appropriateness – a perception that tends to lie theoretically downstream of justice" (Colquitt & Zipay, 2015, p. 76).

Application of General Fairness Theories to HR Contexts

Applicant Reactions to Selection. A more concrete stream of fairness research focuses specifically on applicant reactions to the hiring process and decision (Gilliland, 1993; Hausknecht et al., 2004; Konradt et al., 2017; McCarthy et al., 2017). This research frequently applies the four types of organizational justice described above (Gilliland, 1993; Colquitt et al., 2001), examining the antecedents and consequences of applicant reactions. Reviews of the literature, both meta-analytic and more qualitative reviews, have found general support for Gilliland's (1993) framework of the importance of distributive and procedural justice in applicant reactions to selection processes (e.g., Hausknecht et al., 2004; McCarthy et al., 2017). Studies have consistently found that job-relevant selection procedures, provision of explanations, and availability of feedback were particularly important to fairness perceptions. In their study, Konradt et al. (2017) demonstrated that the importance of different fairness predictors can differ at different points in the selection process, such that interpersonal treatment was more important for procedural fairness perceptions early in the process while availability of explanations was more important later in the process.

The existing research examining applicant perceptions of AI decision tools in selection suggests neutral to negative perceptions of fairness (Acikgoz et al., 2020; Kaibel et al., 2019; Köchling & Wehner, 2020; Langer et al., 2019; Lee, 2018; Newman et al., 2020; Suen et al., 2019) for procedures such as initial applicant screening and asynchronous video interviews. This is consistent with earlier reviews on emerging technologies in selection (e.g., McCarthy et al., 2017) which noted that emerging technologies have efficiency and cost advantages for organizations but there have been mixed results from applicants in terms of their reactions. Some technology-based features such as easy-to-use online applications are viewed positively, but those that degrade the quality of the face-to-face experience or are perceived as invading privacy (e.g., use of social media) have been viewed more negatively. Blacksmith et al. (2016) suggested that negative reactions to online interviews may be due to perceptions of unfairness and frustration because applicants have less ability to manage impressions in online interviews, which are viewed as less personal than face-to-face interviews. Having interviews scored with AI could exacerbate this effect, as applicants could believe they have even less influence over the process (Langer et al., 2019) or less opportunity to perform (Acikgoz et al., 2020), or that the algorithm is reductionistic and cannot consider all the important qualitative information necessary to make a fair decision (Newman et al., 2020). Perceptions of the AI system being responsible for unfairness could lead to some of the negative behaviors described in the literature, such as forming a negative opinion of the organization and communicating that viewpoint to family and friends (Hausknecht et al., 2004).

Decision-Maker Reactions to Selection Processes. Another stream of research has examined the perceptions of the decision makers in the selection process regarding their preferences for algorithmic versus expert decision making (e.g., Diab et al., 2011; Highhouse, 2008; Kuncel et al., 2013; Nolan et al., 2016). The use of standardized selection processes and mechanical decision making is clearly superior from a validity perspective, resulting in improved hiring outcomes for organizations. However, research and anecdotal evidence routinely show that hiring managers prefer clinical methods (subjective, non-standardized decision making that often varies between individuals) for making hiring decisions. They believe that expert decision makers can make better decisions than impersonal algorithms or equations and that their own value as experts in the process is reduced when standardized methods are used (Grove & Meehl, 1996; Highhouse, 2008; Nolan et al., 2016). These findings have not been specifically interpreted in line with the justice and fairness literatures, but we argue they could be extended to suggest decision makers believe it is unfair to hiring managers to be "replaced" with standardized decision-making tools in the selection process. It is also important to note that this research has not been conducted using AI-based decision tools but rather has been conducted with reference to a mechanical combination of data through a generic algorithm or formula (Kuncel et al., 2013) or a computer program (Nolan et al., 2016). Grove and Meehl (1996) clearly state the opinion that using clinical decision making rather than the more accurate mechanical processes would be unethical, as people who are the subjects of such decisions deserve the most accurate decisions that can be made under high-stakes conditions

Summary. The organizational justice and social exchange perspectives offer two broad theories of fairness from which others have developed (e.g., fairness theory). They complement each other such that organizational justice establishes the set of desired rules governing fairness judgments and social exchange specifies under what conditions those rules may be acceptably broken, or when a particular set of rules may be seen as fair in one situation but not another. Organizational justice suitably describes circumstances for fairness with respect to job applicants, but social exchange adds nuance that is necessary to also explain fairness judgments with respect to manager decision making (where we ask, fair to whom?) and general legal issues in HR, where some types of fairness are defined at the group level (adverse impact) and others are defined at the individual level (adverse treatment). Fairness in organizational settings is a complex issue that has been studied for almost a century. From these efforts arose rich, multifocal theories that offer different fairness definitions and situational contingencies for determining when fairness perceptions are likely. While the study of AI is relatively new compared to the organizational sciences, many similar themes are already emerging with respect to fairness theories and definitions. We offer below a brief overview of this emerging research.

FAIRNESS FROM THE AI PERSPECTIVE

Although one might readily dismiss concerns about different definitions of fairness as being unique to psychological and organizational settings, similar concerns have been noted with respect to ML and AI decision-making technologies (D'Amour et al., 2020; Green & Viljoen, 2020; Harrison et al., 2020; Robert et al., 2020). Historically, "algorithmic fairness is grounded in objectivity and neutrality. Fairness is treated as an objective concept, one that can be articulated and pursued without explicit normative commitments" (Green & Viljoen, 2020, p. 24). For instance, many mathematical definitions of AI fairness rely on what is most often called a confusion matrix, which is a two-by-two contingency table such as the one shown in Table 16.1. In such a table, the number of predicted positive and negative outcomes are contrasted against the number of actual positive and negative outcomes, most often with the objective of maximizing the number of true positives and true negatives. A common definition of fairness drawing from the confusion matrix is to maximize accuracy, which is given as the ratio of true positives and true negatives to all observations, given formulaically as $(TP + TN) / (TP + TN + FN + FP)$. For example, in the selection context, we would want to maximize the percentage of correct employment decisions (hired and performed well, not hired and would have performed poorly) relative to all applications. This mathematical approach to assessing fairness does allow some evaluation of the fairness of employment decisions from the distributive justice point of view at the group level (Robert et al., 2020).

Although accuracy may initially seem like an adequate fairness metric, its definition through the confusion matrix requires the transformation of continuous variables (the test scores) into a categorical variable (pass/fail, select/reject). In doing so, the actual relationship between the two variables is oversimplified and such oversimplification obscures meaningful fairness differences in the data, as shown in Figure 16.1. In the top panel of Figure 16.1, scores greater than 0 on cognitive ability were selected (i.e., the horizontal line is the cut score for cognitive ability) and individuals performing higher than 0 were considered successful (i.e., the vertical line is the cut score for successful performance), a decision rule resulting in accuracy of approximately 66 percent. While the bottom panel also has an accuracy of 66 percent, the cognitive ability cut score was set at −1 and the successful performance cut score was set at −0.5. One result of changing the cut scores is that the top panel has a false positive rate of approximately 18 percent but the bottom panel has a false positive rate of approximately 24 percent. While a difference of 6 percent in false positives might seem trivial in general, such a difference becomes much more meaningful were the hypothetical data in Figure 16.1 generated from two different sets of cut scores for selecting among neurosurgeons (i.e., a 6 percent increase in patient deaths could be quite meaningful). In such a case, the first set of decision rules (the top panel) would likely be viewed as much fairer than the second set of decision rules (the bottom panel) even though both situations produced nearly identical accuracy rates.

Table 16.1   Typical confusion matrix

	Predicted Bad Performer	Predicted Good Performer
Actual Good Performer	False Negatives (FN)	True Positives (TP)
Actual Bad Performer	True Negatives (TN)	False Positives (FP)

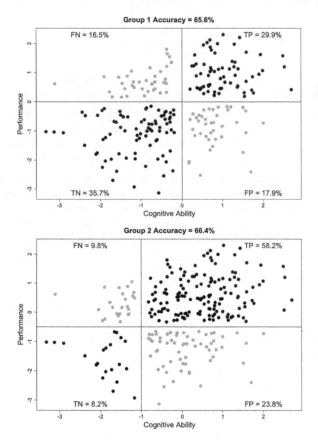

Figure 16.1   Confusion matrix example

This tendency to ignore context (e.g., selecting neurosurgeons vs. selecting writers) and oversimplify the situation in order to create a generalizable, situation-invariant metric is known as the universalism component of formal algorithmic definitions of fairness (see Green & Viljoen, 2020). There is evidence that people observing decisions made with such models perceive that maximizing accuracy may not be perceived as the fairest solution. For example,

Harrison et al. (2020) found that lay individuals prefer ML models with equal false-positive rates across demographic groups to models with equal accuracy rates across groups. Fair, in other words, may mean equal access to opportunities across groups more than equal distribution of outcomes between groups (see also Binns, 2018; Hardt et al., 2016).

Thus, we see that similar to the movement in HR to consider individual perceptions of fairness within particular contexts, the discipline of AI is starting to shift from seeking abstract and context-invariant views of fairness to seeking more concrete and context-sensitive views of fairness (Hutchinson & Mitchell, 2019). Whereas the very concept of an employment test's fairness was once defined mathematically, contemporary employment testing views acknowledge that the foundational aspect of a test's validity is the test's intended use and the scores' intended interpretation (AERA et al., 2014; Kane, 2013; Landy, 1986; Markus & Borsboom, 2013). A more general HR shift amounts to moving away from purely conceptualizing different types (e.g., distributional, procedural) of fairness that should be simultaneously maximized (i.e., the organizational justice view; Colquitt et al., 2001) to understanding the unique combination of individual and situational factors contributing to whether an action is fair, and for whom the consequences of the action are more or less fair (i.e., the social exchange view; Rupp et al., 2014). Within the context of AI, this shift amounts to moving away from formal, mathematical definitions of fairness to understanding the particular situations within which certain fairness tradeoffs are acceptable (e.g., increased false positive potential that also increases diversity; Allen et al., 2006; Green & Viljoen, 2020; Harrison et al., 2020).

APPROPRIATENESS OF AI-BASED DECISION MAKING IN HR

Defining fairness as the general appropriateness of an HR decision (Colquitt & Zipay, 2015) rather than equating it with justice calls for consideration of other judgments about the decision process beyond whether or not the specific justice rules have been followed. For example, research on stakeholder opinions of AI-based decision-making tools suggests that there is general recognition that they can be useful for making decisions quickly and consistently. However, there is also a widely reported perception of algorithm aversion (Berger et al., 2021; Burton et al., 2020; Harrison et al., 2020; Logg et al., 2019) that could lead to employees feeling that AI-based tools are inappropriate for use in HR decision making, thus leading to the negative reactions discussed in the justice and fairness literatures such as reduced intention to accept a job offer, lower job satisfaction and organizational commitment, or higher turnover intentions. Algorithm aversion is a broadly negative reaction to algorithms and a desire to avoid using them (Dietvorst et al., 2015). This aversion is aptly described by Edwards and Veale (2017), who noted "The public has only relatively recently become aware of the ways in which their fortunes may be governed by systems they do not understand, and feel they cannot control; and they do not like it" (p. 19). Algorithmic aversion is partially due to individual characteristics such as the standards for ethics and morality discussed by Leventhal (1980) and affective reactions to specific technologies, such as the construct of creepiness as a reaction to interaction with new technologies (Langer & König, 2018). Below we review several situational and technological characteristics that extend the specific scope of justice and fairness theories and are related to perceptions of the overall appropriateness of algorithmic decision making in HR.

Reliability and Accuracy. Research on algorithm aversion suggests that people are highly sensitive to the reliability and accuracy of algorithmic decision tools, such that they want to avoid algorithms after they observe the tool making an error (Dietvorst et al., 2015; Glikson & Woolley, 2020). Automated decision/action systems need to be very reliable before they can be highly automated (Parasuraman et al., 2000). Strohmeier and Piazza (2015) argue that AI technology should result in not just good decision quality, but an improvement over prior quality levels in order to justify use of AI in HR decision making.

Opacity. The extent to which people understand (or do not understand) AI-based algorithms is related to their acceptance of decisions made by such tools (Edwards & Veale, 2017). Some of this opacity is due to the technical knowledge required to understand how ML algorithms are trained and applied (Burrell, 2016; Kellogg et al., 2020). Opacity is also the result of companies intentionally obscuring how the algorithms work for purposes of maximizing value and competitive advantage (Burrell, 2016; Raghavan et al., 2020). For example, the vendors that market selection systems based on AI decision tools keep their tools proprietary as part of their business model. There have been calls for increasing transparency on the use of algorithms, revealing more information about how they work to the companies that wish to use them and the people about whom decisions are made (Raghavan et al., 2020; Robert et al., 2020). Transparency on how an algorithm works or how a particular decision was made has been found to increase trust across a variety of situations (Glikson & Woolley, 2020).

The HR decision-making literature has revealed some contrasting results on transparency. For example, Langer et al. (2018) found direct negative effects of information provided on organizational attractiveness, but positive indirect effects through perceptions of open treatment. Newman et al. (2020) found that increasing transparency by informing potential interviewees what an algorithm would be doing (i.e., evaluating both the content of their interview responses and their non-verbal cues) resulted in lower perceptions of fairness. However, trust in the algorithm was not assessed. Höddinghaus et al. (2021) demonstrated that transparency was related to trust in an automated decision agent, with higher levels of trust associated with positive fairness perceptions. Laurim et al. (2021) conducted interviews with potential job applicants, recruiters, and managers about the use of AI in recruiting and selection and found that all three stakeholder groups desired greater transparency, reporting that a better understanding of how the AI worked would help increase their trust in the tools. The movement toward algorithmic auditing is an effort to address opacity and increase trust in AI decisions by offering assurance from an objective third party that the algorithm is valid (Robert et al., 2020). We know from the justice literature that people pay more attention to justice and fairness when they experience uncertainty (Colquitt & Zipay, 2015), suggesting that if employees could reduce uncertainty by better understanding AI decision tools there could be fewer fairness concerns.

Control. Managers may lose power in decision making, or be completely removed from a decision process, when AI decision tools are implemented (Kellogg et al., 2020). This concern about control is aligned with the finding in the HR literature that hiring managers prefer clinical or expertise-based decision making over mechanical combination of information, as discussed above. Managers and employees may also make attributions about AI-based decision systems that impact their overall acceptance of such systems. Individuals make attributions about the reasons why organizations are implementing new HR systems, either commitment-focused attributions of service quality and employee well-being, or control-focused attributions of cost reduction and employee exploitation (Nishii et al., 2008).

If managers view that the AI decision system is there to help them improve decision-making quality and perhaps reduce their workload, then they are likely to view it positively and be more accepting of it. In contrast, if they perceive that the system is there to control them for the benefit of the organization, then they are likely to be less accepting of the system. From the applicant perspective, initial research suggests that interviewees may react negatively to highly automated interviews that incorporate AI because they perceive a lack of control over the situation, with less ability to influence the interviewer through social cues (Langer et al., 2019).

Task–Technology Fit. The concept of task–technology fit (Goodhue & Thompson, 1995) is important for the acceptance of AI-based decision agents (Strohmeier & Piazza, 2015). Research has generally shown that people are less likely to accept the decisions made if they perceive that there is a mismatch between the technology and the task. Machines or AI agents are considered more appropriate for technical or mathematical tasks such as analyzing large amounts of data, while humans are more appropriate for social tasks such as facilitating a team or evaluating the performance of an employee (Glikson & Woolley, 2020; Lee, 2018). Kim and Duhachek (2020) found in a series of laboratory studies that people were more accepting of (and persuaded by) AI agents when the system emphasized more concrete suggestions for *how* to perform a task (i.e., how to exercise or how to make soy milk at home) than when the system emphasized more abstract suggestions for *why* someone should perform a task (i.e., why exercise or why make soy milk at home). Thus, there was a match between the persuasive message offered by the AI agent and the perceived appropriateness of that message for an AI agent, resulting in greater intentions to engage in the behavior. However, when the AI was described with more human-like characteristics such as ability to learn or consciousness, this matching effect was reduced and AI agents were able to successfully persuade participants with the more abstract suggestions.

In line with Glikson and Woolley (2020), one explanation for these findings is that providing abstract arguments about *why* someone ought to do something is a purely social task that should be reserved for human (or human-like) agents. Such findings are important to consider in that one major advantage of AI often discussed is autonomous decision making requiring little to no human oversight (Parasuraman et al., 2000; Robert et al., 2020). As noted above, however, people may consider autonomy a fundamentally human characteristic (e.g., Ryan & Deci, 2000) and reserve such autonomous decision making only for human beings, particularly in social contexts or when stating why someone should make a particular decision or take an action.

One such example in an HR context is an employment interview where applicants are asked a series of questions or to perform a series of tasks that will be used to evaluate their employment qualifications. Many interview questions or tasks are inherently social in nature, for example how the interviewee would motivate others. Further, the process of interviewing has historically been a social process involving interpersonal interactions and mutual social influence. These factors suggest that interviewees are likely to expect some sort of social interaction during the interview, and that a human evaluator would be involved in determining if the candidate should be selected. In such situations, a fully autonomous AI would likely engender adverse applicant reactions or decision-maker reactions by creating a task–technology misfit between the social task (employment interview) and AI's more technical nature (Langer et al., 2019). These findings are supported by Lee (2018), who found that individuals perceived greater fairness for hiring and performance evaluation decisions made by a human decision maker than by an algorithm. Similarly, Newman et al. (2020) found that people preferred deci-sions made by humans over algorithmic decisions across a variety of HR functions (selection, promotion, layoffs), suggesting that algorithms are too reductionistic and it is more appropri-ate for such decisions to be made by humans.

User Expertise. Another individual characteristic than can affect perceptions of appropri-ateness for using algorithms is the level of user expertise in the relevant content domain. Logg et al. (2019) conducted a series of experiments comparing the extent to which people valued advice from an algorithm compared to advice from other people, consistently finding that for low-stakes decisions (e.g., determining the weight of someone in a photo, predicting the popularity of a song) people preferred to take advice from an algorithm. This effect, labeled algorithm appreciation in contrast to the earlier reviewed concept of algorithm aversion, held until participants were asked to make decisions about a topic area in which they had expertise, when they found that experts discounted both the advice offered by algorithms and the advice offered by other people. Interestingly, in this situation, even the experts had less accurate results in the decision-making task (Logg et al., 2019). This aligns with the research on man-agerial decision making for selection (Highhouse, 2008; Nolan et al., 2016), where managers prefer to make their own decisions on hiring rather than accept assistance from algorithms or computerized tools. When people lack expertise or view decisions outside of their own area of expertise, they are more likely to appreciate having an algorithm to assist them (Logg et al., 2019).

DISCUSSION

This chapter has focused on the fairness of HR decisions made by humans compared to the use of algorithmic decision tools for the same decisions. We have reviewed literature on justice and fairness in the HR and AI disciplines and examined a wide variety of features relevant to decision-making processes that affect perceptions of fairness both for the affected party and for the human decision maker. From what we see in practice, it is clearly acknowledged that human decision makers are fallible. They have biases, make errors in judgment, and fail to follow procedures that could enhance perceptions of fairness (Gilliland, 1993). And yet, people often prefer the judgments of humans over those of algorithmic decision-making tools that offer great potential for more consistency in decision making. It appears that we apply different standards to people and algorithms when determining what is fair and acceptable in HR decision making, often with a higher standard for the algorithms.

These different standards are related to the varying definitions and criteria for fairness evidenced in the AI and HR decision-making literatures. In the AI literature, fairness has been defined and operationalized from a mathematical viewpoint, optimizing outcomes given a set of clearly defined assumptions. In the HR literature, fairness is typically rooted in human emotions, reactions, and experiences. There is a focus on how individuals react to their expe-rience and what it means to them, regardless of (and sometimes in spite of) the math. Even when something is mathematically fair, given the stated assumptions, people may perceive a decision or experience as unfair based on their own expectations and individual differences. Creating an algorithm that could maximize the fairness perceptions of the hundreds or thou-sands of people in the pool for an HR decision is a very high standard indeed. The need to broaden definitions of fairness has been recognized in the AI research moving toward more context-sensitive definitions (Green & Viljoen, 2020; Harrison et al., 2020). The concept of algorithmic realism (Green & Viljoen, 2020) encourages computer scientists and engineers to consider the context in which the algorithm will be used to better determine the quality criteria, and even ask if an algorithm is the most appropriate intervention. This is consistent with the notion of task–technology fit (Glikson & Woolley, 2020; Lee, 2018; Strohmeier & Piazza, 2015) and its importance for the acceptance of AI-based decision agents. As long as applicants and employees believe it is more appropriate for humans to make decisions about hiring, promotion, performance evaluation, and discipline, this viewpoint suggests that algorithmic decisions will be considered inferior and unfair even if mathematically they produce superior results.

There are some logical reasons for why perhaps we should hold AI to a higher standard (Zerilli et al., 2019), particularly as it reaches higher levels of automation or autonomy. For example, autonomous AI decision agents can make decisions about many more people at one time than a human decision maker can. Second, autonomous AI decision agents cannot be held legally responsible or accountable for their decisions. Managers can be disciplined or fired if they make consistently unfair decisions about who to hire and who to fire. Finally, there are often procedures or committees in place to reduce human bias. Managerial decisions about who to promote or who should receive a raise are often reviewed by a larger group of managers and HR professionals for group-level fairness. This may not be the case for large numbers of decisions made by autonomous AI decision agents.

Part of this higher standard for AI is likely related to broader societal concerns for the impact of technology on our lives in unknown and unexpected ways (Orben, 2020). Orben calls this phenomenon technology panic, "in which the general population is gripped by intense worry and concern about a certain technology" (2020, p. 1144). One possibility for why we seem to be holding AI to a higher standard at this point in time is availability of information as a result of this intense concern about the impact of AI in general, and on workplace decisions specifically. A Google search of "AI decision making" results in hundreds of thousands of articles about how AI is being used in decision making in a variety of disciplines, with potentially inflammatory headlines such as "Is AI taking over?"[2] There may simply be more information available right now to the average person about concerns regarding AI decision making than unfair human decision making. Press coverage and social media coverage of AI certainly exceeds coverage of other potentially unfair HR decisions such as legal cases or U.S. Supreme Court cases.

Another way to frame the issue is to ask why people generally perceive that human unfairness is better, or at least more tolerable, than algorithmic unfairness. Consistency is one hallmark of algorithmic decision making and has been a key piece of organizational justice theory (Leventhal, 1980), but perhaps consistency is overrated as a desirable feature of HR decision making. Several recent research papers have concluded that people value some of the interpersonal and intrapersonal processes that lead to a lack of consistency in decision-making processes, such as social influence and opportunity for self-expression in interviews (Acikgoz et al., 2020; Langer et al., 2019) and qualitative analysis and contextualization (Newman et al., 2020).

We may accept a greater degree of inconsistency in human decision making because human decisions can be interpreted based on an actor's *intentions* (e.g., fairness theory, Folger & Cropanzano, 2001). If decision makers do something intentionally, they should be held responsible for those decisions, but if they intended to make a decision in good faith we are more accepting of unfair outcomes. For example, adverse treatment in selection is determined by the extent to which the organization knowingly and intentionally treats members of a protected class differently than members of the non-protected class. Adverse impact, on the other hand, is not necessarily intentional and thus may not be considered as unfair as adverse treatment. Adverse impact may be legally defensible if using a validated, job-related selection instrument, but adverse treatment is never legally defensible. If it can be determined that the decision maker was intentional, then it is more logical to assign blame and hold that person responsible for the unfair act or decision. Social exchange theory helps us identify when it is acceptable to break the justice rules in service of reaching a good decision. These judgments largely depend on the decision maker's intentions. For example, if humans were making employment screening decisions, they might decide to ignore the requirement for prior job experience if the applicant has other desirable characteristics such as belonging to an underrepresented demographic group or having graduated from the same university as the decision maker. The decision to keep the member of the underrepresented group in the pool could be viewed positively if the intention is to bring greater diversity into the work unit. The decision based on university affiliation could be viewed more negatively if the intention is to provide help to a friend's child who does not have the requisite job skills.

In contrast, AI systems do not have intentions, nor are they likely to in the foreseeable future, if at all (Floridi & Sanders, 2004; Sun, 2016; Hew, 2014). Given that AI and algorithms do not have intentionality, how can applicants or employees determine whether decisions made about them are fair? And how should they react if they judge an algorithmic decision to be unfair? Folger and Cropanzano suggested that "If no one is to blame, there is no social injustice" (2001, p. 1). However, we doubt that dissatisfied applicants or employees would simply shrug their shoulders and accept an otherwise unfair decision gracefully simply because there is no human decision maker to blame. Unfairness of algorithms could be attributed to the human programmers or designers (Martin, 2019), but applicants or employees are unlikely to trace blame all the way back to the programmers and will more likely assign blame to the managers associated with the assessment program. Counterfactual thinking associated with fairness theory could include thoughts that the managers should not be using these unproven and potentially biased computer programs, and this decision is unfair because if the assessment process had proceeded normally (with human assessors) then the employee would have gotten the promotion. However, due to algorithmic opacity, the managers themselves may not understand the algorithms used. As noted by Burrell (2016, p. 10), "the workings of machine learning algorithms can escape full understanding and interpretation by humans, even for those with specialized training, even for computer scientists." If organizational representatives (managers, human resource professionals, or information systems professionals) do not understand how a decision was made, they will probably be unaware if justice rules were broken and therefore unknowingly perpetuate unfair decision processes. Alternatively, employees could blame the organization as a whole, as it developed or purchased the AI agent.

In this context of high opacity and lack of intentionality, one potential path forward is to enhance fairness perceptions through greater trust in AI-based decision agents by giving them more human characteristics. For example, Kim and Duhachek (2020) found that people were more accepting of abstract recommendation messages by AI when they believed it had more human characteristics such as the ability to learn. This suggests that task–technology fit perceptions can be manipulated with how the AI is described to users, perhaps increasing fairness. Robert et al. (2020) also addressed the introduction of more human-like characteristics, raising the question of whether to add expression of emotion or regret in AI decision tools to enhance interactional justice. However, portraying AI decision tools as human may exacerbate the higher standards for AI that cannot be met, as "high expectations of anthropomorphic characters are designed to fail" (Glikson & Woolley, 2020, p. 645). It would be unwise to design AI tools for HR such that they enter into the "uncanny valley" that increases perceptions of creepiness (Caballar, 2019; Langer et al., 2019) and rejection of the technology. Another potential avenue is to explore how we can more effectively pair AI decision support technology with human oversight to combine the best aspects of both in some kind of assisted or augmented decision-making process (Burton et al., 2020), although that approach could reduce the decision-making efficiency of more automated decision making that is so attractive to organizations.

Future Research Directions

There are many exciting research opportunities ahead as we continue to study fairness in the context of algorithmic HR decision making. We observe that much of the literature has been experimental, with participants who imagine they are in the decision situation (e.g., reading a vignette, watching a video). Kaibel et al. (2019) asked participants to engage in some of the assessment procedures, but they were not truly applicants. While this experimental research has helped examine the effects of very specific conditions, we need to better capture the experiences of people really going through assessment and decision-making processes. This type of field research would be challenging, but would obviously be very helpful in understanding reactions of employees or applicants for whom these are truly high-stakes decisions. Research also has not looked at fairness perceptions for algorithms over time. Given the importance of errors in perceptions about AI decision making (Dietvorst et al., 2015), a longitudinal study such as that conducted by Konradt et al. (2017) on justice perceptions of more traditional selection processes would be useful moving forward.

More research is also needed on the different aspects of transparency. What are the different dimensions of transparency related to HR decision making and how much information should be provided? Existing studies have manipulated or measured transparency in a variety of ways (e.g., Höddinghaus et al., 2021; Langer et al., 2018; Newman et al., 2020). To move this research area forward, it would be helpful to identify the different facets of transparency that are related to HR algorithmic decision making such as the nature of the decision maker (e.g., independent algorithm, independent human, human advised by an algorithm), what will be evaluated, how the decision maker conducts the evaluation, and how the process compares to other methods of decision making. More consistent treatment of the transparency construct would help clarify its role in fairness perceptions.

Additionally, we need clarity on the actual role of algorithms and AI in the decision-making tools being used in both practice and research so that we can more effectively compare across studies. For example, some studies refer to automation in decision making (e.g., Höddinghaus et al., 2021) while others (e.g., Newman et al., 2020) specifically refer to AI. Langer et al. (2019) and Laurim et al. (2021) provide examples of clearly defining the technology used. We encourage all researchers to follow suit so we can better draw conclusions across studies.

Managerial Implications

As noted by other researchers in this area, managers need to take note of the varying perceptions of algorithms in HR decision making and actively address this in their decision-making
processes. Managers should participate in appropriate communication about the use of AI
in the decision-making process. While research findings have varied on this topic, overall it
appears that greater transparency about how algorithms are being used results in better fairness
perceptions (Köchling & Wehner, 2020). Efforts at transparency should reduce uncertainty in
order to enhance fairness perceptions (Colquitt & Zipay, 2015). Thus, simply informing job
applicants or employees that algorithms will be used is unlikely to create the intended effects.
More concrete information is likely needed about how information will be combined, how the
organization tries to ensure that the algorithm is fair and unbiased (e.g., describing validation
studies, external and impartial reviews of the process, algorithm audits) and if (or how) human
decision makers will be involved.

While we cannot expect that HR managers will become skilled in the training of AI algorithms, we can encourage managers or other professionals participating in development and
administration of HR decision processes to learn enough about AI to understand the processes,
be able to work with vendors, and ask good questions (Burton et al., 2020; Köchling &
Wehner, 2020; Tippins et al., 2021). This will help ensure that AI-facilitated systems meet
traditional standards for reliability, validity, and job relatedness. Further, organizations have
the ethical responsibility to ensure that the algorithmic decisions really are as good or better
than the human decisions, appropriately weighting criteria such as accuracy, fairness, and use
of resources such as the time of recruiters or managers (Martin, 2019; Strohmeier & Piazza,
2015).

Finally, managers should also make sure there is a mechanism in the decision-making
process to correct mistakes (Martin, 2019; Cheng & Hackett, 2021). This feature is part of
classic organizational justice theory (Leventhal, 1980) and should not disappear with the
implementation of algorithmic decision making. Even when algorithms function on a more
autonomous level, managers must maintain the ability to investigate and rectify mistakes in
order to improve perceptions of fairness. Research on algorithm aversion (Dietvorst et al.,
2015) demonstrates that people lose faith very quickly in algorithms when they make errors,
but showing that the human decision makers can still be responsive and perhaps even help the
algorithm learn could result in less algorithm aversion over time.

Conclusion

AI-based decision tools in HR are being implemented for operational efficiencies and often
with the promise of reduced bias and enhanced fairness. Evidence suggests there are still many
challenges in moving forward with the use of such technologies and in facilitating perceptions
of fairness on the part of people about whom decisions are being made, with AI tools currently
being held to a higher standard than human decision makers. For practice and future research
in this area, a definition of fairness as appropriateness that integrates aspects of organizational
justice theory and social exchange theory will likely help level the playing field.

NOTES

1. We distinguish between the application of mathematical and computational tools to solve social problems (e.g., HRM decision making) as artificial intelligence (AI) and the formal, mathematical study of computational algorithms that inform such social problem solving as machine learning (ML). While AI and ML overlap significantly, our emphasis in this chapter is on the former while acknowledging the latter through more general use of the word *algorithm* (e.g., AI algorithms, AI and associated algorithms).
2. We found this phrase in over 9,600 Google search result items on February 16, 2021.

REFERENCES

Acikgoz, Y., Davison, K. H., Compagnone, M., & Laske, M. (2020). Justice perceptions of artificial intelligence in selection. *International Journal of Selection and Assessment, 28*(4), 399–416.

Allen, C., Wallach, W., & Smit, I. (2006). Why machine ethics? *IEEE Intelligent Systems, 21*(4), 12–17.

American Educational Research Association (AERA), American Psychological Association (APA), & National Council on Measurement in Education (NCME). (2014). *The standards for educational and psychological testing*. AERA.

Berger, B., Adam, M., Rühr, A., & Benlian, A. (2021). Watch me improve – algorithm aversion and demonstrating the ability to learn. *Business and Information Systems Engineering, 63*, 55–68. https://doi.org/10.1007/s12599-020-00678-5

Binns, R. (2018). Fairness in machine learning: Lessons from political philosophy. *Proceedings of Machine Learning Research, 81*, 149–159.

Black, J. S., & van Esch, P. (2020). AI-enabled recruiting: What is it and how should a manager use it? *Business Horizons, 63*(2), 215–226.

Blacksmith, N., Willford, J. C., & Behrend, T. S. (2016). Technology in the employment interview: A meta-analysis and future research agenda. *Personnel Assessment and Decisions, 2*(1), 12–20. https://doi.org/10.25035/pad.2016.002

Burrell, J. (2016). How the machine "thinks": Understanding opacity in machine learning algorithms. *Big Data and Society, 3*(1). https://doi.org/10.1177/2053951715622512

Burton, J. W., Stein, M. K., & Jensen, T. B. (2020). A systematic review of algorithm aversion in augmented decision making. *Journal of Behavioral Decision Making, 33*(2), 220–239.

Caballar, R. D. (2019). What is the uncanny valley? *IEEE Spectrum*. Retrieved October 25, 2020, from https://spectrum.ieee.org/automaton/robotics/humanoids/what-is-the-uncanny-valley.

Carmody, C. (2015). Fairness as appropriateness: Some reflections on procedural fairness in WTO law. In A. Savarian & F. Fontanelli (Eds.), *Procedural fairness in international courts and tribunals*. British Institute for International and Comparative Law.

Cheng, M. M., & Hackett, R. D. (2021). A critical review of algorithms in HRM: Definition, theory, and practice. *Human Resource Management Review, 31*(1), Article 100698. https://doi.org/10.1016/j.hrmr.2019.100698

Colquitt, J. A., Conlon, D. E., Wesson, M. J., Porter, C. O., & Ng, K. Y. (2001). Justice at the millennium: A meta-analytic review of 25 years of organizational justice research. *Journal of Applied Psychology, 86*(3), 425–445.

Colquitt, J. A., & Rodell, J. B. (2015). Measuring justice and fairness. In R. Cropanzano and M. L. Ambrose (Eds.), *The Oxford handbook of justice in the workplace* (pp. 187–202). Oxford University Press.

Colquitt, J. A., Scott, B. A., Rodell, J. B., Long, D. M., Zapata, C. P., Conlon, D. E., & Wesson, M. J. (2013). Justice at the millennium, a decade later: A meta-analytic test of social exchange and affect-based perspectives. *Journal of Applied Psychology, 98*(2), 199–236.

Colquitt, J. A., & Zipay, K. P. (2015). Justice, fairness, and employee reactions. *Annual Review of Organizational Psychology and Organizational Behavior, 2*(1), 75–99.

D'Amour, A., Srinivasan, H., Atwood, J., Baljekar, P., Sculley, D., & Halpern, Y. (2020). Fairness is not static: Deeper understanding of long term fairness via simulation studies. In *Proceedings of the 2020*

Conference on Fairness, Accountability, and Transparency (pp. 525–534). ACM. https://doi.org/10.1145/3351095.3372878

Diab, D. L., Pui, S., Yankelevich, M., & Highhouse, S. (2011). Lay perceptions of selection decision aids in U.S. and non-U.S. samples. *International Journal of Selection and Assessment, 19*(2), 209–216.

Dietvorst, B. J., Simmons, J. P., & Massey, C. (2015). Algorithm aversion: People erroneously avoid algorithms after seeing them err. *Journal of Experimental Psychology: General, 144*(1), 114–126.

Edwards, L., & Veale, M. (2017). Slave to the algorithm? Why a "right to an explanation" is probably not the remedy you are looking for. *Duke Law and Technology Review, 16*(1), 18–84.

Eurostat (2017). *Persons killed in road accidents by type of vehicle (CARE data)* [Data file]. Retrieved June 15, 2020, from https://appsso.eurostat.ec.europa.eu/nui/show.do?dataset=tran_sf_roadve&lang=en.

Floridi, L., & Sanders, J. W. (2004). On the morality of artificial agents. *Minds and Machine, 14*, 349–379.

Folger, R., & Cropanzano, R. (2001). Fairness theory: Justice as accountability. In J. Greenberg & R. Cropanzano (Eds.), *Advances in Organizational Justice* (pp. 1–55). Stanford University Press.

Gilliland, S. W. (1993). The perceived fairness of selection systems: An organizational justice perspective. *Academy of Management Review, 18*(4), 694–734.

Glikson, E., & Woolley, A. W. (2020). Human trust in artificial intelligence: Review of empirical research. *Academy of Management Annals, 14*(2), 627–660. https://doi.org/10.5465/annals.2018.0057

Gonzalez, M. F., Capman, J. F., Oswald, F. L., Theys, E. R., & Tomczak, D. L. (2019). "Where's the I-O?" Artificial intelligence and machine learning in talent management systems. *Personnel Assessment and Decisions, 5*(3), Article 5. https://doi.org/10.25035/pad.2019.03.005

Goodhue, D. L., & Thompson, R. L. (1995). Task-technology fit and individual performance. *MIS Quarterly, 19*(2), 213–236.

Green, B., & Viljoen, S. (2020). Algorithmic realism: Expanding the boundaries of algorithmic thought. In *Proceedings of the 2020 Conference on Fairness, Accountability, and Transparency* (pp. 19–31). ACM.

Grove, W. M., & Meehl, P. E. (1996). Comparative efficiency of informal (subjective, impressionistic) and formal (mechanical, algorithmic) prediction procedures: The clinical–statistical controversy. *Psychology, Public Policy, and Law, 2*(2), 293–323.

Hardt, M., Price, E., & Srebro, N. (2016). Equality of opportunity in supervised learning. In *Advances in neural information processing systems* (pp. 3315–3323). ACM.

Harrison, G., Hanson, J., Jacinto, C., Ramirez, J., & Ur, B. (2020). An empirical study on the perceived fairness of realistic, imperfect machine learning models. In *Proceedings of the 2020 Conference on Fairness, Accountability, and Transparency* (pp. 392–402). ACM.

Hausknecht, J. P., Day, D. V., & Thomas, S. C. (2004). Applicant reactions to selection procedures: An updated model and meta-analysis. *Personnel Psychology, 57*(3), 639–683.

Hew, P. C. (2014). Artificial moral agents are infeasible with foreseeable technologies. *Ethics and Information Technology, 16*, 197–206.

Highhouse, S. (2008), Stubborn reliance on intuition and subjectivity in employee selection. *Industrial and Organizational Psychology, 1*(3), 333–342.

Höddinghaus, M., Sondern, D., & Hertel, G. (2021). The automation of leadership functions: Would people trust decision algorithms? *Computers in Human Behavior, 116*, Article 106635. https://doi.org/10.1016/j.chb.2020.106635

Hutchinson, B., & Mitchell, M. (2019). 50 years of test (un)fairness: Lessons for machine learning. In *Proceedings of the 2019 Conference on Fairness, Accountability, and Transparency* (pp. 49–58). ACM. https://doi.org/10.1145/3287560.3287600

Kaibel, C., Koch-Bayram, I., Biemann, T., & Mühlenbock, M. (2019). Applicant perceptions of hiring algorithms – uniqueness and discrimination experiences as moderators. In *Academy of Management Proceedings, 2019*(1). https://doi.org/10.5465/AMBPP.2019.210

Kane, M. T. (2013). Validating the interpretations and uses of test scores. *Journal of Educational Measurement, 50*(1), 1–73.

Kellogg, K. C., Valentine, M. A., & Christin, A. (2020). Algorithms at work: The new contested terrain of control. *Academy of Management Annals, 14*(1), 366–410.

Kim, T. W., & Duhachek, A. (2020). Artificial intelligence and persuasion: A construal-level account. *Psychological Science, 31*(4), 363–380.

Köchling, A., & Wehner, M. C. (2020). Discriminated by an algorithm: A systematic review of discrimination and fairness by algorithmic decision-making in the context of HR recruitment and HR development. *Business Research, 13*, 795–848.

Konradt, U., Garbers, Y., Böge, M., Erdogan, B., & Bauer, T. N. (2017). Antecedents and consequences of fairness perceptions in personnel selection: A 3-year longitudinal study. *Group and Organization Management, 42*(1), 113–146.

Kuncel, N. R., Klieger, D. M., Connelly, B. S., & Ones, D. S. (2013). Mechanical versus clinical data combination in selection and admissions decisions: A meta-analysis. *Journal of Applied Psychology, 98*(6), 1060–1072.

Landy, F. J. (1986). Stamp collecting versus science: Validation as hypothesis testing. *American Psychologist, 41*(11), 1183–1192. https://doi.org/10.1037/0003-066X.41.11.1183

Langer, M., & König, C. J. (2018). Introducing and testing the Creepiness of Situation Scale (CroSS). *Frontiers in Psychology, 9*, 1–17.

Langer, M., König, C. J., & Fitili, A. (2018). Information as a double-edged sword: The role of computer experience and information on applicant reactions towards novel technologies for personnel selection. *Computers in Human Behavior, 81*, 19–30.

Langer, M., König, C. J., & Papathanasiou, M. (2019). Highly automated job interviews: Acceptance under the influence of stakes. *International Journal of Selection and Assessment, 27*(3), 217–234.

Laurim, V., Arpaci, S., Promegger, B., & Krcmar, H. (2021). Computer, whom should I hire? – Acceptance criteria for artificial intelligence in the recruitment process. In T. X. Bui (Ed.), *Proceedings of the 54th Hawaii International Conference on System Sciences* (pp. 5495–5504). https://doi.org/10.24251/HICSS.2021.668

Lee, M. K. (2018). Understanding perception of algorithmic decisions: Fairness, trust, and emotion in response to algorithmic management. *Big Data and Society, 5*(1), 1–16.

Leventhal, G. S. (1980). What should be done with equity theory? New approaches to the study of fairness in social relationships. In K. Gergen, M. Greenberg, & R. Willis (Eds.), *Social exchange: Advances in theory and research* (pp. 27–55). Plenum.

Logg, J. M., Minson, J. A., & Moore, D. A. (2019). Algorithm appreciation: People prefer algorithmic to human judgment. *Organizational Behavior and Human Decision Processes, 151*, 90–103.

Markus, K. A., & Borsboom, D. (2013). *Frontiers of test validity theory: Measurement, causation, and meaning.* Routledge.

Martin, K. (2019). Ethical implications and accountability of algorithms. *Journal of Business Ethics, 160*(4), 835–850.

McCarthy, J. M., Bauer, T. N., Truxillo, D. M., Anderson, N. R., Costa, A. C., & Ahmed, S. M. (2017). Applicant perspectives during selection: A review addressing "So what?," "What's new?," and "Where to next?". *Journal of Management, 43*(6), 1693–1725.

National Highway Traffic Safety Administration (n.d.). *Fatality analysis reporting system/summary.* Retrieved June 15, 2020, from https://www-fars.nhtsa.dot.gov/Main/index.aspx.

Newman, D. T., Fast, N. J., & Harmon, D. J. (2020). When eliminating bias isn't fair: Algorithmic reductionism and procedural justice in human resource decisions. *Organizational Behavior and Human Decision Processes, 160*, 149–167.

Nishii, L. H., Lepak, D. P., & Schneider, B. (2008). Employee attributions of the "why" of HR practices: Their effects on employee attitudes and behaviors, and customer satisfaction. *Personnel Psychology, 61*(3), 503–545.

Nolan, K. P., Carter, N. T., & Dalal, D. K. (2016). Threat of technological unemployment: Are hiring managers discounted for using standardized employee selection practices? *Personnel Assessment and Decisions, 2*(1), Article 4. https://doi.org/10.25035/pad.2016.004

Orben, A. (2020). The Sisyphean cycle of technology panics. *Perspectives on Psychological Science, 15*(5), 1143–1157.

Orlikowski, W. J. (1992). The duality of technology: Rethinking the concept of technology in organizations. *Organization Science, 3*(3), 398–427.

Ötting, S. K., & Maier, G. W. (2018). The importance of procedural justice in human–machine interactions: Intelligent systems as new decision agents in organizations. *Computers in Human Behavior*, *89*, 27–39.

Parasuraman, R., Sheridan, T. B., & Wickens, C. D. (2000). A model for types and levels of human interaction with automation. *IEEE Transactions on Systems, Man, and Cybernetics – Part A: Systems and Humans*, *30*(3), 286–297.

Plotkin, H. (1993). *Darwin machines and the nature of knowledge.* Harvard University Press.

Raghavan, M., Barocas, S., Kleinberg, J., & Levy, K. (2020, January). Mitigating bias in algorithmic hiring: Evaluating claims and practices. In *Proceedings of the 2020 Conference on Fairness, Accountability, and Transparency* (pp. 469–481).

Robert, L. P., Pierce, C., Marquis, L., Kim, S., & Alahmad, R. (2020). Designing fair AI for managing employees in organizations: A review, critique, and design agenda. *Human–Computer Interaction*, *35*(5–6), 545–575. https://doi.org/10.1080/07370024.2020.1735391

Rupp, D. E., Shao, R., Jones, K. S., & Liao, H. (2014). The utility of a multifoci approach to the study of organizational justice: A meta-analytic investigation into the consideration of normative rules, moral accountability, bandwidth-fidelity, and social exchange. *Organizational Behavior and Human Decision Processes*, *123*, 159–185.

Ryan, R. M., & Deci, E. L. (2000). The darker and brighter sides of human existence: Basic psychological needs as a unifying concept. *Psychological Inquiry*, *11*(4), 319–338.

Strohmeier, S. (2020). Algorithmic decision making in HR. In T. Bondarouk & S. Fisher (Eds.), *Encyclopedia of electronic HRM* (pp. 54–59). DeGruyter.

Strohmeier, S., & Piazza, F. (2015). Artificial intelligence techniques in human resource management – a conceptual exploration. In C. Kahraman & S. Ç. Onar (Eds.), *Intelligent techniques in engineering management* (pp. 149–172). Springer.

Suen, H. Y., Chen, M. Y. C., & Lu, S. H. (2019). Does the use of synchrony and artificial intelligence in video interviews affect interview ratings and applicant attitudes? *Computers in Human Behavior*, *98*, 93–101.

Sun, R. (2016). *Anatomy of the mind: Exploring psychological mechanisms and processes with the Clarion cognitive architecture.* Oxford University Press.

The Society for Industrial and Organizational Psychology (SIOP). (2018). Principles for the validation and use of personnel selection procedures. *Industrial and Organizational Psychology: Perspectives on Science and Practice*, *11*(Supl. S1), 1–97. https://doi.org/10.1017/iop.2018.195

Tippins, N. T., Oswald, F., & McPhail, S. M. (2021). *Scientific, legal, and ethical concerns about AI-based personnel selection tools: A call to action.* https://psyarxiv.com/6gczw/

World Health Organization (2020). *World Health Data Platform: Road safety* [Data file]. Retrieved June 15, 2020, from https://www.who.int/gho/road_safety/mortality/en/.

Zerilli, J., Knott, A., Maclaurin, J., & Gavaghan, C. (2019). Transparency in algorithmic and human decision-making: Is there a double standard? *Philosophy and Technology*, *32*, 661–683. https://doi.org/10.1007/s13347-018-0330-6

17. Accountability of artificial intelligence in human resources

Katharina A. Zweig and Franziska Raudonat

INTRODUCTION

Accountability is a term with multiple facets, but essentially it is about how to find the person or institution responsible for a desired or undesired outcome by using an artificial intelligence (AI) system, regardless of whether the result was intended or not.

In this chapter, we will review the problem of assuring the accountability of "algorithmic decision-making systems", or ADM systems, that are used in human resources (HR) (cf. Strohmeier, 2020) or other work and personnel-related areas in a very broad sense, for example training or support of unemployed people.

In general, ADM systems are software systems that contain algorithms which turn data into a single real number that can be interpreted as scoring or classification. The mechanism by which such an algorithm computes a decision can include human-made decision rules, compiled into a so-called *expert system* or *ontology*[1] (see CHAPTER 8). However, those algorithms based on human decision rules are, due to their construction, in most cases well inspectable and thus accountability is achieved rather easily. Therefore, in this chapter, we focus on ADM systems used in HR that are based on a learned or learning component (see CHAPTER 2). We further restrict ourselves to ADM systems built through *supervised learning*, that is, those in which the statistical model is built based on a training data set with given cases and known results, for example a data set of applications for which it is known whether the applicants were finally successfully recruited.

Furthermore, the term "ADM system" comprises more than just the algorithm: It encompasses the data it was trained on, the method by which it abstracted the decision rules, and all modeling decisions that went into its development and employment, from the selection of data, data cleaning, feature engineering (Zheng & Casari, 2018), the chosen machine learning (ML) method and its precise parameter settings, to the choices made on the quality and the fairness measure by which it was evaluated, to the way feedback is used to evolve the system (Zweig, 2019).

Next to the internal information, which can only be assessed at the system level, there is also the need to understand the interaction between the ADM system and the social process it is embedded in. In this sense, we do not distinguish between an algorithm that only supports a human's decision and one which decides "itself". We define that an algorithm makes a decision "itself" if it triggers some action that has an influence on the person being scored or categorized. One reason to include both uses of a decision-making algorithm is that people may not be independent enough to reject the machine's result. Explanations for this include people in the loop not being adequately trained or powerful incentives to use the machine's decision. A strong reliance on the machine's decision is called *automation bias* (Mosier et al., 1998) and this can lead to *omission* and *commission errors*, that is, overlooking a problem because the system did not warn of it or following the machine's decision even though other systems have warned of it (Skitka, Mosier, & Burdick, 1999). Another reason is that the socio-technical system has to be considered in any case (Zweig, Fischer, & Lischka, 2018; Wieringa, 2020) to evaluate the machine's long-term consequences, that is, to conduct a technology assessment. With this, we now define the term of *accountability*.

ACCOUNTABILITY

Accountability is often used synonymously with transparency (Ball, 2009), and sometimes explainability is considered as a prerequisite for an accountable system (see CHAPTER 15). While both might help to achieve accountability, we follow Wieringa's proposal to lay the foundation of accountability in AI systems.

In her extensive review on the usage of the term accountability in AI, Wieringa (2020) links it to the accountability theory as defined by Bovens (2007):

> Accountability is a relationship between an actor and a forum, in which the actor has an obligation to explain and to justify his or her conduct, the forum can pose questions and pass judgement, and the actor may face consequences.

With this definition, the relationship between *explainability, transparency*, and *accountability* for the use of AI in HR is given as follows: The actor in this definition is a natural or a legal person, for example a person working in HRM (human resource management) or the company itself. The actor is not the machine. In Bovens' definition, he requires that the actor can explain his or her behavior, that is, there needs to be some *explainability* of the person's decision. We thus conclude that the use itself must also be justified, but it does not need an explainable AI system. The forum consists of natural or legal persons but can also contain human institutions like courts, unions, or nongovernmental organizations (NGOs). To ensure that such a forum can pass judgment, we interpret that the definition also requires sufficient *transparency* about the whole process of decision-making, including information regarding the machine's results, to enable this judgment. Thus, the transparency required in using such a system must be consistent with the forum's knowledge to enable an informed decision about possible consequences. Explainability, however, is not necessarily required at all in this definition. Nevertheless, it might be helpful to inform the forum about details of the ADM system.

It is obvious that a company applying an ADM system to support its HR processes becomes an actor in the above sense, accountable to a forum, for example to prove the legitimacy of a hiring decision. One justification could be that the software company asserted a high accuracy of their software's results. In this case, the software company becomes an actor accountable to the company and has to prove that the results of their software are reliable enough to support HR processes. The software company itself might be dependent on the training data it has received from another actor who needs to be accountable for it. We conclude that designing, developing, and operating an ADM system in HR depends on the decisions of multiple actors who have multiple accountability relationships with each other.

Wieringa (2020) mentions that different forums might be necessary. Her review proposes to define the various actors, forums, and their accountability relationships, as well as the associated criteria and consequences of accountability, based on the software development life cycle (e.g. Tsui & Karam, 2011). Wieringa divides the various steps of the software development life cycle into three phases: *ex ante*, *in medias res*, and *ex post*. She also points out questions that should be asked in the different phases to identify, in addition to the actors, the relevant forums, their relationship, and the criteria against which accountability could be measured. In an extensive study of where errors can occur when machines make or support decisions, Zweig, Fischer, and Lischka (2018) provided answers to some of the questions posed by Wieringa using the so-called *Long Chain of Responsibilities*,[2] in which they also named the responsible actors. While this *Long Chain of Responsibilities* details the process of developing an ADM system, there also needs to be a clear picture of the different actors when the ADM system is deployed. The next section outlines the combination of different subprocesses in the software development life cycle and the most common actors for each of these in the *Long Chain of Responsibilities*.

LONG CHAIN OF RESPONSIBILITIES

The *Long Chain of Responsibilities* groups the different tasks of the development process of a ML system. It assigns the different tasks in this process to different actors and can therefore be used as a structure to define different accountability relationships. As mentioned above, the development and deployment of an ADM system is a socio-cultural artifact that needs to be considered as a socio-technical system (cf. Wieringa, 2020). Understanding and evaluating its consequences thus requires making all actors in its development and deployment accountable for their contribution. The *Long Chain of Responsibilities* was shaped by Zweig, Fischer, and Lischka (2018) to describe the different groups of actors responsible for the process of developing and deploying an ADM system (see Table 17.1).

The development of a ML process starts with data collection and selection (see CHAPTER 2). The data collection is often done by a domain specialist – in the case of a ML project in HR, this will in many cases be the company that wants to use AI in its HR processes. If a pre-trained system is used, the data collection can also be done at least partially by a software developer. In both cases, the data collectors make decisions on what to measure and what to store, even if they may not be experts in the field of application. In the *data selection* phase, the so-called *features* of the model are determined, that is, those properties of, for example, applicants that will become the basis for the scoring or classification result.

Some of the features can easily be measured objectively, for example whether a person has a degree in a certain field of study or how many years an employee has worked in the same company.[3] Often, however, a feature represents a so-called *operationalization*. Whenever someone defines how to measure a salient social concept (like "rate of success in a given job" or "education fits the job description"), this definition is said to be an *operationalization*. While such features can end up taking the form of percentages or a number on a Likert scale, they entail many modeling decisions which need accountability as well.

The accountability for decisions made on data selection, data manipulation,[4] and operationalization is not yet well researched. In this respect it is important to note that there is no such thing as "raw data" (Brine & Poovey, 2013). Any measurement made and any data stored follows the decision of a human to measure and store it; thus, it contains a value decision on the importance of that data. Next to this very basic observation, more complex operations incorporate even more values of the data scientists into the ADM system. Examples are feature engineering, the imputation of missing data, any kind of balancing data from different minorities, or the decision to take something easy to measure as a proxy for something difficult to define and measure. The most obvious decisions that show how values are infused into an ADM system are so-called *operationalizations*, the decisions on how to measure socially salient concepts. A simple example of such an operationalization is how a company would define a "successful hire". The best quality-ensuring process would likely be a thorough assessment of the candidates by their colleagues and their supervisors. However, either these assessments already contain a set of simplifying operationalizations, like Likert scales, or they result in unstructured text that is difficult to integrate into ML. An easy proxy, that is, a value that is supposed to be correlated with the difficult concept, could be the question whether a person has received a salary raise since being hired. Depending on the policy of salary increases, the ratio of women and men in different positions in a company, and whether men and women take parental leave comparably often and for approximately the same amount of time, such a proxy could favor one gender over the other. Although such a choice is likely to be made without bad intentions, data scientists correlate salary raises with success and overlook the fact that this correlation could differ by gender.

In the broader area of ADM systems in the social system (e.g. management of unemployment by the state) or education, other players could collect and curate the data, for example governmental institutions or schools and universities. All of these could become actors for the people depending on the decisions based on those data in later phases of the development and deployment of the ADM system.

In parallel with the data collection, new ML methods are being invented by researchers and implemented either by them or by data scientists. Data scientists have become a crucial new group in these projects. They select the ML method and the data that comprises the training and test data set. Since all models contain assumptions, certain conditions are already set with the choice of the model. Additionally, almost all methods of ML come with several parameters, and the team of data scientists finally decides what values these parameters will take. Often, the team also decides on the quality and fairness measure by which the trained decision system is evaluated. The training process of the ADM system is iterative: As long as the desired threshold for the selected quality measure is not reached, changes are made to parameters. In some cases, the input data can also be combined to arrive at more complex features, a process known as *feature engineering* (Zheng & Casari, 2018).

As the quality measure is the guideline for the improvement process, it is crucial to choose it according to the application of the ADM system. As Zweig and Krafft (2018) have shown, there are different quality measures and some of them work best in scenarios where only a few candidates need to be compared to each other (e.g. ROC AUC), while others optimize a scoring algorithm when the best k candidates need to be identified from a large number of candidates (e.g. positive predictive value among the first k predictions, PPV_k). In most cases, the model cannot be trained optimally for both types of selection processes. Identifying the best possible quality measure for the ADM system is therefore of utmost importance. The future operators of the system can either make this decision themselves or, if the data scientists make it for them, the latter must justify why they have chosen the particular quality measure.

Next to the quality, it has to be considered that the decisions made by an ADM system have to be as fair as possible towards all subgroups of a population, for example people of different genders, ethnicities, or religions (see CHAPTER 16). Again, decision-making is of crucial importance. The case of a recidivism risk assessment system called COMPAS by Northpointe Inc. has shown that society can have a different opinion on what a fair system's decision should look like. In a black-box analysis by a team of journalists led by Julia Angwin (Angwin et al., 2016), Afro-Americans were found to suffer more from false-positive decisions than white Americans. When held accountable, it turned out that the software company Northpointe Inc. had chosen a fairness measure which ensured that within a risk class, all groups would eventually have the same recidivism rates. It was later shown that some fairness measures cannot be optimized at the same time (Kleinberg, 2018). Hence, the choice of the fairness measure by which the final decision is made is a decision that needs to be made in an accountable way to reduce harm.

Finally, all actors involved must be held accountable if profound violations of individual rights are identified or if – especially in the case of AI in HR – a disparate impact on groups with sensitive properties protected by the law, such as gender, religion, or age, is reported. But it is probably neither very efficient to identify all possible actors in hindsight, nor practical to discuss accountability aspects with all of them simultaneously, for example in a legal forum. It has been proposed (Krafft, Zweig, & König, 2020) that the main accountable actor from a socio-informatic perspective could be the one who deploys the ADM system in question. This does not mean that this institution or person should be accountable for all decisions in the development process. However, it is the person who is easily identifiable and who can control the accountability process in the sense of a chain of responsibility.

In the broader environment in which the ADM system is applied, three other roles appear, that of the candidate, the data assistant, and the final decision-maker, all of which need to be taken into account, with the pairwise accountability relationships between them being important, as discussed below.

LARGER PICTURE OF THE SOCIO-TECHNICAL SYSTEM USING AN ADM SYSTEM

As already discussed by Wieringa (2020), it is not sufficient to only analyze the different accountabilities resulting from decisions of the ADM system. On the contrary, the embedding of decisions into the whole social process of concern must also be taken into account (cf. Zweig, 2019).

Five Role Model

In general, there can be up to five roles in the socio-technical system created by using an ADM system in HR (for a generalized discussion, see Krafft, Zweig, & König, 2020). Next to the already discussed developer team consisting of researchers, data-providing institutions, and data scientists, as well as the operator, this broader picture brings three new roles into perspective: that of the candidate; that of a possible data assistant, who helps with the input of the candidate's data into the system; and that of the final decision-maker. All persons instantiating a role can be part of either the set of actors or the forum or both in different situations. For example, the operator of the ADM system who prescribes or offers its usage is an actor. However, with respect to the developer team, the company that applies the system is also part of a forum that holds the developers accountable. Similarly, the person who enters the data of a candidate into the system (the data assistant) is an actor who is accountable for some parts of the process and may also be part of a forum while understanding the importance of correct input to decide on borderline cases in it. The person entering the data is possibly distinct from the human-in-the-loop (cf. Citron & Pasquale, 2014, for a typology) who makes a final decision based at least in part on the outcome of the ADM system (see Table 17.2). But the data assistant is an actor who needs to be held accountable, for example by the operator of the ADM system, as well. However, the decision-makers also need to be part of a forum that holds the operator and the developer team accountable for the way the machine's result is computed and how it is brought into the process of decision-making.

In this review, we argue that from a socio-informatic perspective the main responsible actor of an ADM system used in HR should be the operator of the system. This could be an employer or the state making decisions about unemployed people. The person who is to be decided on is the candidate. The decision-maker is the human-in-the-loop making a final decision on the candidate, based on the outcome of the ADM system. The ADM system is developed by a developer team from whom the operator acquires it. In many cases, the person typing in the candidate's data is neither the candidate nor the decision-maker; however, in some cases, the candidate or the decision-maker enters the data into the system. The relationship is further complicated by the fact that the operator leaves some decisions regarding the final design of the ADM system to the developer team and at the same time delegates decisions about the candidate to decision-makers, for example people working in HRM or headhunters. This delegation can be modeled by the principal–agent theory, as discussed by Krafft, Zweig, and König (2020) in a different context. Table 17.1 gives an overview of the different roles and specific aspects of the respective accountability relationships between them.

Table 17.1   *Possible accountability relationships between different roles in the socio-technical system using an ADM system to make decisions about people*

Accountability from → to	Operator	Developer	Decision-maker	Data assistant	Candidate
Operator	–	Requirements, communication of decision rules	Delegation, communication of decision rules	Delegation	Lawful decision
Developer	E.g. truthful implementation, documentation, optimal decision transparency, explainability, reproducibility of results	–	E.g. transparency, explainability, reproducibility of results	Documentation of input types	Optimal decisions
Decision-maker	Best possible decision as an agent for the principal	–	–	–	Lawful and optimal decision
Data assistant	Truthful input	–	Truthful input	–	Truthful input
Candidate	Truthful insight into data	–	Truthful insight into data	Truthful insight into data	–

Combining the Different Process Models

In the following, we will show that the *Long Chain of Responsibilities* can be understood as a refinement of Wieringa's process structure. It can thus help to distribute the different components of accountability in a more detailed way.

In Wieringa's view, the *ex ante* phase includes processes of domain understanding, data understanding, and, as its prerequisite, data collection. For example, data preparation, model generation, and model evaluation belong to the *in medias res* considerations. The model application as well as the resulting adaptations to the system are finally part of the *ex post* considerations (Table 17.2). Based on the questions collected by Wieringa, we will discuss below which actor–forum relationships are relevant in the HR domain and which accountability relationships exist in each case.

Table 17.2   *HR process model and Long Chain of Responsibilities divided into three phases*

Wieringa (2020)	HR process model by Strohmeier (2020)	*Long Chain of Responsibilities* by Zweig, Fischer, and Lischka (2018)	
phases	tasks	subprocess	possible actors
ex ante	domain understanding and data understanding	data collection, data selection	operator, other company/government, data scientists
		operationalization	operator, data scientists
		choice of quality and fairness measure	operator, data scientists
		method selection	data scientists
in medias res	data preparation, model generation, and model evaluation	choice of parameter values	data scientists
		data selection, operationalization	data scientists
		feature engineering	data scientists
		model evaluation (quality measures, fairness measures)	operator, data scientists
		interpretation of results	operator, likely by delegation to employee
ex post	model application and feedback loop	decision of action	operator, likely by delegation to employee
		feedback	operator, data scientists

In principle, the actors of one phase or subprocess are accountable to those using their results. Therefore, any pair of subprocesses with a change of actor can lead to a new accountability relationship. Before discussing those, we need to make a last distinction between explicit and embedded software development.

Accountability in Explicit and Embedded Software Development Processes

As illustrated by the process model for ML in HR (see CHAPTER 2, Figure 2.1), all the steps of the process can occur in the company (explicit process) or the essential steps can be carried out by a software provider (embedded process). In cases where both processes occur within the software development, it is then possible to expand the concept to include the accountability that arises from the involvement of a third party. All questions that arise within the organization can also be transferred to an embedded process, but there will be a need for additions and tightening. For example, it is necessary to ensure that the values of the organization are taken into account by the service provider during development (e.g. Saurwein, Just, & Latzer, 2015).

IDENTIFYING POSSIBLE ACCOUNTABILITY RELATIONSHIPS IN THE DEVELOPMENT AND DEPLOYMENT OF ADM SYSTEMS

We have now discussed different process models: the simple one by Wieringa with three phases, namely, *ex ante*, *in medias res*, and *ex post*; and the more detailed one consisting of the *Long Chain of Responsibilities* in the development of the ADM system and the five-role model in the deployment phase. We have furthermore referred to Strohmeier's process model of ML in HR (see CHAPTER 2, Figure 2.1). Real development and deployment processes can be organized with respect to any of these models and to the main actors who are active in the respective phase. In those cases, where more than one distinct actor is involved, it may be necessary to detail the structure such that each subprocess is clearly assigned to one actor. Bear in mind that an "actor" can also be a team or an external company as long as this is the best organizational unit to take responsibility for the outcome of the subprocess.

Once this assignment is made, accountability relationships need to be established whenever the actors change from one subprocess to another. Since the different applications of AI in HR can be very diverse, we will outline below the most likely actors and forums for a typical application, that is, one in which employees or applicants are scored or classified by an ADM system with a human decision-maker who makes the final decision.

Actors

In an explicit process, all the steps of process development occur in the company, but different actors are involved. Currently, very few HR managers have the necessary expertise to carry out the data preparation or the development of the ML models themselves. Even for the application of the ML software, the acquisition of additional technical expertise is required (e.g. Knobloch & Hustedt, 2019). Actors can therefore act as developers (often data scientists) or as users (employees in the personnel department, i.e. those who apply the ADM system operationally) and, in addition, as decision-makers (management level) (cf. Wieringa, 2020).

In the phase of *ex ante* consideration of the ML model, data scientists act as developers who, with the help of HRM specialists, have to form a picture of the tasks to be completed and the objectives to be met. Based on this picture, they can derive the required input data and suitable algorithms for modeling, that is, requirements engineering (e.g. Pohl, 2010). Depending on whether the decision of the algorithm and the data basis is left to the data scientist, or whether these decisions are (co-)made by a higher authority, the data scientist can also act as a decision-maker in addition to his/her developer role. An additional decision-maker (e.g. head of HRM) can take this role as well.

If the subprocesses, as defined in the *Long Chain of Responsibilities*, are even more dispersed across different parts of the company, there could be more actors, especially in the data collection and the operationalization of important concepts. Such concepts are, for example, satisfaction with the work of an employee or categorization of the knowledge and experience of an employee. These additional actors would then be accountable to the data scientists working with this database.

In the following phase *in medias res*, a similar picture emerges. While the manipulation of the data, the partitioning of the test data, or the choice of quality measures (see CHAPTER 2) can be carried out autonomously by the data scientist, the management level can also set the parameters here, as discussed above. The more decisions the developer makes, the more responsibility he/she takes for the process and the more important it is that this person becomes aware of his/her moral responsibility in the process (Martin, 2019).

In the *ex post* consideration of the development of the ML model, the users finally appear as actors in the system. In the HR context, the company itself is the legal person that makes decisions, for example to hire or promote someone. However, this decision-making is delegated to the employees of the company, for example the employees of the HRM department. Currently, the most common approaches in HR are in the area of support systems (human-in-the-loop). It must therefore be ensured that the supported decision-makers know how to deal with the decisions of the system, especially if their own expertise leads them to a different decision. At this point, they can act to a limited extent as decision-makers. Or if they are not qualified to do so or overwhelmed with the decision, they can pass it to their superiors, which again results in a switch of actors. It is also up to them to decide whether a system needs to be revised. As shown, the following actors can act in the appropriate roles in the context of HR (Table 17.3).

Table 17.3   *Roles of actors in the HR context*

Roles of actors	Management	Data scientist/ Software developer	Employees in HRM
Decision-maker	x	x	x
Developer		x	
User			x

Forums and Accountability Relationships

Before defining accountability criteria, it must first be determined which groups (forums) the actors are accountable to (cf. Wieringa, 2020). While the actors of a system can easily be identified based on the development process of the model, this is only partly true for the forums. Wieringa, therefore, suggests approaching this problem in the *ex ante* phase, with the question "who is affected?". Basically, in the HR context, employees, applicants, and unions are crucial forums, as they are directly affected by the decisions of the model. However, other forums such as the company itself, society, competitors, suppliers, customers, competitors, politics, or the government are also conceivable if they have an interest in the processes of the company (Leicht-Deobald et al., 2019; Bovens, 2007). Bovens (2007) distinguishes five different types of accountability relationships: political, legal, administrative, professional, and social relationships. In the domain of HR, political accountability relationships that also give affected people the opportunity to address violations through legal channels and social relationships seem to be the most relevant. Additionally professional relationships, for example in an audit community of companies, could lead to a nonobligatory way to establish accountability processes (e.g. Kemper & Kolkman, 2019).

While most people only notice the application of a ML model when it is in use, it is still important to focus on when the forums are relevant within the development process. In the moment when a person wants to make the operator of an ADM system accountable for a possibly wrong or even illegal decision-making, it is too late to organize the accountability structure. For example, discrimination of certain candidate groups can be based on incomplete or biased data, the wrong ML method, the wrong quality/fairness measure, or wrong decision-making by humans based on a wrong interpretation of the machine's results. To understand who is accountable, every change of the actors is likely a good place for an accountability relationship with the actor of the next subprocess, as we already mentioned above. Finally, the management level can obtain justifications from developers and users for the decisions made regarding the ML model, and check if they fit with company norms and values.

To ensure a smooth process, it is good practice to involve unions or the staff council early in the development process as part of a forum for the deployment of the ADM system (see CHAPTER 19). However, at this early stage it is unlikely that any members of the staff council will be able to foresee all potential consequences; rather, this process needs to be repeated at various points. Further research is needed to identify how best to structure the involvement of unions and staff councils in the development and usage of ADM systems.

Finally, external accountability might need to be established: Employees and applicants who come into direct contact with the ML model have a right to an explanation according to the General Data Protection Regulation of Europe (EU GDPR) (European Parliament and Council of European Union, 2016) if the decision is fully automated (see CHAPTER 18). The state could demand the fulfillment of transparency criteria in the form of a political accountability relationship or systematic use of benchmarks, evaluations, or black-box tests to learn more about the ML model behavior (cf. Diakopoulos, 2016). On the other hand, networks could be established with other companies within which the ML models are mutually audited.

EXAMPLE OF DEFINING ACCOUNTABILITY RELATIONSHIPS

In the last years, we have tried hard to find companies that would talk to us about their usage of AI in HR – and could not find any. In a survey we conducted together with the German Association for Human Resource Management (DGFP), 93 percent of the companies that responded said they were positive about the usage of AI in HR, but only 3 percent said they already use it in their company (Borgert & Zweig, 2019). Internationally, there have been some scandals around AI systems used in HR processes like hiring. Since they were only anecdotal and no official report has been released by the companies involved, we won't repeat them here. Instead, we want to give an example of how accountability can be organized around the use of an ADM system in a related area. The Austrian Public Employment Service supports unemployed people and has recently deployed a very simple logistic regression to categorize unemployed people into three different classes: those who are likely to find a job quickly, those who are very unlikely to find any job in the future, and the rest (Holl, Kernbeiß, & Wagner-Pinter, 2018). The software was designed by SynthesisForschung. Together with its software, the company published a technical report that communicates very transparently various choices in the software development process (Holl, Kernbeiß, & Wagner-Pinter, 2018). In addition, a set of rules for "social acceptability" (*Sozialverträglichkeitsregeln*) was published by the company (Holl, Kernbeiß, & Wagner-Pinter, 2019). These rules encompass requirements that data scientists need to fulfill, for example to only use features that are causally related to the prediction and that can be explained to a candidate. One rule requires the operator of the system to recompute the statistical model every year to make sure that it contains the most current information. Other rules refer to the recruitment phase, with the company stating that the result of the ADM system needs to be discussed with the candidate and that the human decision-maker needs to be able to overwrite the classification by the system at any time. However, in this case, the company wants to have feedback on why the human decision-maker made a different decision to feed this information back into the next development round of the model (Klingel, Krafft, & Zweig, 2020).

While none of these rules specifies explicitly an accountability relationship in the sense it is used by Bovens, most are clearly assigned to an actor. However, all of them can be turned into such an accountability relationship by defining a forum and a process by which the latter can hold the actors accountable. While the application of the resulting model is heavily discussed and currently lacks a legal basis (Hierländer, 2020), the transparency of the statistical model and the addition of the *social acceptability rules* mentioned in this example could be one step towards the development and deployment of ADM systems in an accountable way.

FUTURE RESEARCH

Society, politics, and science have just started to investigate the implications resulting from employing AI in HR, especially the accountability for the high number of necessary decisions and the diffusion of responsibility for those decisions in the software development. Disciplinary and interdisciplinary research in different areas will be needed to fully flesh out the concept of accountable AI in HR. Social, legal, and technical sciences will have to combine their knowledge to identify those processes that enable accountable AI in HR. In the following we outline three directions that further research could take.

In order to make ADM systems accountable, the problems identified concerning the basis of data selection, data manipulation, and operationalization need to be addressed first. There is not yet a comprehensive framework to help data scientists identify their own subjective choices in all these operations, to communicate their choices to others in the process, or to deduce the possible harm inflicted by these decisions. In a very confined field of data science called *complex network analysis*, initial considerations on the choice of an operationalization, a measure, and an application have been made under the term *network analysis literacy* (Zweig, 2016). It is time to search for similar frameworks in the broader context of data science and ML. The same holds true for the data basis itself: More research is necessary to identify general conditions for suitable databases (ground truth) and non-discriminatory algorithms that improve decisions in HR in an objectively measurable way.

Further research could also address the differences in accountability relationships, resulting in different software development models. Classical waterfall models are carefully planned and easy to reconstruct. Therefore, it is more straightforward to find the accountable person for a specific issue. On the other hand, the fast and efficient development process of agile models is more complex and contains many loops. Such a model requires much greater efforts towards a detailed documentation of the development to ensure accountability. On the other hand, core concepts of agile software development like "testing first" or the "four-eyes principle" could also lead to a higher level of responsibility if socio-informatics issues are considered from the start.

With respect to Wieringa's three-phase approach (2020), in this chapter we have detailed how to transfer Bovens' accountability definitions by using the *Long Chain of Responsibilities*. However, it is an open question as to how these relationships need to be structured, and especially how the forums can exert their power to actually induce consequences on the actor.

SUMMARY

Wieringa's proposal to use Bovens' definition of an accountability relationship to render the development and deployment of ADM systems accountable integrates different views of which person makes decisions in the software development life cycle and where in the cycle this decision is made. It is too early to say whether any of the reviewed process models is sufficient as a basis for identifying the necessary actor relationships. The field is lacking success stories of useful, accurate, fair, and accountable ADM systems in HR for which any details are known. In particular, we do not know of any such system where the company using it is transparent about its technical details and the persons that are accountable for its correct usage and its decisions. Due to the known problems of other ADM systems that predict human behavior, such as the COMPAS system discussed above, it is not likely that successful, accurate, and fair ADM systems able to assess job applicants or match people to job profiles in an accurate and fair way will be achievable soon. It is all the more important then to accompany all trials of such systems with a clear process that defines the accountability of all persons involved in the development, deployment, and evaluation of these systems.

NOTES

1. An *ontology* is an "explicit specification of a conceptualization", where a *conceptualization* "is an abstract, simplified view of the world that we wish to represent for some purpose" (Gruber, 1993). In most cases, it is represented as a network of terms that are connected by relationships like: "A is a subset of B" or "X creates Y".
2. In general, a problem associated with accountability in any kind of chain, for example in production, which contains many different actors, is called the *problem of many hands*.
3. Note, however, that even these seemingly simple cases provide some pitfalls of borderline cases that need to be decided in some way. Consider, for example, an international applicant with an academic degree very similar but not quite the same as the respective field in one's own country. Does he/she match the criterion? What if a person was hired by company A that is later acquired by company B, or if he/she starts a new job in one of A's subsidiaries? Are all those years counted as spent in the same company or not?
4. In computer science, the term *data manipulation* is inherently neutral. It just means that the data is transformed, for example by combining features into more complex features or by replacing a missing value with the mean value of this feature.

REFERENCES

Angwin, J., Larson, J., Mattu, S., & Kirchner, L. (2016). Machine bias – there's software used across the country to predict future criminals. And it's biased against blacks. ProPublica. Retrieved November

13, 2020, from https://www.propublica.org/article/machine-bias-risk-assessments-in-criminal-sentencing.

Ball, C. (2009). What is transparency? *Public Integrity, 11*(4), 293–308.

Borgert, S., & Zweig, K. A. (2019). *Künstliche Intelligenz in der Personalabteilung: Unternehmen haben positive Erwartungen, setzen KI bisher aber kaum ein.* Study on a survey conducted together with the DGFP. Retrieved December 1, 2020, from https://www.dgfp.de/fileadmin/user_upload/DGFP_e.V/Medien/Publikationen/2019/Befragung-KI-in-HR_September-2019.pdf.

Bovens, M. (2007). Analysing and assessing accountability: A conceptual framework. *European Law Journal, 13*(4), 447–468.

Brine, K. R., & Poovey, M. (2013). From measuring desire to quantifying expectations: A late nineteenth-century effort to marry economic theory and data. In L. Gitelman (Ed.), *"Raw data" is an oxymoron* (pp. 61–75). MIT Press.

Citron, D. K., & Pasquale, F. A. (2014). The scored society: Due process for automated predictions [Research Paper No. 2014-8, U of Maryland Legal Studies]. *Washington Law Review, 89*(1), 1–33. https://ssrn.com/abstract=2376209

Diakopoulos, N. (2016). Accountability in algorithmic decision-making: A view from computational journalism. *Communications of the ACM, 59*(2), 56–62. https://doi.org/10.1145/2844110

European Parliament and Council of European Union (2016). *Regulation (EU) 2016/679.* Retrieved November 13, 2020, from https://eur-lex.europa.eu/eli/reg/2016/679/oj.

Gruber. T. R. (1993). A transition approach to portable ontology specifications. *Knowledge Acquisition, 5*(2), 199–220.

Hierländer, J. (2020). Das vorläufige Ende des AMS-Algorithmus. *Die Presse.* Retrieved December 1, 2020, from https://www.diepresse.com/5855950/das-vorlaufige-ende-des-ams-algorithmus.

Holl, J., Kernbeiß, G., & Wagner-Pinter, M. (2018). Das AMS-Arbeitsmarktchancen-Modell. *SynthesisForschung.* Retrieved December 1, 2020, from https://www.ams-forschungsnetzwerk.at/downloadpub/arbeitsmarktchancen_methode_%20dokumentation.pdf.

Holl, J., Kernbeiß, G., & Wagner-Pinter, M. (2019). Personenbezogene Wahrscheinlichkeitsaussagen ("Algorithmen") – Stichworte zur Sozialverträglichkeit. *SynthesisForschung.* Retrieved December 1, 2020, from http://www.synthesis.co.at/images/Personenbezogene_Wahrscheinlichkeitsaussagen_Algorithmen_Mai2019.pdf.

Kemper, J., & Kolkman, D. (2019). Transparent to whom? No algorithmic accountability without a critical audience. *Information, Communication and Society, 22*(14), 2081–2096.

Kleinberg, J. (2018). Inherent trade-offs in algorithmic fairness. In *Abstracts of the 2018 ACM International Conference on Measurement and Modeling of Computer Systems* (pp. 40–40). ACM. https://doi.org/10.1145/3292040.3219634

Klingel, A., Krafft, T. D., & Zweig, K. A. (2020). Mögliche Best-Practice-Ansätze beim Einsatz eines algorithmischen Entscheidungsunterstützungssystems am Beispiel des AMS-Algorithmus. In M. Hengstschläger (Ed.), *Digitaler Wandel und Ethik* (pp. 190–215). Ecowin.

Knobloch, T., & Hustedt, C. (2019). Der maschinelle Weg zum passenden Personal. Zur Rolle Algorithmischer Systeme in der Personalauswahl. *Bertelsmann Stiftung.* Retrieved December 1, 2020, from https://www.bertelsmann-stiftung.de/fileadmin/files/BSt/Publikationen/GrauePublikationen/SNV_Robo_Recruiting_final.pdf.

Krafft, T. D., Zweig, K. A., & König, D. P. (2020). How to regulate algorithmic decision-making: A framework of regulatory requirements for different applications. *Regulation and Governance.* https://doi.org/10.1111/rego.12369

Leicht-Deobald, U., Busch, T., Schrank, C., Weibel, A., Schafheitle, S., Wildhaber, S., & Kasper, G. (2019). The challenges of algorithm-based HR decision-making for personal integrity. *Journal of Business Ethics, 160*(2), 377–392.

Martin, K. (2019). Ethical implications and accountability of algorithms. *Journal of Business Ethics, 160*(4), 835–850.

Mosier, K. L., Skitka, L. J., Heers, S. & Burdick, M. (1998). Automation bias: Decision making and performance in high-tech cockpits. *The International Journal of Aviation Psychology, 8*(1), 47–63.

Pohl, K. (2010). *Requirements engineering: Fundamentals, principles, and techniques.* Springer.

Saurwein, F., Just, N., & Latzer, M. (2015). Governance of algorithms: Options and limitations. *info, 17*(6), 35–49. https://doi.org/10.1108/info-05-2015-0025

Skitka, L., Mosier, K. L., & Burdick, M. (1999). Does automation bias decision-making? *International Journal of Human-Computer Studies, 51*(5), 991–1006.

Strohmeier, S. (2020). Algorithmic decision making in HRM. In T. Bondarouk & S. Fisher (Eds.), *Encyclopedia of electronic HRM*, (pp. 54–59). De Gruyter Oldenbourg.

Tsui, F., & Karam, O. (2011). Software process models. In F. Tsui & O. Karam (Eds.), *Essentials of software engineering* (pp. 73–80). Jones and Bartlett Publishers.

Wieringa, M. (2020). What to account for when accounting for algorithms: A systematic literature review on algorithmic accountability. In *Proceedings of the 2020 Conference on Fairness, Accountability, and Transparency* (pp. 1–18). ACM. https://doi.org/10.1145/3351095.3372833

Zheng, A., & Casari, A. (2018). *Feature engineering for machine learning: Principles and techniques for data scientists*. O'Reilly Media.

Zweig, K. A. (2016). *Network analysis literacy*. Springer.

Zweig, K. A. (2019). *Ein Algorithmus hat kein Taktgefühl*. Heyne.

Zweig, K. A., Fischer, S., & Lischka, K. (2018). *Wo Maschinen irren können* (Working Paper No. 4, series "AlgoEthik"). Bertelsmann Foundation. Retrieved November 13, 2020, from https://www.bertelsmann-stiftung.de/fileadmin/files/BSt/Publikationen/GrauePublikationen/WoMaschinenIrrenKoennen.pdf.

Zweig, K. A., & Krafft, T. D. (2018). Fairness und Qualität algorithmischer Entscheidungen. In R. Mohabbat Kar, B. Thapa, & P. Parycek (Eds.), *(Un)berechenbar? Algorithmen und Automatisierung in Staat und Gesellschaft* (pp. 204–227). Kompetenzzentrum Öffentliche IT.

18. Legitimacy of artificial intelligence in human resources – the legal framework for using artificial intelligence in human resource management

Kai von Lewinski and Raphael de Barros Fritz

INTRODUCTION

The appearance of algorithmic systems, artificial intelligence (AI), and machine learning in the workplace (see CHAPTER 2) will have an impact comparable to the introduction of the steam engine in factories over 200 years ago. It is not difficult to see that AI is about to change the world of labor and the organization of production fundamentally. AI is a (comparatively) new phenomenon, and it will have a global impact. Both the newness of AI and its global impact are challenging for lawyers.

First, taking a global perspective on questions of law is difficult because there is no such thing as a uniform and universal set of rules. What the reader of this chapter must not expect is a comprehensive encyclopedia of all legal systems in the world and how they interact; this would be the subject of a whole set of volumes of legal treatises. Instead, this chapter takes a two-step approach. In the first step it will outline how to determine the applicable jurisdiction in the field of AI and human resources (HR) (see "How to Identify the Applicable Law"). In the second step general rules and regulatory ideas will be described and illustrated by examples (see "Fields of AI Regulation in HR").

Second, law – it is said – is the rear-guard of progress. Therefore, nowhere in the world does a comprehensive "AI Code of Law" yet exist. This chapter will thus focus on the three most relevant fields of law pertaining to AI and HR (labor law, data protection law resp. privacy law,[1] and anti-discrimination law) on three analytical levels (technology as such, implementation of technology in an HR context, and application to employees) (see "Fields of AI Regulation in HR"). At the end of this chapter, the future regulatory perspectives for AI will be briefly addressed (see "Future Developments in the Field of AI Law").

HOW TO IDENTIFY THE APPLICABLE LAW

AI will not only affect the world of HR, but it will affect HR worldwide. Nonetheless, a worldwide law does not exist. We do not have uniform and universal legal standards, neither for HR nor for AI nor for most other aspects of life.[2] This means in practice that in the first place the applicable law has to be identified. The field of law responsible for determining the applicable law in a given case is commonly known as "choice of law". Thus, before embarking on an outline of the rules of substantive law setting forth the general framework for the deployment of AI in the workplace (see "Fields of AI Regulation in HR"), this first section will give a general overview of the choice of law rules which are used to ascertain the law applicable to AI in the workplace.

This overview will be limited to an outline of the choice of law rules which are relevant when determining the applicable substantive law. Questions of cross-border procedures and cross-border enforcement will not be discussed because the focus is on a compliance perspective. This perspective reflects how law-obedient businesses address legal questions; they do not ask whether and how they might get away with violations of standards and regulations, but first and foremost want to comply.

As already mentioned, the deployment of AI in the workplace touches mainly three areas of the law: labor law, data protection law (resp. privacy law), and anti-discrimination law. The determination of the applicable law varies in these three areas of law.

Labor Law

As a general rule, the parties to an employment contract – as parties to a contract in general – are free to choose which law shall apply to their contract.

> In the European Union (EU), for example, Article 8 of the Rome I Regulation allows the parties to choose the law applicable to an individual employment contract.

The same is true in the United States, where pursuant to § 186 of the Restatement 2d on Conflict of Laws issues in contract are determined by the law chosen by the parties in accordance with the rule enshrined in § 187.

Many labor law provisions aim, however, at protecting the individual interests of the employee, who is seen as being in a weak and vulnerable position vis-à-vis his or her employer; in some jurisdictions, their protection is regarded to be in the public interest. As a consequence, the parties to an employment contract are usually not given an unrestrained right to choose the law applicable to their employment contract.

> The Rome I Regulation of the EU, for instance, restrains the freedom of choice insofar as it provides in its Article 8 that a choice of law may not have the result of depriving the employee of the protection afforded to him or her by provisions that cannot be derogated by agreement under the law that, in the absence of choice, would have been applicable pursuant to paragraphs 2, 3, and 4 of Article 8. By the same token, several labor law provisions (as, for example, provisions concerning working hours[3]) are deemed to be overriding mandatory provisions within the meaning of Article 9 of the Rome I Regulation. Thus, the parties are not allowed to opt-out of them.

In the absence of a choice of the applicable law by the parties, the connecting factors used to determine the applicable labor law are manifold.

> Within the ambit of application of the EU Rome I Regulation, Article 8 section 2 sets forth that an individual employment contract shall be governed by the law of the country in which, or failing that from which, the employee habitually carries out his or her work in performance of the contract. Furthermore, where the law applicable cannot be determined pursuant to the preceding choice of law rule, the contract shall be governed by the law of the country where the place of business through which the employee was engaged is situated (Article 8 section 3 of the Rome I Regulation).

On the other hand, many jurisdictions in the United States have departed from such black-letter rules and prefer instead an approach which focuses on determining the state having the "most significant relationship" to the employment contract in question based on a wide range of factors such as the relevant policies of the forum and the protection of the parties' justified expectations.

Data Protection Law

A fundamental difference exists between the choice of law regime of an (EU) data protection approach and a (Common Law) privacy approach (for further references see Kift, 2013, pp. 1–7). Privacy – especially under a market privacy perspective – is seen as a personal asset to be traded and, consequently, is governed by the principle of a free choice of law. Data protection, on the other hand, follows a more regulative approach which might include restrictions on options to choose the applicable law.

> Since the enactment of the General Data Protection Regulation (GDPR) in the EU, Article 3 GDPR has become the most important choice of law rule from the perspective of European law to determine the applicable data protection law. According to this provision, the GDPR applies to the processing of personal data in the context of the activities of an establishment of a controller or a processor in the EU, regardless of whether the processing takes place in there or not. Furthermore, it applies to the processing of the personal data of data subjects who are in the EU by a controller or processor not established there, when the processing activities are either related to the offering of goods or services, irrespective of whether the payment of the data subject is required, or related to the monitoring of a data subject's behavior within the EU. Despite its pivotal importance, Article 3 GDPR only sets forth the GDPR's territorial scope. Thus, it is silent on the issue of whether and to what extent the data protection laws of Member States are applicable. This can become a problem, especially in those cases where Member States have used one of the many[4] opening clauses contained in the GDPR such as Article 6 section 2 GDPR or Article 88 section 1 GDPR. In those cases it is up to the Member States themselves to set forth the scope of application of their own data protection law. This creates, however, the risk of application of multiple national data protection laws and, concomitantly, the risk that a controller or processor is simultaneously bound by different data protection laws (see Svantesson, in: Kuner et al., 2020, Article 3 GDPR, no. 5). In order to avoid this, the GDPR should – at least in intra-European cases – be interpreted in a manner that renders applicable the law of the country of origin (Thon, 2020, pp. 24, 44–47).
>
> Conversely to the situation in the EU, the United States lacks a central choice of law rule on privacy law. The reason for this is that the absence of overarching (federal) legislation is one of the main features of American privacy law, where federal data protection law is merely sectoral and must be complemented by data protection statutes existing at a state level (see Mulligan & Linebaugh, 2019, pp. 2, 7, 36–37). Thus, one must look into the specific data protection or privacy statute the person wants to apply to determine its exact scope of application in a case having connections to different jurisdictions.

Anti-Discrimination Law

As with labor law and data protection law provisions, the scope of application of many anti-discrimination rules of substantive law go beyond the territory of the countries or states which enacted them due to the overriding public interests underlying them.

> In Germany, for example, § 2 AEntG (Arbeitnehmer-Entsendegesetz, German Emplyee Assignment Act) expressly provides that rules of law concerning equal treatment of men and women and other

anti-discriminatory provisions are applicable to employment contracts between an employer situated abroad and an employee who is a German resident.

By the same token, 42 U.S.C. § 2000e(f) overruled the court decision EEOC v. Arabian American Oil Co (1991) and sets forth that Title VII applies to any employee in a foreign country who is a citizen of the United States.

Summary: The Importance of the Public Interest in Determining the Applicable Law

Because of overriding public interests and to protect employees, many provisions of substantive law which are relevant to the deployment of AI in the HR context are applicable beyond national borders and are immune to a choice of law by the parties to an employment contract. Nevertheless, employers and employees are still given the right to choose the law applicable to their contract to the extent that these rules of law are not involved.

FIELDS OF AI REGULATION IN HR

Law tends to lag behind technological developments. Comprehensive and specific AI regulations do not yet exist in the jurisdictions of the world. But important aspects of AI in the workplace are already covered by data protection law and anti-discrimination regulations. Additionally, (varying local) labor law provisions have to be observed.

Three levels of regulation can be distinguished in each of the aforementioned fields of law – regulation of technology, implementation of technology in an employment context, and operating such technology – addressing and/or protecting individual employees.

General Regulatory Framework for Technologies Based on Algorithms

There is currently no general set of rules regarding AI as a technology. AI is neither forbidden nor explicitly allowed.

In the EU, in the meantime, initiatives have been put in place to set up a regulatory framework for AI. The European Commission published a White Paper at the start of 2020 (Commission of the European Union, 2020) and is following a roadmap of consultations.

Labor law
In a labor context, algorithms are not considered to be something as inhuman as slavery. Therefore, AI as such is not universally banned from the workplace.

Data protection law
Data protection law as a regulatory concept to protect informational privacy originates from the EU.[5] In addition to the material prerequisites for personal data processing, data protection law has always had a (admittedly somewhat less developed) side shoot of technical data protection and data security (see Article 32 GDPR). Despite the efforts to achieve technology-neutral regulation, there are also algorithm-specific provisions and regulatory links.

No Ban on Specific Technologies. Conversely to the step pertaining to processing of personal data, data protection law does not in principle prohibit a specific technology. On the contrary, it is the aim of modern data protection legislation to be technology-neutral (see Recital 15 sent. 1 GDPR). As a result, AI and other similar technologies as such are not subject to regulation.

> Data protection through technology design, which is taken up in Article 25 GDPR (see Wrigley, 2018, pp. 199 et seq.), is also intended to contribute to the principles of lawful data processing in the EU. Taking into account state-of-the-art technology, the protection of personal data should be located as early in the process as possible, it being considered decisively in the development of the technology (and also of the underlying algorithms). Thus, the entire life cycle of a product is covered by data protection law (see Bygrave, in: Kuner et al., 2020, Article 25 GDPR, C.1).
> In the United States, a resolution (House Resolution 153, 2019) has been introduced in the House of Representatives concerning the development of guidelines for the ethical development of AI. Nonetheless, it is not nearly as precise as the GDPR as it only contains aims, not regulations.

Intervention of Human Beings. As we are at the beginning of the age of AI, some jurisdictions stipulate that algorithmic decision-making systems shall not have "the final word". Commonly, this requirement is fulfilled by a human checking, verifying, and confirming automated decisions.

> Linguistically put in the form of a subjective right, EU's Article 22 GDPR contains the principle that no automated individual decisions based on personal data may be taken without the intervention of humans. Two things must be considered when fleshing out this provision: On the one hand, it follows from its meaning and purpose that it presupposes that the person intervening can actually influence the result or at least essential aspects of the data-processing process. On the other hand, a right of the data subject to intervention by a person is only to be recognized if justified reasons support this in the individual case. Otherwise the exception under Article 22 para. 2 and 3 GDPR would be reversed in that Article 22 GDPR intends (as a general rule) to make a fully automated decision possible from a technical-law perspective.
> In the United States, the "Right to a Human Decision" is more hidden in the law as there is no equivalent to Article 22 GDPR. However, Article 6 of the U.S. Constitution grants the right to a (human) jury. Similarly, the Algorithm Accountability Act, if passed, could allow people to sue against the usage of algorithms (Huq, 2020, pp. 625–627).

Data Protection Impact Assessment. The implementation of AI technology can be subject to compulsory risk assessment. This is explicitly decreed under EU law. Article 35 GDPR specifically stipulates a duty to conduct a data protection impact assessment (DPIA).[6] According to Article 35 para. 1 sent. 1 GDPR, the data controller is obliged to carry out a DPIA when "a type of processing in particular using new technologies,[7] and taking into account the nature, scope, context and purposes of the processing, is likely to result in a high risk to the rights and freedoms of natural persons."

> In the United States, a bill (Algorithmic Accountability Act 2019) has been introduced which would require certain companies to conduct an automated decision system impact assessment. Section 2 Article 6 of the bill defines such an impact assessment as a "study evaluating the extent to which an information system protects the privacy and security of personal information the system processes". Similar to EU law, these assessments will only be mandatory if the automated decision system is deemed to be of "high risk".

Algorithm Transparency. Sunlight is said to be the best disinfectant. This is true not only in relation to government and the prevention of corruption, but also in relation to the acceptance and the control of new technologies. Therefore, legislations include duties to inform the persons concerned, the workforce, or the public about certain aspects of AI use or implementation.

> Article 13 para. 2 lit. f, Article 14 para. 2 lit. g, Article 15 para. 1 lit. h GDPR, which address the rights of data subjects in the EU, are examples of technical regulations as they are aimed at the communication of information on the "logic involved" in automated decision making.

Anti-discrimination law

Finally, the use of AI may in certain cases give rise to discriminatory results. Nevertheless, legislators generally refrain from enacting statutes prohibiting it as a technology, preferring instead an approach which focuses on the avoidance of discriminatory effects brought about by the usage of AI.

Summary: no general ban on AI technology

Rules of law addressing algorithms are generally restrictive rather than promotive. The reason for this is the fact that algorithmic systems are means and tools that anyone can use within the framework of his or her (general) freedom of action or his or her freedom to work. So, if the use of algorithms is basically permitted, then the law contains primarily restrictions as an exception to this basic rule. Nevertheless, none of the fields of law analyzed in this chapter contain a general ban on AI as a technology (as there is on weapons of mass destruction, a.k.a. ABC weapons), and there have been no legal "swing riots".[8] Thus, as a basic rule of thumb, it is noted that AI technology can be used for any purpose.

Implementation of AI in HR

Between technology (see "General Regulatory Framework for Technologies Based on Algorithms") and its effects on individuals (see "Effects on Individual Employees"), the specific implementation in an HR context and its effects on the company's workforce as a whole may be located. The following section of this chapter will address measures which are directed at entire workforces and situations in which the entire workforce is observed, especially in order to identify (behavioral) patterns.

Labor law

Rules of law that apply to entire workforces are most commonly found in labor law.

   Co-Determination. The work councils' or trade unions' co-determination rights are an example of such rules of law which can also be of importance for algorithmic procedures. If labor law applies to the introduction and implementation of AI technology at the workplace, it is not narrowed to the processing of personal data (as is the scope of data protection law; see "Effects on Individual Employees" and "Data Protection Law") but encompasses the development of algorithms and correlations (often by means of machine learning).

> Most EU countries have some form of board-level employee representation which then might have a voice on technology issues. An example for such co-determination in relation to technology can be found in German law (see § 87 para. 1, § 94 para. 2, § 95, § 111 BetrVG [Betriebsverfassungsgesetz, (German) Works Constitution Act]).
>
>   Quite recently, the Accountable Capitalism Act (2018) has been introduced in the U.S. Senate, which would implement some parts of the German co-determination law such as employees being able to elect 40 percent of the board members (Dammann & Eidenmüller, 2020). However, since

co-determination has yet to be introduced in U.S. companies, it is unclear if and how it will apply to the implementation of AI technology.

Similarly, in 2017, the UNI Global Union, which represents more than 20 million workers from the service industry all over the world, released 10 Principles for Workers' Data Privacy and Protection (UNI Global Union, 2017), giving companies proposals on how they should design the transition towards a more "technical" workplace where AI and algorithms are going to play a huge role. Nonetheless, it is important to highlight that the UNI Global Union principles are not binding legislation.

Workers' Protection. The risks posed by algorithms are largely due to their technical design. Therefore, in the area of labor law, one could at first glance consider using regulations on technical labor safety to protect employees who come into contact with algorithmic systems during (and as a result of) their work. Nevertheless, the provisions pertaining to technical labor safety generally only protect against harm to the body or health (such as provisions to "cage" industrial robots). Harm to body or health resulting from the use of algorithms in the context of HR decisions is, however, hardly conceivable. Therefore, regulations on technical labor safety will generally play no role in protecting employees from algorithms. This is a difference between the regulation of algorithms and the regulation of robots and automatization.

In California, it is illegal (Cal. Penal Code, Section 637.7) for employers to track their employees' whereabouts using the Global Positioning System (GPS) unless they are given notice and are able to consent. Additionally, employers cannot use audio or video monitoring in restrooms or locker rooms (Cal. Labor Code, Section 435).

Data protection law
Data protection law includes some instruments which address the implementation of technology.

Appointment of a Data Protection Officer. Most prominent and visible is the obligation to appoint a "data protection officer" (in practice sometimes called "chief privacy officer").

Under EU law, the data protection officer must monitor compliance with data protection regulations with regard to entire workforces (in particular with regard to the list of tasks contained in Article 39 GDPR). The data protection officer was introduced for the first time on a European level by Articles 37–39 GDPR. Nevertheless, this should not obscure the fact that the appointment of a data protection officer will remain largely optional for the non-public sector throughout Europe, since only a limited number of companies are covered by Article 37 para. 1 lit. b and c GDPR. The scope of this duty can be broadened by European Member States in that Article 37 para. 4 GDPR allows them to enact provisions on a national level making the appointment of a data protection officer mandatory in a larger number of cases (for an example of such a Member State provision, see § 38 para. 1 BDSG [Bundesdatenschutzgesetz, (German) Federal Data Protection Act]).

Data Protection Impact Assessment. It should also be noted that the DPIA pursuant to Article 35 GDPR can also be applicable in those cases in which risks arise for entire workforces through the use of algorithmic systems (especially in the context of a Big Data procedure). Thus, this provision can certainly also be understood to have the intention of protecting employees' groups and not only single individuals. This is demonstrated by Article 35 para. 9 GDPR, which refers to this collective dimension by speaking of "data subjects and *their* representatives".

Accountability. Some jurisdictions connect special duties in relation to documentation and observation to the implementation of new technologies.

Under EU legislation, the controller of personal data must not only comply with data protection regulations but must also be able to demonstrate such compliance (Article 5 para. 2 GDPR). This means keeping records, setting up and enforcing internal guidelines, and asserting external (contractual) obligations (Zwenne and Steenbruggen, in: Gijrath et al., 2018, Article 5 GDPR, no. 2).

Anti-discrimination law

Anti-discrimination law also contains certain provisions designed to protect entire workforces. The legislator may prescribe a "competent body" inside or outside an enterprise for receiving employees' complaints about discriminatory behavior.

An example for such a provision is § 13 AGG [Allgemeines Gleichbehandlungsgesetz, (German) General Equal Treatment Act]. A similar rule can be found in Article L422-1-1 du Code du travail (French labor code).

In addition, the legislator may also set forth different mechanisms to enhance the private enforcement of employees' anti-discrimination rights.

This is usually done by creating anti-discrimination associations or agencies (like the U.S. Equal Employment Opportunity Commission or the French Défenseur des droits) which support employees when they seek to enforce their rights in court.

Summary: group-related AI regulations

As far as measures which are directed at entire workforces or situations where the entire workforce is observed are concerned, a variety of regulative concepts and institutions exists. They largely vary from jurisdiction to jurisdiction, depending on the specific legal and political traditions. The implementation of AI technology will have to take into account this diverse global legal landscape.

Effects on Individual Employees

AI does not only affect the workforce as such. Rather, it also (and, actually, primarily) affects the individual employees. As far as regulations already exist, they address the directly palpable effects on individual employees rather than the indirect effects on the workforce as a group of persons.

Labor law

Labor law contains a number of provisions which are intended to protect the health of employees (in particular prior to the occurrence of the damage). Regulations on workplace safety and employment health protection are included here. However, as far as can be seen, there is no general regulatory framework for algorithms and intelligent systems in HR.

In the United States, a bill (Workers' Right to Training Act 2019) has been introduced to the Committee on Finance which would require an employer to provide training to employees who may risk losing their jobs because of AI (and other technologies).

Similarly, in 2017, it was set forth in the Italian national collective agreement for the manufacturing sector that employees have a specific individual right to training in cases where their jobs are automized (De Stefano, 2018, p. 9).

In this context, labor law provisions concerning working hours can lead to a restriction on the use of algorithms in the workplace. Rules of law setting forth a minimum number of rest hours between an employee's shifts and a ban on working Sundays can, for example, result in difficulties for an employer in deploying algorithms in the fourth industrial revolution (Industry 4.0), where algorithms are used to adapt employees' working hours or shifts to the actual work demands by using information about the production environment.

Data protection law
The regulatory approach of data protection law is to generally restrict the processing of personal data to minimize the probability of violations of the private sphere. The main difference – in very general terms – between the concept of data protection and the concept of privacy is that data protection law applies to any processing of (personal) data, whereas privacy law only addresses the actual violations of privacy, not threats or abstract dangers.

Requirement to Identify a Legal Basis for Data Processing. Data protection prohibits processing of personal data as a general rule. Nevertheless, data protection legislation also sets forth specific cases and circumstances where the processing of personal data is allowed by exception.

> That is – in a nutshell – what Article 6 GDPR is about. It covers algorithmic processing of personal data, with or without AI. The GDPR offers in Article 6 section 1 a range of six alternatives to justify the processing of personal data: consent (lit. a), performance of a contract (lit. b), legal obligation of data controller (lit. c), vital interests of the data subject (lit. d), public interest (lit. e), and a balance of interests (lit. f).

Consent. Processing of personal data may be based on consent. This is common ground for more or less every jurisdiction in the world, whether or not they possess an EU-style data protection regime.

> In Australia, an employee has – according to a court decision (Jeremy Lee v Superior Wood Pty Ltd (2019)) – to be asked for his or her consent if the employer wants to obtain sensitive personal information such as biometric data or health information.
> Consent can also play an important role in the hiring process. For example, Illinois passed the Video Interview Act (2019), forcing employers who are using AI to analyze video interviews submitted by job applicants to not only inform applicants of the process, but also explain how the AI works and obtain their consent to the procedure.

A crucial aspect is that consent has to be given freely (see Article 4 No. 11 GDPR, Article 7 section 4 GDPR). As Recital 42 sent. 5 GDPR puts it: "Consent should not be regarded as freely given if the data subject has no genuine or free choice or is unable to refuse or withdraw consent without detriment."

> Due to the hierarchical nature of employment relationships and the employee's social and financial dependence on his or her job, this requirement becomes particularly relevant in the employment context. Recital 155 GDPR shows that in the EU the employee's consent (see Article 6 section 1 lit. a GDPR) is in general a permissible legal justification in employment relationships. Nevertheless, because of the special circumstances just mentioned surrounding an employment relationship, the element of voluntariness must be carefully considered when dealing with an employee's consent. As a rule of thumb, an employee's consent will be deemed to have been granted voluntarily when the employee has in effect a freedom to choose whether to grant his or her consent, especially if he or she

has a realistic option not to consent. Another indicator for the voluntary nature of consent is that it is associated with a financial or legal advantage to the employee (see especially § 26 section 2 BDSG [Germany]). Examples for such advantages are the implementation of corporate health care schemes in the workplace and the private use of the firm's electronic equipment. Another important aspect to be considered when obtaining an employee's consent is the point in time at which it is given. Prior to signing an employment contract, employees will normally be more vulnerable to the employer's influence and less inclined to refuse to grant their consent. Thus, the employee's consent is more likely to be considered by a court to have been given freely when it is obtained after and not before the signing of the employment contract.

Although the element of voluntariness plays an important role when obtaining an employee's consent, practitioners must also be mindful of other legal requirements when drafting contract clauses relating to an employee's consent to the processing of personal data.

Article 7 section 2 GDPR, for example, sets forth that, if the data subject's consent is given in the context of a written declaration which also concerns other matters, the request for consent shall be presented in a manner which is clearly distinguishable from the other matters, in an intelligible and easily accessible form, using clear and plain language. This provision addresses cases such as the one where the employee's consent is included in a clause of the employment agreement. Thus, lawyers must take Article 7 section 2 GDPR into consideration when drafting a clause in an employment agreement requesting the employee's consent. For practitioners, highlighting the consent declaration in color or by bolding (Dienst, in: Rücker & Kugler, 2018, marginal no. 458) and refraining from including it in the paragraph where the information pursuant to Articles 13, 14 GDPR is provided to the employee has been suggested. Furthermore, the use of the word "consent" in the clause's heading might be advisable, whereas the use of the wording "I know that …" is discouraged (Data Protection Working Party, 2017, p. 14 fn. 36).

Performance of a Contract. It only seems sensible that – unless the law wants to contradict itself – data processing that is necessary to establish and maintain an employment relationship must be permissible.

Labor law is very much a nation-specific subject (as is data protection). Therefore, additional regulation might exist. Article 88 GDPR gives leeway to country-specific regulation of workplace data protection within the EU. As Recital 155 of the GDPR puts it:
"Member State law or collective agreements, including 'works agreements', may provide for specific rules on the processing of employees' personal data in the employment context, in particular for the conditions under which personal data in the employment context may be processed on the basis of the consent of the employee, the purposes of the recruitment, the performance of the contract of employment, including discharge of obligations laid down by law or by collective agreements, management, planning and organisation of work, equality and diversity in the workplace, health and safety at work, and for the purposes of the exercise and enjoyment, on an individual or collective basis, of rights and benefits related to employment, and for the purpose of the termination of the employment relationship."
   German law, for example, specifies these requirements by applying the rule of (strict) necessity ("Erforderlichkeit") in a labor context (§ 26 BDSG).

In order to combat the practice of employers asking employees to give them their social media passwords to essentially monitor them even outside of work and eventually generate data for further analysis by AI systems, a substantial number of U.S. states have introduced laws banning it.
   Legal Obligation of Data Controller. Employers have many legal obligations and most of them result in data processing and documentation which often also includes the process-

ing and documentation of employees' personal data. Again, if the law does not want to be self-contradictory, necessary processing of personal data must be allowed.

This is explicitly laid down in Article 6 para. 1 lit. c GDPR for the processing of personal data in the EU.

But even today it is very rare that the law requires that AI systems process such data, although this aspect might become relevant to risk control systems in the financial industry.

The European Commission has recently published a White Paper (Commission of the European Union, 2020) concerning AI. It mentions the finance sector (p. 15) as one of many industries using AI in need of further legislation, and proposes a risk-based approach to AI, to ensure that the regulations are proportionate, and requirements for high-risk AI applications such as human oversight and training data as well as robustness and accuracy (pp. 18 et seq.).

Vital Interests of the Data Subject. Of only minor practical relevance is the justification for maintaining and safeguarding the vital interests of employees. One of the few cases where data processing might be justified by the employees' vital interests is the case where AI technology is deployed to assess patterns of risk and danger in dangerous workplaces (e.g., nuclear plants or virus laboratories).

This and similar cases are addressed in the EU by Article 6 para. 1 lit. d GDPR.

Public Interest. Of course, data processing is allowed for the protection of public interests and by public bodies.

Balance of Interests. In business contexts, especially towards consumers, the balance of interests is generally regarded to be a fall-back option to base the processing of personal data on if you do not have more specific legal justifications. But because employment relationships are usually based on detailed contracts and are governed by a dense network of regulations, the balance of interest clause in data protection laws does not have any significance in an employment context (see "Performance of a Contract").

Additional Requirements for Automated Decision Making. Beyond general data protection law requirements, some jurisdictions provide for additional requirements for automated decision making. Such provisions do not address the processing of data, but the decisions stemming from a (certain) data-processing process. This prevents an individual becoming a "mere object" of data processing with perhaps even limited accuracy (see the contributions of Hänold and Wrigley in: Corrales et al., 2018, pp. 123 et seq. resp. pp. 193 et seq.).

The EU's Article 22 GDPR contains such requirements for "scoring" and "profiling", including the duty to "implement suitable measures to safeguard the data subject's rights and freedoms and legitimate interests, at least the right to obtain human intervention on the part of the controller, to express his or her point of view and to contest the decision" (Article 22 section 3 GDPR).

Some jurisdictions have even more additional requirements, for example for the "scoring" of individuals (see § 31 section 1 BDSG).

Information and Rights of the Data Subject. Finally, auxiliary claims should be mentioned, which, in the case of processing of personal data by algorithms, enable the data subject to better protect and enforce his or her rights and interests. The effectiveness of data protection is enhanced if the data subject is informed about the processing of personal data concerning him or her by means of algorithms.

> This is the aim of Article 13 para. 2 lit. f, 14 para. 2 lit. g, 15 para. 1 lit. h GDPR in the EU, whose provisions are tailored to the processing of personal data by algorithms in fully automated procedures. Accordingly, the data subject must be provided with information on the existence of automated decision making, including profiling as defined in Article 22 GDPR, and – at least in these cases – meaningful information on the logic involved and the scope and intended effects of such processing on the data subject. When applying these rules, it should be noted in particular that the term "logic involved" does not mean the disclosure of the algorithm. This is because, according to Recital 63 sent. 5, the right to information under Article 15 GDPR should not affect the rights of third parties, which may include business secrets (see Parliament of the European Union, 2019, pp. 26 et seq.) The algorithm is protected as a trade secret, so does not have to be disclosed, at least within the scope of Article 15 GDPR (Schrey, in: Rücker & Kugler, 2018, marginal no. 638). As the wording of Article 13 and Article 14 GDPR coincides with that of Article 15 GDPR, the same must apply to Articles 13 and 14 GDPR. Consequently, the person concerned should only be provided with a general, comprehensible description of the basis for calculation and the calculation's methodology (Schrey, in: Rücker & Kugler, 2018, no. 620).
>
> In China, data subjects also have to be informed about automated decision making and profiling, specifically which personal information is going to be collected and for what purpose (Yang, 2019, p. 125).

Other Safeguard Mechanisms. Although rights to receive information are important, data protection cannot be achieved by mere information rights of the data subject. In a figurative sense, one can speak here of a "right to a fair trial".

> The GDPR provides, therefore, for other protective mechanisms to protect the data subject from algorithmic procedures.
>
> On a European level, Article 22 para. 3 GDPR mentions the right of the data subject to obtain human intervention. Although the wording suggests a subjective right, this provision in fact addresses to a great extent merely technical-organizational measures. Furthermore, Article 22 para. 3 GDPR also includes an (auxiliary) right subsequent to the actual processing in so far as it expressly provides for a right to present one's own point of view. This teleologically includes the duty of the controller to actually take into account the aspects presented, and a right of appeal, which gives the individual the right to have the decision taken reviewed (see Schrey, in: Rücker & Kugler, 2018, marginal no. 697 ("right to review")).
>
> In the EU Member States, there are – generally speaking – four approaches to implementing the GDPR and the measures taken to regulate certain cases of automated decision making according to Article 22 para. 2 lit. b GDPR. Most countries do not allow any automated decision making under this rule, for example Italy, Sweden, or Finland; Germany and to a certain extent Belgium and Austria have no specific safeguard measures in place even though they have implemented Article 22 para. 2 lit. b GDPR. The United Kingdom (before Brexit), Ireland, and in parts Slovenia require data controllers to take certain procedures when using automated decision making or an algorithm impact assessment. Finally, France and Hungary have chosen to implement new and more intrinsic safeguards to specify Article 22 para. 2 lit. b GDPR (Malgieri, 2019, pp. 8 et seq.).

Anti-discrimination law

With regard to provisions intended to protect individual employees against discrimination in connection with algorithmic processes, the first provision to be addressed is Article 9 GDPR. Article 9 GDPR aims at avoiding discrimination by prohibiting the processing of data commonly referred to as "sensitive data" (Feiler & Forgó, 2018, Article 9 GDPR, note 6). It is modeled on Article 8 of the EC Data Protection Directive 95/46/EC and its first paragraph prohibits in principle the processing of sensitive data. The following paragraphs provide for exceptions, whereas Article 9 para. 4 GDPR opens up the possibility for Member States to enact additional conditions for the processing of genetic data, biometric data, or data concerning health on a national level.

> Also, on a national level there is a wide range of provisions which can be important in avoiding discrimination due to the use of algorithms. In German law, for example, § 12 AGG should be mentioned. This provision sets forth that an employer is obliged to take the necessary steps to avoid discrimination pursuant to § 1 AGG. In the United States, on the other hand, Title VII of the Civil Rights Act of 1964 protects employees against discrimination due to the deployment of algorithms (see Bornstein, 2018, pp. 519 et seq.). Additionally, the United States' "Algorithmic Accountability Act of 2019", if passed, will require large companies to (internally) assess whether or not the AI they are using is discriminating against certain employees. Additionally, discrimination in the hiring process due to AI is already covered by the Employment Equality Act (Foale, 2020, p. 179).

Summary: protection of individual rights

All jurisdictions contain rules of law to protect the rights and interests of individual employees. Whereas labor law provisions and anti-discrimination laws do not generally address AI issues directly yet, data protection laws do – if and when they exist in the respective jurisdiction.

FUTURE DEVELOPMENTS IN THE FIELD OF AI LAW

AI – at the workplace and beyond – will be a dominating trend in this century, as will other related technologies such as machine learning, bots, and other man–machine interfaces. Law will gradually catch up in an experimental (and often situational) style. In some decades, global standards and a certain degree of harmonization will have occurred. To give an idea of what is probably ahead, some developments will be briefly outlined below.

Labor Law

Algorithms and AI will remove many jobs, and new occupations will arise. It will be the task of national politics to react and manage this technological and social process. Societies will experiment with employment politics and unconditional basic income to adapt people to the new technological environment.

Data Protection Law

Data protection law primarily addresses the relationship between the "data subject" and the "controller". Although the GDPR focuses more on procedures and technology, data protection law lacks a holistic approach. This could include the (direct) restriction of "algorithmic power" (see von Lewinski, 2014, pp. 74 et seq.).

Socialization of Risks

AI is a risk technology. Therefore, future legislation might not only address the implementation and use of this technology as such, but also the allocation of liability. If law makers decide to categorize AI as a "general risk of life", the risk of such a technology becomes socialized. Such a solution may be just and sensible if individual attribution of damage is not possible at reasonable costs.

Restriction of Algorithmic Power

Progressing digitalization is likely to result in a shift of power to the disadvantage of employees. Decartelization in general might help or not help against data giants. But such anti-trust measures definitely do not help protect employees against a shift of power within the employment relationship because they do not depend on the size of the employing company.

Declaring AI a Legal Person

A rather futuristic regulatory option is to award algorithmic systems the quality of a legal entity (a person). AI would then be treated as being responsible (and liable) for its acts. But this might only become an option for systems with strong AI (see CHAPTER 2) and leads to further questions beyond the scope of this handbook, for example a right to "algorithmic self-determination" and digital co-determination at the workplace.

NOTES

1. The denomination of the field of law varies in different jurisdictions. The EU (and EU-inspired) legislation usually chooses to name it "data protection", but in Common Law countries, especially the United States, the term "privacy law" is common.
2. Even the Universal Human Rights (laid down in the United Nations' Universal Declaration of Human Rights and specified by the International Covenant on Civil and Political Rights and the International Covenant on Civil and Political Rights, all three together sometimes referred to as the Universal Bill of Rights) do not have a uniform universal effect because they lack a uniform enforcement mechanism.
3. For German law see § 2 AEntG [Arbeitnehmer-Entsendegesetz; (German) Employee Assignment Act].
4. The GDPR contains approximately 70 opening clauses.
5. Data protection law is generally traced back to 1970 and a state-law in the German State (*Land*) of Hesse. From today's perspective, perhaps surprisingly, the respective political debates are rooted in the United States in the 1960s (only cf. Vance Packard, *The naked society*, 1964).
6. In other jurisdictions, which do not follow the (European) concept of "data protection", the term "privacy impact assessment" (PIA) might be more in use.
7. The term "new technologies" does not refer to the technology as such (as in "new media") but to the specific context where such technology is implemented. This becomes clear when Article 35 GDPR is read together with Recital 89 sent. 4 GDPR, where reference is made to the circumstance that "no data protection impact assessment has been carried out" yet. As a result, at least the first time AI is implemented in a certain context, a DPIA has to take place.
8. This refers to a movement and unrest in 1830s Britain against the mechanization of agriculture, culminating in the destruction of (threshing) machines. The German equivalent of such *Maschinenstürmerei* is the Weavers' Uprising, which took place in Silesia in 1845.

REFERENCES

Bornstein, S. (2018). Antidiscriminatory algorithms. *Alabama Law Review*, *70*(2), 519–572.

Commission of the European Union (2020). *On artificial intelligence. A European approach to excellence and trust* [White Paper]. European Commission. https://ec.europa.eu/info/publications/white-paper-artificial-intelligence-european-approach-excellence-and-trust_en, accessed November 12, 2021.

Corrales, M., Forgó, N., & Fenwick, M. (Eds.). (2018). *Robotics, AI and the future of law*. Springer.

Dammann, J., & Eidenmüller, H. (2020). *Codetermination: A poor fit for U.S. corporations* (Law Working Paper No. 509/2020). European Corporate Governance Institute.

Data Protection Working Party (2017), Opinion 2/2017 on data processing at work – (Working Paper (WP) 249), adopted on 8 June 2017.

De Stefano, V. (2018). *"Negotiating the algorithm": Automation, artificial intelligence and labour protection* (Working Paper Nr. 246). International Labour Office.

Feiler, L., & Forgó, N. (2018). *EU-Datenschutz-Grundverordnung*. Verlag Österreich.

Foale, N. (2020). Back to the future: How well equipped is Irish employment equality law to adapt to artificial intelligence? *Trinity College Law Review*, *23*, 170–198.

Gijrath, S., van der Hof, S., Lodder, A.R., & Zwenne, G.-J. (Eds.). (2018). *Concise European data protection, e-commerce and IT law*. Wolters Kluwer.

Huq, A. Z. (2020). A right to a human decision. *Virginia Law Review*, *106*(3), 611–688. https://www.virginialawreview.org/articles/right-human-decision/, accessed November 12, 2021.

Kift, P. (2013). Bridging the transatlantic divide in privacy. *Internet Policy Review*, *2*(3). https://doi.org/10.14763/2013.3.190

Kuner, C., Bygrave, L. A, & Cocksey, C. (Eds.). (2020). *The EU General Data Protection Regulation (GDPR). A commentary*. Oxford University Press.

Malgieri, G. (2019), Automated decision-making in the EU Member States. The right to explanation and other "suitable safeguards" for algorithmic decisions in the EU national legislations. *Computer Law and Security Review*, *35*(5), Article 105327.

Mulligan, S. P., & Linebaugh, C. D. (2019). *Data protection law: An overview*. CRS. https://www.hsdl.org/?view&did=823585, accessed November 12, 2021.

Parliament of the European Union (2019). *Report on a comprehensive European industrial policy on artificial intelligence and robotics (A8-0019/2019)*. European Parliament. https://www.europarl.europa.eu/doceo/document/A-8-2019-0019_EN.html, accessed November 12, 2021.

Rücker, D., & Kugler, T. (Eds.). (2018). *New European General Data Protection Regulation. A practitioner's guide*. C. H. Beck/Hart/Nomos.

Thon, M. (2020). Transnationaler Datenschutz: Das Internationale Datenprivatrecht der DS-GVO. *RabelsZ [Rabels Zeitschrift]*, *84*(1), 173–177. https://doi.org/10.1628/rabelsz-2020-0019

UNI Global Union (2017). *Top 10 principles for workers' data privacy and protection*. www.thefuturew orldofwork.org/media/35421/uni_workers_data_protection.pdf, accessed November 12, 2021.

von Lewinski, K. (2014). *Die Matrix des Datenschutzes*. Mohr Siebeck.

Wrigley, S. (2018). Taming artificial intelligence bots: The GDPR and regulatory approaches. In M. Corrales, N. Forgó, & M. Fenwick (Eds.), *Robotics, AI and the future of law* (pp. 183–208). Springer.

Yang, H. (2019). *The privacy, data protection and cybersecurity law review: China*. The Law Reviews.

PART IV

RESEARCH ISSUES OF ARTIFICIAL INTELLIGENCE IN HUMAN RESOURCES

19. Design considerations for conducting artificial intelligence research in human resource management

Richard D. Johnson and Dianna L. Stone

RESEARCH DESIGN CONSIDERATIONS FOR AI RESEARCH IN HRM

Organizations are justifiably interested in applying new artificial intelligence (AI) techniques in human resource management (HRM) in order to (a) streamline burdensome processes (e.g., initial screening of applicants), (b) decrease costs, (c) enhance decision making (e.g., selection decisions), and (d) improve overall HRM processes. As a result, AI vendors have started touting the many benefits of AI for supporting HRM (e.g., AI decreases biases in selection decisions, helps organizations attract the best applicants) (Davenport & Ronanki, 2018). However, given that the application of AI techniques to HRM is relatively new, there has been little objective empirical research examining its effectiveness (Tambe et al., 2019; Johnson et al., 2021).

The effectiveness of AI can be judged on several criteria. For example, one criterion is whether the implementation of AI improves the ability of organizations to attract, select, motivate, and maintain employees in their roles. A second criterion that can be used is whether AI improves the satisfaction among employees, HRM professionals, and managers. Finally, organizations can assess the impact on HRM processes (decrease timeline, increase efficiency, better decision making). Whatever criterion is utilized, it is important that HRM researchers assess the validity of the claims made by AI vendors and those touting the value of AI in HRM (Stone, 1978) prior to implementing these new systems.

To ensure that AI vendors and organizations make valid inferences, researchers must begin by properly designing their studies. A research design is an a priori plan for conducting research so that researchers can answer key questions about the applications of AI (Stone, 1978; Stone-Romero, 2011). The type of design utilized by a researcher should be based upon the type of research question(s) that the researcher wishes to answer. This is because the research design utilized affects the insights and generalizations that can be made by the researcher (Shadish et al., 2002). Therefore, a researcher must match the research questions of interest to an appropriate research design. In the sections that follow we consider some of the advantages and limitations of various research designs that can be used to examine the effectiveness of AI applications in HRM. We then discuss examples of studies examining the role of AI in HRM to illustrate the research designs in action, highlighting the relative strengths and weaknesses of each. Space limitations preclude a discussion of all the studies, but we briefly summarize the full set of studies in Table 19.1. We first turn to a discussion of the importance of validity to the interpretation of AI research in HRM.

Table 19.1   Research designs of HRM studies with an AI focus

Paper	Research design	Study focus
Fletcher & Morrison (2014)	Experiment	Design of an intelligent tutor to improve training outcomes. Findings suggest that individuals using the tutor had stronger learning outcomes and subsequent job performance than those who did not.
Kurilovas et al. (2015)	Experiment	Comparison of two e-learning systems: one with personalization capabilities and one without personalization capabilities.
Langer et al. (2019b)	Experiment	Compared applicant reactions to the selection interview using a 2 (innovative vs. established firm) × 2 (AI-enabled anthropomorphic character vs. human interviewer) experiment.
Langer et al. (2019a)	Experiment	Compared applicant reactions to the selection interview using a 2 (high stakes vs. low stakes interview) × 2 (AI-enabled anthropomorphic character vs. human interviewer) experiment.
Langer et al. (2016)	Experiment	Compared job interview performance of groups that received AI-enabled feedback during training vs. traditional interview training.
Langer et al. (2018)	Experiment	Compared individuals' assessments of an avatar-based interview using a 2 (major: computer science vs. non-computer science) × 2 (low vs. high information about the interview system) experiment.
Langer et al. (2020)	Experiment	Compared applicant reactions to videotaped interviews under two conditions: human evaluated and AI evaluated.
Ötting & Maier (2018)	Experiment	Compared individuals' reactions to a 2 (justice: fair/unfair) and 3 (decision agent: human, AI robot, and computer system) in the employment context (e.g., allocation of resources, job assignments).
Suen et al. (2019)	Experiment	Compared individuals' reactions to three types of selection interview (synchronous, asynchronous, and asynchronous AI evaluated).
Chen et al. (2016)	Qualitative non-experimental design	Design of an AI-enabled e-learning system that can recognize human affective states to improve metacognitive awareness.
Chien & Chen (2008)	Qualitative non-experimental design	Design of an AI-enabled tool to improve employee selection.
Gebhard et al. (2018)	Qualitative non-experimental design	Development an AI-enabled gamified training system for improving interview skills.
Hemamou et al. (2019a)	Qualitative non-experimental design	Development of an AI-enabled system for real-time analysis of non-verbal behavior in asynchronous selection interviews.
Hemamou et al. (2019b)	Qualitative non-experimental design	Development of an AI-enabled system for real-time analysis of verbal and non-verbal behavior in asynchronous selection interviews.
Hwang (2003)	Qualitative non-experimental design	Design and evaluation of an AI-enabled digital tutor to provide performance feedback to students.
Lykourentzou et al. (2009)	Qualitative non-experimental design	Design of an AI-enabled system to more effectively identify potential performance deficits in learners.
Naim et al. (2016)	Qualitative non-experimental design	Development of an AI-enabled system to quantify verbal and non-verbal behavior in job interviews.
Leong et al. (2019)	Quantitative non-experimental design	Assessing whether an AI-enabled selection tool may contain bias based on the data which it is trained on.
Van Esch & Black (2019)	Quantitative non-experimental design	Examined reactions to the use of AI-enabled recruiting technology.
Van Esch et al. (2019)	Quantitative non-experimental design	Examined potential applicants' likelihood of applying for a job when AI technology was used as part of the recruitment process.

VALIDITY

Validity reflects the extent to which the evidence from a research study supports the inference(s) being made by the researcher (Shadish et al., 2002). It important to understand that validity is not a property of the research design, but of the inferences being made (Shadish et al., 2002). However, the way a specific study is designed can affect the validity of the inferences made. In this section, we focus on four key types of validity that are important to consider when choosing a research design: construct validity, internal validity, statistical conclusion validity, and external validity.

Construct validity refers to the extent to which the measures and sampling procedures accurately reflect the higher order constructs they purport to measure (Straub, 1989; Shadish et al., 2002). For example, if we were interested in how computer self-efficacy (CSE) (Marakas et al., 1998) affects trainees' responses to an AI-enabled e-learning tutor, we would need to ensure that the items reflecting CSE fully represent the construct rather than representing only part of the construct (Straub, 1989). *Internal validity* reflects the extent to which the observed covariation between a treatment variable and an outcome variable reflect a causal relationship. *Statistical conclusion validity* refers to the extent to which statistical methods are appropriately applied so that researchers can make inferences about the relations (e.g., covariation or correlation) between the treatment variable(s) and the outcome variables. Finally, *external validity* refers to the extent to which the findings from the study generalize to other populations, settings, and treatments.

Although validity is not a property of a research design, the choices a researcher makes when choosing a research design can affect the extent to which valid inferences can be made from the results. Some designs are stronger on internal validity, but weaker on external validity. In addition, the research design chosen can affect statistical conclusion validity and construct validity. In the following sections, we discuss the different types of research designs, considering their strengths, weaknesses, and relative effectiveness in ensuring valid inferences are made by researchers.

RESEARCH DESIGNS

The effectiveness of any research design depends on the extent to which researchers can control variance, and make valid inferences that scores on a dependent variable (e.g., outcome) are a function of scores on the study's independent variables (e.g., predictors), and not scores on other extraneous variables (Stone, 1978; Kerlinger, 1986). For example, if a researcher wants to determine if AI results in biases in selection decisions then he/she must design a study that shows that selection scores based on AI algorithmic decisions are less biased than scores based on human decision making, and not a function of other factors. In order to make these inferences, the researcher must control the variance associated with the independent variable (e.g., AI-enabled vs. human decisions), the variance associated with other variables (e.g., human biases programmed into AI algorithms), and the variance associated with measurement error (Stone, 1978; Kerlinger, 1986).

In order to control these three sources of variance, studies must be designed to maximize systematic variance due to AI, minimize error variance (e.g., human programming of AI), and control extraneous variance (e.g., decision maker'ss prior knowledge of applicant) (Kerlinger,

1986). In other words, to make valid inferences regarding the influence of AI, researchers must ensure that extraneous factors are not affecting the theorized relationship between the use of AI and outcomes of interest to the researcher. There are multiple ways that research can be designed, but they can be broadly categorized as non-experimental and experimental and we discuss examples of these below.

Non-Experimental Research Designs

In non-experimental or ex post facto studies, researchers typically measure or observe the independent and the dependent variable at the same point in time and examine the extent to which they are related to one another (Stone, 1978; Kerlinger, 1986). In these types of designs the researcher has little or no control over the study's independent variables, and these variables are not manipulated. Despite these limitations, non-experimental designs have historically been the most widely used research strategies in organizational behavior (OB) and HRM, comprising between 61 and 90 percent of published studies (Stone-Romero et al., 1995; Scandura & Williams, 2000). These types of designs often fall into two categories, (a) quantitative and (b) qualitative (Stone-Romero, 2011), and we will consider each of them below.

Quantitative non-experimental studies

In quantitative non-experimental studies, a number of variables including independent, moderating, and dependent variables are measured and quantitative estimates of population parameters are estimated for individuals in one or more groups (Stone-Romero, 2011). Researchers who use these strategies typically collect data on the study's independent and dependent variable (or moderating variable), and assess the strength of the relationship (e.g., correlation) between them (Stone, 1978; Kerlinger, 1986). For example, a researcher might collect data on employees' reactions to the use of an AI-based virtual intelligent tutor, and their performance (e.g., learning) in an online training course. The rationale for a study like this is that online training is often very isolating and is less engaging than traditional face-to-face learning, and virtual intelligent tutors can enhance learning by making individuals feel more connected with others (Johnson et al., 2021). In non-experimental studies, the use of a virtual intelligent tutor is not randomly assigned to two groups of trainees in an online training course, but researchers assume that measured variables (e.g., trainee learning) are attributable to the study's independent variable. However, the researchers have no way of knowing about other variables that might affect learning in such a course (e.g., employees' prior learning, motivation, learning style, self-efficacy) (Johnson et al., 2008), and researchers need to rule out confounding variables that might influence the study's results.

Advantages of quantitative non-experimental studies

One of the major advantages of quantitative non-experimental studies is that the use of experiments in organizations may, at times, be unethical, interfere with the normal functioning of the organizations, or create harm for individuals (Kerlinger, 1986). For example, if a researcher truly believes that AI-based selection algorithms are less biased against ethnic minorities than human selection decisions then assigning job applicants to AI algorithm versus human decision-making conditions may result in denial of employment or harm to ethnic minority applicants. In other cases, researchers may not be able to manipulate independent variables (e.g., studies of employees' demographic or personality differences). Thus, manipulating the variables using an experiment may not be possible or may be unethical in organizational settings. As a result, researchers often use non-experimental strategies because they are less likely to cause harm to individuals or organizations.

Another advantage of quantitative non-experimental studies is that the results from these types of studies can extend our knowledge about human behavior in organizations, and that knowledge can be used to generate new theories or new hypotheses that can be tested by more rigorous research studies (Stone, 1978). Thus, a key advantage of using non-experimental research to study AI applications is that it generates knowledge that might not be studied otherwise, and results of non-experimental studies can help us gain a better understanding of the factors that are related to AI effectiveness (Stone, 1978). The results of studies may also offer insights on practical applications in organizations that can be tested using experiments or quasi-experimental designs in the future (Reio, 2016).

A third advantage of non-experimental designs is that they require lower effort and less funding on the part of researchers than true experimental designs (Kerlinger, 1986). For example, if researchers are interested in how job applicants react to chatbot based interviews or other AI applications (e.g., the use of virtual tutors) they can easily use questionnaires to gather the information rather than manipulate the use of these techniques in organizations. Thus, this type of research requires minimal funding and few researchers to conduct the study. In summary, non-experimental research designs make an important contribution to our understanding of organizational phenomena because they can be used for conducting research when experimentation is not possible (Reio, 2016). They can be used also to make tentative recommendations for practice and serve as the basis for future experiments (Reio, 2016).

Disadvantages of quantitative non-experimental research designs

However, quantitative non-experimental designs do have disadvantages. One of the major disadvantages is that researchers cannot make inferences that one variable causes another (Stone, 1978; Kerlinger, 1986). Stated differently, just because two variables are correlated does not mean that the independent variable causes the dependent variable. For instance, if a study suggests that trainees' reactions to virtual intelligent tutors are related to learning in an online course the results do not necessarily mean that virtual tutors cause learning in these contexts.

Another disadvantage of non-experimental designs is that researchers are placed in the position of ruling out rival or extraneous hypotheses that may affect the study's results. For example, based on the example above, it may be that an individual's prior knowledge, motivation, or learning style affects their learning in online courses rather than the use of virtual intelligent tutors (Johnson et al., 2009). Thus, when researchers use non-experimental designs, they cannot always control extraneous or confounding variables. Those who use these designs are in a position where they must rule out competing hypotheses for their results (Stone, 1978). However, researchers are only able to rule out confounding variables that were measured and they may have no idea of how many other unmeasured variables may influence their results (Stone, 1978).

A third disadvantage of non-experimental is that many published articles in our field use unwarranted causal language (e.g., use of terms like causes, effects, influences) to describe research results. For example, Stone-Romero and Gallaher (2006) found that 79 percent of articles that used non-experimental or quasi-experimental designs and that were published in the major journals in our field (e.g., *Academy of Management Journal*, *Journal of Applied Psychology*, *Personnel Psychology*, and *Organizational Behavior and Human Decision*

Processes) used inappropriate causal language (Stone-Romero, 2011). Thus, many researchers make unwarranted claims about cause and effect in published research, which can lead organizational leaders to implement new interventions (e.g., AI applications in HRM) believing that they will have a direct effect on outcomes (e.g., employee performance, learning, retention). However, given the nature of these designs, it is not possible for the researcher to claim that one independent variable (e.g., virtual intelligent tutors) caused the dependent variable (e.g., trainee learning). In addition, when researchers use these designs, they may not be able to state with confidence that an observed relation between variables is legitimate and not spurious (Stone, 1978).

Examples of AI/HRM survey research
We are aware of two examples of quantitative non-experimental research. First, van Esch and Black (2019) used a crowdsourcing platform to survey 293 individuals about their perceptions of AI-enabled recruitment. They found that participants' perceptions of the fairness of AI-enabled recruitment were related to their intentions to complete the recruitment process. In addition, participants' beliefs about AI as a trendy tool were positively related to their intentions to complete the recruitment process.

In a second study that used a quantitative non-experimental research design, van Esch et al. (2019) surveyed 532 individuals using a crowdsourcing platform to assess the relations between participants' attitudes about an organization's use of AI-enabled recruitment, and the likelihood that they would complete a job application with that organization. The findings suggest that the attitude a potential job candidate has toward the use of AI as well as the extent to which the participants believed AI to be novel were positively related to the likelihood they would complete a job application.

These studies illustrate the strengths and weaknesses of the use of quantitative non-experimental designs. For example, by utilizing a quantitative non-experimental design, both studies were able to reach out to a broad set of individuals rather than relying on only those within one organization. In addition, by utilizing a survey, they were able to conduct their study in a more cost-effective fashion than if they had to design and implement an experiment. In addition, in the context of using AI-enabled recruitment and selection, an experiment using actual applicants could be perceived as (or could actually be) unethical. For example, if the researchers had designed an experiment so that half the applicants interacted with an AI-enabled chatbot and the other half with a live recruiter, it is likely that those receiving one of the two conditions would perceive themselves as at a disadvantage when applying for a job, or would be less satisfied with the experience. Thus, they may view the hiring organization less positively, and be less likely to apply for a job. This could cost the hiring organization the chance to hire strong applicants and could potentially disadvantage actual applicants. In addition, if the organization believes that one condition is more positive or beneficial to applicants, then it may be unethical to subject individuals to the less positive condition as part of the recruitment process.

Finally, these studies provide insights that organizations can use to design future experiments. For example, based upon the findings of van Esch et al. (2019), researchers could design an experiment that considers applicant reactions to AI, e-recruitment website design (Allen et al., 2007; Dineen et al., 2007), and the use of social interfaces (Johnson et al., 2006; Hess et al., 2009). Specifically, researchers could manipulate variables such as the use of AI, website aesthetics, organization reputation, the ability to customize an applicant experience, and the social character of the technology; these variables could then be examined to determine how they interactively affect applicant reactions and their intention to apply for a job.

These studies also illustrate several weaknesses associated with quantitative non-experimental designs. For example, although van Esch et al. (2019) found a number of interesting relations between the variables in their model and use causal language in reporting on these relations, the nature of survey research means that causality cannot be inferred. Further, by not utilizing an experiment, the authors were unable to control for factors that may serve as alternate explanations for the findings or which may have materially affected the findings. Finally, as discussed by Stone (1978), the use of a quantitative non-experimental design means that the researchers cannot state with confidence that an observed relation between variables is legitimate and not spurious.

Qualitative non-experimental designs

A second type of non-experimental design is a qualitative non-experimental research strategy (Lee et al., 2011). There are several types of qualitative non-experimental designs that are used in the organizational sciences, including case studies, ethnographies, and grounded theory (Locke & Golden-Biddle, 2002). As case studies are the mostly widely used qualitative research strategy, we consider these types of studies below.

Case studies are in-depth investigations of a single person, group, event, organizational application, organizational unit, or community (Lee et al., 2011; McLeod, 2019). Data for case studies are typically collected using a variety of methods including observations, interviews, diaries, memos and letters, or archival documents (McLeod, 2019). Once the data are collected, the researcher provides a detailed description of the events, and interprets the processes and outcomes associated with them (McLeod, 2019). For example, a researcher may observe how AI is implemented in one or more organizations and collect data on the most effective or ineffective ways of implementing these new systems. Case studies may take place over extended periods of time so that processes and changes can be studied as they happen (McLeod, 2019). These types of studies generally provide rich qualitative data and have been widely used to study new technologies used in HRM (e.g., HRIS or eHRM) (Ruël et al., 2004). One reason for this is that these systems are new, and researchers need to more fully understand how they are implemented and in turn develop theories that explain how they influence organizational functioning.

A second form of qualitative non-experimental design is reflected in the design science paradigm. The design science paradigm focuses on the creation, building, and evaluation of technology artifacts that address real-world problems (Hevner et al., 2004; March & Smith, 1995; Strohmeier, 2014), such as the design of AI-enabled HRM systems. Unlike the other research designs discussed in this chapter, the design science paradigm is focused on the design of the artifact itself rather than the people and organizations that use them (Hevner et al., 2004). Design science focuses on the design of a system from conceptualization to realization, and on the evaluation of the new artifact (Peffers et al., 2007). That is, rather than utilize traditional social science research designs, design science draws its methods from engineering (March & Smith, 1995). Researchers utilizing design science often present their results in the form of a qualitative study where the design of the artifact is discussed along with a case study of its evaluation (e.g., Naim et al., 2016; Chien & Chen, 2008).[1]

Advantages of case studies
Case studies have several advantages when examining the implementation and use of AI in HRM. For instance, case studies are typically exploratory and can be used to understand a new phenomenon or gain insights about new applications or interventions (Yin, 2017; McLeod, 2019), and generate new theories and hypotheses that can be used to explain the factors that affect the success of AI applications in HRM. Case studies allow researchers to investigate a topic in detail, and typically provide qualitative data or a verbal description rather than quantitative measurement (Yin, 2017; McLeod, 2019). However, researchers may include quantitative data if they are available. Case studies may also help researchers understand a phenomenon or application from a multiple stakeholder point of view and give researchers information about how it affects the organization, unit, managers, employees, or job applicants. For instance, a case study may allow researchers to gather data on reactions to AI applications from employees, managers, job applicants, and other stakeholders. Case studies are an excellent mechanism for gathering rich data about a phenomenon, which can then be used to generate future empirical research work.

Disadvantages of case studies
Although there are several advantages of case studies for generating new ideas, theories, and hypotheses, they also have a number of disadvantages. For instance, they lack the statistical rigor associated with empirical studies and researchers may not be able to generalize the results to a wider population (Lee et al., 2011; Yin, 2017).[2] Given that case studies typically deal with only one organization or one unit, researchers may never be sure that the results reflect the broad range of outcomes associated with an application or intervention. As a result, the conclusions may not be generalizable to other organizations or contexts (Lee et al., 2011). In addition, because the data are qualitative and based on the researchers' interpretation of events, they may be biased by the researchers' point of view or their subjective feelings about a phenomenon (Yin, 2017). For instance, if a researcher believes that AI will benefit HRM decisions, he/she may report that the new systems decrease biases and enhance HRM selection decisions based only on managers' reactions to AI rather than evidence that they improve decision making.

Apart from these limitations, case studies are also very time-consuming, expensive, and difficult to replicate (Yin, 2017). They also generate a large amount of information that is difficult to analyze in a limited period of time. This may mean that information gained from case studies are especially susceptible to researchers' subjective opinions, which may bias the conclusions drawn from these types of studies.

Examples of AI/HRM case studies
In this section, we briefly discuss two case studies that focus on the use of AI to support HRM. However, unlike traditional case studies, which often longitudinally study the impact of a technological innovation or the effects of a technology change within a firm (Ruël et al., 2004), these case studies focus on the development of an AI-enabled tool and how its effectiveness was assessed. First, Chien and Chen (2008) examined the development of an AI-enabled data mining tool designed for a high-technology organization in Taiwan. The goal of this new system was to help an organization better identify the factors that were related to successful job-related outcomes (e.g., job performance, retention, and reasons that an individual employee left the firm). Specifically, the researchers considered variables such as age, gender,

marital status, degree, school from which the employee graduated, major, experience, and successful job outcomes.[3] Using the findings from this study, they developed a set of hiring rules the organization could use to increase the likelihood that a new hire would succeed on the job.

A second study (Gebhard et al., 2018) focused on the development of a gamified, AI-enabled, tool to help younger, less professionally mature, job candidates better understand the socioemotional content of job interviews. In this study, they described the process through which the tool was designed as well as the interactive and immersive capabilities of the tool. They further discussed how the simulation allowed participants to experience different levels of conflict or challenge and how much control the system gave learners over the learning experience. Finally, they presented an overview of four studies designed to refine and examine the capabilities of the system to improve interview behavior and reduce interview anxiety. These studies also provided insights for system design, which were examined in a laboratory experiment (Langer et al., 2016).

These studies illustrate the strengths and weaknesses of case studies. Both provide a rich description of the technology, how it was designed, its strengths and weaknesses, how organizations used the software, how it was received by those using it, and its potential benefits. This richness would not have been possible with experimental or survey designs.

These studies also provide some of the first insights into how AI is being used to improve hiring outcomes. For example, Chien and Chen (2008) used data mining to identify several factors that are related to better employee outcomes. Researchers could use the results of this case study to extend theory and determine if the newly identified factors are theoretically sound, add incremental validity over existing selection methods, and are legally defensible.

However, these studies suffer from weaknesses associated with all case study designs. First, they report limited measurement information, and that which is reported is often non-theoretically developed. For example, Chien and Chen (2008) do not clearly describe how "employment success" was measured nor its measurement properties. Similarly, Gebhard et al. (2018) present only scant measurement information and instead rely on comments and observations to describe how individuals responded to the AI-enabled tutor. Because of this, it becomes impossible to investigate the strengths of the relationships assessed in the model or to ensure that the findings were not simply an anomaly of the data within that firm. Thus, these studies suffer from a lack of statistical conclusion validity.

Second, it is not possible to assess causality because all variables were measured simultaneously, and no manipulation occurred. Thus, we cannot tell if the relationships found are causal and valid, or if they are spurious, or the result of a missing factor. Finally, neither of these papers draw upon theory to explain how or why the variables *should* be related. This makes it challenging for researchers to make inferences about other samples, settings, or organizations. Thus, these case studies suffer from a lack of construct validity, internal validity, statistical conclusion validity, and external validity.

Experimental Research Designs

We consider two types of experimental designs in the following sections: experimental and quasi-experimental designs. Experimental research design strategies have three major attributes. First, they allow researchers to manipulate a study's independent variables. Second, the units of interest to the researcher (e.g., individuals, teams, organizational interventions) can be assigned to the study's conditions. Third, levels of the dependent variables or outcomes are measured (Shadish et al., 2002; Stone-Romero, 2011). The ability to manipulate variables and randomly assign units to conditions strengthens the degree to which researchers can make inferences that one variable causes another. The primary reason for this is that when an experimental design is used, a researcher can be confident that the causes precede an effect in time, and he/she can be assured that the changes in dependent variables are a result of the manipulations rather than confounding variables (Stone-Romero, 2011).

For example, if a researcher wants to determine if the use of a virtual intelligent tutor causes or enhances learning in an online training course, then he/she would manipulate whether or not a trainee received a virtual intelligent tutor during online training, and would randomly assign trainees to those two conditions. Note that all other aspects of the online training would be exactly the same for all trainees. Once the training has been completed, the researcher would assess or test learning in the online course. If the trainees in the virtual intelligent tutor condition had higher test scores (i.e., learned more information) than those with no tutor then the researcher can infer that virtual tutors increase learning in online courses. Researchers should also examine the validity of the manipulation by measuring trainees' beliefs about the manipulation (e.g., a manipulation check on trainees' beliefs about virtual tutors vs. no tutors) (Stone-Romero, 2011).

Advantages of experimental research designs

The major advantage of using an experimental design is that researchers should be able to make the inference that an experimental treatment had an effect (e.g., the use of a virtual intelligent tutor enhances learning in an online course). To make this inference, experimental research designs allow researchers to rule out the effects of other, confounding, variables (e.g., history, maturation, testing effects). Thus, experimental designs allow researchers to have a great deal of control over extraneous variables. Another advantage of experimental designs is that they enable researchers to control the degree to which the groups assigned to conditions are as equal as possible with respect to the manipulated and measured variables (e.g., reduces extraneous within-group variance) (Stone, 1978). For example, if a study examines the effects of a virtual tutor on learning in an online course then scores on final tests of learning could be due to trainees' prior learning or attitudes toward technology. However, when trainees are randomly assigned to experimental conditions, their prior learning or attitudes toward technology are measured, so these two variables and others can be ruled out as confounding variables (Stone, 1978). A third advantage of experimental designs is that the results of the study can be replicated to determine if the effects are potentially generalizable.

Disadvantages of experimental designs

Even though experimental designs have a number of advantages, they also have several limitations (Shadish et al., 2002). One of the primary limitations is that it may be difficult or impossible to use this type of design to study the effects of AI-based interventions in organizational settings. For example, it is not possible to manipulate, or control for, some types of independent variables that may affect reactions to new AI-based interventions (e.g., applicants' or employees' personality, age, ethnicity, gender). Further, it may not be ethnical to manipulate variables in organizations that are likely to be beneficial to one group but harm others.

For instance, if a researcher firmly believes that AI-based selection algorithms decrease biases in selection decisions then applying these algorithms to only one subset of applicants may result in one group being hired and not the other. This would create harm to both job applicants who are denied jobs and organizations which may not hire the most qualified individuals. Another limitation is that it may not be possible to isolate one unit from another or control the degree to which employees learn about the manipulated variables (e.g., information may spread that virtual tutors are used to benefit one group of trainees and not others) (Stone-Romero, 2011).

The final set of limitations is that experiments may be subject to artifacts that bias the study's results. One artifact is that the sample used in the study may not be representative of those in the population (e.g., student participants are used to examine hiring decisions when they have no experience or there are no consequences of these decisions in the experimental context). This limits the external validity of the results. Another artifact is that participants may learn about the nature of the experimental conditions and respond in socially desirable ways or ways that jeopardize the study's results (Rosenthal & Rosnow, 2008). Other artifacts are experimenter expectation effects. Experimenters can affect a study's results if they pay more attention to one experimental group or treat one more positively than another. If these experimenter effects are present, then the results of the study may be due to self-fulfilling prophecies rather than the experimental treatment. Researchers have to be cautioned to control these artifacts in experimental research.

Examples of AI/HRM experiments
In our review of the literature, we found nine studies that utilized an experimental research design. These included five studies that are part of a program of research focused on the use of AI in the employment interview by Langer and colleagues (see Table 19.1). Space limitations preclude a full discussion of all the articles, but we briefly review two of them here. First, Langer et al. (2018) conducted a 2×2 laboratory experiment to better understand the attitude of potential job applicants to novel technologies. Specifically, all participants watched a video of an interview conducted by a humanlike virtual character (e.g., an avatar) and then the researchers measured their reactions to this interview. The two conditions were computer experience (computer science students vs. non-computer science students) and information provided (low vs. high). Those in the low-information condition were told that they would be interviewing with a virtual character. Those in the high-information condition were also provided with information about the capabilities of the virtual character to analyze facial expressions, body language, and speech patterns. The results indicated that individuals who received more information about the capabilities of the virtual character had more positive perceptions of the virtual character than those who received limited information. However, computer experience did not have a statistically significantly influence on participants' perceptions of interviewing with a virtual character.

Second, Langer et al. (2020) conducted a laboratory experiment to better understand how potential applicants would react to the use of AI-enabled evaluation of selection interviews. The research design included two conditions. In the first condition participants completed an online one-way interview and were notified that their responses would be evaluated by a human rater. In the second condition, participants completed an online one-way interview and were notified that their responses would be evaluated by an advanced computer program. The results suggest that compared to evaluation by a human, potential applicants were less likely to engage in impression management and more likely to feel that their ability to perform was constrained when evaluated by AI.

These two studies illustrate the strengths and weaknesses of experiments. By using experiments, Langer and colleagues (Langer et al., 2018; Langer et al., 2020) were able to demonstrate causality and make inferences that their treatments affected their outcomes of interest. For example, in the former study, the researchers were able to show that providing more information about the virtual character influenced their attitudes toward AI-enabled selection interviews. In the latter, the researchers were able to demonstrate that perceptions of the selection interview differed based upon how the interview was evaluated (e.g., human or AI). In addition, by creating a controlled environment the researchers were able to control for potential extraneous or confounding variables (e.g., history, maturation, testing effects). Finally, these studies can provide the basis upon which other researchers can build by replicating and extending these works to determine if these effects are generalizable across different samples and environments.

Despite the rigorous nature of experiments, these studies also illustrate potential disadvantages of experiments. First, this study was not conducted in an organizational setting under realistic conditions. This makes generalizability of the study to these environments more difficult. In addition, the use of students who were not actively engaged in seeking employment means that the sample was less representative than if it consisted of those who were actively seeking employment. As noted earlier, using student participants to examine hiring decisions when they have no experience or there are no consequences for their decisions risks that their responses may not represent how professionals would respond. This reduces the generalizability of the findings.

Quasi-experimental Research Designs

As noted above, it is not always possible to use a completely randomized experimental design in an organizational setting. Thus, researchers may use quasi-experimental designs that allow them to make stronger inferences than non-experimental designs, but weaker inferences than randomized experimental designs (Stone-Romero, 2011). Quasi-experimental designs can be very useful in organizational settings because they allow researchers to control two major research factors: (a) who or what is measured, and (b) when such measurement takes place (Stone, 1978). They do not allow researchers to randomly assign people or units to experimental conditions, but they do allow them to determine who gets the experimental treatment and when the treatment is administered.

According to Shadish et al. (2002), there are five types of quasi-experimental designs (i.e., single-group design without a control condition, time series designs, a regression discontinuity design, multiple-group design which lacks one or more pre-test measures, and non-equivalent control group design). Space limitations preclude a complete review of each design, and for a full description of each design, readers should refer to Shadish et al. (2002). In the section below, we consider one exemplar of a quasi-experimental design, the non-equivalent control group design, and provide examples to show how it might be used in AI research. In a non-experimental control group design, researchers use two groups: a treatment and a control group (Stone, 1978).

Given that assignment to these groups is not random, researchers typically first measure pre-test values of a dependent variable, then introduce the treatment to one group and not the other. After the treatment, they measure post-test values of the dependent variable for both groups. For example, if researchers want to determine if the use of AI-based chatbots increases employees' satisfaction with benefits enrollment, then they would first measure all employees' current satisfaction with benefits enrollment. Then they would give employees in one department, and not the other, the opportunity to use an AI-based chatbot to help them with benefits enrollment (e.g., answer benefits questions, give advice on the most effective benefits plan that has the lowest cost). Next, they would assess satisfaction with self-service benefits enrollment for employees in both departments. If the employees who were given the opportunity to use an AI-based chatbot for benefits enrollments had higher post-test measures of satisfaction than pre-test measures but the control group did not, then researchers can cautiously infer that the use of AI-based chatbots is related to satisfaction with self-service benefits enrollment.

It merits noting that the non-experimental control group design is widely used to examine the effectiveness of organizational interventions. However, although it does have advantages for the researcher, it may also pose threats to certain types of validity (Stone-Romero, 2011).

Advantages of quasi-experimental designs

Quasi-experimental designs have a number of potential benefits. First, they enable researchers to manipulate variables, and that strengthens the validity of inferences made from the study's results (Stone-Romero, 2011). Second, they are appropriate when randomization is viewed as unethical or impossible in organizations. For example, as discussed above, if actual job applicants were randomly assigned to two conditions (e.g., AI-enabled chatbot vs. live recruiter), the researchers would have a priori assumptions about which condition would be more beneficial to applicants and the organization. Thus, randomly assigning individuals to the "inferior" condition would place them at a disadvantage in finding employment with the firm and would be unethical.[4] In addition, even if these individuals were not disadvantaged in the recruitment and selection process, they may still perceive their condition to be inferior and may be less likely to accept a job offer. This in turn could cause the hiring organization to miss out on quality employees.

Third, this design controls several threats to internal validity including history, maturation, and testing (Stone, 1978). Another advantage of quasi-experimental designs is that they are often less costly than experimental studies and require fewer resources than randomized experiments. They are also pragmatic because they can be used to evaluate real-world interventions, which influences the external validity of the study's results (Schweizer et al., 2016).

Disadvantages of quasi-experimental designs

However, there are several validity threats that are not controlled by this design (i.e., interaction of testing and the experimental variable) (Stone, 1978). For instance, when researchers introduce a measure of satisfaction with benefits enrollment prior to the treatment condition, employees who are involved in the study may guess the study's hypotheses and respond in a socially desirable way to support the hypothesis. Thus, the use of a pre-test measure of satisfaction may serve as a threat to the validity of the inferences made from the study.

Examples of AI/HRM quasi-experiments

We are not aware of any studies that have focused on the use of AI in HRM, and which utilized a quasi-experimental design. However, there have been a number of eHRM studies that have utilized a quasi-experimental design. We briefly discuss one that examined the equivalence of proctored web-based and paper-and-pencil-based employee selection tests (Ployhart et al., 2003). The sample consisted of over 5000 applicants and incumbents who worked in, or were applying for work in, a call center. The participants were separated into three groups. The first group consisted of incumbent employees and they received a paper-and-pencil version of the selection battery (personality, biodata, and a situational judgment test). The second group consisted of applicants and they received the paper-and-pencil version of the battery. Finally, a third group consisted of applicants that received the web-based version of the battery. In this study, the researchers examined the equivalence between the two types of batteries (paper-and-pencil and web-based) and the two types of samples (e.g., incumbent vs. applicant). They compared these groups on response distributions, variance, means cores, internal consistency reliabilities, and intercorrelations.

This study illustrates several of the advantages and disadvantages of quasi-experiments. First, because this study was conducted with actual employees and applicants, using existing testing methods, the researchers were able to evaluate real-world interventions (e.g., selection batteries), which increases the generalizability of the results. Second, the researchers were able to manipulate the variables (e.g., incumbent vs. applicant, paper-and-pencil vs. web-based). This allowed them to make inferences about causality. Third, as the study was conducted as part of ongoing hiring and validation processes within the organization, it did not require the organization to dedicate substantial resources to a formalized lab experiment.

However, this study also has limitations. First, the researchers were unable to truly randomize the participants to conditions. As the authors noted, randomization was not truly possible because the sample consisted of individuals who were applying for a specific job at a specific firm. Thus, it is possible that the characteristics of each group may have affected the results.

DISCUSSION

AI has the potential to fundamentally alter the practice of HRM and revolutionize how we attract, hire, evaluate, and manage employees. However, because the application of AI techniques to HRM is relatively new, empirical research examining its effectiveness is needed to ensure that vendors and organizations make valid inferences. Therefore, this chapter focuses on the importance of a priori decisions regarding research design to ensure that valid inferences are made about the effectiveness and risks of AI. Specifically, it focuses on how the chosen research design can affect the insights gained and generalizations made by the researcher.

In this chapter, we considered four types of empirical research designs that can be used to examine the effectiveness of AI applications in HRM. These were the quantitative non-experimental designs (e.g., surveys), qualitative non-experimental designs (e.g., case studies), experiments, and quasi-experiments. Each research design has relative strengths and weaknesses that affect the validity of the inferences that are made by researchers. For example, case studies allow for rich data and deep analysis of a specific department, division, or company. However, because the findings are interpreted by the researchers, the results can be biased by the researchers' perspectives. In addition, because they are focused on one organization, and do not rigorously measure variables, generalizability of findings is lower than with other research designs.

In comparison, controlled laboratory experiments are much more rigorous in terms of internal validity. Experiments allow variables to be precisely defined and measured, manipulations can be rigorously designed, and researchers can account for other variables that may affect the theorized relations. However, in some cases, where the characteristics of the sample are not representative of the population of interest (e.g., undergraduate students vs. HRM managers), research findings may not generalize.[5] It is also important that researchers understand that if there is a mismatch between the research questions of interest, the types of data available, and the research design, their ability to make valid inferences will be eroded.

In closing, we wish to reiterate that this chapter should not be viewed as a call for selecting one research design over the others. Each research design has its own strengths and weaknesses that the researcher must consider. Ultimately, the use of all the research designs by many different researchers will help us build a cumulative research tradition and will help inform AI vendors and organizations about the promise and pitfalls of AI in HRM. We encourage researchers to use these research designs to tackle the interesting and challenging research questions revolving around the use of AI in HR. It is our hope that this chapter will help researchers design studies that inform organizations how to effectively design, implement, and use AI to benefit HRM decisions and improve both organizational and individual outcomes.

NOTES

1. A full discussion of design science research methodology is beyond the scope of this chapter. However, interested readers are encouraged to look at the work by March and Smith (1995), Hevner et al. (2004), and Peffers et al. (2007) for its use in information systems and the work by Strohmeier (2014) for its use in HRM.
2. It is important to note that the authors of this chapter are quantitative researchers who adhere to the logical positivistic research paradigm. In general, this paradigm subscribes to the philosophy that objective reality exists apart from the researcher and can be examined through rigorous observation or experimental design and statistical analyses (Weber, 2004). As such, measurement and experimental validity are critical to the truth of the inferences made by researchers. It merits noting that researchers may adopt other philosophical research paradigms such as interpretivism. The interpretivist paradigm subscribes to the philosophy that reality and the researcher cannot be separated, and that knowledge of the world is reflected through lived experience and cannot be interpreted outside of the researchers' lived experience (Weber, 2004). Thus, quantitative analyses are not typically used by interpretivist researchers, who instead rely on qualitative research to derive meaning and understanding about the phenomena that can be extrapolated to other, similar environments (Hoepfl, 1997; Patton, 2002). For qualitative researchers, validity as we use it in this chapter is not applicable. Instead qualitative researchers focus on the "quality, rigor, and trustworthiness" of the findings (Golafshani, 2003, p. 602).

    For this reason, it is important to understand that when we discuss the limitations of qualitative research, we are focusing on those limitations considering our philosophical perspective. Not all AI researchers may concur with our worldview, but even if they do not, they still need to ensure the trustworthiness and generalizability of research findings. One such way is through triangulation using other research methods, such as quantitative research (Golafshani, 2003). For more information on the different philosophies underlying research, and guidelines for conducting high-quality interpretive research, we encourage readers to look at the work of Walsham (2006), Klein and Myers (1999), Lee et al. (2011), or Patton (2002).
3. It is important to note that several of the factors of interest to the researchers (e.g., age, gender, marital status) are ill-advised to consider in the United States because they can lead to a prima facie case for unfair discrimination.
4. For more information on the legal and ethical issues associated with the use of AI-enabled HRM, interested readers can refer to Part IV of this book.
5. Scholars have begun turning to Amazon's Mechanical Turk (MTurk) as a source for research participants. Although one motivation for using MTurk is to reduce costs, its use also helps generate a large and diverse sample which may be more representative of the general population than

students (Aguinis et al., 2021). This can help with generalizability of research findings but brings with it a new set of threats to validity for which researchers must account. Discussing these in detail is beyond the scope of this chapter. However, for interested readers, Aguinis et al. has an excellent review to assist researchers in properly utilizing MTurk in research.

REFERENCES

Aguinis, H., Villamor, I., & Ramani, R. S. (2021). MTurk research: Review and recommendations. *Journal of Management, 47*(4), 823–837. https://doi.org/10.1177/0149206320969787

Allen, D. G., Mahto, R. V., & Otondo, R. F. (2007). Web-based recruitment: Effects of information, organizational brand, and attitudes toward a web site on applicant attraction. *Journal of Applied Psychology*, 92(6), 1696–1708. https://doi.org/10.1037/0021-9010.92.6.1696

Chen, J., Luo, N., Liu, Y., Liu, L., Zhang, K., & Kolodziej, J. (2016). A hybrid intelligence-aided approach to affect-sensitive e-learning. *Computing*, 98(1–2), 215–233.

Chien, C. F., & Chen, L. F. (2008). Data mining to improve personnel selection and enhance human capital: A case study in high-technology industry. *Expert Systems with Applications*, 34(1), 280–290.

Davenport, T. H., & Ronanki, R. (2018). Artificial intelligence for the real world. *Harvard Business Review*, 96(1), 108–116.

Dineen, B. R., Ling, J., Ash, S. R., & DelVecchio, D. (2007). Aesthetic properties and message customization: Navigating the dark side of web recruitment. *Journal of Applied Psychology*, 92(2), 356–372. https://doi.org/10.1037/0021-9010.92.2.356

Fletcher, J. D., & Morrison, J. E. (2014). *Accelerating development of expertise: A digital tutor for Navy technical training*. Institute for Defense Analyses.

Gebhard, P., Schneeberger, T., André, E., Bauer, T., ... & Langer, M. (2018). Serious games for training social skills in job interviews. *IEEE Transactions on Games*, 11(4), 340–351. https://doi.org/10.1109/TG.2018.2808525

Golafshani, N. (2003). Understanding reliability and validity in qualitative research. *The Qualitative Report*, 8(4), 597–607.

Hemamou, L., Felhi, G., Martin, J.-C., & Clavel, C. (2019a). *Slices of attention in asynchronous video job interviews*. arVix. https://arxiv.org/abs/1909.08845

Hemamou, L., Felhi, G., Vandenbussche, V., Martin, J.-C., & Clavel, C. (2019b). *Hirenet: A hierarchical attention model for the automatic analysis of asynchronous video job interviews*. arVix. https://arxiv.org/abs/1907.11062

Hess, T. J., Fuller, M. A., & Campbell, D. (2009). Designing interfaces with social presence: Using vividness and extraversion to create social recommendation agents. *Journal of the Association for Information Systems*, 10(12), 889–919.

Hevner, A. R., March, S. T., Park, J., & Ram, S. (2004). Design science in information systems research. *MIS Quarterly*, 28(1), 75–105.

Hoepfl, M. C. (1997). Choosing qualitative research: A primer for technology education researchers. *Journal of Technology Education*, 9(1), 47–63.

Hwang, G. J. (2003). A conceptual map model for developing intelligent tutoring systems. *Computers and Education*, 40(3), 217–235.

Johnson, R. D., Gueutal, H., & Falbe, C. M. (2009). Technology, trainees, metacognitive activity and e-learning effectiveness. *Journal of Managerial Psychology*, 24(6), 545–566.

Johnson, R. D., Hornik, S., & Salas, E. (2008). An empirical examination of factors contributing to the creation of successful e-learning environments. *International Journal of Human-Computer Studies*, 66(5), 356–369.

Johnson, R. D., Marakas, G. M., & Palmer, J. W. (2006). Differential social attributions toward computing technology: An empirical investigation. *International Journal of Human-Computer Studies*, 64(5), 446–460. https://doi.org/10.1016/j.ijhcs.2005.09.002

Johnson, R. D., Stone, D. L., & Lukaszewski, K. (2021). The benefits of eHRM and AI for talent acquisition. *Journal of Tourism Futures*, 7(1), 40–52.

Kerlinger, F. (1986). *Foundations of behavioral research*. Harcourt Brace & Company.

Klein, H. K., & Myers, M. D. (1999). A set of principles for conducting and evaluating interpretive field studies in information systems. *MIS Quarterly*, *23*(1), 67–93.

Kurilovas, E., Zilinskiene, I., & Dagiene, V. (2015). Recommending suitable learning paths according to learners' preferences: Experimental research results. *Computers in Human Behavior*, *51*(Part B), 945–951.

Langer, M., König, C. J., & Fitili, A. (2018). Information as a double-edged sword: The role of computer experience and information on applicant reactions towards novel technologies for personnel selection. *Computers in Human Behavior*, *81*, 19–30.

Langer, M., König, C. J., Gebhard, P., & André, E. (2016). Dear computer, teach me manners: Testing virtual employment interview training. *International Journal of Selection and Assessment*, *24*(4), 312–323.

Langer, M., König, C. J., & Hemsing, V. (2020). Is anybody listening? The impact of automatically evaluated job interviews on impression management and applicant reactions. *Journal of Managerial Psychology*, *35*(4), 271–284.

Langer, M., König, C. J., & Papathanasiou, M. (2019a). Highly automated job interviews: Acceptance under the influence of stakes. *International Journal of Selection and Assessment*, *27*(3), 217–234.

Langer, M., König, C. J., Ruth-Pelipez Sanchez, D., & Samadi, S. (2019b). Highly automated interviews: Applicant reactions and the organizational context. *Journal of Managerial Psychology*, *35*(4), 301–314.

Lee, T. W., Mitchell, T. R., & Harman, W. S. (2011). Qualitative research strategies in industrial and organizational psychology. In S. Zedeck (Ed.), *APA handbooks in psychology®. APA handbook of industrial and organizational psychology*, Vol. 1. Building and developing the organization (pp. 73–83). American Psychological Association. https://doi.org/10.1037/12169-003

Leong, C. W., Roohr, K., Ramanarayanan, V., Martin-Raugh, M. P., … & McCulla, L. (2019). *To trust, or not to trust? A study of human bias in automated video interview assessments.* arVix. https://arxiv .org/abs/1911.13248

Locke, K., & Golden-Biddle, K. (2002). An introduction to qualitative research: Its potential for industrial and organizational psychology. In S. G. Rogelberg (Ed.), *Handbook of research methods in industrial and organizational psychology* (pp. 99–118). Blackwell Publishing.

Lykourentzou, I., Giannoukos, I., Mpardis, G., Nikopoulous, V., & Loumos, V. (2009). Early and dynamic student achievement prediction in e-learning courses using neural networks. *Journal of the American Society for Information Science and Technology*, *60*(2), 372–380.

Marakas, G. M., Yi, M. Y., & Johnson, R. D. (1998). The multilevel and multifaceted character of computer self-efficacy: Toward clarification of the construct and an integrative framework for research. *Information Systems Research*, *9*(2), 126–163.

March, S. T., & Smith, G. F. (1995). Design and natural science research on information technology. *Decision Support Systems*, *15*(4), 251–266.

McLeod, S. A. (2019, August 3). *Case study method.* Simply Psychology. https://www.simplypsychology .org/case-study.html, accessed 9/3/2020.

Naim, I., Iftekhar Tanveer, M., Gildea, D., & Hoque, M. E. (2016). Automated analysis and prediction of job interview performance. *IEEE Transactions on Affective Computing*, *9*(2), 191–204.

Ötting, S. K., & Maier, G. W. (2018). The importance of procedural justice in human–machine interactions: Intelligent systems as new decision agents in organizations. *Computers in Human Behavior*, *89*, 27–39.

Patton, M. Q. (2002). *Qualitative evaluation and research methods* (3rd ed.). Sage Publications.

Peffers, K., Tuunanen, T., Rothenberger, M. A., & Chatterjee, S. (2007). A design science research methodology for information systems research. *Journal of Management Information Systems*, *24*(3), 45–77.

Ployhart, R. E., Weekley, J. A., Holtz, B. C., & Kemp, C. (2003). Web-based and paper-and-pencil testing of applicants in a proctored setting: Are personality, biodata, and situational judgment tests comparable? *Personnel Psychology*, *56*(3), 733–752.

Reio, T. G. (2016). Nonexperimental research: Strengths, weaknesses and issues of precision. *European Journal of Training and Development*, *40*(8–9), 676–690.

Rosenthal, R., & Rosnow, R. L. (2008). *Essentials of behavioral research: Methods and data analysis.* McGraw-Hill.

Ruël, H., Bondarouk, T., & Looise, J. K. (2004). E-HRM: Innovation or irritation. An explorative empirical study in five large companies on web-based HRM. *Management Revue*, *15*(3), 364–380.

Scandura, T. A., & Williams, E. A. (2000). Research methodology in management: Current practices, trends, and implications for future research. *Academy of Management Journal*, *43*(6), 1248–1264.

Schweizer, M. L., Braun, B. I., & Milstone, A. M. (2016). Research methods in healthcare epidemiology and antimicrobial stewardship-quasi-experimental designs. *Infection Control and Hospital Epidemiology*, *37*(10), 1135–1140.

Shadish, W. R., Cook, T. D., & Campbell, D. T. (2002). *Experimental and quasi-experimental designs for generalized causal inference*. Houghton, Mifflin and Company.

Stone, E. F. (1978). *Research methods in organizational behavior*. Goodyear Publishing.

Stone-Romero, E. F. (2011). Research strategies in industrial and organizational psychology: Nonexperimental, quasi-experimental, and randomized experimental research in special purpose and nonspecial purpose settings. In S. Zedeck (Ed.), *APA handbooks in psychology®. APA handbook of industrial and organizational psychology,* Vol. 1. Building and developing the organization (p. 37–72). American Psychological Association. https://doi.org/10.1037/12169-002

Stone-Romero, E. F., & Gallaher, L. (2006, May 5–7). *Inappropriate use of causal language in reports of nonexperimental research* [Paper presentation]. Annual Meeting of the Society for Industrial and Organizational Psychology, Dallas, TX, United States.

Stone-Romero, E. F., Weaver, A. E., & Glenar, J. L. (1995). Trends in research design and data analytic strategies in organizational research. *Journal of Management*, *21*(1), 141–157.

Straub, D. W. (1989). Validating instruments in MIS research. *MIS Quarterly*, *13*(2), 147–169.

Strohmeier, S. (2014). Research approaches in e-HRM: Categorisation and analysis. In F. J. Martinez-López (Ed.), *Handbook of strategic e-business management* (pp. 605–632). Springer.

Suen, H. Y., Chen, M. Y.-C., & Lu, S. H. (2019). Does the use of synchrony and artificial intelligence in video interviews affect interview ratings and applicant attitudes? *Computers in Human Behavior*, *98*, 93–101.

Tambe, P., Cappelli, P., & Yakubovich, V. (2019). Artificial intelligence in human resources management: Challenges and a path forward. *California Management Review*, *61*(4), 15–42.

van Esch, P., & Black, J. S. (2019). Factors that influence new generation candidates to engage with and complete digital, AI-enabled recruiting. *Business Horizons*, *62*(6), 729–739.

van Esch, P., Black, J. S., & Ferolie, J. (2019). Marketing AI recruitment: The next phase in job application and selection. *Computers in Human Behavior*, *90*, 215–222.

Walsham, G. (2006). Doing interpretive research. *European Journal of Information Systems*, *15*(3), 320–330.

Weber, R. (2004). The rhetoric of positivism versus interpretivism: A personal view. *MIS Quarterly*, *28*(1), iii–xii.

Yin, R. (2017). *Case study research and applications: Design and methods*. Sage Publications.

20. Employing artificial intelligence in human resources research

Chulin Chen and Richard Landers

EMPLOYING ARTIFICIAL INTELLIGENCE IN HUMAN RESOURCE MANAGEMENT RESEARCH

Although it has great potential for human resource management (HRM) research, machine learning (ML) is most directly intended to solve general statistical problems, including the prediction of categorical outcomes (i.e., classification), the prediction of continuous outcomes (i.e., regression), the identification of groupings of variables or cases (i.e., clustering), and pattern detection (e.g., association rule learning). Use of these techniques has seen many broader data science applications, in areas like natural language processing (NLP), automatic recommendation systems, and image recognition, which can in turn be used in applied contexts. HRM research applications are much more recent, even as algorithm-rated interviews and the development of automatic recruitment/selection systems are being used in a growing number of organizations.

Mirroring practical applications, it has been mostly computer science researchers who have been using ML in HRM areas, including recruitment (e.g., Pessach et al., 2020), selection (e.g., Chien & Chen, 2008), training and development (e.g., Borghini et al., 2017), performance management (e.g., de Oliveira et al., 2019), and turnover (e.g., Frierson & Si, 2018), to enable new insights into old problems. For instance, ML-based prediction of organizational outcomes such as employee performance and turnover has led to the discovery of additional factors associated with these outcomes which were not previously documented. ML can even provide answers to new problems which are otherwise difficult to investigate using traditional methodologies, such as in the study of transient organizational or psychological processes. ML-based methods allow the analysis of a huge quantity of variables and samples associated with dynamic processes in a single study, beyond what can be reasonably analyzed with traditional modeling, which could in turn deepen our understanding of more fine-grained microprocesses.

Despite widespread enthusiasm among computer scientists for applying ML methods to HRM problems (Berhil et al., 2020), interdisciplinarity has been poor. Much current ML research within the HRM domain has been done by computer scientists, with little or no input from HRM researchers, creating numerous interpretability problems related to validity, reliability, and adverse impact. Interdisciplinary collaborations between such computer scientists and HRM researchers are essential for establishing standards for measurement and research based on ML techniques. Examples of such challenges and potential solutions will be explored later in this chapter.

The general aim of this chapter is to introduce HRM researchers to the potential of ML-based methods for the investigation of HRM problems and the development of HRM theories. We will plainly describe the limitations of traditional HRM research data collection strategies and statistical approaches that can be reasonably addressed using ML while preserving the psychometric standards of traditional research methods. We will then review existing HRM studies using ML methods, address challenges associated with using ML in HRM research, and recommend future research directions on the interface between HRM and ML.

CHALLENGES IN HRM RESEARCH ADDRESSED BY MACHINE LEARNING

Traditional research designs used in HRM research that rely heavily on survey-based data collection exhibit two major methodological weaknesses that limit scope and generalizability in ways that are potentially addressed by the focus on "big data" common in much ML-related research. First, because the effects tested in HRM research tend to be small, conventional data collection methods often gather samples that are too small to reliably detect those effects due to associated time and other costs. This leads to low statistical power for inferential tests, which in turn results in publication biases. Second, due to the small effect sizes of interest, researchers can only reasonably study a limited number of variables in any one collection effort without overburdening the information provided by the small samples they collect. These two issues together restrict the types of research questions that HRM researchers investigate, encouraging confirmatory research that is highly limited in scope. This has become even more counterproductive as theories of HRM and organizational phenomena have become increasingly complex, dynamic, and multilevel (Kozlowski & Klein, 2000), requiring even larger sample sizes to reasonably test them. Additionally, the relatively small convenience populations from which data are collected cast questions on the generalizability of the conclusions draw by HRM research, a problem exacerbated by the general lack of replication studies in the entire domain (Campbell & Wilmot, 2018).

Another problematic aspect of current HRM research potentially addressed by ML methods is its reliance upon statistical methods optimized for small sample sizes. Recent technological advancements have enabled organizations to accumulate HR-relevant data across many different organizational functions and across long periods of time at very low cost (Angrave et al., 2016). These internal data can also be combined with external data from the broader socioeconomic context in which the organization is located (e.g., unemployment rates), communication between the organization and external members (e.g., emails), and employee activities outside of work (e.g., location data) to generate insights that are difficult or impractical to assess using questionnaires. Currently, 80 percent of organizational data can be categorized as unstructured data, including text, images, and videos (Shilakes & Tylman, 1998), much of which cannot be easily analyzed using classical statistical approaches. Such data cannot be easily or comprehensively modeled with conventional statistical analyses, due to their general lack of ability to handle high p-to-N ratios, a major aspect of such data.

ML not only overcomes the abovementioned shortcomings associated with these established research methodologies, but also enables research designs that can address meaningful HRM research questions in new, powerful ways. Although researchers have traditionally relied on inference-focused statistical approaches, there is an increasing recognition of the value of prediction as a meaningful way to build theory (Yarkoni & Westfall, 2017). Although drawing causal conclusions about human behaviors remains important, Yarkoni and Westfall argued that predictive ML approaches can overcome many problems with traditional statistical data modeling, which include p-hacking, low research efficiency, and a lack of consensus metrics of model performance for radically different models, while still maintaining a degree of explainability. The effects of common p-hacking practices may be somewhat mitigated by several common practices in ML that balance analytical flexibility and predictive performance. One of these is cross-validation, a method of estimating out-of-sample generalizability of models, which increases research efficiency and reproducibility by providing some of the benefits attributed to replication research. Another is regularization, a method to improve out-of-sample generalizability by penalizing complex models. Using techniques like these, ML could even drive a new era of inductive theory-building by uncovering unanticipated relationships between variables in a way that does not suffer from the same drawbacks as classic data-mining techniques, using predictive models as the first stage in a larger mixed-methods research program. This is because ML-based methods can more meaningfully identify generalizable variance within large theoretically-relevant predictor groups than is possible with traditional data mining. This kind of optimization also improves the chances of discovering theoretically meaningful predictors that were not previously known. Given such findings, researchers can generate more refined research questions and hypotheses for triangulating inferential research. Such procedures are particularly useful for creating theory from quantitative investigation of new topics that are difficult to study deductively and inferentially (e.g., predicting job applicants' competency based on video interviews) and triangulating upon existing topics from a different perspective to assess the generalizability of theory (e.g., predicting team performance from moment-to-moment team interactions).

AN INTRODUCTION TO ML IN HRM

Broadly speaking, there are two classes of ML methods that HRM researchers will find most useful: supervised and unsupervised ML. Supervised ML is used to generate an algorithm that will accurately predict a criterion in newly collected data. In supervised learning, much like in linear regression, model parameters, rules, and functions are estimated to create a generalizable predictive formula, a process referred to as "training a model" by ML practitioners. Unsupervised ML, on the other hand, is used for reducing the dimensionality of data by generating factors or clusters from datasets without pre-assigned labels. More details about supervised and unsupervised learning will be presented in the following sections.

SUPERVISED LEARNING METHODS

Introduction

Supervised ML is arguably the most useful ML method for most HRM research questions, especially considering its conceptual similarities to linear regression, one of the most common statistical techniques already in use. Some of the most commonly used supervised learning methods include decision trees, naïve Bayes classification, support vector machines, artificial neural networks, and regularized regression (please refer to CHAPTER 6 for a more detailed introduction of specific algorithms and modeling techniques). The selection of algorithms for a specific study should depend on a joint consideration of data characteristics (including size, noise, redundancy, interaction, and nonlinearity), explainability, and predictive accuracy.

Because algorithms differ in terms of their suitability for different data patterns and explainability, and because these differences can be quite subtle, researchers generally do not know which specific algorithm will result in the best prediction among a set of plausible options. Therefore, a standard practice in an ML research project is to select a group of algorithms that are appropriate to each research problem and then estimate and compare the results of several different algorithms applied to the same data.

Challenges Associated with Supervised Learning Methods

Predictors for use in supervised learning models can be identified using a top-down, bottom-up, or hybrid approach, and the choice between these is often not straightforward. With a top-down approach, predictors are created according to existing theories and the literature using a variety of methods. Quantitative predictors can be used without pre-processing, as they would be used in traditional regression-based approaches. However, for unstructured data such as text, audio, and videos, additional steps need to be taken to create valid and reliable measures of target constructs. For textual data, NLP techniques should be used to create useful quantitative variables from the text (for a detailed discussion of the application of NLP techniques in HRM, please refer to CHAPTER 3 and CHAPTER 12). Audio and video data must be similarly treated (refer to CHAPTER 4 for a discussion on specific techniques). Conversely, a bottom-up approach means that predictors that are not addressed by relevant theories and the literature are generated from data directly or after dimension reduction methods are applied. For example, from inductive methods such as artificial neural networks, interaction and nonlinearity can be discovered and scrutinized to determine if these effects are theoretically meaningful and can therefore be incorporated in the prediction model. Similarly, data clusters can be generated from a large number of individual predictors, which can then be interpreted to see if they are meaningfully related to the target criterion (see the section titled "Unsupervised Learning Methods" below for a discussion on specific techniques). As a result, bottom-up predictors often explain additional variance in criteria beyond top-down predictors. Therefore, a hybrid model combining both types of predictors might be useful to achieve better prediction than either alone. These two types of predictor also make different contributions to HRM theory. The inclusion of top-down predictors has implications for theory testing, whereas bottom-up predictors can help researchers to discover novel predictors of a criterion which can contribute to theory building and expansion.

Another challenge associated with supervised ML methods is that the models often involve a huge number of predictors that, by using a process called feature engineering, need to be reduced to a smaller number to prevent overfitting on the training dataset. This is usually done with two methods. The first method is to select algorithms for their feature generation or selection techniques. These functions also serve as inbuilt mechanisms to control the extent to which model parameters are optimized on the local dataset or constrained so that the prediction model become more generalizable. Second, feature generation or selection techniques may be applied directly to the dataset before running the prediction model. These techniques themselves can generally be classified into three types: methods that remove redundant predictors based on predictor interdependence, approaches that select a subset of predictors based upon predictive contribution toward the criterion variable, and approaches that involve the creation of new summary predictors based upon existing data. There is no best way to select features, as the ideal approach varies by dataset composition and research goals; feature selection methods should instead generally be chosen by experimenting with different techniques and subsets of predictors within a cross-validation framework.

Cross-validation is a process used to avoid overfitting by striking a balance between local optimization and generalization. Cross-validation in HRM is typically done by applying a prediction model obtained from one sample to another independent sample to see how well the model predicts out-of-sample. Such attempts are necessary before one can conclude that the conclusion drawn from an empirical study can be generalized to a wider population, as the model parameters and R-squared statistics derived from a sample are optimized on that dataset. However, for ML models that are usually more complex and require larger independent samples to validate, more sophisticated techniques such as k-fold cross-validation are required to ensure that the model development does not capitalize on chance variation in the local data. Such techniques work by splitting the dataset into k "folds" and developing k models on every possible combination of k-1 folds and cross-validating them using the held-out fold. Summary statistics, such as mean and SD of R^2 are then calculated across the models to estimate model generalizability. This process is typically crossed with a procedure called hyperparameter tuning, which involves systematically varying hyperparameters (i.e., configuration options for each algorithm) and observing the effects of that variation during cross-validation. The ML literature has devoted significant effort to developing cross-validation strategies far beyond what is commonly seen in HRM. The best cross-validation approaches for a particular research problem should be chosen depending on the characteristics of the predictors used in the problem (for a more detailed discussion, see Arlot & Celisse, 2010).

UNSUPERVISED LEARNING METHODS

Introduction

In contrast to supervised learning, unsupervised ML is more conceptually similar to factor analysis or traditional cluster analysis in its focus on identifying unlabeled latent groups within unstructured data, whether across variables or across cases. These analyses involve the identification of latent groups within a dataset such that objects within a group will be similar to one another (i.e., intra-cluster distances are minimized) and dissimilar from the objects in other groups (i.e., inter-cluster distances are maximized). The most widely used measure of intra-cluster distance is the Euclidean distance (i.e., sum of squares of differences on each dimension between two objects), but other proximity measures are also used. Sets of clusters can generally be classified based on two distinctions: partitional versus hierarchical and exclusive versus non-exclusive. Partitional clustering refers to the division of objects into non-overlapping clusters, whereas hierarchical clustering refers to a set of nested clusters organized in a hierarchical structure. For example, employees can be organized into non-overlapping clusters based on their knowledge, skills, abilities, and other characteristics (KSAOs), from which researchers can discover different subgroups of employees that are similar to each other in terms of KSAOs; on the other hand, data about different jobs profiled in a job analysis can be clustered hierarchically to not only discover clusters of jobs that are similar to each other, but also higher-level job families to which each job cluster belongs. Exclusive clustering means that each object can only be in one cluster whereas non-exclusive clustering allows objects to belong to multiple clusters. Non-exclusive clustering is more suitable when objects are supposed to have multiple memberships. For example, in more modern organizational settings, employees are more likely to be members of multiple work teams simultaneously (Mathieu & Chen, 2011). In this case, non-exclusive clustering techniques could be applied to estimate overlapping organizational clusters based on social interaction data or other such metrics among employees. Before conducting a cluster analysis, researchers should select an appropriate technique by considering the intended relationships between clusters as well as the type of cluster most suitable for a focal research question. For example, K-means and agglomerative clustering algorithms are commonly used to generate exclusive prototype-based clusters and hierarchical clusters, respectively. When analyzing text data, latent Dirichlet allocation (LDA) is another popular unsupervised technique which generates clusters of lexico-semantically related terms to form interpretable topics. As with supervised ML, unsupervised algorithms should be selected according to data requirements and research goals.

Challenges Associated with Unsupervised Learning Methods

Unsupervised learning is best used in HRM research for dimension reduction and quantifying similarity or dissimilarity between latent groups. Reducing the dimensionality of data can be important for understanding data structure or deriving high-level features. For example, résumés contain a myriad of information which could be grouped into a smaller number of clusters or topics. Exploratory factor analysis and principal components analysis serve similar purposes but are less accurate, especially when group membership signals are weak or when the number of true latent grouping is very large. High-level clusters extracted from such analyses can also serve as predictors for later supervised learning models (e.g., models that predict selection outcomes based on résumé content/groupings). Unsupervised learning can also provide information about the extent to which two objects or groups of objects are similar or dissimilar to each other.

Many of the concerns when using supervised learning in HRM research apply to unsupervised learning too. For example, the number and pattern of data clusters produced by unsupervised learning vary as a result of hyperparameter values, and the interpretation of hyperparameter appropriateness is often a matter of professional judgment. The validity of data clusters must be established by contrasting results produced by different algorithms and/ or parameters through cross-validation and by mapping clusters to existing theories to see which approaches produce most theoretically meaningful results. This can be done by applying expert judgment on the meaning of each data cluster and mapping clusters to theoretical concepts.

CONSTRUCT VALIDITY EVIDENCE IN BIG HRM DATA FOR ML

Unlike most pure ML researchers, HRM researchers must consider the construct validity of data examined using ML, which introduces concerns that are thus far only lightly explored in the HRM literature. HRM researchers typically follow a much stricter standard for developing and evaluating psychological measurements to establish construct validity, defined as the extent to which an operationally defined test is measuring the latent theoretical construct that the test is intended to measure. Loevinger (1957) emphasized the importance of construct validation for psychological theory development as it provides evidence for not only the validity of the measurement itself but also the validity for the construct it claims to measure. The Standards for Educational and Psychological Testing (American Educational Research Association et al., 2014) is the gold standard in psychological test validation principles worldwide. This section will therefore organize our discussion on how to obtain validity evidence using ML approaches in the framework provided by this standard. These standards approach construct validation as a process of "accumulating relevant evidence to provide a sound scientific basis for the proposed score interpretation" (American Educational Research Association et al., 2014, p. 11). It delineates various sources of evidence including evidence based on test content, response processes, internal structure, and relationships with other variables. It is not necessary to obtain all types of evidence to support a validity argument, and not all types of evidence apply well to ML-based measurement. Thus, decisions about which types of evidence are critical for measurement quality in each study should be made by developing explicit construct validity propositions to make assumptions clear. For example, if an ML-based measure of neuroticism was developed using individuals' behaviors on social media as indicators, the following propositions could be relevant: (1) behaviors in the social media environment reflect individual differences in neuroticism; (2) the content domain of the indicators is consistent with existing theory on neuroticism; (3) scores on the measure can be generalized to other populations and across time; and (4) scores on the measure are not confounded by ancillary variables. Once these propositions have been identified, they can be individually evaluated by examining relevant literature or obtaining empirical evidence within a primary study, as described below.

Validity Evidence Related to Content

Content-related validation evidence can be built by asking experts to evaluate the conceptual associations between model features, or groups of features, and intended constructs. Additionally, experts may be asked to evaluate differences between theory-expected and theory-unexpected content. Measures used by an ML study typically develop features associated with a specific construct in either a deductive or an inductive manner. The deductive approach is similar to the traditional content validation procedure in which test items are designed to represent the content domain of a specific construct before generating test content. For instance, Pennebaker et al. (2015) used a procedure commonly used in NLP, developing a semantic dictionary to link constructs to the content of text. The procedure starts by creating a list of words that are potentially relevant to the intended construct by consulting existing psychometric scales, reference books, and brainstorming. Then, several rounds of expert judgments are collected to rate each word's relevance to the content domain, adding new words that were not included in the initial list. Similar procedures have been used for behavior data as well. For example, in a high-fidelity simulation designed for training emergency medical teams, Grand et al. (2013) developed team process behavior indicators across team process dimensions based on Marks et al. (2001)'s behavioral process taxonomy. These indicators were mapped onto the event structure of the scenarios and content validated by subject matter experts. In contrast, an inductive approach involves the extraction of features associated with a construct after the data is collected. In ML research, this is usually done by applying ML algorithms on large datasets to identify latent variable groups.

This type of content validation is relatively rare in ML (Bleidorn & Hopwood, 2019). In addition to difficulty matching the conventional concept of content-related validity evidence to the inputs and outputs of ML methods, a major reason for this rarity is that ML approaches often result in very large quantities of identified features, which makes content validation very labor-intensive. However, a content validation procedure similar to the deductive approach can still be applied to evaluate inductive features, after feature-engineering techniques are applied to select a smaller subset of features that are most highly associated with the intended construct. The content validation process can start with an accurate definition of the intended construct based on existing literature, which includes finding theoretically-relevant indicators of behaviors, thoughts, and feelings associated with the construct. These theoretical specifications can then be used to guide expert ratings on the relevance, representativeness, specificity, and clarify of the content of the ML-based measure, to serve as content-related validity evidence. These ratings also help in identifying overrepresented, missing, or irrelevant content (Haynes et al., 1995). Some aspects of a construct may be overrepresented in an ML-based measure because of repeated features or multicollinearity in the dataset, which can be remedied by applying appropriate data cleaning or feature selection strategies. Missing content can reflect deficiency of the measure, the cause of which should be scrutinized to identify problems associated with the dataset or the measure itself. Theoretically-irrelevant features may be included by chance; alternatively, they might represent overlooked aspects of the target construct, which could expand or refine understanding of alternative structures or novel content to drive inductive theory-building. Therefore, seemingly irrelevant features should be tested on new samples to assess their generalizability. A feature may be deemed relevant if it is consistently related to the targeted construct across different samples.

Validity Evidence Related to Response Processes

One of the most compelling kinds of validity evidence for ML-derived measurement comes from analysis of response processes, but it is also often the most complex and expensive to collect. For example, if a researcher believed intentions to quit were reflected by a certain semantic dictionary created from comments on Twitter, the researcher might ask a sample of Twitter users to explain why they wrote comments that were scored highly by the semantic dictionary. If those users described all their comments about wanting to quit their jobs as being "only jokes" or "venting," this would be interpreted as evidence against accurate representations of turnover on Twitter with that dictionary; however, if they reported their comments reflected an authentic desire to quit, this would be viewed as positive evidence.

Similarly, for data collected from individuals' responses to a data-driven game-based assessment, the scores reflecting in-game behaviors that serve as features in ML-based scoring models should be aligned to constructs the game is intended to measure. For instance, if an assessment game is designed to measure leaders' communication skills through leaders' behaviors in team interactions, it is important to determine whether the leaders' performance is an accurate reflection of their abilities instead of being affected by irrelevant factors such as typing skills. Evidence related to response processes of this more technical nature can be gathered from analyses of response strategies from different subgroups. An inspection of records of different aspects of performance (e.g., response time, eye movement) could reveal the extent to which respondent performance is affected by capabilities irrelevant or ancillary to the intended construct. If subgroup differences in response processes were found, the appropriateness of these processes to the intended interpretation or construct definition would need to be reconsidered.

Validity Evidence Related to the Nomological Net

Convergence of and differentiation between ML-derived scores and those from theoretically linked measures can also be examined using a multimethod approach comparing ML-based measurements to other measures of similar and different constructs. This type of evidence is provided by testing the association between ML-based measurements and other established measures designed to assess the same or similar constructs, whereas discriminant evidence is obtained by a lack of associations between ML-based measures and other measures intended to assess different constructs within the same general domain.

The current literature on ML-based measurement of psychological constructs has largely focused on assessing the convergence between ML-based measures and questionnaire-based measures (self- or other report) of the same constructs and use the degree of convergence alone as an index of the quality of the ML-based measure. The underlying assumption is that established questionnaires represent the true scores of intended psychological constructs, so ML-based measures should be optimized to achieve better prediction of scores generated from questionnaires. Although such an approach enables the development of ML-based measures with high convergence, this presumption excludes the measurement of new or previously unmeasured aspects of the intended construct that are not captured by existing instruments and theoretical frameworks, the discovery of which could advance understanding of the underlying structure of those constructs. It is therefore useful to analyze the factorial structure of the ML-based measure and compare it to multiple measures and theoretical models of the same construct to identify the dominant factors associated with the construct as well as factors possibly overlooked by established questionnaires.

Evidence of differentiation between ML-based measures using similar methods is largely unexamined, although existing evidence suggests that common method variance is prominent among certain types of ML-based measures. For example, Park et al. (2015) found that the average discriminant validity coefficients of measures of Big Five traits based on social media language was significantly higher than that of self-report questionnaires, which may be a result of common linguistic correlates of different traits. A high correlation between social media based measures of conscientiousness and agreeableness might be due to their common relationships with positive and negative evaluations rather than the true relationship between those personality constructs. Differentiation could be increased by eliminating shared features among measures of different construct, but this would likely simultaneously decrease the measures' associations with self-report measures and targeted criteria. Therefore, the extent to which differentiation validity is traded with convergence or criterion relationships should be considered based on specific applications.

Validity Evidence Related to Consequences

Evidence of relationships between scores on an instrument and a relevant criterion has been widely used in HR settings for the purpose of assigning individuals to different treatments (jobs, training, etc.), although causal tests are more uncommon. The most compelling evidence related to consequences comes from experimentally testing the implementation measures linked to criteria and observing the effect on those criteria. Similarly, ML-based HRM research has generally focused on predicting a targeted criterion using supervised learning models without significant attention paid to causality. Similar patterns of relationships were found between ML-based measures and more traditional assessments with external criteria. Although the former typically displayed better predictive abilities (Bleidorn & Hopwood, 2019), it is generally unclear to which constructs these increases are attributable.

Reliability

Reliability for ML-based measures is conceptually similar to reliability of traditional psycho-metric tests. Scores derived using ML should still consistently reflect the constructs they are intended to reflect. If variability of scores from one occasion to another is inconsistent with the definition of the construct being measured, this is evidence of unreliability, meaning that variation in scores is attributable to measurement error. There are multiple potential sources of variation which are captured by different estimation approaches for reliability. Inter-rater reli-ability estimates assess the extent to which multiple rating sources agree on score estimates; test-retest reliability estimates assess the degree to which test scores are consistent across time; internal consistency estimates assess the relationships between estimates within the same measure. For studies concerning ML-based measures, test-retest reliability is reported most frequently, often by using artificially defined cut points. For example, Park et al. (2015) calculated test-retest reliability by splitting each user's timeline into four 6-month intervals, applying personality estimation methods to each interval, and calculating correlations between each pair of intervals assessing the same trait. Stability of each trait was then calculated as the average of pairwise correlations. Other forms of reliability estimation are seldom reported in the literature.

HR DATA SOURCES FOR DEVELOPING THEORY BY APPLYING ML

Although most ML methods do not require massive datasets, they still benefit from them in making increasingly accurate predictions, making the acquisition of "big data" a high priority. In contrast to traditional HRM research in which data collection methods are typically designed to focus on measures that reflect predetermined constructs, big data are often collected with less consideration of construct representation, if any. For instance, in a conventional approach of building a prediction model for turnover, data may be collected from assessments of rele-vant KSAOs and archived demographic profiles of a group of employees in an organization. In contrast, an ML-based approach can leverage large structured and unstructured datasets internal and/or external to the organization (job interview videos, emails, national databases, etc.), and incorporate all meaningful variance from all sources in the creation of predictive models. There are many potential sources of such data, which vary in both the degree to which they require advanced programming skills and the intensity of ethical concerns related to data governance, which we explore next.

Records from Human Resource Information Systems

Archival records in HR systems have been frequently used in HRM research and are often collected in combination with other data collection procedures such as surveys (Sackett & Larson, 1990); however, the drastic increase in volume and variety of data stored in organizational data vaults and the speed with which data are now generated bring new challenges to HRM researchers regarding data acquisition and data management, as well as new legal/ ethical considerations. In contrast to traditional HRM "small" data methods, ML-based methods typically require large datasets integrated from multiple data warehouses managed by different units in one or more organizations. This means that researchers need to obtain data from different parties that often have different rules and restrictions regarding data access and sharing, requiring appropriate programming skills to collect and integrate with varying database and data format standards.

From a technical perspective, harvesting such data requires knowledge about data structures, database operations, and at least one type of programming language. Big data stored in organizational data vaults are always at least somewhat structured, but those structures are generally decided upon according to the technical requirements of the specific information systems being used and their purposes, which may not coincide with researcher needs. Most commonly, data are stored within relational databases, a format in which all data are stored tabularly with complex interrelationships between tables to indicate nesting and intervariable associations. A major advantage of relational databases for HRM researchers is that they can often be exported in unencrypted plain text, such as in a comma-separated values (CSV) format, which makes them easy to import into statistical analysis programs and suitable for use with statistical programming languages. Popular database engines include Oracle, MySQL, MS SQL Server, PostgreSQL, and MongoDB. Thus, if HRM researchers wish to access massive quantities of organizational data, they often need to learn one or more of the database languages used. Database manipulation libraries available for programming languages like R and Python can also provide alternative data-wrangling strategies.

Researchers also need to ensure compliance with more specific requirements imposed on different data sources by professional organizations, nations, regions, organizations, and even units within those organizations related to data access, storage, and sharing of such data, Generally accepted standards for such decision-making do not currently exist. For example, in large-scale data collection, it is often impossible to obtain informed consent from all employees on a particular research use of their personal data, the legality of proceeding without consent varies by locality, and the ethics of it are unclear at best.

Biometric and Sociometric Sensors

Biometric and sociometric sensors are wearable devices that automatically collect continuous streams of physiological and social interaction data in an unobtrusive manner. Wearable biometric sensors detect real-time variations in physiological and behavioral indicators such as heart rate, blood pressure, sleep pattern, physical location, and number of steps taken. They have similar characteristics to more conventional physiological measures based on EEG, fMRI, and heart rate/blood pressure monitors, all of which have been used to research topics related to occupational health. However, the portable nature of personal biometric sensors enables data collection over a prolonged time period, enabling the study of long-term physiological profiles for different individuals, which enables new research questions. Similarly, sociometric sensors capture behavioral data relevant to social interactions including conversational time, physical proximity, amount of face-to-face interaction, and tone of voice, which can be used to quantify employee behavior, social interaction, and organizational dynamics (e.g., Olguín-Olguín et al., 2008). Sociometric sensors can be viewed as a substitute for behavioral observations, which are more labor-intensive, more obtrusive, and subject to more obvious biases. Employees' social behaviors captured this way have been associated with a variety of organizational phenomena and outcomes, such as job satisfaction (Olguín-Olguín et al., 2008), sales performance (Olguín-Olguín & Pentland, 2010), and team creativity (Tripathi & Burleson, 2012).

Internet and Social Media

As websites and social media profiles house an enormous amount of descriptive and behavioral data created by organizations and individuals, web content and social media mining resembles data collection based on archived organizational records but adds a few distinct advantages. Compared to its conventional counterpart, a much greater quantity of data can be downloaded from websites and social media in an efficient, automatic, and unintrusive way and with negligible financial cost. This can drastically decrease time, effort, and expense associated with HRM research while increasing the quantity of data that can be collected.

To provide researcher access to such data, some companies such as Bing, Wikipedia, Twitter, and Facebook provide application programming interfaces (APIs) to enable easier extraction of data from their website databases and automatic enforcement of their data access and privacy policies. Researchers have also created code libraries to make access even easier in both R and Python. Twitter has been the most popular API-accessed data source for social media research. Murphy (2017) provided a step-to-step guide for collecting Twitter data for psychological research using R, while Hernandez et al. (2016) gave an instruction on how to collect data from Twitter for organizational research using Python.

When looking at the broader universe of websites, most do not provide APIs, in which case web scraping is used, which refers to the use of algorithms to extract content from a website (Braun et al., 2018; Landers et al., 2016). This process can be automated, as the web content of modern websites is hierarchically structured using a scripting language called Hypertext Markup Language (HTML), and patterns within HTML can be tracked to target the collection of data systematically from any page of interest. Web scraping generally follows a number of set steps: (1) raw HTML is examined to understand how raw data are organized; (2) a data model is created to map the raw data in its original HTML format to the desired structure; (3) a crawler and a scraper are executed using scraping software or packages are used to write crawling and scraping code in R or Python; (4) the code is executed to convert raw content into a structured dataset.

Website and social media mining are subject to consent and privacy issues similar to those faced during data collection from organizational databases when personal data are collected; additionally, intellectual property and cybersecurity regulations should be considered when original content is copied without approval from the authors. One key ethical controversy around collecting behavioral data on the internet is whether content shared openly by individuals should be viewed as public or private. Although this type of information is indeed presented in a public space, there is evidence that some social media users do not believe their social media content to be public (e.g., O'Brien & Torres, 2012). Therefore, there is still an ongoing debate on whether web data mining is equivalent to observing individual behaviors in private or public. Website owners also vary in the extent to which they are willing to let their content be replicated, used, and shared by unauthorized parties. For example, many websites enforce anti-crawling mechanisms to stop algorithms from harvesting their content. Although there are technical solutions to circumvent such restrictions, such actions may still be a breach of research ethics. Much as before, researchers should consider the legal context of scraping in their location, especially in relation to website user agreements. Although using web content for research purposes is considered fair use in most regions around the world, researchers should still be mindful of factors that impact the evaluation of fairness (e.g., impact on the copyrighted work's market value; Madison, 2004).

Public and Open Source Datasets

Beyond collecting primary data, HRM researchers can also leverage relevant public datasets published by nations, public/private organizations, and research institutions; as more and more scientific research and data has become open access, these datasets have become increasing valuable. For example, in the United States, data.gov acts as a clearing house for government data, providing information regarding both individuals and groups, locally and nationally. Datasets shared by organizations and research centers often focus on more specific topics. For example, organizations, groups, and individuals can make their data public though the support of Amazon Web Services Open Data Registry. Pew Research Center allows public access to datasets covering a wide range of topics including social media, online privacy, politics, and technology. Yelp Open Dataset houses a subset of its businesses, reviews, and user data, which might also be relevant to HRM research. It is also worthwhile searching for open access research data related to a topic of interest before data collection. For instance, many researchers who collected large corpora of tweets to train their ML models have made their datasets public.

EXAMPLES OF HRM RESEARCH USING ML

Although most existing ML-based research in HRM focuses on prediction, more attempts have been made to increase the interpretability of ML-based predictions recently, in order to mitigate many of the issues created by the "black box problems" of unreadable ML-based methods. HRM researchers should attend to this advancement for two reasons: First, algorithmic explainability is crucial if ML-based prediction is to be used as an initial inductive step in a triangulation approach toward future deductive, inference-based research. Second, it provides new research opportunities for HRM researchers. In this section, we will review the status quo of research in various subareas of HRM, discuss the latest approaches to improve algorithmic explainability, and suggest ways in which HRM researchers can use ML to test and build upon HRM theories.

Recruitment and Staffing

To date, ML-based research in the domain of recruitment and staffing have mostly sought to build automated job recommendation systems (JRS) by estimating relationships between job candidates and positions via a number of different technical approaches (Hong et al., 2013). In general, these approaches rely upon similarity measures either within supervised ML frameworks or within unsupervised ML frameworks, but sometimes they combine the two.

Approaches to JRS that involve the application of supervised learning models include content-based recommendation (CBR) and knowledge-based recommendation (KBR). CBR is used to predict matches between job candidates and jobs by comparing text content. For example, Roy et al. (2020) applied a linear support vector machine (SVM) classifier on the text of a résumé dataset to classify résumés into different industrial categories. Then, lists of résumés that were conceptually closest to job descriptions provided by employers were obtained by computing cosine similarity between job descriptions and the content of the résumés. Résumés nearest to the provided job descriptions were identified using K-nearest neighbors (KNN). Paparrizos et al. (2011) trained a naïve Bayes classifier to predict a candidate's next job transition based on the candidate's past job transitions and personal information as well as general information about companies affiliated with the candidate's profile. In contrast, KBR predicts relationships between candidates and jobs based on patterns and rules obtained from the functional knowledge of how a specific candidate/job meets the requirements of a particular job/candidate. This can be done using association rules generated from data, theoretical taxonomies, or subject matter expert (SME) expertise. For instance, based on a corpus of job description text labeled by experts as requiring one of seven kinds of general competency, Guohao et al. (2019) built a convolutional neural network model to automatically classify job descriptions into different competency requirements. The same approach was then used to extract the competency qualities of candidates from their résumé text, which could be matched to the competencies extracted from job requirements. Faliagka et al. (2012) used SVM with a nonlinear kernel to predict an expert recruiter's judgment of the candidate's relevance score for the applied position based on education, work experience, average number of years spent per job, and extraversion.

Unsupervised ML is sometimes used for JRS to generate job and/or candidate clusters, followed by matching jobs with candidates by calculating the degree of similarity between individuals and existing clusters. The approach of finding clusters of users who have the same preference/experiences and then predicting relationships between items and a new user based on what the similar users like/experience is called collaborative filtering recommendation (CFR). In the domain of job recommendation, a user-item rating matrix generated from job candidate behaviors, opinions, or subjective ratings is usually used to calculate similarities between job candidates. Ajoudanian and Abadeh (2019) applied fuzzy clustering to both work projects and users on GitHub to form project and user clusters. Then, lists of projects that were the most interesting to undocumented users could be predicted based on Pearson correlations generated from a user-project rating matrix constructed from opinions of users in the training set. Clustering techniques can also be combined with other techniques such as association rules mining based on users' implicit interaction records with items (e.g., browsing history of candidates on a recruitment website) to overcome the common sparsity problem associated with a user-item rating matrix to achieve better performance (e.g., Najafabadi et al., 2017). This last system is also an example of a hybrid recommendation (HyR) system in which KBR and CFR are incorporated to combine their strengths.

Although these approaches to JRS emphasize maximizing allocation success to individual positions, additional steps could be taken to predict staffing success on an organizational level. For example, Pessach et al. (2020) constructed a variable-order Bayesian network (VOBN) model for a large dataset of recruitment records collected over a decade, diversified over roles and job descriptions and representing a wide range of heterogenous populations, in order to predict recruitment success (i.e., performance and turnover) based on rich pre-hire data. Because VOBN is a generalized version of a Bayesian network model, it could be easily interpreted to see how the probability of recruitment success was dependent on specific features, which enabled a high degree of interpretability. An optimization process was then implemented to balance between different staffing objectives (i.e., workforce demand, accuracy of placement, and diversity) across different business units and positions within the organization.

Although some JRS approaches like KBR incorporate knowledge from the HRM literature, research in this area is almost universally conducted by computer scientists with a practical focus and relatively little citation or reference to HRM literature (for a detailed discussion of the application of ML in HR practice, please refer to CHAPTERS 6 and 7). This leads to concerns about whether the clusters of and relationships between job candidates and jobs mined from data is theoretically meaningful. Therefore, this represents a great opportunity for HRM researchers to incorporate relevant HRM theories into the JRS framework, in order to map clusters and associations to meaningful concepts. JRS approaches also tend to overlook more general HR strategies associated with staffing and workforce planning. Pessach et al. (2020) provided a good example of balancing optimization of specific job allocations and broader organizational goals, a strategy future HRM researchers would do well to replicate.

Selection and Assessment

ML algorithms have been used to improve prediction of selection outcomes either directly through modeling historical performance data using incumbent data or indirectly through the prediction of KSAOs. There are numerous examples of each. In the case of direct modeling of performance, Aiolli et al. (2009) provided an example of the former approach by building a preference learning model implemented by an SVM classifier to rank new candidates based on past selection decisions. Mahmoud et al. (2019) also predicted job performance directly by building decision trees based on employee information collected in the selection process (gender, degree, skills, experience, health condition, etc.). Illustrating another approach, Chien and Chen (2008) developed a data-mining framework based on decision trees and association rules for selection, which were evaluated by domain experts in the company to justify them rationally.

In the more frequent case of KSAO prediction models, researchers use textual, graphical, visual, and audio data derived from a variety of assessment methods, including résumés and game-based assessments. Hernandez et al. (2020) built convolutional neural networks using visual résumé features and found that these features predicted individual differences in cognitive ability and Big Five traits. In a game-based assessment context, a series of ML models has also been used to predict both cognitive and non-cognitive abilities (Auer et al., 2020).

One particularly prominent area for KSAO prediction models is using video interviews. Bekhouche et al. (2017) modeled facial feature data using five nonlinear support vector regression models to predict Big Five personality traits scores, which were in turn fed into an interview score regression to predict applicant performance in interviews. Because techniques like this do not provide clearly interpretable coefficients, making their internal functions a "black box," researchers and policy makers have recently raised concerns about the necessity of developing explainable ML algorithms for automatic decision making applications (refer to CHAPTER 15 for more details). Some effort has been made to explain the decisions of such ML models and to identify important features. For instance, The CVPR 2017 Job Candidate Screening Challenge was conducted using 3000 videos annotated for Big Five traits and an "invite for interview" decision. Competitors were asked to provide both an accurate prediction of the "invite for interview" variable and a justification for the decision with verbal/visual explanations (Escalante et al., 2017). The winner of the challenge carried out predictions in two stages: The first-level predictions included separate channels of extreme learning machine (ELM) classifiers (which is a type of neural network) that evaluated audio, scene, and facial features. These predictions were then combined in a second modeling stage, a stacked random forest classifier, that gave the final prediction and also information about the path of a decision including the system dynamics, the learned features, and the weights of the individual ELM classifier.

Although many of these approaches showed high predictive accuracy, they bring new validity and ethical concerns. Algorithms that are optimized upon decisions made by the existing selection system or existing SMEs likely replicate and reinforce existing biases, such as against minority groups. ML done using such approaches can simply formalize deficiencies and biases in human judgment. Furthermore, constructing ML models based on a myriad of different predictors without clear theoretical links to outcomes mimics the dustbowl empiricism era of performance prediction, likely leading to the use of predictive features that are not theoretically related to the quality of job applicants but are selected by the algorithm due to systemic biases. This also raises questions about the necessity of job-related predictors and the ability of the whole selection model to cross-validate across contexts. Selection researchers are therefore encouraged to explore algorithm explainability in tandem with the value of ML techniques, as the use of explainable algorithms enables insight into potential biases and the building of evidence related to construct validity. Interested researchers could also read CHAPTER 8 for the application of ML in selection practice.

Training and Development

Although ML has begun to be studied by education researchers, these techniques have generally not reached training and development. However, just as rich behavioral and interaction data can be gathered from learners in educational settings and models, using data generated by technologies like massively open online courses and virtual learning environments, ML-based technologies may enable deeper insight into learning behavior and learning processes for organizational learners. For example, Borghini et al. (2017) proposed an ML algorithm based on a metric created from brain activity to quantify a user's skill level within a series of training sessions, considering the level of task execution, behavioral stability, and cognitive stability between consecutive sessions. The proposed methodology proved to be useful in quantifying and tracking learner processes. Extending such methods further into workplace contexts, and considering similarities and differences between those contexts and existing work in education, will be a vital next step toward integration of ML into training and development.

Performance Management

In general, existing studies on performance management that used ML focused on building prediction models of employee performance either from data stored in HR information systems or using self-report data. Some of these performance prediction models have already been explored in the earlier discussion of recruitment and selection (Pessach et al., 2020; Chien and Chen, 2008; Mahmoud et al., 2019). Beyond these, de Oliveira et al. (2019) trained a series of ML algorithms on 241 predictors which involved personal data, behavioral data, and data from internal questionnaires. Similarly, Valle et al. (2012) predicted sales performance based on socio-demographic attributes using a naïve Bayes classifier.

Apart from problems related to validity and adverse impact, much as with recruitment and selection, several additional issues are encountered with performance prediction models. First, collected predictor variables are generally limited to demographic variables. Many studies have incorporated variables such as gender and age in their models (e.g., Chien & Chen, 2008; Mahmoud et al., 2019), without significant exploration of adverse impact. Future studies should be more cautious with the selection of demographic predictors so that the feature set is theoretically relevant to and justifiable for the particular research topic. Second, the collection of data is usually constrained within a single organization, which inevitably limits the generalizability of predictive models. Sample sizes in prior studies have also tended to be small given the number of variables they sought to model, which in turn has limited the number of predictors that could be included in ML models without causing instability, possibly signaling overfitting. Researchers should therefore explore alternative data sources to collect a more representative sample of the general working population and also to build more robust prediction models.

Turnover and Retention

Turnover studies frequently use the same general analytic approach as performance management studies (e.g., Frierson & Si, 2018; Moyo et al., 2018; Alduayj & Rajpoot, 2018; Jain & Nayyar, 2018; Rombaut & Guerry, 2018; Fan et al., 2012; Sajjadiani et al., 2019). In fact, job performance and turnover frequently occur in the same study and are used as criteria in paired ML models. For example, Sajjadiani et al. (2019) applied naïve Bayes classifiers on résumés and job application form content to predict both job performance and turnover.

These methodological similarities also bring similar problems, especially related to feature selection and sampling. Zhao et al. (2019) reviewed recent studies in the application of ML to predict turnover. All the study samples they identified were collected in one organization. The majority of the studies had a sample size of less than 1000 and modeled less than 20 features, signaling the potential for both underfitting given the full potential landscape of relevant variables and overfitting given the particular features chosen. To overcome such problems, alternative data sources like social media could be used to collect a large quantity of turnover-related samples as well as data on a richer variety of predictors. For example, Chen and Chan (2020) collected a sample of 25,842 Twitter users who recently turned over and built a prediction model of turnover types based on over 10,000 language features including semantic dictionaries, n-grams, and LDA topics extracted from user timelines. The combination of top-down and bottom-up predictors boosted the predictive accuracy of the model and enabled both the testing of turnover predictors named in turnover theories and the discovery of new turnover antecedents not previously known.

CONCLUSION

This chapter provided a current review of existing ML research in HRM contexts, as well as a description of how ML research can be done using conventional HRM standards across research design concerns, including data collection, analytic, measurement, validation, and ethics. There is much research on HRM, although mostly not done by HRM researchers, showing that ML models can achieve more accurate prediction compared to more traditional models or make recommendations that mirror human judgment, depending upon the purpose of the modeling. Within HRM, ML studies using inductive approaches have contributed to the understanding of organizational phenomena and helped to develop HRM theory. These promising results demonstrate ML's potential to advance HRM research. However, the lack of explainability and potential biases associated with most of the modeling approaches impair ML models' validity and practical application, especially when done without sufficient expertise in both ML and HRM. Existing HRM theory on assessment, ethics, and bias is particularly relevant and is needed to address key issues in the ML research literature. For more thorough discussions of explainability and fairness of ML, please refer to CHAPTER 15 and CHAPTER 16 respectively.

We conclude with three major recommendations to facilitate more widespread adoption of ML methods in HRM in both academia and practice. First, ML methods should be employed in such a way that model predictions, or at least model comparisons, are explainable in terms of constructs. Second, interdisciplinary teams of HRM and ML experts are needed to develop methods to quantify and mitigate bias in a way that is practically meaningful and self-evidently legal, such as in relation to adverse impact laws around the world. Third, ethical standards and codes of conduct for ML-based research in HRM are needed to reduce pressure on researchers to develop and navigate their own personal ethics when it comes to data collection related to these issues. We hope that this chapter will serve as a useful starting point for researchers using ML methods, providing an initial set of guidelines that will help them to better understand HRM-related problems that stem from the issues raised.

REFERENCES

Aiolli, F., De Filippo, M., & Sperduti, A. (2009). Application of the preference learning model to a human resources selection task. In *2009 IEEE Symposium on Computational Intelligence and Data Mining* (pp. 203–210). IEEE.
Ajoudanian, S., & Abadeh, M. N. (2019). Recommending human resources to project leaders using a collaborative filtering-based recommender system: Case study of gitHub. *IET Software*, *13*(5), 379–385.
Alduayj, S. S., & Rajpoot, K. (2018). Predicting employee attrition using machine learning. In *2018 International Conference on Innovations in Information Technology (IIT)* (pp. 93–98). IEEE.
American Educational Research Association, American Psychological Association, & National Council on Measurement in Education (Eds.). (2014). *Standards for educational and psychological testing*. American Educational Research Association.
Angrave, D., Charlwood, A., Kirkpatrick, I., Lawrence, M., & Stuart, M. (2016). HR and analytics: Why HR is set to fail the big data challenge. *Human Resource Management Journal*, *26*(1), 1–11.
Arlot, S., & Celisse, A. (2010). A survey of cross-validation procedures for model selection. *Statistics Surveys*, *4*, 40–79.
Auer, E. M., Marin, S., & Landers, R. N. (2020, April). Predicting non-cognitive traits using trace data from a cognitive ability GBA. In S.-C. Codreanu (Chair) & F. Leutner (Chair*), *Game-based*

assessments: Fad or sound psychometrics assessments? [Symposium]. Society for Industrial and Organizational Psychology, Austin, TX, United States.

Bekhouche, S. E., Dornaika, F., Ouafi, A., & Taleb-Ahmed, A. (2017). Personality traits and job candidate screening via analyzing facial videos. In *Proceedings of the IEEE Conference on Computer Vision and Pattern Recognition Workshops* (pp. 10–13). IEEE.

Berhil, S., Benlahmar, H., & Labani, N. (2020). A review paper on artificial intelligence at the service of human resources management. *Indonesian Journal of Electrical Engineering and Computer Science*, *18*(1), 32–40.

Bleidorn, W., & Hopwood, C. J. (2019). Using machine learning to advance personality assessment and theory. *Personality and Social Psychology Review*, *23*(2), 190–203.

Borghini, G., Aricò, P., Di Flumeri, G., Sciaraffa, N., Colosimo, A., Herrero, M. T., ... & Babiloni, F. (2017). A new perspective for the training assessment: Machine learning-based neurometric for augmented user's evaluation. *Frontiers in Neuroscience*, *11*, Article 325.

Braun, M. T., Kuljanin, G., & DeShon, R. P. (2018). Special considerations for the acquisition and wrangling of big data. *Organizational Research Methods*, *21*(3), 633–659.

Campbell, J. P., & Wilmot, M. P. (2018). The functioning of theory in industrial, work and organizational psychology (IWOP). In D. S. Ones, N. Anderson, C. Viswesvaran, & H. K. Sinangil (Eds.), *The SAGE handbook of industrial, work and organizational psychology: Personnel psychology and employee performance* (pp. 3–38). Sage Reference.

Chen, C., & Chan, D. K. S. (2020, April). *Classifying and predicting voluntary turnover on Twitter with machine learning* [Poster presentation]. Society for Industrial and Organizational Psychology, Austin, TX, United States.

Chien, C. F., & Chen, L. F. (2008). Data mining to improve personnel selection and enhance human capital: A case study in high-technology industry. *Expert Systems with Applications*, *34*(1), 280–290.

de Oliveira, E. L., Torres, J. M., Moreira, R. S., & de Lima, R. A. F. (2019). Absenteeism prediction in call center using machine learning algorithms. In Á. Rocha, H. Adeli, L. P. Reis, & S. Costanzo (Eds.), *New knowledge in information systems and technologies* (pp. 958–968). Springer International Publishing.

Escalante, H. J., Guyon, I., Escalera, S., Jacques, J., Madadi, M., Baró, X., ... & Van Lier, R. (2017). Design of an explainable machine learning challenge for video interviews. In *2017 International Joint Conference on Neural Networks (IJCNN)* (pp. 3688–3695). IEEE.

Faliagka, E., Ramantas, K., Tsakalidis, A., & Tzimas, G. (2012). Application of machine learning algorithms to an online recruitment system. In *Proc. International Conference on Internet and Web Applications and Services* (pp. 215–220). IARIA.

Fan, C. Y., Fan, P. S., Chan, T. Y., & Chang, S. H. (2012). Using hybrid data mining and machine learning clustering analysis to predict the turnover rate for technology professionals. *Expert Systems with Applications*, *39*(10), 8844–8851.

Frierson, J., & Si, D. (2018). Who's next: Evaluating attrition with machine learning algorithms and survival analysis. In F. Y. L. Chin, C. L. P. Chen, L. Khan, K. Lee, & L.-J. Zhang (Eds.), *Big Data – BigData 2018* (pp. 251–259). Springer International Publishing.

Grand, J. A., Pearce, M., Rench, T. A., Chao, G. T., Fernandez, R., & Kozlowski, S. W. (2013). Going DEEP: Guidelines for building simulation-based team assessments. *BMJ Quality and Safety*, *22*(5), 436–448.

Guohao, Q., Bin, W., Bai, W., & Baoli, Z. (2019). Competency analysis in human resources using text classification based on deep neural network. In *2019 IEEE Fourth International Conference on Data Science in Cyberspace (DSC)* (pp. 322–329). IEEE.

Haynes, S. N., Richard, D., & Kubany, E. S. (1995). Content validity in psychological assessment: A functional approach to concepts and methods. *Psychological Assessment*, *7*(3), 238–247.

Hernandez, I., Kim, S., Sanders, A., & Towe, S. (2020, April). Deep selection: Inferring employee's traits from résumé style. In M. Q. Liu (Chair), *Machine-learning for I-O 2.0* [Symposium]. Society for Industrial and Organizational Psychology, Austin, TX, United States.

Hernandez, I., Newman, D. A., & Jeon, G. (2016). Twitter analysis: Methods for data management and a word count dictionary to measure city-level job satisfaction. In S. Tonidandel, E. B. King, & J. M. Cortina (Eds.), *Big data at work: The data science revolution and organizational psychology* (pp. 64–114). Routledge/Taylor & Francis Group.

Hong, W., Zheng, S., Wang, H., & Shi, J. (2013). A job recommender system based on user clustering. *Journal of Computers, 8*(8), 1960–1967.

Jain, R., & Nayyar, A. (2018). Predicting employee attrition using XGBoost machine learning approach. In *2018 International Conference on System Modeling & Advancement in Research Trends (SMART)* (pp. 113–120). IEEE.

Kozlowski, S. W. J., & Klein, K. J. (2000). A multilevel approach to theory and research in organizations: Contextual, temporal, and emergent processes. In K. J. Klein & S. W. J. Kozlowski (Eds.), *Multilevel theory, research, and methods in organizations: Foundations, extensions, and new directions* (pp. 3–90). Jossey-Bass.

Landers, R. N., Brusso, R. C., Cavanaugh, K. J., & Collmus, A. B. (2016). A primer on theory-driven web scraping: Automatic extraction of big data from the internet for use in psychological research. *Psychological Methods, 21*(4), 475–492.

Loevinger, J. (1957). Objective tests as instruments of psychological theory. *Psychological Reports, 3*(3), 635–694.

Madison, M. J. (2004). A pattern-oriented approach to fair use. *William and Mary Law Review, 45*, 1525–1690.

Mahmoud, A. A., Shawabkeh, T. A., Salameh, W. A., & Al Amro, I. (2019). Performance predicting in hiring process and performance appraisals using machine learning. In *2019 10th International Conference on Information and Communication Systems (ICICS)* (pp. 110–115). IEEE.

Marks, M. A., Mathieu, J. E., & Zaccaro, S. J. (2001). A temporally based framework and taxonomy of team processes. *Academy of Management Review, 26*(3), 356–376.

Mathieu, J. E., & Chen, G. (2011). The etiology of the multilevel paradigm in management research. *Journal of Management, 37*(2), 610–641.

Moyo, S., Doan, T. N., Yun, J. A., & Tshuma, N. (2018). Application of machine learning models in predicting length of stay among healthcare workers in underserved communities in South Africa. *Human Resources for Health, 16*(1), Article 68.

Murphy, S. C. (2017). A hands-on guide to conducting psychological research on Twitter. *Social Psychological and Personality Science, 8*(4), 396–412.

Najafabadi, M. K., Mahrin, M. N. R., Chuprat, S., & Sarkan, H. M. (2017). Improving the accuracy of collaborative filtering recommendations using clustering and association rules mining on implicit data. *Computers in Human Behavior, 67*, 113–128.

O'Brien, D., & Torres, A. M. (2012). Social networking and online privacy: Facebook users' perceptions. *Irish Journal of Management, 31*(2), 63–97.

Olguín-Olguín, D., & Pentland, A. (2010). Sensor-based organisational design and engineering. *International Journal of Organisational Design and Engineering, 1*(1–2), 69–97.

Olguín-Olguín, D., Waber, B. N., Kim, T., Mohan, A., Ara, K., & Pentland, A. (2008). Sensible organizations: Technology and methodology for automatically measuring organizational behavior. *IEEE Transactions on Systems, Man, and Cybernetics, Part B (Cybernetics), 39*(1), 43–55.

Paparrizos, I., Cambazoglu, B. B., & Gionis, A. (2011). Machine learned job recommendation. In *Proceedings of the Fifth ACM Conference on Recommender Systems* (pp. 325–328). ACM.

Park, G., Schwartz, H. A., Eichstaedt, J. C., Kern, M. L., Kosinski, M., Stillwell, D. J., ... & Seligman, M. E. (2015). Automatic personality assessment through social media language. *Journal of Personality and Social Psychology, 108*(6), 934–952.

Pennebaker, J. W., Boyd, R. L., Jordan, K., & Blackburn, K. (2015). *The development and psychometric properties of LIWC2015*. University of Texas at Austin.

Pessach, D., Singer, G., Avrahami, D., Ben-Gal, H. C., Shmueli, E., & Ben-Gal, I. (2020). Employees recruitment: A prescriptive analytics approach via machine learning and mathematical programming. *Decision Support Systems, 134*, Article 113290.

Rombaut, E., & Guerry, M. A. (2018). Predicting voluntary turnover through human resources database analysis. *Management Research Review, 41*(1), 96–112.

Roy, P. K., Chowdhary, S. S., & Bhatia, R. (2020). A machine learning approach for automation of résumé recommendation system. *Procedia Computer Science, 167*, 2318–2327.

Sackett, P. R., and Larson, J. (1990). Research strategies and tactics in I/O psychology. In M. D. Dunnette & L. Hough (Eds.), *Handbook of industrial and organizational psychology* (2nd ed.) (pp. 435–466). Consulting Psychologists Press.

Sajjadiani, S., Sojourner, A. J., Kammeyer-Mueller, J. D., & Mykerezi, E. (2019). Using machine learning to translate applicant work history into predictors of performance and turnover. *Journal of Applied Psychology, 104*(10), 1207–1225. https://doi.org/10.1037/apl0000405

Shilakes, C. C., & Tylman, J. (1998). *Enterprise information portals*. Merrill Lynch Inc.

Tripathi, P., & Burleson, W. (2012). Predicting creativity in the wild: Experience sample and sociometric modeling of teams. In *Proceedings of the ACM 2012 Conference on Computer Supported Cooperative Work* (pp. 1203–1212). ACM.

Valle, M. A., Varas, S., & Ruz, G. A. (2012). Job performance prediction in a call center using a naive Bayes classifier. *Expert Systems with Applications, 39*(11), 9939–9945.

Yarkoni, T., & Westfall, J. (2017). Choosing prediction over explanation in psychology: Lessons from machine learning. *Perspectives on Psychological Science, 12*(6), 1100–1122.

Zhao, Y., Hryniewicki, M. K., Cheng, F., Fu, B., & Zhu, X. (2019). Employee turnover prediction with machine learning: A reliable approach. In K. Arai, S. Kapoor, & R. Bhatia (Eds.), *Intelligent systems and applications* (pp. 737–758). Springer International Publishing.

Index

Abadeh, M. N. 384
Abdulsalam, W. H. 78, 81
ABox 172, 173, 180–82
Abraham, A. 210, 212, 213
absenteeism 127–30, 132, 139, 251
accountability 14, 17, 323–5, 327–34, 341, 343
  actors 330–31
  development and deployment, ADM systems
    330
  example of defining 332–3
  in explicit and embedded software
    development processes 329–30
  forums and 331–2
  future research 333–4
  relationships 324, 325, 329–34
accuracy 34, 58, 59, 74, 116–18, 137, 138,
    140–42, 244, 309, 312
actors 305–7, 324–34
AdaBoost 70, 74, 76, 77
additional information 57, 58, 111, 160, 171, 290,
    294
Affectiva 73, 79, 245
affective computing 4–5, 16, 243–55
  assessment center exercises and situational
    judgment tests 248
  challenges 253–4
  current state of 243
  and diversity training 250
  emotional speech synthesis 245–6
  facial emotion expression synthesis and body
    language 246
  facial expressions and body language 244
  interviews 246–8
  leadership training and development 249
  methods 246, 247
  multimodal emotion sensing systems 245
  physiological emotion monitoring 244–5
  producing emotions 245
  research 254–5
  selection 246
  sensing emotions 243–5
  speech processing 244
  systems 243, 248, 250, 251, 254
  talent management 251–3
  technology 243, 246, 250–54
  training and development 248–9
  training in emotional intelligence 249–50
Aggarwal, C. C. 110
aggregate skill 173

AI-based approaches 106, 110, 111, 118
AI-based chatbots 364, 365
AI-based decisions 285–7, 291, 292, 294–9, 303
  processes 291, 295
  tools 308, 318
AI-based personnel selection 149, 296, 298
AI-based recommendations 285–7, 297
AI-based recruiting 118, 119
AI-based selection algorithms 356, 362
AI-based systems 157, 265, 285–8, 291–9
Aickelin, U. 217
Aiolli, F. 385
AI opacity 35, 285, 286, 288, 296, 297, 299
AI understandability 286, 287, 289–92, 295–9
Ajoudanian, S. 384
Alamro, S. 175
algorithm aversion 35, 36, 38, 157, 270, 311, 312,
    314, 318
algorithm category 29, 35, 197
algorithm development 31, 342
Algorithmic Accountability Act 341, 349
algorithmic bias 76, 82
algorithmic decision making 38, 40, 61, 195, 303,
    305, 311, 315, 317, 318
"algorithmic decision-making systems" (ADM)
    systems 323–30, 332–4, 341
  different process models, combining 329
  five role model 327–8
algorithmic decisions 38, 40, 61, 303, 305, 311,
    314–18
  tools 312, 314
algorithmic explainability 383
algorithmic HRM 197, 276
algorithmic management 196–8, 203, 271, 272,
    274, 275
algorithmic power 349, 350
algorithmic procedures 342, 348
algorithmic processes 290, 291, 348
algorithmic systems 271, 337, 342, 343, 350
algorithmic transparency 289, 290
algorithm literacy 36, 40
algorithms 27, 37, 97, 98, 108, 131–3, 141, 151,
    152, 159, 267, 289, 312, 314, 318, 323,
    343, 374
algorithms usage 268, 341
Ali Shah, S. A. 137, 139
Alom, M. Z. 72
Amandi, A. 215, 219
Angrave, D. 274